REA

A Laboratory for Anthropology

Cliff Dwellings in Mancos Canyon, W. H. Holmes watercolor, 1876.
Courtesy of the Library of Congress.

DON D. FOWLER

A Laboratory for Anthropology

SCIENCE AND ROMANTICISM
IN THE AMERICAN SOUTHWEST,
1846–1930

Published in cooperation with the
University of Arizona Southwest Center

University of New Mexico Press
Albuquerque

Design and composition by B. Williams & Associates

Library of Congress Cataloging-in-Publication Data
Fowler, Don D., 1936–
A laboratory for anthropology : science and romanticism in the
American Southwest, 1846–1930 / Don Fowler.—1st ed.
        p.   cm.
"University of Arizona Southwest Center book"—T.p. verso.
"Published in cooperation with the University of Arizona Southwest Center."
Includes bibliographical references (p.   ) and index.
ISBN 0-8263-2036-8 (cloth : alk. paper)
1. Anthropology—Southwest, New—History.   2. Ethnological expeditions—Southwest,
New—History.   3. Indians of North America—Southwest, New—Public opinion.
4. Anthropology in popular culture—Southwest, New.   5. Indians in popular culture—
Southwest, New.   6. Indians of North America—Southwest, New—Public opinion.
7. Public opinion—Southwest, New.   8. Southwest, New—Discovery and exploration.
9. Southwest, New—Description and travel.
I. University of Arizona. Southwest Center.   II. Title.
GN17.3.S67F68 2000
301'.0979—dc21
00-009359

A University of Arizona Southwest Center Book

Joseph C. Wilder, Series Editor

For Kay,

Whose Southwest Has Always Been a Special Place

Contents

Preface

Half a century ago and counting, Mexican historian Edmundo O'Gorman wrote: "America is an idea which was invented by Europeans and in the reality of which the Americans themselves have come to believe."[1] A central theme of this book is that the "American Southwest" is an idea invented by Euro- or Anglo-Americans (henceforth, "Anglos"), an invention they have come to believe is reality. Indeed, the invention of the Southwest derives in part from the same processes that earlier led to the invention of America. A second theme is that the invention of the Southwest was intertwined with the invention of "ethnology" as a field of inquiry in the 1840s, and its metamorphosis into the scholarly discipline of "anthropology" after 1880.

My approach to these themes combines biography with social and intellectual history. The principal characters are the women and men who described, and spun theories about, the "native" peoples of the Southwest between about 1846 and 1930. Of central interest are the social and cultural milieux—"the times"—in which the characters lived and conducted their studies. We are interested as well in the institutions in which they worked—the museums, universities, and schools of research, whose goals were the making, dissemination, and display of knowledge about the natural and cultural worlds. The intent, then, is to tell a story about the social and intellectual history of a cultural construct—the Southwest—and those who created that construct.

The characters include Anglo anthropologists, archaeologists, bureaucrats, military officers, politicians, traders, entrepreneurs, philanthropists, historians, philosophers, poets, painters, novelists, and "yearners." There are also Spanish and Mexican (collectively "Hispanic") administrators, scholars, soldiers, and missionary friars. Finally, and most centrally, there are the Indian peoples, resident in the land for millennia, and Hispanic villagers, resident for centuries, who were the "objects" of attention and study by the Anglos.

Point of View

The philosopher Ludwig Wittgenstein pointed to the important distinction between "seen" and "seen as." This is the distinction between simple perception of the world around us through the senses ("seeing"), and interpreting the world from a particular perspective ("seeing as"). The distinction extends into the metaphorical realm as well.[2]

Wittgenstein's "seen versus seen as" is central to a dichotomy seemingly common to all human groups: the distinction between "we and they," "us and them," or in postmodern lingo, in conceptions of "Alterity," or the "Other." How are "we" *seen as* by ourselves? How are other social groups—"ethnic," "tribal," "racial," or "national"—*seen as* by *us* ? Are they *commensurable with* us ? If not, how and why not, and what are the implications of the differences?[3] My theses, that the Southwest is an idea invented by Anglos, and that the development of ethnology *cum* anthropology was in large part an exercise in exploring and defining "otherness," both ultimately derive from the "seen versus seen as" distinction.

The "Southwest" implies a directional orientation vis-à-vis an assumed geographical center. However, this is not geographical or cartographic placement, but an *intellectual* directional orientation, a *point of view*. Thus, a vaguely bounded area of land—a "region" defined by interleaved cultural constructs, geographical, sociopolitical, literary, artistic, anthropological—is, *as seen from* Boston, New York, Philadelphia, and Washington, D.C., directionally and intellectually southwest of the "Center" of the Anglo world.

This is as it should be, for all of the Indian peoples of the Southwest have strong intellectual directional orientations of their own. The Zuni, of western New Mexico, live in the "great ant heap" at the center of their world. The origins stories of other Pueblos tell of migratory wanderings as each people sought, or dispersed from, their center. The neighboring Navajos tell of Dinetah, a sacred central place east of their present-day reservation lands.[4] Anglos, Pueblos, Navajos, then, all have intellectual directional orientations that influence how they think about and interpret themselves and their neighbors. Our concern is primarily with Anglo conceptions, however, especially those of anthropologists and archaeologists whose self-appointed task was to interpret the "native" Southwest to fellow Anglos and the world at large.

A Laboratory for Anthropology

In 1870, explorer, geologist, and nascent anthropologist John Wesley Powell spent a month in the American Southwest. He was attracted by the mix of peoples and cultural traditions. This mix later led him and others to think of the Southwest as an ideal "laboratory" for the "science of man" they hoped to develop. In 1879, as the newly appointed director of the Bureau of Ethnology of the Smithsonian Institution, Powell sent an anthropological expedition to the Southwest, marking the beginnings of Smithsonian studies there which lasted until the 1950s. The equation "Southwest equals anthropological laboratory" culminated in the founding of the "Laboratory of Anthropology" in Santa Fe in 1927.

"Laboratory" implies scientific research, "objectified" study and analysis of "specimens"—objects and beings—and the ongoing search for "natural laws" thought to "govern" the processes and behaviors in the natural world. From the 1730s on, the hope for a "science of man" has been driven by the conviction that humans are integrally part of the natural world, hence governed by natural laws; find those laws and the science of man becomes a reality. It was this search that drove the development of anthropology during the decades of our concern.

Whether there is, can be, or ought to be a "science of man" has been a matter of concern and dispute for three centuries. The existence of the dispute is implicit in my subtitle "Science and Romanticism . . ." which also refers to various tensions, images, categories, and stereotypes in Anglo constructs of "native peoples." As *Prologue* to this story we first look briefly at the geography of the area defined as the American Southwest, then sketch an overview of the peoples and places encountered by the Anglos when they began visiting after 1806. The following *Introduction* is a historical look at some images and stereotypes of "New World native peoples" which began to be formed almost as soon as Christopher Columbus mistakenly called them "Indians" in the 1490s. These images centered on commensurability: are "they" the same as "we" Europeans? That question partly turned on others: how and from whence did native peoples come into the Western Hemisphere; that is, what were their "origins"? These concerns, variously framed, were the basis for early American anthropology, together with the Enlightenment ideas of natural laws, science as a method to search out and explicate those laws, and the concept of "absolute" linear time. We then discuss how these ideas informed the "research agendas" in American anthropology, from the time of Thomas Jefferson until 1846 and beyond. In the following chapters, we turn to the main part of the story: the development of American anthropology and how it was intertwined with the developing idea of the Southwest.

Finally, a word about the origins and purposes of this book. One of my long-standing interests is in the history of ideas, particularly those ideas underlying and giving form to the disciplines of anthropology, history, and philosophy. Ideas, like clothing and architecture, are subject to fads, fashions, and recycling. In a culture slavishly haunted by a need for "the new," clothing styles, building facades, and ideas come into fashion, wane, are oftimes forgotten, and then revived, or reinvented, as something "new" yet again. This book is in part about such recycling and grows out of three decades of teaching courses and seminars in the history of ideas. Since 1970, I have enjoyed the status of Research Associate in Anthropology at the Smithsonian Institution, an affiliation that began when I and my spouse and colleague, Catherine S. Fowler, went to the Smithsonian to edit John Wesley Powell's anthropological manuscripts in 1967–68.[5] In 1980, we became part of the Smithsonian's "road show," an innovative outreach program originated by Charlene James-Duguid, which brought Smithsonian staff and research associates to cities across the country to present lectures, concerts, workshops, and seminars jointly sponsored by the Smithsonian Associates Program and local cultural institutions. It was our pleasure, from 1980 through 1996, to visit numerous cities and towns nationwide with Charlene and staff coordinators Maurine Connelly, Amy Kotkin, Mary

Beth Mullen, Betsy Pash, and Ann Post, to give lectures and seminars in company with a varied and congenial band of fellow presenters.

At the request of several individuals connected with cultural institutions in Arizona, Colorado, and New Mexico, I developed two lectures, and later two seminars, on the history of early anthropology in the Southwest. These were kindly received, not only in Albuquerque, Boulder, Phoenix, and Santa Fe, but in such diverse venues as Greenwich, Connecticut; Midland, Austin, and San Antonio, Texas; Omaha, Nebraska, and San Diego, California. At some point, they began to metamorphose into a book, with the encouragement of Charlene, Daniel Goodwin, and others. It has been a long process, sandwiched in between a plethora of teaching, administrative, national, and international professional duties, and frequent visits to Phoenix, Albuquerque, and Santa Fe, over more years than it should have taken.

True to its origins, this book is specifically written first for a public audience, represented by those hundreds of people whom I enjoyed meeting while "on the road" for the Smithsonian. Indeed, the form of the book was shaped in large part by questions and comments from people who heard the lectures and seminars. If one so desires, the book can be read without recourse to the endnotes. The second audience is students, providing background and context for more formal courses in Southwestern anthropology or history. For them, the endnotes and bibliography will allow entrée to additional information on the many necessarily terse, often oversimplified, statements in the book, and to see where I have shamelessly borrowed, recycled, and perhaps misconstrued the ideas therein.

My involvement with the Southwest and Southwestern anthropologists began in the fall of 1957 when, as a junior majoring in anthropology at the University of Utah, I found myself working under the watchful eye of James Gunnerson, a superb field archaeologist, helping excavate a small Anasazi archaeological site in a tributary of the Escalante River, itself a tributary of the mighty Colorado River. Construction of the Glen Canyon Dam was just beginning, and the University of Utah and the Museum of Northern Arizona were conducting salvage archaeological surveys and excavations in advance of the filling of Lake Powell. The Utah project was under the direction of the late Professor Jesse D. Jennings, who was to be a teacher, mentor, boss, taskmaster, colleague, and friend for forty years. Doing archaeology in remote side canyons, bouncing across dunes and slick rock in jeeps, on mule and horseback, and running rivers was not in my original game plan. As a youth I had studiously avoided the Boy Scouts and the whole idea of camping out, let alone its reality. My idea of roughing it was a boarding house I had inhabited the previous summer in Jackson Hole, Wyoming, where I worked at various jobs alternately serving and bilking tourists. Nonetheless, there I was, trowel in hand. In November, we returned to the archaeology lab in Salt Lake City. There I met Robert and Florence Lister, consummate scholars and famed Southwestern archaeologists, who were working for the Glen Canyon Project that year. It was the beginning of another four decade–plus friendship that I shall always cherish. The next summer, William D. Lipe, as crew chief, I as assistant, and a small crew of other students became personally acquainted with every sandbar and rapid in the Colorado River from its confluence with the San Juan to the dam site as we boated up and down the river recording and sampling archaeological sites. At the famous Crossing of the Fathers, where the friars Domínguez and Escalante forded the Colorado in 1776, I met Alexander (Lex) J. Lindsay, Jr., working for the Museum of Northern Arizona. Bill and Lex both became major Southwestern archaeologists, and friends whose knowledge and wit I have valued over the years.

In August 1958 our crew traveled to Albuquerque, by way of the Hopi Mesas, the Navajo Reservation, and the Gallup Indian Ceremonials to attend the Pecos Archaeological Conference. I was amazed and delighted by all I saw. At that conference and those that followed, I met numerous already well-known Southwestern anthropologists, many of whom be-

came long-time friends and mentors, especially Richard and Nathalie Woodbury, Raymond and Molly Thompson, Douglas K. Schwartz, and the late Fred Eggan, Emil H. Haury, Julian Hayden, Erik K. Reed, Albert R. Schroeder, Charlie Steen, and Joe Ben Wheat. I was hooked. I remained with the Glen Canyon Project through three years of graduate work. That also enabled me to court Catherine (Kay) Sweeney, a fellow student who was working for the Glen Canyon Project doing what would later be called ethno-archaeology. Kay had been introduced to the Southwest during her Girl Scout years by the late Bertha Dutton, who took young women on field trips for a number of years and imparted to them her own unparalleled knowledge of the Southwest, as well as her sense of professionalism and the idea that women, too, could enjoy careers as scholars. We made our first trip to the Southwest together in 1962, the year before we were married. We attended the Society for American Archaeology meeting in Tucson where I gave my first professional paper in front of seemingly every Southwestern archaeologist in existence. They had little interest in me; but I had been in charge of a crew that did the first-ever excavations on the Kaiparowits Plateau, and everyone wanted to see the slides. Kay and I have spent many weeks and months in Arizona, New Mexico, and southern Utah and Colorado ever since, and have come to know and learn from dozens of Southwesternists—archaeologists, ethnographers, linguists, historians, and museum professionals— many of whom have become close friends as well.

Many people who work for numerous institutions have assisted in the research for this book over the years. (Individuals are listed under the organization they worked for at the time I was visiting or requesting information and assistance.) All gave unstintingly of their time and knowledge, for which I am most appreciative. They include: at the American Museum of Natural History, New York, Stanley Freed, Lorann S. A. Pendleton, Anibal Rodriguez, Lisa Stock, Niurka Tyler, and David Hurst Thomas; the Arizona Historical Society, Tucson, Susan Sheehan; the University of Arizona, Center for Creative Photography, Diane

Nilsen and Marsha Tiede; the Bancroft Library, University of California, Berkeley, Susan Snyder; The Brooklyn Museum of Art, Diana Fane; the California Historical Society, San Francisco, Emily Wolff; the Amon Carter Museum, Fort Worth, Courtney De Angelis and Barbara McCandless; the Chicago Field Museum of Natural History, Jonathan Haas, Terry Novak, Phyllis Rabineau; the Colorado Historical Society, Deborah Neiswonger and the staff of the Colorado State Historic Preservation Office; the University of Colorado Museum, Deborah Confer and Linda S. Cordell; the Denver Public Library, Western History Collection, Augie Mastrogiuseppe and David Myers; the Thomas Gilcrease Institute of American History and Art, Tulsa, Sandra Hilderbrand; the Hispanic Society of America, New York, Marcus Burke and Renée Nisivoccia; the Huntington Library, San Marino, Brooke M. Black; the Mennonite Library and Archives, Bethel College, Newton, Kansas, John D. Thiesen; the Mesa Verde National Park Research Center, Steve Grafe, Robert C. Heyder, and Jack Smith; the Milwaukee Public Museum, Susan Otto; the Missouri Historical Society, Stephanie Klein, Emily Miller, Jill Sherman, Duane R. Sneddeker, and Barbara Stole; the Nevada State Library, Carson City, Mona Reno. Staff members of the various divisions of the Museum of New Mexico were helpful. They include: in the History Division, Thomas Chaves; at the Laboratory of Anthropology, Laura Holt, Marsha Jackson, Stuart Peckham, Willow Powers, Curtis Schaafsma, and Rosemary Talley; at the Museum of Fine Arts, Joan Tafoya; at the Museum of Indian Arts and Cultures, Mary Elizabeth King Black; and in the Photographic Archives, particular thanks to Arturo Olívas and Richard Rudisill. Special thanks also to the University of New Mexico/National Park Service Chaco Project, W. James Judge, Steven Lekson, Frances Joan Mathien, and Thomas Windes; the New York Historical Society, Laird Ogden and Nicole Wells; the City of Omaha Public Library, Thomas Heenan; the Peabody Museum, Harvard University, Hillel Berger, Leah McChesney, Stephen Williams, and the staff of the Tozzer Library; the University of Pennsylvania Museum, Jeremy A. Sabloff and Charles S. Kline; William H. Holmes and staff of the Pioneers Museum, Colorado Springs; the Rhode Island Historical Society, Serina Gunderson; the School of American Research, Santa Fe, Douglas K. Schwartz, Duane Anderson, and Michael Hering; the Smithsonian Institution National Anthropological Archives, Margaret Blaker, Paula R. Fleming, James Glenn, John Homiak, Vyrtis Thomas, and Herman Viola; the Southwest Museum, Los Angeles, Patrick Houlihan, Craig Klyver, Steven Le Blanc, Daniela Moneta, and Kim Walters; the Stanford University Libraries, Special Collections, Polly Armstrong, Margaret Kimball, and Patricia White; the University of Nevada, Reno (UNR) Getchell Library, the staffs of the Interlibrary Loan, Reference and Special Collections departments have been graciously and enthusiastically helpful for many years; a collective thanks to all of them. At UNR, Office Managers Ella Kleiner, Susan Rodriguez, and Marion (Bonnie) Salter over the years have, with aplomb and amused good humor, managed me, my travels, research accounts, and schedules, and aided immeasurably in the production of this book. Numerous research assistants have helped with library and bibliography tasks, especially Alyce Branigan (who deserves special thanks for her excellent help with illustrations), Angela Christensen, Julie Tipps, and Heather Van Wormer.

Many individuals have contributed information, ideas, and encouragement including Richard Ahlstrom, Todd Bostwick, David Brugge, Catherine Cameron, Christopher Chippindale, Carol Condie, Linda Cordell, B. Sunday Eiselt, Robert C. Euler, Richard I. Ford, Douglas R. Givens, Daniel Goodwin, Curtis M. Hinsley, Ira Jacknis, Thomas W. Kavanaugh, Alice Beck Kehoe, Carl Kuttruff, Steven Lekson, R. Lee Lyman, William Longacre, Donald McVickers, Betty J. Meggers, William Merrill, Stephen Nash, David M. Pendergast, Peter Pilles, Jonathan Reyman, Jeremy A. Sabloff, Michael B. Schiffer, Brenda Shears, James E. Snead, William C. Sturtevant, Raymond H. Thompson, Elisabeth Tooker, Neal L. Trubowitz, Gwinn Vivian, Dorothy K. Washburn,

Patty Jo Watson, David R. Wilcox, Stephen Williams, Nathalie F. S. Woodbury, Richard Woodbury, Barton Wright, and Ezra Zubrow.

At the Smithsonian Institution, the late Clifford Evans, John C. Ewers, and Waldo and Mildred Wedel were mentors and kindly critics who stimulated my interest in the history of the Institution and those who carried out James Smithson's mandate to "increase and diffuse knowledge." Through the good offices of Betty Meggers and Clifford Evans I was privileged to know the late Neil M. Judd, and talk with him about his Southwest, and archaeological sites he had seen in the 1910s and 1920s and I in the 1960s.

Many others contributed ideas, suggestions, and help; to all my general thanks. Needless to say, all the sins of ommission and commission herein are mine alone.

Carol Condie, Nancy J. Parezo, and David Hurst Thomas read versions of the manuscript and gave me much useful and insightful advice and criticism for which I'm especially grateful. Special thanks to Durwood Ball, of the University of New Mexico Press, for his excellent advice and help throughout the process of making this into a book. Equally special thanks to Amy Elder and Floyce Alexander for helping me turn my turgid prose into more or less respectable English, to Nancy Ford for the index, and to Dawn Hall and B. Williams & Associates for making such a handsome book. Particular thanks to Patty DeBunch for drafting the maps. My gratitude is also to David R. Wilcox, whose knowledge of Southwestern archaeology and its history is unparalleled and with whom I've most profitably shared and argued ideas over the years.

This book is for Kay Fowler. Our personal lives and professional careers have been intertwined with the Southwest, and we would not have missed any of it. We both owe special thanks to Carol Condie, M. Kent Stout, and Rosemary Talley, whose friendship and gracious hospitality know no bounds, and who have made the Southwest a special place for us.

The Land and the People

The Land

In 1884, Charles Fletcher Lummis walked from Chilicothe, Ohio, through the Southwest to Los Angeles to become the city editor of the *Los Angeles Times*. During his "tramp across the continent," Lummis became greatly enamored of the Southwest. He devoted the next four decades to touting its scenery, its archaeological ruins, and its native peoples. He was the first Anglo to define "the Southwest" (Map 1) in the general anthropological sense it is used herein.[1]

The line Lummis drew was an impressionistic one, derived from his sense of cultural characteristics; it included the general area defined by the Spanish crown in 1776 as the "Interior Provinces" of Mexico. In 1951, archaeologist Erik Reed defined a "Greater Southwest," extending roughly from "Durango [Mexico] to Durango [Colorado] and from Las Vegas [New Mexico] to Las Vegas [Nevada]." Mexican scholars refer to the region as the "Greater Northwest," the "Mexican American West," or the "Gran Chichimeca," as seen from Mexico City and the perspective of the preconquest civilizations of Mesoamerica.[2]

Portions of two physiographic provinces lie within the Southwest (Map 2). The first is the Colorado Plateau, a 390,000 sq. km. area of sedimentary geological formations with an elevation generally above 1,250 meters, deeply dissected by the Colorado River and its tributaries. The plateau is dotted by various features of volcanic origin, such as Navajo Mountain, the San Francisco peaks, and Ship Rock.[3]

South and west of the Colorado Plateau lie portions of the Basin and Range province characterized by block-fault mountain ranges and intervening alluvial-filled valleys, or basins. To the east are the San Juan and Sangre de Cristo ranges of the Southern Rocky Mountains. The Continental Divide meanders across the region, dividing the waters of the Rio Grande and the Colorado. East of the Sangre de Cristos are the High Plains. The Pecos River heads in the

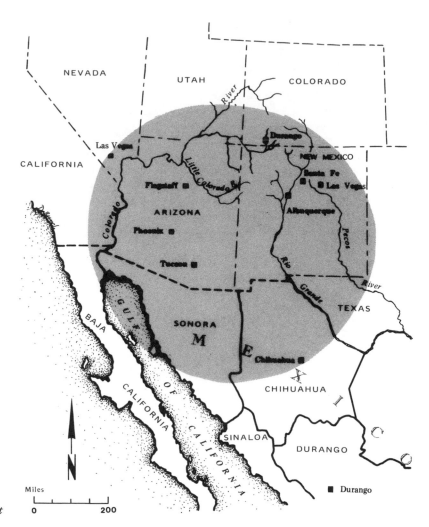

1. The Anthropological Southwest

southern end of the Sangre de Cristos, flowing ultimately into the Rio Grande in west Texas.

The Southwest is divided ecologically into a High Desert province centered on the Colorado Plateau and Low Desert (Sonoran and Mohavian) provinces, each with characteristic xerophytic floras. Annual precipitation varies from scant to some, giving the region an "arid to semi-arid" climate. Short- and long-term climatic change is characteristic and has deeply influenced the fluctuating distributions of plants, animals, and humans across the landscape over time.

"Mounds" and "Ruins"

The first Anglo reports on New Mexico in 1806 (see Chapter 1), and all subsequent reports, noted the thousands of "mounds" or "ruins" dotting the landscape. They were sources of great mystery and became focal points for investigation beginning in 1846. The first Spanish description was in 1694 by Father Eusebio Kino of the "Casa Grande" ruins south of present-day Phoenix, Arizona. Many descriptions and much speculation about the ruins was to follow.

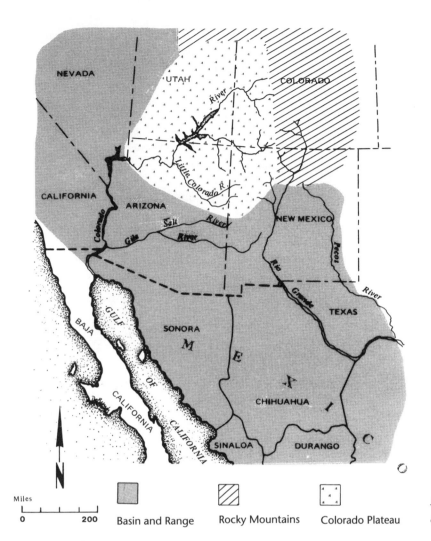

NEVADA

UTAH

COLORADO

River

CALIFORNIA

ARIZONA

Little Colorado R.

NEW MEXICO

Colorado

Gila

Salt

River

River

Rio

Pecos

BAJA

GULF

Grande

TEXAS

River

SONORA

M

OF

E

CALIFORNIA

X

CHIHUAHUA

I

CALIFORNIA

C

SINALOA

DURANGO

O

Miles

0   200

Basin and Range   Rocky Mountains   Colorado Plateau

2. Major Physiographic Provinces of the Southwest

Pre-Spanish Demographics

The number of Indian people living in the Southwest, or for that matter in North America, just prior to the Spanish *entrada* is simply unknown. Estimates vary wildly, with none rooted in any sort of demonstrable demographic data, as David Henige has shown. The matter is complicated due to the introduction and spread of Old World diseases after 1492. Some demographers assert that many Indian populations in Mexico and northward were reduced or decimated long before the survivors ever saw a European, but the evidence is ambiguous.[4] For post-Spanish demographics, see Table 3.

Historic Indian Populations

By 1846 most of the Indian groups in the Southwest occupied what are now regarded as their "traditional" territories, those in which Anglo observers from 1806 to 1860 saw, described, and mapped them (Map 3). Both Spanish and Anglo observers distinguished

Table 1[5]   Pueblo Languages and Dialects

I. **Uto-Aztecan**
   Hopi
II. **Zunian**
   Zuni
III. **Keresan**
   Acoma-Laguna (Western Keresan)
   Rio Grande Keresan (Eastern Keresan) (Zia, Santa Ana, San Felipe, Santo Domingo, Cochiti)
IV. **Tanoan**
   Towa: Jemez (Jemez and Pecos)
   Tiwa: Northern Tiwa (Taos and Picuris), Southern Tiwa (Isleta and Sandia)
   Tewa: Rio Grande Tewa (San Juan, Santa Clara, San Ildefonso, Pojoaque, Nambe, and Tesuque) and Tano (Arizona Tewa)

Table 2[6]   Non-Puebloan Languages and Dialects

I. **Apachean**
   Western Apachean: Navajo, Western Apache (Tonto, Cibeque, San Carlos, and White Mountain), Mescalero-Chiricahua
   Eastern Apachean: Jicarilla, Lipan, Kiowa Apache
II. **Yuman**
   Pai: Paipai, Upland Yuman (Havasupai, Walapai, Yavapai)
   River Yuman: Mohave, Quechan, Maricopa (Maricopa, Kavelchadom, Halchidhoma)
   Delta-California: Diegueño (Northern, Southern, and Mexican Diegueño); Cocopa (Cocopa, Halyikwamai, Kahwan)
III. **Uto-Aztecan**
   Southern Numic: Ute (Chemehuevi, Southern Paiute, Ute)
   Tepiman: Upper Piman (Pima, Papago [Tohono O'odham], Névome), Lower (Mountain) Piman (Yepachi, Yécora-Maycoba), Northern Tepehuan, Southern Tepehuan
   Tarahumaran: Tarahumara, Guarijío
   Optan: Opata, Eudeve, Cahitan (Yaqui and Mayo)

between the Pueblo and the "wild," or nomadic groups.

Southwestern Pueblos are divided by anthropologists into "Eastern Pueblos," along the Rio Grande and its tributaries, and "Western Pueblos:" Laguna, Acoma, Zuni, and the Hopi villages, including the Hopi-Tewa village of Hano. Pueblo peoples speak languages of four widely divergent language families (Table 1).

In 1540, there were over one hundred pueblos along the Rio Grande, and a dozen or more to the east on the edge of the High Plains. By 1846, there were about twenty pueblos along the Rio Grande and none to the east (Map 3). In 1540 there were six or seven Zuni villages (sources vary); by 1846, there was one. The Hopi lived in at least seven villages, most on terraces below the three mesas. After the Pueblo Revolt of the 1680 (see below) the Hopi moved their villages to the defensible mesa tops, where Father Garcés, in 1776, and later Anglo observers encountered them.

Other Tribal Groups

The major non-Pueblo Indian groups in the Southwest are the Apacheans, the Yumans, and the Pimans (Table 2).

The Apacheans

There are six Apachean-speaking tribal clusters: Navajo, Western Apache, Mescalero-Chiricahua, Jicarilla, Lipan, and Kiowa-Apache, with the latter two centered in the Southern Great Plains. Apachean is related to the Athapaskan-Eyak languages of Alaska and northwestern Canada. The Apacheans seemingly were late arrivals in the Southwest, perhaps only a few decades before the Spanish. The derivation of the word *Apache* is uncertain. Ongoing hostilities and Apache mobility led to a confusing proliferation of Apachean band names during both Spanish and Anglo times.[7]

By the early 1700s, the Spanish distinguished between "Apaches del Nabaxu," or "Apaches of the Fields," and other Apachean groups. The "Nabaxu," or Navajo, were then concentrated in the Gobernador

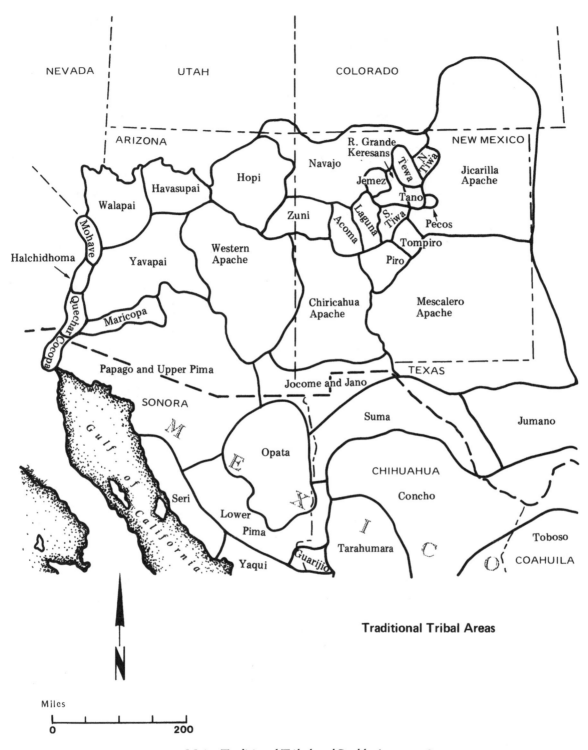

NEVADA   UTAH   COLORADO

ARIZONA   NEW MEXICO

Walapai

Havasupai

Hopi

Navajo

R. Grande
Keresans

Tewa

N. Tiwa

Jicarilla
Apache

Jemez

Zuni

Tano

Halchidhoma

Mohave

Yavapai

Western
Apache

Laguna

Acoma

S. Tiwa

Pecos

Tompiro

Piro

Quechan

Cocopa

Maricopa

Chiricahua
Apache

Mescalero
Apache

Papago and Upper Pima

Jocome and Jano

TEXAS

SONORA

M

E

X

I

C

O

Gulf of California

Opata

Suma

Jumano

CHIHUAHUA

Concho

Seri

Lower
Pima

Tarahumara

Toboso

COAHUILA

Yaqui

Guarijio

N

Traditional Tribal Areas

Miles

0   200

3. Major Traditional Tribal and Pueblo Areas ca. 1850

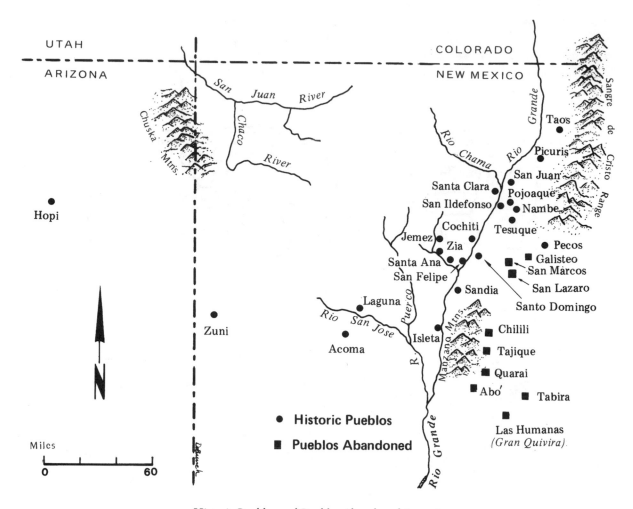

4. Historic Pueblos and Pueblos Abandoned Late 1600s

region of northern New Mexico (Map 3). This region is *Dinetah,* the traditional homeland of the Diné, the Navajo people.[8]

Navajos spread west as far as the Grand Canyon by the early 1700s. Contacts with Pueblos and Spanish led them to become part-time farmers, as well as sheepherders and weavers. They became famous for the blankets that were widely traded to the Spanish and to other Indians. Prince Maximilian, the German naturalist, collected one from a Blackfeet man on the Upper Missouri River in 1834.[9]

"Pimas Altos"

The Indian peoples centered in the Gila River drainage were called by the Spanish, "Pimas Altos," the Upper Pimas, to distinguish them from the Pimas Bajos, the Lower Pimas, in present-day lower Sonora.[10] The Spanish distinguished between Pima ("River People") and Papago ("Desert People"). The latter now call themselves Tohono O'odham. The Pimas along the Gila River were farmers. For a variety of reasons, they managed to escape domination by the

Spanish. At the same time, they added European wheat and livestock and became strong middlemen and traders. They also developed an effective military organization to combat the Apaches. Early Anglo army officers greatly admired the Pimas for their well-provisioned and maintained villages and their business acumen.

The Yumans

Yuman-speaking peoples centered in present-day northwestern Arizona and along the lower Colorado River.[11] The River Yumans (the Cocopa, the Quechan, or Yuma, and the Mohave), were along the lower Colorado and Gila rivers. The Maricopa were centered along the Middle Gila (Map 3). Endemic warfare led to movement and merger of some groups. The River Yumans were farmers, growing crops on the floodplains of the lower Colorado, supplemented by wild plants and game.

The sparse populations of the Upland Yumans, the Walapai, Havasupai, and Yavapai, were located in present-day northwestern Arizona. The Havasupai farmed in the summer in remote Havasu Canyon, a tributary of the Grand Canyon. In the winter they foraged on the Coconino Plateau along the south rim of the Grand Canyon. The Walapai and Yavapai were hunter gatherers ranging south of the Havasupai (Map 3).

The Numic Peoples

Finally, there were various Southern Numic groups, speakers of one language of the tripartite Numic branch of the Uto-Aztecan language family.[12] Known historically as Southern Paiute and Southern Ute, they were hunter gatherers living in the southern Great Basin, the northern reaches of the Colorado Plateau, and throughout the Southern Rocky Mountains. With the advent of horses (see below), some Southern Utes moved into the mountains north of the Rio Grande and the San Juan valleys.

The Advent of Horses

The Spanish brought many new artifacts, technological processes, plants, and animals with them. All had major impacts on Indian peoples, but none more so than horses. The cultural, economic, military, and demographic impacts of the spread of horses on North American Indian groups were immense.[13] The Spanish tried hard to keep both horses and guns out of Indian hands. They were more successful with guns than horses. By the 1640s, some Apaches east of the Rio Grande were using horses to hunt and raid. Horses spread rapidly after the Pueblo Revolt of 1680 and transformed Plains Indian cultures and those of the adjacent Rocky Mountain and Columbia Plateau tribes. The Apaches, Navajos, Comanches, Kiowa-Apaches, Utes, and others within and adjacent to the Southwest all became horse users during the late seventeenth century. Horses were used in hunting, transport, and raiding the Hispanic and Pueblo settlements of New Mexico, northern Mexico, and Texas. Indians also raided each other, as well as non–horse using Indians such as the Southern Paiutes, for captives to be sold as slaves to the Spanish in New Mexico and later in California.

Spain in the New World

The Spanish who came to the Southwest beginning in 1540 brought a very long tradition of military and spiritual conquest.[14] The reconquest to drive the "Moors," the adherents of Islam and its brilliant civilization, from Iberia had ended only in 1492, after seven hundred years. The Spain of 1540 was a society led by land-based *hidalgos*, strongman coercion specialists, who had organized armies and led the reconquest, often under contract with regional rulers, sharing the booty and using it to subsidize further warfare. Wealth was crucial to social advancement: hereditary titles and lands, hence noble status, were granted by the crown to those who brought wealth to the kingdom. The split was often 90/10 for crown and hidalgo.

Once ennobled, it took much wealth to keep up with the Cortés and Mendozas.

Thus from the very beginning in the New World, a central Spanish concern was wealth. It was said that the Spanish "lusted" for gold. In 1519, the emissaries of Moctezuma, ruler of the Aztecs, met Cortés and his men at the pass leading into the Valley of Mexico and laid before them

> golden streamers, quetzal feather streamers, and golden necklaces. . . . The [Spanish] appeared to smile, to rejoice exceedingly, and to take great pleasure. Like monkeys they seized upon the gold. It was as if then they were satisfied, sated, and gladdened. For in truth they thirsted mightily for gold; they stuffed themselves with it, and starved and lusted for it like pigs.[15]

By 1521, the Spanish had conquered the Aztecs and soon after, the Incas in South America. Both had gold aplenty, by the ton. The gold of the Antilles and the great wealth of the Aztec and Inca empires spurred the Spanish on—if in those places, why not elsewhere? In South America, they sought in vain for El Dorado, the kingdom of the Golden Man, the empire of the Amazon women, and the Enchanted City of the Caesars. In Mexico, they pushed northward into the "Gran Chichimeca," the vaguely defined "barbarian" area beyond the sphere of Aztec influence (Map 5). Others chased chimerical "Seven Golden Cities" across "Florida"—the present-day southeastern United States.[16]

One disastrous expedition to peninsular Florida, led by Panfilo de Narváez, started in Spain in 1527 with several ships and six hundred people. It ended in 1536 when the sole survivors, Alvar Núñez Cabeza de Vaca, Alonso de Castillo, Andrés Dorantés, and the latter's black slave, Estéban, wandered into Culiacán, in northwestern New Spain, after an incredible sojourn of perilous journeys in makeshift boats along the Gulf Coast, captivity by Texas Indians, and a long trek across Texas and northern Mexico. They were soon in Mexico City telling the viceroy, Antonio de Mendoza, their story, which included rumors of "seven cities" in the far northern reaches of the Gran Chichimeca.[17]

In 1539, Mendoza purchased Estéban from Dorantés and sent him to guide the Franciscan Fray Marcos de Niza in search of the seven cities. By the time the party came to the Gila River, Estéban had pressed on ahead, collecting an entourage as he went. He reached Zuni and was killed by the inhabitants. Fray Marcos got to the Zuni area, possibly saw the Zuni villages from a distance, then turned and fled southward after claiming "Cibola"—the Zuni villages and the territory around them—for the Spanish crown.[18]

Back in Mexico City, Marcos's experiences grew as they were told and retold by others. An expedition to the "Province of Cibola" seemed warranted. Mendoza chose Francisco Vásquez de Coronado to lead it.[19] With Coronado went a number of "gentlemen" cavaliers—high born but otherwise unemployed soldiers of fortune—plus foot soldiers and nearly one thousand Indian and Black servants, together with a remuda of one thousand horses and hundreds of pack mules. Marcos de Niza acted as a chaplain and guide.

In midsummer 1540, Coronado and the vanguard of his expedition arrived half-starved at one of the Zuni pueblos, either Hawikuh or Kiakima. To their utter disgust they found a terraced, multistory stone and adobe pueblo, rather than one of the seven wealthy "cities of Cibola." They also found some three hundred very angry Zuni warriors and were soon engaged in pitched battle; in the end, the Spanish prevailed, and hungrily plundered the foodstores of the Zuni. The long and complex relationship between Hispanic and Indian peoples of the Southwest had begun. It would continue for three centuries, in an atmosphere of fear, conflict, and cross-cultural misunderstanding.

Coronado consolidated his hold on Cíbola. He sent Captain Pedro de Továr to investigate the "Province of Tusayan." Továr found the Hopi, but no wealthy cities. The Hopi told him of a great river to the west. Coronado sent Captain Lopez de Cárdenas to investigate. He and his men reached the south rim of the Grand Canyon and tried to climb down to the river, but could not. Meanwhile, Coronado moved his party to the Province of Tiguex—the Rio Grande pueblos—for the winter. There was intermittent conflict, marked by numerous atrocities against the Indian people.

The Search for Quivira

The Spanish were lured onto the High Plains in 1541, seeking the rumored wealth of the Province of Quivira. They encountered vast herds of bison, as well as hunter-gatherer Querechos, probably Apaches. Coronado and thirty-six soldiers finally reached Quivira, somewhere in central Kansas. They found numerous grass houses, but a singular lack of great cities or precious metals. The bitterly disappointed men returned to Tiguex, and the following year, trailed back to Mexico in disgrace.

Between 1542 and 1590, the Spanish slowly pushed farther and farther north into the Gran Chichimeca, finding some gold and silver. They were followed by the Franciscans and, after 1589, by the Jesuits. The native peoples fiercely resisted attempts to subjugate them. To cope, the Spanish developed a pattern of territorial expansion, pacification, and control using soldiers and priests. The presidio and the mission were successfully used for the next two centuries.[20]

Back to "New Mexico"

With missions and presidios established on the northern frontier, the Spanish once again began looking toward the Rio Grande Valley, which in the 1580s was called "Nuevo México." The first permanent settlers, led by Juan de Oñate, arrived in the Rio Grande Valley in July 1598. Missions were quickly established and strict control extended over the Pueblos. In 1610, the year Santa Fe was founded, New Mexico became a royal colony, with Pedro de Peralta as governor. The colony's principal purpose was to save souls for the glory of the Spanish Catholic Church.[21] The Franciscans were to do the saving. There were no diocesan

priests, and no bishop. The royal governor was administrator, legislator, and judge. But friars and the governors came into deep conflict over control of Indian labor, lands, and tribute. The Indians, caught between the two, suffered. The friars sought to suppress the indigenous religions by various means; in response, the Pueblos took their religious practices underground. The Spanish governors often were rapacious, since whatever wealth they gained in New Mexico had to come from the land and the Indians. To the Pueblos, the result was the same: increasingly intolerable oppression.

By 1680, the Pueblos had had enough; they rose in concert, killing some 380 Spaniards and 21 friars, and driving the rest to El Paso. Spanish buildings and artifacts were destroyed, especially the missions and churches. The Pueblos tried to erase all traces of Spanish hegemony: crops, language, Spanish ways of doing things. Kivas were rebuilt, and the kachinas danced again in the plazas of the pueblos.[22]

But it did not last. In early 1691, Don Diego José de Vargas was appointed governor of New Mexico and took command of the miserable exile community at El Paso. Between 1692 and 1696, Vargas reestablished Spanish control of New Mexico by diplomacy, duplicity, and classic divide-and-conquer tactics. Some Rio Grande Pueblos fled west to Acoma, to the Navajos, or to the Apaches. A group from Tano in the Galisteo Basin, probably from San Cristóbal and San Lázaro (Map 4), fled to the Hopi on First Mesa, where, as the Hopi Tewa, their descendants remain at the village of Hano.[23]

By the end of 1696 there was uneasy peace. The Franciscans reestablished themselves among the pueblos, except at Hopi. The Hopi village of Awatovi had welcomed the friars back. But other Hopi would not permit the reintroduction of Christianity and all that it meant. In the winter of 1700–1701, the other Hopi attacked Awatovi and, legend says, killed the men, captured the women and children, and distributed them among the other villages. All further attempts at Spanish intrusion into the Hopi world were successfully resisted.[24]

5. *Northern Provinces of New Spain, ca. 1750*

Eighteenth-Century New Mexico

Eighteenth-century New Mexico (Map 5) was a place of almost constant misery and discord.[25] The Pueblos were, as before, caught between the civil and ecclesiastical authorities; both wanted labor and tribute. The latter also wanted souls and demanded renunciation of "pagan idolatry"; as before, the Pueblos took their religion underground. Spanish and Mexican-Indian settlers trickled up from the south and encroached on traditional Pueblo lands. But the dominant problems for Pueblo and Spaniard alike after 1700 were created by the mounted nomadic tribes. For the latter, the dominant problems were the Spanish, and sometimes their Pueblo auxiliaries. All parties engaged in slave raiding and trading. The "market forces" driving the raiding were the labor requirements of the Hispanic haciendas and villages.

Raiding and pillaging increased in tempo and severity throughout the eighteenth century.[26] The nomadic groups regarded the settlements as provisioning points, sources of food, clothing, tools and utensils, livestock, and human captives. They rarely stole all the livestock, or all the food, or took a whole village captive. They simply "harvested" some of each periodically; "root stock" was left to be further harvested another time. From the villagers' perspective, of course, the process amounted to an endemic reign of terror and deprivation.

In 1763, Spain acquired the Louisiana Territory, vastly enlarging the "Interior Provinces of New Spain," an ungovernable area of several hundred thousand square miles from the Mississippi to the Pacific. The Spanish were faced with continuing warfare on the Plains and in New Mexico, potential threats from the British *cum* Yanquis across the Mississippi and the Russians pushing down the Pacific Coast from Alaska.[27]

In New Mexico, the raiding and killing went on, and on. There was a kind of peace after about 1775 with the Comanches. By 1800, Hispanics were raiding Navajos for slaves and the Navajos were retaliating both by taking slaves and raiding villages. The Apache simply conducted their raiding-harvesting business as usual. It did not end until the 1860s, when the Navajo were finally corralled, literally, by Kit Carson and his militia in the Bosque Redondo; until the 1870s, when the Comanches and other Plains tribes were finally settled in Indian Territory; and until the 1880s, when the Apaches were at last subdued.

The Hispanic Population

When Anglos arrived in 1821 to open the Santa Fe trade, there were perhaps twenty-nine thousand culturally Hispanic occupants of the Province of Nuevo México; by 1846 there may have been fifty thousand. The Hispanic population was never very large until about 1800 (Table 3). There was nothing approaching an accurate census until 1749; earlier figures are simply guesses. Estimates of Pueblo Indian populations were often wildly high, inflated by the Franciscans as propaganda to generate support from the Spanish crown for their missionary activities: the more souls ostensibly saved or to be saved, the more pesos.

The Province of Nuevo México (Map 5) in actuality was essentially the drainage basin of the Rio Grande from its headwaters to El Paso. The Hispanic settlements, as elsewhere in the Gran Chichimeca, formed small islands of governmental control amid vast expanses of land sparsely populated by part-time farmers and hunter gatherers.[28] Along the Rio Grande most of the Spanish haciendas and people lived in Rio Abajo, from Socorro to La Bajada Hill, where the Rio Grande Valley is broad and the sheep industry was most developed. The region northward to Taos was called Rio Arriba with settlements along the Rio Grande and Rio Chama, and in the high country to the east and northeast.

The principal economic base was sheep and weaving, although large-scale sheepherding began only late in the eighteenth century.[30] Since the New Mexicans had little other than animal hides, piñon nuts, and salt that could be sent to Mexico to earn cash or to trade for finished goods, woolen textiles were very important. Information on early textile production is sparse, but by 1638 some nineteen hundred *varas* (a vara is approximately a meter) of coarse woolen fabric were exported yearly from Santa Fe to Chihuahua. Sometime during the eighteenth century, the Navajos began herding sheep and weaving. They adopted the upright loom of their Pueblo neighbors, and women (rather than men, as among the Pueblos) became the weavers. By the beginning of the nineteenth century, Navajo blankets were famous and widely traded.

The Jesuits in the Southwest

Spanish colonization of Pimería Alta, Baja California, and, ultimately, Alta California followed a somewhat different course than in the Rio Grande Valley, due to the nature of the country, proximity to the Pacific Ocean, and European geopolitics. After 1591, the principal agents of expansion were Jesuit missionaries, aided by soldiers—symbolized by the presidio and mission.[31]

In 1540, Pope Paul III approved the constitution of the Society of Jesus, with its founder, Ignatius of Loyola, as "General." "Society" was used in a Spanish sense of "military company." The Jesuits saw themselves as the elite troops of the Church Militant. They recruited from the upper ranks of European society: well-born, well-connected, bright, and energetic young men. Their academic and spiritual training was rigorous and long. They vowed poverty, chastity, obedience, and ultimate loyalty only to the pope. Their aims were education, conversion of the heathen in foreign missions, and "reconquering" Protestant Europe for Catholicism.

Table 3[29] **New Mexico Population Estimates, 1600–1850**

	Spanish	Pueblo
1600	700	80,000
1609	60	——
1620	200	17,000
1638	800	40,000
1680	1,470	17,000
1749	4,353	10,568*
1800	19,276	9,732*
1820	28,436	9,923*
1842	46,988	16,510*

* Does not include the Hopi.

From the outset, the Jesuits were a power in intra-Catholic politics, as well as European and Eurocolonial politics, diplomacy, and foreign affairs. Ultimately, they were accused of a great international conspiracy to dominate the world and the Society was suppressed between 1759 and 1767.[32] Jesuits arrived in Mexico in 1572, serving first as teachers. In 1591 they began their mission activities on the Northwest frontier, slowly establishing a tightly organized and closely controlled chain of missions northward into Sinaloa and Sonora. Their ranches and farms produced surpluses to support new endeavors on the expanding frontier.

Father Eusebio Kino, a highly educated native of the Tyrol, arrived in Sonora in 1685 and founded a mission, Nuestra Señora de los Dolores, his base of operations for the next quarter-century.[33] To the northwest lay Pimería Alta, as Kino would name it. Kino ranged widely throughout Pimería Alta, exploring and establishing missions and cattle ranches to feed both missionaries and Indians. In 1694 he was joined by Juan Matheo Manje.[34] Manje was the crown's representative and accompanied Kino on many of his explorations between 1694 and 1701. Kino made over forty trips into and across Pimería Alta, often traveling immense distances in a twenty-four-hour day. Both Kino and Manje kept diaries of their expeditions and produced numerous reports.

In late 1694, Kino visited Casa Grande; both he and Manje were there again in 1697:

> The *casa grande* is a four-story building, as large as a castle. . . . It is said that the ancestors of Montezuma deserted and depopulated it . . . and left for the east or Casas Grandes, and that from there they turned towards the south and southwest, finally founding the great city and court of Mexico. Close to this *casa grande* there are . . . the ruins of many others, which make it evident that in ancient times there had been a city here. . . . further to the east, north and west there are seven or eight more of these large old houses and the ruins of whole cities, with many broken metates and jars, charcoal, etc. These cer-

tainly must be the Seven Cities mentioned by the holy man, Fray Marcos de Niza.[35]

Spanish historians in the eighteenth century used Kino and Manje's reports extensively. They seemed to validate the "common knowledge" of the time about prehistoric population movements and the relation of Southwestern ruins to the Aztecs or Toltecs (see Chapter 2). Kino continued his missionary and ranching labors until his death in 1711. His importance to the Southwest is symbolized by the state of Arizona placing a statue of him in the Hall of Statuary in the United States Capitol.

After Kino's death the Jesuits continued to operate the missions he had established. Some, such as Jacobo Sedelmayr, Ignaz Pfefferkorn, and Juan Nentvig, traveled widely over the country, and left reports of their activities and descriptions of various Indian tribes.[36]

The Franciscans in Pimería Alta

When the Jesuits were expelled in 1767, they were quickly gathered together and sent to Mexico City and finally to Europe. Their "missionary empire" in Sonora and Baja California lay abandoned. They were replaced by the Franciscans, who faced exceedingly difficult tasks, particularly in those areas most subject to Apache raids; but the Franciscans held on for nearly eighty years. They produced a lasting monument in Arizona, the church and *convento* at San Xavier del Bac, begun in 1777. It remains as the most striking example of New World Spanish Baroque architecture in the United States, and continues to delight the eye, especially after a restoration in the 1980s.[37]

Garcés and Alta California

The final surge of Spanish exploration was stimulated by the geopolitical reshuffling after 1763 and Russian expansion down the Pacific Coast. To thwart the Russians, in 1769–70, Spain sent settlers and missionaries into Alta California to occupy San Diego and Monterey, under the direction of Fray Junípero Serra and

Governor Gaspar de Portolá. In late 1773, the commander of Tubac presidio, Juan Bautista de Anzá, and Fray Francisco Garcés, based at San Xavier del Bac, quickly established an overland supply route to California. Like Kino, Garcés had traveled widely over the northern frontier since his arrival in 1768.[38]

Anzá was next assigned the task of leading a group of settlers to San Francisco Bay. Garcés accompanied the Anzá party to the Colorado River, then turned north up the Valley of the Colorado, where he met Mohaves and Chemehuevi. After crossing the Mojave Desert to California to visit San Gabriel and the Central Valley, he returned, crossed the Colorado, and started eastward south of Grand Canyon, where he encountered various groups of Yavapai and Hualapai and visited the Havasupai.[39]

On July 2, 1776, Garcés reached the Hopi village of Oraibi on Third Mesa. He was rebuffed and left to camp in the street. A Spanish-speaking Zuni man entreated him to return to Zuni with his party; Garcés refused. On July 4, 1776, a group of rebellious English colonists were concerned with a particularly important document in the Old State House in Philadelphia. Some two thousand miles to the southwest, a large crowd of irate Hopi Indians, dressed in traditional ceremonial regalia, forced Father Garcés out of Oraibi after he had witnessed part of a ceremony.[40]

Learning from the Zuni man that Fray Silvestre de Escalante was at the Zuni mission, Garcés sent a letter to him describing the routes he and Anzá had found to California. He finally returned to San Xavier del Bac, having covered over two thousand miles. Garcés continued his peripatetic missionizing on the frontier for five more years. But in July 1781 he won the martyr's crown; he and three companions were killed by Indians on the lower Colorado River.[41]

Domínguez and Escalante

In addition to an overland route from Sonora to California, Spanish officials wanted a route connecting New Mexico and California. The first effort in that direction was taken by a young Spanish-born Franciscan

recently stationed at Zuni Pueblo, Fray Silvestre Vélez de Escalante, together with Fray Atanasio Domínguez, who was in New Mexico as a canonical visitor investigating the conditions and problems of the missions. Domínguez was, seemingly, a perfectionist. His massive report on the missions of New Mexico was thorough, highly critical, and earned him the deep enmity of many local friars and officials. He received the standard bureaucratic treatment given, then as now, to whistle blowers: his report was buried in "the files" and he was assigned to a series of hardship posts as chaplain at remote presidios. Sometime before 1805 he died, an embittered man.[42]

But in the latter half of 1776 Domínguez and Escalante made the journey for which they are principally remembered, seeking an overland route to Monterey from New Mexico. Based on scant information from Spanish traders, the friars thought they should travel through present-day Colorado, Utah, and Nevada. The entire region was *terra incognita,* at least officially, and largely in fact. Just before they were to leave, Domínguez and Escalante received the letter from Garcés, telling of his route from California to the Hopi mesas.[43] But they set out anyway; the more data on potential routes, the better. They took along a local man, Bernardo Miera y Pacheco, whose map of the region traversed would be important for the next seven decades.

Their route took them through southwestern Colorado, across the Uintah Basin in eastern Utah and on into Utah Valley. From there they turned south along the Wasatch Front. But by September they decided that the lateness of the year precluded a journey westward to Monterey. Instead they turned south, finally found a way across the Colorado in Glen Canyon, at the famed "Crossing of the Fathers," and arrived at the Hopi mesas in mid-November 1776. They were given a civil reception, and were able to buy some desperately needed food supplies. They arrived "extremely cold" and "extremely exhausted" at Zuni on November 24, 1776.[44] Unlike Domínguez's mission report, Escalante's diary and Miera's map became important documents for Spanish planners. Escalante, always in poor health, finally set out for Mexico City to recuperate. He died en route at Parral in April 1780.

Even though Domínguez and Escalante did not find their way to California from New Mexico, others soon did. A branch of the "Old Spanish Trail" followed their route to about present-day Cedar City, Utah, then turned southwestward to Las Vegas, across the Mojave Desert, and through the San Bernardino Mountains into California. For over seventy-five years, pack-train caravans passed over the trail, as did Spanish and Indian slave raiders.[45] After 1847 the portion of the trail from Utah Valley southwestward became a major emigrant trail and wagon road— roughly the route of present-day Interstate 15.

The Province of New Mexico was the "uttermost" portion of the Spanish empire, far away indeed from Seville and Madrid, its administrative and power centers, and from Mexico City, the nerve center of New Spain. Don Diego de Vargas, who led the Reconquest of New Mexico in 1692, summed it up neatly. From El Paso del Río del Norte, he wrote to his son-in-law, "I could have done no more than to have exiled myself to this kingdom, at the ends of the earth and remote beyond compare." The Spanish Borderlands historian Herbert Bolton called Father Kino's Pimería Alta the "Rim of Christendom." Both phrases convey the geographical and intellectual distances as seen from the centers of the Spanish world. For three centuries in faraway New Mexico, life for both Indian and Hispanic people was extremely difficult, full of "misery and discord," full of conflict wrought by the desperate need to survive. Out of it came a unique set of cultures, which the Anglos encountered after 1805 and more fully after 1846.[46]

Origins of American Anthropology

ANTHROPOLOGY IS concerned with how humans came to be, and with their *commensurability*—how and why they are alike and different in their physical makeups, psyches, languages, societies, and cultures. Anthropologists know that all cultural traditions have a cosmology, sets of taken-for-granted assumptions—sometimes called "principles of order"—about the origin of the universe, and the nature of the beings, things, and processes within it. All known cosmologies account for the origin(s) of humans, their perceived differences, and the nature of those differences. In other words, they contain an "anthropology." All anthropologies account for differences between males and females; most account for differences between "our group" and "others," however defined. Most cultures have stories, either as parts of an origin myth, or as legends about peoples' migrations from place to place, that tell when, how, and where they acquired their technologies, religions, or other social and cultural practices.

What does all this have to do with the development of American anthropology in the Southwest? Well, everything. Contemporary European and American anthropology is rooted in the cosmological anthropologies of the so-called Western cultural tradition. The specific concerns of American anthropology grew out of five centuries of speculation and inquiry about the commensurability and culture histories of "indigenous" peoples in the Western hemisphere. After 1846, many of these questions were posed, and answers attempted, in the Southwest. To understand the form the questions took, and what constituted "acceptable" answers, requires a brief review of some Western intellectual history. The premise is, to paraphrase Aristotle, "She who sees things from the beginning will have the best view of them."

"In the Beginning, All the World Was America"

Christopher Columbus died believing he had found the "Indies." Others soon concluded he had encountered a "New World." It was a troublesome place, filled with previously unknown plants, animals, and peoples. The immediate questions were: how had the people come there, and from whence; what were their *origins*? And are they commensurable with Europeans? Thus, from the start, in European and Eurocolonial discussions of this "New World," two major anthropological questions were posed: commensurability, and culture history.

Origins of the "Indians"

The "Indians" were a puzzle. Neither biblical nor classical sources provided any clear answers as to their origins. They were said to derive from nearly every national or ethnic group known in Europe, Asia, the Pacific isles, and Africa, or from the "Ten Lost Tribes" of biblical Israel, or Alexander's lost fleet, or those who managed to abandon the sinking continent of Atlantis for the Antilles, or all of the above. There was much speculation as to routes and means of travel, ranging from ships to angelic assistance. The more sober-minded, such as Joseph de Acosta in 1590, thought the route must have been by way of some as-yet undiscovered land bridge.[1]

Europeans had long known of the legends of the bejeweled kingdom of Prester John, said to be far to the east, perhaps near a great queendom of Amazon women; hairy wild men were said to live in the forests near fabled peoples such as the Blemmyae, with faces in their chests, and the dog-headed Cynocephali. All these fabled folk lived on the edges of the (Old) World, at least in European imaginations.[2] There were tales of Iberians fleeing westward across the Atlantic from the Moors, and a host of related stories about "golden cities." After 1492, these legendary creatures, kingdoms, and places were said to be in the Western Hemisphere, and searches were made for them.[3]

The questions of origins and the timing of migration(s) from Eurasia to the Western Hemisphere were of more than academic interest. European international law held that ownership of a "heathen land" fell to the country whose representatives first "took posses-

sion of it" in the name of their sovereign. Hence, any assertion that Indians might be derived from a European nation had geopolitical implications.[4]

Like the matter of prior discovery, the issue of commensurability of Indian peoples vis-à-vis Europeans was deadly serious. Between the 1550s and 1580s, Spanish savants engaged in a great debate as to whether the Indians were "fully human," or bestial, or "natural slaves." If they were seen as less than human, that might somehow justify the cruelty, enslavement, and ethnocide visited upon them by conquistadors and missionaries. The British engaged in similar sophistry in the 1600s and 1700s.[5]

The Guises of Natural Man

In his excellent survey of Indian-White relations, Robert Berkhofer wrote: "For most Whites throughout the past five centuries, the Indian of imagination and ideology has been as real, perhaps more real, than the Native American of actual existence and contact."[6] In North America, the Indian of French and British imagination and ideology was "natural man," draped in various "savage" stereotypical guises, which we shall call "ignoble savage," "*le Bon Sauvage*" ("noble savage"), "vanishing savage," "analogical savage," and "managed savage." These images became very important in European and American political philosophy, anthropology, and popular culture and were carried into the American Southwest after 1846.[7]

From whence natural man and his guises? In the 1930s the intellectual historian Arthur Lovejoy defined an "old and deep" complex of beliefs in Western thought he called "primitivism"—that is, widely held beliefs by discontented members of "highly evolved, complex" societies that the optimal human condition, the "good, simple life," existed either in the distant past, or exists among contemporary "primitives:" savages, peasants, or lower-class "folk." These beliefs are tied to one of the "most potent and persistent" ideas in Western thought, that "nature" provides the ultimate standard of goodness and source of human morality. *Good* equals that which is "natural," "according to nature," and "authentic." Since early humans lived in "a state of nature," they were good. As humans became "civilized," they became corrupt, artificial, inauthentic. Contemporary "primitives" living closer to nature are ipso facto inherently good, more "in tune with" the good of their "natural environment." They are seen as the original deep ecologists.[8]

It somehow follows that to study, appreciate, merely to be around, any group of "authentic" people, however labeled—folk, primitives, natives, savages, or indigenes—is to share in their "natural inherent goodness." *By association,* one is somehow cleansed of the corrupt artificialities and discontents of civilization. If there are no authentics available, one can become a pretend natural by "playing Indian," in many formats from Boy Scouts and Campfire Girls to visiting the powwow circuit. Or one can sing folk songs, or hang out with "those who work with their hands."[9]

The idea that "native peoples" are both "authentic" and "naturally good" was and is a major reason for Anglo interest in and study of Indian, and sometimes Hispanic, peoples of the Southwest. Anglo yearners and some anthropologists "found" in Southwestern native peoples the "naturalness" they sought. Yearners, in particular, came to the Southwest to "learn about themselves" by painting or writing about, or just hanging around, the "natural others." All hoped for palliation by proximity.

But how and when were the guises of natural man created? They began with the advent of French and English settlement in North America. The French came to engage in the fur trade. They learned Indian languages and married Indian women. The Jesuits came in 1632. They too learned the local languages and tried to gather the Indians into settlements similar to the theocratic *reductions* their fellow Jesuits later established in South America, Mexico, and Baja California.[10]

Between 1632 and 1674 the Jesuits published annual reports in France on their missionary activities. These *Jesuit Relations* were primarily "truthful propaganda" designed to solicit financial and political support. A constant theme was *le Bon Sauvage,* living

morally and justly in an idyllic natural world, echoing themes earlier established in French letters by Michel Montaigne's essays on Brazilian Indians.[11] Those who attended Jesuit schools or knew of the work in New France heard endlessly about the good savages and their wondrous world. The image of the *noble savage,* which figured so prominently in eighteenth-century French social philosophy, was basically formed by Jesuit propaganda and pedagogy.[12] Verbal images were strengthened by published illustrations. However they were described, the Indians often looked like Greek gods and goddesses in the pictures.[13]

Things were very different in the English colonies.[14] There, families came to settle as farmers and planters. The natural landscape, the forest, was a feared "howling wilderness" to be cleared, planted, dominated, and civilized as soon as possible. In general, "natural man *in* nature" was a pejorative notion and the derivative stereotypes were negative. The Indian peoples of Virginia, Massachusetts, New York, Carolina, and Georgia colonies, who were battling for their lives and their lands, were seen as bad guys—ignoble savages. The sooner they "vanished," one way or another, the better. Those who remained had to be managed, placed out of the way on reservations, to be Christianized and taught simple trades so they might be of some economic use. The basic principles of United States Indian policy from 1780 to 1934 were formulated in Massachusetts Bay Colony in the 1600s.[15] So too were the images of "the Indian" seen as Ignoble Savage, Vanishing Savage, and Managed Savage.

Natural Man on Stage

Stereotypes of Indians were also formed in popular culture, travel literature, novels, and short stories. Even more pervasive were images formed in theatrical productions, pageants, galas, masques, and plays. By 1502 there were several hundred Indians in Europe, primarily slaves; they were also exhibited from time to time and drew eager crowds. Real and pretend Brazilian Indians appeared in pageants at Rouen in 1547 and

Bourdeaux in 1565.[16] Stereotypical Indians began to appear on the English stage by the time of William Shakespeare's *The Tempest* of 1611, featuring the "savage and deformed" Caliban, based on reports about Indians from Jamestown in Virginia.[17]

By John Dryden's time in the 1670s, Noble and Ignoble Savages, and a character Eugene Jones calls the "Pathetic Dusky Heroine"—the Indian woman who loves or helps White males, but always is tragically betrayed or killed—were stock characters on the English stage. It was Dryden who coined the phrase "noble savage," in his 1672 play *The Conquest of Granada,* when the character Alamanzor asserts his personal freedom and rejects an imposed death sentence:

> No man has more contempt than I, of breath;
> But whence hast thou the right to give me death?
> Obey'd as Sovereign by thy subjects be,
> But know that I alone am King of me.
> I am as free as Nature first made man
> 'Ere the base Laws of Servitude began
> When wild in the woods the noble Savage ran.[18]

Dryden first introduced his Indian characters in 1664, in the heroic tragedy *The Indian Queen,* wherein noble, ignoble, and pathetic heroine savages move through a convoluted plot filled with love, honor, and death during a major pre-Columbian war between the Incas and the Aztecs! Dryden used Indian characters in later plays performed for many years on the London stage.[19]

The noble, ignoble, and pathetic heroine characters were frequently seen in eighteenth-century French and British satires and tragedies, and in nineteenth-century melodramas in the United States. They then segued into Wild West shows and pageants at world's fairs after 1870 and finally into the movies. But, as William Turnbaugh points out, the appeal of these characters, especially the noble and heroine characters, "usually was in a rough inverse relationship to the proximity in space or time between [the characters] . . . and his or her staunchest admirers. The most es-

timable Indians consistently appeared just beyond the frontier line or were recalled from a respectable distance in the past."[20]

Savages in the Service of Political Philosophy

By the 1600s, "natural man" began to appear in treatises on political philosophy. Most authors took a historical approach, tracing their version of the development of human society from the "first ages" of the world onward. The first was the Dutch legalist Hugo Grotius in the 1620s, followed by Thomas Hobbes in the 1650s, and John Locke and others in the 1670s and 1680s. Later, in France, there was the work of Montesquieu, beginning with the *Persian Letters* in 1721 and *The Spirit of the Laws* two decades later, and followed by a host of others.[21] In eighteenth-century Britain, there were the "Scottish moralists," Adam Smith, Adam Ferguson, John Millar, and others. All agreed that humanity first existed in a natural state. There was consensus that New World peoples were analogues of, or surrogates for, that state, hence John Locke's (1632–1704) famous phrase "in the beginning all the World was *America,*" and later, "America . . . is still a Pattern of the first Ages in Asia and Europe."[22]

Since British writers centrally influenced the thinking of nineteenth-century European and American anthropologists, a review of their major ideas is needed.[23] First was the idea of the Commons—humans living close to nature and holding property in common, or "primitive communism." Second, either by ratiocination or from an innate impulse, some humans by their industry begin to convert portions of the commons to private property. Third, private property gives rise to civil society, the accumulation of wealth, and the development of money. Fourth, ultimately some ideal form of government will arise: an enlightened monarchy, according to some; an elected representative government according to Locke.

In general, the state of nature and natural man was not good. Thomas Hobbes, in *Leviathan* (1651), famously and sourly describes the "Naturall Condition of Mankind" as a "state of Warre," lacking all that is estimable in civilized life, farming, architecture, geography, arts, letters,

> and which is worst of all, continuall feare, and danger of violent Death; And life of man, solitary, poore, nasty, brutish, and short.
>
> It may peradventure be thought, there never was such a time, nor condition of warre as this; . . . but there are many places, where they live so now. For the savage people . . . of *America,* except the government of small Families, the concord whereof dependeth on naturall lust, have no government at all; and live at this day in that brutish manner.[24]

John Locke, writing in 1683, held that those who had moved beyond the state of nature and developed a civil society with a money economy were the ones to make proper use of the Commons.[25] Locke is remembered as the doyen of natural law and natural rights in the formation of representative government. But he was also in the entourage of the Earl of Shaftesbury, who was much involved in the colonization of the Carolinas. Locke owned four thousand estates of land in the Carolina charter colony.[26] Hence, part of his concern in his *Treatises on Government* was to justify colonization.

Thus, "in the beginning all the world was America," and the first humans had natural rights to the Commons. But if they did not convert the Commons to private property through agriculture and a money economy, they had no continuing rights in them. In the real America, it was somehow "naturally right" for others to take the Commons and develop them.[27] Locke simply reified practices already in place in Virginia, Massachusetts Bay, and other colonies. The argument would continue to be made by Anglos throughout the eighteenth and nineteenth centuries all across North America. By 1846, when the United States "Army of the West" marched into the plaza of Santa Fe, the argument was called "Manifest Destiny."

Enlightenment Anthropology

Some major roots of modern anthropology lie in the Enlightenment era, usually dated from 1637 to about 1800.[28] The intellectual hallmark of the Enlightenment is the application of reason through the scientific method to investigate the universe. It is assumed that knowledge is ever-expanding, and knowledge production an open, cooperative enterprise subject to ongoing public scrutiny. The purpose of science is to investigate the things, beings, processes, and relationships within the universe and to discover the natural laws governing their operation.[29]

Absolute Time and Literal History

As Enlightenment science developed, there was a parallel development of world history. Intellectual historians Frank Manuel and Donald Wilcox have cogently discussed the "invention" of world history during the Enlightenment.[30] By "invention" they mean the expansion of history beyond the confines of Europe and the political doings of its rulers. They also mean the development of a universal time scale and the periodization of named "epochs" or "eras," with assumed specific cultural features, such as the familiar Classical, Dark Ages, Middle Ages, and Age of Discovery.

A key difference between Catholic and Protestant theology, especially in the sixteenth and seventeenth centuries, was the Protestant belief in the literal truth of the Bible and the history chronicled therein. Ever since Augustine, Catholics had seen biblical history as largely allegorical and metaphorical. Whether literal or allegorical, history occurs in time. An important part of the quantification of reality during the Enlightenment was the invention of "absolute" linear time. In some cosmologies, such as those of Hinduism, time is seen as circular, recursive, folding back upon itself. In Judeo-Christian cosmologies time "began" with the creation of the universe; it will continue unidirectionally ("time's arrow") until "the end," after which there will be the timeless forever of eternity. But a concept of generic, unmarked, ever-ongoing linear time is different than a periodized scale along an "absolute" time line, on which agreed-upon chronometric and epochal markers can be hung. Dates *anno Domini* (A.D.) were introduced in 525 by Dionysius Exiguus (Dennis the Short) and the B.C. sequence by Petavius in 1627, but the B.C./A.D. scale was not generally adopted until Isaac Newton's *Chronology* of 1728. The B.C./A.D. scale extends both backward and forward infinitely from the "zero" of the division point. It allows one to "quantify the relationship between any two events with . . . precision . . . and express this precision with a single number," something no other chronology had done. Newton linked the scale to astronomical "absolute, true and mathematical time," as he called it in his *Principia Mathematica* of 1686, and wove it integrally into his cosmology. Linear time was taken for granted until Einstein's theory of relativity. It is still taken for granted in the "historical sciences" of geology, paleontology, evolutionary ecology, and archaeology, and hence is of central concern to our story.[31]

For Protestant historians, an accurate chronology was a crucial issue: *how much* time before "now" had there been for human history assuming that the Bible is literally, not allegorically, true? Several subsidiary assumptions were made. One, the Bible is the most authentic history in the world; two, the kingdom of Israel was the first large-scale political society with all the trappings of civilization; three, all other civilizations *derived from* Israel.[32]

To demonstrate these assumptions it was necessary to establish an *accurate historical chronology,* since naysayers held that Egypt and China were earlier than, and culturally superior to, Israel. (We need to recall here that the civilizations of Mesopotamia before the "Babylonia" of the Bible had been totally forgotten.) Others said that Greece and Rome were of much higher achievement than Israel. The civilizations and cultures of the New World were of unknown age. If they were older than, or even contemporaneous with, biblical Israel, the whole assumption of biblical truth was threatened. The stakes were high.

The first step, a chronology of world history since the creation, was provided by James Ussher (1581–1656), the Anglican Archbishop of Armagh in Ireland, a leading antiquarian, and one of the great scholars and bibliophiles of his time. The chronology was contained in his *Annals of the World; Deduced from the Origin of Time . . .* , a 907-page magnum opus first published in Latin between 1650 and 1654. It has been called "one of the greatest ancient histories of its era, an opus of dumbfounding erudition," and now totally forgotten. Ussher concluded that the world was created and time began on the evening of October 22, 4004 B.C. Subsequently, a Cambridge University scholar, Dr. John Lightfoot, slightly amended Ussher by placing the creation and the beginning of time on October 23, 4004 B.C., at 9:00 A.M.[33] In 1701, Ussher's chronology (sometimes with Lightfoot's amendment) began to be printed in the margins of the authorized (King James) version of the English Bible. It continues to be printed in some Bibles. Since Ussher's chronology is "in the Bible," it too has come to be regarded as literally true by fundamentalist Protestants.

Given an established chronology, the next task was to *synchronize* the events of Egyptian, Assyrian, Babylonian, Persian, Greek, and Roman annals with the chronology of biblical history in order to demonstrate that Israel was the founding civilization. Isaac Newton worked for forty years on this task, finally producing his *Chronology . . .* in 1728. He used every device he could, from mathematics to astronomy, to misinterpreting historical documents and fudging data, to distort and twist world culture history into the Ussherian chronology and make ancient Israel out to be the basic world civilization from which all others were derived.[34] But despite Newton's efforts and his great prestige as a founding genius of the Enlightenment, others remained unconvinced—guided as they were, like Newton, by the light of their own reason. They read the evidence differently and found the tasks of chronology building and establishing cultural-historical connections very difficult.

In the eighteenth and nineteenth centuries, as the

writing of world history became secularized, the concerns with chronology and intercultural connections remained; tying it all to biblical Israel fell by the wayside. The importance of Newton's work was not his erroneous *Chronology,* but his linking of linear time to astronomical time, thus creating an "absolute" scale on which historical chronologies could be hung—histories of the universe, of the earth, of life, and of human societies.

In the later eighteenth century the practice of dividing the past into named periods, stages, eras, or epochs and stringing them along the now-agreed-upon time line became increasingly common. The practice soon spilled over into the nascent field of archaeology, giving us, for example, Old Stone Age, New Stone Age, Bronze Age, etc., as well as the Eras, Epochs and Periods of historical geology and paleontology.[35]

By 1800 it seemed to some geologists who were of a "uniformitarian" bent, such as James Hutton, that Ussher's chronology was far too short to allow for the geological processes they observed. An untold number of eons were required. Once Darwinian evolution appeared in the 1850s, "deep time" seemed even more important to allow the processes of organic evolution to do their work. Time and chronology were central research questions in organic evolution, paleontology, historical geology, astronomy, and archaeology throughout the nineteenth and on into the twentieth centuries.[36]

As we will see, time and chronology were very important in North American archaeology throughout the nineteenth and twentieth centuries. Deep time issues centered on the "origins" question: when had people first entered the New World? In the Southwest, building chronologies and linking them to absolute time was the central concern of the "new archaeologists" of the 1910s and 1920s, as were attempts to establish connections between prehistoric cultures. Though they were not aware of it, Southwesternists were applying methods used by Sir Isaac Newton for similar, yet very different purposes.

The Savage and the Comparative Method

One of the burning issues of the Enlightenment, both for those concerned with some sort of moral reform of contemporary society and for those seeking to justify the status quo, was the question of "original" human nature.[37] It made a great deal of difference to moral philosophers whether early humans and the lives they lived were "originally" good or bad, as we saw in our quick glance at Hobbes, Locke, and others. As the civilizations of China and India, and especially their highly complex religions, became understood in Europe, concern shifted to the nature of "original" religion. The issue, once again, was critical to Protestant fundamentalists. What was the "original" religion like? How to account for apparent religious aberrations, such as paganism and polytheism? Enlightenment deists, such as Voltaire, tended to argue that early humans were polytheists, and only as reason developed did (some) humans progress to Christianity. Isaac Newton argued that polytheism, all savage religions, classical Greco-Roman pagan religions, and "wrong Christianity," that is Catholicism, resulted from people falling into "idolatry," and forgetting the *original true religion* of the premier civilization of Israel.

While many could understand how non-Europeans might fall into religious error, how could such superior beings as the European ancients do so? The answer might lie in determining what ancient European religions and societies were "really" like. This brings us back to our old friend "Natural Man," now in the guise of "Analogical Savage." John Locke's phrase "In the beginning all was America" implied that original humans were like, *or analogous to,* American Indians. In 1724, the analogical savage took stage center in Joseph-Francois Lafitau's monumental *Customs of the American Indians.*[38] Lafitau was a Jesuit missionary in New France for several years. He saw the religious and other practices of the Iroquois of northeastern America as direct *analogues* of the practices of "the Ancients" of the Old World, in effect saying, "as they are now, so our ancestors once were." Other works followed, seeing living savages, as Bernard McGrane points out, as analogues for *both* generic natural men *and* the European ancients: "In a complex, obscure and confusing modification, the *savage* was mixed with the *ancients* (pagans and Jews) to became the *primitive*. The savage took on the value and the status of *representing* the ancients."[39]

This conflation had several results. First, it downgraded classical Greeks from the pinnacle of civilization to the status of rude barbarians. Second, it led to the general idea of "psychic unity"—*that all human minds are basically the same everywhere and every-when*. Third, and for our purposes of central importance, it firmly fixed the equation of living "savages" with *original, or first, humans*. Thus, living savage peoples, especially those who were foragers or hunter gatherers, came to be seen as *proxy primitives,* where "primitive" equals "original." A close study of the lifeways of living savages, it was thought, would provide insights into the "origins" of all forms of social and cultural practices *by analogy.* Histories of social and cultural practices could be formed by *comparing* them cross-culturally and through time. The analogical savage and the "comparative method" became basic tools of modernist anthropology.[40]

A "Science of Man"

Since the Enlightenment was the "age of science," there was an attempt to create a "science of man," based on a chain of assumptions which said: if humans are part of the natural world, and the natural world is governed by natural laws, then the laws governing human behavior *ought to be* discoverable. Or put another way, the "unknown causes" of human behavior are potentially knowable through scientific investigation. In the rarefied atmosphere of the Enlightenment the prospects were heady: if the natural law processes/causes "governing" or "driving" human behavior could be ascertained, then human behavior could be "truly" understood—and once understood, predicted.

In France, the quest for a science of man took on a moral tone as social philosophers, from Montesquieu to Rousseau to Condorcet and Chavannes, sought to reform a corrupt French society through reason and science. If laws of human behavior could be formulated, and morally worthy commonalities derived therefrom, both might be used to reform society and make it "good." Enter morally good natural man. And who is natural man? Why, *le bon sauvage* of New France, created by the Jesuits in the 1600s, now seen as the moral archetype by Rousseau and others in the 1700s.[41] Additional *bon sauvages* were found inhabiting the idyllic South Sea isles, as described by Bougainville and Cook; they too became analogical savages.[42] All were studied in search of the "original" moral human nature.

Although the French sought much among analogical savages, they did not find "original" human nature, nor did they achieve social reform through reason. But they began the search for an inductive anthropology based on the premise that "to know humanity we must know all humans." That is, we must know the range of variability of humans and human behavior in order to achieve any real understanding of commensurability.

Finally, the French Enlightenment philosophers are good examples of Arthur Lovejoy's "discontented members of highly evolved, complex societies," who sought goodness and morality of natural man in the guise of the noble savage. Their quest did much to keep the image of the noble savage alive within European and Eurocolonial culture.

A "science of man," or "science of society," continued to be a desideratum pursued by those in the 1800s and 1900s who developed the "social sciences" —economics, sociology, political science, psychology, anthropology, and their various auxiliaries. Despite this extended pursuit, no "laws" comparable to those in physics or chemistry have yet appeared, although the quest continues.

From Four Stages to Three

By the 1760s many of the strands we have been following were brought together in the works of various

European political economists, especially the "Scottish moralists" Adam Ferguson and John Millar.[43] Both saw humanity as passing through four stages of development: 1) hunters/fishers; 2) pastoralism; 3) agriculture; 4) commerce, or civilization. Both agreed that American Indians were the exemplars of stage 1. Both thought that some Indians had passed from stage 1 to stage 3, recognizing that, except in South America, there were no domesticated herd animals.

Ferguson first asserts the idea of psychic unity; given that, he notes that peoples with the same mode of subsistence in the same general environment will have similar social forms, institutions, and ideas. But what is the *change mechanism*? What *causes* social and cultural change? For Ferguson, as for Hobbes and Locke, it is the development of private property. Humans, says Ferguson, have an *innate propensity* to acquire and accumulate private property, and as they do so, they move from one stage of society to another.

John Millar agreed: the "natural impulse to create and accumulate property" leads to commerce, wealth, social ranking, and legal systems; wealth leads to "science and literature, the natural offspring of ease and affluence." There is a "natural progress" from the stage of savagery to the stage of civilization. Cultural variability is the result of "various accidental causes," which cause differing and "peculiar manners" that are carried down through time. "This appears to have occasioned some of the chief varieties which take place in the maxims and customs of nations equally civilized."[44]

The four-stage theories of Ferguson, Millar, and others are the lineal ancestors of nineteenth-century three-stage schemes of human cultural development: savagery, barbarism, and civilization, usually with subdivisions. They are important *because they propose a process or mechanism of social and cultural change*; all subsequent developmental schemes have done likewise. They all assume the operation of "natural laws" in some form: the universal unfolding of reason through stages of mind (for example, Hegel and Auguste Comte); the operation of a cosmic evolutionary "force" of progress (for example, Herbert Spencer); the universal unfolding of innate "germs of thought" (for example, Lewis Henry Morgan); the dialectical operation of material processes (for example, Karl Marx and the multitudes of Marxist camp followers); cultural-ecological interactions (for example, Julian Steward); expressions of genetically controlled behavior (for example sociobiologists, such as E. O. Wilson); synergistic and cybernetic interactions of nature, humans and machines (for example, George Dyson); and such imponderables as inventive genius, free will, and God's will.[45]

Finally, the Act One stars of all these schemes are the analogical savages. Nineteenth-century anthropologists studied them avidly, seeking in their behavior "the origins" of social and cultural customs of all sorts, from religion to the family. In the twentieth century, renamed "hunter gatherers," they are still studied by those seeking clues, "ethnographic analogies," to interpret archaeological finds and spin theories about the origins and processes of protohuman and early human behavior.[46]

Beginnings of American Anthropology

The image of Indian people in the British colonies of North America was essentially negative—the ignoble savage. The colonials' view in the 1600s was that Indians should vanish, by whatever means were required. Most did; some, however, remained. Pious Puritans felt obliged to convert the remaining few to Christianity and to move them aside. The reservation system was instituted soon after the Puritans reached Massachusetts, thus creating another stereotype, the *managed savage*.[47]

Out of the conversion efforts came the first studies of Indian languages. A basic fundamentalist Protestant tenet was that everyone should be able to read the Bible in their own language. Hence, learning Indian languages was a necessary step to translating the Bible so that potential converts could read it for themselves or have it read to them. There were several Bible translations, some catechisms, psalters, and related religious materials, by John Eliot and others in the 1660s and 1670s. There was also Roger Williams's *A Key into the Language of America . . .* , published in 1643, which contains valuable linguistic and ethnographic data, especially on the Narraganset Indians.[48] While Puritans felt a Christian duty to "convert the heathen," there was little thought of studying Indian languages and cultures for broader intellectual purposes. That came a century later.

Eighteenth-century colonial Americans—Benjamin Franklin, David Rittenhouse, Benjamin Rush, Thomas Jefferson, and many others—were actively involved in Enlightenment science. Following European precedent, they formed volunteer scholarly societies to advance their interests. Franklin was a moving force behind the creation of the American Philosophical Society in 1743 (and its resuscitation in 1769), just as John Adams was of the American Academy of Arts and Sciences in Boston in 1780.[49]

Early American anthropological studies emerged in the context of the scholarly societies after about 1770, and were focused on Indian peoples. "Gentlemen scholars," government officials, and missionaries all had reasons to study the Indians and their cultures and languages. There was still the matter of commensurability. The famed French naturalist Georges Louis Leclerc, Comte de Buffon, and his apologist, Cornelius de Pauw, asserted that New World environments, plants, animals, and native peoples were "weak," and "immature" vis-à-vis those of the Old World. This "Dispute of the New World," as it has been called, was a major stimulus for Thomas Jefferson's *Notes on Virginia* and Clavigero's *History.* The pointless dispute finally petered out about 1900, apparently from terminal boredom.[50]

While American Enlightenment scholars generally agreed that Indian people were fully human and in no way inferior to Europeans, they also found them rapidly vanishing, as had their forebears. "Civilization or death to all American Savages" was a common theme throughout the nineteenth century.[51]

But this dwindling database posed problems for inductively oriented scholars who wanted as large a sample of human variation as possible. Natural man, as *vanishing savage,* took on additional meanings. Laments that Indians and other native peoples were disappearing before their languages and cultures were properly recorded became a theme that echoed through nineteenth- and twentieth-century American anthropology.

Origins Revisited

The question of the origins of Indian peoples was still unresolved in the 1770s. By then the problem was one of "hard" evidence. Comparative studies of languages seemed to be an answer. The idea of language "families," comprised of "mother" languages with descendant "daughter" languages, had long been known, for example, in the case of Latin and its Romance-language descendants, Italian, Spanish, French, and so on. The discovery of Sanskrit and the formulation of the Indo-European language family, including the Romance and Germanic languages among others, gave further credence to the concept.[52] By the 1770s scholars in Europe were busily collecting word lists worldwide and comparing them for cognates in attempts to develop a comprehensive "genetic" classification of world languages. The assumption of common origin and later divergence within a language family had important implications for tracing historical origins and migrations of peoples in both the Old World and New World. This brings us to Thomas Jefferson's research agenda.

Jefferson's Research Agenda

Thomas Jefferson actively studied American Indians. He thought that they would vanish and tried to see to it that their languages and cultures were recorded beforehand.[53] But he was also interested in developing knowledge of the Indians for diplomatic and management purposes as the nascent United States expanded to fulfill his vision of westward empire. Treating with and managing the Indians would require ethnographic, linguistic, and demographic information about them. Hence, as in much he did, Jefferson had both intellectual and practical reasons to encourage and support studies of Indians. In his attempts to put Indian languages and cultures "on the record," Jefferson set much of the research agenda for American anthropology for the next century and more. He did so in concert with his fellow members of the American Philosophical Society (APS).[54]

By the late 1700s, it was clear that there were several hundred Indian tribes in North America. A central problem was how to establish some sort of standardized *classification* of the tribes. What criterion should be used as the basis for such an ordering? The most likely was a genetic language classification, which also offered a potential resolution of the origins question. In his *Notes on Virginia,* Jefferson called for the collection and systematic comparisons of standardized vocabulary lists of all Indian languages spoken in North and South America so that a genetic classification could be developed. Such information "would furnish opportunities to those skilled in the languages of the old world to compare them with the new, and hence to construct the best evidence of the derivation of this part of the human race."[55]

Benjamin Smith Barton made such an attempt in 1797, in his *New Views of the Origin of the Tribes and Nations of America,* but it was unsuccessful.[56] Part of his problem was the lack of lists of comparable words. The use of Jefferson's standardized lexicons or vocabulary lists was already common practice in Europe. Jefferson circulated his own printed list in the 1790s, which included words for body parts, numbers, simple astronomical and meteorological phenomena, etc.[57] He collected much information, unfortunately later lost. Thus, the first items on Jefferson's agenda were the development of a comprehensive classification of Indian languages and a resolution of the origins question. American scholars continued to pursue this agenda throughout the nineteenth century, including in the Southwest.

As Euroamericans began spilling across the Appalachians in the late eighteenth century, they encountered in the Ohio and Mississippi valleys thousands of "mysterious" burial mounds and enormous

earthen structures of the "Mound Builders."[58] But "who were the Mound Builders, and where had they gone, and when?" How did those complex works relate to the origins question? Did the ancestors of the current Indians build the "mounds," or had some other people(s) done so? Jefferson's second contribution to the agenda of American anthropology was to help initiate systematic archaeological studies of the "mounds." There was a small burial mound on one of Jefferson's properties. He had it excavated, noted the stratigraphic layers therein, described the artifacts it contained, and presented a straightforward report on his findings, together with some hypotheses about the mound's content, in his *Notes on Virginia.*[59] This is often regarded as the first scientific "site report" in American archaeology.

In 1799 Jefferson and his colleagues in the APS distributed a *Circular* which, together with Jefferson's discussions in his *Notes on Virginia,* are regarded as "charters" for American anthropology. The circular called for systematic compilations of linguistic, ethnographic, and historical data relating to the Indians, and the collection of archaeological data including maps, plans, and detailed verbal descriptions.[60] Over the next four decades, various interested persons collected such data as they could and deposited them with the APS or the American Antiquarian Society.

The APS and Indian Languages

The APS continued to be a focal point for Indian language studies until the 1840s. Indian languages were of particular interest to several APS members, including Jefferson, Barton, Peter Stephen Du Ponceau, and Albert Gallatin. They and others pursued the collection of vocabularies and grammatical data toward a systematic classification. Du Ponceau's 1838 memoir on the Delaware and Onondaga languages was a major contribution. There, he noted that "the general character of the American languages is that they unite a large number of ideas under the form of a single word, what American philologists call *polysynthetic languages.*" He went on to assert that all languages, "from Greenland to Chile," are of the polysynthetic form. The implications of Du Ponceau's statement were still being explored by linguists at the end of the twentieth century.[61]

But the collection of linguistic data was seriously hampered by problems of orthography. Indian languages contain sounds and sound combinations not heard in European languages. How should those sounds be represented orthographically? Every student of Indian languages struggled with the problem. In 1820, John Pickering developed an orthography that was widely used, although it was not entirely satisfactory.[62]

A further question remained. Was the comparison of word lists adequate to determine genetic connections? Or should grammatical structures be compared?[63] Whatever position was taken, throughout the nineteenth century lexicons were the principal forms of data collected, as a matter of simple expediency. An adequate understanding of the grammar of a language requires sophisticated training and a high degree of knowledge of the language. Most vocabularies were collected by soldiers, traders, Indian agents, and missionaries who had little, if any, linguistic background, but could readily collect more or less useful lists of words. The accuracy of the lists varied greatly; but such information was better than nothing.

Lewis and Clark

Jefferson's final contribution to the development of American anthropology was the set of instructions he provided to Lewis and Clark. Even before the acquisition of Louisiana Territory, Jefferson had planned an expedition to "stake a claim" in the West before the British could do so. With Louisiana in hand and Lewis and Clark signed on to explore it, Jefferson saw an opportunity to collect a wide range of information about its geography, natural history, and Indian inhabitants for both scientific and management purposes. At its inception in 1660, the Royal Society of London, the first modern scholarly society, developed "heads of inquiry"—detailed questionnaires sent with

those going to foreign climes. The society and its counterparts on the Continent continued the practice for the great government-sponsored voyages of exploration, such as Captain Cook's, sent out by Britain, France, Holland, and Spain in the mid-1700s.[64] Jefferson and his colleagues followed suit: they drew up a detailed list of questions and sent them with Lewis and Clark, who answered them in detail in their journals and reports.[65]

Providing detailed questions became standard practice for all subsequent federally sponsored parties of exploration to the West. In 1818, an APS committee, headed by Peter Du Ponceau, drew up extensive instructions for Lt. Stephen Long's expedition to the Rocky Mountains. Long also employed naturalists and artists to help collect information, thus continuing the practice of the European voyagers, and setting a precedent for future U.S. exploration. The Wilkes naval expedition to the Pacific in 1838–42 was also guided by lists of questions drawn up by an APS committee.[66]

Albert Gallatin

By 1820, work toward a linguistic classification of American Indian languages was well under way. After Jefferson and Du Ponceau, the leader of Indian language studies was the venerable Albert Gallatin (1761–1849) (Fig. In.1). In the 1780s, as a young man newly arrived in Maine from Switzerland, he knew some Abenaki and other Indians and learned much traditional knowledge from them. He later had some contact with Miami and Shawnee people in the upper Ohio Valley. His acquaintance with Jefferson quickened his interests and led to further studies of Indians, sandwiched in between his duties as a congressman, Secretary of the Treasury under both Jefferson and Madison, U.S. minister plenipotentiary in negotiating the end of the War of 1812, and later U.S. minister to France and England.[67]

In 1823, following his return from France, Gallatin began systematically working on a "synopsis" of Indian tribes, collecting vocabulary lists through various

In.1. Albert Gallatin, 1843, by William H. Powell. Courtesy of the New-York Historical Society.

The American Ethnological Society

The American Antiquarian Society was the first "anthropological" scholarly society in North America. In 1842 Albert Gallatin and others founded the American Ethnological Society, with Gallatin serving as its first president. In a March 17, 1846, letter to W. C. Marcy, Secretary of War, Gallatin wrote that "the modern appellation 'Ethnological' has been substituted for that of 'Antiquarian.' Its seat is at New York; that of the American Antiquarian Society is at Worcester, Massachusetts; the object of both is the same."[71] Gallatin, then in his eighties, settled in New York City in 1840 as a banker after his long and illustrious career of public service. There, he became doyen of a group interested in American Indians and archaeology. Members of the group often met informally at Bartlett and Welford's Bookstore in the Astor House, across the street from P. T. Barnum's famed museum. The group included Gallatin; Henry Rowe Schoolcraft (Fig. In.2); E. G. Squier; John Russell Bartlett (Fig. In.3); John Lloyd Stephens, famous for his travel books on the Middle East and Middle America; artist John Mix Stanley; and literary figures such as Edgar Allan Poe.[72]

The Ethnological Society met around Gallatin's dinner table. He also paid the costs of publishing the first two volumes of the Society's *Transactions* and contributed two major papers to them. The breadth of the group's interest can be gauged by Bartlett's "Progress of Ethnology" paper in the series reviewing the current state of ethnological knowledge worldwide.[73] We shall meet Bartlett again later.

The term *ethnology* seemingly was first used in 1787–88, by the French scholar Alexandre André Chavannes, to mean roughly "the history of human progress in civilization." In 1841 a French group interested in questions relating to the abolition of slavery and amelioration of abuses of colonial peoples formed the Société d'Ethnologie de Paris. The group redefined ethnology as "the study of human races," and emphasized the "place" of each race in the larger scheme of things.[74] The society issued a field manual based on a remarkable ethnographic inquiry written in

channels. Pulling together all published and manuscript sources, Gallatin published his famous *Synopsis of North American Indian Languages* in 1836 through the American Antiquarian Society. It became the standard classification of American Indian language, superseded only by the Powell classification in 1891.[68]

The American Antiquarian Society was founded in 1812 by Isaiah Thomas and located at Worcester, Massachusetts. Its "immediate and peculiar design . . . [was] to discover the antiquities of our own continent . . . natural, artificial and literary."[69] The first two volumes of the Society's *Transactions* contain several papers speculating on the origins of American Indians. Besides Gallatin's *Synopsis,* there is the first systematic description, with maps, by Caleb Atwater, a resident of Circleville, Ohio, of a number of the great Hopewellian (as they are now called) earthworks of the Ohio Valley.[70]

In.2. Henry Rowe Schoolcraft, ca. 1850.
Courtesy of the Library of Congress.

In.3. John Russell Bartlett, ca. 1855; engraving by J. C. Buttre.
Courtesy of the Rhode Island Historical Society.

1799–1800 by Joseph-Marie Degérando for a French expedition to the Pacific. Degérando insisted that observers should learn native languages and live with the people for extended periods in what would later be called "participant observation."[75] Not to be outdone, the British formed an Ethnological Society of London in 1842; Gallatin and his compatriots created the American Ethnological Society the same year.

The constitution of the American society states that "the objects of this Society shall comprise inquiries into the origin, progress, and characteristics of the various races of man."[76] These were loaded words in the context of the time. Complex issues relating to African slavery, forced-labor practices in the South Pacific, the brutal treatment of other native peoples, including American Indians, were roiling in France, Britain, and the United States. The old issue of commensurability was again center stage as Euro-

peans and Eurocolonials wrestled with the ongoing problem of somehow morally and ethically justifying the exploitation of lands and peoples, especially slavery, as they increased the size of the bottom line on their corporate ledgers. In all this, "race" was the key term.

Whatever "racial" issues may have been discussed around Albert Gallatin's dinner table, or in the easy setting of Bartlett and Welford's bookstore, the publications of the American Ethnological Society centered on Indian culture history and languages. Gallatin published two major papers in the series on the "semi-civilizations" of Mexico and New Mexico (see Chapter 2). After Gallatin's death in 1849, the Society became quiescent; it was revived briefly in the 1870s under a different name, fell moribund again, and was finally revived in the early 1900s and, with some fits and starts, has continued since.

Inquiries and Synonymies

Degérando's was the first systematic anthropological field manual in 1800. The first detailed ethnographic *Inquiry*, or field manual, focused on American Indians was published in 1823 by Lewis Cass (Fig. In.4). The lists of questions and explicit instructions for recording data reveal Cass's extensive firsthand knowledge of Indian languages and cultures and their complexities. His *Inquiry* became a model for later manuals used throughout the nineteenth century in the United States.[77]

Cass played a key role in the development of early American anthropology. He was appointed governor of the Michigan Territory and *ex officio* Superintendent of Indian Affairs for the Northwest Territory in

In.4. Lewis Cass, 1851. Courtesy of the Library of Congress.

1818. He used his field manual to try to learn more about the Indians in his charge. In 1826 Cass added an item to the American anthropological research agenda by calling for a comprehensive collation of American Indian tribal names, languages, and cultures. In an article in the *North American Review,* he noted that most Indian tribes were known by many different names. A collation, or *synonymy,* of tribal names was required, he thought, if ever a linguistic classification was to be properly developed, or a comprehensive history of the tribes written.[78] Many tribes, living and extinct, were known by numerous names, which opened the possibility of major errors on the part of unwary scholars. Many had been (or would be) moved, some several times, from their original homelands, "vanished" beyond the frontier. Many were called differently in French, English, and Spanish historical literature, some by as many as two dozen or more names. To take a Southwestern example, the Pueblo of Picuris, north of Santa Fe, has over thirty names in the historical literature, from Acha to Welatah.[79] The proliferation of tribal names required a systematic collation if any historical studies were to be made, hence Cass's proposed synonymy.

Cass had a long career of public service, over nearly fifty years. As Secretary of State in 1861, he was instrumental in circulating Lewis Henry Morgan's kinship schedules worldwide (see Chapter 6). Although he produced no scholarly works on Indians, except several extensive book reviews and his *Inquiries,* he stimulated the work of others, especially Henry Rowe Schoolcraft.

Schoolcraft (1793–1857) was born in upstate New York.[80] In 1821, he joined Cass as geologist and mineralogist for the latter's famous exploration of the Great Lakes area. In 1822 Cass appointed him as Indian agent at Sault St. Marie, a position he held until 1841. In 1823 Schoolcraft married an Ojibwa woman, Jane Johnston. Urged on by Cass, Schoolcraft actively pursued studies of Ojibwa language and culture, gathering information from his in-laws and others. He wrote dozens of books and articles on Indian languages, culture, antiquities, and mythology. In 1845, the state of New York hired him to make a census of the Iroquois tribes. This led to a meeting with Lewis Henry Morgan and an association of the two men until Schoolcraft's death.

Schoolcraft expanded Cass's idea of an Indian synonymy into that of an encyclopedia, a "Cyclopedia Indianensis." In 1846, with support from Cass and others, he began a campaign for congressional support for a project to "collect and digest such statistics and materials as might illustrate the history, present condition and prospects of the Indian tribes in the United States." In 1847 Congress appropriated twelve hundred dollars to begin the project. Schoolcraft developed both a census questionnaire and an ethnographic inquiry based on Cass's model, and sent them to Indian agents, traders, army officers, and missionaries.[81] Over the next decade, although suffering from a debilitating and at times paralytic illness, he compiled the replies, including a few from the Southwest (discussed later), together with his own essays, and various historic material, pell-mell into six massive and largely unusable folio volumes, at an overall cost of some 130,000 dollars.[82] The need for a useful synonymy and encyclopedia of Indians remained on the agenda.

Schoolcraft used his magnum opus to express his biases and opinions on a wide range of topics, some actually related to Indians; others not. Scattered through the work there is also a culture-history model of North American Indians: Humans were originally created by God as farmers; hunter gatherers were the result of moral degeneration from the original state. American Indians originated in Mesopotamia by at least 1500 B.C. and made their way through Tartary and North East Asia, thence across the Bering Strait into the New World. They then moved along the West Coast of North America to Mexico. From there, some groups migrated northeast back into North America and declined into hunter gatherers. But one group, the Toltecs, developed a semicivilization in Mexico. About A.D. 1100, some elements of the Toltecs also moved northeast to establish the mounds and earthworks of the eastern United States. They later succumbed in drawn-out and bloody wars with the local tribes. The story of "advanced" tribes coming into the present-day northeastern United States and being done in by "bad guy" local tribes was in wide circulation in upstate New York in the 1830s and 1840s. Joseph Smith, who grew up in the area, incorporated it into the *Book of Mormon*.[83]

While Schoolcraft's massive tomes are rarely consulted, he occupies an important place in the history of American anthropology. He was a founding member of the American Ethnological Society; he was partly responsible for stimulating the researches of Lewis Henry Morgan; and he established a precedent for federal support of extensive studies of American Indians.

By coincidence, in the summer of 1846, as Schoolcraft was lobbying for funds in Washington, a new organization—the Smithsonian Institution—was being created by Congress, and the United States "Army of the West" was marching toward New Mexico. A whole new era of American institutionally based science, as well as the creation of the Anglo Southwest, were about to begin.

CHAPTER I

Documenting the Southwest, 1540–1846

AS BACKGROUND to the story of Anglos in the Southwest, it is useful to briefly review what was known about the region prior to 1846. "Known" here means published information widely available to interested persons. As many budding writers find to their dismay, just because something is published does not mean anyone except the author and editor have read it, hence the vague, but useful, "widely available."

Spanish Documentation of the Southwest, 1521–1821

According to historian John Bannon, "The Spaniards in the Americas at no time and in no area enjoyed the boon of salutary neglect. The frontier, as all else, was carefully planned, minutely organized, and regularly oversupervised."[1] The Spanish empire was a consummate bureaucracy, comparable to the most complex and inefficient structures of any Chinese dynasty, the Byzantine Empire, or modern nation-state. The or-

ganization of the empire was carefully crafted to create imbalances of power and levels of insecurity that left the crown in control.

The oversupervision generated vast numbers of records, both sacerdotal and secular. Activities in the Spanish New World were governed by the Council of the Indies in Seville. All expeditions to explore, missionize, or colonize required approval of the crown through the Council. Expedition leaders were required to keep detailed diaries or journals. Routine official actions anywhere in the empire required documentation—in triplicate, with one copy remaining at point of origin, one sent to a central archive in Mexico City, and one to Seville or Madrid. The major missionary orders, the Franciscans, Dominicans, and Jesuits, required their own reports and documents. The result was an enormous archival (and hence historical) record.

Some Spanish friars collected historical and ethnographic information about preconquest traditional cultures. The official rationale was, "You can't combat 'pagan ways' if you don't understand them." But much material was collected by scholar-priests out of sheer intellectual curiosity and admiration for the previous lifeways. The most notable example was the great historical and ethnographic study of the Aztecs by Fray Bernardino de Sahagún, *General History of the Things of New Spain,* carried out over more than a half-century in the 1500s, but not available to the world until the late 1700s.[2] Various friars wrote "General Histories of the Indies," or histories of some portion thereof, such as New Spain, or Baja California. All drew upon the manuscript resources of archives in Mexico City or Seville and often uncritically copied, added to, and amended earlier works as they saw fit.

One of the great scholarly tasks undertaken by nineteenth- and twentieth-century Anglo, Mexican, and Spanish historians and ethnohistorians was the systematic investigation of these masses of archival and published documents. Some of those efforts are chronicled in later chapters. Here some published sources are noted that were available in the early decades of the nineteenth century.

Scholars and the educated public in Europe began reading about the Southwest in the 1540s. A report of Coronado's expedition was widely circulated. In his 1554–59 compilation, *Some Navigations and Voyages . . . ,* the Italian Gian Batista Ramusio included Cabaza de Vaca's *Relation,* Marcos de Niza's and Coronado's reports on Cibola, and Hernando Alarcón's report of his voyage up the Sea of Cortés. Antonio Espejo's *New Mexico* (historically the first published use of the term) appeared in Spanish and French in 1586 and in English in 1587. In the *Foreign Voyagers* section of his *Principall Navigations,* published between 1589 and 1600, Richard Hakluyt presented English translations of the sources just listed. The Spanish originals were printed or capsulized by Antonio Herrera, official chronicler of the Indies at the Spanish court, in his *General History,* which appeared in Spanish in 1601, in English in 1726, and in a new Spanish edition in 1730, giving it wide circulation among European scholars.[3]

The best known general history of New Spain was the Franciscan Juan de Torquemada's *Monarquia Indiana,* published in 1615. He had learned the Nahuatl language and for twenty years traveled widely in Mexico, although not into New Mexico. In 1609 he was commissioned to write a history of Franciscan missions and a description of native customs. For the latter he drew heavily on Sahagún and other sixteenth-century compilers. The result is regarded as "one of the great colonial monuments in the ethnohistory of Middle America." It includes brief accounts of Spanish activities in the Southwest from Cabeza de Vaca to Oñate. While Torquemada added nothing new to the history of New Mexico, his work was widely known, often through other sources.[4]

Finally, there are the works of Francisco Javier Clavigero (1731–1787) which had a major impact on Anglo interpretations of Southwestern and Mexican culture history. Clavigero was a Creole, born in Veracruz in 1731. He joined the Jesuit Order in 1748. A brilliant scholar, he studied theology, languages, philosophy, Mexican history, and the Nahuatl language, producing a detailed grammar, *Rules of the Aztec Language.*[5] Clavigero taught at various colleges for native students, continuing to study Nahuatl and preconquest history. When the Jesuits were expelled from New Spain in 1767, Clavigero settled in Italy. He published his *History of Mexico* in Italian in 1780–81; an English edition appeared in London in 1787 and a German edition in Leipzig in 1789. The English edition was reprinted in Philadelphia, Richmond, Virginia, and again in London, in at least four separate editions between 1804 and 1817.[6]

Thomas Jefferson had a copy of Clavigero's *History* in his library. It was widely read in Mexico and was an important source for the "Neo-Aztecism" of burgeoning eighteenth- and nineteenth-century Mexican nationalism. It was carefully studied by Alexander von Humboldt, William Hickling Prescott, and Albert Gallatin. It was the principal source for the idea that the Toltecs and Aztecs had migrated from the Southwest.[7]

Clavigero provides detailed descriptions of Mexican geography, Aztec society and culture, and the conquest. The main body of the work is a history of the Toltecs and their successors. He first reviews the various theories of the origins of the indigenous people and animals of the New World. He derives the ancestors of the Toltecs and their successors from "the most easterly part of Asia" across the (then recently discovered) Bering Strait. He derives the Indians of northeastern America from northern Europe, and those in South America from Africa by way of a now-submerged connection between Africa and Brazil.[8]

He then turns to the histories of the Toltecs. They came from the original kingdom of Tollan, vaguely located "to the north-west of Mexico," beginning in A.D. 596. After 104 years of intermittent wandering, they arrived east of the Valley of Mexico and founded Tollantzinco, then later "founded the city of Tollan or Tula, after the name of their native country." They flourished until A.D. 1052, when, decimated by famine and disease, they dispersed to Yucatán, Guatemala, and cities such as Cholula.

The Toltecs were succeeded by the "Chechemecas," barbarian hunters who "were originally . . . [in] the North of America." The "Chechemecas" ultimately were integrated into various city-states in the highlands. Finally, about A.D. 1160, the "Aztecas or Mexicans" left

> the province of Aztlan, a country situated to the north of the gulf of California. . . . Having passed . . . the Red [Colorado] River from beyond the latitude of thirty-five, they proceeded towards the southeast, as far as the river *Gila,* where they stopped for some time; for at present there are still remains to be seen of the great edifices built by them [there]. . . . From thence having resumed their course toward the south-southeast, they stopped in about twenty-nine degrees of latitude, at a place which is more than two-hundred and fifty miles distant from the city of Chihuahua, towards the north-northwest. This place is known by the name of *Case grandi* [*sic*], on account of an immense edifice still existing, which, agreeable to the universal tradition of these people, was built by the Mexicans in their peregrination.[9]

The Aztecs then proceeded southward into the Valley of Mexico, where they built their great city of Tenochtitlán and expanded their political hegemony over much of Mesoamerica. Clavigero's explicit linking of the Aztec migration to the "casas grandes" of the Gila Valley and Chihuahua carried the weight of great authority in later interpretations of Southwestern prehistory by American scholars (see Chapter 2).

British, German, and American Histories

One of the leading eighteenth-century British historians was William Robertson. In developing his great *History of America,* first published in 1777, he had copies made in Seville and Madrid of numerous Spanish documents relating to histories of the Aztecs and other indigenous groups.[10] When Clavigero's *History of Mexico* appeared a decade later, Robertson incorporated his materials into later editions of his work. Robertson's *History* was often reprinted, until at least 1850, and was widely known in North America.

During his great five-year expedition to Spanish America, Alexander von Humboldt studied manuscript histories in Mexico City, and later in the Vatican Library in Rome. In his description of the New World, Humboldt, borrowing directly from Torquemada and Clavigero, lays out a detailed "history" of preconquest Mexico. It differs from Clavigero's only in details of dates.[11]

By the 1830s there was a quickening of interest in Spanish American history. In Britain, Edward King, Lord Kingsborough, became obsessed with the Mexican past. He hired artists to make copies of Aztec and Maya codices in European libraries. He published these and related documents in nine lavish volumes between 1830 and 1848, vainly hoping to prove that the inhabitants of Mesoamerica were descendants of the Ten Lost Tribes of Israel. The project bankrupted him and he spent his final years in a Dublin prison. During the same time, the French bibliophile and scholar Henri Ternaux-Compans began collecting and publishing numerous documents relating to Spanish America, including Mexico and its provinces.[12]

The American historian William Hickling Prescott published his great biography of Ferdinand and Isabella in 1837, and went on to his equally famous *Conquest of Mexico* of 1843. Both were best-sellers.[13] In the latter, Prescott had planned a major chapter on pre-conquest Mexico, but relegated his data and some speculations to an appendix. He drew on Clavigero, numerous unpublished manuscripts he had had copied in Mexico and Spain, as well as on Humboldt, Lord Kingsborough's compilation, and published and manuscript sources provided to him by Ternaux-Compans. Prescott's *Conquest* was well known to the army officers and others who came to the Southwest in 1846 and after.

Anglo Descriptions of New Mexico, 1806–1846

In 1811 Pedro Bautista Pino, scion of a leading New Mexican family, was sent to Spain to plead for help for his beleaguered province. He asked for a bishop, hence diocesan status for New Mexico; a church-operated seminary and school system; a high court in Chihuahua so people would not have to travel all the way to Guadalajara to settle legal matters; and finally, increased numbers of military garrisons to afford protection from Indians and foreign powers. Pino noted that no bishop had visited New Mexico in fifty years; no one had been confirmed during that time. The crown made some promises. But Spain was in the midst of its incessant European geopolitical struggles and beset by rebellions brewing in South America. The promises came to naught. Along the Rio Grande people said, "Don Pedro Pino fue, don Pedro Pino vino" ("Don Pedro went, don Pedro returned").

Pino presented his pleas in a published memorial, as was the fashion. It contains a cogent description of the New Mexico of 1810. Besides internal problems, it expresses concerns about an emerging threat from the East—the Yanquis, the Anglos. Jefferson's purchase of the Louisiana Territory brought the vague boundary between U.S. territory and New Mexico Province to within 150–200 miles of Taos and Santa Fe. Pino notes that in 1806 a U.S. Army officer, Lt. Zebulon Montgomery Pike, and his party were captured well inside New Mexico territory; they had not strayed there accidentally (see below). Pino warned that the Americans might soon move to take over New Mexico. The Spanish had maintained a stout policy of closed borders and exclusion of foreigners. After the Pike incident, the policy stiffened in New Mexico. But a trail already had been opened between Missouri and Santa Fe in 1805. Soon Anglo trappers and traders followed; sometimes they were jailed, sometimes not.[14]

Pino's fears were well-founded. The Anglos had a sense of mission, nurtured since the seventeenth century, based on the idea that their actions were in some sense approved, if not planned, by God. By 1810 there was a conviction that the nascent United States *by right* should control the destiny of North America. In 1845 the New York publisher John O'Sullivan gave a name to the conviction: Manifest Destiny—a providential "expansion, prearranged by Heaven, over an area not clearly defined."[15] To some, the area was westward to the Pacific Coast; to others, all of North America from the Arctic to the Isthmus of Panama; to still others, the Western Hemisphere. To arch-expansionists, such as Thomas Hart Benton, whose 1821–51 career in the U.S. Senate was devoted to promoting westward expansion and settlement, the slogan came to symbolize a literal godsend. He saw the Mexican-American War, so carefully nurtured into existence by the master geopolitician President James K. Polk, as an expression of Providence.[16]

The 1821 Mexican Revolution ended Spanish rule and, with it, the exclusionist policy. The Missouri trader William Becknell found himself welcome in Santa Fe in 1821; the Mexicans had silver dollars to exchange for American goods. Thus began the Santa Fe trade, which flourished between 1821 and 1846 along the famed trail from Missouri to New Mexico. Josiah Gregg, in his 1844 *Commerce of the Prairies,* estimated the value of the trade at 450,000 dollars for the year 1843. Anglo traders and trappers took up residence in New Mexico, particularly in Taos. By the early 1840s the "American party," led by Charles Bent, Kit Carson, Antoine Le Roux, the Robidoux brothers, and Ceran St. Vrain, held considerable economic and political power, solidified by marriages into prominent New Mexican families.[17]

Mexico's open-border policy led to an influx of Anglo settlers into Texas. These "Texians" were soon agitating for independence from Mexico or annexation by the United States. The 1836 battles at the Alamo and San Jacinto resulted in the Republic of Texas, since antislavery forces in Congress kept Texas from being annexed to the United States. In 1845, President John Tyler managed to get the annexation through Congress, and the stage was set. The United States formally declared war on Mexico on May 13, 1846.[18]

Describing New Mexico

There were various published sources of information about New Mexico and its inhabitants available to Anglos prior to 1846, especially newspaper reports about the fur trade, the Santa Fe trade, and political doings in Texas (which often involved New Mexico). Scattered and partial fur trappers' accounts appeared in the 1820s in various American magazines and newspapers. There were also three widely read books: Pike's *Account,* published in 1810, R. W. H. Hardy's *Travels,* published in 1829, and Josiah Gregg's *Commerce of the Prairies,* published in 1844. The information they contain about Southwestern Hispanic and Indian peoples and ruins is based on casual observation and hearsay, reflecting the "common knowledge" current in New Mexico at the time each person was there.[19]

In 1806, Lt. Zebulon Pike was sent on an expedition to seek the headwaters of the Arkansas and Red rivers, a probable cover for a spy mission into New Mexico (Map 6). On the way, he described, but did not climb, the famous peak in the Colorado Rockies later named for him by John C. Frémont. Pike and his men came to the headwaters of the Rio Grande, thus entering Spanish Territory. They were arrested and placed in rather comfortable captivity in Santa Fe and then Chihuahua for several months before being escorted to U.S. Territory near Natchitoches, Louisiana, and released.[20]

R. W. H. Hardy was one of many agents for British business interests who flocked to Mexico after 1821. He traveled as far as the southern portion of the Southwest. Josiah Gregg joined a wagon train to Santa Fe in 1835 to regain his health. He did so, and remained in the trading business for nine years.

Travel narratives by three others appeared in 1847–48: G. A. F. Ruxton's *Adventures* and *Life in the Far West*; Lewis Garrard's *Wah-to-Yah*; and a report by a German-American physician and natural historian, Frederick Adolph Wislizenus, published by the U.S. Congress in 1848.[21]

George Augustus Frederick Ruxton's (1821–1848) life is epitomized by the old country-western song "Live Fast, Die Young and Leave a Beautiful Memory." The son of a British army surgeon, he entered the Royal Military Academy at Sandhurst in 1835. Expelled in 1837, he became a mercenary in Spain. After two years and many battles he returned to England, a seasoned and decorated veteran of seventeen. He traveled in Canada and South Africa before heading for Mexico in 1845, probably as a British spy. In 1846 he traveled from Mexico City to Taos. His description of Santa Fe is famous: "a wretched collection of mud houses. . . . The appearance of the town defies description, and I can compare it to nothing but a dilapidated brick kiln or a prairie-dog town. . . . The inhabitants are worthy of their city, and a more miserable, vicious looking population it would be impossible to imagine."[22]

Ruxton spent the winter of 1846–47 with various mountain men in the Southern Rockies, then joined a wagon train headed for Missouri from Bent's Fort. One of his fellow travelers was Lewis H. Garrard. Ruxton was back in England by August 1847, where he published his *Adventures*; his *Life in the Far West* appeared in installments the next year. He returned to the United States, arriving in St. Louis in August 1848 in the midst of a dysentery epidemic. He died from it on August 28, aged twenty-seven. The last installment of *Life in the Far West* appeared in November of 1848; it was followed by his obituary.

Ruxton was favorably disposed to the "partly civilised . . . most industrious" Rio Grande Pueblo Indians he met and was struck by their religious compartmentalization: "Although the Pueblos are nominally *Cristianos,* and have embraced the outward forms of *la santa fe Catolica,* they . . . still cling to the belief of their fathers, and celebrate in secret the ancient rites of their religion. . . . They are careful, however, not to practice any of their rites before strangers."[23]

Ruxton notes that fur trappers thought the Hopi to be "Welsh Indians," because "they are much fairer in complexion than other tribes, and have several individuals amongst them perfectly white, with light hair." He thought this was due to albinism, not Welsh ancestry (see Chapter 2). Reflecting Clavigero, he gives credence to the theory of the northern origins of the Aztecs, as evidenced by numerous ruins "from the shores of the Great Salt Lake of the north towards the valley of the Gila," and on into Mexico, as well as similarities in "many of their customs and domestic arts." The Aztecs, he thought, were driven farther and farther south by "violent volcanic convulsions."[24]

Ruxton's traveling companion from Bent's Fort in April 1847 was seventeen-year-old Lewis H. Garrard, who had spent a few months at the fort, living for much of the time with a band of Cheyenne Indians. His descriptions of their lifeways are vivid and compelling. After the "Taos Revolt" he was among those who rushed to Taos to render aid, not knowing that the revolt had been squelched by U.S. Army troops, and remained during the trial and execution of several of the insurrectionists. He visited Taos Pueblo and wrote a vivid, if secondhand, description of the battle there during the insurrection. He had little contact with the Taos Indians—and none with other Southwestern Indians; his remarks about them are brief and condescending.[25] While Garrard's readers learned very little about Indian people (except the Cheyenne) from him, they found his, and Ruxton's, style thrilling and adventurous, and their descriptions of the country

and the people fascinating. Both were widely read. The invention of the "romantic" Southwest begins in the work of the two young authors.

Finally, among the travelogue reports on New Mexico available to Anglo readers was one by Frederick Adolph Wislizenus (1810–1889), whose "Memoir of a Tour in Northern Mexico . . . in 1846 and 1847" was published by the U.S. Congress in 1848. Wislizenus was born in Germany, came to the United States in 1835 after receiving a medical degree in Zurich, and settled near St. Louis. In 1839, he accompanied a party of trappers on a tour of the Rocky Mountains, later writing a book about his adventures.[26] He returned to St. Louis and entered into medical practice with George Engelmann, who was just seriously embarking on the botanical studies for which he is deservedly famous.

In 1846 Wislizenus joined a caravan headed for Santa Fe and Chihuahua. He apparently drove a horse-drawn ambulance, outfitted with "an adequate scientific outfit," and was accompanied by a servant.[27] In September 1846 he was incarcerated, together with six other Anglo traders, at a small mountain town west of Chihuahua. Allowed to wander during the day up to two leagues from the town, he spent his time making collections of plants and studying the land, the climate, and the people. In March 1847 Wislizenus and his compatriots were freed. He returned to St. Louis and turned his botanical collections over to Engelmann, who found numerous new species among them. Senator Thomas Hart Benton saw to the printing of his *Memoir.*

The *Memoir* is both a chatty travelogue, filled with personal observations and secondhand gossip, and a thorough geographical and economic review of New Mexico and northern Mexico. Like Ruxton, he thought the Santa Fe of the 1840s "more a prairie-dog village than a capital." He retailed versions of the legends of Montezuma, Pecos Pueblo, and Gran Quivira (see Chapter 2). He sardonically noted the "harvesting" raids by Apaches and others on the settled communities: "the raising of stock has been crippled by the invasions of the hostile Indians, who consider themselves secret partners in the business and annually take their share away." Wislizenus, like others, had a generally positive view of the Pueblo Indians, considering them good farmers, although "generally poor, frugal and sober. . . . Their religious rites are a mixture of Catholicism and Indian paganism."[28]

In sum, most of the published information that eastern Anglo readers received on the Southwest between 1806 and 1846 consisted of verbal snapshots derived from informal observation and the hearsay of local "common knowledge." Some of it, especially in the works of Garrard and Ruxton, was framed in the romantic genre already established by James Fenimore Cooper and others. Thus, from the outset, the Anglo Southwest had a strong romantic tinge to it.

CHAPTER 2

The Topographical Engineers in the Southwest

The ideal or typical form taken by natural science in nineteenth-century America was description of frontiers. The Great American fact of the time was not intellectual, like Darwin's theory in England and Huxley's preaching of it. It was geographical, the apprehension of a whole new world of creatures and places. All energies of the explorers and settlers of that world were turned, first, to knowing it well, and, second, to setting a wide knowledge of it.[1]

Exploration Science in the Southwest

The first systematic scientific studies of the Southwest, including anthropology, were undertaken by members of the Corps of Topographical Engineers of the United States Army. The corps was formally created as a separate unit in 1838, with a status equal to the regular Corps of Engineers. Its commander was the politically adroit Colonel John James Abert, who had nurtured the corps into existence over several years out of the earlier Army Topographical Bureau. Limited to thirty-six officers, the corps had its pick of the best and brightest graduates of West Point. They were simultaneously scientists, civil engineers, cartographers, natural historians, and explorers. They surveyed the national boundaries of the country, laid out

wagon roads and railroad routes, and directed "the apprehension of a whole new world of creatures and places." They were, as William Goetzmann has said, an "instrument of self-conscious nationalism," and a "department of public works for the West."[2] As the United States expanded westward between 1843 and the Civil War, the corps did the mapping and scientific studies that allowed the infrastructure of expansion to be built.

The work of the Topographical Engineers in the West took place during the ever-deepening North-South crisis over slavery, states' rights, and related issues symbolized by the Compromise of 1850, the Kansas-Nebraska Act of 1854, and the subsequent guerrilla warfare between proslavery "Ruffians" and antislavery "Free-Soilers," culminating in the outbreak of the Civil War in 1861. The crisis gave a distinct political spin to nearly everything the engineers were instructed to do.

Then there was the sheer size of the new land in which the engineers worked. The annexation of Texas in 1845, the settlement of the Oregon Territory boundary with Britain in 1846, and the Treaty of Guadalupe Hidalgo in 1848 increased the territorial domain of the United States by nearly 1,200,000 square miles. Another 30,000 square miles was added by the Gadsden Purchase in 1853. The magnitude of the new territory had only just begun to be comprehended when word arrived of the discovery of gold in California, precipitating the rush westward in the following years.

Thus, between about 1840 and 1859 the federal government was faced with several immediate major tasks: surveying wagon roads and railroad routes across the West; planning for a general opening of the vastly expanded U.S. territory to trade and settlement; dealing with numerous Indian tribes whose lands began to be crossed, usurped, and appropriated at ever-accelerating rates; surveying and settling the U.S./Canadian and U.S./Mexican borders; sending an army against the Mormons in Utah in 1857–58 in the confused and embarrassing "Utah War," or "Mormon War." The Topographical Engineers played key roles in all these activities and more. In the process, they collected an impressive array of scientific and natural history data on the country, the biota, the Indians, and archaeological sites throughout the West, and presented that information in various reports published by the government.

The first major western expeditions by the Topographical Engineers were those led by Lt. John C. Frémont to South Pass in 1842, and in 1843–44 to the mouth of the Columbia River, southward into the Great Basin, westward into the Central Valley of California, and back to Missouri. The trips, and his reports, romantically written (from his dictation) and

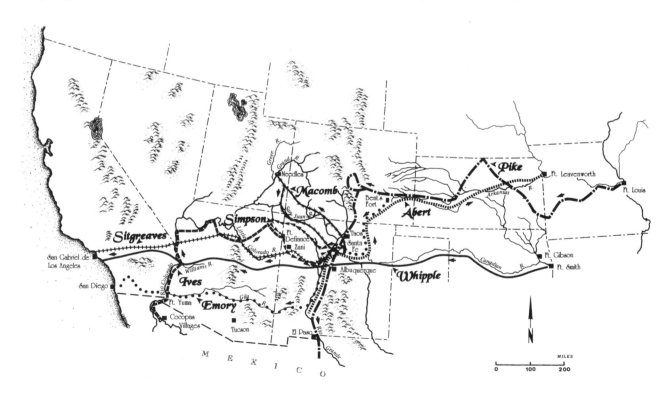

6. Major Routes of Exploration by U.S. Topographical Engineers, 1846–1859

edited by his wife, the beautiful and brilliant Jessie Benton Frémont, daughter of Senator Thomas Hart Benton, made him a hero.[3] They also fueled the expansionist dreams of Senator Benton and others.

In 1845, as war with Mexico became more likely, Colonel Stephen Watts Kearny led a dragoon reconnaissance along the Oregon Trail to South Pass, then south to Bent's Fort and back to Fort Leavenworth —a two-thousand-mile trip in ninety-nine days. Second Lieutenant James W. Abert, the son of Colonel Abert, made a mapping reconnaissance from Bent's Fort south and southeast into the Canadian River drainage and onto the Llano Estacado.[4] Both expeditions gave the military much useful information for later operations.

Frémont headed west again into the Central Valley of California. There, in January 1846, a courier from Washington, Lieutenant Gillespie, of the U.S. Marines, caught up with Frémont and gave him a message. Frémont was transferred from the Topographical Engineers and commissioned as a lieutenant-colonel in the Mounted Rifles. He and his men were soon involved in the "Bear Flag Revolt," which helped gain control of California as the United States moved toward war with Mexico.[5]

The United States formally declared war on Mexico on May 13, 1846. In June, Kearny was put in command of the "Army of the West" and given the mission of seizing New Mexico and Alta California provinces. On August 18, 1846, Kearny led his army into Santa Fe. Acting Governor Juan Bautista Vigil y Alarid turned New Mexico Province over to the United States without a fight. Kearny established a new legal code and appointed Charles Bent, of Taos, as governor, then started for California on September 25. In January 1847, dissident Hispanics and some Taos Indians staged a "revolt" in Taos against U.S. rule, killing Charles Bent in the process. This "Taos Revolt" was quickly and brutally quelled by the army.[6]

By 1846, raiding and slave-taking between the Navajos, on the one side, and the Mexicans and Pueblos, on the other, had reached a high level in New Mexico. There were no innocent parties, but full blame was unjustly laid on the Navajos. Kearny sent Colonel Alexander Doniphan to meet with a contingent of Navajos, but no lasting truce resulted. An expedition into Navajo country in 1849, discussed below, was a disaster. Continued conflict was in the interests of the Hispanic slave traders, who used it as an excuse to take additional Navajo slaves. The "Navajo problem" was not resolved until 1864, when the draconian measures taken by Kit Carson resulted in the Navajo captivity at Bosque Redondo (discussed below).[7]

Topographical Engineers in the Southwest

The army sent out numerous reconnaissance and survey parties in the Southwest between 1846 and 1859. Most were led by topographical engineers, others by line officers. Sometimes army physicians went along. The engineers and officers were trained to observe and describe the topography, biota, mineral resources, and Indian people they saw. The army doctors were usually well trained in natural history in addition to medicine. Both officers and doctors were aware of the nascent "science of ethnology," and most were familiar with the works of Clavigero, Humboldt, and Prescott. All the officers were trained in drawing and sketching, both freehand and using the *camera lucida*. Photography was in its infancy; a daguerreotype outfit was carried by Frémont in 1848, but it was not successful. Whenever possible, professional artists were employed.[8]

The various army expeditions in the Southwest prior to the Civil War are well documented and works about them readily available.[9] Here thumbnail sketches of the expeditions are provided to place them in context. There were four topographical engineers with Kearny in 1846: First Lieutenants William H. Emory and William H. Warner, and Lieutenants James W. Abert and William G. Peck. Abert and Peck had fallen ill and were left behind by Kearny when he started toward California from Santa Fe in September 1846; upon recovery they were assigned to conduct a "survey of New Mexico."[10] They made a reconnais-

2.1. *Abó, watercolor by James Abert, 1846. Courtesy of John Galvin and John-Howell Books, San Francisco.*

sance of the Rio Grande and Puerco River valleys (Map 6), developed a useful map, and visited Laguna and Acoma, as well as the Salinas region east of the Manzano Mountains, where Abert sketched and described the ruins of Abó and Quarai (Fig. 2.1). Abert mistook Acoma, Laguna, and some adjacent pueblos and ruins for Clavigero's "Aztec" cities. He made casual observations of various pueblos, especially Acoma, and provided valuable information on the political organization and demography of New Mexico. Abert returned to Washington to complete his report and map and never returned to the Southwest. He served in the Civil War, then retired from the army, and taught at the University of Missouri at Rolla for thirty years.[11]

William Hemsley Emory (Fig. 2.2) was the scion of an old Maryland family. His grandfather and father had distinguished themselves in the Revolutionary War and the War of 1812, respectively. He entered West

2.2. William Helmsley Emory, 1850s. Courtesy of the Library of Congress.

Point at age sixteen with his longtime friends Jefferson Davis and Henry Clay, Jr., graduating in 1831. He married Matilda Wilkins Bache, a great-granddaughter of Benjamin Franklin. Emory had a keen interest in science and natural history; in later years he was close friends with several prominent scientists, including William Bond, the builder and first director of the Harvard Astronomical Observatory; John Torrey, the famed botanist; Joseph Henry; Asa Gray; Louis Agassiz; George Engelmann; and Spencer F. Baird.[12] He had a brief but important connection with Albert Gallatin (see Chapter 3).

Emory served in the Southwest for nine years. He was Chief Astronomer for the Boundary Commission

2.3. Richard Hovenden Kern, daguerreotype, ca. 1845. Courtesy of the Huntington Library.

from 1848 to 1853, and after the Gadsden Purchase, was both astronomer and commissioner, finishing that work in 1857. He wrote two reports that contain his ethnographic and archaeological observations on the Southwest. The first, with illustrations by John Mix Stanley, is a narrative of the march west with Kearny; the second describes his work with the Boundary Commission.[13] Emory participated in numerous Civil War campaigns and later commanded various army districts. He retired as a brigadier general in 1876, and died in 1887.

The first systematic descriptions of the great ruins of Chaco Canyon were made by Lt. James Hervey Simpson and two artists, Richard (Fig. 2.3) and Edward (Ned) Kern, in a report on the so-called Navajo Expedition in 1849 (see Chapter 3). Simpson graduated from West Point in 1832, transferring to the Topographical Engineers in 1848. In early 1849 he was part of a team to survey and construct a wagon road from Fort Smith to Santa Fe along the south bank of the Canadian River. He reached Santa Fe in June 1849, completed his report on the wagon-road route, and then accompanied the Navajo Expedition to Chaco Canyon.[14]

Edward and Richard Kern's presence in New Mexico in 1849 was due to the enigmatic charisma of John Charles Frémont. They were artists and art teachers from an old Philadelphia family; brother Benjamin was a physician. In 1845, Ned Kern became artist for Frémont's third expedition.[15]

By 1845 Frémont was a national hero. After California was secured for the United States, he got into a complex bickering match with Commodore Robert Stockton and General Kearny that resulted in his arrest and court-martial in Washington, D.C. Despite great public outcry, Frémont was found guilty and sentenced to dismissal from the army in January 1848. President Polk remitted the sentence; however,

2.4 (left). Zuni woman weaving. Drawing by Richard Kern. Sitgreaves (1853).

2.5 (below). Zuni forge. Drawing by Richard Kern. Sitgreaves (1853).

Frémont felt his honor had been impugned and resigned his commission.[16]

Talk of a transcontinental railroad had begun in 1844, even before the United States invaded Mexico. Now Frémont saw a chance to regain his honor, renew his hero status, and further Benton's dreams of westward expansion. He proposed an expedition to prove the feasibility of an all-weather railroad route to California near the Thirty-eighth Parallel. Ned Kern, together with brothers Richard and Benjamin, signed on.

The Thirty-eighth Parallel crosses some of the highest mountain ranges in the Southern Rockies. In late November, against all advice and in the face of blinding snowstorms and subzero weather, Frémont led his party across the Sangre de Cristo range into the San Luis Valley and on into the rugged San Juan Mountains of southern Colorado. On December 17, 1848, the party finally turned back. The retreat was a disaster. Twenty-one men, including the Kern broth-

ers, finally reached Taos after incredible suffering. Frémont abandoned his party and hastened on to California by a more southerly route, leaving the mountains strewn with the bodies of fifteen men who had frozen to death to satisfy his megalomania. Ben Kern was later killed by Ute Indians.[17]

Ned and Richard Kern met Simpson in Santa Fe. Simpson immediately hired them to make a map and draft illustrations for his wagon-road report. Later, when the Navajo Expedition was forming, Simpson was assigned to it and the Kern brothers were employed as mapmakers and artists.

In 1851, Captain Lorenzo Sitgreaves led an expedition westward from Zuni Pueblo to investigate both a wagon road and the possibility of navigation on the Colorado River and its tributaries (Map 6). Simpson's 1849 report had provided information on the area between the Rio Grande and Zuni Pueblo, but the country west of Zuni was little known. Richard Kern signed on as expedition artist.[18]

Sitgreaves started at Zuni Pueblo, where Kern made the first published sketches of Zuni people (Figs. 2.4 and 2.5). The party followed an ancient trail —more or less the later Route 66—westward to the San Francisco Mountains, then southwest to the Colorado River. On the way, they passed through the Petrified Forest area of eastern Arizona, noted various ruins along the Little Colorado River, and crossed through the area covered by volcanic ash from Sunset Crater. Sitgreaves noted the ruins that are now in and adjacent to Wupatki National Monument. The trip from the San Francisco peaks to the Colorado River was very difficult. Barely enough water was found to keep men and animals alive. There was little food for men or mules; finally the latter became food for the former. The party reached Camp Yuma just before the mule supply gave out.[19]

The Boundary Survey

The treaty ending the war between the United States and Mexico established a joint Boundary Commission. Each country was to appoint a Boundary Commissioner; they jointly would direct a binational staff in drawing the line. On the U.S. side, the commission was immediately immersed in turmoil. The first commissioner, Ambrose Sevier, died before he could be confirmed by the Senate. The second, John B. Weller, lasted six months, did little, and returned to Washington. The third appointee was John C. Frémont, who sought the appointment to soothe his wounded ego

after his court-martial and the disastrous expedition into the Southern Rockies. Receiving the appointment, and thereby an ego reinflation, he refused it and instead became the first senator from the newly created state of California. That led to the appointment of a very unlikely, although eager, candidate for the job, John Russell Bartlett (see Fig. In.3), coproprietor of Bartlett and Welford's Bookstore in New York City and active participant in the American Ethnological Society.

By 1850 Bartlett longed to see other places and peoples rather than simply read of them in books or in letters from John Lloyd Stephens and E. G. Squier. He sought help from friends in Washington, hoping for a consulate in an interesting place. He knew from Stephens and Squier that a consulship, or some other vaguely defined diplomatic post, left ample leisure time for archaeological or ethnographic explorations in exotic climes.[20] Bartlett's friends said there were no available consulships, but would he consider the post of Mexican Boundary Commissioner, then vacant? Bartlett, with "a great desire for travel, and particularly for exploring unknown regions" as well as "a deep interest in the Indians," thought that "to be thrown among the wild tribes of the interior," would be a splendid ethnological opportunity.[21] As it turned out, he was thrown among several tribes—Apaches, Maricopas, Yumas, and others. He was also thrown among wild politicians, deeply enmeshed in the sectional North-South schisms of the time. In the end, the politicians threw him to the wolves.

Bartlett's appointment as Boundary Commissioner came because he was a Whig, had a "scientific reputation," and because his supporters, including Stephen A. Douglas, Thomas Hart Benton, John C. Calhoun, Jefferson Davis, and others, prevailed in the pork-barrel appointment process. The other candidate was Major Foliet Lally, a Topographical Engineer, a Whig, and a minor hero of the Mexican War. Lally was strongly supported by the Topographical Engineers, especially William H. Emory and Amiel Weeks Whipple, who were staff members of the Boundary

Commission. Bartlett started with two strikes against him.

Both Emory and Whipple had served under Weller. Despite political machinations and much military-civilian friction, they completed the section of the boundary from San Diego to the Gila/Colorado confluence. The joint commission had agreed to meet again on November 1, 1850, in El Paso. Bartlett, rather than Weller, kept the appointment.

Bartlett's adventures and misadventures cannot be fully described here, but some details are necessary to make sense of his anthropological observations. His appointment was not ratified by the Senate until June 19, 1850, leaving him little time to hire over one hundred men, purchase and arrange to ship one hundred tons of supplies, and still meet his Mexican counterpart, Pedro Garcia Conde, in El Paso on the appointed day. He made some good appointments to the scientific staff, and Whipple stayed on; Emory strategically withdrew.

Bartlett sailed from New York to the Texas coast, then traveled overland to El Paso, armed to the teeth, riding in a rockaway coach and four. There was immediate internal dissension, a couple of murders, and rampant drunkenness. Little was accomplished until the following June. Meanwhile, Bartlett and his staff made excursions into the surrounding country.

For a variety of financial, supply, and health reasons, Bartlett strayed far away from the border, south to Acapulco and all the way to Clear Lake, California, north of Napa Valley. He contracted typhoid fever; his counterpart, Garcia Conde, was also afflicted, and died. Bartlett and party finally started east from San Diego in late May 1852. There was more dissension and yet another murder. Crossing the Colorado River, the party traveled up the Gila Valley. Bartlett made numerous observations of the Pima and the Maricopa during a two-week stay at the confluence of the Salt and Gila rivers—his most sustained and useful ethnographic observations. He also visited and studied Casa Grande and other archaeological sites in the Salt River Valley. Turning south, Bartlett visited Tucson, San Xavier del Bac, Tubac, and Tumacacori, then detoured to Casas Grandes in Chihuahua. He finally reached El Paso in mid-August 1852. Emory, reassigned to the Survey, had arrived in El Paso some months previously and found matters in chaos.[22]

Bartlett and Conde were to fix the "initial point" at which the New Mexico boundary reached the Rio Grande. They picked a point thirty miles above El Paso at 32 degrees, 22 minutes north latitude. A line projected west from that point placed the only southern railroad route then thought to be feasible in Mexican territory. Southern U.S. expansionists were outraged over Bartlett's "wrong" placement of the point, and began clamoring for his head. He finally decided to return to Washington to defend himself and get the commission reorganized. On his way back he learned that Democrat Franklin Pierce had defeated Whig Millard Fillmore for the presidency and that Congress had appropriated more money for the Survey, but only on condition that the Bartlett-Conde line be renounced. His tenure was over.[23]

In Washington, Bartlett defended himself as best he could against vicious charges, and began writing his *Personal Narrative*, which became a best-seller.[24] He had the misfortune to try to act honestly and fairly, according to his lights, in the miasma of U.S. expansionist politics. He became the scapegoat for those who finally got what they wanted by brinkmanship and the Gadsden Purchase. W. H. Emory, promoted to major, became the Boundary Commissioner and Chief Astronomer. Work on the new boundary line went quickly and was finished by mid-October 1855.

Bartlett's mauling by the Washington wolves did not affect him in his home state. In 1855 he became Secretary of State for Rhode Island, a post he held until 1872. He was much involved with archival and library work, and after 1856 helped John Carter Brown amass his great collection of early Americana. He continued to update his famous *Dictionary of Americanisms*,[25] but turned away from ethnology toward local history. He died, full of years and honors, in 1886.

The Railroad Surveys and the Southwest

In 1844, Asa Whitney, an American with extensive business interests in Asia, launched a campaign for construction of a "national railroad" from Lake Michigan to the Columbia River. The aim was to appreciably shorten the sea connection between Asia and the United States. Even the fastest of the great clipper ships of the day took seventy-seven days from Hong Kong to New York; others were far slower. A "West Coast connection" was highly desirable, even though, at the time Mexico and Great Britain controlled the West Coast.[26]

Whitney's proposal was taken up with alacrity and immediately engulfed in sectionalist controversy. After 1846, the United States controlled the West Coast and the intervening land. The issue then became which route should be followed? The Gadsden Purchase of 1853 recouped the Thirty-second Parallel route. But by then congressional wrangling over other routes had reached an impasse. It appeared at the time that only one line would be built. Hence, the stakes were enormous for those at or near the eastern terminus of the line, for the various potential builders of the line, for potential land developers along the chosen westward route, and for determining whether Northern or Southern political interests would control the line.

Finally, a compromise turned the problem over to the Corps of Topographical Engineers by creating the Pacific Railroad Surveys in March 1853. They would conduct "scientific" investigations and reach an "impartial" judgment as to the "best route." The assignment was impossible—the corps was to report back within ten months with a determination of the "most practicable and economical route for a railroad from the Mississippi River to the Pacific Ocean." Despite hopes of impartiality, the undertaking was immersed in partisan politics from the outset; it could hardly have been otherwise.[27]

Four official surveys were funded (there were two unofficial surveys, backed by Thomas Hart Benton and others). One was between the Forty-seventh and

Forty-ninth Parallels in the north, a second between the Thirty-eighth and Thirty-ninth Parallels, a third along the Thirty-fifth Parallel, and a fourth in California seeking passes through the Sierra Nevada to connect with the more southerly east-west routes. A route roughly along the Forty-first Parallel through South Pass in Wyoming and on westward across Utah and Nevada was not surveyed, since it was thought that earlier explorations by Frémont, and by Captain Howard Stansbury in 1849, provided sufficient data. Each party was headed by a Topographical Engineer and included civilian engineers, scientific personnel, and one or more artists.[28]

The Thirty-fifth Parallel survey across the Southwest (Map 6) was commanded by Lt. Amiel Weeks Whipple, already familiar with the area through his work with the Boundary Commission.[29] Whipple's party included the artist-naturalist Heinrich Balduin Möllhausen, who was born near Bonn, Germany, in 1825. He came to America in 1849 and linked up with a natural history expedition to the Great Plains led by Duke Paul Wilhelm von Wurttemberg. He became separated from the party and spent several months living with bands of Oto and Omaha Indians before rejoining the duke along the lower Mississippi.

In January 1853, Möllhausen was back in Germany where he met Alexander von Humboldt, who liked the young man and his sketches of the American West.[30] Humboldt encouraged him to return to the United States to seek further opportunities for exploration and gave him a letter of introduction. The letter, and a recommendation from the Prussian ambassador, gained Möllhausen an appointment as topographer and Smithsonian Institution naturalist with Whipple's survey.

Following the Whipple expedition, Möllhausen returned to Germany and became a member of Humboldt's entourage. Humboldt used his influence with King Friederich Wilhelm IV to get Möllhausen appointed custodian of the libraries of Potsdam, a post he held for the rest of his life. His *Diary* of the Whipple expedition appeared in 1858 in German, Dutch, and English.[31] Meanwhile Möllhausen had been invited by Lt. Joseph C. Ives to go on the Colorado River expedition; he accepted with alacrity (see below).

After the Colorado River trip, Möllhausen returned to Potsdam and settled down. He published a second account of his American explorations in 1861. While continuing to catalog books, he began writing novels, short stories, and essays. For some two decades he was the most popular novelist in Germany, producing at least thirty-nine novels and numerous short stories. Nearly all of his fictional works were set in a very romanticized America. He is sometimes called the German Fenimore Cooper.[32]

Whipple began the survey near Fort Smith, Arkansas, in late July 1853, and reached Los Angeles in March 1854. Since both Whipple and Möllhausen were interested in Southwestern ruins and in the Indian people they encountered, Whipple's official report and Möllhausen's *Diary* are particularly important sources on early Southwestern anthropology. Whipple had collected ethnographic data during his Boundary Commission work. Now, he took seriously the part of his official instructions directing that attention be paid to "the location, character, habits, traditions, and languages of the Indian tribes."[33]

At the onset of the Civil War, Whipple, now a captain, was placed in charge of the Union Army hot-air observation balloon project, used to spy on the Confederates from aerial vantage points. He was mortally wounded in the Battle of Chancellorsville in May 1863. On the day he died he was promoted to brevet major general "for gallant and meritorious service during the Rebellion."[34]

Exploring the Colorado River

The lower reaches of the Colorado River were the focus of attention by the U.S. Army from 1849 until the Civil War, primarily because of transport concerns. The wagon route roughly paralleling the Gila crossed the Colorado at about the confluence of the two rivers. Tens of thousands of Forty-niners passed that way, and many eager emigrants followed in subse-

quent years. The Indian people along the lower Colorado had always stoutly defended their homelands against intruders—Father Garcés and other Spanish were killed by them.

A ferry across the Colorado was established in 1849 at the "Yuma Crossing." To protect the crossing, the army established Fort Yuma in late 1850. Supplying the fort was a major problem, especially by pack mule trains overland from San Diego; costs were an exorbitant five hundred to eight hundred dollars a ton. One alternative was to bring supplies by water from San Diego to the Colorado delta via the Gulf of California, then ship them upriver to the fort. A regular steamboat service upriver began in early 1854 with a sidewheel steamboat, the *General Jesup*. Soon there was a second steamboat and talk of running all the way upriver to the mouth of the Virgin River to trade with the Mormons in Las Vegas.[35]

In 1856 Congress appropriated seventy thousand dollars to fund a steamboat expedition up the Colorado to determine the head of navigation. The owner of the steamboats on the river, George Johnson, planned to be in charge of the expedition. But 1856 was a presidential election year and James Buchanan won. Buchanan named John B. Floyd of Virginia as Secretary of War, as a reward for his campaign support. Floyd appointed his niece's new husband to head the exploration party up the Colorado River. The foppish and very ambitious new nephew-in-law was Lt. Joseph Christmas Ives, of the Corps of Topographical Engineers.

Ives graduated from West Point in 1852 and served on the Pacific Railroad Survey under Whipple. He spent 1854–57 in Washington helping prepare the Survey report. There he met Cora Semmes, who with her sister Clara were two of the "regnant beauties" of antebellum Washington and John B. Floyd's nieces. The "dashing" Ives wooed and won Cora. They became "noted as the handsomest pair in Washington society."[36]

George Johnson expected to head the Colorado expedition himself, or at least rent a steamboat to the government at thirty-five hundred to forty-five

CHAPTER 3

Legends and Ruins, 1846–1859

EARLY ANGLO OBSERVERS briefly described, measured, and mapped archaeological ruins. They were aware of the works of Clavigero, Humboldt, and Prescott, and speculated about the direction of north to south or south to north migrations or the flow of cultural influences between Mexico and the Southwest. Their reports mark the beginning of systematic study of Southwestern archaeology. They described six groups of ruins: Pecos Pueblo and church; the so-called Salinas Ruins east of the Manzano Mountains; those along the Salt and Gila rivers in central Arizona; the spectacular sites in and adjacent to Chaco Canyon; ruins near Sunset Crater, now called Wupatki Ruin, and others; and scattered ruins elsewhere, including White House in Canyon de Chelly.

Clavigero provided dates for north to south migrations of Aztecs and Toltecs, but not everyone agreed with the migration concept or the dates. But if not Aztecs or Toltecs, then who built the towns and villages now lying in ruins? And when were they occupied, when abandoned, and where did the occupants go? Whatever the origins and fates of their builders, the ruins seemed to be mute evidence for larger populations and perhaps more complex societies than the historic Pueblos. Issues of demography and social complexity are still current in Southwestern archaeology.[1]

The *Oxford English Dictionary* defines a legend as "an unauthentic or non-historical story, especially one handed down by tradition from early times and popularly regarded as historical."[2] Some suppose that legends contain "kernels" of historical truth. Early Anglos heard legends aplenty that accounted for some aspect of culture history, a set of ruins or a group of people. One was the "legend of Montezuma." Another was the legend of "White" or "Welsh" Indians.[3] Both figured in pre–Civil War speculation about Southwestern ruins. After 1880, Pueblo Indian legends were closely studied for what they might reveal about pre-Hispanic migrations and the possibilities of linking specific ruins to historic Pueblos (see Chapter 14).

By 1846, the legend of Montezuma was "common knowledge," well established in the minds of Hispanic and Anglo residents. Whether Pueblo Indians believed it, or simply retailed it when asked, is an open question. The Pueblos had for centuries practiced all sorts of dissimulation to protect their religious beliefs and practices from suppression by the Spanish, and the Montezuma legend may have been used in that deception. On the other hand, "Montezuma" had become entangled with an indigenous myth figure, and perhaps was "real" to many Pueblo people.

The Montezuma legend was most closely attached to the Pueblo of Pecos on its mesa overlooking the Santa Fe Trail (Map 4). Pecos Pueblo had been there for a long time. It is now known that it was established in the 1300s, and after about 1450 took on the form it had when Coronado arrived—a large, multi-storied pueblo with a central plaza and kivas and

perhaps two thousand inhabitants. Pecosians were middlemen in the Plains-Pueblo trade. Flint, tobacco pipes, and bison hides from the Plains were exchanged for corn, beans, pottery, and obsidian from the Rio Grande pueblos.

The Franciscans built a church and convento at Pecos in the 1620s. Pecos participated in the Pueblo Revolt of 1680, but sided with the Spanish during the Reconquest of the 1690s. In the 1700s, Pecos continued to be a trading center, but suffered from continuing attacks by the Comanches and at least three major epidemics. By 1786 there were fewer than two hundred Pecosians left; by the 1820s there were about forty. The last thirty-eight inhabitants moved to Jemez Pueblo in 1838, leaving the pueblo and the church complex to the elements and firewood pillagers.[4]

Emory reported the pueblo and the church to be in fair condition in 1846 (Fig. 3.1), but by 1858 the church roof had been removed and the adobe walls of church and pueblo were melting. The site continued to fall

3.1. Pecos Mission, 1846; drawing by William H. Emory. Emory (1848).

into ruin until A. V. Kidder began excavations there in 1915 (see Chapter 25). Although seen by many early observers, no one made a detailed measured description of the site, perhaps because it was too recently abandoned: there was no mystery about who the occupants had been. But there was mystery surrounding the decline of the Pecos population.

One explanation was contained in the Montezuma legend, a mélange of Pueblo, Spanish, and Anglo elements merged with an Aztec name—Montezuma. There were two Montezumas (or Moctezumas) in Aztec history. Montezuma I became ruler in 1440. He guided the expansion of military and political domination, built an aqueduct from Chapultepec to Tenochtitlán, and expanded the city. Montezuma II was the ruler when Cortés arrived in Mexico in 1519 and died in Cortés's hands the next year.[5]

The name "Montezuma" was carried north by Spanish colonists and their Indian servants, especially the Aztec-speaking Tlaxcalans. Probably, as Adolph Bandelier later speculated, the Southwestern "Montezuma" was partly a fusion of Aztec legends about Montezuma I and distorted historical information about Montezuma II. Probably there were some elements of the legend of Quetzalcóatl, the bearded, fair-skinned cultural hero-god, who had gone away to the east, promising to return at some future time. Whether the Quetzalcóatl legend was preconquest, or a Spanish rationalization for the inevitability of the conquest, the idea of a cultural hero who goes away with a promise to return at some indefinite time became part of the Montezuma legend.[6]

Apparently the Mexican "Montezuma" became intertwined with a traditional pan-Pueblo cultural hero Poseyemu. Poseyemu is similar to Prometheus, at least in the role Aeschylus gave Prometheus, as bringer of the arts, agriculture, and technology to humanity. Poseyemu is identified with fertility and rain, central concerns in the Pueblo world. After the Spanish arrival, Poseyemu apparently came to be called "Montezuma" by some Pueblo groups, with the name achieving common usage among Pueblo Indians, Mexican Indians, and Hispanics.[7]

The version of the Montezuma legend set at Pecos is most completely presented by Josiah Gregg in his *Commerce of the Prairies* in 1844. He notes that Pecos had dwindled and the survivors had moved to Jemez, then recounts the principal elements of the legend: that Montezuma told the people to keep a sacred fire going in a kiva "until he should return to deliver his people from the yoke of the Spaniards," and that the people daily watched the sunrise hoping to see Montezuma return (Fig. 3.2). The Pecosians never lost hope until the fire was extinguished, but the task of tending it took its toll; the people died from exhaustion and asphyxiation trying to keep it going. Their corpses were fed to "a monstrous serpent, which kept itself in excellent condition by feeding upon these delicacies. . . . This huge snake was represented as the idol they worshipped, and as subsisting entirely upon the flesh of his devotees: live infants, however, seemed to suit his palate best." While only Pecos had the great reptile, all other Pueblos "held Montezuma to be their perpetual sovereign."[8]

A variant had been published in 1840 in the New Orleans *Picayune* by Matthew (Matt) C. Field, a journalist who visited Santa Fe in 1839. In his version, the last of the Pecosians were a romantic young couple stricken by a "pestilential disorder." They took a brand from the sacred flame and fired the prairie and the mountainside so that Montezuma's flame "shall tell the world how Montezuma's children have passed away!" Having set the conflagration, the lovers died locked in each other's arms, "kissing death from each other's lips, and smiling to see the fire of Montezuma mounting up to heaven."[9]

The "giant snake" and "eternal fire" elements of the legend derived from Pueblo practices and beliefs. Fires were kept burning for long periods in kivas; snakes figure prominently in Southwestern Indian legend, mythology, and iconography. The great Pecos serpent may have been Spanish and Anglo inter-

3.2. *"Watching for Montezuma."* Scribner's Monthly Magazine *1885.*

pretations of the water serpent Avanyu (or Awanyu), who figures prominently in Pueblo mythology and iconography.[10]

Other variants of the legend recorded by Balduin Möllhausen in 1853, and elaborated by the pseudo-traveler the Abbé Emmanuel Henri Domenech, have Montezuma predicting the coming of the Anglos who will "destroy the power" of Hispanic oppressors. Montezuma will return and "then should the earth be fertilized by abundant rain, and the nation be enriched by the treasures buried in the midst of the mountains."[11] This version is a wondrous mix of Puebloan and European elements: deliverance from oppression, rain and fertility and treasure. Treasure buried in mountains is a prominent element in European folklore, which Domenech probably added.

The ubiquity of the legend was suggested by Emory as he proceeded with Kearny's army down the Gila River in October 1846:

> We are now in the regions made famous in olden times by the fables of Friar Marcos, and eagerly did we ascend every mound, expecting to see in the distance . . . the fabulous "Casa Montezuma."
> . . . The Indians here do not know the name Aztec. Montezuma is the outward point in their chronology; and as he is supposed to have lived and reigned for all time preceding his disappearance, so do they speak of every event preceding the Spanish conquest as the days of Montezuma.[12]

Emory's claim of the ubiquity of the legend is more rhetorical than factual; nonetheless it suggests that it was widespread.

Hopis, Welshmen, and Mormons

There was also the legend that began in 1580 as a geopolitical ploy in the court of Elizabeth I, came with British colonists to North America, found its way to the Great Plains, and finally to the Southwest: the legend of the Welsh Indians. The simplest version is that in 1170 Prince Madoc, of Wales, led a group of colonists across the Atlantic to a "western land," left them there, and sailed back to Wales, promising to return. Madoc seems to have been conjured up, Merlin-like, from old legends of Arthurian conquests in western lands for geopolitical purposes by the English. Queen Elizabeth's advisors, especially the brilliant alchemist, "Arch Conjurer," and philosopher Dr. John Dee, used the Madoc legend to assert prior discovery, hence legal possession, of North America by England. A "Title Royal" submitted to Queen Elizabeth, in 1580, asserted that "The Lord Madoc, sonne to Owen Gwynedd, Prince of Northwales, led a Colonie and inhabited in Terra Florida or thereabowts" in 1170. Therefore the English held title to "all the Coasts and Islands beginning at or abowt Terra Florida . . . unto Atlantis going Northerly." Presumably the 1536 merger of England and Wales made Madoc retroactively English. Later courtiers made similar arguments. Sir George Peckham cited a purported speech to his Aztec subjects by "Mutuzuma . . . made in the presence of Hernando Curtese" about a noble king and captain, "Prince Madocke." Therefore, "Mutuzuma's" speech clearly established "the undoubted title of her Majestie" to North America.[13]

The Madoc legend thus became a minor part of the propaganda campaign that England waged against Catholic Spain for two centuries and more. But, as good legends do, it came to have a life of its own. After the English came to North America, there were rumors and purported sightings of "White Indians," and interpretations of Indian languages or words as "Welsh." As Welsh historian Gwyn Williams says, sardonically: "By the twentieth century, at least fifteen Indian languages had been identified as Welsh, often by linguists of such uncommon capacity as to be able to recognize the Welsh language without knowing it."[14]

The Tuscarora in Virginia, the Mandan of the Upper Missouri, and the Comanches of the Southern Plains were all said to be "Welsh." George Catlin, the famed Indian painter, avidly sought Welsh Indians throughout the prairies and Plains in the 1830s and 1840s. He thought he had found remnants of them among the Mandan, whose ancestors, he said, had migrated from a landing somewhere along the Gulf Coast. Others were skeptical.[15]

In the 1840s and 1850s, however, enthusiasts took new hope: Welsh Indians were alive and well in the Southwest, disguised as Zunis, or Hopis, or Navajos. Ruxton, in 1846, noted stories about the Hopi being of Welsh derivation. The Abbé Domenech described "a great many" Zuni Indians, whom he never saw, as having "white skin, fair hair, and blue eyes" derived from Welsh women who followed their miner husbands into Zuni country and married Indian men after their husbands "were all massacred by the Indians. . . . What strengthens this tradition is, that we could cite [but he does not do so] numerous Zuni words which are quite analogous to English [i.e., Welsh] ones, having just the same signification; yet the Indians deny this story, which does not do credit to their hospitality." P. G. S. Ten Broeck, an army physician stationed at Fort Defiance, also heard of the Zuni-Welsh connection: "They [Zuni] are supposed to be descended from the band of Welsh, which Prince Madoc took with him on a voyage of discovery, in the twelfth century; and it is said that they weave peculiarly and in the same manner as the people of Wales."[16]

The purported Hopi-Welsh connection interested the Mormons in the early 1850s, and became intertwined with questions about the Southwestern ruins in relation to the *Book of Mormon*. Brigham Young, the indomitable Mormon leader, probably heard the Hopi-Welsh story from members of the Mormon Battalion who passed through the Southwest in 1846, trailing behind Kearny's army.

In 1858 Young sent Jacob Hamblin to the Hopi Mesas to scout out the country and look into the possibility of doing some missionizing, as prelude to Mormon settlement in Arizona after 1876, particularly along the Little Colorado and Salt rivers. With Hamblin was James Durial Davis, a native Welshman, whose task it was to learn if the Hopi spoke a Celtic tongue.[17]

Young's curiosity about the Hopi-Welsh connection had a theological basis. The *Book of Mormon* tells how "Nephites" and "Lamanites" migrated from the eastern Mediterranean to South America, then northward through Mexico into North America. After their mutual Armageddon at the Hill Cumorah in New York, only the bad-guy Lamanites supposedly remained to become the Indians of historic times, marked for their wickedness by their "red skins." The Mormons also believed that when the Lamanite/Indians were all converted to Mormonism, their red skins would metamorphose and they would become a "white and delightsome" people. The Mormon Battalion troops brought to Salt Lake City tales of ruins they had seen along the Gila River. These "ruined cities" seemed to confirm the *Book of Mormon*: they must have been occupied by the Nephites during their northward migrations.[18]

In Mormon eyes, the Hopi were at a higher level of development than the surrounding "wild tribes." Perhaps they were a surviving Nephite island amid a sea of Lamanites. But if the Hopi spoke Welsh, then either they were not remnant Nephites, or the Nephites came from Wales and not ancient Israel, as the *Book of Mormon* asserted. Davis found no trace of the Welsh tongue in Hopi speech. He did pick up local stories that the Hopi were worshipers of Montezuma and had migrated from Mexico. That seemingly strengthened the Nephite connection, but left the Welsh connection up in the air. In 1863 Hamblin brought three Hopi men to Salt Lake City. They were besieged by Welshmen wanting them to utter Celtic words, but the beleaguered men failed the test, and there the matter rested.[19]

But the Welsh connection did not die. While scholars found no Welsh-Indian connections, nor a New World landfall for Prince Madoc, the Daughters of the American Revolution (DAR) found both. On November 10, 1953, the Virginia Cavalier Chapter of the DAR erected a plaque at Fort Morgan on the shores of Mobile Bay, Alabama, which reads: "In memory of Prince Madoc, a Welsh explorer who landed on the shores of Mobile Bay in 1170 and left behind, with the Indians, the Welsh language."[20]

While the Montezuma and Welsh Indian legends are entertaining, they are noted for another reason. In the period 1800–1860, modern historiography and ethnohistory (the study of European documents relating to indigenous ethnic groups) were nascent; archaeology was even more so. Comparative linguistics was well under way, especially in Europe, but with the exception of Albert Gallatin and William Turner, few in the United States understood the principles on which it was based, or commanded the data to make any systematic comparisons. Over the next half-century, these fields all developed procedures and canons of evidence to test claims of historical connections inherent in the Montezuma and Welsh Indian legends. At the same time, scholars in the Southwest developed methods for studying Indian legends in relation to Pueblo culture histories. Such legends were a focus of attention from about 1880 until the "New Archaeology" was introduced in 1914.

Salinas Ruins

The so-called Salinas Ruins attracted the attention of early Anglo observers (Map 7). When the Spanish arrived, they found as many as twenty pueblos situated along the east flanks of the Manzano Mountains and out to the edges of the High Plains (Map 4), some near saline playas, long a source of widely traded salt. The Spanish established missions at several pueblos including Chilili, Tajique, Tabirá, Abó, Quarai, and Las Humanas, the last later known as Gran Quivira. By 1846 all of them had long been abandoned (Map 4).

As part of his reconnaissance of New Mexico in 1846, Lieutenant Abert passed through the Salinas region. At Quarai, he found "yet standing the walls of a time-worn cathedral," and a similar structure at Abó. He made extensive measurements,

as well as watercolor sketches (see Fig. 2.1). He could gather little local information about the sites: "They view our inquisitiveness with jealous eyes, for they can only account for it by supposing we are in search of gold which tradition has said is buried beneath the altars and floors of these old churches and other ruins." Abert had encountered the legend of the Salinas Pueblos.[21]

The second venture into the Salinas country was in December 1853. Major James Henry Carleton led one hundred dragoons from Albuquerque "as an expedition to explore the country around the ruins of Gran Quivira, New Mexico, and for other objects connected with the bands of Apache Indians who often infest that portion of the territory."[22] Carleton's diary of the trip was published in 1854 by the Smithsonian Institution. He too measured and described the ruins at Abó and Quarai, but he also closely inspected Humanas, or Gran Quivira (Fig. 3.3).

In the 1850s, Coronado's route of march to the Great Plains in 1541 was still unclear. Over time, the ruins of the pueblo and mission complex at Humanas had become identified with his Gran Quivira (and are still so called), and they, together with the ruins of

3.3. Humanas (Gran Quivira) Church; photograph by Don Fowler, 1985. Don Fowler Collection.

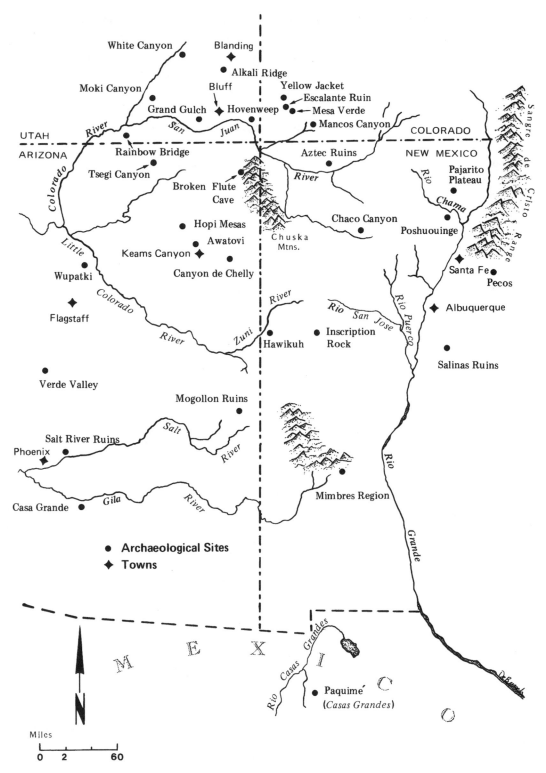

White Canyon

Blanding

Moki Canyon

Alkali Ridge

Bluff

Yellow Jacket

Grand Gulch

Hovenweep

Escalante Ruin

Mesa Verde

Mancos Canyon

UTAH

COLORADO

ARIZONA

NEW MEXICO

Rainbow Bridge

Aztec Ruins

Colorado

Tsegi Canyon

Rio

Pajarito
Plateau

San

Juan

River

Chama

Broken Flute
Cave

Chaco Canyon

Poshuouinge

Hopi Mesas

Rio

Awatovi

Chuska
Mtns.

Santa Fe

Keams Canyon

Pecos

Little

Canyon de Chelly

Wupatki

River

Albuquerque

Colorado

Rio

Rio San Jose

Rio Puerco

Flagstaff

River

Zuni

Hawikuh

Inscription
Rock

Salinas Ruins

Verde Valley

Mogollon Ruins

Salt

Salt River Ruins

River

Phoenix

Rio

Casa Grande

Gila

River

Mimbres Region

Grande

● **Archaeological Sites**

✦ **Towns**

M   E   X   I   C   O

Rio Casas Grandes

N

Paquimé
(*Casas Grandes*)

De Rancho

Miles

0   2   60

7. Major Southwestern Archaeological Sites and Site Areas

Abó and Quarai, were linked to the Aztec migration legends. Carleton carefully measured and described the mission complex and associated pueblo at Gran Quivira. As have others since, he puzzled over the seeming lack of irrigation or potable water, rejecting Josiah Gregg's earlier claim of aqueducts and cisterns serving the complex. Carleton refuted the claim that Humanas was Coronado's Gran Quivira, concluding that Pedro de Castañeda's description of "round houses roofed with straw," and a hunter-gatherer lifeway did not fit Humanas. Nor did he think that the sites were remnants of the Aztec southward migration. He rightly concluded that the three sites had been Spanish missions, but wrongly thought that they were destroyed at the time of the 1680 Pueblo Revolt.[23]

Carleton also heard the Salinas gold legend. "Old Mr. Chavez" told him that the "Pueblos of Quivira" were missionized by Spanish priests. At the time of the 1680 Pueblo Revolt, "there were seventy priests and monks . . . all of whom were butchered except two, who contrived to make their escape." Sensing danger, the priests had buried "not only . . . immense treasures . . . , but had concealed likewise the bells of the churches." Ultimately all the "Quivira" Indians died or moved away, but, as is usual with legendary treasure troves, there was a "paper" with directions to the treasure and the bells, "as given from the lips of the last cacique of Quivira." Later, various treasure maps appeared. By 1853 the site had already been thoroughly dug over, as Carleton notes (and as late as the 1950s, the National Park Service was still trying to stop treasure seekers from digging). The principal reasons for Carleton's excursion, the Apaches, slipped away: "We found that the Mescalero Apaches, with whom we had some business of interest, had all gone far towards the south."[24]

The Salinas Ruins languished for many decades after Carleton's visit. The National Park Service finally gained control of Abó, Quarai, and Gran Quivira in the 1970s and thereafter conducted archaeological and ethnohistorical studies. The picture that emerged is one of marginal pueblos subsisting by farming, hunt-

ing bison, and collecting piñon nuts from trees which, then as now, blanket the slopes of the mountains. They traded with Plains groups and were active in collecting and trading salt from the playas. Their situation was always tenuous and water was always scarce. Over time, drought, disease, Spanish oppression, and Apache raiding took their toll. By the 1670s the survivors had moved to the Rio Grande Valley; there was no one left to participate in the Pueblo Revolt, and no priests to bury bells or treasure.[25]

Gila River Ruins

Father Kino and others briefly described ruins along the Gila River Valley in the 1690s and 1700s (Map 7). Lieutenant William Emory was the first Anglo to closely observe the ruins and discuss their possible origins, as he rode westward with Kearny's army. In Santa Fe, Kearny had signed on John Mix Stanley as artist and mapping assistant. Self-taught, by 1846 Stanley was a well-known painter of Indians; he had been in Santa Fe in 1842 and 1845. His drawings of ruins and the Indian people he encountered while traveling with the army were among the first images widely seen by Anglos in the East.[26]

In the Upper Gila drainage, Emory encountered the first evidence of the "long sought ruins . . . immense quantities of broken pottery, extending for two miles along the river." At the confluence of the Gila River and San Simon Valley, Emory described a very large site with a 270 foot-in-circumference circular wall, another enclosure 400 yards in circumference, and remains of rectangular houses from 20 to 100 feet long. More sites were seen in the days following, including "very large ruins which appeared . . . to have been the abode of five or ten thousand souls."[27] On November 10, Emory investigated and described Casa Grande (Fig. 3.4), although he did not name it. Emory's descriptions of the ruins were of great interest to Albert Gallatin (see below) and helped the latter formulate his hypotheses about Southwestern culture history.

3.4. Casa Grande, 1846; drawing by J. M. Stanley. Emory (1848).

Emory described Casa Grande as "a large pile . . . the remains of a three-story mud house, sixty feet square, pierced for doors and windows. The walls were four feet thick, and formed by layers of mud, two feet thick. . . . it was, no doubt, built by the same race that had once so thickly populated this territory, and left behind the ruins. We made a long and careful search for some specimens . . . but nothing was found except the corn grinder, always met with among the ruins . . . The marine shell, cut into various ornaments, was also found here, which showed that these people came either from the seacoast or trafficked there."

From a Pima man, Emory recorded a legend about the origin of Casa Grande and other nearby ruins:

In bygone days, a woman of surpassing beauty resided in a green spot in the mountains, near the place where we were encamped. All the men admired, and paid court to her. She received the tributes of their devotion, grain, skins, &c. but gave no love or other favor in return. Her virtue, and her determination to remain unmarried were equally firm. There came a drought which threatened the world with famine. In their distress, people applied to her, and she gave corn from her stock, and the supply seemed endless. Her goodness was unbounded. One day, as she was lying asleep with her body exposed, a drop of rain fell on her stomach, which produced conception. A son was the issue, who was the founder of a new race which built all these houses.[28]

John Russell Bartlett and the Casas Grandes

In the summer of 1852, John Russell Bartlett made his leisurely way from San Diego to El Paso by way of the Gila River and northern Chihuahua. There was pressing Boundary Survey business, by then nearly a year behind schedule, but for Bartlett ethnology came first. He visited Casa Grande, spending "three hours . . . at the ruins, the hottest, I think, I have ever experienced," and described the site in detail. He quoted from a manuscript copy of Father Pedro Font's description of 1775 and noted Manje's description of 1694 at the time of Father Kino's visit to the site (see Prologue). Bartlett collected and illustrated potsherds from the site, recognizing their potential as cultural markers.[29]

Nearly a month later, Bartlett eagerly arrived at Casas Grandes (now called Paquimé), in Chihuahua, one of the purported Aztec stopping places (Map 7). In 1584, the historian Baltasar Obregón wrote that Casas Grandes was a

large city . . . [with] buildings that seemed to have been constructed by the ancient Romans. . . . There are many houses of great size, strength and height. They are of six and seven stories, with towers and walls like fortresses for protection and defence . . . The houses contain large and magnificent patios paved with enormous and beautiful stones resembling jasper. . . . The walls of the houses were whitewashed and painted in many colors and shades with pictures of the building.[30]

Obregón obviously never saw the site, but his description whetted Bartlett's appetite. What he found was a very large building complex built entirely of puddled adobe. He made several sketches and unsuccessfully attempted an overall ground plan. His detailed description of the ruins were the first to be published, despite the prominence of the site in Spanish and Mexican histories for two centuries. Bartlett again collected potsherds and a few whole vessels. "I collected a number of specimens exhibiting various patterns . . .

The ruins of Casas Grandes . . . face the cardinal points, and consist of fallen and erect walls, the latter varying in height from five to thirty feet, and often projecting above the heaps of others which have fallen and crumbled away. . . . From a close examination of the building or buildings, I came to the conclusion that the outer portions were the lowest, and not above one story in height, while the central ones were from three to six stories. . . . every portion of this edifice is built of adobe, or mud . . . nowhere, as far as I could trace the foundations, could I discover any walls of stone. . . . Although there is less order in the *tout ensemble* of this great collection of buildings than in those of the north, the number of small apartments, the several stages or stories, the courts within . . . resemble in many respects the large edifices of the semi-civilized or Pueblo Indians of New Mexico.[31]

They will also serve for comparisons with the pottery of the Moquis, Zuñis, and other Pueblo Indians. . . . When so little remains of a people, the smallest fragments of their works of art become important."[32]

Casas Grandes, or Paquimé, continued to be a major enigma to Southwestern archaeologists for a century. In 1958, the Amerind Foundation of Dragoon, Arizona, began a major excavation program, led by the late Charles DiPeso, who produced a magisterial eight-volume study of the site and its place in the cultural history of the Gran Chichimeca.[33]

Chaco Canyon and the Navajo Expedition

The name *Chaca,* at the proper location for Chaco Canyon, appears on a map drawn around 1774 by Bernardo de Miera y Pacheco, mapmaker for the Domínguez-Escalante expedition in 1776. The first published reference to the Chaco ruins is seemingly by Josiah Gregg in 1844. He concluded that the Chaco ruins, the Hopi villages, and Casas Grandes all were built by "founders . . . descended from the same common stock," that is, early Aztecs.[34]

In 1846, General Kearny promised the citizens of New Mexico protection from the Navajos, but conflict continued and by the spring of 1849 was a serious problem. In August 1849, Lt. Colonel John Macrae Washington led a large contingent of troops and Pueblo, Mexican, and Anglo volunteers into Navajo country to try and force an abiding treaty. There was a Mexican guide, known only as Carravahal, together with Francisco Hosta, the civil governor of Jemez Pueblo, and the Kern brothers as topographers and artists. Lieutenant James Hervey Simpson was the topographical engineer assigned to the expedition.[35]

After visiting and describing Jemez Pueblo, the troops crossed the Continental Divide and started down the Chaco drainage (Map 8). They soon encountered the easternmost of the great pueblo Chacoan ruins:

[There] could be seen in the distance on a slight elevation, a conspicuous ruin called, according to some of the Pueblo Indians with us, *Pueblo de Montezuma,* and according to the Mexicans, *Pueblo Colorado.* Hosta calls it *Pueblo de Ratones;* Sandoval, the friendly Navajo chief with us, *Pueblo Grande;* and Carravahal, our Mexican guide, who probably knows more about it than anyone else, *Pueblo Pintado.*[36]

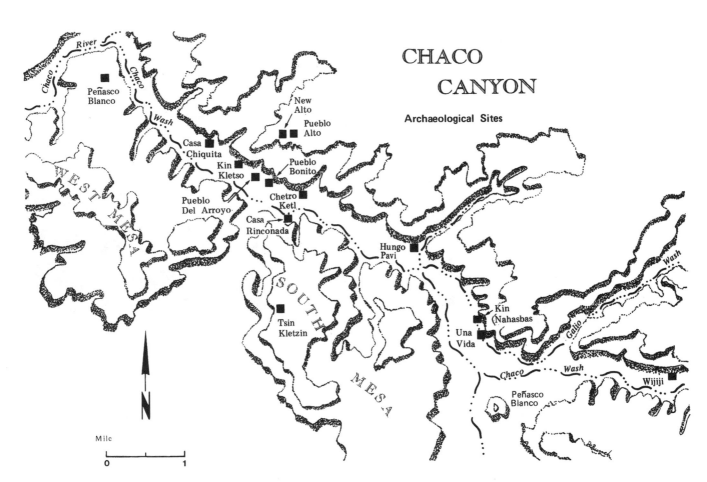

8. Principal "Great House" Ruins in Chaco Canyon

3.5 (left). Pueblo Pintado, Chaco Canyon; drawing by R. H. Kern. Simpson (1849).

3.6 (below). Reconstruction of Hungo Pavi Pueblo, Chaco Canyon; drawing by R. H. Kern. Simpson (1849).

Simpson adopted Carravahal's name, as he did for the other ruins (Fig. 3.5). Simpson and the Kerns were particularly struck by the fineness of the masonry in the ruins. The fine, rubble-core, dressed-face masonry of Chacoan houses has been noted by all students of the Chacoan culture ever since. Simpson described the ground plan, the rooms, the floor/roof beams of the upper stories, the post-and-lintel door construction and the presence of kivas.[37]

The troop entered Chaco Canyon proper and soon came to "Pueblo Wege-gi [Wijiji] . . . The number of apartments on the ground floor, judging from what was distinguishable, was probably ninety-nine." The next day, Simpson, Richard Kern, and Carravahal

The ground plan shows an extent of exterior development of eight-hundred and seventy-two feet, and a number of rooms upon the ground floor equal to seventy-two. . . . The main walls of the building are at base two and three-quarter feet through, and at this time show a height of about thirty feet. The ends of the floor beams, which are still visible, plainly showing that there was originally, at least, a vertical series of four floors, . . . and as the debris at the base of the walls is very great, it is reasonable to infer that there may have been even more. The floor beams, which are round, in transverse section, and eleven inches in diameter, as well as the windows, which are as small as twelve by thirteen inches, have been arranged horizontally with great precision and regularity.[38]

continued on down the canyon and recorded Pueblo Una Vida, which they found to be 994 feet in circumference, with four kivas and two, possibly three, stories.[39] They next came to the "Hungo Pavi . . . Crooked Nose" (Fig. 3.6) which Kern reconstructed.

Next came "Pueblo Chetro Kettle [Chetro Ketl], the Rain Pueblo," which still had rooms with plastered walls and intact ceilings, and what were later called "tower kivas": "The [six] circular estuffas [kivas] . . . have a greater depth than any we have seen, and differ from them also in exhibiting more stories, one of them showing certainly two, and possibly three . . ."[40]

Just downstream from Chetro Ketl, they came to what was to become the most famous of the Chacoan ruins, Pueblo Bonito. "The circuit of its walls is about thirteen hundred feet. Its present elevation shows that it has had at least four stories of apartments. . . . it is not unreasonable to infer that the original number of rooms was as many as eight-hundred." Simpson counted four kivas, "the largest being sixty feet in diameter, showing two stories in height and having a present depth of twelve feet." He also noted "several

rooms in a very good state of preservation—one of them . . . being walled up with alternate beds of large and small stones, the regularity of the combination producing a very pleasing effect."[41]

The day was wearing on; other ruins were only briefly noted: "Pueblo del Arroyo," and two other ruins not named, but later called Kin Kletso (Yellow House) and Casa Chiquita. Finally, they noted "Pueblo de Peñasca Blanca" [Peñasco Blanco, White Bluff], and correctly noted that it was second only to Pueblo Bonito in size. Having measured and described the individual ruins, Simpson devoted some space to a discussion of construction details, correctly concluding "that these pueblos were terraced on their inner or court side," as Kern interpreted Hungo Pavi in his reconstruction.[42]

Simpson's and Kern's descriptions and illustrations of the Chaco Canyon ruins, published in 1850, brought them to the attention of the Anglo world. Since then, the ruins have excited the interest of both archaeologists and the public and are among the most studied sites in the Southwest. Yet the "Chaco Phenomenon," a term coined in the 1970s to describe not only the ruins in and adjacent to the canyon, but numerous sites away from the canyon, called "Outliers," as well as the enigmatic "road system" centering on the canyon, remains with more questions unanswered than answered.[43]

The troops moved northwestward away from Chaco Canyon, met a large party of Navajo, and parleyed with them. But an argument led to the killing of Narbona, a powerful Navajo elder and leader, and six others. Colonel Washington's peace campaign was off to a miserable start. Undaunted, the troop moved on, finally entering Canyon de Chelly, where they met with more Navajos (Map 7). Simpson and Kern explored Canyon del Muerto and Canyon de Chelly proper; like all those to follow, they were amazed and delighted by the geology of the canyons. They described and sketched, but did not name, White House ruin (Fig. 3.7).[44]

The Navajo people in Canyon de Chelly treated Colonel Washington and his entourage with great respect, agreeing to treaties with diplomatic aplomb. But they also managed to convince him that Apaches had attacked Zuni Pueblo and he turned his troops thereto, arriving after several days' march to discover the rumor was untrue.[45] Simpson described Zuni in some detail. The troop then turned eastward, stopping, as had innumerable others, for the cool water found at the base of Inscription Rock. For untold centuries individuals had recorded their passing by inscribing symbols, names, dates, etc., on the Rock. Simpson and the Kerns copied many of the inscriptions before adding their own names (Figs. 3.8, 3.9, and 3.10).

Sunset Crater and Wupatki

The Sitgreaves survey passed near, but did not see, Sunset Crater. However, Sitgreaves described "ridges of lava and a black dust, the detritus of the lava, covering the ground in many places . . . all the prominent points occupied by the ruins of stone houses of considerable size, and in some instances of three stories in height. . . . they occurred at intervals for an extent of eight or nine miles, and the ground was thickly

3.7 (above). "Ruins in Canon De Chelly [White House]"; drawing by R. H. Kern. Simpson (1849).

3.8 (right). Inscription Rock; drawing by R. H. Kern. Simpson (1849).

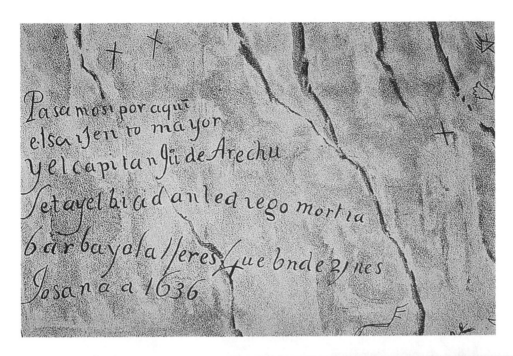

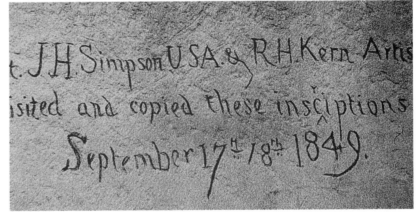

3.9 (above). Inscription on Inscription Rock; drawing by R. H. Kern. Simpson (1849).

3.10 (right). Simpson and Kern signature inscription on Inscription Rock. Drawing by Richard Kern. Simpson (1849).

strewed with fragments of pottery in all directions."[46] Some of these ruins are now included within Wupatki National Monument (Map 7).

The Four Corners Area

The final military expedition before the Civil War was that led in 1859 by Captain John N. Macomb from Santa Fe to the confluence of the Grand and Green rivers in Utah. Macomb was accompanied by the geol-

ogist John Strong Newberry, who had earlier been with Ives. Their reports of the trip were shelved as attention turned to the impending war, and finally appeared in 1876, by which time Newberry was an eminent professor of geology at Columbia University.

Newberry's report contains geological observations and a journal of the trip, enhanced by a large number of his watercolors of landscapes. The route of travel was from Santa Fe up the Chama River Valley, then across the Continental Divide into the drainage of the

San Juan River. The party circled, but did not climb onto, the Mesa Verde, explored the Dolores River Valley, and then marched to the Colorado River, which they tried to reach by way of a lateral canyon, but failed to do so. They returned along the San Juan Valley and by way of Jemez Pueblo.[47]

Newberry provided the first detailed descriptions of several ruins. Near Abiquiu he noted "the ancient ruins which crown the bluff" above the Chama River. This is the site now known as Poshouinge, an ancestral Tewa village occupied between 1250 and 1550 (Map 7). It may contain as many as twelve hundred rooms and eight or more kivas. He also described a site south of Abiquiu, now known as Tsiping, or Cañones Ruin, now known to have been occupied in the late 1200s and early 1300s. According to Tewa tradition, it was the duty of Tsiping to block raids of enemies from the northwest.[48]

Newberry provided the first detailed description of, but did not name, Aztec Ruin (Map 7): "The principal structures are large pueblos, handsomely built of stone, . . . The external walls are composed of yellow Cretaceous sandstone, dressed to a common smooth surface without hammer-marks; in some places they are still 25 feet in height." He thought that the pottery and the architecture indicated occupation by the "common aboriginal race of this region, now generally known as the Pueblo Indians."[49]

In the Dolores River Valley (Map 7), Newberry described the site noted in 1776 by Father Escalante, and now called "Escalante Ruin." He also described the extensive ruin now called Yellow Jacket Pueblo: "There is every evidence that a large population resided here for many years, perhaps centuries . . . How they managed to exist here, and how their town was depopulated, are questions that suggest themselves at once, but certainly the former is more puzzling; . . . where a population of many thousands once existed, now as many hundreds could not be sustained . . . The remains of *metates* (cornmills) are abundant about the ruins, and corn was doubtless the staple article of their existence, but none could be raised here now. The ruins of several large reservoirs, built of masonry,

may be seen . . . and there are traces of acequias, which led to these, through which water was brought perhaps from a great distance."[50]

During the return trip at the confluence of the San Juan and Animas rivers, Newberry noted the "remains of a large, but very ancient town . . . the foundations of many buildings of considerable size still remaining, and traces of an acequia through which water was brought from a point some miles above on the Animas." The site no longer exists, lying either under the Farmington, New Mexico, city hospital or the sewage disposal plant.[51]

Although Newberry's report did not appear until 1876, he provided the first descriptions of a number of Southwestern ruins. Some, such as Aztec Ruin, came to have prominent places in the development of Southwestern archaeology at the beginning of the twentieth century.

Gallatin's Research Agenda

In 1843, William Hickling Prescott published his best-seller *The Conquest of Mexico,* various Spanish documents were being published by Ternaux-Compans, and the great compilation of pre-Columbian Mesoamerican paintings by Lord Kingsborough was completed in 1848.[52] All this stimulated the venerable Albert Gallatin to pull together and sift the available information on Mexico and the Southwest, and formulate a series of sharply focused research questions, most of which are still under investigation 150 years later. In 1845 Gallatin summarized what he knew and conjectured in a paper on the "Semi-Civilizations" of Mexico. In late 1847, he was finishing an extensive *Introduction* to the linguistic materials collected by Horatio Hale during the Wilkes Expedition of 1840–42. Keenly interested in the Southwest, Gallatin wrote to Lt. William Emory for information in advance of the publication of Emory's report. Drawing on Emory's letter, and other materials, Gallatin inserted a forty-four-page "Ancient Semi-Civilization of New Mexico" into his introduction to Hale's work. Soon after the Abert and Emory reports appeared, E. G. Squier published an extensive summary of them in the *American Review,* together with his own interpretation of available Spanish documents and a critique of Gallatin's two papers.[53]

The publications by Gallatin and Squier are the founding documents in the history of Anglo Southwestern anthropology, marking the beginning of systematic analysis of ethnographic, archaeological, historic, and ethnohistoric data in the region. Gallatin advanced a series of hypotheses concerning intertribal relationships, the origin and spread of agriculture, and the question of Mexican-Southwest relationships; and Squier reacted to them. Both drew on Spanish documents to sort out early histories of the Pueblo and non-Puebloan tribes. Both raised issues relating to Spanish-Indian acculturation, and acculturation between tribes. Squier challenged some of Gallatin's assertions. In short, modern analytical scholarship on the Southwest was under way. This was Gallatin's final contribution; he died soon after, almost ninety years old.

The "origins" issue and the Mexican-Southwest connection as subset of it was noted earlier. By the 1780s, it was assumed that the most probable Old World-New World connection was in the north across the Bering Strait, discovered in 1741. This meant that the Western Hemisphere likely was populated from north to south, either overland or coasting by boat along the coasts of Asia, the Aleutians, and western North America. There was still the question of acceptable evidence. Jefferson, Gallatin, and others agreed that linguistic affinity was the primary hard evidence by which connections between "races," "tribes," or "nations" could be firmly established.

In his *Synopsis* of 1836 and his two "semi-civilization" papers, Gallatin steadfastly maintained, as did DuPonceau, that *all* American Indian languages have "a uniformity of character indicat[ing] a common origin," despite a great divergence into an estimated one hundred-plus distinct languages. He assumed that linguistic affinities will be demonstrated between Indian and Asian languages in due time. In his 1845 paper, Gallatin cites physical data to firm up his case: Indians

and East Asians share a "similarity of physical type," which would tend to "prove a general, though perhaps not universal, common origin."[54]

Although he does not refer to the eminent German anatomist Friedrich Blumenbach's works, Gallatin probably was familiar with them. In the 1780s Blumenbach had written of "the extreme probable origins of the Americans from northern Asia," and speculated that there likely had been migrations at different times, with the Eskimo peoples being the last—essentially the same proposal advanced by linguists and physical anthropologists in the 1980s and 1990s.[55]

If Indian peoples derived from Northeast Asia, the first question was: when? Gallatin argues for a long, though indeterminate, length of time, given the great diversity of known Indian languages, which had occurred, he thought, after people reached the New World. He then turned to the hoary issue of *commensurability.* Were the "semi-civilizations" of America (as he called them) indigenous, or derived from elsewhere? Commensurability, Gallatin notes, "involves two most important questions in the history of man: that of the presumed inferiority of some races; and whether savage tribes can, of themselves, and without any foreign assistance, emerge from the rudest and lowest social state, and gradually attain even the highest degree of civilization known to us." He thought the answer lay in the abilities of peoples in different cultures to independently develop astronomy, mathematics, and a calendar system. Thus he examined the Mesoamerican calendars and their underlying astronomy in some detail. He concluded that many cultures worldwide had independently figured out the "annual motion of the sun." Having achieved that, further advances in astronomy and mathematics followed, and the path to civilization lay open.[56]

A related issue was the origin of agriculture. Gallatin agreed with Humboldt that "maize is exclusively a plant of American origin" and "tropical" derivation, and that its cultivation ultimately led to civilization. He concluded that both New World agriculture and astronomy were indigenous, and hence, so too were the "semi-civilizations" of the New World.[57]

Gallatin then turns specifically to the Southwest, drawing principally on Castañeda's account of the Coronado expedition, recently published by Ternaux-Compans. He notes that the "villages" of Cibola (Zuni), Tusayan (Hopi) and Tiguex (central Rio Grande Pueblos) are agricultural, planting the same crops—maize, beans and pumpkins—as the Mexicans, proof that the Pueblos derived agriculture from the Mexicans. But connections beyond food crops are another matter. "Clavigero, who makes the Aztecs to come from the Rio Gila, appears to have embraced that opinion . . . on account of the ruins of buildings, on the banks of that river and others farther south, generally called 'casa grandé,' and which are supposed to have been built by the Aztecs." Then comes the clincher: what, he asks, is the hard evidence? "No trace of the Mexican language has been discovered in any part of [present-day New Mexico and Sonora, hence,] it seems probable that the Indians of New Mexico and of the country south of it . . . were not of the same stock or family as the Mexicans or Toltecs, though they may have received their agriculture from those nations."[58]

Gallatin's final statement on the Mexican-Southwest connection came in 1848. By then, he had Abert's and Emory's data, and was better able to sort out the Pueblo tribes. He again rejects the supposition that the Aztecs came from the Southwest: "It is indeed contradicted by the Mexican traditions, which place the Aztlan of the Azteques [sic], not in some unknown remote country, but adjacent to Michoacan." If linguistic evidence ultimately warrants, it is "most probable that the civilization of the river Gila, and of New Mexico, must be ascribed to an ancient Toltec colony." But "if the languages should prove different from the Mexican proper or any of the other spoken between the tropics, we will not be able ever to ascertain how this northern civilization originated."[59]

In summary, Gallatin's conclusions can be stated as a set of hypotheses that helped shape Americanist anthropology for the next half-century—and, in some instances, to the twenty-first century.

First, the Western Hemisphere was peopled from north to south, either across the Bering "bridge," or by coasting in water craft. The same possibilities continue to be debated.[60]

Second, the first migrants were hunter gatherers who spread quickly southward, aided by an explosive increase in population. This issue also continues as the timing of the earliest New World north-south migrations, by land or by sea, is more closely examined.[61]

Third, the "semi-civilizations" of Mexico and Peru were indigenous developments, with no appreciable influence from the Old World. The issue of significant "influences" on the development of pre-Columbian Mesoamerican and Highland South American civilizations from Europe, Asia, Africa, the Pacific Islands, or all four, has remained in controversy to the present day, in contributions ranging from mainstream science to fantasy.

Fourth, agriculture, and possibly other elements of "semi-civilization," diffused *from* the Mesoamerican core *into* the Southwest. It is presently accepted that agriculture indeed entered the Southwest from Mesoamerica. The nature of other connections, including migrations, remains in contention.[62]

Fifth, the purported "northern" point of derivation of the Toltecs, Aztecs, etc., could *not be* the Southwest, because there was no hard evidence of linguistic connections. This assertion was challenged by Balduin Möllhausen in 1858, who was aware of the work of his fellow German, the linguist Johann Karl Buschmann, on what came to be called the Uto-Aztecan language family and connections within it, including Sonoran and some Southwestern languages. Linguists continue to refine their understanding of Southwestern and Mexican languages and their implications for cultural history.[63]

Albert Gallatin, then, expanded the American anthropological research agenda to include the five hypotheses listed above. Within the Southwest, in the two decades following his death in 1849, interest focused on the Southwest-Mesoamerican connection. The other questions, however, remained central.

The Southwest-Mesoamerican connection was a subset of the larger north-south connection, already discussed for decades. In 1820, Caleb Atwater speculated that some of the Mound Builders had left Ohio, moved toward the Gulf, and then on into Mexico. The massive *Ancient Monuments of the Mississippi Valley,* by Ephraim G. Squier and Edwin H. Davis, published in 1848, favored some sort of north-south connection, but the authors were not sure which way it ran. As David Meltzer notes, Squier and Davis opined that, "Whichever way the moundbuilders had migrated, they either began or ended 'in the gorgeous semi-civilization of Mexico and Peru.'"[64]

The purpose of Squier's 1848 article was to organize and critique what was then known about the Southwest. He also made a prophetic statement about the future Southwest. Referring to early Spanish descriptions of the "Moquis" [Hopis], he notes:

> They have never been subjugated, and no doubt retain their primitive habits, impaired in no essential respect by the changes which have been going on in the other parts of North America during the past three hundred years. They therefore afford to the intelligent explorer an opportunity, never again to be enjoyed, of investigating aboriginal semi-civilization under its original aspects. Included now within the territory of trading, land-absorbing America, it will not be long before their fastnesses will be penetrated by the "Surveyor of Public Lands," and the advantageous sites for mill seats and future cities be duly displayed in lithographic splendor, upon the walls of the office of the "*Moqui Universal Improvement and Land Investment Association,* No.—Wall street, New York!" Farewell then to the peace, simplicity, and the happiness of this Californian [*sic*] Arcadia![65]

Squier could not know just how prescient his jest would be over the next 150 years in both the real "Californian Arcadia," and next door in the Southwest.

The Abbé Domenech and the Southwest

Finally, as a coda, there was a French priest, the Abbé Emmanuel Henri Diedonné Domenech (1824?–1886), who summarized most everything known about American Indian ethnology in his widely disseminated, 910-page *Seven Years' Residence in the Great Deserts of North America,* published in two volumes in 1860 in French, German, and English.[66] His writing style has led some commentators to believe he traveled widely throughout North America. In fact, he spent two years in St. Louis and five years in west Texas and northern Mexico, having been recruited from France as a missionary by the famous French-born vicar-apostolic (later bishop) of Texas, John Mary Odin. Domenech did not reside, nor travel, in any other "Great Deserts" of North America. He did do his homework. He used many sources, including Schoolcraft and "those of the Smithsonian Society [*sic*] and of the Ethnographical [*sic*] Society of New York, as likewise the reports of the scientific expeditions made by order of the government of the United States." Despite the title, the book is a major summary of the routes of travel of the several Pacific Railroad Surveys, some of John C. Frémont's travels, and all the Topographical Engineers expeditions.[67]

Like the sixteenth-century Spanish savant Gregorio Garcia, Domenech found room for many Old World peoples in the "community of origin" of the Indians, including Scythians, Hebrews, Tartars, Scandinavians, Welsh, and various Africans and Asians who arrived by "voluntary or accidental emigrations." These diverse groups intermarried and because of "the difference of the climates, the change in their mode of living, they . . . formed this heterogeneous combination of colors, habits, tastes, languages, and religions, which baffles science and the antiquary's researches."[68]

Domenech's debt to the army reports is patent. His "narration" of a journey from the Mississippi to New Mexico is from Whipple's report, but is presented in an "I [Domenech] was there" manner. At Rocky Dell Creek, on the edge of the Llano Estacado, Whipple describes "a sort of cave, which the Indians have converted into a gallery of fine arts." Domenech has "a sort of grotto that the Indians have turned into a kind of gallery of fine arts"; and so on.[69] His description of Gran Quivira is taken from Carleton; that of Santo Domingo and Laguna from Whipple and

Möllhausen; of Jemez, Chaco Canyon, and Canyon de Chelly from Simpson; of Zuni and the route west to California from Simpson, Sitgreaves, and Whipple. His compilation is a tour de force, neatly laying out what was known about western and Southwestern Indians and archaeology, as well as some natural history, as of about 1857. No American produced anything comparable for several decades. Certainly Domenech's presentation is better organized than Schoolcraft's massive six volumes of anthropological confusion compiled in the 1850s, and used by Domenech in his own work.

CHAPTER 4

Army Ethnographic Observations,
1846–1860

IN ADDITION TO descriptions of ruins, a few army officers published brief ethnographic observations on the Indians. "Observations" include firsthand descriptions, as well as hearsay from Anglo, Spanish, or Mexican sources, the "common knowledge" of the day. The observations are valuable for what they say about Indian cultures between 1846 and 1870, simply because they are all we have.

The Anglos brought their own biases and prejudices with them. They were firmly convinced of their own northern European, and especially Anglo-Saxon, superiority and the rightness of Manifest Destiny. Protestant Anglos were heirs to a long tradition of Hispanophobia, fueled in part by the so-called Black Legend.[1] In its extreme forms, the legend made the Spanish out to be brutal, cruel, rapacious, treacherous, dull-witted, and "hot blooded." By 1846, what began as political propaganda had entered the implicit folk beliefs of many Protestant Anglos. Parts of it were diffusely focused on Catholics in general. The

1840s was a time of particularly strong anti-Catholic sentiment in the United States, itself partly fueled by English Protestant propaganda against the Catholic Irish. The great St. Patrick's Cathedral in New York City was deliberately begun in 1847 as a symbolic counter to the rampant anti-Catholicism of the day.

New Mexicans, as Catholic colonial subjects of the Spanish, were seen by many Anglos to be "as bad as" or even "worse than" the Spanish themselves. Indeed, as David Weber has shown, Anglos held similar stereotypes of Californios and Mexicans in general, symbolized by Texan settler Noah Smithwick's phrase, "I looked upon the Mexicans as scarce more than apes."[2] In Emory's Boundary Survey report, published in 1857, he describes with admiration the presidio and mission system strung across the northern frontier of New Spain. The "downfall" of the frontier, "this magnificent cordon of military and ecclesiastical establishments, and the return of the Indians to a savage life tenfold more ferocious than ever," Emory says, was due to the Mexican Revolution. It was also due to "intermarriage of the whites and Indians," which accounts "for the decline and retrograde march of the population." Beneficial change only occurs when both White men and women come into a country where, "with proper guards upon morals," they can breed freely and become dominant. This "results in exterminating or crushing out the inferior races, or placing them in slavery." Such a view is hardly surprising from the scion of a Maryland plantation family, fixated by "racial color."[3]

Ethnographic Observations, 1846–1859

While many Anglos in New Mexico had a strong negative bias toward the Hispanic population, their views of the Indian peoples were mixed. They quickly came to distinguish Pueblo tribes from the "wild" tribes, as noted earlier. Nearly all Anglo observers spoke highly of the Pueblos, extolling their work ethic, farming abilities, and quiet and serious demeanor, while disparaging the "wild" tribes or "inferior" Hispanics.

The Rio Grande pueblos, from Taos in the north to Isleta in the south, were the most frequently observed and described, especially the architecture, kivas, details of dress and ceremonial, the agricultural fields, and *acequias*, the irrigation canals. Santo Domingo Pueblo was well known since it was situated along the Camino Real between Santa Fe and Albuquerque. The pueblo described by the early chroniclers no longer exists; it and its church were washed away in a flood during the 1880s. The present village and church were built on somewhat higher ground and farther east. Balduin Möllhausen, in 1854, provided the most extensive description of the pueblo, including house construction and details of interior furnishings. He also visited the church (Fig. 4.1) and noted details of interior decoration, including numerous paintings.[4]

4.1. Santo Domingo Pueblo Church, 1853; drawing by H. B. Möllhausen. Möllhausen (1858).

The Zunis

The Zunis were visited by various army survey parties beginning with Simpson and Kern in 1849. Kern's sketches of Zuni were the first visual depictions available to Anglo readers. Although Sitgreaves provided minimal description of Zuni pueblo and people, Kern's accompanying illustrations (see Figs. 2.4 and 2.5) provided vivid depictions of Zuni daily life. Whipple described Zuni in some detail, and Möllhausen provided various illustrations.

The Hopis

Two army parties briefly visited the Hopis in the 1850s, and provided the first substantive descriptions since Father Garcés in 1776. In April 1852 a scouting party including army physician P. G. S. Ten Broeck visited Sichomovi for four days. In May 1857, the Ives party visited Mishongnovi for two days during their trek from the Colorado River to Fort Defiance. Both Ives and Ten Broeck noted the harshness of the environment, the spring-fed reservoirs, the terraced gardens, and sand-dune horticulture. Both noted herds of sheep and cotton cultivation. Both described terraced house construction and remarked on the neatness of the interior rooms, whitewashed with clay (Fig. 4.2).[5]

Ten Broeck's report, in Schoolcraft's compendium, contains the first Anglo mention of kachina dolls. "Hanging by strings from the rafters, I saw some curious and rather horrible little Aztec [sic] images made of wood or clay, and decorated with paint and feathers, which the guide told me were 'saints'; but I have seen the children playing with them in the most irreverent manner."[6] He also provides an extensive description (including sketches of costumes) of a kachina dance, seemingly the first ever published. Although he saw the dance in early April, it was apparently a performance of the Hemis Kachina, now danced in July as part of the Niman, or Home Dance, the time when the kachinas go home to the San Francisco mountains for the remainder of the ceremonial year.

The next day, Ten Broeck met with the governor and principal men of the village. They "smoked, and had our 'big talk,' obtaining from them as much information as possible, relative to their history, customs, origin, religion, crops, &c." He seemingly was following the instructions in Schoolcraft's *Inquiry*. He estimated the population of the seven Hopi villages at about eight thousand, noting that disease had reduced numbers in recent years, briefly described marriage arrangements, divorce, and farming practices, and visited a kiva and saw the men weaving cotton cloth. He notes that inhabitants of "Harno" [Hano] on First Mesa have their own language and customs. He recorded a simplified origin myth, recounting how "their

4.2. "Interior of Moquis house," 1858; drawing by H. B. Möllhausen. Ives (1861).

There were twenty men and as many women, ranged in two files. . . . they wear on their heads large pasteboard towers painted typically and curiously decorated with feathers; and each man has his face entirely covered with a vizor made of small willows with the bark peeled off and dyed a dark brown. The women all have their hair put up in the manner peculiar of virgins; and immediately in the center, where the hair is parted, a long, straight eagle's feather is fixed. . . . by far the most beautiful part of their dress is a tilma of some three and a half feet square, which is thrown over the shoulders, fastened in front, and, hanging down behind, reaches half-way below the knee. This tilma is pure white . . . and it has one or more wide borders of beautiful colors. . . . The dancers furnished their own music, and a most strange sound it was, resembling very much the noise, on a large scale, of a swarm of blue-bottle flies in an empty hogshead. Each one was rolling out an aw, aw, aw, aw, in a deep base tone, and the sound, coming through a hollow visor, produced the effect described. . . . After dancing awhile in the mode described, the ranks were opened, and rugs and blankets being brought, the virgins squatted on them. . . . Every third or fourth female had . . . a large hollow gourd placed before her, on which rested a grooved piece of wood, shaped like an old-fashioned washboard; and by drawing the dry shoulder-blade of a sheep rapidly across this, a sound was produced similar to a watchman's rattle.

Ten Broeck also describes young men dressed as Tcuku and Koshare clowns and Chaveyo, or Ogre Kachinas, who catch and whip the clowns:

Such horrible masks I never saw before—noses six inches long, mouths from ear to ear, and great goggle eyes, as big as half a hen's egg, hanging by a string partly out of the socket. They came and vanished like a dream, and only staying long enough to inflict a signal chastisement on the unfortunate clowns.

After watching food being "distributed by the virgins among all the spectators," Ten Broeck was surprised to learn "that those whom I supposed to be young virgins, were in fact young men, dressed in female apparel for the occasion."[7]

great Mother . . . from her home in the west," brought nine 'races' of men in the following forms: deer, sand, water, bear, hare, prairie wolf (coyote), rattlesnake, tobacco-plant, and reed-grass. Having placed them on the spot where their villages now stand, she transformed them into men, who built the present Pueblos, and the distinction of the races is still kept up." Although not recognized as such, Ten Broeck provided a partial listing of Hopi clans, apparently the first notice of the Hopi kinship system that would preoccupy later anthropologists.[8]

Finally, Ten Broeck notes a "sacred fire . . . kept constantly burning by the old men . . . Some great misfortune would befall their people if they allowed it to be extinguished." But "they know nothing of Montezuma, and have never had any Spanish or other missionaries among them." He is incorrect concerning Spanish missionaries; his hosts did not tell him about the missionaries before the Pueblo Revolt or the fate of Awatovi.[9]

Ten Broeck's report is important for two reasons. First, it and that of another army physician, Dr. Jonathan Letterman on the Navajo (below), were responses to Schoolcraft's inquiry, hence part of the nascent cooperative effort to document Indian cultures and histories. Second, it provides the first description of a Hopi dance and details on kinship and marriage practices, yet is generally overlooked in histories of Southwestern studies.[10]

Observations on the "Wild" Tribes

Following Hispanic precedent, Anglos labeled all non-Pueblo tribes as "wild," most notably the Navajos and Apaches. Kearny's army encountered their first Apaches along the Rio Grande south of Albuquerque; they met others along the Gila River. The meetings were tense, but peaceful. In fact, the Apaches provided the army with desperately needed mules to continue their march to California. Emory noted that "the women . . . rode a la Duchesses de Berri [that is, astride, rather than side-saddle] . . . Some of the men had fire-arms, but the greater part were armed with lance and bow. They were generally small legged, big bellied and broad shouldered."[11]

On the headwaters of the Gila River they met the famed Apache leader Mangas Coloradas. Emory wrote:

> By this time a large number of Indians had collected about us, all differently dressed, and some in the most fantastical style. The Mexican dress and saddles predominated, showing where they had chiefly made up their wardrobe. . . . Several wore beautiful helmets, decked with black feathers, which, with the short skirt, waist and belt, bare legs and buskins, gave them the look of pictures of antique Grecian warriors. Most were furnished with the Mexican cartridge box, which consists of a strap round the waist, with cylinders inserted for the cartridges. . . . The light and graceful manner in which they mounted and dismounted, always on the right side, was the admiration of all. The children are on horseback from infancy.[12]

Schoolcraft printed a report from an army physician, Dr. Charleton Henry, "who has been several years stationed in the country of the Apaches." Henry's sketch of Apache origins and history is a pastiche of supposition and misinformation, the com-

mon hearsay knowledge of 1850s New Mexico. He did, however, answer the questions in Schoolcraft's *Inquiry* as best he could. Thus, his factual ethnographic information based on observation, rather than hearsay, is much better. He lists three western bands, as well as the Mescalero and Jicarilla. He briefly describes techniques of arrow manufacture, horse training and horse gear, dress and body decoration, cradleboards, and the buckskin helmets mentioned by Emory. He also notes, as would others, that women's noses were cut off for "infidelity."[13]

The Navajos

One of Kearny's first actions after reaching New Mexico was to promise relief from Navajo raiding, and he sent Colonel A. W. Doniphan to attempt a peace treaty. At the parley, one of the Navajo leaders, Sarcilla Largo, reportedly said:

> Americans! You have a strange case of war against the Navajos. We have waged war against the Mexicans for years. We have plundered their villages, killed many of their people and have taken many prisoners. Our cause was just. You have lately commenced a war against the same people. . . . You . . . have conquered them, the very thing we have been attempting to do for many years. You now turn upon us for attempting to do what you have done yourselves. We cannot see why you have cause to quarrel with us for fighting the New Mexicans on the West, while you do the same thing on the East . . . [14]

Doniphan explained that since the Mexicans were now conquered, they were entitled to protection by the army. Whatever the Navajo thought of such logic, a treaty was duly signed and Doniphan marched off into Mexico.

Conflict erupted almost as soon as Doniphan's troops were out of sight. Emory cast an interesting light on the conflict in his 1848 report, claiming that Governor Armijo used the Navajos as hit squads to keep the New Mexicans in line. He, like others, noted the Navajo and Apache "harvesting" pattern: "They [the Navajo] are prudent in their depredations, never taking so much from one man as to ruin him."[15]

As the conflict continued, the U.S. Army established Fort Defiance in Navajo territory, commanded by Colonel Electus Backus. Although the presence of the fort did not stop the raiding, it did change the relationship of the army with the Navajos, who came to the fort for rations, with some acting as guides and interpreters. This made it possible for officers and doctors to observe and describe something of Navajo society and culture. In 1853, Backus, Ten Broeck, and Lt. Colonel J. B. Eaton sent reports to Schoolcraft. In 1855, Jonathan Letterman, an army doctor, sent an extensive "Sketch of the Navajo tribe" to the Smithsonian; it was published the following year (his name is misspelled as "Letherman"). Letterman (1824–1872) was stationed at Fort Defiance in 1854–55. His system of mobile field hospitals and ambulances completely revamped the way that battle casualties were handled during the Civil War and thereafter. In 1911 the hospital at the presidio in San Francisco was named for him.[16]

These reports constitute the first Anglo accounts of the Navajo based on close observation and inquiry, although they vary in content and tone. All briefly describe Navajo sheep, corn, beans, melons, and some wheat. Hogans, called "log shanties," or "lodges," are described, as is the abandonment of a hogan after someone dies therein. Eaton correctly notes that the Navajos call themselves "Tenuai" [Diné] and that "the appellation Navajo was unquestionably given them by the Spaniards." Letterman describes "pure-blooded" Navajos as "good size, nearly six feet in height, and well proportioned." But "mixed-bloods," that is, Navajos mixed with "Utahs, Apaches, Moquis and Mexicans," are generally smaller.[17]

All three convey some idea of the primary Navajo extended family unit. Ten Broeck notes that wealth was measured in terms of horses and sheep, and that rich men have large numbers of "retainers and servants" to tend the animal herds.[18] Both Backus and Letterman noted the practice of bride-price payment

of horses to the bride's parents, and the practice of polygyny. Letterman was puzzled by Navajo property relationships and women's roles:

> The husband has no control over the property of his wife, their herds being kept separate and distinct; from which, doubtless, arises the influence of the women not only in their own peculiar sphere, but also in national matters, which it is well known they often exert. . . . Property does not descend from father to son, but goes to the nephew of the descendent, or, in default of a nephew, to the niece; so that the father may be rich, and upon his death his children become beggars.[19]

Such a system was indeed foreign to a man imbued with the canons of English property law as practiced in the United States. To Letterman, the Navajo matrilineal system of descent and inheritance and the roles of the senior mothers was indeed mystifying.

The Navajo were already known for their weaving, a fact noted by both Backus and Letterman. The latter provides a fairly comprehensive description of dyeing and weaving processes. He also notes that "occasionally a blanket is seen which is quite handsome, and costs . . . the extravagant price of forty or fifty dollars; these, however, are very scarce, and are generally made for a special purpose."[20]

The complex, subtle, and sophisticated Navajo myths, legends, and religion were also mystifying. Letterman thought little of all of it: "Nothing can be learned of the origins of these people from themselves. At one time they say they came out of the ground; and at another, that they know nothing whatever of their origin; the latter, no doubt, being the truth." Ten Broeck recorded fragments of the Navajo origin myth relating the emergence through the various underground levels, the placement of the stars, and the origins of Pueblo and Anglo people. His narrative is the first published version of part of the Navajo origin myth, the first small step toward Anglo understanding and explication of the complex sophistication of Navajo ideology.[21]

The reports of Backus, Easton, Letterman, and

Ten Broeck, as brief as they are, are the baseline studies of Navajo ethnography. They are especially useful since they provide something of a picture of Navajo life and culture prior to the captivity at Bosque Redondo in 1864–68.

The Yuman Tribes

The Yuman-speaking groups centered on the lower Colorado River and its delta were described by the various military expeditions in some detail since their lands were crossed by emigrant routes and located along the Colorado River. Sitgreaves and others engaged in the wagon-road and railroad surveys of the 1850s passed through "Pai" territories south of the Grand Canyon, but had only occasional, and usually fleeting, encounters with them. In 1856 Ives and his party met some Hualapais. A few days later, Ives, Egloffstein, and some soldiers found their way into Havasu Canyon. They observed only "fields of corn and a few scattered huts," and perhaps "all told . . . no more than two hundred persons." Egloffstein broke a ladder leading down from a ledge and fell to the canyon floor. The Havasupai seemed more bemused than startled by the sudden appearance of fifteen white men peering at them from a ledge and one floundering about near their village. Egloffstein was lifted back to the ledge with difficulty.[22]

The Piman-speaking peoples who live along and adjacent to the Gila River and its tributaries received much more attention since they were along a major east-west route of travel. Nearly all Anglo observers were favorably impressed by the Pima, probably because they were farmers and well versed in commercial exchange. They kept herds of cattle, horses, mules, donkeys, and sheep; had some oxen; and were using Spanish, or Spanish-derived, implements, including axes, harrows, shovels, plows, and fences. They were also able warriors. To the Anglos, steeped in an agrarian-mercantile background, the Pimas seemed very different from the "wild" Indians and the secretive Pueblos.

Downstream from the Pima were their close allies, the Maricopa. Emory reported that Maricopa farming, commercial, and military activities were essentially the same as the Pima. He was very impressed with both groups. After describing the agricultural system, the houses, implements, and people in detail, as well as a boisterous and merry trade fair between the Indians and the soldiers, he wrote:

> To us it was a rare sight to be thrown in the midst of a large nation of what is termed wild Indians, surpassing many of the Christian nations in agriculture, little behind them in useful arts, and immeasurably before them in honesty and virtue. During the whole of yesterday, our camp was full of men, women and children, who sauntered amongst our packs, unwatched, and not a single instance of theft was reported.[23]

John Russell Bartlett collected considerable information on Maricopa and Pima dress and adornment, religion, marriage, division of labor, the irrigation and field systems, food production, processing and storage, and weaving, pottery, and basketry.[24]

Linguistics

The ongoing effort to collect data on American Indian languages, and the use of vocabulary lists to do so, was undertaken by several individuals. William Carr Lane, the territorial governor of New Mexico in 1854, sent Schoolcraft a letter outlining a linguistic classification of Southwestern Indians that is relatively correct in terms of modern understanding:

Kes whaw-hay [Keresan languages] Laguna, Santo Domingo, San Felipe, Santa Ana, Cochiti, and Sille [Zia], [plus Acoma].
E-nagh-magh [Northern Tiwa languages] Taos, Vicusis [Picuris], Zesuqua [Tesuque; Tesuque is a Tewa language], Sandia, Yslete [Isleta], and two Pueblos of Texas near El Paso [Southern Tiwa].
Tay-waugh [Tewa languages] San Juan, Santa Clara, Pojuaque [Pojoaque], Nambe, San Il de Conso [San Ildefonso], and one Moqui Pueblo [Hano].

Those of Jemez and Pecos speak the same language [Towa]. Those of Zuni speak a different language. In six of seven Moqui [Hopi] Pueblos, the same language is spoken.

Apaches, the Navahoes and the Seepans [Lipans] of Texas, speak dialects of the same language. The Jicarillas, Mescaleros, Tantos [sic], and Coyoteros, are bands of the Apaches.[25]

During the railroad survey, Whipple was able to collect a fair amount of linguistic information. These data, together with other vocabulary items he had gathered earlier, were turned over to William W. Turner for analysis. Turner (1810–1859) was immensely interested in languages from a precociously early age, and ultimately mastered Hebrew, Latin, Greek, Arabic, and various Oriental languages. In 1842 he was appointed professor of Oriental languages at Union Theological Seminary in New York, and in 1852 became librarian in the U.S. Patent Office. He also took charge of the Smithsonian Institution library. When he died in 1859, his sister, Jane Wadden Turner, whom he had trained, became the Smithsonian librarian and served in that position for thirty years. Turner not only studied Southwestern Indian languages, but wrote on the "trade language" Chinook Jargon from along the Columbia River, Lakota from the Great Plains, and Yoruba from West Africa.[26]

Turner combined Whipple's materials with some vocabularies from Bartlett and other sources and was able to review what was then known about Southwestern Indian languages. He could not clearly link Zuni to any other language (it is now regarded as an isolate, or perhaps remotely related to Penutian). He did reaffirm his earlier discovery, that Apachean (collectively the various Apache dialects and Navajo) is closely related to the Athapaskan languages of northern Canada and interior Alaska. Horatio Hale had earlier demonstrated pockets of Athapaskan-speaking groups along the Northwest Coast. A vocabulary published by Schoolcraft established Hupa in northwestern California as Athapaskan. Turner noted this widespread distribution, but did not comment on its potential implications for North American culture history. It became, however, a major topic of concern later in the nineteenth century and throughout much of the twentieth century in attempts to use linguistic connections to write New World cultural history.[27]

CHAPTER 5

The Great Surveys

Prelude: The Smithsonian Institution

In the summer of 1846, as Henry Rowe Schoolcraft was lobbying Congress for funds to support his "cyclopedia" of American Indians, the denizens of Capitol Hill had some other matters on their minds. In May, Congress had declared war on the sovereign nation of Mexico and soon General Kearny was marching his army toward Santa Fe. The festering slavery issue and its attendant divisive sectionalism continued to rankle, as did numerous other items on the congressional agenda.

One item, which had been before the Congress for a decade, was what to do about a bequest of monies left to the United States by one James Smithson (ca. 1754–1829), of England. Smithson was an acknowledged natural son of Hugh Smithson, first Duke of Northumberland. He was educated at Oxford, never married, but had the wealth to pursue the life of a gentleman scholar, making a number of contribu-

tions to mineral chemistry. In his will, Smithson bequeathed his estate to the United States, "to found at Washington, under the name of the Smithsonian Institution, an establishment for the increase and diffusion of knowledge among men." He had never visited the United States. In July 1836, Congress accepted the bequest, $508,318.46 in gold, together with a library and minerals collection. The funds were deposited at interest in the United States Treasury.[1]

For the next decade, interested citizens and members of Congress fervently debated what sort of establishment should be founded "for the increase and diffusion of knowledge . . ." Some thought it should be a National Museum to house all the collections of the federal surveys. There were also many other proposals, the complex details of which are beyond our scope.[2]

The act finally passed on December 1, 1846, establishing the Smithsonian Institution was broad and vague enough to allow considerable latitude and discretion in forming its purposes. The act created a

Board of Regents which, then as now, includes the vice president of the United States, the chief justice of the Supreme Court, three senators, three congressmen, and several citizen members appointed by joint resolution of Congress. The Regents moved quickly to elect Joseph Henry (1797–1878) as the Institution's first secretary. Henry was a professor of natural philosophy at the (then) College of New Jersey at Princeton, a person of great vision, firm principles, and strong resolve. By request of the Regents, Henry had submitted a plan of organization for the nascent Institution prior to his election. He took his election to be an endorsement of that plan and its unfolding. He clearly saw the Institution as a focal point for original research and the diffusion of knowledge worldwide.[3]

There was intense pressure for Henry to create a National Museum, but he saw that if the Smithsonian was forced to use its own resources, the interest on the 500,000-dollar Smithson bequest, for museum purposes, it would founder and die. In 1857 Henry finally got Congress to agree to provide funding for curating collections and related museum functions in perpetuity.[4] He achieved a situation in which the Smithsonian Institution housed and administered, on behalf of the government, a National Museum, but the two were separate entities. *Legal* establishment of a National Museum did not come until 1876, when appropriations were made for a National Museum building.

The critical point in all this was Henry's unwavering insistence that the purposes of the Smithsonian Institution, as he saw them, would not be compromised, and that the funds from the Smithson bequest *not* be mixed with public monies. Although the bequest was deposited in the U.S. Treasury, the interest was seen as *private money*. This "private side/public side," or "trust funds/public funds," distinction has continued ever since. The precedent of the Smithsonian as a quasi-autonomous organization managing another organization created and funded by Congress would allow John Wesley Powell in 1879 to get his Bureau of Ethnology lodged under the administrative shelter of the Smithsonian (see Chapter 6).

In 1846, science and natural history were largely avocational activities of "gentleman scholars" who earned their living in medicine or business, such as botanists George Engelmann, John Torrey, and Asa Gray. Only Gray at Harvard was a full-time scientist. Engelmann, Gray, and Torrey employed professional collectors, or trained the collectors who were attached to the Topographical Engineers' parties of exploration to bring them specimens.[5] There was a network of ethnologists centering around Albert Gallatin and the American Ethnological Society, and other networks of individuals interested in physics, chemistry, mineralogy, and so on.

The Royal Society and the American Philosophical Society became models, throughout the nineteenth century, for dozens of local "academies of science," formed by interested and enthusiastic amateurs. Members of these organizations, many of whom belonged to the overarching American Association for the Advancement of Science, were the "correspondents" on which the Smithsonian Institution relied to help increase knowledge, and through whom and to whom it diffused that knowledge through its publications. In addition, these organizations and individuals, together with popular interest in natural history within the larger public, generated the political support for the Smithsonian and a "National Museum" related to it.

Beginnings of the "Great Surveys"

The horror of the Civil War ended in 1865 with a ruptured but not severed Union. Many eyes turned again to the American mythic West. Manifest Destiny became Progress. Great corporations were organized to finally build the transcontinental railroad along the central route, figuratively a "second opening" of the West. "Opening" meant converting the public domain to private property, exploiting natural resources, producing foodstuffs, and making fortunes. All that required teams of surveyors to plot the distribution of western resources and arable lands on accurate maps.

It also meant resolution of "the Indian problem"; making the people into managed savages on reservations, or turning them into vanished savages if they resisted. The Bureau of Indian Affairs and the U.S. Army undertook those tasks. The continuing apparent phenomenon of the vanishing savage again stimulated calls to study the Indians in their "natural state" before extinction or reservation life changed them into "good Christian farmers in overalls."[6] Anthropology as a profession grew out of the new western surveys and attempts to study the Indians for management and scholarly purposes.

Origins of the Great Surveys

Until 1861, the Topographical Engineers were in charge of exploring the West, but they were merged into the regular Corps of Engineers during the Civil War. In postwar pork-barrel politics, new government-funded, but civilian-led, surveys were created.[7] The army was unwilling to retire completely, and managed to develop one survey of its own. There were ultimately three civilian surveys, led by politically savvy scholar-entrepreneurs—Clarence King, Ferdinand Vandiveer Hayden, and John Wesley Powell. The army's survey was led by a young, ambitious, and well-connected officer, George M. Wheeler. The four surveys they led are called the "Great Surveys."

The King Survey

The first survey was led by Clarence King. Fresh from the Yale Sheffield Scientific School, in April 1863 King went to work for J. D. Whitney in the California Geological Survey. One result was his classic *Mountaineering in the Sierra Nevada*.[8] By 1866 King was dreaming of a survey along the Fortieth Parallel, the route of the soon to be built transcontinental railroad. In January 1867, just twenty five years old, King went to Washington. He arrived with letters of introduction from prominent individuals and soon gained powerful political support from Edwin McMasters Stanton, the Secretary of War; Spencer F. Baird, of the Smithsonian; and others. All were taken by King's bold plan and captivated by his ebullience, charm, wit, and brain-

power. A measure authorizing the Secretary of War "to direct a geological and topographical exploration of the territory between the Rocky Mountains and the Sierra Nevada" was passed in March 1867, and King was named Geologist in Charge of the Geological Exploration of the Fortieth Parallel. He was to get 100,000 dollars for three years; funding was subsequently supplemented and extended through 1878.[9]

King put together an excellent team of geologists and topographers. He had learned the value of photography for geological work in California, and so hired a "wet-plate artist," Timothy O'Sullivan, who was one of Mathew Brady's battlefield photographers in the Civil War.[10]

King conducted his survey with great panache and scientific exactitude. By 1874, the fieldwork was finished and he and his staff were at work in offices in New York City. There, King moved as easily in the interlocking circles of high financial and artistic society as he moved in the circles of literature and politics in Washington. Everywhere, his multitude of powerful and accomplished friends and admirers enjoyed his brilliant wit and the bon mots of the great raconteur he had become. King finished his survey reports in 1878.[11] He did not do anthropology nor did he work in the Southwest, but his survey was the model for others who did.

The Hayden Survey

The second survey was led by Ferdinand Vandiveer Hayden (Fig. 5.1).[12] He enrolled in Oberlin College in 1847 and studied with John Strong Newberry (see Chapter 2). Newberry sent him on to James Hall at the Albany Medical College, where he absorbed enough medical training to receive an M.D. degree in 1853. But Hall's, and by then Hayden's, real interest was paleontology and Hayden joined an expedition to the Dakota Badlands. Between 1853 and 1858, Hayden ranged widely across the High Plains, making several basic contributions to historical geology.[13]

During the Civil War, Hayden served as an army surgeon. In 1866 he was appointed professor of geol-

5.1. Ferdinand Vandeveer Hayden, ca. 1877. Photograph by W. H. Jackson. Courtesy of the Library of Congress.

ogy *in absentia* at the University of Pennsylvania. The post was strictly honorary and Hayden required support for himself and his continued explorations. In 1867, soon after King's survey had been approved, and with the help of Spencer Baird, O. C. Marsh, the Yale paleontologist, and others, Hayden was granted five thousand dollars to conduct a geological survey in Nebraska under the auspices of the General Land Office. He hired an aspiring young geologist named James Stevenson, whom he had met in 1856. Stevenson (1840–1887) was fascinated by geology and Indians. During the Civil War he rose to the rank of brevet colonel, a title he later retained. He was a competent field topographer, but an even better administrator and became executive officer of Hayden's Survey.

Hayden's Survey highlighted aspects of geology,

minerals, soils, water, and climate that could be of immediate economic importance. In 1869 his appropriation was doubled to ten thousand dollars and he transferred to the Department of the Interior, as the U.S. Geological and Geographical Survey of the Territories.

In 1870, Hayden's appropriation was increased to twenty-five thousand dollars. He hired William Henry Jackson (1843–1942), a teamster and stock drover who had decided that photography was easier and more lucrative than bull-whacking.[14] By the end of 1868, he co-owned two photographic studios in Omaha, Nebraska. Omaha was booming as the eastern terminus of the Union Pacific Railroad, which was then being built. Jackson began to produce stereopticon "views," then all the rage, of the railroad, its construction, and the country it crossed, as well as regular wet-plate photographs. He began photographing Plains Indians at every opportunity; like other photographers of the time, he wished to "document" them, and make a profit before they "vanished."

Jackson apparently met Hayden in 1870. Hayden signed him on for "your keep and your kit"—rations and camera gear. Jackson would own all the photographs and keep the profits from their sales. Hayden would get a competent craftsman to make photographs for scientific, as well as political and publicity, purposes. Hayden knew that continuation of his survey depended on good publicity and the favor of the Congress. Many copies of Jackson's photographs and stereographs passed into the hands of congressmen and others over the next decade, as did Timothy O'Sullivan's photographs from the King Survey. John Wesley Powell and George M. Wheeler would later follow this politics-through-photography policy.

By 1870, talk of the wonders of the Yellowstone region were circulating. Hayden jumped at an obvious opportunity. He received a forty-thousand-dollar appropriation from Congress for a large expedition to the region. Stevenson and Jackson signed on and Hayden invited the famed landscape artist Thomas Moran. By July 25, 1871, the party members were gazing at the wonders of Yellowstone. Hayden explored,

Moran sketched, and Jackson photographed for over a month. By early October Hayden was back in Washington. The suggestion that Yellowstone ought to be set aside as a public park was raised. A quick but concerted campaign was launched; Jackson's brilliant photographs and Moran's sketches helped immeasurably.[15] The bill passed both houses of Congress by unanimous consent, and President Ulysses S. Grant signed it on March 1, 1872. Thus was created the first national park in the United States—and the world. The congressional action of setting aside a portion of the public lands for the benefit of the people was a highly significant precedent for subsequent environmental and cultural preservation.

Congress upped Hayden's 1872 appropriation to seventy-five thousand dollars. He was thus able to hire new men. One was a twenty-six-year-old artist named William Henry Holmes (1846–1933).[16] In 1871 Holmes went to Washington to study art and there met Mary Henry, daughter of Joseph Henry, secretary of the Smithsonian. She invited Holmes to see the Institution. During his first visit, Holmes was making some sketches, caught a staff member's eye, and found himself doing scientific illustrations for Spencer Baird and other staff members. Hayden was planning another expedition to the Yellowstone region, the Teton Mountains, and Jackson's Hole, and Holmes signed on. It was the beginning of his career as perhaps the greatest master ever of geologic illustration in the United States.[17]

The Cliff Dwellings

In 1873 Hayden turned his attention to the Territory of Colorado, where good topographic maps were needed for railroad, agricultural, mineral, and timber development. There were several field parties, each with a geologist, a topographer, mule skinners, and cook, plus assorted naturalists, guests, journalists, and congressmen's young sons or nephews. Jackson led a separate photographic party with an assistant and a faithful mule lugging his heavy wet-plate camera equipment up and down innumerable mountains and canyons.

As Hayden's men spread out over Colorado, they began hearing frequent rumors of "cliff dwellings"— long abandoned Indian ruins in the southwestern part of the territory. In 1874 Jackson was guided by a mining engineer, John Moss, to Mancos Canyon, which cleaves through the eastern section of Mesa Verde. The two then went westward to Aztec Springs, down McElmo Creek and into the Hovenweep area in southeastern Utah. They saw numerous "cliff dwellings," ruins of pueblos, and the enigmatic "watch towers" of Hovenweep. Jackson's brief report, "Ancient Ruins in Southwestern Colorado,"[18] provided succinct and intriguing descriptions of many small "cliff houses" high in the ledges of Mancos Canyon (see the frontispiece), large open pueblo ruins, as at Aztec Springs, and the Hovenweep towers.

In 1875, Hayden sent both Jackson and Holmes to the Four Corners region. Holmes made a more detailed survey around the Mesa Verde, but did not follow up any of the side canyons off the main stem of Mancos Canyon, thus leaving the great cliff dwellings there to be discovered by others. Jackson's assignment was to photograph more ruins, to visit and photograph the Hopi villages, and to make plan maps and measurements of various ruins and pueblos as the basis for plaster models. Hayden wanted the photographs and models for his survey's exhibit at the Philadelphia Centennial Exhibition of 1876. Jackson made some of the photographs with a giant 16 × 24-inch wet-plate camera. The results, as later exhibited in Philadelphia, were sensational.[19] Jackson's and Holmes's reports on the cliff dwellings and other sites created great interest. The reports, and Jackson's photographs, established the term *Cliff Dwellers* in both the archaeological and popular literature and art of the Southwest.[20]

In 1877 Jackson traveled to Chaco Canyon to photograph the ruins and make plat maps and measurements, as the basis for expanding the series of scale models. He was guided to Chaco Canyon by Hosta, the now elderly former governor of Jemez, one of Simpson and Kern's guides in 1849. In the canyon Jackson discovered "a line of steps and handholes hewn out from the rock, back of the Pueblo Chetro Kettle [*sic*], by which I easily gained the summit."[21] On the canyon rim, he described and named Pueblo Alto. The steps, now called "Jackson's Steps," are thought to be part of the extensive prehistoric "road" system that radiates out from Chaco Canyon.[22]

The Wheeler Survey

In the aftermath of the Civil War, western exploration was not an immediate priority for the U.S. Army. The Union had assembled the largest army in history, a million-plus men by 1865. By 1867 there were only twenty-five thousand regular army soldiers spread thinly at 169 posts, 130 of them west of the Mississippi. Most of the underpaid and often ill-disciplined soldiers were engaged with "the Indian problem." Although the army was not what it had been, there was still great pride among the career officers. Western exploration had been a prestigious activity of the army since 1818, and being outdone in that field by civilians rankled, especially Brigadier General A. A. Humphreys, commander of the Corps of Engineers.

The young officer thrust into the breach was Lt. George Montague Wheeler (1842–1905). He was, as William Goetzmann put it, "a newly minted second lieutenant at a time when experienced officers were the most abundant commodity on the national labor market."[23] Soon after graduating from West Point, Wheeler married Lucy Blair, a granddaughter of Francis Preston Blair, Sr., the fiery editor of the *Congressional Globe* and political kingmaker from Jackson to Lincoln, and niece of Francis Preston Blair, Jr., the brilliant congressman, later senator and Civil War major general from Missouri.

Wheeler was sent to California. In 1869, he was promoted to first lieutenant and assigned to lead a reconnaissance across southeastern Nevada. In his report, Wheeler laid out a grandiose scheme to map the entire West at a small-enough scale, yet at a level of detail useful both to military tacticians and civilians concerned with the general development of the country; the army liked the idea. Good maps would aid its

major task of "pacifying" the Indians scattered over the Plains and the West. The civilian surveys were producing large-scale topographical maps, of little use for rapid military operations. Then, too, the operation would put the army back in the survey business. General Humphreys threw his full weight behind the plan, as did the Blair family. In 1871, Wheeler was assigned the task of exploring "parts of eastern Nevada and Arizona south of the Central Pacific Railroad," to make "accurate maps of that section" and to find out "as far as practicable, everything relating to the physical features of the country, the numbers, habits and disposition of the Indians . . . [and] the facilities offered for making rail or commonwealth roads."[24]

Wheeler's surveys of 1871 and subsequent years were driven by megalomania and greed. He assembled an excellent team of civilian experts, especially Grove Karl Gilbert, the geologist; Edward D. Cope, the paleontologist; and Timothy O'Sullivan, the photographer who came over from King's survey. Wheeler became obsessed with showing up the civilian surveys. This led him in 1871 to tow and row boats up the Colorado River into the lower Grand Canyon as far as Diamond Creek, ostensibly seeking military wagon routes and a "true" head of navigation, but apparently also to somehow one-up John Wesley Powell's epic river trip (see below). The trip was perilous and nothing of military or scientific value was gained, except to give Gilbert a view of the geology of the Colorado Plateau.[25]

In 1873, Wheeler sent a party into the Glen Canyon area where Powell had been mapping for two years. This, however, had also to do with Wheeler's hidden agenda—seeking gold. The zigzagging across the landscape by his survey teams from 1871 to 1874 puzzled his contemporaries, but had much to do with the search for gold and silver deposits. Wheeler seemingly had a quiet under-the-map-table agreement with various San Francisco financiers to use his survey as a federally subsidized prospecting expedition.[26]

Also in 1873, Wheeler sent parties into Colorado where Hayden was already at work. A fight between a Hayden party and a Wheeler party over mapping led to a congressional investigation in which Hayden and Powell and their civilian compatriots made Wheeler look very bad indeed. But a cloakroom compromise was reached, and all parties emerged with generous appropriations for the following year.[27] In 1874–76 some of the Wheeler Survey's best work was done, including its anthropological work in the Southwest. And his survey did, in fact, produce usable maps for military and land-office purposes.

Although his survey was abolished by the 1879 reorganization that created the U.S. Geological Survey, Wheeler did put his results on record in seven royal octavo volumes, the last published in 1889.[28] Volume VII of the final report is on "Archaeology," edited by Frederic Ward Putnam, of the Peabody Museum at Harvard.[29] Most of the papers are a miscellany of hasty and offhand archaeological, ethnohistorical, linguistic, and ethnographic observations and collections from southern California and the Southwest, such as brief notes on Acoma, Taos, and San Juan, and sketches of dances at Zuni and Jemez. There is a brief but important paper on ruins in the Gallinas region in New Mexico by Edward D. Cope. Like other observers, Cope was struck by the large number of ruins in relation to the scarcity (as of the 1870s) of surface water. Like others before and after, he speculated on the possibility of climatic change as a factor in Pueblo abandonment. He tried to estimate the rate of erosion around the ruins. An assistant cut a piñon tree growing in a ruin and counted its annual growth rings, arriving at 640. While Cope reached no definitive conclusions, he was among the first to try to define objective factors and establish a chronology relating to pueblo abandonment.[30]

Putnam briefly described artifacts collected by Wheeler's parties. Among these were prayer sticks removed from "Sacred Places" (Putnam's quotation marks) on Corn Mountain at Zuni and on Mt. Taylor. Both places are indeed sacred, the former to the Zuni, the latter to the Navajo and others. But the places were "sacred" only in the pagan, not the Christian, sense. Hence, the prayer sticks were "objects of curiosity," not "real" sacred objects. Their removal reflects the scientific orientation of the time. The most substantial contribution was by Albert Gatschet, presenting a linguistic classification of data from some forty vocabulary lists collected by the survey.[31] Gatschet was a philologist connected with Powell's survey, and later with the Bureau of Ethnology (see below).

Anthropology was not a major concern to the Wheeler Survey, simply part of the "natural history" orientation of the surveys in general. Hence, such observations as were made were included as part of the record. In the end, Wheeler's major contributions were the individuals he employed, among them C. C. Abbott, Edward D. Cope, Henry C. Yarrow, Henry W. Henshaw, and especially Grove Karl Gilbert. Abbott, Yarrow, and Henshaw would go on to make further contributions to anthropology and other natural-history fields. Gilbert, arguably the most brilliant American geologist of the nineteenth century, joined John Wesley Powell in 1875, and moved to the U.S. Geological Survey in 1879. His studies of the laccolithic structure of the Henry Mountains in Utah and Pleistocene Lake Bonneville in the Great Basin are classics.[32]

The Powell Survey

The fourth of the Great Surveys was led by John Wesley Powell (1834–1902). Powell was born in Mt. Morris, New York, the oldest son of English emigrants Joseph and Mary Dean Powell.[33] The Powell family moved west in the 1840s, finally settling in Illinois. Young John Wesley was vastly interested in natural history and an education; he got the latter catch as catch can, finally managing about two years of college in 1855–57. In the summers of 1856 and 1857 Powell made natural-history excursions down the Mississippi and Ohio rivers. He also met cousin Emma Dean, newly arrived from England, twenty years old and vivacious. In 1858 he became secretary of the Illinois Natural History Society.

Powell joined the Union Army in May 1861 as a private. By August he was a captain, supervising the fortifications around Cape Girardeau, Missouri, under Ulysses S. Grant. Grant gave Powell a week's leave to get married. Powell went to Detroit, married Emma, and returned with her to Cape Girardeau. On April 6, 1862, in the thick of the battle around the meeting house at Shiloh, Tennessee, Powell's right arm below the elbow was shattered by a Confederate minié ball, and had to be amputated just below the elbow. Emma nursed him back to health. He returned to his command on June 30. He was at Vicksburg during the long terrible siege there, but in the lulls found time to study the local geology and collect mollusks in the ever-expanding trench network the Union sappers were placing around the city. He was promoted to major in August 1863, serving in Mississippi and participating in the battle at Nashville in late September 1864.

Professor Powell and the West

Powell returned to Illinois in January 1865, known ever after as Major Powell. He became professor of natural history at Illinois Wesleyan University and then at Illinois Normal University. He was a popular and innovative teacher who took his students on frequent field trips. Like many others, Professor Powell turned his eyes westward. In late 1866, the Illinois legislature granted him twenty-five hundred dollars and appointed him "general commissioner and curator" of a museum at Normal. He proposed an expedition the next summer to the Rocky Mountains to make collections. The Illinois Board of Education, which oversaw his museum, allocated five hundred dollars for field expenses.

More money was needed; Powell went to Washington and called on his old commander, General Grant. Grant issued orders for Powell to receive government rations from army posts. He also called on Joseph Henry, secretary of the Smithsonian, who loaned him some equipment and asked him to collect whatever specimens he could.[34] He then petitioned the railroads for free passes and received them. Returning to Illinois, he raised additional funds from public institutions in return for promised duplicate collections. All

this was the first of his many forays using institutional and personal connections to tap public financial resources, a practice he came to master.

Powell, Emma, and a party of students and relatives headed for the Front Range of the Rockies. Later, Powell, Emma, and some mountain-men guides traveled northwestward to the headwaters of the Colorado River. The Powells were back in Normal by mid-November 1867 and he was already planning a second expedition. He again put together a package of institutional funding. The summer was spent around North Park and Long's Peak. In the fall the party moved to the White River in northwestern Colorado. A camp was established at a place now called Powell Bottoms. Powell spent the winter exploring the upper Green River area and getting to know a local band of Ute Indians from whom he collected ethnographic and linguistic data and material-culture items. Probably at this time he was given the name of "Kapurats," meaning "Right Arm Off," a name by which he was long remembered among Indian people.[35] He also determined to his satisfaction that he could run boats down the Green River and on down the Colorado.

In March 1869 Powell went to Washington seeking congressional support for his river trip. He failed, but did receive authorization to draw army rations, and again was loaned some equipment by the Smithsonian. He received some financial support from various institutions in Illinois. He had four boats built and shipped to Green River Station, Wyoming Territory, on the just-completed transcontinental railroad.

Powell recruited a crew of relatives and mountain men for the boat trip. On May 24, 1869, after a hearty breakfast and a last shot of red eye, the party set off down the river on their epic ninety-nine-day adventure. During the trip three of the men left the river party, climbed out of the Grand Canyon, and were killed by Indians. The entire party was reported drowned at various times during the summer.[36]

Powell returned to the East a hero; like Mark Twain he could say that reports of his death were greatly exaggerated. He went to Washington where, aided by his friends Salmon P. Chase, then a senator, and James A. Garfield, then a congressman, and both Regents of the Smithsonian Institution, he received a twelve-thousand-dollar appropriation from Congress. The money was to be used for "completing the Survey of the Colorado of the West and its tributaries, under the direction of Professor Powell . . ."[37]

Powell's survey had various names, but was most commonly known as the Geographical and Geological Survey of the Rocky Mountain Region. He was placed administratively under the Secretary of the Interior, in direct rivalry with Hayden. Powell planned a second trip down the Green and Colorado rivers for 1871–72. In 1870 he returned to Utah to arrange for supply drops for the trip, to make peace with the Indians who had killed the men who left the river party, and to see the country he planned to study and map. Powell hired Jacob Hamblin, the Mormon explorer and Indian missionary, as a guide. Powell met with the Shivwits Indians who had killed his men, heard their side of the story, and made peace.

In October 1870 Powell accompanied Hamblin to the Hopi Mesas. He spent nearly two months studying Hopi language, architecture, social organization, religion, dress, myths and tales, etc. He was permitted to observe and participate in some kiva ceremonies. In an 1875 article in *Scribner's Monthly,* Powell described the seven Hopi villages and life there in some detail.[38]

In late November Powell and Hamblin went to Fort Defiance, where they met a number of Navajos. Powell then returned to the East via Santa Fe and Denver. The trip was crucial for the development of Powell's general interests in Indians and anthropology, but particularly in the peoples of the Southwest. He was attracted by the region as a kind of anthropological "laboratory" where different peoples living in the same environment could be studied. Also, the Pueblos were in their home territories and not on reservations far from their traditional homelands, thus offering more "authentic" societies and cultures.

Powell's second river trip was essentially a scientific expedition, although the river rapids were no less exciting than before. Just before he left Salt Lake City to begin the boat trip, Powell hired Jack Hillers as a boat-man. By the next year, Hillers had become Powell's photographer and would work for Powell for the next twenty-five years, becoming one of the great nineteenth-century photographers.[39]

Powell established his survey in southern Utah to map the Kaibab and Wasatch plateaus, and to do geology and anthropology when he found the time. In 1873, he was appointed a Special Commissioner of Indian Affairs to look into problems of the Numic-speaking peoples of the Great Basin and northern Colorado Plateau (Fig. 5.2). Powell, Hillers, and an Indian agent, George W. Ingalls, spent the summer and fall with various Indian groups in Utah and Nevada. Hillers made some of his first ethnographic photographs. Powell and Ingalls submitted a detailed

5.2. *John Wesley Powell and Kaibab Paiute man, Kanab, Utah, 1872. Photograph by J. K. Hillers. Courtesy of the National Anthropological Archives, Smithsonian Institution.*

report on Indian problems; few of their recommenda-tions were heeded.[40]

Powell and Anthropology, 1874–1879

Powell's various activities and publications established him as an expert on western Indians. Whenever he could, he collected data from Indians, particularly the Numic-speaking peoples of the West. He planned a general "Report on Indians of the Numa Stock," but his increasing involvement in other matters precluded its completion during his lifetime.[41]

Powell began nurturing plans for a federal ethno-logical bureau. The agenda for the study of American Indians set by Thomas Jefferson, Lewis Cass, and Al-bert Gallatin included a genetic classification of In-dian languages, a "synonymy" of tribal names, and detailed studies of Indian tribes. Gallatin managed a partial language classification; Schoolcraft transmuted Cass's synonymy into an encyclopedia and produced his ponderous and minimally useful *History*; yet a syn-onymy was still lacking. Others continued to collect information piecemeal. It could hardly be otherwise, given the limited private resources available and the magnitude of the tasks. Powell planned to use the re-sources of the federal government to carry out the work in a comprehensive manner. He justified re-search in linguistics, ethnography, and demography in terms of "better knowledge for better governance," that is, the old "managed savage" argument. Even though Sitting Bull and his compatriots prevailed at the Little Big Horn in July 1876, it was clear by then that the "Indian problem" was one of reservations and wardship. Therefore, the management argument was received sympathetically in Washington. On the scholarly side, there was an invocation of the equally old image of the vanishing savages, whose cultures ought to be recorded as part of "the human record" before they disappeared.

Powell capitalized on his "Indian-expert" image. In January 1875, the Commissioner of Indian Affairs, on the advice of Special Indian Commissioner Powell, asked that the Secretary of the Interior undertake an ethnological classification of the Indians of the United States. Powell was requested to "undertake the work" by the Secretary. Anthropological research thus became an authorized function of the Powell Survey. This enabled Powell to request funds in the annual federal budget, and to arrange deals with other agen-cies to carry on the work. His scholar-entrepreneur talents continued to emerge.

Powell immediately began work on a map of the distribution of Indian tribes west of the Mississippi. In early 1876, the Smithsonian turned over to him some 650 vocabulary lists of Indian languages, col-lected from correspondents over many years, and he took up the linguistic classification of North Ameri-can Indian languages where Albert Gallatin had left off in 1848. The 1876 Philadelphia Centennial Exhibi-tion provided additional opportunities for Powell to further his anthropological plans, and he took advan-tage of them.

The Philadelphia Centennial Exhibition

The success of the great Crystal Palace Exhibition of 1851 in London set a pattern for similar large-scale fairs. Soon other countries began planning and hold-ing exhibitions to demonstrate their participation in nineteenth-century Progress (see Chapter 17). The centenary of the Declaration of Independence pro-vided a fitting occasion for the United States to pro-duce a fair to surpass the efforts of the Europeans.

In 1875 an exhibition commission was formed with Spencer F. Baird representing the Smithsonian Institu-tion and also generally in charge of American Indian exhibits. Both Powell and Hayden seized the opportu-nity to showcase the work of their surveys. Baird, Powell, Hayden, and Bureau of Indian Affairs repre-sentatives planned extensive exhibits relating to North American archaeology and ethnography. Several arti-fact collectors were dispatched to the Midwest, West, and Alaska to bring back materials for the exhibits. Jack Hillers was sent to Indian Territory in May 1875 to photograph Indians, just as Jackson was sent to the Southern Rockies and Hopi villages.[42]

The planners of the exhibition outdid all previous efforts. Most previous world-class exhibitions were in one or two large buildings; there were 160 in Philadelphia. The main building enclosed 21.5 acres of floor space. During the run of the exhibition, over 9.7 million people thronged onto the grounds to gaze at the wonders provided by more than 31,000 exhibitors from fifty countries.

The U.S. government building had four acres of floor space and three acres of outside exhibit area. It was jammed with a potpourri of objects and displays from various federal agencies. At the west end, there were displays by the Smithsonian, the Bureau of Indian Affairs, and the Powell and Hayden surveys. Contemporary accounts indicate that various "Indian" exhibits were rather jumbled. The Smithsonian exhibited archaeological materials including a "collection of stone implements and weapons . . . believed to be the largest and most complete ever formed."[43] The hundreds of artifacts stuffed into glass cases, arranged in presumed evolutionary sequences, were mind-numbing.

There was a plan to create a sort of ethnographic zoo: "real Indians" camped around the government building in traditional houses, wearing traditional clothes, and, presumably, conducting traditional activities for the edification of the fairgoers. However, Congress balked at the proposed 115,000-dollar price tag, so manikins were substituted.[44] There was a live "Esquimaux" couple, dressed in traditional parkas and mukluks, undoubtedly suffering in the humid heat of a Philadelphia summer.

The Southwest was well represented. Both Hillers and Jackson exhibited their photographs, many mounted as glass transparencies in the windows of the building. Jackson and Holmes produced a series of models including a Mancos Canyon "cliff house," a Hovenweep tower, a ruin from Canyon de Chelly, and Acoma Pueblo. There was also a display of archaeological pottery from both the Mississippi Valley and the Southwest.[45] As an aside, Hayden's plaster models, as well as others that Jackson and Holmes later produced—Taos, a restoration of Pueblo Bonito, and

Montezuma's Castle in the Verde Valley of Arizona—were purchased by Henry A. Ward, founder of the still-extant Ward's Scientific Establishment.[46] They were duplicated, nicely encased in polished mahogany, and widely sold to museums in the United States and elsewhere. Examples were still on exhibit as late as the 1970s at the Peabody Museum at Harvard and the late 1980s at the Carnegie Museum in Pittsburgh. Generations of museum goers learned about Southwestern pueblo architecture from the Hayden-Ward models.

The Philadelphia Exhibition was very useful to the Smithsonian. The judges recommended the Smithsonian exhibit for the highest award and took the liberty of telling the government to support a National Museum so the Smithsonian funds could be used for their original purposes. This recommendation, probably written by Baird, was very useful to him and Henry in their successful fight to obtain funding for the U.S. National Museum building, which opened in 1878.

Enlarging the Anthropological Agenda

Powell, through his survey display, received international attention, further establishing his position as a leader of the budding science of anthropology. He used the occasion to announce a new publication series, the *Contributions to North American Ethnology*, as an outlet for his authorized anthropological research, and for the works of collaborators.[47] King and Hayden had set a precedent of publishing elaborately illustrated research reports. Powell's reports had been much smaller. Now he tossed his own large-format series into the arena of prestige and competition for attention, both within the scientific world and the world of Washington-appropriations politics.

Powell's First Philologists

Powell soon began to make additional arrangements to further his anthropological work. He hired Albert Gatschet in April 1877 to work on Indian language vocabularies. Gatschet was born in Switzerland in 1832, and studied there and in Berlin, specializing in languages. He came to the United States in 1868 and found work as a language teacher in New York City. His analysis of Indian vocabularies from the West and Southwest collected by the Wheeler Survey brought him to Powell's attention.[48]

Powell soon was able to get Gatschet to Oregon to study the Klamath Indians. Congress made an appropriation of twenty-five hundred dollars to the Department of the Interior "for continuing the collection of statistics and historical data respecting the Indians of the United States"—Schoolcraft's terminology of three decades earlier. It was Powell's doing in concert with J. Q. Smith, the Commissioner of Indian Affairs. Powell made it seem to be a continuation of his previously authorized anthropological work. Now he needed further support to continue the work, especially linguistics, ethnography, and demography, and especially in Oregon. He recommended that the appropriation be used to employ Albert Gatschet to pursue "the desired investigation in Oregon." The arrangement was continued in 1878 and 1879, much to Powell's satisfaction. He had a competent person doing anthropology under his direction, "without expense to my appropriation."[49]

Powell also began working with James Owen Dorsey in 1877. A polyglot, Dorsey had been an Episcopal missionary to the Ponca Indians since 1871. In 1878 Powell put Dorsey on the payroll and sent him to Nebraska and Indian Territory to work with the Omaha and the Ponca. Dorsey continued with Powell as an "ethnologist" until his death in 1895. His works on the Ponca, Omaha, and others are classics.[50]

Powell also proposed to "review . . . a large body of literature in English, German, French and Spanish," that is, to compile bibliographies of published and unpublished materials needed to complete the linguistic classification and the synonymy. He gave this assignment to his faithful clerk James Constantine Pilling. In addition to his duties as Powell's chief clerk, first in the Rocky Mountain Survey, then in the Bureau of Ethnology, and finally in both the Bureau

and the Geological Survey, Pilling labored on exhaustive bibliographies of books and manuscripts on the various Indian language "stocks." By the time he died in 1895, he had compiled nine published volumes and played a major role in creating the Bureau of Ethnology library, now part of the J. W. Powell Library in the National Museum of Natural History.[51]

By the end of 1877, Powell had made major strides in taking up the linguistic classification and the synonymy and launching new ethnographic and linguistic studies. But the data-collecting tasks were still enormous. Following the long tradition of developing "inquiries" and vocabulary lists, discussed earlier, Powell had an extensive vocabulary list printed and circulated in 1877. It brought him much data for the eventual linguistic classification.[52]

Consolidation of the Surveys

By 1877–78 Powell was increasingly engrossed in anthropology, although his survey continued geological and topographic work. But there was congressional dissatisfaction with the perceived overlapping work of the surveys. In 1877, the stakes were raised. The economy was shaky and there was a strong move to retrench. To some in Congress this meant abolishing the surveys; both Powell and Hayden were threatened. Each marshaled his forces and, after a bitter fight, monies were restored.[53] But there was a rider clause calling for a study by the National Academy of Sciences of some form of survey consolidation. O. C. Marsh was acting president of the Academy and personally chaired the study committee. Interestingly, Carl Schurz, Secretary of the Interior, asked Powell, but not Hayden, to submit recommendations to the committee. Powell's report advocated a consolidated survey under civilian control, dedicated to appropriate geological research and accurate topographic mapping as the basis for a rational policy of land classification of the public domain. It also argued for a federally supported program to study American Indians.[54] The committee presented its report to the Academy in November 1878. The report called for a reorganization of the Coast and Geodetic Survey, a consolidated Geological Survey, and a revamped Public Lands Office.

Portions of the academy proposal were incorporated into a House appropriations bill early in 1879, minus the proposed changes in the Public Lands Office and the Coast and Geodetic Survey, but a Public Lands Commission was added to study allocation of resources and disposition of public lands. Once the bill was written, the issue of the directorship of the Geological Survey sparked intense infighting. Hayden desperately sought the job. Powell appeared to be after it, but was quietly supporting Clarence King. The story is long and complex; in the end, King's supporters won.[55]

Meanwhile, Powell was quietly frying his own fish. In a February 20, 1879, letter to an old friend, J. D. C. Atkins, chairman of the House Appropriation Committee, Powell outlined the need to "complete" the *Contributions to North American Ethnology* publication series and suggested that such a task could best be accomplished under the Smithsonian Institution.[56] This is the only letter to tip Powell's hand. He undoubtedly continued his discussions of an "ethnological bureau" with Spencer Baird and their compatriots at the newly founded Cosmos Club (see Chapter 6).

On March 3, 1879, Congress passed the Civil Sundry Bill for fiscal 1879–80. It provided for a consolidated Geological Survey, a Public Lands Commission, and the organization of the Tenth Census. Buried far in the back of the bill was a long sentence:

> For completing and preparing for publication the Contributions to North American Ethnology, under the Smithsonian Institution, $20,000: *Provided,* that all the archives, records, and materials relating to the Indians of North America, collected by the Geographical and Geological Survey of the Rocky Mountain Region [Powell's survey], shall be turned over to the Smithsonian Institution, that the work may be completed and prepared for publication under its direction: *Provided,* that it shall meet the approval of the Secretary of the Interior and the Secretary of the Smithsonian Institution.[57]

With the exception of the last clause, the sentence came straight from Powell's letter to Atkins. Thus did Powell achieve his "ethnological bureau."

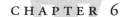

CHAPTER 6

The Bureau of Ethnology:
Organizing Anthropological Research in America

"It is the purpose of the Bureau of Ethnology to organize anthropologic research in America."
—John Wesley Powell, 1880[1]

O N JULY 9, 1879, Spencer F. Baird, secretary of the Smithsonian Institution, implemented the provisions of the legislation for "completing" the *Contributions to North American Ethnology*. He appointed John Wesley Powell to "take charge of the work and also to act as the disbursing officer of the appropriation for the purpose," and requested a program of operations. On July 22, Carl Schurz, Secretary of the Interior, authorized the transfer of "archives, records, and materials relating to the North American Indians" from the Interior Department to the Smithsonian.[2]

Although the legislation provided monies to *complete* work in hand, Powell saw it as the *beginning* of his ethnological bureau, as did Baird. Powell immediately sent James Stevenson (accompanied by his wife Matilda), Frank Hamilton Cushing, and Jack Hillers to Arizona and New Mexico to *begin* a survey of Pueblo Indian villages and ruins, and to make collections for the U.S. National Museum (see below). He

placed his chief clerk, James Pilling, in charge of the office, had some *Bureau of Ethnology* letterhead stationery printed, listing him as "Director," and left for the West to serve on the Public Lands Commission, which he had helped create.

As he traveled, Powell continued to formulate plans for his ethnological bureau. He had broad support in Congress and within the growing scientific community in Washington. His relationship with Baird was congenial; Baird had not sought to have the Bureau placed within the Smithsonian, but he shrewdly saw its utility to the National Museum. The legislation clearly placed Powell's operation "under" the Smithsonian Institution. Baird's price for this accommodation was a piece of the appropriation. He "reserved" up to five thousand dollars to be used at his discretion to purchase museum collections. Powell had no choice; he was on shaky legal ground after 1880 in seeking continued funding for his self-declared "Bureau." The matter came to a head in a vituperative standoff in the early 1880s, but Baird prevailed and until he died in 1887, exacted the five thousand dollars yearly.[3]

The twenty-thousand-dollar appropriation, even without the five-thousand-dollar "bite," was not sufficient for Powell's plans. There was a science of man waiting to be nursed beyond infancy. The task was enormous and pressing: visions of the vanishing savage danced in Powell's head, and in the letters and reports he wrote to get his appropriation increased.

Powell saw himself not as *the* creator of a science of anthropology, but *a* creator *and* orchestrator of the *development* of the science. All his previous experience, as intellectual, explorer, and soldier, could be brought to bear. He called his staff the "Corps of Ethnologists." In the first annual report of the Bureau of Ethnology, he boldly stated his intentions in the epigraph at the head of this chapter.

In 1876 Powell had taken up the basic, long-pending scholarly tasks needed to put anthropological studies of American Indians on a firm footing: the synonymy, the linguistic classification, and the bibliographies to back them up. These were central Bureau tasks until finally completed. But there was the larger task of *organizing* anthropology. Powell chose "Bureau of Ethnology" as a name for his organization because "ethnology" was a long-established and familiar term to scientists and even to some congressmen. But it was "anthropology" in the modern sense, embracing archaeology, physical anthropology, linguistics, and social and cultural anthropology, that Powell and his collaborators pursued. By 1879 numerous isolated scholars were working on anthropological questions, but there were few publication outlets for their results. Since 1846, the Smithsonian had provided a general focus and publication outlet for correspondents and collaborators; Powell adopted the model.

Powell requested fifty thousand dollars for fiscal year 1880–81 to implement a comprehensive plan for research on North American Indians, including "somatology, philology, mythology, sociology, habits and customs, technology, archaeology, and the history of Indian affairs (treaties, land cessions, etc.)." He evoked the vanishing savage image: "Rapidly the Indians are being gathered on reservations where their original habits and customs disappear, their languages are being modified or lost and they are abandoning their savagery, and barbarism and accepting civilization. If the ethnology of our Indians is ever to receive proper scientific study and treatment the work must be done at once." In a letter to Henry G. Davis, chairman of the Senate Appropriations Committee, Powell invoked the managed savage image, stressing the need for accurate knowledge of Indians as the basis for "wise" management: the appropriation, he said, was small in "comparison with the value of the work . . . to science and . . . wise legislation and administration of Indian affairs."[4]

Congress did not share Powell's view and continued the funding at twenty thousand dollars for 1880–81; he got the message. The appropriation for fiscal 1881–82 was for twenty-five thousand dollars, but five thousand dollars of that was a line item for Mound Builders exploration (discussed later). By 1884, the appropriation was up to forty thousand dollars, but part of that was a second line item of three thousand dollars a year was for the work of Charles C. Royce on Indian treaties and "cessions of land."[5]

Powell was able to secure a fair amount of extra support for his fledgling corps by placing his people on the payrolls of other agencies, as he had previously done. From 1880 through 1883, he had some of his staff on the Census Bureau payroll. The legislation creating the Tenth Census provided for the collection of many new sets of data—economic, agricultural, manufacturing, mining, etc.—as well as the enumeration and distribution of the population. The Constitution excludes "Indians not taxed" from the census. Francis Amasa Walker, superintendent of the Tenth Census, thought that was no longer appropriate. Since most Indian people were on reservations by 1880 they could, in theory, be subject to taxation. Further, it behooved the government to know how many Indian people were in its charge. He got around the constitutional wording by a bit of legislative sophistry that allowed special agents to collect "such information as to [Indians'] condition as may be obtainable," which included counting them.[6]

Powell sent Walker a plan to collect such information, and was appointed a Special Agent of the Census, in charge of "Statistics of Indians not taxed," with a budget, over three years, of 25,800 dollars. Four of Powell's staff were placed on the census payroll to do the work. "Information as to their condition" was seen to include ethnographic and linguistic data. Powell did some work himself. In the fall of 1880, as Indian Census Special Agent, he managed a few days of ethnographic work, his last, with the Wintun of northern California, and the Northern Paiute and Western Shoshoni of Nevada. The arrangement lasted until January 1883, when the Census Office decided that an ambitious new 28,500-dollar plan presented by Powell to collect "historical" data on the Indians was outside its purview; Powell had to scramble to get his people back on the Smithsonian payroll.[7]

The Bureau and the Survey

While Powell was struggling to keep his ethnological bureau alive, Clarence King was growing increasingly unhappy as director of the Geological Survey. He liked the socializing part, especially with Henry and Clover Adams and their friends in Washington, but he loathed the day-to-day work. His brilliance and his many interests made it impossible for him to endure the trench warfare of Washington politics. Powell was content with, indeed relished, political influence and the growing prestige of science in the capital city. King felt otherwise; he sought wealth and *la dolce vita*. He had done well in a very difficult situation. He had organized the Geological Survey, and gamely fought for and won continued appropriations for 1880–81. But he wanted out.[8]

On March 6, 1881, King called upon newly inaugurated President James A. Garfield and submitted his resignation. He recommended that Garfield's old friend, John Wesley Powell, be his successor. So too did Joseph Stanley-Brown, a young clerk whom Powell had loaned to Garfield to help him in his presidential campaign. Brown became Garfield's private secretary, and, later, son-in-law. On March 11, 1881, Garfield forwarded Powell's nomination to the Senate. He was confirmed on March 18, and permitted to remain, concurrently, as director of the Bureau of Ethnology, thereby in effect legitimizing the Bureau.[9]

A lesser person might have been crushed under the weight of running two organizations, one of which soon became the focal point of intense controversy over the classification and disposition of the public domain, the other dedicated to developing a science of man. Powell approached his dual task with a calm determination, tempered with scientific ebullience. He restructured the Survey, and combined the administration of both agencies in one office, with James Pilling as chief clerk and disbursing officer of both. By controlling both agencies, Powell obtained some flexibility to pursue his anthropological interests.[10]

At the beginning of fiscal year 1882, Powell's corps of ethnologists included Stevenson, Pilling, Hillers, and Powell on the Geological Survey payroll; Henry W. Henshaw, W. J. Hoffman, Charles C. Royce, and Albert Gatschet on the Census Office payroll; and James Owen Dorsey and Garrick Mallery on the Bureau payroll. Henry C. Yarrow received some expenses, but his salary was paid by the Army Medical Museum. Powell, the scholar-entrepreneur, was doing well: he was on his way to "organizing anthropological research in America" and using other agencies' funds and staff in the process.

Powell, Morgan, and the Southwest

While Powell achieved his Bureau of Ethnology through the political process, he had support from the larger scientific community, especially through the networks of the Philosophical Society of Washington and the National Academy of Sciences, to which he was elected in 1880, and the American Association for the Advancement of Science, which he had joined in 1875.

Powell's most important and ardent supporter was

Lewis Henry Morgan, whose agenda for the development of American anthropology meshed with Powell's own. Morgan was the key person in the development of American anthropology from 1860 until his death in 1881. Without his prestige and quiet behind-the-scenes support, Powell may not have sustained his bureau beyond the first two years. It also was Morgan who provided Powell with a theoretical framework, and who reset the anthropological research agenda for the American Southwest, an agenda that Powell and others followed for two decades.

Lewis Henry Morgan (1818–1881) was born in Aurora, in upstate New York (Fig. 6.1).[11] He graduated from Union College in Schenectady in 1842, then read law and moved to Rochester in 1844 to practice. Secret fraternal orders flourished in nineteenth-century America, a fad noted by Alexis de Tocqueville as an American peculiarity. Morgan joined one such, the "Grand Order of the Iroquois," became the "grand To do da ho," and assumed the ritual name of "Skenandoah." Soon there were "tribes" (chapters) in several New York towns, each named after a real Iroquois tribe: Seneca, Mohawk, Onondaga, and so on.[12]

The members "played Indian." They dressed in Iroquois costumes, carried tomahawks, made elaborate speeches mimicking Iroquois leaders, who were well known for their public oratory, and carried out various pretend rituals while engaging in male-bonding behavior around "council fires." Morgan and his fellows sought authenticity and some form of covert legitimacy by attempting to learn how to behave from real Iroquois. In 1844, Morgan chanced to meet a young Seneca, Ely S. Parker, who introduced him to some tribal elders.[13]

Morgan, in his youthful enthusiasm, saw the Order as a catalyst for a national organization, which would be a "vast repository of all that remains to us of the Indian . . . his antiquities, customs, eloquence, history and institutions."[14] He sent letters seeking help for his vanishing savage cause to numerous prominent individuals, including Henry Rowe Schoolcraft, who responded and encouraged his efforts.

The Grand Order soon went defunct, but Mor-

6.1. Lewis Henry Morgan, ca. 1877. Courtesy of the National Anthropological Archives, Smithsonian Institution.

gan persevered in his work with Iroquois elders. He helped establish the New York State Museum in Albany and contributed many Iroquois artifacts to it. His *League of the Ho-De-No Sau-Nee, or Iroquois,* published in 1851, is still regarded as a major source on the League. Powell called it "the first scientific account of an Indian tribe given to the world."[15]

Morgan married, had a family, and grew wealthy as an attorney for railroads and other businesses. In 1847, Joseph Henry and others prominent in United States science founded the American Association for the Advancement of Science (AAAS), modeled on the British association created a few years earlier. The associations were (and are) divided into lettered "sections," reflecting the proliferating disciplinary segmentation, as natural philosophy metamorphosed into modern science. In 1856, Morgan attended a meeting of the association in Albany where he met Jeffries Wyman, Louis Agassiz, Asa Gray, James Dwight Dana, and, most critically, Spencer Baird, all of whom encouraged him to return to his Iroquois studies.

The Iroquois are matrilineal; they trace descent and transmit titles, rights, and property from one generation to another through women, who also choose the sachems, the council leaders. Their kinship terminology reflects the matrilineal organization.[16] These practices puzzled Morgan. One immediate question was, did other Indian tribes, or tribes elsewhere, have similar terminological systems? He sent an inquiry to missionaries in the United States and abroad, and to U.S. Indian agents, asking them to collect kinship terms of reference, ranging from "What do you call your father?" to "What do you call the daughter of the daughter of a brother to the son of the son of the son of the brother's sister?"[17] Many answered with the equivalent of "Huh?" But some understood, especially missionaries who had a better grasp of Indian languages and family organization than Indian agents. Stephen Return Riggs, who had published a landmark *Grammar and Dictionary of the Dakota Language* in the *Smithsonian Contributions to Knowledge* series in 1852, sent an extensive description of Dakota patrilineal social organization and kinship terminology—in effect a "mirror image" of the Iroquois matrilineal system. But Morgan required much more information and made several field trips to Kansas, Nebraska, Minnesota, and up the Missouri River.[18]

Systems of Consanguinity and Affinity

By 1862 Morgan had become obsessed with the complexities of kinship systems; his wealth allowed him to devote nearly full time to his research. A completed inquiry arrived from a missionary who had worked among a Tamil-speaking group in southern India. The group was matrilineal and the kinship terminological system was identical with that of the Iroquois. This led Morgan to the much larger origins issue. Jefferson, Du Ponceau, and Gallatin thought that linguistic affinity would provide the key to linking Indians to the Old World. But the effort had stalled after Gallatin's work, and no usable data on the languages of northeastern Asia had been forthcoming.

Morgan took another tack: perhaps there were different basic "types" of family organization, each with a specific form of descent and inheritance, each reflected in a specific type of kinship terminological system. Perhaps a systematic comparison of these family types would provide the "hard data" to link Old World and New World societies. Not only might kinship data resolve the "origins" issue, but larger cultural-history questions as well: "With a thread as delicate as a system of relationships, we may yet reascend the several lines of the outflow of generations, and reach and identify that parent nation, from which we are . . . all alike descended."[19]

Heady stuff! But many data were needed. Joseph Henry and Spencer Baird agreed to send out Morgan's kinship inquiry under Smithsonian auspices. Lewis Cass, then Secretary of State, contributed a letter to American foreign diplomats asking for cooperation in distributing the schedule and getting it returned. Schedules came back from around the world, again primarily from missionaries. Morgan compiled all his data into the massive *Systems of Consanguinity and Affinity in the Human Family*, finally published by the Smithsonian in 1871.[20]

On the Road to Ancient Society

Eighteenth-century culture historians, from Lafitau to Millar, used the analogical savage to speculate about the origins of human nature, society, and religion: as they (living savages) are now, so our (European) ancestors once were. Many cultural histories contained a "stage theory" of human development. The "engine," or "historical dynamic," of this development varied. As more schemes were proposed in the nineteenth century, so too were the proposed engines driving historical change, from the lust for private property to the inevitable unfolding of dialectical processes, idealist or materialist.[21]

By the 1860s various European anthropologists, such as John McLennan, Johann Bachofen, and Edward Burnett Tylor, began putting together the concepts of origins, stage theories of evolutionary development, and the analogical savage into universal culture histories. In 1870 Morgan and his family made an extended tour of Europe, where he met Charles Darwin, John Lubbock (Lord Avebury),

Thomas Henry Huxley, Sir Henry Maine, and John F. McLennan.[22] All were concerned with social and cultural origins, using the customs of analogical savages as proxy data for origins and the progressive evolution of humanity through various technological and social stages. The full title of Lubbock's 1865 book says it all: *Pre-historic Times, as Illustrated by Ancient Remains, and the Manners and Customs of Modern Savages.*[23]

Morgan absorbed all these ideas and meshed them with his kinship data in *Ancient Society*, published in 1877. There, he assumed human psychic unity past and present, and assumed that all human social and cultural forms developed from the unfolding over time of a few panhuman elementary ideas. The unfolding had proceeded at different rates, due to environmental and historical factors; hence the existence of living "savages" and "barbarians." But the process is inevitable, beginning with primitive communism and promiscuity and culminating in nineteenth-century Victorian and American civilization. The stages are Lower, Middle, and Upper Savagery; Lower, Middle, and Upper Barbarism; and Civilization. Each substage exhibits specific forms of the family, descent, kinship, government, concepts of property, and technology. Any one society has to develop *all* the features of the next substage to advance.

Finally, in Morgan's view, *all* American Indians represent "the great period of barbarism"; *none,* past or present, had achieved "civilization." All the same, living peoples need to be studied now. Archaeological "remains buried in the earth will keep for the future student, the remains of Indian arts, languages and institutions will not. They are perishing daily and have been . . . for upwards of three centuries."[24]

Ancient Society made Morgan famous, but even before it appeared he was developing some other ideas that relate directly to the Southwest. In 1876, he published two articles in *The North American Review*. One, "Montezuma's Dinner," is discussed in Chapter 15. The second, "Houses of the Mound Builders," made two points. First, the Mound Builders of the Mississippi drainage migrated from the Southwest. Second, the great linear earthworks (now related to

the Hopewell Culture) in the Ohio Valley were platforms on which very long Iroquoislike longhouses were built: "The movement of the tribes who constructed the earth works . . . can be explained as a natural spread of Village Indians from the valley of the Rio Grande, or the San Juan, to the shores of the Gulf of Mexico, and thence northward to the valley of the Ohio." Further, these Village Indians, or their descendants, finding themselves unable to build adobe or stone houses, as they had in the Southwest, *"might have raised these embankments of earth, enclosing rectangles or squares, and constructed long houses on them,* which, it is submitted, is precisely what they did."[25] Such houses were joint tenement houses occupied by peoples at the requisite level of Lower to Middle Barbarism. No evidence of the Hopewell embankments serving as longhouse platforms has been found by later archaeologists.

Morgan's concern with houses had to do with his theory of social development: like kin term systems, houses and house life, as he would call them, reflect the forms of the family units living there. House types then were another data set to be used in support of his model of social evolution.

The development of Morgan's theories has been discussed in some detail. The reasons are obvious; he was the pivotal figure in the development of nineteenth-century American anthropology. His great work on kinship, published in 1871, made the study of kinship a central concern within modern anthropology worldwide until at least 1950.[26] He then used kinship data as "hard evidence" to validate his theory of universal human social evolution. Finally, his concern with "houses and house life" reset the anthropological research agenda in the American Southwest from 1880 to about 1910.

Morgan, Powell, and Bandelier

In 1875 Morgan helped create Sub-Section D, the "Permanent Sub-section of Anthropology," of the AAAS, and became the section's first chairman (status as a full section, Section H, Anthropology, came later).

Morgan's long term involvement with scholarly societies gave him the institutional links and intellectual cachet to get the sub-section created. By doing so he institutionalized anthropology in the eyes of the American scientific community. Soon after the AAAS meeting, Morgan became the sixtieth member of the National Academy of Sciences; he had arrived.[27] But the strain of the intensive work to which he had subjected himself for eighteen years had begun to seriously affect his health. It was time for a vacation.

Morgan in the Southwest

In the summer of 1878, Morgan made a trip to Colorado and northern New Mexico, accompanied by two grandnephews and two of their friends. He kept a journal of the trip, and a partial journal was kept by one of the nephews, William Fellowes Morgan. The party traveled by train to Canyon City, Colorado, then by wagon and horseback through the Rocky Mountains, including South Park, Leadville, and finally to Silverton. From there they traveled down the Animas River to the Aztec ruins and adjacent sites.[28]

Morgan spent several days exploring, measuring, and sketching the Aztec Ruins. He thought that the arrangement of rooms reflected occupation by "a gens [clan], a group larger than a family." He had already convinced himself that the ruins of Chaco Canyon were Coronado's Seven Cities of Cibola. He speculated that Aztec and adjacent ruins were "built by the tribes of Cibola after Coronado captured their villages and the Indians deserted them." Chaco Canyon was not Cibola, although his posited connection between Chaco and the Aztec Ruins site is correct: the latter is a Chacoan outlier.[29]

The party then moved to the Mancos Valley to see the "cliff houses," reported three years earlier by Holmes and Jackson. They visited and measured one, which nephew William Morgan described in a paper presented later that summer, before the AAAS.[30] They then skirted the north end of Mesa Verde and traveled to the head of McElmo Canyon, where they examined a number of cliff houses, open sites, and towers.

Morgan was struck by the variety of plant life in the San Juan region, as well as the number of ruins. This led him to speculate "that the San Juan was not only the Aztlan of the Mexican tribes, but the [original] native region of corn." He speculated that corn "originated in the Rocky Mountains" and then was propagated and differentiated "along the tributaries of the San Juan itself."[31]

Morgan visited Taos Pueblo and was given access to a kiva and apartments. The room arrangements he thought to be the same as his conjecture about Aztec Ruin. Finally, he wrote, "It is now evening, and . . . we hear the boys singing [and] dancing. They are Iroquois all over. I am going out to be on the spot."[32] Given Morgan's theoretical bent, the "Iroquois all over" could refer to a perceived similarity in the music, or it could mean that the Taosians and the Iroquois were, in his mind, at the same level of cultural development.

On the return east, Morgan stopped at St. Louis to attend the AAAS meeting, where he gave papers on Southwestern Indian architecture, later folded into his *Houses and House Life* volume. Powell was there and they spent much time talking anthropological shop with Frederic Ward Putnam, Adolph Bandelier, and Otis T. Mason. Bandelier made his debut at big-time scientific meetings with a paper, "On the Sources for Aboriginal History of Spanish America." Like everything else Bandelier produced, it was long winded, but stuffed with information.[33] Powell also met a young geologist from Iowa, W J McGee (among McGee's many affectations was that of no periods after his initials, which stood for William John). McGee later became Powell's right-hand sycophant in the Geological Survey and the Bureau of Ethnology.

Powell and Morgan

By 1876 Powell and Morgan had became close friends. When Morgan's *Ancient Society* appeared in 1877, Powell ordered copies for all his employees and collaborators as required reading.[34] Powell and his family visited the Morgans in Rochester. Morgan was present at the 1877 meeting of the National Academy of Sciences when Powell delivered his bombshell "Public Domain" speech, an abstract for his revolutionary *Arid Lands Report,* published the following year. The speech and the report propelled Powell into the forefront of national efforts to reform land and natural-resources allocation in the American West.[35]

Powell and Morgan spent long hours discussing how to develop anthropology in the United States. Morgan, meanwhile, was receiving encouragement from Henry Adams. There was an urgent "need," Adams wrote, "of a careful scientific inquiry into the laws and usages of the village Indians and to collect in a complete form all the material which is still in existence but will not last much longer." Adams thought Morgan's "influence might be decisive in organising such an undertaking. . . . If you will take the lead in it, I believe something might be accomplished."[36]

Morgan in turn encouraged Powell, and urged through the networks of scholarly societies the need for a systematic program of American anthropology. All this helped Powell get his Bureau of Ethnology going. In a November 1880 letter, Morgan wrote to Powell, "I congratulate you and myself on our great Republican victory [James Garfield's election as president]. It will give four years of steady encouragement to your work and enable you to get it on a solid foundation. . . . Hurra for Garfield and the Ethnological Bureau." When Garfield's nomination of Powell to head the Geological Survey was made public, Morgan wrote to James Pilling, "Tell Powell I . . . wish him congratulations on his promotion, but the promotion consists in the higher trust and the greater pay. The work in Ethnology is in fact the superior work."[37]

Though relatively brief, the relationship between Morgan and Powell was very important for Powell. Morgan used his considerable prestige to help make the Bureau of Ethnology a reality. Powell became a champion of Morgan's brand of societal evolution, in the end doggedly forcing data into its constricting theoretical framework. And finally, they both played key roles in getting Adolph Bandelier started on his work in the Southwest.

Adolph Bandelier

Adolphe (or Adolph, or Adolf) Françoise Alphonse Bandelier (1840–1914) (Fig. 6.2) was born in Bern, Switzerland, and emigrated with his family to Highland, Illinois, in 1848.[38] His father was a lawyer who became involved in banking, mining, and a foundry. Young Adolph grew up in a rich intellectual milieu and was a voracious reader. He was put to work in the family bank at age fourteen; in 1861 he married Maria Josepha (Josephine) Huegy, a daughter of one of the bank's partners. By the late 1860s, he had become engrossed in both pre- and post-conquest Latin Ameri-

6.2. Adolph Bandelier, ca. 1885. Courtesy of the Museum of New Mexico.

can history. Growing up speaking French, German, and English, he taught himself Latin and Spanish.

In 1873 he made a trip to Rochester, New York, and was introduced to Lewis Henry Morgan. They talked away an evening about Spanish historians and histories and their descriptions of Indian peoples in Mexico and the Southwest. Thus began the discipleship of the thirty-three-year-old businessman and midnight-oil scholar with the fifty-five-year-old wealthy lawyer turned full-time scholar. They became close friends, although they actually saw one another on only four occasions between 1873 and 1879, and soon entered into a breathless correspondence (at least from Bandelier's end) lasting until Morgan's death in 1881.[39]

By late 1873 Morgan was deep into his work on *Ancient Society*, including his reanalysis of preconquest Aztec culture that would emerge in the "Montezuma's Dinner" article in 1876. Bandelier, steeped in the Spanish sources, was not initially convinced of Morgan's view that the Aztecs had only risen to the stage of Middle Barbarism, but he was gradually "converted." Morgan, said Bandelier, finally "opened my eyes," allowing him to "see the light," and Bandelier became a "disciple" of his "revered teacher." But even though Bandelier "crusaded" for Morgan's ideas, he retained a healthy scholarly skepticism.[40]

The constant theme in Bandelier's letters is his increasing disgust with the business world and frustration with family responsibilities. He is in Highland, Illinois, but no longer of it; his head is in Tenochtitlán, and New Spain and New Mexico. Morgan arranged to have Frederic Ward Putnam publish three of Bandelier's major papers on Aztec life and culture in the *Annual Reports* of the Peabody Museum at Harvard University, as well as reviews and comments in magazines such as *The Nation*.[41] In the winter of 1879–80, Bandelier suffered a breakdown from overwork and began seeking ways to devote full time to scholarship. Unbeknownst to him, committees were being formed and decisions made in Boston that would grant his wish, and transform his life as well as the study of anthropology in the Southwest.

Morgan, Powell, Bandelier, and the AIA

In April 1879 Charles Eliot Norton and eleven other prominent persons in the Boston area issued a circular proposing the establishment of a society "for the purpose of furthering and directing archaeological investigation and research."[42] Norton (1827–1908) was one of the most influential scholars of the nineteenth century. He had a long and distinguished career as an independent scholar, editor, and critic. In 1873 his cousin, the young and innovative president of Harvard, Charles W. Eliot, appointed him to a professorship in art history. His brilliant lectures were crowded with students during the twenty-four years he taught. He was also famous for editing Thomas Carlyle's letters, the poems of John Donne and of Anne Bradstreet, and a prose translation of Dante's *Divine Comedy*.[43]

Over one hundred scholars and wealthy patrons, primarily from the New England region, heeded the call to the meeting held on May 10, 1879. A week later, the Archaeological Institute of America (AIA) was incorporated and Norton became its first president. The immediate aim of the Institute was to support archaeological work in the Mediterranean region. Longer-range goals included the establishment of a school of classical studies in Athens, to be followed later by a similar school at Rome, and the establishment of a scholarly journal in archaeology; all were ultimately realized.

Norton had scant regard for Americanist studies. In an 1880 letter to Morgan, Frederic Ward Putnam wrote that although Norton lived three minutes' walk from the Peabody Museum, he had never been in it since it opened in 1865.[44] In a letter to Thomas Carlyle, Norton wrote:

> I don't care much for our American Archaeology (though as president of the society I must say this under my breath), but it is worth while to try to get what exact information we can about the semi-barbarians concerning whom so many wild fancies

have been current, ever since the days of the Spanish conquest which the amiable Prescott confirmed by his pieces of romantic narrative. But I do care much for the Greeks.[45]

But some powerful members of the new institute *did* care much for American archaeology, including Putnam, Francis Parkman, and Lewis Henry Morgan; hence Norton's *sotto voce.* Parkman, Norton's longtime friend and intellectual compatriot, was a fellow of Harvard, near his peak as a major nineteenth-century American historian, and much interested in the cultural history of American Indians. He was also a member of the Institute's executive committee, which was given full power to decide what sorts of research would be done and how it was to be accomplished.[46]

Parkman and the committee turned for advice to Lewis Henry Morgan. Morgan responded with a plan that set a new research agenda for the American Southwest. The committee responded favorably and the plan was published in the first annual report of the Institute.[47] Institute members felt that some sort of an Americanist program should be launched, perhaps as a cooperative venture. On January 17, 1880, the committee voted "that correspondence be opened with gentlemen of the Bureau of Ethnology at Washington and with officers of the United States Army and others, in order to learn what aid and cooperation may be expected from persons already in the field."[48] A week later, Morgan wrote to Powell giving him a general idea of his research plan, and urging Powell's involvement: "I urged upon them the importance of an exploration and interpretation of the house architecture in New Mexico and the San Juan regions, to be followed by a second expedition to Yucatan and Central America. . . . I have shown them," Morgan went on, "that there was but one system of house architecture from the San Juan to Panama; . . . That a false interpretation has been put upon this architecture from the beginning from not understanding the institutions and plan of life of the Indian tribes. That we must look to the present occupied pueblos in

New Mexico for a part of the means of explaining the object and uses of the houses in ruins in Yucatan, etc. . . . I have mentioned you, [Frederic Ward] Putnam and Bandelier as three great Ethnologists who would made a good joint Commission for both explorations."[49]

Powell saw an opportunity to further his plans to "organize anthropologic research in America." He responded, outlining his and the Bureau's previous and present work in the Southwest, and indicated his willingness to cooperate. Morgan replied, again urging Powell's involvement in the project and telling him, "You can have the main oar as well as not. . . . with the position you have gained you can't afford to be out of it. I see no objection to you managing the working part of the expedition at the expense of the Institute, and under their auspices, and in reporting the results to them; or in cooperating with them as head of your Bureau in which case it would be at your own expense." Morgan also wrote to Bandelier, telling him what was in the wind. Back came bubbling and detailed letters laying out Bandelier's plans.[50]

Powell was invited to attend the second annual meeting of the Institute in Cambridge on May 15, 1880. He gave a detailed report of the Bureau's work in the Southwest and his plans. There was a long discussion; ultimately the executive committee voted to "appropriate $1,500 [it turned out to be $1,200] for the expenses of an expedition to New Mexico and the Southwest, to be arranged by consultation with Major Powell." Parkman then wrote to Powell seeking his cooperation in developing a specific plan to gain "such information as may help to determine the ethnographic position of the pueblo tribes, and the relation of their languages, mythology, and social life to those of the savage tribes of Mexico. As to methods, the Institute would leave them to your judgment." Bandelier desperately wanted the job; he wrote to Norton, introducing himself as Morgan's protégé. Morgan had first suggested Frank Hamilton Cushing as a possibility, since he was already at Zuni, but now threw his full weight behind Bandelier's appointment.[51]

Matters moved quickly. Powell indicated his cooperation and submitted a plan of work to Parkman, outlining a comprehensive study of the Southwestern Pueblos, including linguistic, ethnographic, architectural, and archival studies, all preliminary to later, extended studies in Mexico. Norton immediately accepted Powell's plan. Powell invited Bandelier to Washington to discuss matters, then sent him to Boston with letters recommending him as "the gentleman chosen by me to make the investigation in New Mexico for the Archaeological Institute." Bandelier spent two weeks in Boston, talking with Norton, Putnam, and others. On July 19, 1880, Norton informed Powell that the Institute had hired Bandelier.[52]

But even as the cooperative venture between Norton's Institute and Powell's Bureau was aborning, the ground shifted. Before Bandelier left Illinois, he wrote to Norton laying out his plan of work. The letter foreshadows Bandelier's independent actions once he reached New Mexico, and probably reflects Norton's second thoughts about handing over control of an AIA project to Powell and a determination to keep the fledgling Institute in his own hands. Norton, and others in his circle, were quite aware of the vagaries of Washington politics and that Powell's nascent Bureau might not exist by the following year, despite Powell's magnetism, political savvy, and organizational abilities. The letter also reflects Bandelier's clear realization where his funding (meager though it was) came from: "I believe that a quite respectable basis is laid for *documentary* evidence—Not every ethnologist may see the bearings of the dry accumulations of data.—thus friend Powell has asked me whether I really intended to go into old history instead of into Ethnology—but I am responsible to *You alone* for such preparatory work."[53]

Bandelier finally arrived in the Southwest in late August 1880, and was launched at last, at age forty, on a career as a scholar. He spent only about three months in New Mexico in 1880. He was then sent by the AIA to Yucatán to join the Lorillard-Charney expedition. He arrived to find the expedition abandoned, but stayed on for the year 1881, surveying ruins

and studying archives. In 1882 he was back in New Mexico.

Clearly miffed, Powell wrote rather brusquely to Francis Parkman, complaining that his program of "intensive ethnographic inquiry and linguistic study based on participant-observation" had not been followed, that Bandelier had agreed to such a program but "he then left to visit Boston and while there the entire plan of investigation was changed. Since that time he has been sent to Mexico. I have a low estimate of the poor results obtained by traveling anthropologists. The only results of value at the present time in any of these fields of research comes from years of well directed labor." Powell went on to hope that "some of your Boston people" would see the light and "enter this field of research where substantial results can be obtained," that is, by applying Powell's methods.[54] Although Frederic Ward Putnam continued to interact with Powell, there was no more talk of cooperative anthropological ventures between Boston and Washington.

Morgan's Research Agenda

In early 1880, as Morgan and Powell mulled over the potential Archaeological Institute-Bureau of Ethnology project, Morgan was finishing his final magnum opus, the *Houses and House Life* volume, which Powell would publish. The research plan Morgan sent to Norton was extracted from the manuscript. The plan, together with some additional statements from *Houses and House Life,* became the research agenda followed by Powell, his staff, and Bandelier in the Southwest. Morgan envisioned Southwestern studies within a larger Americanist whole:

> There are reasons for assuming that all the tribes
> of the American aborigines were of one common
> stock; that their institutions, plan of life, usages and
> customs were similar; and that the houses in ruins
> in the various places named can be explained, by
> comparison with those now inhabited in New
> Mexico, as parts of a common system of house

architecture. If this be so, *it follows that the facts of American archaeology must be studied ethnologically; i.e., from the institutions, usages, and mode of life of existing Indian tribes.*[55]

Morgan believed that a study of Pueblo house ground plans would reveal a hemisphere-wide pattern of communal living "in [the] ruins in Yucatan and Central America, as well as on the San Juan, the Chaco, and the Gila. From Zuni to Cuzco, at the time of the Spanish conquest, the mode of domestic life in all these joint tenement houses must have been substantially the same."[56]

A research program for the Southwest and beyond "should ascertain by actual exploration and investigation: 1. The architectural style and extent of the ruins, and the ground plans of the principal structures; 2. The condition of the art of masonry and of house construction, . . . ; 3. The object and uses for which the houses were erected; 4. The social organization, usages, and customs of the native tribes in New Mexico, Yucatan, and Central America, and, so far as possible, those of their ancestors, who constructed the houses."[57]

Finally, in *Houses and House Life* Morgan combined his stage theory of sociocultural development with the older "north to south connection," and "Southwest as point of origin" model he had proposed in his Mound Builders article of 1876, and his speculations in his journal of the 1878 trip to the Southwest. He argued that the San Juan Basin "ruins and those of similar character in the valley of the Chaco . . . suggest "that the . . . [Basin] held a prominent place in the first and most ancient development of Village Indian Life." Further, "the evidence of Indian occupation and cultivation throughout [the northern Southwest] suggest[s] the hypothesis that the Indians here first attained to the condition of the Middle Status of barbarism, and sent forth the migrating bands who carried this advanced culture to the Mississippi Valley, to Mexico and Central America, and not unlikely to South America as well." Morgan further argued that maize agriculture *originated in and was carried from* the San Juan Basin by the "migrating bands" as they moved into the Mississippi Valley and south into Mexico and South America. In a very real sense, Morgan's research agenda replaced that put forth by Albert Gallatin in the late 1840s. Modern anthropology was now under way in the Southwest.[58]

Morgan struggled against deteriorating health to finish his *Houses and House Life.* In mid-June 16, 1880, he shipped it off to Powell, saying, "It is undoubtedly the best I shall ever make."[59] He was able to preside over the opening of the 1880 AAAS meeting, but thereafter was increasingly confined to his home with "nervous exhaustion." He soon was in serious decline; even Bandelier, on his way back from Mexico in late 1881, was not allowed to see him. He died December 17, 1881, just before *Houses and House Life* came off the press.[60] He left an enormous intellectual legacy, not only for American and European anthropology, but in the research agenda for the Southwest that Bandelier and those working under Powell pursued for the next two decades.

CHAPTER 7

The Bureau and the Southwest

JOHN WESLEY POWELL managed to keep his fledgling Bureau alive after the first year. The language of the 1880–81 appropriation read, "to continue to complete the *Contributions to North American Ethnology* series." The next year it simply read, "for the normal operations of the Bureau of Ethnology."[1] By then the Bureau had been given de facto recognition when Congress ordered the printing of its first annual report, and the Senate confirmed Powell as director of the Geological Survey and allowed him to remain as director of the Bureau of Ethnology.

Powell also used professional and social organizations to achieve his goals. The Anthropological Society of Washington was founded in February 1879. Powell was its first president, serving nine terms. He was elected to the National Academy of Sciences in 1880. Both organizations were useful in generating support for his plans. But of more immediate use was the Cosmos Club, which came into existence in Powell's

living room on November 16, 1878; he was its first president.[2]

The Cosmos Club had a social function, but its real purpose was to develop support for the burgeoning Washington scientific community by providing a setting in which the intellectuals, the powerful, and the power brokers could interact over good food, good whiskey, and fine cigars. "By 1879 the intellectuals [in Washington] had provided themselves with a firm . . . structural base from which to exert—if not power—at least the next best thing to power, influence," usually at the Cosmos Club.[3] One example will suffice. In March 1881, Edward M. Gallaudet, the director of the Columbia Institution in Washington, who had revolutionized teaching methods for deaf children, went to the Cosmos Club "to take dinner with Major J. W. Powell. I found at his table Robert Lincoln, Secretary of War, Gov. [Samuel J.] Kirkwood, the [newly appointed] Secretary of the Interior,

Senators [Cushman K.] Davis, [John A.] Logan and [James D.] Cameron . . ."[4]

The years 1881–92 were Powell's heydays in Washington. With the addition of a single legislative phrase, he moved the Geological Survey into a complex program of research and mapping of the entire United States. In 1882, friends on the House of Representatives Appropriations Committee added the words, "and to continue the preparation of a geologic map of the United States," to the Geological Survey organic act of 1879. This master stroke of "authorizing legislation," as it is called, allowed Powell to argue for and receive very large increases in the Survey budget for several years. Powell always adhered to cardinal rule number one in government bureaucracy: Never do anything you cannot demonstrate that you've been authorized by Congress to do, even if such demonstration has to be both elastic and creative. Geological mapping requires accurate topographic base maps; topographic maps require numerous teams of surveyors and cartographers to do the mapping; geological mapping also requires field teams of trained geologists and paleontologists; they in turn need laboratories and photographic darkrooms, and so on. All that costs lots of money.[5] Powell tried to use the mapping program as a tool to instill rationality, as he saw it, in U.S. land policy in the West. What worked "east of the 100th meridian,"—homesteading of 160-acre farm plots—did not work west of that line, where control of water sources meant control of tens, if not hundreds, of thousands of acres. He got legislation passed limiting further opening of the public domain until it was properly mapped and hydrographic studies completed. For a time this put him in a position of great influence over further settlement and exploitation of natural resources in the much of the West. That infuriated western congressmen and their powerful constituents, and they went after him with a vengeance. He was vilified in the press and finally brought down through the time-honored congressional technique of drastically cutting an agency's budget to lop off its head. Powell signaled in 1892 that he would resign, carefully picked his successor, Charles D. Walcott,

and in 1894 retreated to the newly renamed Bureau of *American* Ethnology. The story of Powell's battles over land-use policy are well chronicled by his biographers William Darrah, Wallace Stegner, and Donald Worster and need not be pursued further here.[6]

Organizing Anthropology in the Southwest

By becoming director of the Geological Survey and retaining the Bureau directorship, Powell was able to expand his anthropological operations. Jack Hillers was transferred to the Survey payroll as chief photographer, at a salary of eighteen hundred dollars, but was available to photograph delegations of Indians visiting Washington, or to accompany anthropology parties to the field. James Stevenson, the Bureau's "executive officer," at a salary of three thousand dollars, became the Survey's executive officer at the same salary. But he was "detailed" for anthropological collecting. Pilling's 2,100-dollar salary was paid from Survey funds, but he did triple duty as chief clerk for both the Survey and the Bureau as well as continuing the compilation of his massive bibliographies on American Indian languages. Powell drew only a six-thousand-dollar salary as director of the Survey. These arrangements freed nearly twelve thousand dollars of Powell's Bureau appropriation, and lessened the impact of Baird's five-thousand-dollar annual "tax."

Despite this boost, Powell's avowed purpose of "organizing anthropologic research in America," never came to full fruition; given available resources, it could not. Powell took up the still-pending linguistic classification and synonymy, recognizing their central, undergirding importance to the development of an anthropology of American Indians. Beyond those long term tasks, the research problems the Bureau undertook were strongly conditioned by the winds of politics, the realities of congressional funding, and the personal inclinations and expertise of its staff and collaborators. Henry W. Henshaw, originally an ornithologist, assisted by W. J. Hoffman and Albert Gatschet, worked on the linguistic classification. James Mooney's initial assignment was to help with the linguistic classification, but he soon began working with the Cherokee and went on to his famed studies of Plains Indians. Garrick Mallery labored on his studies of sign language and rock art, Henry C. Yarrow on mortuary practices, Charles C. Royce on Indian land cessions, and James Owen Dorsey on Omaha and Dakota societies and languages. All these studies are classics and still frequently consulted, but they did not result from any coordinated anthropological research program, despite Powell's avowed purpose for his Bureau.[7]

In 1881, Powell was forced into a Mound Builders archaeology program by Spencer Baird, who used congressional pressure to get the program going on the grounds that foreign and private museums were busily carting off wagon loads of artifacts. That Cyrus Thomas, preacher turned entomologist, turned lawyer, turned archaeologist (and an old friend of Powell's), was able to carry the program off as well as he did was rather extraordinary.[8]

In the Southwest, things became a bit more focused, thanks to Lewis Henry Morgan's research agenda as it was implemented by Bandelier and Cushing after 1880. Morgan's trip to the Southwest the previous year had convinced him of the importance of the region for his theories. And he agreed with Powell that the Southwest was possibly the best place in the United States in which anthropology could be done, due principally to the presence of the Pueblo Indians. They had managed to retain much of their cultural integrity, and were not being herded onto reservations by the U.S. Army, as was happening elsewhere at the time.

The Corps of Ethnologists in the Southwest

The years 1879–91 were halcyon ones for the Bureau of Ethnology and the National Museum in the Southwest. By various means, Powell had as many as eight researchers in the Southwest during most of the 1880s. During this time, the National Museum acquired tens of thousands of ethnographic and archaeological specimens from the region; major ethnographic stud-

ies were undertaken, and the concept of an interdisciplinary anthropological research project was brought into existence.

When the first appropriated funds became available on July 1, 1879, Powell hastened to get a team into the field. Spencer Baird, secretary of the Smithsonian, was always anxious to increase the collections of the National Museum. James Stevenson (Fig. 7.1), Powell's new administrative officer, saw himself as a "man of action," and was always ready to head west, if possible with his wife, Matilda (Fig. 7.2). John K. (Jack) Hillers, Powell's amiable and accomplished photographer, went wherever Powell assigned him to go and produced superlative photographs. Finally, there was a

7.1. James Stevenson, 1870s. Courtesy of the National Anthropological Archives, Smithsonian Institution.

7.2. Matilda Coxe Stevenson, 1870s. Courtesy of the National Anthropological Archives, Smithsonian Institution.

In 1879, the railhead of the Atchison, Topeka and Santa Fe Railway was at Las Vegas, New Mexico. From there the group traveled by wagon into the Rio Grande Valley, collecting artifacts from several pueblos. They then moved to Fort Wingate, roughly 150 miles west of Santa Fe, arriving on September 16, 1879, with "a six mule wagon, a four mule escort wagon and an ambulance," and Cushing astride a mule. During this and subsequent trips, the group was often aided by the army. Horses, mules, wagons, and sometimes a military escort were made available as a courtesy, and rations were provided at cost.[11]

The four, accompanied by an escort of soldiers, arrived in Zuni on September 18, 1879. Cushing and Hillers set up a camp and Hillers quickly began making photographs (Fig. 7.3). The Stevensons rented two rooms in the pueblo for living and trading. By October 12, the Stevensons and Hillers were back at Fort Wingate. Cushing remained in Zuni and had sought permission from Baird to stay for two extra months. James Stevenson and Jack Hillers then made a quick trip to the Hopis to collect artifacts and make photographs. Matilda remained at Fort Wingate. Stevenson wrote to Pilling: "Mrs. S. is here at Wingate with Mrs. Brull [*sic*, George P. Breull], the Commandant's wife—Genl. [Edward] Hatch, Commander of the District of New Mexico insisted on her coming here, where she will remain till I am ready to come home."[12]

Stevenson acquired several wagon loads of artifacts at Hopi, with assistance from Thomas Keam (see Chapter 10). He returned briefly to Zuni in early November to do some final collecting and tell Cushing that Baird and Powell had agreed he could stay on. Stevenson clearly had done well. He wrote to Pilling, "The total weight of our collection is 10,512 lbs." Before he left Fort Wingate, in another letter to Pilling, Stevenson wrote: "I secured from the Old Church of Zuñi two large altar images 4 ft. high, carved out of one block of wood, and the center piece of the altar representing a crown with a large heart carved on it below. Got them in the dead hours of night."[13]

Stevenson's letter contradicts some rewriting of history by his wife. In April 1881, Tilly Evans Stevenson,

twenty-two-year-old brilliant but bumptious curatorial assistant in the National Museum, Frank Hamilton Cushing (see Fig. 8.1), who yearned mightily for a chance to go west and study the Indians. These four comprised the Smithsonian team.[9]

Stevenson's orders read: "You are hereby placed in charge of the party organized to make ethnological and archaeological explorations in south-western New Mexico and contiguous territory. Mr. J. K. Hillers has been instructed to report to you as photographer and Mr. F. H. Cushing of the Smithsonian Institution will assist you in making collections and in other ethnologic work."[10]

7.3. *Schoolchildren at Zuni Pueblo, 1879. Taylor Ealy, missionary-teacher at right; Jenny Hammaker, assistant teacher, at left; tall individual in center is We'wha, Zuni berdache. Photograph by Jack Hillers. Courtesy of the National Anthropological Archives, Smithsonian Institution.*

as Matilda then called herself, circulated a privately printed booklet, "Zuni and Zunians," in which she described Zuni and Hopi, implying she had visited both "during the summer of 1879." In 1904 she wrote: *"The whole of the six months devoted to field work in 1879 was spent at Zuñi; and though the writer accompanied Mr. Stevenson to the meetings of the various secret organizations, and though her relations with the Indians were of the most cordial nature, she obtained at this time but the merest suggestion of their inner life."*[14]

In 1879, Matilda Stevenson was at Zuni slightly over three weeks, according to her husband's letters. She was not at Hopi, and there is no evidence that she and James attended meetings of Zuni secret organizations, nor would they have been allowed to do so. Of more immediate interest is James's statement about

looting the church: "Got them in the dead hours of the night." In Stevenson's 1881 paper she described "the old Spanish Church, . . . still remarkably preserved, even to the wooden carvings about the altar." There are "two well-erected wooden statues of saints, each about three feet in height, or rather these were to be seen there, until removed with other relics to Washington." One of "the statues from Zuñi, . . . is remarkable for the enamel finish on the limbs and face."[15]

In February 1883, Adolph Bandelier visited Zuni and wrote in his diary: "In the aft[ernoon] went to see the church, which is not quite as large as that of Acoma, but after the same style, abandoned, plundered by the Washington party [as Bandelier called Stevenson's group] in the most shameless manner, and falling to ruin in consequence."[16]

In 1896, in a Bureau of American Ethnology *Annual Report,* Frank Hamilton Cushing wrote:

A few years since a party of Americans who accompanied me to Zuñi desecrated the beautiful antique shrine of the church, carrying away "Our Lady of Guadelupe of the Sacred Heart," the guardian angels, and some of the painted bas reliefs attached to the altar. When this was discovered by the Indians, consternation seized the whole tribe; council after council was held, at which I was alternately berated (because people who had come there with me had "plundered their fathers' house"), and entreated to plead with "Wasintona" to have these "precious saints and sacred masks of their fathers" returned to them.[17]

In 1904, Matilda Stevenson countered Cushing's statement (he could not reply since by then he was dead):

Two images of saints and portions of the altar of the old Catholic Church were obtained, . . . The church objects were in the custody of one Mauritio, and in order to determine whether they might be removed a council of religious and civil officers was held. It was finally decided that it would be well to have these objects go with other Zuñi material to the 'great house' (National Museum) in Washington, where they would be preserved.[18]

This is rather at odds with James Stevenson's "Got them in the dead hours of the night."

What he got was most of the altar screen. The missionary church at Halona (present-day Zuni) was destroyed in the 1680 Pueblo Revolt, but was rebuilt in the early decades of the eighteenth century. In his 1776 report on the missions in New Mexico Province, Fray Francisco Domínguez described the church and its equipage: "It has a small new altar screen, as seemly as this poor land has to offer, which was paid for by Father Vélez and the Indians of the pueblo." The screen includes, he continues, "a large oil painting on canvas . . . of Our Lady of Guadalupe . . . Below this painting is a very old lacquer Child Jesus vested as a priest, the clothing also old. The lower niches at the

sides contain St. Michael on the right and St. Gabriel at the left, new middle-sized images in the round." The statues are plainly visible in a watercolor of the altar screen done in 1851 by Richard Kern and a photograph taken by Timothy O'Sullivan in 1873.[19]

The altar objects, although assigned numbers, do not appear in Stevenson's catalog of Zuni artifacts. By 1898, however, they were on display in the National Museum as part of an exhibit of mission artifacts; in the 1950s, St. Gabriel and the cartouche were incorporated into an exhibit in the North American Indian Hall.[20]

In 1887, while the Stevensons were at Zia pueblo, James was shown two ollas with snake designs on them, carefully hidden in a talus slope far from the pueblo. They were of central and major importance to the Zia Snake Society. He tried to buy them, but was refused. Later, according to Matilda Stevenson, one of the leaders of the Snake Society came in the dead of night and "took from [a] sack one of the vases, he being in the meanwhile much excited and also distressed. He would not allow a close examination to be made of the vase, but urged the packing of it at once; he deposited a plume offering in the vase, and sprinkled meal upon it and prayed while tears moistened his cheeks. The vase was brought to Washington and deposited in the National Museum."[21] The implication is that the priest brought the olla to the Stevensons on his own. However, given Matilda Stevenson's dissimulation about the altar pieces from Zuni, it is more likely that James acquired the olla "in the dead of the night," or bribed the priest to sell it to him. Given the picture that Stevenson painted of poverty and endemic food shortages at Zia in the introductory chapter of her monograph, the latter explanation may have validity.

In his summary of the 1884 field season, Powell noted that the Stevensons collected eighty-five hundred specimens, including "many objects relating to the outdoor ceremonies of the Zuni. Specimens of these were secured from their sacred springs, caves and shrines . . . representative specimens of their fetishes, plume sticks and other objects connected with their mythology and religious practices."[22] Like the figures from the Catholic Church, the "sacred" objects were simply appropriated.

Two such objects were Zuni Ahayu:da, wooden carved and painted statues of the "Twin War Gods" created by Sun Father during the Zunis' epic search for Middle Place in cosmogonic times.[23] The twins helped the Zunis overcome enemies and find Middle Place, but also continue to use their powers to bring rain and protect them. Each year during the initiation of a new Bow Priest, the Deer Clan leaders carve a statue of Elder Brother, Ahayu:da, Uyeyewi, and the Bear Clan leaders carve an image of Younger Brother, Ahayu:da, Ma'a'sewi. The images are seen as the living embodiments of the twins and are taken to special shrines and ritually placed next to Ahayu:da from previous years. In 1881, James Stevenson removed an Elder Ahayu:da from its cave shrine on Corn Mountain; Frank Hamilton Cushing also took one from the same shrine during his sojourn at Zuni. Both men kept the figures as part of their personal collections; they came to the National Museum after the two had died. The fact of their removal from the shrine did not lessen the power nor importance of the Ahayu:da fig-

7.4. Acoma and Zuni pottery collected by James Stevenson, 1879–1883, in storage at U.S. National Museum of Natural History, 1979. Courtesy of the National Anthropological Archives, Smithsonian Institution.

Thank you for visiting the
Allen County Public Library.

Item ID: 31833045153860
Title: Harvard Yard
Author: Martin, William, 1950-
Date due: 9/12/2009,23:59

Item ID: 31833057576925
Title: The lost throne
Author: Kuzneski, Chris.
Date due: 9/12/2009,23:59

Item ID: 31833056757724
Title: A tale out of luck
Author: Nelson, Willie, 1933-
Date due: 9/12/2009,23:59

Item ID: 31833041299519
Title: A laboratory for anthropology : s
cience and roman
Author: Fowler, Don D., 1936-
Date due: 9/12/2009,23:59

Summer hours begin
Sunday, May 24!

WEBSITE RENEWAL
www.acpl.lib.in.us
↳ MY LIBRARY ACCOUNT
↳ RENEW MATERIALS

ALLEN COUNTY PUBLIC LIBRARY
HAVE YOUR LIBRARY CARD AND MATERIAL READY

TELEPHONE RENEWAL
(DURING MAIN LIBRARY BUSINESS HOURS ONLY)
(260) 421-1240

WEBSITE RENEWAL
www.acpl.lib.in.us
↳ MY LIBRARY ACCOUNT
↳ RENEW MATERIALS

ALLEN COUNTY PUBLIC LIBRARY
HAVE YOUR LIBRARY CARD AND MATERIAL READY

TELEPHONE RENEWAL

ures to the Zuni people. They were finally returned to Zuni in 1987.[24]

The collecting practices of the Stevensons were no different than those of other Anglos in the nineteenth century who bought or appropriated what is now called "traditional cultural property" to enhance museum or personal collections. The practices followed from the scientistic view of the time: indigenous peoples and their artifacts— "sacred" or no—were objects to be studied and collected "in the interests of science," or as "objects of curiosity."

7.5. *Taos Pueblo, north room block, 1880. Photograph by Jack Hillers. Courtesy of the National Anthropological Archives, Smithsonian Institution.*

The Stevenson Team

The Stevensons returned to Washington from the first collecting trip in late December 1879, and James began the tedious work of describing the collection (Fig. 7.4) in between administrative duties. Matilda, meanwhile, had been rethinking her career possibilities. Given the likely prospect of James returning for several more years to the Southwest, there was an opportunity to do anthropology, and she began to move in that direction.

Matilda Coxe Stevenson (1849–1915) was a daughter of Alexander Hamilton Evans and Maria Coxe Evans.[25] Evans was an attorney and journalist and a close friend of Joseph Henry. Matilda was tutored at home and then spent five years in a fashionable Philadelphia finishing school. It was expected she would marry well and become a society wife and mother. But Matilda wanted more from life. She returned to Washington in 1868 and began to read law in her father's office; she also began studying chemistry and geology with Dr. N. M. Mew, of the Army Medical Museum, hoping to be a mineralogist and do field-

work in interesting places in the West. She met the dashing and well-liked James Stevenson in 1872, and after a whirlwind courtship they married. Her hopes were realized and she found herself in the West during the field seasons of 1872, 1875, and 1878, collecting fossils and birds and studying the geysers in Yellowstone. During the 1875 trip she gained some initial experience with Indians by briefly interviewing some Ute and Arapaho people in Wyoming and Colorado.

When Powell sent Cushing, Hillers, and James Stevenson to New Mexico in 1879, Matilda went along as "volunteer coadjutor in ethnology," her own polite euphemism for gofer.[26] But she was not just a gofer, nor simply "the wife" of James. In 1879 she actively helped him with the trading for artifacts at Zuni. In subsequent seasons, she was with James or at Zuni beginning her own research program.

In 1880, the Stevensons, with two assistants, spent their field season in the Rio Grande Valley collecting artifacts while Jack Hillers made his now-classic photographs of the pueblos (Fig. 7.5). The Stevensons' modus operandi was to trade, rather than buy. Cloth, needles, tools, building materials, and much more were exchanged for pottery vessels, ceremonial regalia, bows and arrows, woven textiles, and whatever other implements the people were willing to trade. But the major items of interest were pottery vessels, especially the painted bowls and jars, many of them heirlooms.

At Santa Clara Pueblo, the Stevensons found that polished blackware pottery was still being made and provided perhaps the earliest description of its production.[27] The "revival" of this ware at Santa Clara and San Ildefonso pueblos early in the twentieth century was an important factor in the development of the Indian art and crafts market in New Mexico (see Chapter 27).

In 1881, the Stevensons and Hillers returned to Zuni and established a base of operations, collecting there but also at Hopi and again in Canyon de Chelly, with assistance in both places from Thomas Keam. Matilda had decided to begin serious ethnographic work of her own at Zuni, to Cushing's great annoyance. By the summer of 1881, Cushing had been at Zuni for nearly two years, and Matilda Stevenson's "invasion" of "his" pueblo was most unwelcome. Despite that, she was determined to become an ethnographer, by force of will if necessary.

There was much animosity between the two, due in large measure to Cushing's egotism and Matilda's overbearing disposition. On the back of a photograph of a painting of Cushing, there is a note in Matilda Stevenson's hand, "Frank Hamilton Cushing in his fantastic dress worn while among the Zuni Indians. This man was the biggest fool and charlatan I ever knew. He even put his hair up in curl papers every night. How could a man walk weighted down with so much toggery?"[28]

At Zuni Matilda Stevenson began studying women and children. Given Victorian mores and standards of modesty, and indeed, Indian mores and standards of modesty, it was regarded as unseemly for Anglo men to inquire into matters of women's daily work, pregnancy, childbirth, and sex—"women's knowledge." Given Victorian mores, it was beneath the dignity of

Anglo men to study children; that too was "women's knowledge." Matilda did pursue women's knowledge among the Zuni and published an insightful paper thereon.[29] But she used that knowledge to move on into religion, economics, agriculture, government— into "men's knowledge."

The Stevensons returned to the Southwest every season from 1882 through 1887, except 1886.[30] Matilda spent much of her time at Zuni, but made various trips with James to other pueblos. He ranged widely, to Hopi, Acoma, and the Rio Grande pueblos. In 1882, James and Hillers returned to Canyon de Chelly to investigate and dig in White House ruin. They named a tributary Cañon de los Muertos, after finding some mummies in what came to be called Mummy Cave. In 1883, James was at Awatovi and in the Flagstaff, Arizona, area collecting archaeological materials. In 1884, both James and Matilda spent the season at Zuni and collected some eighty-five hundred artifacts. Charles A. Garlick, John Wesley Powell's brother-in-law, was employed for the season and managed to collect thirty-five hundred items at Acoma.

In 1885, Powell and Jack Hillers came out to the Southwest for most of the field season. They visited sites along the Little Colorado River and made a trip to Havasupai in the Grand Canyon. It was the last trip to the Southwest for Hillers. He had finally married in 1883, and the flare-up of a back injury sustained in the Civil War, together with a near-geometric increase in workload in the Geological Survey photographic darkroom, which Hillers supervised, kept him in Washington.[31]

The Stevensons went to Hopi. At Oraibi, they encountered stiff resistance to their being in the village, an incident sensationalized some months later by *The Illustrated Police News* (Fig. 7.6).[32] They arrived at Keams Canyon, east of the Hopi Mesas, in time to witness one of the major Navajo chantway ceremonies, the Hasjelti Dailjis, as James Stevenson called it, better known as the Night Chant. His report on the ceremony, edited by Matilda, was published by the Bureau after his death.[33]

In 1887, Powell managed to get away to the South-

7.6. *"Cowed by a woman. A Craven Red Devil Weakens in the face of a resolute White heroine—exciting adventures in an Indian village in Arizona." Matilda Coxe Stevenson at Oraibi, 1886.* Illustrated Police News, *Mar. 6, 1886.*

west again for a few weeks to join Stevenson in what Powell billed as archaeological research around the Rio Grande pueblos and some geology in the Jemez Mountains, but it was primarily an R&R trip for him. By then, he was deep in his battles over the management and disposition of the public domain and the expansion of the Survey. Worse, the stump of his right arm had begun to be seriously and constantly painful. Part of a summer in New Mexico was far preferable to part of a summer in the heat and humidity of Washington, D.C.

In October, after Powell returned to Washington, the Stevensons spent six weeks at Zia Pueblo making collections and doing ethnography. In 1885 in Arizona, James had contracted a serious case of "mountain fever," presumably Rocky Mountain spotted fever. He managed to overcome the infection, but now was again infected and his condition became complicated by heart problems. He was seriously ill by December 1887, and died on July 25, 1888.[34]

Matilda Coxe Stevenson, Assistant Ethnologist

By the time of James's death, Matilda Stevenson was becoming an accomplished ethnographer and had done a fair amount of fieldwork at Zuni. But there was an immediate task: to complete the research and the report on Zia Pueblo that she and James had begun in the fall of 1887.[35] Powell took an extraordinary step: he put Matilda on the Bureau payroll, at first temporarily and then permanently in 1890. Matilda Stevenson thus became the first woman employed as an anthropologist anywhere. Her salary, interestingly, was always less than the men around her: fifteen hundred dollars a year from 1890 until 1907, when it was raised to eighteen hundred dollars. She never had an office in the Bureau until 1902, and she was the only woman anthropologist ever hired on a permanent basis by the Bureau from its inception until 1964, when it became part of the National Museum.

Stevenson returned to fieldwork in 1890, at Zia. She was accompanied by May Clarke, a Bureau stenographer who doubled as a novice photographer. She was at Zuni from August 1891 to March 1892, from July to December 1896, and finally, July to November 1902, after her major report on the Zuni was finished. Other years were spent writing; she was ill for varying periods throughout the 1890s.

Stevenson's relationship with Powell, and Powell's sycophant alter ego, W J McGee, was tempestuous.

Between bouts of illness and trips to the field, she labored on her Zuni manuscript, which Powell and McGee thought was taking far too long. They tried many different stratagems to get her to finish; finally they put her on furlough, without pay. They also had another agenda; they wanted to use Stevenson's salary to hire Frank Russell, a young Harvard Ph.D., to work with the Pima in Arizona (see Chapter 26). It was a serious tactical and political mistake. Stevenson was *very* well connected in the power structures of Washington. The story is complex, but in the end she prevailed and was reinstated.[36] In 1903, when McGee was subjected to a witch-hunt internal Smithsonian investigation Stevenson got her revenge (see below).

After 1902, Stevenson tried very hard to develop a research program that would allow her to do a comparative study of religion among the Rio Grande pueblos. But her attempts to gain entrée to the pueblos were generally thwarted. The pueblos had spent three centuries protecting their indigenous beliefs and ceremonies from Spanish and Anglos. As formidable as she was, Matilda Stevenson was no match for the polite, yet very firm Puebloans. Stories abound of her attempts to intrude where she was not wanted. One has it that she arrived inside the compound at Taos Pueblo by wagon. She declared her intention of staying in the pueblo while she began work there; the Taosians demurred. Stevenson sat firmly down on her trunk to wait them out. At dusk, she and the trunk were bodily picked up and placed outside the gate of the compound. She met similar resistance elsewhere. She managed to meet secretly with a few people from one or two pueblos and did gain some minimal information on scattered topics.

Stevenson finally purchased and moved to a small ranch adjacent to San Ildefonso Pueblo, apparently hoping that proximity might help her cause; it did not. Instead, she became embroiled in enervating court battles with Clara True, a BIA schoolteacher, and True's sister and mother, over fraud in relation to the ranch and later over charges of libel. Stevenson finally won all the lawsuits, but they ruined her financially and emotionally.[37] Her last few years were spent in New Mexico, where she was generally perceived by the anthropological community and others as a disagreeable old woman, sliding into alcoholism. She was never able to develop her planned study of comparative religion. Some of her Zuni consultants did come to work with her, and out of that collaboration came her final contribution, a study of Zuni ethnobotany.[38]

Stevenson and We'wha

Stevenson's key consultant and friend among the Zuni was We'wha, a berdache. The Zunis, like most Indian tribes, had well-defined social categories for individuals who are of one sex, but who assume cross-gender roles and, often, dress. The early French explorers in North America used the term *berdache* to label Indian males who did "women's work" and usually dressed in women's clothes. By extension, anthropologists use the term *female berdache* to indicate an Indian female who assumed male roles of warrior or chief, or did "men's work." Most Indian tribes had their own terms for such individuals. In Zuni, a male berdache is *lhamana*, a female berdache *katsotsi*.[39]

We'wha was born at Zuni in 1849. As he grew up he received male religious training and, as an adult, took numerous roles in religious rituals. But as his berdache orientation became apparent he was trained in women's traditional activities—food preparation, housekeeping, gardening, pottery making, and weaving. The Presbyterian minister, doctor, and teacher Taylor F. Ealy, his family, and assistant teacher Jennie Hammaker arrived at Zuni in October 1878. We'wha apparently worked as a domestic helper in the Ealy household and as matron in the school. Jack Hillers's 1879 photograph (see Fig. 7.3) of Ealy, Hammaker, and their Zuni pupils has We'wha prominently placed in the center. He was then thirty years old, the tallest person in Zuni, and by every account very intelligent.

When Stevenson arrived at Zuni in September 1879, she was faced with the problems of establishing a temporary household in two rooms rented from the Ealys. She had grown up surrounded by domestic help to do household chores. Her celebrated description of her attempt to teach We'wha how to do laundry says much about her and We'wha:

> [We'wha] was averse to the work, and at first refused to wash. He looked on in silence for a time while the writer worked. Never having had any experience in that work herself, she soon had most of the water from the tub on the floor and was drenched to the skin. The pupil exclaimed, "You do not understand that which you would teach. You do not understand as much as the missionary's wife; she keeps the water in the tub and does not make a river on the floor. Let me take your place."[40]

The incident was the beginning of a friendship. When Matilda returned to Zuni in 1881, We'wha became not only a consultant, but a go-between with other Zunis to help her collect information, often at some personal risk. Given Stevenson's often overbearing demeanor, We'wha was of great help in smoothing matters over and getting people to cooperate.

Stevenson apparently did not realize that We'wha was male for many years, perhaps until he died in 1896 and she saw him laid out for burial. The two had a close personal friendship and a mutual intellectual respect. At the end of the 1885 field season, the Stevensons invited We'wha to return to Washington with them for a visit of several months. At that point, We'wha spoke little English and Matilda about the same amount of Zuni. The United States had continued a British practice of taking Indian people to their capital to impress them with the might of the nation.[41] There were dozens of delegations to Washington in the nineteenth century as the United States struggled with its vacillating and often duplicitous "Indian policy." By the 1880s Washingtonians had a very blasé attitude toward such visits. But among all the hundreds of delegates, very few were women. Hence, We'wha, dressed and presented as a Zuni woman (Fig. 7.7), was a minor sensation, immediately styled "an Indian princess of the Zuni tribe" by the press.[42]

Matilda Stevenson saw to it that We'wha met members of Congress and attended many of the re-

7.7. We'wha, Zuni berdache in Washington, D.C., 1886. Photograph by Jack Hillers. Courtesy of the National Anthropological Archives, Smithsonian Institution.

ceptions and parties given during the social season. The Anthropological Society of Washington had chauvinistically chosen to reject Stevenson's application for membership, and remain an old boys' club (James was a member). Thereupon, she and a number of other prominent and accomplished women had formed the Women's Anthropological Society of America.[43] The society met several times in Stevenson's home while We'wha was a guest. In March 1886 the society held a reception, attended by We'wha, various senators, congressmen, Powell and other anthropologists, "and many other members of society," according to newspaper reports.[44] As an aside, in 1899 the members of the women's society were finally

7.8. Matilda Coxe Stevenson, ca. 1910.
Photographers Harris and Ewing, Washington, D.C.
Courtesy of the National Anthropological Archives,
Smithsonian Institution.

belt or blanket under the eye of the camera." We'wha and Stevenson spent much time at the National Museum where he posed for his portrait (see Fig. 7.7) and a series of photographs taken by Jack Hillers relating to weaving and other crafts and activities.[45]

Finally, not long before returning to Zuni, We'wha and Matilda Stevenson called upon President Grover Cleveland. The six-foot-tall We'wha, in traditional Zuni women's dress and a feather headdress, and the very rotund Cleveland undoubtedly were one of the more picturesque pairs ever to grace the Green Room of the White House.[46] We'wha returned to Zuni, where he played many prominent roles in Zuni ceremonial and political life and used his knowledge of Anglo society, technology, and English to help his people. We'wha and Stevenson remained close. She was at Zuni when he died in 1896, witnessed the preparation of his body for burial, and participated in the burial rites.[47]

Matilda Coxe Stevenson was a determined woman, as the classic portrait made in her later years reveals (Fig. 7.8). Nancy Parezo says Stevenson was "an intelligent, self-sufficient, proud, serious, humorless, opinionated woman. . . . She wanted others to judge her on the basis of her work."[48] Some did, others did not, preferring to dwell on her perceived personality as somehow lessening the quality of her work—a common male-chauvinist ploy. Powell's Corps of Ethnologists produced a number of major, classic studies of various aspects of the lives and cultures of Indian peoples. One of those is Matilda Stevenson's massive, six-hundred-plus-page *The Zuñi Indians: Their Mythology, Esoteric Fraternities, and Ceremonies.* Along with her rival Cushing's several works, it formed the principal base on which the next generation of Southwestern ethnographers would begin their studies of the Zuni people.

invited to join the Anthropological Society of Washington, principally because the latter was financially strapped and needed the extra dues.

We'wha continued to be a consultant for Matilda Stevenson. According to Otis T. Mason, "For six months this woman has taught her patroness the language, myths, and arts of the Zuñis,—now explaining some intricate ceremony, at another time weaving a

CHAPTER 8

Cushing, Matthews, Bourke, and Compatriots

THE STEVENSONS were only two of a group of anthropologists at work in the Southwest during the halcyon decade of the 1880s. All had ties to Powell's Bureau of Ethnology, either on its payroll, or being in the field in whole or part because of his influence. The other members of the group were Frank Hamilton Cushing, already briefly introduced; Washington Matthews, an army physician and ethnographer; John Gregory Bourke, an army officer and ethnographer; and Victor Mindeleff, an architect, and his brother Cosmos Mindeleff. The work of all these individuals was facilitated greatly by an English seaman turned U.S. cavalryman, turned Indian interpreter, turned Indian trader, Thomas Varker Keam, and his longtime house guest, soldier turned prospector, turned linguist and ethnographer, Alexander McGregor Stephen. The lives of these seven were intertwined for greater or lesser periods in the 1880s and early 1890s. They produced basic studies of Zuni,

Hopi, Navajo, and Apache ethnography, and Pueblo and Navajo architecture.

Frank Hamilton Cushing

In the twentieth century, the hallmark of cultural anthropology is an extended stay with and intensive study of people of another culture. Arnold van Gennep's famous phrase, "rite of passage," coined in 1909, has long since passed into general usage.[1] In some societies, individuals pass through a puberty rite and emerge with new personae; they are new social beings, ready to assume assigned social roles associated with adulthood and marriage. For cultural anthropologists, the change in persona is wrought by the rite of "going to the field." Nascent ethnographers, armed with field guides, notebooks, pencils, tape recorders, cameras, video recorders, and lap-top computers, as well as a large box of unguents and balms, go to the field. There, ideally for a year or more, they impose on the patience and good humor of a host group, ask endless questions, make numerous social and cultural faux pas, hopefully learn the local language, and begin, slowly and painfully, to understand something about the subtleties and complexities of the ways and thoughts of their hosts. After returning home and publishing suitable evidence of their rite of passage through the field, they are accorded the status of "cultural anthropologist."

Many anthropologists return periodically (often every seven years, as academic sabbatical leaves accrue) over long periods of time, literally intellectually growing up, as they grow older with, "their" people. Their hosts often come to regard them as friends, helpmeets, and finally elders.[2] But there is the delicate matter of reciprocity. The host peoples give of their time, knowledge, patience, and often material culture. The anthropologists are from colonialist or world-power societies, and therefore of them, in their hosts' eyes. In return for knowledge and time given, host peoples rightfully expect help in articulating their lives with, or deriving some advantage from, the power society. Many anthropologists have played this role, some with success; others have not. In the eyes of host peoples, the latter take time and knowledge and give nothing in return. Such "anthros" were properly castigated years ago by Vine Deloria, Jr., in his *Custer Died for Your Sins*.[3]

The issue of reciprocity between "anthro" and "native" was central in the life and career of Frank Hamilton Cushing, the first professional anthropologist to "go to the field" and function as a "participant observer." And the first host people to give of their time, knowledge, and patience were the Zuni. Cushing faced all the complexities of reciprocity just touched on, and more. He was the most unique member of Powell's corps of ethnologists. Powell and others thought him a genius; to still others he was a hypochondriac, and was twice accused of scholarly fraud. He has always been an enigma in American anthropology, although his actions, particularly during the

Hemenway Expedition, discussed later, are only coming into proper focus after a century.[4]

Cushing (1857–1900) was born prematurely; he grew up as a frail loner in upstate New York. By age eight he had become fascinated with archaeology and Indians, as many young Anglo boys and girls did, and do. His fascination became a consuming passion. He read voraciously, collected arrowheads, built a bark wigwam in the woods near his home, and taught himself to make stone tools. He read the works of Lewis Henry Morgan and corresponded with him. In 1874, at age seventeen, he submitted a paper to the Smithsonian Institution on archaeology near his home, which so impressed Joseph Henry and Spencer Baird that they published it.[5] Cushing and Baird began corresponding. In the fall of 1875, Cushing entered Cornell University, but in November Baird offered him a job as an assistant in the National Museum. Cushing accepted with alacrity and immediately began working on materials for the Smithsonian exhibit at the 1876 Philadelphia Exposition. He was then appointed assistant curator of the Department of Ethnology in the National Museum and given a combination office and sleeping quarters in the south tower of the Smithsonian "castle."

Cushing became increasingly interested in the Southwest, but was assigned some archaeological work in nearby Virginia and Maryland. He chafed at routine curatorial chores in the museum. Then, as Cushing told it:

One hot summer day in 1879, as I was sitting in my office in the ivy-mantled old South Tower of the Smithsonian Institution, a messenger boy tapped at my door and said: "Professor Baird wishes to see you sir." The professor, picking up his umbrella and papers, came toward the door as I entered. "Haven't I heard you say you would like to go to New Mexico to study the cliff houses and Pueblo Indians?" "Yes sir." "Would you still like to go?" "Yes sir." "Very well then, be ready to accompany Colonel Stevenson's collecting party, as ethnologist, within four days. I want you to find out all you can about some typical tribe of Pueblo Indians. Make your own choice of field, and use your own methods; only, get the information. You will be gone three months. Write me frequently. I'm in a hurry this evening. Look to Major Powell, of the Bureau of Ethnology, if you want further directions. Good day."[6]

Cushing chose Zuni, as we saw earlier. His three months grew into a stay of nearly four and one-half years, during which time he became a member of the tribe's Bow Priest Society and as "Zuni-ized" as the governor of the pueblo could make him. In his first year Cushing was beset by distrust and hostility. His insistence on making sketches of the pueblo and of ceremonials in the plaza, and his intrusions into secret ritual areas displeased the people. But he gradually gained the favor of the governor, who took him under his personal protection and resolved to remake Cushing into a true Zuni. Cushing's frail constitution suffered from bad water and the food. In an 1880 letter to Spencer Baird he wrote:

> my life here has been: physically, so far as the appetites are concerned, paralyzed; Socially, exile; ethically, theoretically, a feast, a peace of mind unapproached in all my previous experience. And as to results: probably impaired health during life; a strengthening and development of moral character in *every respect,* and mentally aside from a more practical and cosmopolitan view of humanity and its Institutions, I hope, pray (through rather dubiously) that it make *a worker* of me.[7]

By his second year Cushing was faring better. He was rapidly learning the language and in late 1881 was invited to join the Priesthood of the Bow, one of the secret societies. To gain admittance, he had to present evidence of his prowess by presenting scalps to the society. He claimed to have acquired one from an Apache battlefield; others came in the mail from his father and Henry Yarrow at the Army Medical Museum. These "enabled me to get a hearing in the secret

8.1. *Frank Hamilton Cushing; painting by Thomas Eakins, ca. 1896. Courtesy of the Thomas Gilcrease Institute of American History and Art, Tulsa.*

council and be named a candidate for entrance into the Order of the '*Apithlan Shiwani*' or 'Priests of the Bow.'"[8] Later, Cushing became a Zuni War Chief and adopted the title of "First War Chief of Zuñi, U. S. Assistant Ethnologist." He was given the Zuni name of "Tenatsali," or "Medicine Flower." He participated in appropriate ceremonies and created a rather dandified costume, which led the Zuni to call him, in jest, "Many Buttons" (Fig. 8.1).

In May 1881 at Fort Wingate, Cushing met John Gregory Bourke (Fig. 8.2), an army officer and ethnologist in his own right, and Sylvester Baxter and

8.2 (above). John Gregory Bourke, 1890s.
Courtesy of the Library of Congress.

8.3 (right). Washington Matthews, 1880s.
Courtesy of the National Anthropological Archives, Smithsonian Institution.

Willard L. Metcalf. Baxter was a journalist for the *Boston Herald*; Metcalf, an artist working for *Harper's* magazine. The latter two were traveling through the Southwest on the newly opened railroads, and were headed to Zuni to do a story on them. Bourke was at the fort to make travel arrangements as part of a whirlwind ethnographic survey he was making of western tribes (see below). The three met in the fort officer's club.[9]

A few days later, there was a "literary evening" at the home of General and Mrs. Luther Bradley, the commandant of Fort Wingate. The guests were Bourke, Baxter, Metcalf, Dr. Washington Matthews (Fig. 8.3), and several officers and their wives. They were gathered to hear Cushing read and explain the poetics of a Zuni song. Palowahtiwa (also called Patricio Piño), the governor of Zuni and Cushing's self-appointed mentor, sang a song to the antelope, in

Zuni.[10] That evening, Bourke, Matthews, and Cushing, fellow ethnologists, began a mutual friendship that continued throughout their lives. Baxter and Metcalf were entranced by Cushing. Metcalf drew portraits of him, and Baxter and Cushing began a friendship that would flower in the context of the Hemenway Expedition of 1887–89 (see Chapter 13).

Baxter filed the first of many stories he wrote about Cushing with the *Boston Herald*. He was among the first to begin the invention of the Southwest as a place of Romance, inhabited by Natural Man in his guise of Noble Savage.

There are several layers to Baxter's article. Some deal with the scenic splendor of the Southwest and the savage, but gentle and colorful, "original folk"; themes soon to be taken up by Charles Lummis and many yearners. Other layers reflect Baxter's image of Cushing as the wise-beyond-his-years, pretend-help-

Fort Wingate seems to me a grandly situated post, facing from its mountain side the marvellous natural creations of sandstone architecture to the north, an architecture constantly changing its aspect with the changing light of day, and glowing with vividly varying colors. It seems some enchanted city of the gods. . . . While just outside the gates of the fort blaze the camp-fires of the Navajos, the plaza-like parade ground is bordered by neat cottages of gray adobe—the quarters of the officers and their families—and within may be found pleasant rooms, as tastefully furnished and decorated as the aesthetic homes of the East; the adornment of Navajo blankets, Pueblo pottery, and the skins of animals shot in the mountains giving a peculiar charm of local color. . . . [T]he cañons roundabout [are] . . . full of the unexplored ruins of the Aztec cliff-dwellers—ruins of unknown antiquity. The . . . region [is] perhaps one of the oldest inhabited parts of the earth, and still peopled by the original folk.

It was here at Fort Wingate . . . that I had the rare good fortune to meet Mr. Frank H. Cushing, a young gentleman whose name will soon rank with those of famous scientists. . . . As a result of Mr. Cushing's labors Aztec [sic] history will have to be rewritten. Much of what has hitherto been received as such falls to the ground, a mass of rubbish. There are no other people so distrustful of strangers as are the Indians, so reticent about everything concerning themselves. Therefore, when questioned by strangers about their religion, their past and their traditions, they have answered, to be sure, but these answers, accepted as sober truth, have been uniformly a pack of very ready and ingeneous lies. Mr. Cushing, therefore, adopted the only sensible method of getting to the bottom of the facts; that of becoming one with the Zuñis, learning their language and living with them. Hence, we see him, a slender, light complexioned young man—he is not yet 24 years old—with long, flowing blond hair, confined by the Indian head band, and dressed in the picturesque full costume of the tribe—every item of native manufacture. . . . He has gained his cause by the use of pluck, tact and adaptability to circumstances worthy of both a general and a diplomatist. In the first place he put himself at their mercy and entirely in their power. Savages, finding a stranger under such circumstances, seldom fail to be merciful. Thus, gaining their confidence by his helplessness, Mr. Cushing was made one of them and formally adopted into the tribe of the Zuñi. Gradually gaining influence among them he has obtained [entrée] into their most secret councils, and has now been made one of their chiefs, the second man of influence in their city, standing next to their governor in authority.[11]

less-but-not-hapless, hero enduring much in the interests of science. At the same time, there is a note of duplicity, a tricksterlike game in which the ethnographer becomes a member of the tribe to learn its secrets, enduring hardships and deprivation in the process. Cushing was increasingly aware of this problem, one shared by all participant-observer ethnographers, and the moral and ethical dilemmas it poses. Baxter's article ends with a trial balloon, floated by Cushing, which paid off the following year: "Mr. Cushing hopes to be able to bring four or five of the principal men of Zuñi East with him when he returns to Washington. . . . It is to be hoped that he will, for they are a remarkable race, and have a wonderful, fascinating history that still holds the key of many grand secrets."[12] It was a good publicity ploy, and it soon paid off.

In February 1882, Cushing and several Zuni leaders,

8.4. Cushing and Zunis during 1882 trip to East Coast. Courtesy of the Southwest Museum.

including Palowahtiwa, made a trip to the East Coast (Fig. 8.4). They visited Washington and called upon President Chester A. Arthur. They traveled to Boston where they were a media sensation and feted by the intelligentsia. Boston Brahmins were very keen on visiting Indians. Two visiting Ponca lecturers in 1879 stimulated Helen Hunt Jackson's crusade for Indian rights. The year following the Cushing-Zuni visit, 1883–84, Sarah Winnemucca, a Northern Paiute Indian activist and author from Nevada, was lionized by the Bostonians.[13]

The Zunis were able to collect water from the Atlantic Ocean for use in their ceremonies. They subsequently traveled to the Seneca Indian Reservation in upstate New York, where they and Cushing were formally adopted into the tribe. Cushing cut a unique figure during the trip since he wore his Zuni garb. He had, however, cut his long hair, with the Zunis' permission, so he could be properly dressed for his Anglo wedding in Washington, D.C.

Cushing married his fiancée, Emily Tennison Magill, the eldest daughter of Emma Whitehead and John W. Magill, a prominent Washington banker. He was motivated to marry partly to avoid pressures on him

to marry a Zuni woman. Emily returned to Zuni with him, and they were soon joined by her sister, Margaret Whitehead Magill, and a black cook, Abram. Just before Cushing left Zuni on his eastern trip, Powell and Baird agreed to transfer him from the payroll of the National Museum to that of the Bureau of Ethnology, though he maintained a close correspondence with Baird until the latter's death in 1887.[14]

Once back at Zuni, Cushing continued his work. But he also became embroiled in attempts to block a grab of Zuni lands by Whites. His efforts provoked the displeasure of Senator John A. Logan of Illinois, whose relatives were involved in the scheme. For a time, the affair threatened Cushing's position at Zuni, since Senator Logan, though previously one of Powell's supporters, demanded that Powell recall Cushing or he, Logan, would destroy the Bureau. But Cushing managed to stay on and the matter was finally settled, in favor of the Zuni, in 1885.[15]

Cushing took his dual roles of surrogate Zuni and ethnographer of the traditional Zuni ways very seriously. This led to numerous run-ins with Bureau of Indian Affairs agents, various Mormon missionaries, and the Presbyterian missionary/schoolmaster at the pueblo, Taylor F. Ealy. After Ealy had attended a theological seminary and graduated from the University of Pennsylvania medical school, he married Mary Ramsey and the two became Presbyterian missionaries. In February 1878, the Ealys found themselves in eastern New Mexico just in time for the harrowing first five months of the infamous Lincoln County War. In the fall of 1878 they were assigned to Zuni Pueblo. Under the so-called Grant Peace Plan of 1869, Protestant churches sent missionaries to Indian reservations to serve as agents or schoolteachers. They were on the government payroll, but, it was expected, they would do their utmost to turn the Indians into "good Christian farmers in overalls." Learning that the Mormons had designs on the Zunis and their lands, the Presbyterians hastened to send a medical missionary and teacher there in 1877, who was then replaced by the Ealys. They arrived on October 12, 1878, "just," as Ealy wrote, "at the closing exercises of a Devil's Dance. The noise was hideous. Perhaps there were one hundred people looking down on us from the roofs."[16] In June 1879, a young teacher's assistant, Jennie Hammaker, arrived. School was opened in September 1879; among the pupils was We'wha, the berdache. On September 19, Ealy noted in his diary the arrival of "Major Stephenson [sic] & lady from Washington . . . Francisco [sic] Cushing from the Smithsonian Institute here, an artist."[17] A few days later he wrote: "All or many of the old pieces of pottery are being bought up, to be sent to Washington; every nook and corner of the Pueblo are being photographed. There will be a complete model of the town placed in the Smithsonian. . . . It will perhaps measure 10 x 15 feet."[18]

At first, Cushing and the Ealys got along. But the Ealys were overwhelmed by their failure to convert the Zunis and resolve health problems in the pueblo. There were frequent clashes. Cushing strongly championed the Zunis' right to practice their own religion and control their own children. Ealy accused Cushing of having a "reputation for licentiousness," and the Missionary Board filed charges against him.[19] The Ealys left Zuni in June 1881 and retired from the fields of the Lord.[20] Jennie Hammaker stayed on, but died

in September 1881 of typhoid fever in Albuquerque. Ealy entered medical practice in Pennsylvania and later grew wealthy from the sales of T. F. Ealy Baby Powder.[21]

Although Cushing weathered the various accusations against him, he suffered from nearly continual ill health throughout most of 1883. He finally decided that his health would be improved if he built himself some better living quarters and did so, without any clear authorization from Powell. When Cushing found himself in debt, he appealed to Powell for a salary advance or a loan. This, coupled with Cushing's other problems, was enough, and Powell recalled him to Washington. Cushing finally left Zuni in late April 1884.[22]

Although his years at Zuni had been stormy ones, made worse by his chronic ill health, Cushing's accomplishments were considerable. We cannot do full justice to Cushing's Zuni sojourn, but it is instructive to highlight some aspects of his experiences in his own words and briefly note his major works on Zuni. The first has to do with Cushing and the governor of the pueblo, Palowahtiwa, or Patricio Piño. In 1879, when the Stevensons and Hillers left Zuni for Fort Wingate, they "abandoned" Cushing, or so he said: "Of provisions I had almost none; of money almost none, as it chanced; resources aside from these, none whatsoever."[23] The governor took pity on him and brought him a meal of highly spiced mutton and venison, corn cakes and he-we, the flat "paper bread."

Cushing elaborated on the first part of the story in *My Adventures in Zuñi*: the governor took away his clothing and made him dress as a Zuni and sleep on sheepskins on the floor, and generally took steps to "harden his meat." Cushing's relationship with the governor was clearly complex: mentor/student and father/son combined, with all the potential strains of such relationships. Some have wondered how much of the relationship was real, and how much Cushing was drawing on an old motif in American literature, a variation on the theme of the Indian as Noble Savage. A mature or elder Indian warrior, chief, or shaman befriends, adopts, and becomes a mentor to a White

"Here," said the old man, plainly motioning his meaning. "Now sit down with me and eat food fit for *men*!" . . . I put forth my hand (there were neither spoons, knives nor forks), took a morsel in my fingers and was about to taste it, when the old man grabbed my wrist and pointed to the fire, then to the food, and then lifting his palm upward: "They," said he, "must always be remembered." He took a tiny morsel of each kind of food, breathed on it, held it near his heart, and uttered a short prayer; after which he cast the food into the fire and again breathed from his hand.

"There now," he said, or seemed to say, "you are a barbarian, and no wonder your people forsook you. Did they? Are you poor? Very poor? Well," he managed to explain, "unless you are a fool, you shall be poor no longer. You shall have brothers and sisters; I and mine; uncles and aunts; fathers and mothers; and where such are, no man need be poor. Now will you be a Zuñi? Or will you still be a fool?—in which case"—he pointed toward the northern mountains [in the direction of Fort Wingate]—"you will have to live beyond with your kind. Zuñis live here, not fools." I meekly acquiesced.

[To further "Zuni-ize" Cushing, his ears were pierced, followed by a prayer.] I could not understand the whole prayer; but it contained beautiful passages, recommending me to the gods as a "Child of the Sun," . . . At its close, the old man said—"And thus become thou my son, Té-na-tsa-li," and the old woman followed him with, "This day thou art made my younger brother, Té-na-tsa-li." . . . my father . . . explained that I was "named after a magical plant which grew on a single mountain in the west, the flowers of which were the most beautiful in the world, and of many colors, and the roots and juices of which were a panacea for all injuries to the flesh of man. That by this name,—which only one man in a generation could bear,—would I be known as long as the sun rose and set, . . . as a *Shi wi* (Zuñi)."[24]

male, a neophyte, if not chronologically, then psychologically and certainly in cross-cultural understanding. The White man learns not only Indian "ways and lore," and sometimes even the language, but the wise Indian's perspective on Nature, Life, Being a Man, and "What it all means."

The theme seemingly first appears in Alexander Henry's *Adventures,* published in 1809, describing a relationship he purportedly had with a Chippewa named Wawatam in the 1760s, who adopted him, protected him, and taught him wisdom and "Indian ways." In the 1840s, Henry Rowe Schoolcraft unsuccessfully attempted to establish the historical existence of Wawatam. Historical personage or no, Wawatam lived on in Henry's popular narrative, and later as the archetypal exemplar of cross-cultural friendship in Henry David Thoreau's ruminations of life and the metaphors of the Indian in American thought. So too did he live on in the relationship between Natty Bumppo and the Indian sage Chingachgook in James Fenimore Cooper's *Leatherstocking Tales*; between the elderly Cheyenne shaman Old Lodge Skins and the impecunious and bumptious James Crabb in Thomas Berger's *Little Big Man*; finally, the theme reappeared in the 1990s retelling, *Dances with Wolves,* in which a disaffected Union Army officer, Lt. John Dunbar, finds life and love with a band of Lakota, and gains understanding and wisdom from the holy man Kicking Bird.[25]

Cushing, steeped in "Indian lore" and literature from childhood, became a Zuni-ized Alexander Henry to Governor Piño's Wawatam. Piño apparently did what he could to teach Cushing how to behave like a Zuni, and Cushing, despite his complaints and illnesses, real and imagined, learned avidly. But in Cushing's *telling of the tale,* the whole affair becomes another example of the long-established Romantic motif in the Indian-White mythos in American letters.

While Cushing romanticized his situation, the "My Adventures in Zuni" articles were a remarkable achievement. The stories are told in the first person in a lively style and at the same time convey a great deal of information about Zuni society, customs, practices, rituals, and beliefs at a level never before achieved in American ethnography. The only similar published narrative at the time was John Wesley Powell's "Province of Tusayan" in 1875, which may have partly been a model for Cushing's work.[26] But Powell was simply able to observe and describe what he saw; he did not learn Hopi. Cushing's facility in Zuni was well along, hence his understanding of nuance and meaning was at a much deeper level, evident in his descriptions and interpretations.

Cushing's "Adventures" appeared in the *Century Illustrated Monthly Magazine* in the fall of 1882, after he and his Zuni companions had concluded their eastern visit. His articles were preceded by two introductory articles written by Sylvester Baxter, "Father of the Pueblos" in the June 1882 issue of *Harper's New Monthly Magazine,* and "An Aboriginal Pilgrimage" in *Century.*[27] Cushing's articles were illustrated—for example, Fig. 8.5—by the well-known Cincinnati artist Henry Farny, who specialized in Indian subjects. Farny went to Washington, D.C., to meet Cushing and the Zunis. He used the Zunis as live models, but also used several of Jack Hillers's photographs of Hopis, redrawn and relabeled as Zunis, and some of Cushing's sketches, as the bases for the illustrations signed by him in the three articles.[28]

The Nation of the Willows

In June 1881, shortly after Cushing met Bourke, Baxter, and Metcalf, he embarked on a pack trip to visit the "Kuhni kwe," the Havasupai, who lived, as they still do, in Cataract Creek Canyon, a tributary of the Colorado River on the south rim of the Grand Can-

yon. The Havasupai were visited by Father Garcés in 1776 and again by Lt. Joseph Ives's party in 1857. The Zunis told Cushing of these people with whom they traded for buckskins and a high-quality red pigment. There was a well-established trail from Zuni to the Hopi Mesas and on westward to the edge of Cataract Creek Canyon. There, the steep and perilous trail that Garcés and the Ives party negotiated led down to the Havasupai village.

The Havasupais had been in their territory for hundreds of years, and were just beginning to have any sustained contact with the Anglo world. Literally days before Cushing arrived, Colonel William R. Price, from Whipple Barracks near Prescott, had visited the Havasupai and laid out some lines for a reservation within the canyon, as well as another reservation for the Walapais to the west. Price was accompanied by Dr. Elliott Coues, an army surgeon, but better known as one of the top ornithologists in the United States and personal friend of Spencer Baird.[29]

Cushing determined to visit the "Kuhni kwe" and started off with a Zuni guide, and a young Cheyenne man, Tits-ke-mat-se, who had gone to school at the Hampton Institute. Tits-ke-mat-se wanted to work with Cushing, and Baird had arranged it.[30] After a very difficult trip, Cushing arrived at the head of Cataract Creek Canyon, expecting to meet Coues and Price, but found that they had been and gone.

Cushing spent four days with the Havasupai, during which time he gathered an amazing amount of ethnographic data, a task made more difficult because he had to work through his Zuni guide, who apparently translated from Havasupai to Zuni. Cushing was able to put together an ethnographic sketch still regarded as a useful contribution to Havasupai ethnography.[31]

In July 1883, the Dutch ethnologist and world traveler Herman ten Kate met the Cushings and Margaret Magill in Albuquerque, presenting a letter of introduction from Powell. Cushing invited ten Kate to Zuni. He arrived in September from Hopi, where he had witnessed the Snake Dance at Walpi and

Mishongnovi in the company of Dr. Jeremiah Sullivan, the Keams Canyon agency physician, and Thomas Varker Keam (see below). Cushing and ten Kate got on famously; they spent time with various Zuni dignitaries and witnessed a dance. The Zunis named ten Kate "man with the pointed mustache." When ten Kate left, he and Cushing visited Washington Matthews at Fort Wingate. It was the beginning of another mutual friendship centering on Cushing that would be renewed in the context of the Hemenway Expedition (see Chapter 13).[32]

Cushing and Zuni Anthropology

Cushing spent most of five years at Zuni and learned a great deal about Zuni society and culture. A common complaint is that, despite his long sojourn and accumulated knowledge, he never produced a "complete" ethnography. He is also said to have "withheld" much of what he knew about ritual and the Zuni "sacred world." This has to do with the questions posed earlier about ethics and reciprocal obligations between an anthropologist and her or his host group. It also has to do with an issue raised in the Introduction: the general Western assumption that all knowledge is part of the universal commons. This assumption drove Cushing, as he says at various points, to surreptitiously observe, to intrude in places where he should not be from the Zunis' perspective. The Zuni assume that knowledge is powerful, dangerous in uninitiated hands, and will not be efficacious if witnessed or used by those not "authorized" by supernatural powers or beings to know about it or use it. In extreme cases, the stability of the world, or at least the health and well-being of the tribe, is threatened if certain rituals are wrongly observed, or certain knowledge falls to those who should not be involved.

Cushing, and all the ethnographers who followed after, devoted much time and effort to understanding and describing the cosmologies and myths and rituals that articulate and give meaning to them. The cosmologies of Southwestern Indian groups are highly complex, subtle, philosophically sophisticated, and provide frameworks for understanding the nature of the universe and how it, and the things in it, came to be. After a century of study, anthropologists have recognized that there are some basic similarities in at least the Pueblo and the Navajo cosmologies, similarities shared with many groups well into the heartland of Mesoamerican civilization.

Basic cosmological similarities center on an emergence process in which protohumans move upward through successive color-coded underworlds by the agency of deities or forces, finally emerging into the present, usually fourth, world. The specific place of emergence is identified in each cosmology; for example, a particular spot in the Grand Canyon for the Hopi, a lake in the San Juan Mountains for the Navajo, a lake west of Zuni for the Zunis, and so on. Key events or actions during mythical time turn protohumans into humans and give form and "hardness" to the world. Events and actions often create different types of people—Pueblos, non-Pueblos, Mexicans, and Anglos. The world has six directions, usually the cardinal points, plus zenith and nadir, each color-coded and associated with specific sacred mountains, as well as guardian animals and/or supernatural beings. There are stories accounting for death, evil, sickness, and disarray, and misfortunes often attributed to the trickster Coyote. There are also twins, sometimes called "war gods," immortal sons of the sun, who play various roles in slaying monsters and setting the world aright. Finally, there is a female deity, Whiteshell Woman, sometimes Changing Woman, who may be the sun's wife and who has various roles in creating humans and properly organizing and giving a moral dimension to the world.[33]

Some snippets of the cosmologies and their validating myths were collected by the early army officers and physicians prior to the Civil War. But it was Cushing, in his first paper on "Zuni Fetishes," published in 1883, who first grasped and described the complexities and sophistication of Zuni cosmology, thus laying the groundwork for all subsequent Anglo attempts to understand the cosmologies of Zuni and other Southwestern groups.[34] Cushing's achievement was to relate a central part of Zuni cosmology, embodying the elements listed above, and demonstrate the importance of the small stone fetishes made by the Zuni as symbols of their world, its directions, and the forces and beings within it. He also described, insofar as he knew about them, some of the cosmological rituals, and how the fetishes and the masked kachina dancers and other figures related to and were integral parts of the rituals. For example, he discusses the occupants of what later anthropologists call "Kachina Village," located beneath a lake west of Zuni. Here live most of the Zuni kachinas, including the koyemshi, or mudheads, and the six famous ten- to twelve-foot-tall Shalakos (Fig. 8.5), "monster human bird forms," as Cushing calls them, who are couriers for the priests of Kachina Village during winter-solstice ceremonies. The occupants of Kachina Village, most of whom are spirits of dead Zunis, dance constantly to help bring rain; Cushing refers to the village as the "Dance Hall of the Dead." At appropriate times in the ritual year their masked personators dance in Zuni itself.

After Cushing, Zuni religion and ceremonialism fascinated numerous anthropologists, including Matilda Stevenson, Elsie Clews Parsons, Ruth Benedict, and Ruth Bunzel, who we will meet later; and since the 1970s, Barbara and Dennis Tedlock.[35]

Cushing followed his "Adventures" articles with a series of eighteen articles in 1884–85 published in *The Millstone,* an Indianapolis trade journal for the cereal-grains industry. Collectively called *Zuni Breadstuff,* and later republished in book form, they are regarded by many as an ethnographic tour de force.[36] As in "Zuni Fetishes," Cushing wove together cosmological myths, tales, social organization, and ritual activities with farming, food processing practices, and cuisine and their attendant rituals and beliefs. The result is a delightful gastro-centric picture of Zuni life and the importance of corn, as breadstuff. It surely must have

8.5. *Zuni Shalako figure; drawing by Henry Farny. Cushing (1883).*

pleased the magazine's readership—the wheat and corn farmers of the American Midwest—just as it delights readers to the present time.

Cushing's third major contribution, a volume of folk tales, which he never saw in print nor perhaps knew about, is discussed in Chapter 13. Frank Hamilton Cushing is a legendary figure in both anthropology and in Zuni, even being caricatured by the late Zuni artist and cartoonist Phil Hughte, giving a historical interpretation of Cushing from a Zuni perspective.[37]

CHAPTER 9

Washington Matthews

WASHINGTON MATTHEWS (1843–1905) (see Fig. 8.3) was born in Ireland, but was brought to the United States at an early age and grew up in Dubuque, Iowa. He studied medicine with his physician father and at the University of Iowa, graduating in 1864. He was an army surgeon until his retirement in 1895. In 1865, he was assigned to Fort Berthold on the Upper Missouri River. There he became interested in the Mandan, Hidatsa, and Arikara Indians who lived nearby, and began an extensive study of their languages and customs. His interest apparently was aided by a liaison with a Hidatsa woman, who bore him a son but died soon after of tuberculosis. In 1877, he married Caroline Witherspoon, the daughter of an army doctor, but very little is known about her. Although many of his ethnographic notes burned in a fire at Fort Berthold in 1871, Matthews produced a major study of the Hidatsa.[1]

Matthews served at various army posts between 1871 and 1880 and participated in the campaigns against the Bannock and the Nez Perce. Wherever he went, he continued to study Indian cultures and languages. He contributed to Garrick Mallery's study of Indian sign languages and Charles Darwin's study of the expression of emotions. This, and his Hidatsa work, brought him to the attention of John Wesley Powell.[2]

Powell sought good field-workers wherever he could, especially if they were on some other agency's payroll and he could borrow them. In 1880 Powell, aided by Spencer F. Baird and Carl Schurz, Secretary of the Interior, got Matthews transferred to Fort Wingate, New Mexico, to study the Navajo; he remained for four years. His ethnography was in addition to his medical duties: "I have here a large garrison with many children and other camp-followers, there is much sickness and in consequence my official duties take up most of my time."[3] But Matthews managed to pursue his work, at first studying Navajo silversmithing and weaving. As he gained the confidence of ritual specialists, he was invited to attend chant performances, and the complex world of Navajo myth and ritual, with its attendant "sand paintings," began to open to him. In 1884, he secured the services of a "soldier photographer," Sergeant Christian Barthelmess, who accompanied him on trips to Navajo ceremonials and actively assisted in the studies. After his work with Matthews, Barthelmess continued for many years to document photographically the life of Indians and soldiers at frontier posts in the West.[4]

In late 1884, Matthews was transferred to the Army Medical Museum in Washington, where he conducted osteological studies and wrote up his Navajo materials, especially his monograph on the Mountain Chant. In the fall of 1885, with Powell's help, Matthews was able to bring the Navajo singer Tall Chanter to Washington to work on legends and on texts relating to the Night Chant.[5]

In 1890, Matthews returned to Fort Wingate and continued his work until 1892, when he was stricken by an "insidious disease," possibly a stroke, with subsequent physical degeneration. The malady advanced rapidly; unable to continue active fieldwork or fully carry out his medical duties, he was transferred back to Washington in April 1894, and retired in September 1895, "on account of disability incident to the service."[6] Though racked by pain and finally unable to hear, Matthews continued his ethnographic and folklore work for ten years, producing his classic description of the Navajo Night Chant ceremony, some articles, and several pieces for the *Handbook of North American Indians*.[7]

Late in his life, Matthews planned to destroy his notes and papers, but was dissuaded by Frederic Ward Putnam. Putnam had earlier arranged for the publication of the *Night Chant* by the American Museum of Natural History. In 1902–3, in his capacity as chairman of the newly formed Anthropology Department at the University of California, Berkeley (see Chapter 18), Putnam persuaded Phoebe Apperson Hearst to purchase Matthews's papers for thirty-five hundred dollars. The arrangement was that Matthews would continue working on his materials, but if he died before finishing the work, his papers were to be trans-

ferred to California and the materials would be completed by Pliny Earle Goddard. After Matthews's death in 1905, Goddard actually finished only one report. Access to Matthews's papers, however, gave a major boost to his work with the Navajo, which he pursued until his own death in 1929 (see Chapter 19).[8]

Matthews and Navajo Studies

The Navajos, of all the Southwestern Indian groups, have held the most fascination for anthropologists, in part because they have been more accessible than the secretive Pueblos. Gary Witherspoon, a major scholar of Navajo life and language for several decades, estimates that over two hundred individuals worked with the Navajo, some for two decades or more, in the century after Washington Matthews began in 1880.[9] There is a tired joke among anthropologists, and probably among the Navajo people, that every Navajo family camp group consists of parents, children, various other relatives—and an anthropologist.

Navajos in 1880

When Matthews arrived at Fort Wingate, the Navajos had only been back in their home country for twelve years. From 1846 on there had been no peace between Anglos, Hispanics, and Navajos for the complex reasons previously discussed. In 1862 Kit Carson implemented a scorched-earth policy under General James Carleton's direction, which resulted in 1864–65 in the imprisonment of some seven thousand Navajo people at Fort Sumner in the Bosque Redondo on the east bank of the Pecos River. The Navajos, and some Apaches, were held in near death-camp circumstances until 1868, when General William Tecumseh Sherman negotiated a treaty that returned the Navajo to a three-million-acre reservation straddling the New Mexico-Arizona line. Over the next century, the reservation boundaries were expanded several times, ultimately engulfing the Hopi Reservation, exacerbating an already brewing land dispute between Hopis and

Navajos that is still hotly contested at the turn of the millennium.[10]

The Navajos returned to their practice of a mixed economy of farming and herding sheep. Like Morgan's Iroquois, Navajos reckon descent and inheritance through women. The basic family unit is a cooperative economic and residence group with a customary land-use area, organized around a head mother.[11] Traditionally, residence unit members herd their sheep in common. While sheep and farming provided basic subsistence, after 1868 Navajos were increasingly brought into the larger Anglo economy by traders. Since about 1880 the Navajos have become world famous as weavers and silversmiths.

Silversmithing and Weaving

When Matthews arrived at Fort Wingate, he found some Navajo men engaged in silversmithing and blacksmithing. Although records are sparse, it appears that some Zunis, and possibly some Navajos, learned blacksmithing and the working of copper and brass from the Mexicans perhaps as early as 1830–40. Navajo legend says that a Navajo man, Atsidi Sani, learned silversmithing from a Mexican man, Nakai Tsosi, sometime after 1853, but perhaps after the return from Fort Sumner. Atsidi Sani taught his relatives and others both ironworking and silversmithing. By 1873 some Navajos had taught silversmithing to a Zuni. The Hopi apparently learned from the Zunis.[12]

Matthews provided the first detailed study of Navajo silversmithing practice, including the making of a forge and tools and their use to manufacture buttons, rosettes, and bracelets. A few skilled smiths had begun to make powder-chargers, round beads, tobacco cases, concho belts, and bridle ornaments. Ever thorough, Matthews hired a Navajo silversmith and set him up in a building at Fort Wingate, later hiring two other smiths for the same purpose. He notes that the Navajos had difficulty making good crucibles and hence oftimes picked up potsherds from Pueblo ruins for the purpose. Molds were made in soft sand-stone. He notes the use of Mexican dollars as the principal source of silver. Matthews's appreciation of the smiths' craftsmanship is apparent. They "display much ingenuity in working from models and from drawings of objects entirely new to them."[13]

Matthews also provided the first systematic description of Navajo weaving. He speculated that Navajos learned to weave from the Pueblos, which was probably the case, although it was the Navajo women who took up weaving whereas among most Pueblos the men weave. The Chaco Canyon area Navajo have a tradition that they learned weaving from a Pueblo slave woman, perhaps a Zuni, since, unlike the other Pueblos, both men and women weave at Zuni. After the 1680 Pueblo Revolt, Tewa, Jemez, and possibly other Pueblo people fled to the Navajo. The Pueblos apparently brought their own weaving practices and tools, as well as some derived from the Spanish. By the early 1700s the Navajos were herding sheep, spinning wool, and weaving blankets. By the 1770s Navajo blankets were being traded to the Mexicans and were moving through the trade networks extending northward into the High Plains and southward into Mexico.[14]

Matthews describes in concise detail the preparation of the wool and its carding, spinning, and dyeing. He notes that the churro sheep produce wools of three natural colors—white, rusty black, and gray. He recognized the long-standing use of unraveled bright red bayeta cloth for weft, and the recent, as of 1882, introduction of Germantown wool. He describes in detail specific dye plants and mordants, and the construction of the upright loom and the processes of weaving various designs. He notes in passing that Navajo saddle blankets "are in great demand among the Americans for rugs."[15]

Matthews on Navajo Religion

Army physicians Letterman and Ten Broeck recorded snippets of Navajo cosmology in the 1850s. But it was not until Matthews's work became available that Anglos began to appreciate the full complexity and philosophical subtlety of Navajo cosmology and associated religious practices.[16]

Matthews was the first Anglo to grasp the key concepts in Navajo philosophy of harmony, balance, and reciprocity. The core idea is "the belief that the universe is an orderly, all-inclusive, unity of interrelated elements in which the principle of reciprocity governs man's relations with these elements, which include other people."[17] Illness and bad things happen when people or events advertently or inadvertently disrupt balance and harmony. Individual illness is cured through performances of lengthy ceremonies called "chants," or "chantways," the purposes of which are to bring dangerous elements under control and restore harmony. The key is "knowledge and correct performance of orderly procedures: that is, control by ritual. . . . the Holy People, the supernatural beings invoked, are the judges of the completeness and correctness of [a chantway] ritual, and if satisfied, . . . are compelled by the ethic of reciprocity to restore universal harmony and thus cure the patient. Hence, prayers and offerings in Navajo ceremonials are invocatory and compulsive, to attract and obligate the holy ones, not to glorify or thank them."[18]

While the immediate purpose of a chantway ceremony is to cure a specific person, the ceremonies are also public performances held over several nights that serve as mnemonic rituals to remind all participants of core Navajo values and beliefs. This is done by the singer or chanter recounting the cosmological myths about the nature of the universe and the emergence of the Navajo and others from the various underworlds. At an appropriate point, the account branches off to recount legends appropriate for the chant being performed. The legend for each chant establishes its supernatural authenticity and lays down the rules for proper ritual procedures and equipment. If a chant includes sandpaintings, the legend includes directions for their proper construction. The paintings often reflect key incidents in the legends. As Leland Wyman says, "The Navajos' mythology, like their pantheon

and, indeed, their universe, is a unit composed of interlocking parts, filled with vivid word imagery, fine ritual poetry, keen humor, and great imaginative power."[19]

Matthews called the ceremonial complexes "chants," by which he meant all constituent parts of a ceremony: the extended verbal recitations of myths, legends, songs, and prayers; the various activities of the "singer"—the ritual specialist who guides the entire affair and does most of the reciting; the ritual paraphernalia used by the singer, including his "medicine bundle," or "jish"; the activities of various masked figures; public dances in some instances; and the production of sandpaintings, or dry paintings, under the direction of the singer at appropriate times in the ceremony. The leading twentieth-century synthesizer of Navajo chant studies, Leland C. Wyman, prefers the term *chantway* since "it implies a somewhat wider range of practice—the whole of a specific ceremonial complex rather than one specific performance."[20]

Matthews was uncertain as to how many chants or chantways there were in his day. A century later, students have concluded that there were between twenty-four and thirty practiced during the nineteenth century. Of these, perhaps thirteen to fifteen were extinct or obsolescent by the 1980s. Chantways are conducted by specialists called "singers," because singing is a central and integral part of each ceremony. Singers specialize in one or two chants, because of their inordinate complexity. Chants may run two, five, or nine nights. Families of the person to be treated pay for the ceremony and the related feasting and dancing (if they are part of the ceremony).[21]

When Matthews returned to Washington, D.C., in late 1884, he began writing up his Navajo materials, especially the Mountain Chant, which he had witnessed. In the spring of 1885, he gave two illustrated lectures on the complex, nine-night ceremonial, the Night Chant, and its associated dry paintings.[22] James Stevenson heard Matthews's lecture. Some months later at Keams Canyon, Stevenson witnessed a full Night Chant ceremony. His description, done with the assistance of A. M. Stephen, appeared after his death, dated 1891, but did not actually reach print until 1893.[23] According to James Faris, a leading student of Navajo ceremonials, Stevenson's is the *best* actual description of a specific Night Chant ceremony.[24] Matthews was only able to put together a composite description; he never saw a complete ceremony. He saw the final night of the ceremony just two months after he arrived at Fort Wingate and then spent many years piecing together his description. Despite being piecemeal, Matthews's classic account, published in 1902, is the magisterial description from which all subsequent studies of the ceremony begin.[25]

Matthews also made the first systematic attempt to link Navajo myth, legend, and ceremonial practice with the Pueblos, especially the Zuni and the Hopi. A. M. Stephen thought the Navajos had learned from the Hopis. Matthews thought not, at least not the Night Chant. Rather, he suggested, "the ancient Cliff Dwellers, and not the inhabitants of the great pueblos, were the principal instructors of the Navahoes. It is more probable that Navahoes and Mokis [Hopis] derived from a common source." Matthews thought "that the Cliff Dwellers still flourished when the first small bands of Athapascan wanderers strayed in . . . from the north. It is not unlikely, too, that these poor immigrants, . . . may have regarded the more advanced Cliff Dwellers as divine beings, and as such, transmitted their memory in legends," since there is a close association between the Yeis or Holy People in the chantway myths and various "Cliff Dweller"

ruins; for example, White House in Canyon de Chelly.[26]

At the time Matthews was writing, in the 1890s, the relationships between the "Cliff Dwellers," the historic Pueblo tribes and the Navajos had yet to be sorted out archaeologically (see Chapter 24). After a century of study, modern students of Navajo religion acknowledge some influence from Pueblo sources, but also elements already part of their cosmology and practice before they arrived in the Southwest.

Matthews's presentation of the *Mountain Chant,* the *Night Chant,* and *Navajo Legends* are major contributions to the description and understanding of Navajo ceremony and philosophy. Collectively, they are the baseline documents for all subsequent studies of Navajo ideology and associated practice. *Navajo Legends,* published in 1897, was a revelation to anthropologists and folklorists. The scope and complexity of the stories and the subtlety of the underlying philosophy were fascinating to Anglo readers, and have remained so. Contemporary summaries of Navajo philosophy, legends, and ritual practice are presented by John Farella, James Faris, Jerrold Levy, and Paul Zolbrod.[27] All begin with Matthews's work, as did the next generation of scholars after him, Pliny Earle Goddard, Gladys Reichard, Father Bernard Haile, and Leland Wyman. Washington Matthews was a major figure in Southwestern anthropology, a keen observer and excellent analyst who set the highest of standards for everyone who followed him in Navajo studies.

CHAPTER 10

Bourke, Keam, and Stephen

BESIDES CUSHING, the Stevensons, the Minde-leffs, and Matthews, there were three other, very diverse individuals actively involved in Southwestern anthropology in the 1880s. They were a career army officer, John Gregory Bourke; a soldier and interpreter turned Indian trader, Thomas Varker Keam; and a rather mysterious Scotsman and self-styled ethnographer, Alexander McGregor Stephen. They all had links to the Bureau of Ethnology and the Smithsonian. We begin with Bourke.

John Gregory Bourke (1846–1896) (see Fig. 8.2) was born into an Irish Catholic emigrant family who owned a bookstore in Philadelphia.[1] His early education included a Jesuit tutor in Gaelic, Greek, and Latin, in addition to parochial school. He attended St. Joseph's College where he excelled in classics and languages, but left before graduation in a dispute with a priest over another student's cheating; Bourke knew he was right. As his biographer says, "Bourke . . . developed a strict—some might say inflexible—sense of

moral rectitude that frequently won him more respect than friends. He never doubted his own values; rather [in later years] he became disillusioned with a world in which his code seemed increasingly quaint and archaic."[2]

In 1861, he lied about his age and joined the Fifteenth Pennsylvania Volunteer Cavalry. In December 1862 some in Bourke's unit mutinied when ordered into battle at Stones River, Tennessee, but Bourke rode into the fray. In 1887 he was belatedly awarded the Congressional Medal of Honor for "gallantry in action," rallying his fellow soldiers after all their officers were killed and leading a successful charge against the Confederate forces.[3] He was at Chickamauga, the siege at Chattanooga, and entered Atlanta with Sherman.

He was mustered out of the volunteer army with the rank of private in July 1865, age nineteen, and received an appointment to West Point. He graduated in 1869 and was commissioned a second lieutenant in the Third Cavalry. The military was to be his life, and out of that came his interest in Indian peoples and anthropology. He was highly respected by his fellow officers, even by grizzled sergeants, which is saying a great deal, for his courage, wry wit, and abilities as a raconteur. In his diary he commented on a church luncheon in Prescott, Arizona, in the 1870s: "It has always struck me as a queer combination, this mingling of lunch and liturgy, pumpkin and Presbyterianism, doughnuts and dogma."[4]

Bourke's first assignments were in the Southwest at various posts established to contain the Apaches. He quickly learned Spanish from local Hispanics and Apache from the scouts. In June 1871, General George Crook was assigned to the Department of Arizona and soon made Bourke his principal aide-de-camp, a position he held for fifteen years. Bourke "became adviser, confidant, amanuensis . . . henchman . . . and press agent to the silent, austere Crook."[5] Crook was deeply involved throughout his career, from the 1850s to the 1880s, in the struggles between the army and numerous Indian peoples for control of the West. He was alternately praised and vilified by the press, as Indian fighter or "Pacificator." Crook and, in time, Bourke came to respect and admire many of the Indian people they sought to "pacify." They, in turn, were respected by their foes. Bourke chronicled their years together in his famous *On the Border with Crook*.[6]

In 1872 Bourke began keeping a combination diary and field notebook, with almost daily entries of considerable length, some twenty thousand pages in all.[7] Most of his notes are about the manners, customs, folklore, and languages of the Sioux, Cheyenne, Nez Perce, Apache, Pueblo, and other Indian people he met. As time went on he systematized his inquiries, finally printing a ten-page memorandum to guide his work.[8]

In 1880, Crook was assigned to the Ponca Commission, and Bourke accompanied him as recorder. The commission was appointed by President Rutherford Hayes to investigate the disastrous removal of the Ponca tribe from Dakota Territory to Indian Territory

in 1877, and the controversy that followed their removal. During this time Bourke met James Owen Dorsey, who was serving as interpreter for the Ponca, and Edward Everett Hale; both encouraged him to continue his studies.[9]

In January 1881 Bourke met Dorsey and Stephen R. Riggs during a train trip. He discussed his ethnographic work with them and his desire to study the Indians of the Southwest. Dorsey wrote to Powell about Bourke's notebooks and work; Powell invited Bourke to call on him "to show you the material we have collected and to talk with you concerning your ethnologic studies." Bourke accepted the invitation. Powell asked him to join the Bureau team the following summer in the Southwest.[10]

Soon after, Bourke returned to Fort Omaha, Nebraska, where he was stationed. He probably met his wife-to-be, Mary Horbach, fifteen years his junior and a daughter of an Omaha banker and financier, at that time. Powell continued to urge Bourke to join the Bureau expedition. Bourke vacillated, but after consulting with Generals Sheridan and Crook, finally decided he could work better alone. Sheridan agreed, and had orders written giving Bourke carte blanche to carry out his studies and draw army rations, equipment, and personnel as needed.[11]

Bourke in the Southwest

In March 1881, Bourke set out on what can only be described as a marathon reconnaissance by railroad and army mule. He scouted, collecting information on the run. He used the railroads the way airplanes were used in the twentieth century, as the quickest way to get to all the places one needs to be to get the job done. Aided by two or three orderlies, he dashed to the Shoshone and Bannock at Fort Hall, in Idaho Territory, then to Santa Fe and several of the Pueblos up and down the Rio Grande. He moved on to Zuni, Fort Defiance, and Fort Wingate, where he met Washington Matthews, Frank Hamilton Cushing, and Sylvester Baxter (See Chapter 13). In June he was off to northwestern Nebraska to witness the Ogalala Sun

Dance at the Pine Ridge Agency, where Red Cloud and Little Big Man saw to it that he was given information and access to the entire ceremony. In July, he made a quick trip to New York City to serve on a court-martial, then hurried back to New Mexico.[12]

On August 1, 1881, Bourke was joined at Santo Domingo Pueblo by illustrator Peter Moran, brother of the famed artist Thomas Moran. The two boldly marched into a kiva to witness a ceremony—and were promptly thrown back out onto the plaza. They gathered themselves up with what dignity they could muster, and left for Fort Wingate.[13] Cushing and Matthews had arranged for Thomas Keam, the trader at Keams Canyon, to meet Bourke and guide him to First Mesa to witness the Snake Dance at Walpi. Keam and Bourke struck up a friendship that lasted until the latter's death. At Keams Canyon, Bourke also met Alexander McGregor Stephen.

Bourke's Snake Dance

Bourke, Keam, Stephen, two of Bourke's orderlies, and two of Keam's assistants attended the Snake Dance at Walpi on August 11–12, 1881. Bourke used everyone as note takers and recorders. He and Moran were grudgingly allowed to visit all the kivas, including the kiva of the Snake Order, where Bourke fought his dread of snakes and took notes for four hours as many large rattlesnakes were herded by their handlers on the floor at his feet. He and Moran then fled to a rooftop to watch the public parts of the ceremony, including dancers carrying snakes in their hands and in their mouths.[14] Bourke was rather surprised by his access to the kivas. Two months later at Zuni, he learned from Nanje, a member of the Snake Order at Walpi, why he was given access at all:

The reason you were allowed to see so much of the Dance [Nanje told Bourke] was because Cushing had been in there [Walpi] a short time before and told [us] . . . that you were coming to write all of this down for the Great Father and that he (Cushing) was coming back to be with you. . . . We didn't

like to have you down there; no other man has ever shown so little regard for what we thought, but we knew you had come there under orders and that you were only doing what you thought you ought to do to learn all about our ceremonies. . . . So we concluded to let you stay. No man, no man (with much emphasis) has ever seen what you have seen, and I don't think that any stranger will ever see it again.[15]

Bourke's *The Snake Dance of the Moquis of Arizona* appeared in 1884. Thomas Keam tried his hand at ethnographic reporting and published a brief magazine article on the dance in 1883. Keam's article, together with secondhand newspaper accounts and Bourke's book, created a minor sensation that stimulated hordes of yearners, tourists, and photographers to visit the dances, to the great discomfiture of the Hopi.[16]

Bourke visited the Hopi villages on Second Mesa, but was coolly received. In October he tried to visit Oraibi, but encountered much hostility and spent only a day there, with a "bodyguard" of Navajos, which undoubtedly made the Hopi even angrier. He could not get to Havasupai for a variety of reasons, hence turned back to Fort Wingate. From there, he ranged among the Rio Grande pueblos, as far south as El Paso, then went to Zuni, where he witnessed the "Urine Dance," described later. He finally returned to Omaha in December 1881, after nine months on train and trail.

In Omaha, there was a little time to court Mary Horbach; conflict between Anglos and Apaches was again heating up. Crook was placed in command again, and he and Bourke, now promoted to captain, were ordered to Whipple Barracks, near Prescott, Arizona. With the exception of a six-month leave, July–December 1883, to get married and honeymoon in Europe, Bourke was in the Southwest with Crook until 1886. He participated in all the campaigns, including the operation into Mexico and Crook's abortive negotiations with Geronimo, Chihuahua, and Nachez in March 1886.[17]

The so-called Apache wars are well chronicled and need not be rehearsed here.[18] Suffice to say it was the time of the final struggle between the Apaches and the Anglos; of hit-and-run warfare and fragile and complex negotiations which often collapsed; of Anglo duplicity and vacillating policies in Congress and the War Department; of shrill newspaper hysteria, often serving to keep the conflict going for the benefit of army contractors; of venal and corrupt (or sometimes simply confused and fearful) Indian agents. Geronimo and Chato, two prominent Apache leaders, simultaneously became media heroes and bogeyman household words throughout the country. Crook and Bourke worked incessantly to achieve a peace that would leave the Apaches with some economic security and autonomy. Both they and the Apaches were defeated in the end. Many of the Apaches, including Geronimo and Chato, were sent off to prison in Florida, then in Alabama, then resettled in Oklahoma, and never allowed to return to Apacheria.

Crook finally asked to be reassigned, defeated by his own army, Congress, and the press. Through it all, Bourke kept up his inquiries, especially regarding the practices and beliefs of Apache medicine men. He asked for an assignment in Washington, D.C., to write up his ethnographic data. He arrived in 1886 and stayed five years. There was time, however, in November 1884 for a Bourke and Crook trip to visit the Havasupai in Grand Canyon.[19]

Although Bourke steered clear of an official attachment to the Bureau of Ethnology, he maintained close ties with Powell and members of the Bureau and participated actively in the affairs of the Anthropological Society of Washington, the Cosmos Club, and other scientific groups in the capital. It is not clear what role, if any, Powell played in Bourke's transfer to Washington in 1886, but an exchange of letters between Bourke and Powell in 1885, regarding Apache medicine men, suggests that Powell had a hand in the matter. Of more direct help was the support of Francis Parkman, at the behest of Cushing; Bourke later dedicated *On the Border with Crook* to him.[20]

During his Washington years, Bourke completed his biography of Crook and his monograph on Apache medicine men.[21] He also turned his attention

to a subject for which he is best known in psychoanalytic circles—scatology. His interest was kindled by a dance at Zuni which he, Cushing, and Victor Mindeleff attended in November 1881. The dance, held by the "Nehue-Cue" society, began with a broad parody of the Catholic Mass, followed by a feast of tea, hardtack, and sugar. Then, to Bourke's amazement:

> A . . . squaw entered, carrying an 'olla' of urine, of which the filthy brutes drank heartily. I refused to believe the evidence of my senses, and asked Cushing if that were really human urine. "Why certainly," replied he, "and here comes more of it." This time, it was a large tin pailful, not less than two gallons. I was standing by the squaw as she offered this strange and abominable refreshment. She made a motion with her hand to indicate to me that it was urine, and one of the old men repeated the Spanish work *mear* (to urinate), while my sense of smell demonstrated the truth of their statements. The dancers swallowed great draughts, smacked their lips, and, amid the roaring merriment of the spectators, remarked that it was very, very good. The clowns were now upon their mettle, each trying to surpass his neighbor in feats of nastiness. . . . Another expressed regret that the dance had not been held out of doors, . . . there they could show what they could do. There they always made it a point of honor to eat the excrement of men and dogs.[22]

Bourke was repelled, yet intrigued, by what he had witnessed. After he got to Washington, he began to research the uses of excrement in ritual contexts. This led to two papers, one printed and circulated by the War Department in 1888 and labeled "not for general perusal." In 1891 he published his famed *Scatologic Rites of All Nations,* a work highly praised by Edward Burnett Tylor, W. Robertson Smith, Havelock Ellis, and Sigmund Freud, who wrote an extended introduction to the German edition.[23]

While Bourke's star rose in the intellectual firmament, it fell in the duplicitous interstices of military and civilian politics in Washington. He was outraged by the treatment accorded the Apaches. He became deeply involved with the Indian Rights Association, a group attempting to promote more humane Indian policies. His protests against the Cleveland administration's treatment of the Apaches earned him the enmity of many, including Cleveland. Meanwhile, he fruitlessly sought promotion and various posts within the War Department; in the end, even General Crook refused to support him. After Wounded Knee, Bourke became increasingly shrill and bitter about U.S. Indian policy and the role of the army. In April 1891, he found himself ordered back to active duty with his Third Cavalry Troop at an obscure post, Fort Ringgold, on the lower Rio Grande in Texas, despite attempts by Powell, Theodore Roosevelt, and others to keep him in Washington. Once in Texas, Bourke became embroiled in Byzantine affairs involving purported Mexican revolutionaries and bandits and double-dealing politicians in Starr County, Texas, all of which made him yearn for the simplicities of Washington. At one point, he was characterized in a local newspaper as the "New Attila, the Scourge of God." He spent most of later 1892 and early 1893 testifying before a grand jury in San Antonio, defending himself against baseless accusations from politicians, the sheriff, and other worthies.[24]

Bourke escaped through the agency of a friend, William E. Curtis, director of the Bureau of American Republics (a forerunner of the Pan-American Union). Curtis arranged for him to be detailed to the Latin American Department of the World's Columbian Exposition in Chicago. Bourke arrived in Chicago on March 10, 1893. On March 14 he received a telegram stating that all charges against him in Starr County would be dropped if he promised never to return to south Texas; he fervently did so.[25]

Bourke was subsequently assigned to Fort Riley, Kansas, and then Fort Ethan Allen, Vermont. He was increasingly regarded as an anachronism. His application for full retirement was denied on the grounds that his years in the Civil War did not count; nor, apparently, did his Congressional Medal of Honor. Throughout, he continued his active participation in anthropology and folklore. In 1895 he was elected

president of the American Folklore Society, serving with fellow officers Stuart Culin, Franz Boas, and W. W. Newell. But the end was near; he had always lived on the edge physically and emotionally. A lifelong workaholic, debilitated by chronic insomnia, nervous exhaustion, and a variety of physical ailments, it finally all caught up with him. He died in Philadelphia on June 8, 1896, and was buried, as he had requested, in Arlington National Cemetery, without services or ceremony. He was forty-nine years old.[26]

Thomas Keam of Keams Canyon

Thomas Varker Keam (1842–1904) (Fig. 10.1) was born in Truro, England, where he completed a few years of common school before going to sea in 1857.[27]

10.1. Thomas Varker Keam. Courtesy of the Arizona Historical Society, Tucson.

After five years before the mast, he found himself in San Francisco, where in January 1862 he joined cavalry Company C in James Henry Carleton's California Volunteers. Carleton first came to New Mexico in 1846. Now a senior officer, his tasks were to "subjugate Indians . . . guard [the Southwest] frontier against secessionists . . . [and open] a mail route . . . over which the overland mail can be transported with punctuality and expedition at any and all seasons of the year."[28] Carleton marched his troops to New Mexico, where he helped keep the Confederates at bay and tried to subjugate the "wild" Indians, principally the Navajos and Apaches. He masterminded Kit Carson's campaign that brought most of the Navajos and many Apaches to Fort Sumner.

Thomas Keam spent his army years on routine duty. He was mustered out of the California Volunteers in January 1865, reenlisted as a second lieutenant in the New Mexico Volunteer Cavalry, and was again mustered out in September 1866. He then disappeared, at least from official records, for about two and one-half years. He may have traded with the Utes during that time. In February 1869, he was hired as agency interpreter at Fort Defiance, the administrative focal point for the new Navajo Reservation. During his military (and maybe the silent) years, he had learned sufficient Spanish and Navajo to function well in his new job. He remained in and around Fort Defiance for about ten years, working for the agency in various capacities. He married a Navajo woman, Asdzáán Libá, Grey Woman, of the Salt People clan, in a traditional ceremony; they had two sons. His life during this period was complex, but his activities lie beyond our scope. Suffice to say that his active support of the Navajo people against Presbyterian Missionary Board and Office of Indian Affairs policies finally forced him out of government service. A central charge was that Keam and his wife had not had a "proper Christian" marriage.

Meanwhile, he established two trading posts, one a few miles south of Fort Defiance and a second thirteen miles east of First Mesa, near the Hopi, both operated by employees and his brother William. He

closed the Fort Defiance post when it was engulfed by the Navajo Reservation. The other, Tusayan Trading Post, at what came to be called "Keams Canyon" east of First Mesa, became his base. There he traded with the Navajo and Hopi, raised cattle, and after 1879, hosted anthropologists and tourists. Keam became famous for his knowledge of Indian people and his work on their behalf, his leadership in establishing the role of Indian trader, his gracious hospitality, and his elaborate, plantationlike establishment nestled under the bluffs of the canyon.[29]

Laura Graves, Keam's biographer, correctly points out that between 1879 and the late 1890s Thomas Keam was the principal gatekeeper for those anthropologists, photographers, writers, artists, and tourists who came to the Southwest to interact with the Hopi, and to a considerable extent, with the Navajo.[30] James Stevenson and Jack Hillers first met Keam when he helped them collect artifacts from the Hopi in 1879. He drew the appropriate conclusion that here was a potential market for both him and the Indians.

Traders such as Keam, and later the Hubbell family at Ganado, were indeed critical to the success of the work of Bourke, Cushing, Matthews, the Mindeleffs, the Stevensons, and later, Jesse Walter Fewkes and others introduced in later chapters. Keam spoke both Hopi and Navajo. He arranged for guides and interpreters, provided supplies and food, and extended the hospitality of his table and sleeping quarters. He also either arranged for the purchase, or actually purchased from the Indian people, many of the artifact collections that the anthropologists shipped back to the Smithsonian, the Harvard Peabody Museum, the Chicago Columbian Museum, and elsewhere. He played an early and central role in the revival of Hopi pottery making (see Chapter 17).

Early in 1881, Alexander McGregor Stephen (1845?–1894) arrived at Keams Canyon (Fig. 10.2).[31] Stephen is one of the more fascinating and least-known characters in the coterie of nineteenth-century Southwestern anthropologists. He was born in Scotland about 1845 and may have been educated at the University of Edinburgh. In 1862 he enlisted in the

10.2. Alexander M. Stephen, before 1891.
Frontispiece in Stephen (1936).

Union Army as a private in the Ninety-second New York Infantry; he was mustered out as a first lieutenant in the Ninety-sixth New York Infantry in 1866. According to Bourke, Stephen spent the next fifteen years as a "metallurgist and mining prospector in Nevada and Utah."[32] Nothing else is known about his life until he appeared on Keam's doorstep. Whether or not he attended university, Stephen was well educated and had an extraordinary facility for languages. He married a Navajo woman, quickly began to learn Navajo, and used it as a means to learn Hopi. He lived with Keam at times, but mostly with his wife in various houses on First Mesa until his death, apparently of tuberculosis, in 1894. He is buried in Keams Canyon. He became the resident ethnographer who supplied a great deal of data to the Smithsonian team and others, especially Jesse Walter Fewkes; sometimes they gave him due credit, at other times not.

CHAPTER 11

The Mindeleff Brothers

IN 1881, William Henry Holmes brought one of his neighbors to call on John Wesley Powell. Powell was seeking to implement Morgan's research agenda for the Southwest, especially the relationship between houses and house life. Both Powell and Spencer Baird wanted models of pueblos—similar to but larger than those Hayden had exhibited at the Philadelphia world's fair—to accompany displays of artifacts that James Stevenson was bringing back by the ton. Powell had directed Cushing and Stevenson to "measure" Zuni Pueblo and they had attempted to do so. But the results were not good enough to make accurate plat maps, nor to serve as the basis for a model. Powell needed an architect and surveyor who could measure and map Zuni and other pueblos and create models from the data. The person he sought lived down the street from Holmes in Washington; his name was Victor Mindeleff (Fig. 11.1). On Holmes's recommendation and Mindeleff's apparent ability, Powell hired him. The following year, on Victor's recommendation

and partly at the request of Congressman J. Proctor Knott, Powell hired Victor's younger brother, Cosmos, to assist in the fieldwork and the modeling (Fig. 11.2).[1]

Victor (1860–1948) and Cosmos (1863–19?) Mindeleff were children of Dimitri Victorovitch and Julia Feodorovna Mindeleff who had emigrated from Russia to Washington, D.C., in 1861. Dimitri was a chemist and inventor and Julia an accomplished portrait painter. Victor studied at the Emerson Institute prep school, but it is not known where and how he learned his architectural and mapping skills.

Powell sent Victor to Zuni with the Stevensons in 1881 to make a plat map of the pueblo as the basis for a model. Stevenson was directed to continue collecting artifacts, "make photographs and drawings for illustrative purposes of the Indians, their houses, ground plans of the villages and scenes representative of their daily life . . . make investigations into their languages, customs and habits, mythology, govern-

ment, architecture, etc. . . . To enable you to carry out these objects I have directed Mr. Victor Mindeleff to report to you for duty . . . J. W. Powell."[2]

Victor returned to Washington and began construction of a 1/60 model of Zuni, complete with gardens, sheep corrals, and the Nuestra Señora de Guadalupe Church. The model was mounted on an 11 × 20 ft. base and put on display in the new National Museum Building.[3] In 1882, Victor and Cosmos returned to Zuni to complete some work and then moved on to Keams Canyon in preparation for mapping the Hopi villages on First Mesa. There, they met Alexander Stephen who was in the process of moving to First Mesa. Stephen was later employed by the Bureau to aid the Mindeleffs. Over time, he was able to collect Hopi legends about clan movements and tie them to specific archaeological ruins, information included in the Mindeleffs' report.[4] Following the work on First Mesa, the Mindeleffs went for six weeks with James Stevenson and Jack Hillers to the hauntingly beautiful Canyon de Chelly—the brothers to map ruins, including the spectacular White House and Mummy Cave, Stevenson to dig up artifacts, and Hillers to make photographs.

For the next seven years, except 1886, one or both of the Mindeleff brothers spent three to six months in

the Southwest, mapping the inhabited pueblos and a number of the larger archeological sites, such as Wide Ruin, south of the Little Colorado River in Arizona; Awatovi, one of the larger Hopi villages abandoned in the historic period; Casa Grande, south of Phoenix; sites in the Verde Valley, such as Montezuma's Castle; and the larger ruins of Chaco Canyon, including Pueblo Bonito.

When not in the field, Cosmos labored at the National Museum (Fig. 11.3) producing models of pueblos and cliff dwellings, as well as other archaeological sites, such as the Etowah Mounds in Georgia. Beginning in 1884, there was an "international exposition" somewhere in the United States nearly every year until 1904 (see Chapter 17). The National Museum had exhibits at most of these expositions, and Cosmos was kept busy making models for them, as well as replacements for those damaged in transit and duplicates for sale to other museums. In 1888–89, he produced more than twenty models and duplicates, ranging in size from two by two feet to five by fourteen feet. The early models were apparently made of plaster of paris, but the weight and fragility of the plaster in shipping led him to use papier-mâché. The models were ambitious, including the ruins of Peñasco Blanco in Chaco Canyon, White House and Mummy Cave in Canyon

11.3. Cosmos Mindeleff with
model of Zuni Pueblo at U.S.
National Museum. Century
Magazine, *January 1885.*

de Chelly, the Hopi villages of Shipaulovi on Second Mesa, and Sichomovi and Walpi on First Mesa, among others.[5]

In early 1889, Victor finished his fieldwork and began writing his now-classic *A Study of Pueblo Architecture in Tusayan and Cibola,* which finally appeared in 1893.[6] His relationship with the Bureau seems to have terminated in 1890 after he finished writing. He

remained in Washington and developed an active architectural practice. His works include some structures in the National Zoo and numerous houses and their landscaped settings in and around the District of Columbia. He and Holmes remained close until the latter's death in 1931, fellow habitués of the Cosmos Club and the Washington Watercolor Society. Victor died in 1948, the last, excepting Frederick

Webb Hodge, of those involved in the "Smithsonian anthropological decade" in the Southwest.

Cosmos remained with the Bureau of Ethnology and the Smithsonian until 1895, making distribution maps of archeological sites in the Southwest, helping in the stabilization of the Casa Grande ruin in Arizona, and making further studies of the ruins in Canyon de Chelly and the Verde Valley. He submitted his report on the de Chelly ruins in April 1895, and according to Powell, "with the transmission of the report Mr. Mindeleff's connection with the Bureau terminates," although it took the Bureau several years to publish all of his reports.[7] There is little information to indicate what Cosmos did after 1895. He ap-

parently became connected with a New York publication, *The Commercial Advertiser,* in the late 1890s. It is not known when or where he died.

The Mindeleff brothers completed a task stemming from Lewis Henry Morgan's research agenda, providing detailed maps and plans of Pueblo houses and house blocks, thus contributing to the understanding of houses and house life that Morgan considered so important in his scheme of social evolution. But they also contributed to the development of museology with the models of the various pueblos seen by millions of people in National Museum exhibits and at the numerous world's fairs.

CHAPTER 12

The Bureau after Powell

By 1893 John Wesley Powell was close to resigning from the Geological Survey as congressional pressure became intense. On June 30, 1893, he wrote to Smithsonian secretary Samuel Langley recommending raises for James Mooney, from sixteen hundred dollars a year to eighteen hundred dollars, Matilda Stevenson from fourteen hundred dollars to sixteen hundred dollars, Cosmos Mindeleff from fifteen hundred dollars to sixteen hundred dollars, and F. W. Hodge from fifteen hundred dollars to sixteen hundred dollars. He also had "the honor to recommend that Mr. W J McGee, a native of Iowa, . . . be appointed as Ethnologist at $3,300." Langley approved the appointment the next day.[1]

W J McGee had become Powell's close administrative associate and confidant in the Survey after being hired in 1882. He was a self-taught geologist and archaeologist, and was about to become an ethnologist, at least in his and Powell's eyes. After all, if James Stevenson and Powell could do it, why not McGee?

Langley was opposed to the appointment but could not stop it. He was personally fond of Powell, fully aware of his many strong political connections and that he needed someone to run the Bureau. Powell was emotionally and physically drained by twelve years of battles over control and development of the public domain. The stump of his arm had given him constant pain for years (he finally achieved some relief in 1894 through surgical procedures).

McGee was ambitious and pompous, abrasive to underlings, and a toady to his superiors. He was large of body, head, and ego. Lacking formal training, he worked his way into offices in the numerous scientific organizations in Washington and on the national level. He had gained considerable social status in Washington by marrying Anita Newcomb, daughter of Simon Newcomb, director of the Naval Observatory, to the disgust of Mrs. Newcomb, a descendant of Benjamin Rittenhouse and various Revolutionary War luminaries; she saw McGee as a socially inferior bumpkin.[2] Anita Newcomb was a physician, prominent feminist, and social activist, and member of the Women's Anthropological Society of Washington. She organized and directed the U.S. Army nursing corps during the Spanish American War and after (1898–1900), and the Japanese army nursing corps during the Russian-Japanese War of 1904. She was the only woman officially designated as a veteran of the Spanish American War, and to receive Russo-Japanese war medals.[3] W J McGee's role in the Bureau was signaled in September 1893, when he began signing official letters as "Ethnologist in Charge."[4] His tactics and methods in carrying out Powell's and his plans for research increasingly irritated Smithsonian administrators, especially Samuel Langley. Smithsonian legend has it that Langley was McGee's rival for Anita Newcomb's hand.

By February 1902 it was clear that Powell was failing. Langley saw his chance to gain control of the Bureau and neutralize McGee. He convinced William Henry Holmes to "undertake, at least provisionally, the direction of the Bureau of Ethnology in the event of Major Powell's death," and promised the chairman of the House Appropriations Committee that he would place Bureau affairs "on the same footing as the other bureaus of the Institution in fact as well as in name, which I have foreborne to do under Major Powell."[5]

John Wesley Powell died on September 23, 1902, and was buried in Arlington National Cemetery with full military honors. McGee was aware of his tenuous position. As soon as Powell died, he launched a vigorous campaign to be named as Powell's successor, enlisting many scientists and congressmen in his cause. Langley held firm, and on October 11, 1902, appointed Holmes as "Chief," not "Director," of the Bureau.[6] McGee urged Holmes to accept the position and then launched a behind-the-back campaign to oust him and take over the job. Critical articles appeared in *Science*. McGee wrote numerous letters on official stationery that came back to haunt him. He then inexplicably left on what proved to be an abortive expedition to northern Mexico to study the Seri Indians, attempting to make up for previous trips there in 1895 and 1896 that were themselves largely abortive.[7] He became ill, returned to Washington, and was incapacitated for several months. At about this time, his wife chose to separate from him; they were never reconciled.

In early June 1903 a Bureau clerk, Frank Barnett, was caught forging vouchers and pocketing the funds—some 525 dollars. Langley's chance had come. He appointed a committee to look into the Barnett affair and other "irregularities" in the Bureau. The committee members were Cyrus Adler, librarian of the Smithsonian; W. de C. Ravenal, administrative assistant of the National Museum, and Frank Baker, superintendent of the National Zoological Park. Adler and Ravenal were confidants of Langley's; Baker had an active interest in anthropology and had worked as a collaborator of the Bureau. The committee met for nineteen days between June 29 and July 31, 1903.

It was a classic bureaucratic witch-hunt. The record of testimony runs to 1,021 typescript legal-size pages and there are four additional boxes of related materials.[8] The committee heard testimony from all the members of the Bureau staff, including clerks and stenographers. McGee was the star witness. In his opening testimony he responded to a question about his duties by saying: "My first duty, a self-imposed duty, was to take care of Major Powell to the end of his life. After that I performed administrative work and scientific work."[9]

As testimony continued, fiscal and administrative irregularities were aired or invented, and some old scores got settled, including one by Matilda Coxe Stevenson, who loathed McGee.[10] The most serious questions were: why were the Annual Reports so far behind schedule, and why was the "Cyclopedia of American Indians," begun in 1876, still not finished? The most damaging irregularities centered on Powell's and McGee's handling of deficits, their doing work for commercial publishers on Bureau time, and using stenographers and typists for "unofficial" correspondence.[11]

McGee had befriended anthropologist Franz Boas

during a difficult period for Boas in 1894–95 (see Chapter 18), and had begun buying ethnographic and linguistic manuscripts from him to help him out financially. Bureau staff members charged that McGee bought manuscripts from Franz Boas, who then used the funds to support the fledgling new series of the *American Anthropologist*, the official journal of the American Anthropological Association. The association had been informally organized in 1898 and incorporated in 1902. McGee was the association's first president (1902–3). When the journal was taken over from the Anthropological Society of Washington in 1898, both Boas and McGee had committed themselves to fiduciary responsibility for it.[12] In his testimony, Boas said that the manuscript purchases were legitimate in themselves and none of the committee's business, but then indicated that he used whatever means he could to support the journal. Committee records later showed that the Bureau had paid Boas 4,527 dollars for manuscripts between 1893 and 1903. Boas retained possession of several manuscripts, which seemed to some to be "double-dipping," to use a later slang phrase.[13] Several years later, the manuscript purchases would become an issue in Santa Fe, New Mexico, in battles over the control of regional anthropological institutions that did not even exist in 1903 (see Chapter 22).

When asked about the Bureau's programs and problems, Boas responded that the Bureau was essentially adrift; it was a proper assessment. In the 1890s Powell had devoted much of his time to writing cranky, obscure, and naive essays on epistemology and how properly to classify the subfields of anthropology. In his final years he turned to poetry, publishing lengthy poems on evolution, including one he gave as a commencement address at Limestone College in Gaffney, South Carolina.[14] McGee, said Boas, was caught in the middle, had done the best he could, and should be given the opportunity to head the Bureau. McGee stoutly and loquaciously defended himself to the end, finally concluding, "If my course be approved, good; if I be damned, so much the worse, in my judgment, for the tribunal"; but he knew he had

lost.[15] The committee adjourned at 3:00 P.M. on July 31, 1903. Ninety minutes later McGee handed W. H. Holmes a letter of resignation, saying that he had been offered and would immediately accept the position of "Chief of the Department of Archeology and Ethnology at the Louisiana Purchase Exposition," to be held in 1904 in St. Louis (see Chapter 17). The next day, Richard Rathbun, acting secretary of the Smithsonian Institution, accepted McGee's resignation.[16]

A definitive biography remains to be written to assess the very complex character of W J McGee. There is only a privately printed eulogistic *Life* by his sister.[17] McGee was with the St. Louis Exposition until its close, and then became the first director of the St. Louis Public Museum. In early 1907 he became vice chairman and secretary of the Inland Waterways Commission and remained in that position until his death from cancer and "without worldly goods" on September 4, 1912, at the Cosmos Club in Washington, D.C. The onset of the cancer was apparently in 1895. McGee kept a record of its progress and symptoms and wrote a report thereon; it was published in *Science* a week after he died.[18]

Finally, there was the famous bet between Powell and McGee as to who had the largest and most convoluted brain. A burning issue in nineteenth-century anthropology was the relationship between cranial capacity and level of intelligence. It was generally assumed that the bigger one's brain, the higher one's intelligence, but the issue was not settled. It was a matter of observation that some people with small heads were highly intelligent and others with large ones were not. Perhaps, then, intelligence had to do with the structure or the topography of the brain, as well as relative size.

The story goes that one day Powell and McGee were discussing cranial capacity and intelligence. Powell, who was a relatively small person, looked at McGee's large frame and head and bet him that he, Powell, had a larger brain. McGee took the wager. Each agreed that his brain would be given for study to Dr. Edward Spitzka, a prominent brain surgeon who had studied the brains of unusual people—geniuses, criminals, and the insane. And so it happened. When Powell's body was returned to Washington after his death in 1902, his brain was removed and delivered to Spitzka. When McGee died in 1912, his brain also was excised and sent to Spitzka. Spitzka reports that Powell won the bet, 1,488 grams to 1,410 grams.[19] Powell's brain is in the collections of the Zoology Department of the U.S. National Museum. Where and how the wager was collected remains a matter of speculation.

Whither the Bureau?

Smithsonian administrators quickly got the Bureau's fiscal and business procedures under their control. They moved equally quickly to finish the "Cyclopedia," which had become a major political embarrassment. Frederick Webb Hodge, who had moved from the Bureau into the National Museum a few years earlier, was given the assignment of completing it. He completely reorganized the format, abandoned much of what had been previously produced, hired dozens of individuals to write new articles, and saw the monumental two-volume *Handbook of American Indians North of Mexico* into print in 1907–10.[20] Hodge thus was able to finally complete the task set for American anthropology by Lewis Cass in 1826. A twenty-volume revision of the *Handbook,* begun in 1971, remains half-finished at the turn of the millennium.

The Smithsonian's control over the Bureau was sig-naled by W. H. Holmes's appointment as "Chief" of the Bureau, rather than "Director." In the federal government, titles are clear signals of power and administrative responsibility; "Chief" was a demotion. In 1910, Holmes was succeeded by Frederick Webb Hodge, who resuscitated the title "Ethnologist-in-charge." When Hodge left in 1918 to move to the Museum of the American Indian (see Chapter 24), he was succeeded by Jesse Walter Fewkes, who was "Chief" until he retired in 1928. Matthew W. Stirling was "Chief" from 1928 to 1948, when he managed to get the title of "Director" restored, a title also held by Frank H. H. Roberts, Jr., from 1958 to 1964, and finally by Henry B. Collins, who served as acting director during the 1964 "abolishment by merger" of the Bureau with the Department of Anthropology in the U.S. National Museum.

The Bureau of American Ethnology's long involvement with the Southwest did not end in 1902 when Powell died. It continued in the work of Fewkes and others. The impact of the Bureau of American Ethnology on American anthropology, and especially Southwestern anthropology, was enormous. It is fair to say that without Powell's interest in the Southwest as an anthropological "laboratory," his creation of the Bureau, and his use of its resources in conjunction with the National Museum, the history of Southwestern anthropology would have been very different.

CHAPTER 13

The Hemenway Expedition

FRANK AND EMILY CUSHING ended their sojourn at Zuni and returned to Washington, D.C., in April 1884.[1] Cushing was sick much of the time and worked only intermittently. Finally, in June 1885, he and Emily moved to his father's home in upstate New York, later to Shelter Island on Long Island Sound, and then to Cambridge, Massachusetts, for further medical treatment. In June 1886, the Cushings were invited by Mrs. Mary Tileston Hemenway to visit her at her summer place, Manchester-by-the-Sea, on the North Shore. They accepted with alacrity and soon were installed in one of the houses in the compound, which they named "Casa Ramona" for the heroine in Helen Hunt Jackson's then recent (1884) best-selling novel *Ramona,* which had followed her scathing 1881 indictment of federal Indian policy, *A Century of Dishonor.*[2]

Mary Tileston Hemenway (1820–1894) (Fig. 13.1) was the wife of a Boston shipping magnate, Augustus Hemenway. She devoted much of her time and phil-anthropic interest to education, including physical education for young women (then a novel and controversial idea), social reform, and historic preservation —she donated 100,000 dollars toward the restoration of the Old South Meeting House, one of Boston's great landmarks. Mary Hemenway and her lifelong friend Mary Elizabeth Dewey were also strong advocates of Indian rights.[3] The Cushings had just settled in when three Zuni men arrived; Cushing had been trying to get them to the East Coast for a year. One was Palowahtiwa, the Zuni governor and Cushing's mentor. He had been on the 1882 trip to the East Coast with Cushing; the others, Heluta and Wai-husiwa, had not. The three were invited to stay at the Hemenway compound and spent several weeks working with Cushing during the day on religion and other topics, while Mrs. Hemenway and Margaret Magill looked on and Cushing translated. In the evenings, the Zunis told folk tales to assembled guests, again while Cushing translated. Guests were entranced:

13.1. Mary Hemenway, 1880s. Courtesy of Peabody Museum, Harvard University.

"The language has a pleasant, melodious sound. . . . The charm of the stories, . . . is quite indescribable. They were of various kinds; some, simple childish legends . . . most of them connected with the interposition of the gods in human affairs, and all of them full of the domestic life, the family affections, the woodland adventures, the religious emotions of a people worth reading in print, but nothing can give the effect of this gathering into our very ears these utterances of past centuries had upon us."[4]

As the weeks went by, Cushing began to sense a potential patron. On Sundays, he took tea privately with Mrs. Hemenway and imparted to her deeper, more esoteric interpretations of the tales. Unbeknownst to

Cushing, Mrs. Hemenway had stationed a stenographer behind a screen in the corner of the room, who took down everything he said in shorthand. The stenographer produced a large typescript, which Cushing apparently never saw. After he died, Emily published it with a foreword by Powell.[5]

Cushing also talked about his previous work, and his theories about the origins of the Zuni and possibly the Hopis. He spoke of ancient ancestral cities and how intensive archaeological research in those places would link "lost" pre-Hispanic civilizations with the historic tribes. He talked of comparative studies of material culture of the historic tribes and the archaeological finds to help reconstruct the culture history of the region. At the same time, monuments and sites could be preserved from the ravages of time and vandals. Finally, the results of the studies would provide information that would allow Indian agents and missionaries to arrive at a complete and sympathetic understanding of the Indian people and develop better conditions for them. The latter would be facilitated by a museum and school in Salem, Massachusetts, a "Pueblo Museum" for the empathetic study of American Indians.[6]

It was all there—science, romance, preservation, history, good deeds, and noble—but possibly vanishing and certainly wronged—savages, all wrapped in a warm blanket of humanitarian caring and potential social reform. How could Mrs. Hemenway resist, given her interests? In November 1886, she agreed to provide financial support of twenty-five thousand dollars a year for a large-scale expedition to the Southwest, the Hemenway Southwestern Archaeological Expedition—with Cushing as the director. An advisory board was formed, comprised of William T. Harris, a well-known educator, later (1889–1906) U.S. Commissioner of Education, as president; Mrs. Hemenway's son, Augustus Hemenway, and Edward S. Morse, and Martha Lebaron Goddard as vice presidents; and Cushing's journalist friend Sylvester Baxter as secretary. Edward Sylvester Morse (1838–1925) was a marine biologist and for many years director of the Peabody Museum in Salem, Massachusetts. A man of encyclopedic knowledge and strong opinions, he wrote knowingly on biology, archaeology, anthropology, architecture, folklore, astronomy, and especially Japanese fine arts and folkways (he had lived twice in Japan). Martha Goddard, a close friend of Mary Hemenway's, was the wife of Delano A. Goddard, editor of the *Boston Advertiser*, the newspaper of choice of the Boston Brahmins. She was also actively involved in Indian rights and welfare issues. Baxter was to play a much more active role in the expedition than to simply file the correspondence and keep the minutes of the board meetings.[7]

Sylvester Baxter (1850–1927) was from an old Cape Cod family, the son of a sea captain (also Sylvester Baxter) and the captain's third wife, Rosella Ford. The younger Baxter became a reporter for the *Boston Advertiser* when he was about eighteen. From 1876 to 1878 he was a student at Leipzig University in Germany, but also traveled widely in Europe, soaking up the cultural ambiance. When he returned to Boston he went to work for the *Boston Herald*. He met Cushing during his 1881 trip to New Mexico (see Chapter 8).

Organizing the Expedition

Thoughts of the expedition did wonders for Cushing's health, and he began planning a comprehensive program of archeological, ethnographic, ethnohistorical, and physical anthropological research. John Wesley Powell readily acquiesced to the project and gave Cushing the necessary leave. Cushing began to put together his research team. The Cushings had been visited during the summer by Herman ten Kate, who earlier had stayed with them briefly in Zuni. Ten Kate met Mrs. Hemenway, who was sufficiently impressed to offer to support his research in North America. He declined due to family problems, but returned in the fall of 1887 to join the expedition.[8] Powell and Cushing agreed that a stenographer working for the Geological Survey, Frederick Webb Hodge, should become Cushing's field secretary. Others were Adolph Bandelier, whose relationship with the Archaeological

Institute of America had ended the previous year; Charles A. Garlick, of the Geological Survey and Powell's brother-in-law; Cushing's wife, Emily, and her sister, Margaret Magill.[9]

For Frederick Webb Hodge (1864–1956) the expedition proved to be the beginning of a seventy-year career in anthropology, focused on the Southwest. Hodge was born in Plymouth, England, and emigrated with his parents to the United States in 1871. He attended public schools in Washington, D.C., and graduated from Columbian College (later George Washington University). He worked in a Washington law firm before being hired as a stenographer for the Geological Survey in 1886. During his three years with the Hemenway Expedition he played several key roles, one being active suitor to Margaret Magill, whom he first met at Cushing's father's house in December 1886: "My first impressions—lively, brim full of fun, fond of a joke, good talker. Splendid company. . . . I am of the opinion that I shall like her very much."[10]

Herman Frederick Carel ten Kate, Jr. (1858–1931), was born in Amsterdam, Holland. He was the son of an eminent artist of the same name, who enjoyed the patronage of King William III, and a nephew of a celebrated Dutch poet, J. J. L. ten Kate. Young ten Kate was trained in medicine, geography, non-Western languages, and Indonesian ethnology at Leiden University, and physical anthropology and linguistics in Paris. His first publication was a coauthored memoir on the skulls of decapitated criminals and suicides.

Ten Kate traveled to Germany to work and study with Adolf Bastian and attend the University of Berlin before moving on to Göttingen and Heidelberg, receiving a Ph.D. from the latter in 1882. Ten years later he received an M.D. after study at several German universities. In between degrees, and for the rest of his long and active life, ten Kate was an itinerant scholar. Sponsored by various museums, scholarly societies, the Dutch government, and his father's bank account, he traveled the world studying tribal peoples, collecting artifacts and skeletal materials, and writing numerous papers and books (he spoke and wrote in eight languages). It was during his first trip to survey

North American Indian tribes that he met Cushing. He joined the Hemenway Expedition for about a year. His subsequent career took him to South America, Southeast Asia, Australia, China, Japan, and elsewhere. He ended in Carthage, Tunisia. From there he wrote to Frederick Webb Hodge in 1930: "I am living among 'los Muertos' of the Phoenicians, Romans, Vandals and Byzantines, a very silent crowd, but they suit me much better than . . . ultra-modern . . . worshippers of the Machine." He died the next year.[11]

Powell had suggested Charles A. Garlick. Garlick worked for the Geological Survey as a pack-mule wrangler and assistant mapmaker and had helped James Stevenson make collections. He had logistics skills and knowledge of the Southwest of use to the expedition; he was hired as the general field manager and topographer.[12]

The Cushings, Magill, Hodge, and the three Zunis arrived in New Mexico in mid-December 1886, where they met Bandelier, who would continue his archival work in Santa Fe, but as a salaried member of the expedition. Cushing took Hodge to Zuni for the winter-solstice ceremony on December 21. On January 14, 1887, Mrs. Hemenway arrived in Albuquerque in her private railroad car, on her way to California. Cushing traveled on to Flagstaff with her.

Cushing's original plan was to begin west of Zuni and then gradually move southwestward into the upper Salt River Valley of eastern Arizona, following in reverse what he thought had been the route of the Zunis toward their historic location. But winter weather made that impossible. Hence, the Cushings, Magill, Hodge, Garlick, and two Zunis, Weta and Siwatitsailu, went by train to Prescott and then by wagon to the Phoenix Basin, intending to move from there eastward up the Salt River toward the purported Zuni ancestral homeland.

But upon arrival in the Phoenix-Tempe area, Cushing discovered there were several major mound groups and the remains of extensive irrigation canals —sites later archaeologists would call Classic Hohokam. These *felt* like ancestral Zuni sites to Cushing and he determined to begin in the area. On February 12, 1887, the party established Camp Augustus, named for Mrs. Hemenway's son, opposite Tempe. Tempe and Phoenix were small settlements, but they offered supplies, and by late in the year, a railroad connection.

The Hemenway Expedition in the Salt River Valley

During the first days, Cushing and Margaret Magill made a quick horseback survey and discovered that there were numerous mound groups.[13] Previously, two others had recorded some of the major sites in the Phoenix Basin. Alphonse Pinart, a French anthropologist and linguist, had described Pueblo Grande and another site in 1876, and Adolph Bandelier had recorded and made drawings of Pueblo Grande in 1883. It is unlikely that Cushing knew about Pinart at the time, but was certainly aware of Bandelier's work.[14]

Cushing ultimately recorded several sites, but concentrated on six, which he named El [*sic*] Ciudad de los Pueblitos, La Ciudad de los Hornos, La Ciudad de los Muertos, Las Acequias, and La Ciudad de los Guanacos. Cushing gave the latter site its name based on some small figurines excavated there, which he thought to be images of South American guanacos, the camilid relatives of llamas and alpacas. This seemed to be evidence of some tie between the Southwest and South America; subsequent interpreters have thought otherwise. Los Pueblitos came to be called Pueblo Grande, portions of which continue to exist as a Phoenix city cultural park; the other sites have more or less succumbed to the Phoenix sprawl.[15]

Cushing began digging first in Pueblo Grande on February 21, 1887. A week later he recorded La Ciudad de los Muertos and in March established a side camp there. In May he moved his main camp, now renamed Camp Hemenway (Fig. 13.2), near los Muertos. The site would become the main focus of excavation, but extensive work was done at Las Acequias, los Hornos, and los Guanacos.

Cushing played, indeed overplayed, his role as scientist and director with gusto. He gave numerous

13.2. "Camp Hemenway, nine miles southeast of Tempe, Arizona 1887–88." Left to right: Charles W. Garlick, Dr. J. L. Wortman, E. P. Gaston, Margaret Magill, F. H. Cushing, Sylvester Baxter, F. W. Hodge. Man by mules is Percy Yates. Courtesy of the Southwest Museum.

interviews expounding his theories, relishing the attendant publicity. Articles soon appeared in Arizona and California newspapers, as well as national magazines. To Cushing, in his initial enthusiasm of discovery, the sites had been built by the Toltecs, the "progenitors of the Zuni" as he called them, some of whom had later migrated southward to Mesoamerica, thence beyond to found the Inca civilization in South America. He was probably echoing Lewis Henry Morgan's ideas, which the reporter likely misinterpreted. On May 3, 1887, he was regaling visitors and reporters with his hypothesis that los Muertos had been destroyed by an earthquake. A local objected that earthquakes were unknown in the Salt River Valley. Just then the flags on the tent began to flutter and a slight tremor was felt. "An earthquake, gentlemen," said Cushing. It was the great Sonoran earthquake felt widely throughout the Southwest and northern Mexico.[16]

By the summer of 1887 Cushing was exhausted and suffering severe stomach pains. Word got back to Washington, D.C., and this led John Gregory Bourke and Sylvester Baxter to meet with Mrs. Hemenway

about the problem. They recommended that Washington Matthews be sent out from the Army Medical Museum to take charge of the expedition and treat his old friend Cushing. Mrs. Hemenway communicated with fellow Bostonian and Secretary of War William C. Endicott, who ordered Matthews to Arizona. Matthews arrived on September 1, 1887, and took charge of Cushing's health and the project. He later wrote, "I . . . heard him, in delirious sleep delivering harangues in the Zuni tongue. He dreamed in it."[17] Matthews finally persuaded Cushing to take a vacation in southern California, which he did, not returning until late December.

Matthews also requested that Dr. Jacob Wortman, the anatomist at the Army Medical Museum, be sent out to deal with the excavated skeletal materials, which were deteriorating. Wortman arrived shortly after Herman ten Kate did and they were able to deal with the problem. While all this was going on, Fred Hodge's and Margaret Magill's relationship had become intense, so to say. They were engaged in August 1887 and finally married in 1891.

Once Cushing returned, he plunged back into work. He and ten Kate spent three days at Casa Grande. Cushing was fascinated by the site. He began plans to homestead the site area as a prelude to Mrs. Hemenway buying it for an archaeological field-school location. After Sylvester Baxter arrived the following month, this idea metamorphosed into a plan to persuade Congress to set aside the site as a federal reserve to protect it. Baxter was aware that, at Bandelier's urging, the Archaeological Institute of America and the New England Historic Genealogical Society in 1882 had petitioned Congress to preserve "some of the . . . extinct cities or pueblos" in the Southwest, particularly Pecos Pueblo, which was admitted to be "even older than Boston"! The petition died in committee. Now, with Baxter's help, another petition was sent to Congress, dated January 30, 1889, praying that Congress specifically set aside Casa Grande to protect it "from the depredations of visitors . . . [since] it has suffered more in eleven years from this source than in the three hundred and fifty years preceding." The petition was signed by Mrs. Hemenway; Oliver Ames, governor of Massachusetts; Anna Cabot Lodge, wife of Henry Cabot Lodge, then a member of the House of Representatives, later (1893–1924) one of the most powerful of U.S. senators; Francis Parkman; Edward Everett Hale; John Greenleaf Whittier; Oliver Wendell Holmes; and several others. Within a month, Congress appropriated two thousand dollars for repairs of Casa Grande. But it took until 1892 for President Benjamin Harrison to sign an executive order, recommended to him by the Secretary of the Interior at the request of John Wesley Powell, to reserve the site and 480 acres around it for permanent protection because of its archaeological value. Thus did Casa Grande, known and speculated about for two centuries and more, become the first national archaeological preserve in the United States.[18]

In the early months of 1888, Sylvester Baxter busied himself observing the expedition's activities and generating publicity articles describing and praising its accomplishments.[19] Meanwhile, ten Kate spent some time supervising excavations, but in March began an extended anthropometric survey of the Pima in the Gila River area and the Papago (Tohono O'odham) around Tucson and San Xavier del Bac. His central research question was whether or not the Pima and Papago were the descendants of the people whose skeletons were being excavated. Ten Kate was the first anthropometrist to work in the Southwest. He followed the system of Paul Topinard, which meant making twenty-five to twenty-seven direct measurements on individuals, calculating cephalic indices, and noting about a dozen physical characteristics, such as skin and hair colors. In 1883, he had measured about 130 Pima, Papagos, Maricopas, Yumas, and Zunis. Now he was able to measure an additional 445 individuals from the same groups. He finally concluded that there were some relationships between the current and archaeological populations.[20]

Cushing worked unceasingly for the first few months of 1888, but as the temperatures began to rise, his health again declined. He decided that enough had been accomplished in the Salt River area and it was time to move closer to Zuni. The collections were crated and shipped to Salem, Massachusetts, in mid-May. Thereupon, Cushing, Emily, and Margaret retreated to San Diego and San Francisco seeking surcease once more from Cushing's medical problems. Meanwhile, Mrs. Hemenway was proceeding with the idea of the Pueblo museum and school. In September 1887, she paid sixteen thousand dollars for land on Batchelor's Point in Salem as a site for the buildings. In late May 1888 she hired an architect to begin design work.

By mid-July 1888 Hodge and Garlick had closed Camp Hemenway and established themselves at Zuni. Cushing, Emily, and Margaret arrived on August 2. Cushing began excavations on the edges of Halonawa, adjacent to the main Zuni pueblo, and continued until mid-October. But he was again ill, and left with Emily for the East, leaving Hodge and Garlick in charge. They began excavations in the ruins at Héshota, continuing into early December. By then the expedition had come seriously unraveled. Hodge, in particular, was disaffected with Cushing's handling of things, and resigned in late March 1889. On July 1, 1889, at the start of the new federal fiscal year, John Wesley Powell hired Hodge as assistant ethnologist in the Bureau of Ethnology.[21]

Cushing and the Hemenway Expedition

When Cushing and Emily left Zuni, it was the last time either of them were in the Southwest. Cushing had high hopes of returning in the spring of 1889 to revitalize and continue the expedition. Instead, he was confined to bed in Garfield Memorial Hospital in Washington, D.C., with acute abdominal pain and nervous exhaustion. In Boston, the Hemenway family and their advisors were engaged in damage control. Sylvester Baxter, Cushing's staunch champion throughout, was dismissed as secretary treasurer of the expedition. In May 1889, after the death of Martha Lebaron Goddard, Augustus Hemenway convinced his mother to appoint his old Harvard classmate Jesse Walter Fewkes to replace her on the board. On June 15, 1889, Cushing received a telegram from Augustus: "Please give no further directions and incur no more expense on account of Mrs. Hemenway . . . Commit all matters at camp to the sole charge of Dr. Fewkes."[22] Plans for the Pueblo museum and school in Salem were shelved, then died. The Salt River and Zuni collections languished in Salem until Mary Hemenway's death in 1894, when they were transferred to the Peabody Museum at Harvard. They remained unstudied until the 1930s (see Chapter 29).

As time wore on, the Hemenway Expedition under Cushing's leadership passed into the realm of anthropological folklore and gossip. Cushing was depicted as a failed leader and his archaeology as shoddy and off the cuff. Much of that had to do with Frederick Webb Hodge, who had a complex admire/hate relationship with Cushing in various contexts: employee-employer, brothers-in-law, and fellow assistant ethnologists in the Bureau of Ethnology. For many years, Hodge lost few opportunities to disparage Cushing.

After Cushing died in 1900 (see below), Hodge wound up with many of Cushing's papers from the expedition. Some were ultimately deposited in the Southwest Museum library, where Hodge was director during the last years of his long life. But Hodge also had the official letterpress books (the "file copies" of the day) of the expedition's correspondence, together with extensive field notes, maps, and related materials. He placed some four thousand letterpress pages of official correspondence and many of Cushing's field notes in the Huntington Free Library in the Bronx, New York, which served as the library for the Museum of the American Indian when he worked there in the 1920s (see Chapter 24). Hodge never called anyone's attention to the documents, but he did not destroy them either. Probably the historian and archivist in him prevented that. There they lay forgotten until the late 1980s, when David R. Wilcox and Curtis M. Hinsley resurrected them and began a program of systematically putting the full complexity of the Hemenway Expedition and Cushing's achievements on record.[23]

Cushing's Hemenway Expedition was important for two reasons. One, it was the first organized, multidisciplinary anthropology program in the Southwest, perhaps in the United States. In later decades it was often referred to as a model, but always in an admonitory way, since no major reports were ever written: "You should organize your research program as Cushing did, but make sure you follow through and fully publish your findings!" The only published reports were one on the skeletal materials from the expedition excavations by Washington Matthews, Jacob Wirtman, and John S. Billings; a piece on anthropometry by Herman ten Kate; and Adolph Bandelier's "Outline of the Documentary History of the Zuni Tribe."[24] Otherwise, the Hemenway Expedition made no substantive contribution to the study of Southwestern archaeology until after 1930.[25]

Cushing's one published contribution was a lengthy paper that he sent to the 1888 meeting of the International Congress of Americanists in Berlin.[26] It was his only comprehensive statement of the work of the expedition under his direction. It is a remarkable document for several reasons. Among them, it is the first American statement of what a major archaeological expedition *ought to be*: problem oriented, multidisciplinary, long term, and well funded. It sets out standards for how data and artifacts ought to be recorded and preserved. Cushing suggests that archaeological field procedures should include numbering of excavation units, recording artifact associations, drawing detailed site maps, making daily summaries of work, and formulating daily speculations and hypotheses about relationships:

> Such care . . . in the recording of all facts and in the making of all collections was deemed essential . . . because . . . however great our knowledge might be, however extensive our collections might prove, we could not comprehend, as would be comprehended at some future time, the full value and significance of either the specimens we were gathering, or especially the facts relating to them and their gathering which we were accumulating; that, in other words, we were not collecting merely for ourselves, but for future generations![27]

He goes on to note that artifacts in burials and other contexts did not occur randomly, but were deliberately placed, hence good provenience and even the noting of prior disturbances was requisite for proper understanding of archaeological data. It would be at least three decades before American archaeologists heeded Cushing's advice.

Cushing presents a model of Southwestern culture history undergirded by some British and German ideas, but very much reflecting his conceptions of Zuni cosmology. In the 1880s, the British scholar E. B. Tylor was regarded by many as Europe's leading anthropologist.[28] One of his central concepts was what came to be called the "doctrine of survivals." Like Lewis Henry Morgan, Tylor was an evolutionist who saw all human societies and cultures evolving through a series of stages. But what evidence was there to support the stage theory? Tylor was well versed in geology and archaeology.

By analogy with index fossils in geology and index artifacts in archaeology, Tylor saw social and cultural phenomena, kinship practices, games, items of material culture, legends, myths—any patterned forms of human behavior—as index forms, associated with a particular stage (by analogy, stratum) of human culture history. When these forms "survived" from an earlier into a later stage, they provided evidence of earlier social and cultural practices. But in surviving, they were often "twisted and changed" by time, just as artifacts sometimes are. Tylor thought that legends, myths, and folklore reflect, in a distorted way, past social and cultural phenomena, as well as historical events. The task of the anthropologist was to "reconstruct" or "restore" those phenomena and events by careful analysis of "survivals" living on in legend, myth, and folklore. Cushing's close study of Zuni legends, greatly heightened by his understanding of the language, convinced him that Tylor was correct: myths, legends, and folklore reflect past historical events. Legends relating to migrations, named places, and so on could be verified by archaeological investigation. This was a basic working premise of the Hemenway Expedition.

Cushing's reading of Zuni legends told him that the people had migrated from a place about "one hundred miles, more or less," in the "mountain plateaus" west of present-day Zuni to their historic location.[29] He planned to get to those plateaus by traveling from the Phoenix area eastward up the Salt River. But when he saw the mound groups in the Salt River Valley, he began work there instead, coming to see the sites in a much larger context and arriving at some startling conclusions. These are verbosely presented in his 1890 paper. The following is a rearrangement of ideas sprinkled through its fifty-plus pages.[30]

Cushing's model of Southwestern culture history seems rooted in the German ethnological concept of elementary ideas, and their development by specific people or folk in geographically localized areas.[31] He argues that each culture conceives a central *Idea* during its "incipient stages of culture growth."[32] Hence, each culture's history *begins* "with the general conception or acquisition of and conformity to some special *Idea*." This special Idea is due "to environment." That is, the

Idea is a conceptual plan, or model, of sociocultural space, derived from the perceived and culturally interpreted spatial relationships in, and physical features of, a people's "original" environment. Once developed, the Idea is expressed in forms of social structure, cosmologies, and other concepts that support or justify the social structures, and in *spatial expressions* of the Idea on the ground, in intra- and inter-community settlement patterns. A "people carry through all succeeding environments—relatively unmodified—the impress of the *Idea* of the earliest environment which affected their Culture." "Ever after," the Idea modifies and shapes all ideology and "all the autochthonous Institutions specially characteristic of that culture . . . from the least to the greatest."

The task of the ethnologist is to find "what Idea possessed . . . the primitive group he would study." The search is guided by "*surviving customs among analogous peoples,* . . . [the] distribution of structural remains, sacerdotal or utilitarian, of his [the ethnologist's] dead people," and by burial practices and symbolism in art. Once the ethnologist grasps the "dominant Idea . . . or Culture-soul," then, "but scant evidences" of any one "Institution" need be found to permit the reconstruction of "all or nearly all" other institutions. Further, "no matter how widely severed in time or space . . . [the] remains" derived from a specific *Idea* may be, the knowledgeable ethnologist will be able to predict where the original homeland was; how various groups were once related; how long since a group left the homeland; and "perhaps . . . the true succession of the various periods of their subdivision and dispersal."

Cushing thought that his studies of Zuni and other Southwestern cultures showed that the ultimate homeland of the "*Original* Pueblo, Aridian, or Shiwian-peoples" was the Four Corners/San Juan Basin region, as Lewis Henry Morgan had asserted. The environment of the homeland region shaped an Idea in which "septenary divisions" were central. When the various Shiwians, including ancestral Zunis, migrated outward from the center, they took with them the concept that both ideational and social worlds are divided into *seven* segments, or *six* segments and an encompassing *middle*. The migrations were triggered by earthquakes. Fear of further earthquakes led the Shiwians *always* to settle in the *middle of plains*. This reinforced the "Middle of the World" feature of the "Original Idea."

Cushing thought that the "septenary" segmentation concept is reflected in Zuni "mythico-sociologic subdivisions": the world has *six* directions, north, south, east, west, zenith, and nadir, as well as a center, or "Middle of World"; there are seven priesthoods; in 1539–40, when the Spanish arrived, the Zuni lived in the "Seven Cities of Cibola"; when the Zunis retreated to Corn Mountain during the 1680 Pueblo Revolt, they built seven settlements there. More generally, in their early Southwestern explorations the Spanish "repeatedly" noted "province after province" containing seven cities, or sometimes "Thirteen Cities." The latter were two groups of *six* cities, each sharing the same *seventh* central or "Middle" city.

The Zuni are living examples of the "Shiwian," or "Original Pueblo" peoples. To understand Zuni sociocultural obsession with the six-seven concept, the "*archaeology* of the Zuni or Shiwian peoples should . . . be investigated throughout as much of the Southwest as possible." Evidence of "this characteristic tendency of the Shiwians to a sextenary or septenary division of the world . . . would aid to identify any remains, wherever found, of the same or related peoples."

This was the theoretical basis of the Hemenway Expedition. Cushing's Salt River Valley excavations convinced him that there were two groups of six cities there, as well as a "great city which served probably as the seventh (or 'Middle-world') city of both systems." And there were seven "Temple Mounds" in the "Middle-world" city. The thirteen cities were "contemporaneously inhabited"; hence, there was a very large population. Earthquakes forced abandonment of the cities about fifteen hundred to two thousand years ago, just as they had forced abandonment of the Four Corners region. The population dispersed. Some moved northeastward to found the "Seven Cities of Cibola," and become the historic Zuni. Some became other Southwestern Puebloan groups. Some possibly were ancestral to Mexican groups, and even to the Inca of Peru, again as Morgan had postulated.

Cushing's 1888 model of Southwestern culture history was a brilliant, intuitive leap of imagination, like much else he did. In his "Outlines of Zuñi Creation Myths," written primarily in 1892 and his last major statement on Zuni history and culture, he developed a more specific account of the culture history of the Zuni by combining Zuni mythology with what was then known of the archaeology of the Southwest. Given the lack of chronological information, it is a reasoned attempt to account for various types of ruins, as Cushing defined them. It is also an attempt to merge Morgan's model of Southwest culture history with Cushing's own view from Zuni.[33]

First, Zuni mythology states that the Zunis are a composite group. The "elder nations" came from the north and "were direct and comparatively unchanged descendants of the . . . cliff dwellers" of the San Juan Basin. The "western branch" of the Zunis originated in the Colorado River drainage, moved eastward and ultimately merged with the "elder nations." This acculturation process produced the Zuni people and their culture of historic times.

The northern branch followed a "line of development . . . from cave to cliff, and from cliff to round town conditions of life." The earliest of the northern folk lived in small settlements in the open and used low-lying caves for storage and winter shelter, as do the historic Tarahumara of Sonora, as reported by Carl Lumholtz (see Chapter 18). Later, rock shelters higher in the cliffs were used as dwelling places; terraced houses, occupied by women and children, were built against the (often) rounded back walls of the shelters; round kivas, for men, were built in the front of the shelters.

Ultimately, the cliff dwellers began to move south along the trail leading to the Zuni salt lake, a major source of relatively pure salt. The cliff-dweller areas were abandoned. In the southerly country, there were no rockshelters, but the people built "round towns" mimicking the "round" rockshelter villages of earlier

times. Later villages came to be D-shaped, for example the great Chacoan towns; kivas continued to be round; the people became "true Pueblos, or town dwellers of the valleys and plains."

There was later an amalgamation of the western, or "Midmost," folk, with the northern, round- or D-shaped town folk. The Midmost folk built single rectangular houses and "simple extensions, mostly rectilinear," of the single house units. As the western and northern folk merged, villages at first contained both round and rectangular elements; ultimately the rectangular elements prevailed, including those in kiva construction. Further evidence for the merging of the western and northern folk into historic Zunis is provided by burial practices. West of Zuni, in both prehistoric and historic times, the dead were cremated; the cliff dwellers, and round- and D-shaped town dwellers, buried their dead under house floors or in trash mounds. According to Cushing, the early Spanish observed both cremation and burial among the Zuni. Finally, there is the evidence of Zuni origins accounts.

The origins accounts vary somewhat, but center on an upward emergence through four worlds into the light of Sun Father and onto the surface of Earth Mother, in common with most other Southwestern cosmologies. Some accounts give the Place of Origin, or emergence, as a hole in the Grand Canyon; others at a spot further down the Colorado River. From there, the Zuni, or Ashiwi, began a journey eastward in search of the Middle Place, "the center of the world, the mid-most spot among all of the great oceans and lands, the spot in all the heavens of the universe . . ."[34] The seekers stopped at many places, built villages and remained for a time, then moved on. At the San Francisco peaks, they learned of certain medicine plants. At the Little Colorado River, one group hived off and journeyed southward to the Land of Everlasting Sunshine, never to return. When the journey was resumed, the Zunis split into three groups. One group went to Kachina Lake, thence on to the edge of the Middle Place. There the Twin War Gods, elder brother Uyeyewi and younger brother

Ma'a'sewi, were created by Father Sun, and assisted the Zuni in an epic battle with people already in place. The Zunis prevailed, and assimilated some of those people into the tribe; they then moved into *Halona: Itiwana,* the Middle Place. Another group went south from the Little Colorado River, thence to El Morro, or Inscription Rock, in a village on top of which they dwelt for a time before joining the others at Middle Place. Another group went northeastward from the Little Colorado to the Jemez Mountains, then down the Rio Grande, west to Mt. Taylor, and finally to Middle Place. Along the way, they assimilated some other groups. This latter is presumably Cushing's northern group.

When the Zuni were near the Middle Place, *K'yan'asdebi,* water spider spread out his legs until he touched the four oceans in the east, west, north, and south directions; his back touched the zenith and his underside the nadir. Thus oriented to the six cardinal directions, his heart was directly over the long-sought Middle Place—and there the Zuni finally settled, and there they remain.

This brief summary in no way does justice to the rich Zuni symbolism, poetry, and language that Cushing and later anthropologists were able to present to the Anglo world.[35] Nor should it be worrisome that the summary does not exactly match Cushing's archaeologically based account. According to a recent Zuni religious leader, "These are the places that are mentioned and places that are discussed as a trail, but it is a religious idea, or religious trail that is recited in the prayer and not an actual path of people walking on the trail."[36]

Cushing, Bandelier, the Mindeleffs, and later Jesse Walter Fewkes recognized the symbolic nature of the myths, not only of the Zuni, but of the Hopi and all the other Southwestern groups. But, with Tylor, they believed that kernels of "actual," that is scientifically derived, culture history were embedded in myths and legends. This belief informed an item of the Southwestern research agenda: use the myths and legends to identify "actual" ruins on the ground and thus flesh out Southwestern culture history.

Joan Mark argues that Cushing, beginning about 1882, was the first American anthropologist to use the term *culture* in the sense in which the British anthropologist Edward B. Tylor defined it in 1871: "Culture or Civilization, taken in its wide ethnographic sense, is that complex whole which includes knowledge, belief, art, morals, law, custom, and any other capabilities and habits acquired by man as a member of society."[37] For most Europeans and Eurocolonials in the nineteenth century, "culture" meant the elite refinement of manners, attention to the fine arts, and so on. Tylor's definition was much broader, encompassing all learned (as contrasted with genetically programmed) human behavior. It was close to the German "Kultur," used by Johann Herder and others in the late eighteenth century as more or less synonymous with "civilization," but also in the plural, as the unique outcomes of the interactions of each "folk" and its environment.[38]

In 1882, Cushing described the Zuni as remnants of a vast culture in the Southwest and Sylvester Baxter referred to Zuni as the oldest of the Pueblo families, "the father of the *Kultur,* as the Germans would say, and possessing the most distinctive characteristics." In *Zuñi Breadstuff,* Cushing says Americans are "controlled by a culture totally at variance with that of the Zuñis."[39] Finally, as Mark points out, Cushing's concept of a central dominating *Idea* as an organizing principle that structures each culture reemerged in the 1910s and 1920s in the theories about Southwestern societies and ideas of cultural relativism spun by H. K. Haeberlin and Ruth Benedict (see Chapter 26).[40]

Cushing, then, was using "culture" in several senses that would become common in American anthropology after his death: as patterned sets of behaviors distinctive of, or "carried by" a specific population; as a general term, for example, Southwestern Pueblo culture, with specific variants, such as Acoma, Hopi, Zuni, etc.; as assemblages of material culture items—pottery, lithics, basketry, etc.—made to characteristic patterns. The importance of these several usages will emerge in later chapters.[41]

Cushing after the Hemenway Expedition

When Cushing left the Hemenway Expedition in the fall of 1888, he regarded his role as director as a failure, as did others for a time. Charles Lummis would later write, "This magnificent expedition, which seeded the dry valleys of New Mexico and Arizona with gold eagles and hopes, is generally written a failure." Cushing summed it up by saying, "Mrs. Hemenway honored me with greater confidence in my ability to carry on such work than I possessed of myself."[42]

Cushing had just emerged from the hospital in 1889 when it was announced that Augustus Hemenway had appointed Jesse Walter Fewkes as director of the expedition. The announcement plunged him into a slough of despair and self-doubt. The years of 1889 through 1891 were simply dismal. He was either in a hospital or confined to his bed at home; "he was in physical pain much of the time and in mental anguish almost all of the time."[43] He finally achieved a measure of medical relief in February 1890, when he expelled the last of the tapeworms that had been the source of many of his gastrointestinal problems. He wrote to Washington Matthews that he pickled it in alcohol as a souvenir.[44] Over the next two years, he struggled to write up some of the Hemenway materials, but since, as he claimed, he had no access to his notes, maps, or collections, he could do little.[45] By early 1892 he was much better and threw himself into completing his "Outlines of Zuñi Creation Myths," discussed above.

But new directions were looming. In 1893, Cushing was assigned to supervise installation of the Smithsonian's Southwestern ethnography exhibits at the World's Columbian Exposition—the Chicago world's fair—and was there for three months. During the fair, he and Stewart Culin became close friends. Cushing, Culin, Matthews, Bourke, and Baxter were prominently involved in the anthropological congress that was part of the fair (see Chapter 17). After the fair, Cushing fell into another funk, but continued his office work into the following year. On March 6, 1894, Mary Hemenway died; appropriately, there was a me-morial for her at the Old South Meeting House, which Cushing attended. The next day, the trustees of her estate donated the Hemenway Expedition collection to the Peabody Museum at Harvard, where they were to be permanently exhibited in a "Mary Hemenway Room."[46] Cushing now indeed had no access to the collections—his involvement with the expedition was truly over.

Denouement at Key Marco

Early in 1896, Cushing went to Philadelphia for a medical examination by Dr. William Pepper (see Chapter 18), apparently on the advice of Zelia Nuttall. Cushing had favorably impressed Nuttall, Alice Fletcher, Sara Yorke Stevenson, and Daniel Brinton at the Chicago world's fair. This, and his close friendship with Stewart Culin, ultimately resulted in Cushing leading an expedition to Key Marco, Florida, to excavate Indian mounds in a wetlands context, funded by Pepper and Phoebe Apperson Hearst, and jointly sponsored by the University of Pennsylvania and the Bureau of American Ethnology. The full story of the expedition lies beyond our purview.[47] However, since it involved Cushing in his last major project, and a controversy tied back to the Hemenway Expedition, some details should be noted. Cushing concentrated on a late prehistoric shell-mound village, possibly occupied by ancestors of the historic Calusa Indians. There were many organic artifacts of wood, bone, shell, netting, cordage, and the first known remains in the Southeast of domesticated bottle gourds and cucurbits. The wooden artifacts included atlatls, fishing gear, bowls, anthropomorphic masks, a deer's head with moveable ears, and a beautifully carved "feline figure."[48]

One spectacular piece was a *Macrocallista* shell with a masked dance figure painted in a black pigment on the inside surface. In the fall of 1896, William Dinwiddie, a photographer at the Bureau of American Ethnology, publicly charged that Cushing had painted the figure inside the shell. In the meantime, Frederick Webb Hodge was privately circulating a story that Cushing had faked a famous turquoise mosaic-inlaid frog that he said he found at los Muertos in August 1887. When it was "found," he had spent two days in his tent "restoring" it, Cushing said; faking it, Hodge averred. An internal Smithsonian investigation vindicated Cushing with regard to the shell figure, and Dinwiddie was fired "for neglect of duty."[49] Hodge stuck to his story about the frog. Modern opinions vary. In his los Muertos report Emil Haury does not mention the turquoise frog; Marion Gilliland, who reanalyzed the Key Marco artifacts, thinks the shell may be genuine.[50]

Cushing labored mightily on his Key Marco report between 1896 and 1900, or so he told Pepper and Powell, amid bouts of illness, depression, and rows with the formidable Sara Yorke Stevenson at the University of Pennsylvania Museum over disposition of the Florida collections.

On April 1 or 2, 1900, Cushing dined at home with his wife. They animatedly discussed a new expedition to the coast of Maine to do archaeology near John Wesley Powell's summer cabin at Haven. Cushing thought the climate and the work would rejuvenate him. He had some lectures scheduled in New York the following week and was looking forward to them. He apparently choked on, and then swallowed, a fishbone. On April 5 he wrote to Stewart Culin that "an accident deprived me of all my power—nearly causing my death. A fish-bone, double pointed and sharp-edged lodged in the cardiac aperture of my stomach for two days before it could be withdrawn and I have suffered deliriously every hour since until this morning—several days—and even had to put off my New York lectures which meant loss of much money and favor. But such is my usual fate."[51] The bone, though removed, seemingly caused internal hemorrhaging, and he died on April 10, 1900. He was forty-three years old. A shocked and grieving group of prominent friends and family gathered in Washington, D.C., for a memorial service. Cushing was eulogized as a genius; Powell said, "I loved him as a father loves his son."[52] Only later did the people of Zuni learn that Tenatsali was gone.

CHAPTER 14

Jesse Walter Fewkes:
From Ichthyologist to Ethnologist

By MAY 1889 the Hemenway family and the expedition board had concluded that Cushing and his champion, Sylvester Baxter, must go. The death of Martha Goddard allowed Augustus Hemenway to appoint Jesse Walter Fewkes (Fig. 14.1) to the board and to make him director of the Hemenway Expedition in June 1889. Fewkes's anthropological qualifications were nil, but he was from an old New England family, had a Ph.D. from Harvard, and was an undergraduate classmate of Augustus Hemenway, all of which apparently were sufficient credentials.

Jesse Walter Fewkes (1850–1930) was born in Newton, Massachusetts.[1] He entered Harvard in 1871 and emerged in 1877 with a Ph.D. in zoology, then spent two postdoctoral years at Leipzig University. He became an assistant in the Museum of Comparative Zoology at Harvard, focusing on marine biology. He spent the summer of 1887 with the Hemenway family in Monterey, California, studying medusae, but also somehow became interested in Southwestern Indians

and longed to take up anthropology, or so his later biographers said. "Doctor Fewkes's visit to California proved to be the turning point of his career, for it was then that he came into contact with the culture of the Pueblo Indians, which excited in him an interest still further stimulated by the enthusiasm of Mrs. Mary Hemenway."[2] There was a more pressing reason for Fewkes's interest. Alexander Agassiz, who had succeeded his father, Louis, as director of the museum, had become dissatisfied with Fewkes's work and did not renew his appointment in 1889. Agassiz later accused Fewkes of numerous instances of plagiarism, even threatening legal action. Sylvester Baxter wrote Cushing that Edward S. Morse "says Fewkes is a sneak."[3] Augustus Hemenway came to the rescue, and Fewkes was suddenly in charge of the Hemenway Expedition. He was expected to get the expedition restarted and do anthropological fieldwork in the Southwest.

Fewkes spent a couple of weeks with the Pas-

14.1. Jesse Walter Fewkes, 1898.
Courtesy of the Southwest Museum.

canned foods purchased by Mrs. Hemenway from "the finest grocery in Boston" and shipped out on the railroad. Fewkes was not well received at Zuni. He certainly wasn't anything like Cushing; he spoke neither Zuni nor Spanish and had to rely on a local Indian trader to communicate with the people. Fewkes and Owens were able to observe some summer dances, but they had few clues as to what the ceremonies meant, other than through access to some of Cushing's notes, which Fewkes co-opted and published as his own, according to Cushing, who said: "Not only does Dr. Fewkes pre-empt my field, or rather, jump my claim, but he makes use of my material . . . without even quotation marks when my own words are used."[6] Fewkes and Owens returned to Zuni in 1891, but then moved to Hopi.

Owens and George A. Dorsey (see Chapter 18) enrolled at Harvard in 1890 to do graduate work in anthropology with Frederic Ward Putnam.[7] Owens had graduated from Bucknell University and met Fewkes at a Harvard marine-biology summer school in 1889. In 1890, Fewkes asked him to come along to Zuni, and then to Zuni and Hopi, beginning in February 1891. Later in the year Owens went to Copán as part of the first Peabody expedition to Central America. He returned in time to help Fewkes set up the Hemenway exhibit in Madrid in 1892 (see Chapter 17). He was back at Copán in early 1893, when he died suddenly.

Owens was young and idealistic. Fewkes was uncertain of himself, frantic to prove that he could do ethnography, and often raged at poor Owens. In Fewkes and others, Owens saw the darker side of researchers. In April 1891 he wrote to his fiancée, Deborah Stratton:

> During the last year, I have come in contact with many of what we call "investigators." They are men of eminence, men we all respect, indeed the men who give us the books we quote as "authority" on the different subjects. But, as I get a glimpse into

samaquoddy Indians of coastal Maine, giving himself a crash course in ethnography and recording some songs on a phonograph (see below).[4] He then headed for Zuni to look over the expedition. He decided to become an ethnographer, rather than an archaeologist. He was, after all, a scientist; scientists collect data, whether on squids or on human behavior, so why not change fields? Curtis Hinsley cogently contrasts Cushing's and Fewkes's approaches to ethnography as the difference between "ethnographic charisma and scientific routine."[5] Cushing learned the Zuni language and ways of thought. His interpretations were informed by an empathetic, insightful, romantic humanism. Fewkes bulled ahead, collecting bits and pieces of social and cultural behavior, seeking order, as a good Baconian inductivist should, in the scientistic collages he assembled.

Fewkes began his ethnographic career in the summer of 1890, taking along a new Harvard graduate student, John G. Owens. They moved into Cushing's house, which the Hemenway Expedition had previously paid for. No Zuni cuisine for them; they ate

this class of original investigators, *when they are not on dress parade,* I see stamped on the countenance of almost every one the rankest jealousy. Almost everyone seems to look upon the work of every other one as so much "rot." My course at present is laid for an investigation and very frequently I ask myself: "Will I get that way too?" Must I *acquire* a contempt for every other man's work?" Surely I do not wish to and I wonder if it is impossible to come through unscathed.[8]

One such authority was Washington Matthews, who wrote to Cushing about Fewkes: "Our Boston friend, while in Zuni never spoke a word of Zuni and didn't know a word of Spanish . . . yet he learned all about them in two months. What a pity we have not a few more such brilliant lights in Ethnography!"[9]

Fewkes's insecurity continued as he plunged ahead at Hopi. But there he found an ethnographic savior—Alexander McGregor Stephen. By 1891 Stephen was deep into his studies of Hopi language and culture. He was living on First Mesa with his Navajo wife, and most of the time was financially on the edge. He had worked for the Mindeleff brothers, but they had finished and were gone. He helped out at Thomas Keam's trading post; he got by. But what he really wanted was to get his knowledge of the Hopis out to the world, and be recognized for it. It was Stephen who introduced Fewkes to Hopi people, who got him admitted to Hopi dances and ceremonies, who paved the way for his admittance into the Antelope and Flute societies. It was Stephen's intimate knowledge of Hopi dances and ceremonies that Fewkes published as his own, in return for 115 dollars per month between 1892 and 1894.[10] Fewkes also determined to increase the Hemenway Expedition artifact collections. He bought a major collection from Thomas Keam for ten thousand dollars. It consists of about forty-five hundred pieces, including some prehistoric materials, some textiles, a few kachina dolls, and three thousand eighteenth- and nineteenth-century Hopi pots, one of the largest historic pottery collections ever assembled.[11]

One of the criticisms of Cushing was that he did not publish his findings. Fewkes adopted a "publish or perish" attitude and churned out dozens of short and long papers, some two hundred publications in all over his forty-year career as an anthropologist.[12]

Fewkes as Ethnographer

In their time at Zuni and Hopi, Fewkes and Owens did witness several public ceremonies, and Owens was able to gather information on practices surrounding parturition and naming. Apparently, some of the Hopi women at Walpi were quite willing to discuss childbearing, nursing, and infant care with Owens, to his considerable surprise. He was, he said, "among women whose good-nature is only surpassed by their hospitality." He also noted sympathetically how hard the women worked, and the resulting physical debilities, which he called "inferiorities." These came principally from carrying three-gallon water jugs up the very steep six-hundred-foot-high trail to Walpi from the springs at the base of the mesa, while back and arm problems resulted from the unceasing grinding of cornmeal in the metate troughs. Yet Owens could not escape the pervasive negative stereotype relating to "uncivilized" women: "Notwithstanding the physical inferiority of which I have spoken, she [the Hopi woman] still possesses considerable of that strength in childbirth so remarkable in uncivilized races. A woman about to be confined does not slacken in her daily labors, but works until the moment of parturition. This usually takes place with ease and dispatch."[13]

Fewkes's early papers on public rituals are largely descriptive, based on what he could observe and what little interpretation he was able to extract from other Anglo observers. He seems to have had a good eye for detail in his descriptions of dances, paraphernalia, and setting. Once he had Alexander Stephen as a tutor, his levels of description and understanding grew apace. Stephen's knowledge of Hopi ritual was both deep and extensive, as is reflected in his journals, which were not published until 1936.[14]

Fewkes and the Phonograph

When Fewkes headed to Maine in 1889, he took along an Edison phonograph equipped with a treadle for motive power and a flywheel to keep the wax cylinder turning at a constant speed. He used it to record some folk tales, in English, and five Passamaquoddy songs. He then carried the phonograph with him to Zuni in 1890 and to Hopi the next year, recording a variety of songs in both places.[15] Fewkes turned his Zuni and Hopi recordings over to Benjamin Ives Gilman, a well-known musicologist and secretary of the Boston Museum of Fine Arts. Gilman produced a paper on the Zuni songs in 1891 and in 1908 a major treatise on Hopi music, the latter being the swan song, so to say, of the Hemenway Expedition, long after Fewkes had departed.

Various individuals had written down Indian music before Fewkes, but he was the first to use a phonograph in North America. The honor of first using a phonograph in ethnography seems to have gone to A. C. Haddon and the Torres Strait Expedition in the South Pacific the previous year. Many years later, in 1924, Fewkes and John Peabody Harrington (see Chapter 22) made disc recordings of Hopi "Katcina" and other songs, sung at the Grand Canyon by "Hopi Chanters brought from Walpi," probably at the Fred Harvey Company Hopi House (see Chapter 27).[16]

Fewkes and the Bureau of American Ethnology

Both Mary Hemenway and Alexander Stephen died in 1894. The Hemenway family terminated the expedition and turned the archaeological collections over to the Peabody Museum at Harvard. Fewkes was once again "on the street"; his means of support and his principal mentor in Hopi ethnography were both gone. But he had friends in high places and some of them approached Samuel P. Langley, secretary of the Smithsonian Institution, on his behalf. Langley turned to John Wesley Powell at the Bureau of American Ethnology. Frederick Webb Hodge apparently supported Fewkes, perhaps to spite Cushing. The Smithsonian had no one working in the Southwest. The Mindeleffs had finished their architectural surveys and Cushing was about to embark on his Florida adventure. In May 1895, there was a flurry of correspondence between Langley's and Powell's offices. The upshot was that Fewkes was "commissioned" by the Bureau to begin a program of archaeological research in Arizona at a salary of two hundred dollars per month. The trip was financed by the "reserve" monies that the secretary's office continued to take from Powell's annual appropriation, and by five hundred dollars from the Smithsonian fund.[17] By June 1896, with Cushing supported by the Pepper-Hearst Florida expedition, it was possible to put Fewkes on the Bureau payroll. And there he remained until he retired in 1928.

Fewkes's hiring undoubtedly rankled Cushing and his cronies Bourke, Matthews, and Baxter, but from Powell's perspective it was potentially a good move. True, Fewkes had no training in archaeology; but then he had none in ethnography when he took over the Hemenway expedition, yet had produced a relatively large number of respectable, if pedestrian, publications. That alone would appeal to Powell, who had great difficulty in dragging finished manuscripts from the hands of his staff. Second, Fewkes was well connected in the Boston-Cambridge intellectual nexus and with its senators and representatives in Washington; hence, he was politically useful. Third, the Smithsonian and the Bureau felt they needed to be back in the Southwest. By 1895, the Field Columbian Museum in Chicago was actively involved in the Southwest (see Chapter 18), as were others. Fourth, Fewkes had a working relationship with Thomas Keam, the Indian trader whose influence with both Hopis and Navajos eased the way for researchers to work in Arizona. And finally, Fewkes proposed a research program that extended the work of the Mindeleffs and Cushing: tying the archaeological sites in the Southwest to the migration legends of the Hopi. Cushing had begun to do that with the Zuni; now using the knowledge he had gained with Stephen's help, Fewkes could do the same for the Hopi.

Fewkes and the Archaeology of Tusayan

Beginning in 1895, Fewkes spent several seasons in Arizona Territory surveying known archaeological sites, finding new ones, and excavating in several, seeking to tie Hopi legends to specific sites and places. He described his research plan as follows:

> A study of the ritual and mythology of these people for several years had familiarized me with a rich collection of folklore consisting of tales of cosmogony, heroic stories of supernatural beings, and migration legends. These stories . . . present . . . the only material which is available . . . of their origin and migrations previously to their settlement in their present homes. The legends of cosmogony are manifestly outside the realm of scientific verification, but migration stories are evidently of a much greater import to the student of archaeology. These stories are repeated . . . with an exactness which is highly suggestive of the truth in their general character. The old story-tellers recount with detail the places where their ancestors halted in their migrations, and declare that they built homes or villages near certain springs, mountains, or in well-known valleys, where, they declare, the visitor may still see the ruins. . . . Here we have the opportunity to test the legends by archaeological research. We can visit the sites of villages claimed by the ancients and find out if the evidence supports the legends . . . or whether the stories are true or false.[18]

Fewkes reported that one of the Hopi clans, the Water House People, had legends that they came from the "far south" in "Palatkwabi, Red Land." A fragment of a Pima legend connected ruins in the Gila Valley, such as Casa Grande, with "the ancestors of the Tusayan Indians." The major natural route northward from the

Salt/Gila River Valley is up the Verde River Valley and its tributary Oak Creek; hence, this could be a migration route. But Fewkes's survey of the Verde Valley and Oak Creek indicated the sites were related to the Hohokam to the south and not the Tusayan to the northeast. Only when he got into the "Red Land" country east of Oak Creek did he begin to pick up Tusayan sites.[19]

In 1895–97 and 1900 Fewkes was in the upper Little Colorado River drainage, sometimes accompanied by Frederick Webb Hodge and Walter Hough, of the National Museum. Hopi legends tell of the occupation of various sites there. Farther east along the Zuni River, a tributary of the Little Colorado, Fewkes began to record sites mentioned in both Zuni and Hopi legends, such as the Chevlon group and Kintiel. Finally, he moved south along the Mogollon Rim and into the White Mountains, into what would later be called the Mogollon archaeological region.[20]

Fewkes and Stephen had gathered Hopi legends relating to specific ruins. A century later, Hopi narrators published their own version of legends relating to seven ruins. In 1895, Fewkes excavated in two of those ruins, Awatovi and Sikyatki. Awatovi was the one Hopi village that accepted Spanish friars back after the Pueblo Revolt of 1680. Reacceptance of Christianity was anathema to other Hopis, and Awatovi was attacked by them in 1700. Most of the men, and some women, were killed, and the remaining women and the children were distributed among other Hopi villages. Fewkes's version of the story is rather gruesome, including Awatovi men trapped in kivas and burned alive. When he excavated there in 1895, he did not find such a kiva, but he did find clear evidence of individuals who had suffered violent death.[21]

The other ruin, Sikyatki, is now known to have been occupied and abandoned prior to the advent of the Spanish, sometime between 1425 and 1600. The Hopi narrators' legend says that Sikyatki had become infested by witches, and the chief asked the people of the neighboring village of Qöötaptuvela, closely related to Walpi, to destroy his town. They did so by burning the town and killing the witches, but in the process the village chief was killed as well. Fewkes's version has more to do with political and social conflicts between Walpi and Sikyatki, leading to the burning of the latter and the killing of men.[22]

Tusayan Migrations

Fewkes brought together all his archaeological and legendary data in a paper called "Tusayan Migration Traditions," published in 1900. He drew on his own and Stephen's data, some of which had appeared in the Mindeleffs' volume on Tusayan architecture.[23] He tried to sort out not just Hopi clan migrations, but which ceremonies or parts of ceremonies each clan or group of clans brought with them. His principal focus is on First Mesa, since that is where his consultants lived and where he belonged to the Flute and Antelope societies. His presentation is that of the cautious, inductive scientist: here are the data and here are possible or probable interpretations.

The picture he paints is of clans, or groups of clans, coming at various times from the north, south, and east to "Hopiland." The earliest clans came from the north, perhaps from present-day southern Utah; some came from the upper Little Colorado River after about 1650, driven northward by the increasingly hostile Apache. Others came from the Rio Grande country, some prior to the Spanish, still others as a result of Spanish incursions and the aftermath of the Pueblo Revolt of 1680—especially the Tewa who settled in Hano on First Mesa adjacent to Walpi, where their descendants remain.

Having reviewed the history of Hopi migrations, Fewkes then turned to various Hopi ceremonies. Some, such as the Flute ceremony, he thinks came from the south; others, such as major components of the Snake ceremony, came from the north. Finally, he sees the kachina, or katcina, ceremonies as coming from the Eastern Pueblos, but not with any one clan, nor from any one village:

1. The pueblo of Hano is Tanoan in language and culture; it was transplanted from the upper Rio Grande valley to the East [First] mesa of Tusayan. Its religion is intrusive, and its ritual resembles that of Walpi only in those features which have been brought by kindred clans from the same region.

2. The religious ceremonies of Sichomovi are also intrusive from the east, because the majority of its people are descended from colonists from the same region as those who settled Hano, but the ritual is purely Tanoan. . . .

3. The pioneer settlers of Walpi were Snake and Bear clans. [Later there came] Horn clans [from the north] mixed with Flute clans from the Little Colorado. The majority of the clans and the most distinctive ceremonies in Walpi ritual came from southern Arizona.[24]

Fewkes and Nampeyo

While Fewkes was studying the relationships between legends, ruins, and historic Hopi villages, he became increasingly interested in the pottery from archaeological sites, especially Awatovi and Sikyatki. Thomas Keam had been digging in those and other ruins and removing numerous examples of exquisite yellow- or cream-ware vessels beautifully painted in elaborate stylized figures of people, birds, butterflies, and other zoomorphs. The designs were very different from the geometric motifs of other Tusayan wares. The style, called Sikyatki by archaeologists, is now known to have been made from about 1375 to 1625, at the same time as elaborate kiva murals that have many of the same motifs. Some think the pottery style and the murals were related to the introduction of new cults, including the kachina cult, either of local derivation or somehow brought from northern Mesoamerica into the Southwest around 1400; but there is no consensus.[25] Sikyatki-style pottery is aesthetically pleasing for the fineness of its manufacture and its beautifully painted designs. Fewkes excavated numerous examples, which were soon on display in the National Museum. He also began to interact with the Hopi-Tewa potter Nampeyo.

One of the persistent legends in Southwestern anthropology and the Indian art market has to do with the relationship between Fewkes and Nampeyo and the "revival" of the Sikyatki style of pottery.[26] The standard version of the legend derives from Fewkes's obituary:

> It was during the summer of 1895 that he . . . excavated at the Hopi ruins of Awatobi and Sikyatki. His collection of specimens from . . . [these] sites contains some of the finest examples of the ceramic art ever found in the Southwest. While conducting the Sikyatki investigations Doctor Fewkes fostered the beginnings of a renaissance in Hopi pottery making. Nampeo [sic], a young woman from the village of Hano, was a constant visitor at the scene of the excavations and was so fascinated by the beauty of the pottery being unearthed that she began copying the forms and style of decoration. As a result of Doctor Fewkes' encouragement and advice she was so successful in her endeavors that

other women turned to the ancient wares for their inspiration. From that time to the present day the pottery made in the various villages has been distinctly of the Sikyatki style.[27]

Fewkes, over time, presented a somewhat different picture: "The best potter of the East [First] mesa . . . named Nampio [sic], acknowledged that her productions were far inferior to those of the women of Sikyatki and she begged permission to copy some of the decorations for future inspiration." Two years later, he said: "The most expert modern potter at East Mesa is Nampéo . . . who is a thorough artist in her line of work. Finding a better market for ancient than for modern ware, she cleverly copies old decorations and imitates the Sikyatki ware almost perfectly." Finally, in 1919, he recalled that "in 1895 . . . there was a renaissance of old Sikyatki patterns, under the lead of Nampeo. . . . The extent of her work . . . may be judged by the great numbers of Hopi bowls displayed in every Harvey store . . . There is a danger that in a few years some of Nampeo's imitations will be regarded as ancient Hopi ware . . . and more or less confusion introduced by the difficulty in distinguishing

14.2. Nampeyo and daughter Nellie Nampeyo, 1901. Photograph by S. W. Matteson. Courtesy Milwaukee Public Museum.

her work from that obtained in the ruins."[28] In short, Fewkes took no credit, at least in print, for "encouraging," or "advising" Nampeyo.

Walter Hough was with Fewkes in 1896, during the excavation of Old Cuñopavi on Second Mesa. Nampeyo visited the dig to copy designs. Hough, the consummate museum person, noted her visits and bought examples of her work. Fewkes makes no mention of Nampeyo's visits to Cuñopavi. Hough's two obituaries of Fewkes say nothing of his relationship with Nampeyo, and Fewkes's own autobiographical statement is equally silent.[29]

The story of the "revival" by Hopi potters is more complex than simply Fewkes encouraging Nampeyo, although she played a critical role. Nampeyo (Fig. 14.2) was born about 1860. Her mother was White Corn of the Tewa Corn clan; her father was Quootsva of the Hopi Snake clan of Walpi. She had three older brothers, one of whom, Polaccaca, was later known as Tom Polacca. Nampeyo grew up in Hano on First Mesa, speaking both Tewa and Hopi. She learned all the traditional womanly skills, including how to make pottery, from her mother and her maternal relatives.[30]

In 1875, William Henry Jackson and E. A. Barber of the Hayden Survey visited Hopi (see Chapter 5). They met Tom Polacca, who had learned some English, possibly from the Mormon missionary-explorer Jacob Hamblin, and was fast becoming a translator and cultural broker between the Tewa and Hopi and visiting Anglos. Barber and Jackson also met his sister, Nampeyo, and were taken by her beauty and grace; Jackson made the first of many photographs of her. She was wearing the traditional maiden's whorl hairdo, but soon changed it when she married Lesso, or Lesou, of the Cedarwood clan from Walpi.

In 1879 James Stevenson arrived at Hopi and, with the assistance of Tom Polacca and Thomas Keam, made a very large collection of artifacts, including heirloom pots from many families and archaeological pieces from nearby ruins. He was back again in 1881 and most summers thereafter until 1886. The Mindeleff brothers were also collecting for the Smithsonian. It became immediately evident to all parties that an economic boon had come to Hopi. Stevenson and other collectors were particularly taken with the black-on-yellow and polychrome-on-yellow vessels dug up from ruins near First Mesa.

Keam had excavated in Awatovi and Sikyatki, fascinated by the ceramics. He was equally interested in historic pieces, made from about 1600 to 1860, which variously reflect Zuni, Acoma, Rio Grande, and Spanish influences. Hopi potters during that period were very innovative, experimenting with different design styles as they encountered them. Some apparently experimented with the Sikyatki style they saw on sherds in the ruins, long before Fewkes appeared on the scene. Keam commissioned Hopi potters to reproduce various vessel forms and design styles, including Sikyatki, perhaps as early as 1885. He also encouraged them to make miniature vessels, more easily carried by tourists, as well as small, flat, so-called Polacca ceramic tiles, often with "kachina" figures on them.

Nampeyo and other potters may have begun their own experimentation with what became the "Sikyatki revival" style. Keam's encouragement and the market he developed were added incentives. Fewkes's excavations simply provided a further source of design motifs already familiar to Nampeyo and others. But Nampeyo's great skill and sense of design then came into play, for her ceramics were wonderfully done and appreciated widely.

Fewkes also was fascinated by the designs on the pottery, the Sikyatki style as well as the earlier geometric forms. He discussed the designs at some length in two major papers. Alexander Stephen was equally intrigued and discussed Hopi pottery symbols in his catalog of the Keam collection. Both provide a basis for understanding how Hopi potters used the designs to reflect the central concerns of Hopi cosmology.[31]

Fewkes and the Kachinas

Bourke's and others' reports on the Snake Dance served to focus Anglo attention on Hopi ceremonies. Most of the Snake Dance activities occur in secret over eight days and are as mysterious to uninitiated

Hopi as to outsiders. Dancers with live rattlesnakes in their mouths both fascinated and repelled Anglo observers; hence, they flocked to see the ceremony. Few had any real understanding of how the dance articulated with and expressed the Hopi worldview. By the mid-1890s, at Walpi in particular, there were so many disrespectful tourists and so many photographers jostling each other that the integrity of the dance was threatened and the elders banned photography.[32]

Fewkes was initiated into both the Snake and Flute societies, but was also interested in the rest of the Hopi yearly ceremonial cycle, which starts at the winter solstice. He spent most of the winter of 1899–1900 at Walpi observing and participating in the ceremonies. Henry Voth, a Mennonite missionary (see Chapter 26), had begun working on Third Mesa at about the same time and also was able to observe numerous ceremonies. The publications of the two, together with Alexander Stephen's journal, form the basis for all subsequent studies of Hopi cosmology and ceremonialism.[33]

Cushing was fascinated by the Zunis' complex and highly integrated cosmology and the ritual system through which the cosmology is validated and expressed. Those who came to know Hopi found an equally complex and integrated cosmology and related ritual system. Alexander Stephen was the first to fully appreciate the Hopi worldview and ritual cycle. He passed on some of his knowledge to Fewkes, although his notebooks, not published until 1936, contain a great deal more information.[34]

The Hopi share some of the basic Southwestern cosmological ideas, but framed in a distinctly Hopi perspective. These include myths of emergence from earlier worlds, the need to maintain harmony and balance in the universe, and a six-direction spatial orientation: zenith, nadir, and four cardinal directions. There are specific colors, butterflies, birds, and other beings associated with the cardinal directions. There is not a "middle" or "center place" which situates where the Hopi live, as there is at Zuni. The Hopi entered this world at its middle through Sipapu, the emergence place in the Grand Canyon. Sipapu is symboli-cally represented by a covered hole in the floor of Hopi kivas.[35]

In the Hopi universe there is a dual division of time and space in the upper world of the living and the lower world of the dead. When Hopis die they enter the lower world through the Sipapu in the Grand Canyon. The dead become clouds, hence rain, and their spirits return to this world as kachinas. Given the arid environment and Hopi dependence on subsistence agriculture, rainfall and fertility are of central importance:

> Everything, in Hopi belief, is dependent on rainfall, which, when combined with Mother Earth, is the essence of all things. . . . Through the combination of the rain with the earth and its transformation into corn, the blessings of the kachinas . . . become the essence of our bodies. . . .
>
> In a sense, all Hopi life is based on the ceremonies which assure vital equilibrium, both social and individual, and conciliate the supernatural powers in order to obtain rain, good harvests, good health and peace.[36]

The supernatural powers include the sun, gods of germination and death, Spider Woman, Dawn Woman, the Twin War Gods, and about three hundred named kachinas.

There is an annual ceremonial cycle controlled by the position of the sun and a lunar calendar. Each village has its own cycle: there is no central "ritual clearinghouse," although the sequence is generally the same in the various villages. The cycle consists of two major periods, centered on masked, and then unmasked, ceremonies. The masked, or kachina, period begins after winter solstice and continues until sometime after summer solstice, after the end of planting in the fields. The unmasked period begins with the Snake-Antelope and Flute ceremonies, held in alternate years in each village. There are then "social dances," such as the Butterfly Dance, followed by ceremonies of the women's societies, then the men's societies, and finally Soyal, which marks the winter solstice. The cycle then begins again.

The kachina cycle includes many ceremonies and dances in the kivas; beginning in April there are public kachina dances. The kachinas are said to live on the San Francisco Mountains west-southwest of Hopi, and at various other sacred places. At the start of the cycle, each kiva is ceremonially "opened" so the kachinas can symbolically emerge from the sipapus. From then, until the "Home Dance" in July, kachinas are said to be in and around the villages: "They . . . come often . . . to bring the rain, bless the village, bestow their gifts, and gladden the hearts of people with songs and dances."[37] There are many different kachinas. Some appear each year in specific ceremonies; others appear now and then; new kachinas are added; old ones fade away.

"Kachina dolls" are carved wooden figures of specific kachinas traditionally given to young girls so that they may learn their names and characteristics. As Fewkes began learning about kachina ceremonies, he also learned about the dolls. During his 1899–1900 visit, Fewkes gave several Hopi men paper, pencils, inks, and colored paints and asked them to make drawings of kachinas. They produced a number of drawings that were critiqued by those knowledgeable about kachinas, their masks, and their regalia. This led to the production of more drawings and additional critiques. The drawings were then used as the basis for discussions about the kachina ceremonies, the actions and meaning of specific kachinas, and the ritual cycle. Fewkes published an extended discussion of the kachina ceremonial cycle, as practiced on First Mesa, and sixty-three full-colored plates of the kachina drawings.[38]

Fewkes's study is regarded by some art historians as the beginning of modern Hopi painting on paper, but as J. J. Brody points out, there was a backlash to Fewkes collecting the paintings, and nothing more was done for two decades. When a young Hopi artist, Fred Kabotie, began painting in the 1920s, it was in the context of Santa Fe and its developing Indian art market (see Chapter 26), not at Hopi. On the other hand, Fewkes's study later came to be regarded by

kachina carvers and buyers as a kind of arbiter of "iconographic explanation and authenticity."[39]

Excavation and Restoration

As a result of the brief war between the United States and Spain in 1898, the United States suddenly acquired some external colonies—Puerto Rico and the Philippines. The acquisitions opened up new research possibilities for the Smithsonian Institution. In the Philippines, there were many new candidate tribes for the status of managed savages and the Smithsonian dispatched Frank Hilder to study some of them. Fewkes was able to develop an archaeological program in Puerto Rico and eastern Mexico, which occupied him for the first four or five years of the new century.[40]

In 1906 Congress passed the Antiquities Act, as well as legislation creating Mesa Verde National Park (see Chapter 22). The Antiquities Act gave the president authority to declare national monuments, and several Southwestern ruins were soon set aside, with Chaco Canyon being the first. The new park and monuments required excavation, study, ruin stabilization, and interpretation. Since creation of the National Park Service was a decade away, the Department of the Interior contracted with the Bureau of American Ethnology to do the work. Fewkes was the resident Southwestern archaeologist in the Bureau and he took on the task. From about 1906 until he retired, Fewkes was principally concerned with excavation and preservation of ruins at Mesa Verde and elsewhere. He had gotten involved with ruins preservation while still director of the Hemenway Expedition. During a "hurried tour among the ruins of the Salt River Valley" in April 1891, he fairly carefully studied Casa Grande and produced a report on its "present condition." When the Department of the Interior came calling, Fewkes could point to his article as a credential for developing a preservation program. His methods and interpretations of the sites he worked on have been questioned by later workers. But when he began there were no guidelines and he went ahead in his usual fashion. He repaired Casa Grande and numerous Mesa Verde ruins, and had much to do with getting Navajo, Hovenweep, and Wupatki national monuments created.[41]

In 1918 Fewkes became chief of the Bureau of American Ethnology when Frederick Webb Hodge resigned to move to the Museum of the American Indian (see Chapter 24). By most accounts, he was not an administrator or a leader. On his watch, the Bureau drifted, and staff members did largely as they pleased.[42] In 1914 and again in 1923, Fewkes was in Mimbres country in southwestern New Mexico. People had been digging in the ruins there—later called the Mimbres branch of the Mogollon culture—for several years, collecting the beautiful bowls with mythical anthropomorphic and zoomorphic designs on them (see Chapter 25). Fewkes's task was to amass a collection of the bowls for the Smithsonian before they all disappeared into private hands or the collections of other museums.[43] His last fieldwork was at Elden Pueblo near Flagstaff, Arizona, in 1925 and 1926. In failing health, he retired in January 1928 and died in May 1930.

Fewkes holds a central and complex place in the history of Southwestern anthropology. Along with Edgar Lee Hewett and Byron Cummings (see Chapters 21, 22), he was the last of the self-taught anthropologists to work in the Southwest. His archaeology was derided by the "new archaeologists" centering around Clark Wissler at the American Museum of Natural History in the 1910s and early 1920s, although never in print, given his position. His ethnography of the Hopi was inductive and factual, lacking the insights of Cushing and some later ethnographers. Yet he was able to acquire ritual information that most later ethnographers could not, as the Hopi became increasingly concerned about the sanctity and privacy of their ceremonies and moved to exclude Anglos from them.

CHAPTER 15

Bandelier, Bancroft, and Bolton

THE HISTORY of Indian, Hispanic, and Anglo activities and interrelationships has always been an integral part of Southwestern anthropology. Spanish historians from Sahagún to Clavigero contributed much to what was known, or thought to be known, from the mid-1500s through the 1780s. William Robertson, Alexander von Humboldt, and William H. Prescott drew on those sources, as well as archival materials in Mexico and Spain, in writing their own histories. By the 1820s key Spanish documents were being published, such as the compilations of Henri Ternaux-Compans. These were used by Albert Gallatin, E. G. Squier, and others to discuss Southwestern Indian ethnography and Indian-Hispanic relations and test the veracity of the Aztec and Toltec migration legends.

Modern Southwestern historiography, history, and ethnohistory began in the works of two remarkably dissimilar individuals—Adolph Bandelier and Hubert Howe Bancroft. They were succeeded in the early

1900s by the first academically trained historian to focus on the greater Southwest, Herbert Eugene Bolton. Bolton, his students, and his students' students have dominated "Spanish Borderlands" studies for a century.

Bandelier in the Southwest

On August 20, 1880, Adolph Bandelier boarded a train for Santa Fe and began keeping a *Journal* in which he recorded his life and Southwestern researches for the next twelve years.[1] When he arrived he found a town of just over sixty-six hundred people. The Atchison, Topeka and Santa Fe Railway had reached a point a few miles south (later to be called Lamy) the previous February, and a municipal gas system was being installed. Santa Fe was about to enter the nineteenth century.[2]

Bandelier soon became acquainted with a number of people who would be of help to him. Among them were Archbishop John B. Lamy (see Chapter 28) and General Lew Wallace, the territorial governor and former Civil War hero. Wallace's principal achievement as governor seems to have been helping settle the infamous 1869–1880 "Lincoln County War," an "out-of-door theatrical production of huge proportions," as one historian put it, between contending factions of cattlemen and their hired gunslingers, in which William Bonney, "Billy the Kid," played a role much magnified by the media.[3] Wallace also completed and published his famous novel *Ben Hur, A Tale of the Christ,* which sold an astounding 300,000 copies in its first ten years. Wallace's wife, Susan Elston Wallace, published *The Land of the Pueblos* in 1888, reflecting her not overly happy years in New Mexico. As she wrote to her son: "General Sherman was right. We should have another war with Old Mexico to make her take back New Mexico."[4]

Bandelier made arrangements with two Santa Fe photographers, George C. Bennett and William Henry Brown, who operated a studio on the west side of the plaza from 1880 to 1883. Bennett did most of Bandelier's field photography, especially at Acoma, at Cochiti, and in Frijoles Canyon. George Ben Wittick (see Chapter 28), who also had a studio in Santa Fe in 1880 in partnership with R. W. Russell, accompanied Bandelier at various times as well.[5]

On August 28, 1880, Bandelier arrived at the ruins of Pecos Pueblo (Fig. 15.1). He was forty years old, short, stocky, and somewhat pale, with piercing eyes and a high forehead topped by a swatch of black hair. He eagerly began measuring the ruins and collecting artifacts. It was the long-dreamed-of beginning of his new career in the Southwest and Mexico. The touring public knows his name from Bandelier National Monument, created in 1916. Many visitors to New Mexico buy his novel, *The Delight Makers,* set in Frijoles Canyon (now encompassed within the Monument).[6] It has been a constant seller in Southwestern book stores for many years, although few bought it when it came out in 1890, to Bandelier's grief, since he was, as always, on the edge of financial disaster.

Although Bandelier kept up some contact with John Wesley Powell and the Bureau of Ethnology, he pursued his own course. He visited Frank Hamilton Cushing at Zuni for two weeks in 1883, and they got on famously, but did not then work together.[7] He professed to have little use for what James Stevenson was doing: "These surveys of Major Powell's are really ludicrous. I have but to be grateful, personally, to the gentlemen connected with them, but it is absolutely ridiculous. Not one of Mr. Stevenson's party knows a word of Spanish,—they travel from Pueblo to Pueblo in carriages, with all the apparel of

15.1. Adolph Bandelier at Pecos, probably September 3, 1880. Photograph by George C. Bennett. Courtesy of the Museum of New Mexico Photographic Archives.

comfort, and spend (besides the salaries) $1500—in four months."[8]

Bandelier had written to Morgan: "the key to the aboriginal history of Mexico and Central America lies between the City of Mexico and the southern part of Colorado."[9] He envisioned a grandiose geographic, archaeological, and archival survey, beginning in the Southwest and ending in Mexico City to test Morgan's ideas. One part of the survey would be "to follow the supposed tracks of the Mexican [Aztec] tribe to the 'Casas Grandes' . . . and finally to Michhuacan [*sic*]."[10] Presumably he would find the historical "key" along the way. The survey remained a goal, at least as late as 1885, but happened only in part.

Bandelier held that good research required the localized, intensive, long term commitment that Powell espoused. But, in fact, his fieldwork was superficial. His itinerary for the period 1880 to 1885 is that of a scholarly hummingbird flitting from archival, to archaeological, to pueblo "flowers," sipping a bit from each. In fact, the task Bandelier set for himself was impossible; it has yet to be fully accomplished by the legions of scholars who came after him.

In 1880, Bandelier made a hasty survey of Pecos ruins, then spent about two weeks at Santo Domingo Pueblo. The elders were content to use him as a "scrivener" for some council meetings, but when he began asking questions about traditional life and beliefs, they forced him out. Then, as now, Santo Domingo guards its traditional life jealously from outside eyes and ears. Bandelier was received more hospitably at Cochiti, where he spent several weeks.[11] He made his first visit to Canyon de los Frijoles; he was enchanted with it and the Cochitis' tales of their ancestors' doings there, some of which he incorporated into *The Delight Makers*.

Bandelier was back in Illinois by Christmas 1880, intending to return to New Mexico in a few weeks. But the AIA executive committee had agreed with Allen Thorndike Rice, editor of *The North American Review,* and Pierre Lorillard to have Bandelier join the Charnay expedition in Mexico, as a sort of back-up scholar. Désiré Charnay (1828–1915) was a

French explorer-scholar whose explorations of Mexico, southern South America, Java, and Australia were supported by the French government, beginning in 1857.[12]

Charnay returned to Mexico in 1880 to dig at Tula and in Maya ruins, again sponsored by the French government, but also Pierre Lorillard and Allen Rice. Lorillard, of French descent, was a well-known New York tobacco magnate, sportsman, and breeder of fine racehorses. He and Rice felt that there ought to be an American representative on the expedition; they consulted with Norton who agreed to send Bandelier.[13]

Bandelier arrived in Mexico City on March 2, 1881, just in time to say goodbye to Charnay who had contracted a fever and was returning to France. He remained in Mexico for several months, visiting Teotihuacán, Monte Alban, Mitla, and the great Aztec pyramid at Cholula, and becoming acquainted with the eminent Mexican scholar and bibliographer Joaquín García Icazbalceta. In Cholula, Bandelier met the local priest, Father José Vincente Campos. The two had many conversations about antiquities, native peoples, and Catholic doctrine. On July 31, 1881, Bandelier was secretly baptized into the Catholic Church, with García Icazbalceta as his godfather. The reasons for his conversion were complex. Given his ambiguity toward his father and his Protestant background, perhaps it was partly filial protest. Given his intense desire to carry on his researches, he apparently thought that being a Catholic would make access to church archives easier. He did not tell his wife or his father of his conversion until October 1882. He knew that Morgan was opposed to Catholicism; the latter's death in 1881 resolved the problem. In a letter to Norton, Bandelier hinted that his work would be facilitated because "I have acquired a foothold here of greater importance than you can think, and which I will *tell* you, although I cannot *write* it. It is a most powerful lever, better than any protection."[14] Bandelier's conversion did stand him in good stead later in New Mexico.

Bandelier returned to his home in Highland, Illinois, in the fall of 1881 to write up his Mexican materials.[15] In mid-March 1882, accompanied by Josephine, he returned to Santa Fe and plunged into another round of quick trips to pueblos and ruins. He set out on horseback in January 1883, first to the Salinas region, then westward through Isleta, Laguna, and Acoma to Zuni. There he met Cushing, and spent two weeks "in the most pleasant and profitable manner imaginable." Bandelier and Cushing thought each other to be capital fellows.[16] From Zuni, Bandelier wandered southward through the Mogollon Mountains along the New Mexico-Arizona border.

At Fort Apache, Bandelier met Sergeant Will Barnes, the post telegraph operator. Barnes later reminisced that he and Bandelier were sitting one day in the telegraph room and the line was open. Messages began going back and forth between Whipple Barracks, at Prescott, and Fort Bowie, near the Mexican border. The message from Whipple Barracks said that Bandelier had been reported killed by Apaches, and the commandant at Bowie was ordered to verify his death and recover the body. With his enthusiastic approval, Barnes telegraphed Whipple Barracks, the Archaeological Institute in Boston, and Josephine in Highland that Bandelier was alive and well at Fort Apache. Bandelier wrote several letters humorously denying his demise; like Mark Twain and John Wesley Powell, he was able to say that reports of his death were greatly exaggerated.[17] He ended the trip with visits to Casa Grande and other ruins in the Gila and Salt River drainage.

The following October Bandelier explored the Mimbres Valley; then in February 1884 he started from Tucson, crossed the border into Mexico, and headed into the Sierra Madre. The officers at Fort Huachuca warned him of danger since Geronimo and his band of Apaches were in the region. Bandelier traveled with others whenever possible for safety through portions of northern Sonora and Chihuahua. He spent nearly a month studying and recording Casas Grandes, although he seemingly did not understand its full importance as a major trading center and possible link between the Southwest and the Mexican cultures to the south. Nor, according to his biogra-

phers, did he really grasp the overall importance of northern Mexican archaeology, seeing it as of little interest, thus turning Anglo eyes toward archaeology north of the border.[18] He did not continue on to Mexico City, as planned, traveling no farther than about 150 miles below the border. He was back in Illinois by mid-July 1884. By then he had learned that the AIA was in financial straits and had voted to terminate his support at the end of the year.

After consulting with Norton and Putnam in Boston, and lecturing in several eastern cities, Bandelier traveled to Europe. In Germany he called on Adolph Bastian, then the grand old man of German ethnology, and on Rudolph Virchow.[19] But his major purpose was to discuss money matters with the Swiss creditors of the family bank in Illinois. The bank and the other family businesses were in financial trouble in the shaky economic climate of the mid-1880s. In April 1885 there was a run on the bank, and it closed its doors. Father Bandelier had left town two days previously, ostensibly to visit the New Orleans Exposition; instead, he fled to Venezuela for three years. Adolph, even though he was not a partner in the bank, was arrested, apparently as a sufficient surrogate for his father in the eyes of angry depositors. Fraud charges were preferred against him and his brother-in-law, Maurice Huegy, who was an officer of the bank. The morning of the arraignment, Maurice committed suicide. Bandelier refused bail and was sent to jail, although he seems to have spent the night as a guest in the home of the sheriff in Edwardsville. The next day friends signed his bail bond, and he was released.[20] He immediately left for Santa Fe. The summer was spent visiting pueblos and surveying ruins in northern New Mexico, far from the debacle of the failed bank. The case against Bandelier was ultimately quashed, but his name was anathema in Highland and he moved permanently to Santa Fe. There, he continued his peregrinations among pueblos and ruins despite his perilous financial status.

In the *Sixth Annual Report* of the AIA there is a long laudatory summary of Bandelier's work and notice of his termination: applause and accolades as he is being pushed out the door. The summary ends with the hope that the Institute will be able to publish the final reports of his explorations; "inasmuch as so large a proportion of what the society has already expended upon the investigation of American antiquities has gone to defray the expenses of these very journeyings, it would seem unreasonable that the results thus acquired should be lost to science." The next sentence reveals the Institute's real interests: "While the work described in the preceding statement has been done in America, work still more brilliant in result and still more striking in character has been accomplished in the Old World." That is, excavations at the Greek city of Assos, including "the restoration of its famous temple, a monument of the highest interest in the history of Doric architecture."[21] In the eyes of Charles Eliot Norton and his compatriots, there was no comparison between the splendor of a Classical Greek temple and the adobe and stone of Acoma, Zuni, or Casa Grande.

The report also announced the Institute's reorganization, which would later have implications for Southwestern archaeology. The Institute had been "founded mainly by the efforts of individuals in Boston and its vicinity," who expected support from elsewhere that had not been forthcoming. Yet interest in archaeology was growing nationally. This led the Institute "to fear lest independent societies might be formed in various places, whose efforts would suffer from lack of union and mutual understanding and support." Not wanting to lose control, the Bostonians reorganized the Institute as a structure of "affiliated societies," with Boston as "the mother society" and units in Baltimore and New York.[22]

Meanwhile, Bandelier had to support his family and continue his work. His financial situation was never firm until his death in 1914. As historian Mark Harvey says, "Unfortunately, none of his employers paid him well or offered him a secure living. So Bandelier came to resemble Mozart: while he complained constantly about his financial woes he did not allow material considerations to prevent him from undertaking the work he loved, or from producing a staggering amount of written material."[23] He scraped by selling articles to German and American popular publications and writing eighty-six articles for the *Catholic Encyclopedia*.[24] By May 1886 he had finished his novel, but it did not appear until 1890, in German as *Die Koshare*, and in English as *The Delight Makers*. It was not a success.

In October 1886 matters improved somewhat. December 31, 1887, and January 1, 1888, would be the fiftieth anniversaries of Pope Leo XIII's ordination and first Mass. A Golden Jubilee was planned by the Catholic Church. Archbishop J. B. Salpointe of Santa Fe commissioned Bandelier to write a history of the Spanish missions in the Southwest as part of New Mexico's present to the pope. Bandelier produced a 1,400-foolscap-page manuscript, "Histoire de la colonisation et des missions de Sonora, Chihuahua, Nouveau-Mexique et Arizona jusqu'à l'année 1700," illustrated with 388 watercolor sketches, 96 photographs, 7 blueprints, and 11 maps. All this did not reach the Vatican until perhaps March 1888; it is unclear if the pontiff ever saw the gift. The manuscript later disappeared within the recesses of the Vatican archives, to be rediscovered only in 1964. A catalog of the illustrations and representative samples were published in 1969, and excerpts from the manuscript in 1988.[25] Also in October 1886, Cushing hired Bandelier as historiographer for the Hemenway Expedition. This required handcopying books and documents in libraries in Mexico City and the eastern United States to provide an "accessible archive" for the expedition (see Chapter 13).[26]

Bandelier's Later Years

Support from the Hemenway Expedition ceased in 1889. The AIA again picked up Bandelier's salary to enable him to finish his *Final Report*. But by 1892, with *The Delight Makers* generating few royalties and the *Final Report* finished, Bandelier was chafing at a perceived lack of recognition of his work and decided to move on. Accompanied by Charles Lummis, he made an extended trip to the East Coast. He succeeded in gaining support from the New York financier and philanthropist Henry Villard to collect artifacts and do archival work in South America. Lummis would accompany him for a time as photographer.

Bandelier returned to Santa Fe in mid-May, gathered up Josephine, and entrained for San Francisco. On June 6, 1892, they sailed for South America. On May 20, Bandelier had written in his journal that "the greatest undertaking of my life is done, and, so far, successfully. . . . With this I close this journal."[27] His Southwestern sojourn was over, but his engagement with Spanish America continued for the rest of his life.

Bandelier remained in South America until 1903. Josephine died in December 1892 in Lima, Peru. The Bandeliers had been boarding with a Swiss family named Ritter. A year after Josephine's death, Bandelier married Fanny Ritter, a vivacious and energetic woman some years his junior. She became a partner in his researches and a scholar in her own right.[28] In 1894, Villard deposited the collections Bandelier had made for him in the American Museum of Natural History, in New York City, and that institution assumed his salary. In 1903 Bandelier and Fanny moved to New York. After a publication dispute with the museum in 1906, he moved to the Hispanic Society of America, recently created by Archer Huntington (see Chapter 18). He later received some support from the School of American Archaeology in Santa Fe; his final employer was the Carnegie Institution of Washington.[29]

Although he was failing in both health and eyesight, Bandelier and Fanny traveled to Mexico in 1912, and in October 1913 to Spain. Bandelier died in Seville on March 18, 1914, and was buried there. Fanny completed the planned work before returning to the United States. She continued her own scholarly work, in straitened circumstances. Her major project in later years was the publication of a volume of the Spanish glosses in Sahagún's great Florentine Codex. She died November 10, 1936.[30]

In March 1977, Bandelier's remains were returned to Santa Fe. In 1980 they were cremated, and on October 6, one week shy of the one hundredth anniversary of his first visit to Canyon de los Frijoles, the ashes were scattered in the canyon.[31] He thus symbolically returned to one place in the Southwest that particularly delighted him. It was in Frijoles Canyon that the people of Cochiti Pueblo first told him about their life and past; it was there that he set his novel *The Delight Makers.* In 1916 the canyon and adjacent lands were set aside as Bandelier National Monument.

Bandelier's Contribution

But what of Bandelier's achievements? His *Final Report* ends: "Further than what I have intimated in these pages, I do not venture to go for the present. The time has not yet come when positive conclusions in regard to the ancient history of the Southwest can be formulated." New methods were being developed, he thought, and "these may lead to the solution of questions which at present are perhaps not even clearly defined."[32] His accomplishments reflect Morgan's major methodological principle: "the facts of American archaeology must be studied ethnologically; i.e., from the institutions, usages, and mode of life of the existing Indian tribes."[33]

Bandelier effectively operationalized Morgan's method. There first needed to be a survey of the living Pueblos, especially of house types, given Morgan's argument that they reflect social forms. Second, surveys and catalogs of published and archival resources were required, followed by assessments of their validity as historic documents. The documents could then be used to develop histories of Spanish-Indian interactions. The earliest historic documents could also be used to define an "ethnographic present"—a description of a pueblo or tribe on a hypothetical "day before" the first contact between the Indians and the Spanish.

The next step was to begin detailed ethnographic studies of the institutions, usages, and customs of specific pueblos and tribes by direct observation, as Cushing was doing. The questions were: How have groups changed since the hypothetical ethnographic present? How can ethnographic data be used analogically to interpret archaeological finds? This is an extension of Morgan's assertion that the "facts of . . . archaeology must be determined ethnologically." Finally, ethnographic data, as such, are useful in answering the general question of commensurability: what is the range and variation of human behavior? While Bandelier did not conduct his activities quite in the way the questions are here stated, he was a pioneering practitioner of all the approaches during his years in the Southwest.

He began, quite properly, with Pecos Pueblo. The direct historical approach requires the accurate *placement of places*—how do you know that the site on which you're standing is the *same place* as the one described in a three-hundred-year-old Spanish journal? There is also the general problem of synonymy, first clearly posed by Lewis Cass in 1826. Bandelier and other Anglos knew (and know) Pecos Pueblo as "Pecos." But is it the *same place* as Alvarado's and Coronado's "Ci-cuic," "Ci-cui-ye," or "A-cuique," as described by Castañeda? Yes, as it turns out, but Bandelier, as historian, had to verify that through close scrutiny of a range of documents.[34] The general problem has continued ever since. Whole ethnohistorical and archaeological careers have been spent correlating specific places "on the ground" with names and descriptions in historical records and oral legends. Bandelier's hosts at Cochiti told him of their ancestral homes in and near Frijoles Canyon, and he went there with them to verify what they said. But he also studied all the extant Spanish documents relating to Cochiti to round out his understanding of the places, the peoples, and their histories.

After his survey through Arizona and northern Mexico, visiting some four hundred sites altogether, Bandelier felt that he had arrived at a valid classification of archaeological sites. He distinguished between many-storied "communal" houses and one-storied "small houses." Small houses were widely scattered as isolated occurrences or "in groups forming villages." The communal houses were concentrated and included the modern Pueblo villages. Different forms of pottery were associated with different house types.

During one of his early visits to Pecos, Bandelier observed the buried remains of a small house associated with corrugated and finely painted pottery eroding from an arroyo cut. In a stratum above were other remains and a type of pottery later called "glazeware" widely found on sites with large communal houses. He rightly concluded that the small house type and associated pottery were older than the communal house type and glazeware. On the basis of these observations, he defined three relative time periods: Pre-Traditional, with corrugated and indented pottery as its most conspicuous index artifact, and Traditional and Documentary, both with index glazeware, the latter dating after 1540. This is perhaps the first application of the principles of stratigraphy and index artifacts in Southwestern archaeology.[35]

Bandelier thus produced the first archaeological theory in the Southwest using stratigraphy, classification, and association—together with data from Pueblo traditions. Or, put another way, his was the first anthropological model of how the Pueblos came to be as they are. It also just happened to parallel Morgan's theory of a progression from huts to small houses to communal houses.[36] Bandelier's work anticipated by thirty years the methods of the "New Archaeology" in the Southwest (see Chapter 24). His use of Pueblo oral tradition in relation to the location of ruins and culture history was used more immediately by Frank Hamilton Cushing and Jesse Walter Fewkes of the Hemenway Expedition (see Chapters 13, 14).

Bandelier summed up the accumulated results of his decade of Southwestern labor in his 914-page *Final Report*. There is a long chapter on the "Ethnographic Condition of the Southwest in the Sixteenth Century" (the "ethnographic present") followed by a section on "Present Condition of the Indian Tribes," drawing on the Spanish archival and published sources. He focuses on key issues in Pueblo cultural history: matters of "place" and linguistic affiliation. That is, how many pueblos were there in the 1500s and 1600s, where were they located, how were they linked linguistically, what were they named, how many people lived there, and when were they abandoned?[37]

Bandelier also began documentary research into the demographic history of pueblos during the period after 1540. In 1598, Oñate named 134 pueblos in present-day New Mexico and Arizona, although Bandelier thought the number "must be considerably reduced," due to names "being repeated in more than one idiom" (once again the problem of synonymy). By 1679, 46 are mentioned; by 1846, there were 18 in the Rio Grande drainage, plus Acoma, Laguna, Zuni, and the Hopi villages to the west.[38]

The second part of Bandelier's report contains an extensive survey of antiquities, organized generally by river drainage basin. Here he draws on the documentary record and his own surveys and observations. His descriptions bristle with conjectures and ideas to be tested. Some of his conjectures were taken up by later students and made into specialties.

First, he recognized water as the controlling factor in sedentary occupation of the Southwest. Second, "the small house is probably the germ from which the larger structures [of central Mexico] were evolved. . . . in other words, . . . there was a gradual transformation going on in ancient aboriginal architecture in the direction from north to south. [But] "I by no means desire to convey the idea that such a transition must necessarily imply a common origin of the tribes that inhabited the different regions in former times."[39]

He notes the utility of pottery as cultural and time markers: "the decorations of the pottery all over the Southwest bear a marked resemblance. The symbols are the same on the San Juan River in Northwestern New Mexico as in the Sierra Madre and at Casas Grandes."[40] Since Bandelier's day, Southwestern pottery symbols have been analyzed from many perspectives: as cultural markers, religious iconography, formal art, and for what might be learned about cognitive psychology.[41]

Bandelier also discussed the use of language relationships in culture history: "Modern science recognizes language as the surest ethnographic criterion. It is admitted that when two tribes geographically separated speak the same tongue, or dialects of it, they must have sprung from the same original stock." Given this, Bandelier was intrigued, as others have been since, by the culture-history implications of the mixed distribution of the various Tanoan-speaking and Keresan-speaking pueblos (Map 3). He had no ready explanation and warned against facile generalizations based solely on language distributions.[42]

So too, while myths and traditions sometimes afford means of tracing historical relationships, he warns against the uncritical acceptance of migration legends, such as those of Aztec and Toltec migrations from the Southwest. Uncritical acceptance leads to "misconceptions and honest exaggerations, which have become deeply engrafted upon ethnological thought and have cast a veil over ethnological facts."[43]

Finally, Bandelier can be credited as a real (and dogged) pioneer in historiography and archival research. It is difficult for those who take copying machines and computer scanners for granted to comprehend the long hours, days, and weeks he and others spent painstakingly handcopying manuscripts and books in poorly lit archives and libraries. For example, he copied 341 separate documents, totaling well over one thousand pages for the Hemenway Expedition. These were exhibited in Madrid in 1892. Bandelier's right hand sometimes became so painful he could not write at all for long periods. The advent, in the 1880s, of a practical new word processor called the typewriter helped him some, but did not resolve the problem.[44]

It was Bandelier who began a systematic assessment of local and regional archives, such as those in the Palace of the Governors in Santa Fe, and various church and mission archives in New Mexico, Arizona, and northern Mexico, calling attention to their importance for what would later become "Borderlands" history. But when university-trained historians turned their attention to that history, Bandelier was given short shrift. Historian Herbert Eugene Bolton, who invented Borderlands studies (see below), made no mention of Bandelier in his 1911 programmatic call for cataloging and assessing Spanish archives; nor is Bandelier mentioned as a predecessor in Bolton's intellectual biography. Not too much need be made of this, except to note that Bandelier was self-taught, not university trained, hence not of the academic fraternity.

H. H. Bancroft, Assembly-Line Historian

One of the manias that strikes certain individuals and sometimes has beneficent results for humankind is compulsive bibliophilia. Many persons since the invention of writing systems have been passionately enthralled by books, be they cuneiform tablets, papyrus or vellum scrolls, or bound volumes, and amass them by the thousands.

Book and manuscript collections have often become the basis of major research libraries. The Harley manuscripts and Sir John Cotton's library was the basis for the British Museum Library; Thomas Jefferson's collection was the nucleus of the Library of Congress. The private collections of J. P. Morgan, Henry E. Huntington, John Carter Brown, James Lenox (the New York Public Library) were each kernels of major libraries. The great 140,000-volume collection of Robert Hoe, III, of New York, auctioned in 1911–12, added substantially to the libraries of Morgan, Huntington, Peter Widener, and Henry Folger.[45]

Another collector who not only founded a great library but laid the groundwork for western history was Hubert Howe Bancroft (1832–1918) (Fig. 15.2).[46] At age sixteen he began clerking in brother-in-law George Derby's bookstore in Buffalo, New York. In 1852 Derby sent him to California to sell books, on the theory that Forty-niners needed more than mining pans, picks, and bad whiskey. After various difficulties, Bancroft established H. H. Bancroft & Co., Bookseller, in San Francisco in 1856. By 1859 the company had expanded into all areas of publishing, printing, and bookbinding on a large scale. It was later called A. L. Bancroft & Company, for Hubert's brother who was a partner.

Bancroft contracted a severe case of bibliophilia.

15.2. Hubert Howe Bancroft, 1880s. Photograph by Bradley and Rulofson, San Francisco. Courtesy of the California Historical Society.

His area of interest was the American West, broadly conceived. The top floor of his business building was given over to his collection, but it was not fireproof, so another stand-alone fireproof structure was built nearby. He later said he moved from bibliopolist (bookseller) to bibliophile, and from bibliomania to bibliogenesis (book writer). He toyed with the idea of an encyclopedia of the West, but settled on a comprehensive history of the Pacific States, plus the West Coast north to Alaska, the Great Basin, and the Southwest, all of Mexico and southward to Panama.

The history, thirty-nine large volumes, was done on a production-line basis by copyists, readers, abstractors, and writers, as many as fifty at once, working six-day weeks and ten-hour days. Over thirty thousand books were indexed, outlined, and abstracted. The most talented of the assistants organized the abstracted materials, reached their own conclusions, and wrote the texts. Bancroft's editing of each volume varied from none to considerable, depending on the subject.

Bancroft's original intention was to focus on the history of Europeans and Euroamericans, but he soon realized that he must deal with the Indian peoples as well. He and his staff set out systematically. They used an "ethnographic present" approach, or as Bancroft put it, descriptions of Indian peoples "as they were first seen by Europeans along the several paths of discovery . . . in all their native glory, and before the withering hand of civilization was laid upon them."[47] Histories of Indian-White relations were placed in the various state and country volumes.

Five eight-hundred-page volumes were produced, collectively called *Native Races* and subtitled I. *Wild Tribes*; II. *Civilized Nations*; III. *Myths and Languages*; IV. *Antiquities*; V. *Primitive History*. They added nothing new to the ethnography or archaeology of Indian peoples, but they did synthesize and interpret most of the printed sources in English, Spanish, French, and German through about 1870. The major authors of the volumes were Henry L. Oak, William Nemos, a nom de plume, Albert Goldschmidt, and T. Arundel-Harcourt, another pen name.[48]

In the Southwest section of the *Antiquities* volume, written by Oak, the ruins of northern Sonora and Chihuahua are described, with special attention to Casas Grandes, drawing on Kino, Bartlett, and Emory. The extensive chapter on antiquities of Arizona and New Mexico uses the various reports of the Topographical Engineers and related publications, such as Möllhausen.

The archaeology review is systematic, by river basin. For the Rio Grande Valley, Oak drew on descriptions of historic pueblos, asserting that existing descriptions of ruins indicate they were constructed in the same manner. He shows an awareness of the major research questions as they were framed in the 1860s and early 1870s. He rightly asserts that given available information, dating the ruins is almost impossible. He rejects any connection between the Southwest and either the Maya or the Aztecs on the basis of dissimilarities in "material relics." Finally, he suggests that a large-scale population decline in the pueblos began at least a century before the arrival of the Spanish and "has continued uninterruptedly down to the present time until only a mere remnant in the Rio Grande and Moqui towns is left." The causes of the decline were a combination of "warlike and predatory tribes like the Apaches," and environmental change, probably drought. The southern pueblos, along the Gila River, were abandoned first and some of them moved to "kindred northern tribes." But other, more northerly areas were abandoned as well. Then, "[a]t last came the crowning curse of a foreign civilization, which has well nigh extinguished an aboriginal culture more interesting and admirable, if not in all respects more advanced, than any other in North America."[49]

Bancroft's method for surveying the cultures and societies of historic "wild tribes" was to define several major geographical areas and describe social and cultural similarities among the tribes within each area. For western North America, his areas are: Hyperboreans, north of the Fifty-fifth parallel; Columbians, between the Fifty-fifth and Forty-second parallels; Californians, including the Great Basin; New Mexicans, which includes the tribes of the Lower Colorado River, Baja California, northern Mexico, and west Texas. The plan is similar to "culture area" schemes formulated in the 1890s by Otis T. Mason and William Henry Holmes of the Smithsonian Institution (see Chapter 18).

For each area the climate, topography, and biogeography are described. There is a list of the principal tribes, with descriptions of one or two in detail, moving from physical characteristics to dress, dwellings, food, weapons and tools, government, social organization, amusements, medical practices, and religion. Variations in manners and customs of other tribes, as well as tribal boundaries, are discussed.

The "New Mexican" area has four "families:"

"*Apaches* . . . all the roaming savage tribes"; *Pueblos*, including the "non-nomadic" Pimas, Maricopas, and Papagos; *Lower Californians*; and *Northern Mexicans*. The "Apache family" includes the "Comanches" of west Texas, and others in northeastern Mexico, "by language allied to the Shoshone [now Uto-Aztecan] family." There is also the Apache "nation," grouping those linguistically related to the Navajo with tribes of the Lower Colorado River and the "Pai" tribes of northwestern Arizona.[50] Conflating Yuman-speaking tribes with Apachean speakers as "Apache" was a common error in nineteenth-century Arizona.

There is a general deprecatory description of physical types, dress, ornamentation, houses, foods, and weapons. Navajo blankets are described approvingly, but reflecting the confusion of available sources the author is unclear whether the Navajos learned to weave from the Mexicans or the Pueblos. Many stereotypes and prejudices are peddled, reflecting both the biases of the sources and Bancroft and his staff. For example: "Courtship is simple and brief; the wooer pays for his bride and takes her home. Every man may have all the wives he can buy. . . . Government they have none." And: "As usual, parturition is easy," reflecting the Anglo assumption that "wild savages," being closer to nature, give birth with little difficulty. "Difficult" childbirths were reserved for cultured Victorian women, whose problems often stemmed from the absurd obstetrics practices of the time. Finally, "The Apaches, . . . though naturally lazy like all savages, are in their industries extremely active— their industries being theft and murder, . . . in which they display consummate cunning, treachery and cruelty. . . . [Conversely] the Navajos and Mojaves . . . [are] more peaceful, . . . Professional thievery is not countenanced; . . . They are ever ready to redeem their pledged word, and never shrink from the faithful performance of a contract. They are brave and intelligent and possess much natural common sense."[51]

The "Pueblos" include Pimas and Papagos. The Hopi are described in some detail. There is an assertion that no linguistic relationship exists between the Hopi and the Aztecs, hence they cannot be otherwise

related. The Pueblos are "industrious, honest, and peace-loving . . . Sobriety may be ranked among their virtues, as drunkenness only forms a part of certain religious festivals, and in their gambling they are the most moderate of barbarians."[52] In Oak's eyes, the Pueblos would be more or less acceptable substitute-Anglos.

There is a single volume on mythology and languages, with 550 pages devoted to myths and 250 to languages. The mélange of myths is arranged topically, including cosmology, animal fables, gods and other supernaturals, and the hereafter. Scattered within the topical headings are a dozen or so myths from the Southwest.

In the section on languages, apparently written by Goldschmidt, there is a classification of all the Indian groups from Alaska to Panama, and discussions of a variety of specific linguistic problems. The section provides an interesting overview of the state of linguistic classification in the years immediately preceding Powell taking up the problem. For the Southwest, the classification is in general accord with that shown in the Prologue.

A central theme running through the discussions of Pueblo, Shoshone, and northern Mexican languages is the Aztec connection. Like Gallatin before them, Bancroft and staff thought that linguistics provides the best proof of a link between Southwestern groups and the Aztecs. The Keresan and Tanoan languages "are none of them cognate with any spoken in Mexico. . . . Certain faint traces of Aztec" are detected "in all Shoshone idioms," but not enough to demonstrate any form of Aztec connection; "on the contrary, the evidence of language is all on the other side."[53]

Bancroft was an astute marketer. He curried favorable reviews and written endorsements from prominent pundits, especially those around Harvard, to help launch his series. It was a common practice in nineteenth-century publishing to sell expensive sets of books by subscription and door-to-door canvassing in well-to-do neighborhoods. Bancroft's agents sold about six thousand sets of the thirty-nine volumes for from 175 dollars to 390 dollars per set, depending on bindings; the gross was over 1 million dollars. Each set contains 30,700-plus printed pages, or about 20 million words—an average production of about 1 million words per year over the life of the project, a staggering achievement by any measure.[54]

Bancroft versus Morgan

When the *Civilized Nations* volume appeared in 1876, one of the noncomplimentary reviews was Lewis Henry Morgan's famous "Montezuma's Dinner" in *The North American Review*. Arundel-Harcourt, who wrote the volume, used hundreds of extracts from Spanish sources in a five-hundred-page description of Aztec government, palaces and households, class structure, education, marriage, concubinage, childbirth, feasts and festivals, foodstuffs, dress, commerce, warfare, laws and courts, arts and manufactures, architecture, and medicine.[55] While disparaging Spanish exaggeration, Harcourt nonetheless depicted in dazzling detail the glories of the Aztec "empire," as described by eye-witnesses at the time of the conquest and early Spanish historians.

There is a rhapsodic description of Montezuma's great palace, with hundreds of rooms, huge halls and courtyards, walls faced with polished slabs of marble, jasper, obsidian, and hung with exquisite featherwork tapestries. Montezuma dwelt in the inner sanctum of the palace, served by six hundred lords and clothed in gossamerlike garments worn once and then discarded. He took tidbits from over three hundred dishes served on golden plates that also were discarded after one use.[56]

This fanciful description of the Aztec empire and all its purported wonders infuriated Morgan; he denied essentially all of it. Tenochtitlán, he said, was simply "the pueblo of Mexico." The "lords" were "Aztec chiefs"; the "palace" merely a "large joint-tenement house occupied, Indian fashion, by Montezuma and his fellow-householders." Not only were the first Spanish eyewitnesses wrong, they greatly magnified what they saw in the telling and retelling. The Aztecs were no different than the Iroquois and

the Southwestern Pueblos in all respects because all three were in the Middle Stage of Barbarism. Middle Stage barbarians were organized, acted like, and had cultures like the Iroquois—period. Morgan roundly excoriates Bancroft for his perfidious mis-descriptions of the Aztecs: "This work . . . is in entire harmony with the body of works on Spanish America. It embodies their extravagances, their exaggerations, their absurdities, and runs beyond them in fervor of imagination and in recklessness of statement." Bancroft "*ought* to have known" that all Indian tribes in America were organized as Morgan said they were, none being above the stage of Middle Barbarism. The review drips with sarcasm and a detailed "refuting" of Bancroft's excesses. It is interesting that Morgan had no real knowledge of the Spanish American sources; he relied on Adolph Bandelier for textual ammunition, some of which Bandelier got wrong.[57]

Bancroft fired back in a widely circulated pamphlet, which he, rather than Arundel-Harcourt, apparently wrote. He refutes many of Morgan's assertions, making a strong point that if Morgan had, in fact, *read* any of the Spanish sources, he would have known that the Aztecs were far beyond any stage of barbarism. "Compare," he said, Aztec civilization "with the European civilization or semi-civilization of [the early 1500s] on the one hand, and with the savagism of the Iroquois and Ojibways on the other, and then judge which of the two it most resembled."[58]

The exchange is a marvelous instance of dog-in-the-manger intellectual hyperbole: much heat, very little light. Both Bancroft and Morgan took comfort in righteous umbrage, and Adolph Bandelier felt some elation in having supported his hero. After a century of detailed archaeological and ethnohistorical research, it is clear that neither Bancroft nor Morgan were right. Tenochtitlán was far more than a Southwestern or Iroquoian village filled with "joint tenement" houses. And while quite magnificent, Montezuma's palace was far less than the fevered imaginations of the Spanish writers made it.

Bancroft's *Native Races* is particularly important in American popular history and anthropology. Like many book sets purchased for decoration or fashion, the hefty tomes may or may not have been read. If they were, their readers gained most of what they would ever know about the ethnography of Indian peoples in western North America, the Southwest and Mesoamerica, as well as Indian-Eurocolonial history. Bancroft's and his staff's views on Indian and Hispanic histories and cultures thus became part of the "common knowledge" of American culture. It was those views, together with ideas generated in popular magazines and books, such as the idea of the "Cliff Dwellers" (see Chapters 5, 16), which helped shape the anthropological image of the Southwest in the 1880s and beyond.

Finally, as with the collections of the several other bibliomaniacs previously mentioned, Hubert Howe Bancroft's collection became a great research library. His fireproof, stand-alone library building and its contents survived the San Francisco earthquake and fire of 1906. By then he had finally sold the library to the University of California across the bay in Berkeley.[59] As the great collection, now known as the Bancroft Library, was being ferried across the bay to the university in 1906 and 1907, a young and highly ambitious history professor from the University of Texas was busily making inventories of the archives of Mexico, following in the footsteps of Adolph Bandelier. He later became professor of history and director of the Bancroft Library at the University of California, building the library into an even greater resource. His name was Herbert Eugene Bolton.

Bolton and the Borderlands

Herbert Eugene Bolton (1870–1953) (Fig. 15.3) invented "Borderlands" studies.[60] "Borderlands" refers to the region of North America across which the borders of the Spanish empire shifted vis-à-vis French, British, and Anglo territories after 1540. Bolton took his undergraduate degree at the University of Wisconsin and wrote a Master's thesis there under Frederick Jackson Turner. Turner's famous paper on the implications of the closing of the American frontier, pub-

lished in 1896, set an agenda for three generations of American historical scholarship and debate.[61] Bolton took his doctorate at the University of Pennsylvania, but always regarded himself as a "Turner Man." In 1901, he became an assistant professor at the University of Texas and soon discovered the archival riches of Mexico. Frederick Webb Hodge got Bolton involved in the *Handbook of North American Indians* (see Chapter 12). He wrote about one hundred short articles on Texas and Louisiana tribes for the *Handbook*.[62]

In 1906, the Department of Historical Research of the Carnegie Institution of Washington hired Bolton

15.3. Herbert Eugene Bolton, ca. 1905. Courtesy of the Bancroft Library, University of California, Berkeley.

to develop a *Guide to Mexican Archival Materials Relevant to United States History.*[63] Andrew Carnegie established the Institution to encourage and support basic research in numerous fields. The Institution's historians saw their basic task as surveying all original materials, printed and unprinted, relating to the history of the United States. The focus was on unpublished archival materials, especially outside the United States. By 1906 work had begun in Britain and Spain; France and Mexico were next up. "Mexico, because . . . no archive of similar importance to our history has been so little explored."[64] Bolton spent most of 1907 in Mexico. When his *Guide* was published in 1913, it established him as a major scholar in Mexican-U.S. history. He moved in 1911 to the University of California as a professor, and for twenty-five years was director of the Bancroft Library. Bolton directed 104 doctoral dissertations and some 350 Master's theses, a phenomenal output for an entire university department, let alone a single individual.

In 1907 in Mexico City, Bolton discovered the journals of Father Eusebio Francisco Kino, the peripatetic Jesuit missionary to Pimería Alta (see Prologue) and published it in 1919. Bolton literally set out on Kino's trail from his birthplace in the Italian Alps to his various missions in Sonora and Arizona. "By water on ocean liner and Gulf steamer, by land on horseback, on muleback, by team, by automobile, and *á pie,* by air in a monoplane, I have retraced nearly all his endless trails and identified most of his campsites and water holes—all this in an endeavour to see Kino's world as Kino saw it."[65]

For Bolton, archives were not enough. He could not write about Kino's, or later, Coronado's or Escalante's and Domínguez's travels unless he had followed their footsteps over the ground.[66] In this, he was very much like his great colleagues at California the geographer Carl Sauer and anthropologist A. L. Kroeber: one must go "into the field" to properly understand where others had been and what they did.[67]

Bolton defined a new field of study, the "Spanish Borderlands." One theme of the present book is the setting of research agendas. Once an agenda is set,

various "worker bees" pursue the problem or problems it defines and compile great quantities of relevant information. This continues until someone sets a new agenda, and the worker bees buzz off in the new direction. Bolton's guide set the Spanish Borderlands agenda and two of his papers gave direction to it: "The Mission as a Frontier Institution in the Spanish-American Colonies" (1916) and "Defensive Spanish Expansion and the Significance of the Borderlands" (1930). The mission and the presidio were the key institutions that the Spanish used to try to control their enormously lengthy northern frontier.[68]

While Bolton and his students took the lead in finding, translating, and publishing documents relating to the history of Spanish activities and Spanish-Indian relations, others were involved. The Bureau of American Ethnology in 1896 published Castañeda's report of the Coronado expedition of 1540–42, translated and edited by George Parker Winship (1871–1952), a project he undertook during his senior year at Harvard. Winship was one of the great bibliophiles of the twentieth century who was centrally involved in the development of the great library at Brown University and of the Widener and Houghton libraries at Harvard.[69]

J. Franklin Jameson was the director of the Department of Historical Research at the Carnegie Institution and managing editor of the *American Historical Review* from 1905 to 1929.[70] He started an "Original Narratives of Early American History" series. Frederick Webb Hodge and T. H. Lewis, in 1907, edited a volume of documents relating to early Spanish exploration from 1528–1543. Bolton followed, in 1916, with documents dating between 1542 and 1706.[71]

Thus, by 1920 one of the projects Adolph Bandelier had begun—finding, evaluating, translating, editing, and publishing Southwestern archival materials was well established. "Borderlands" studies have continued robustly ever since. Bolton's students, led by the Jesuit scholar John Bannon, have greatly expanded the knowledge base.[72] Published documents made possible such classic studies of Indian-Eurocolonial relations as Edward Spicer's *Cycles of Conquest,*

Elizabeth John's *Storms Brewed in Other Men's Worlds,* and John Kessell's *Kiva, Cross and Crown.*[73] At the turn of the millennium, the field is very much alive and well in the hands of David Weber and his students and associates.[74] When Adolph Bandelier, seeking to satisfy his intellectual curiosity and escape the drudgery of the family business, arrived in New Mexico to start a new life at age forty, he began a field of study that a century later has expanded far beyond his wildest dreams. His spirit, perhaps hovering over Frijoles Canyon, should be well pleased with what his successors have done.

CHAPTER 16

The Wetherills and Nordenskiöld

I N 1880, a family of Quakers, Benjamin Kite Wetherill, his wife Marion, daughter Anna, and sons
Richard, Benjamin Alfred ("Al"), John, Clayton, and
Winslow (Fig. 16.1) arrived in the Mancos Valley in
southwestern Colorado.[1] In 1882 they homesteaded
160 acres along the Mancos River—and named their
place the Alamo Ranch. By 1891 they owned 1,000
acres, 300 of them under cultivation, and had a "com-
modious" house and numerous ranch buildings. The
great cliffs of the Mesa Verde provide a breathtaking
backdrop to the west and south, as do the San Juan
Mountains to the north and northeast.

The Wetherills ran their cattle in Mancos Canyon
and atop the Mesa Verde. They saw small archaeological ruins and began exploring for others, having heard
stories of "big ruins, high, high in the rocks" of the
mesa.[2] Others were exploring the Mesa Verde as well.
A prospector, S. E. Osborn, may have seen Cliff Palace
in the winter of 1883–84, and Al Wetherill glimpsed it
from the canyon bottom below sometime after that.

16.1. Wetherill Brothers. Left to right: Benjamin Alfred,
Winslow, Richard, Clayton, John. Courtesy of the
Colorado Historical Society.

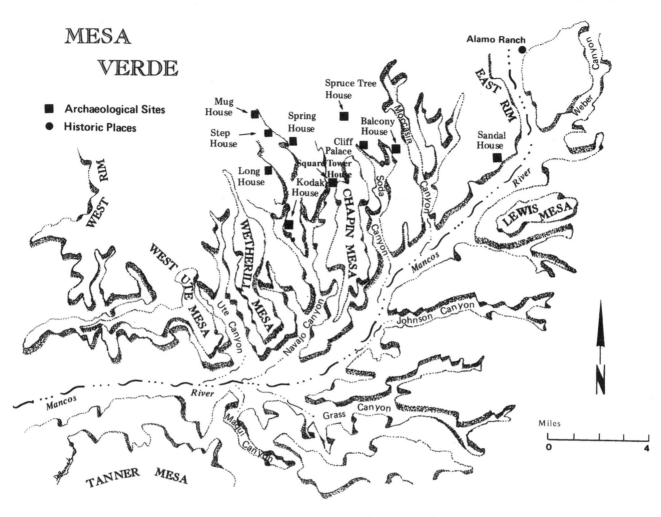

MESA
VERDE

■ Archaeological Sites
● Historic Places

Mancos ●

Alamo Ranch

9. Major Ruins on the Mesa Verde

The "official" discovery is credited to Richard Wetherill and Charles Mason, Anna Wetherill's husband, while hunting cattle on Chapin Mesa on a snowy December day in 1888. They saw a large ruin, made their way to it, gazed wondrously, and decided on the name Cliff Palace. That day and next they also found and named Spruce Tree House and Square Tower House (Map 9).[3]

During the next several months, Richard and John Wetherill and three locals formed a loose partnership

and began digging for artifacts in the ruins. Their collection was exhibited in the spring of 1889 in Durango, Pueblo, and Denver. The newly formed Colorado Historical Society bought the collection for three thousand dollars.[4]

The Wetherills continued to explore and dig. They located and named most of the known major ruins and many of the minor ones, over 180 in all. They turned a barn into a makeshift museum. In 1891 their collection was purchased by Charles D. Hazzard for the H. Jay Smith Exploring Company of Illinois; Smith also purchased a similar collection from C. M. Viets of Cortez, Colorado. Both were exhibited in Minneapolis in 1892 and at the Chicago world's fair in 1893 (see Chapter 17). In 1892, the Wetherills made a third collection, this time for the state of Colorado. That collection also was exhibited at the Chicago fair, with Richard in attendance for some weeks to answer questions.

The Wetherill ranch carried a heavy mortgage, and income from cattle and wheat sales was not enough to meet the payments. Additional income came from selling artifacts and guiding tourists to see the ruins. Between 1889 and 1901, approximately one thousand people visited the ranch and were taken to see the cliff dwellings.[5] Among the tourists in the summers of 1889 and 1890 was Frederick H. Chapin, a well-to-do partner in a large pharmaceutical firm in Connecticut, who began visiting the Rockies in the 1880s. His article "Cliff Dwellings of the Mancos Canyon" appeared in 1890 in both a mountaineering journal and the *American Antiquarian and Oriental Journal*. These apparently were among the first national notices of Cliff Palace and other major Mesa Verde ruins. Chapin then wrote a sketch of Spanish and Anglo explorations in the Southwest, threw in some observations on the Rockies, expanded his "Cliff Dwellings . . . " paper and published *The Land of the Cliff Dwellers* in 1892.[6] It sold widely and attracted national attention to the Mesa Verde.

Gustaf Nordenskiöld

Another tourist was a twenty-three-year-old Swede, Gustaf Nils Adolf Nordenskiöld (1868–1895) (Fig. 16.2), scion of a prominent Finnish-Swedish family.[7] His father, Nils Adolf Erik Nordenskiöld, was head of the mineralogical department of the Swedish Royal Academy of Science and a famed Arctic explorer. In 1878–80 he led an expedition on the ship *Vega* through the Northeast Passage across the top of the Eurasian continent. He was awarded the title of baron by King Oscar II. A tall column topped with a golden

16.2. Gustav Nordenskiöld. Courtesy of Gustaf O. Arrhenius.

sculptured sailing ship commemorating the voyage stands on the grounds of the Swedish National Museum of Natural History in Stockholm. Gustaf's mother, Anna Maria Mannerheim, was the aunt of Carl Gustaf Mannerheim, field marshal and president of Finland. Gustaf's younger brother, Nils Erland Nordenskiöld, made significant ethnographic studies in Central and South America.[8]

Gustaf took his bachelor's degree in geology and chemistry at the University of Uppsala, but soon thereafter contracted tuberculosis. He decided to go on a world tour to regain his health. He arrived in Denver in late June 1891. There, he met schoolteacher and natural historian, Alice Eastwood. She had made extensive botanical surveys in the Four Corners region, knew the Wetherill family well, and gave Nordenskiöld a letter of introduction. He arrived at the Alamo Ranch on July 2.[9]

Nordenskiöld's Excavations

Nordenskiöld intended "to stay only about a week in the neighborhood of Mancos, to which place I had come as a tourist in order to see the objects of interest in the vicinity." But the Wetherills showed him "some of the most remarkable and largest ruins," which "inspired me with a strong desire to examine them more closely."[10] The Wetherills were for hire to help out.

Nordenskiöld began cautiously. He, Richard, and Al excavated a small site in Cliff (Soda) Canyon containing about eight rooms and two small kivas. There were lots of artifacts: sherds, stone axes, projectile points, and a variety of perishables including maize ears, cotton cloth, and yucca sandals. Nordenskiöld was entranced. He decided to begin extensive excavations in sites on Wetherill's (now Wetherill) Mesa, which Nordenskiöld named for the family, while at the same time naming Chapin's (now Chapin) Mesa for Frederick H. Chapin. John Wetherill and two locals assisted. For two months, Nordenskiöld and crew excavated in Mug House, Long House, Kodak House, Step House, and Spring House (Map 9).

In early September, Nordenskiöld and Clayton Wetherill delivered seven boxes and two barrels of artifacts to the Durango railroad station to be shipped to the Swedish consulate in New York and then on to Stockholm. They were back in Durango on September 16 with a second shipment, to find the first had been seized and impounded and that Nordenskiöld was being roundly vilified by Durango and Denver newspapers. The following day he was arrested on a warrant sworn out by the local Indian agent. He posted a thousand-dollar bond and was released.

The incident is significant in the history of attempts within the United States to prevent archaeological remains from being looted or leaving the country. A motivating factor in the Bureau of Ethnology's Mound Builders program of the 1880s was to prevent foreign museums from acquiring all the good specimens. Nordenskiöld's troubles arose partly because the boundaries of the Ute Indian Reservation, drawn in 1868 but often realigned thereafter, were ill defined across the Mesa Verde. During his excavations, Nordenskiöld became concerned that he was on reservation land, although the Wetherills thought not. Nonetheless, in August Nordenskiöld went to Durango to confer with the Indian agent. Through a lawyer, he received a letter from the agent stating "that as long as the buildings [in the sites] were not damaged, no one would disturb him in his work."

Considerable negative sentiment had built up about commercial exploitation of archaeological sites by the Wetherills. The idea that Nordenskiöld's collection would go out of the United States exacerbated feelings and led to the seizure of the artifacts. When Nordenskiöld appeared in Durango District Court, the complaints were dismissed. There were no state or federal laws prohibiting the excavation of archaeological objects on public lands, nor their removal from Colorado or from the United States. The collections were released and shipped to Sweden. Although he had won legally, Nordenskiöld, the soul of propriety, ceased excavations and devoted his remaining time to mapping and photographing sites.

The ruckus highlighted the issue of "exploitation" of the Cliff Dweller ruins. That Nordenskiöld would produce a model scientific report could not have been foreseen by the local citizens, nor would it have mattered much. The issue was not scientific knowledge, but exploitation of the sites by someone associated with the Wetherills, and the export of the artifacts out of Colorado and out of the country. Indeed, the Indian agent brought similar charges against the Wetherills, but they too were dismissed. On February 29, 1892, Richard Wetherill wrote to Nordenskiöld: "no witnesses appeared when our trial come off [sic] and so we are at liberty to continue as before till the 'Locoed Agent' sees fit to make a fuss again. We have applied to the proper authorities for permission to do this kind of work regardless of the local croaking element."[11] In time, the "local croaking element" would help support the passage of the Antiquities Act and establishment of Mesa Verde National Park, both in 1906 (see Chapter 22).

To Hopi and the Grand Canyon

After his Mesa Verde work, Nordenskiöld made a horseback trip to the Hopi Mesas and the Grand Canyon. He wanted to see the Hopi, whom he took to be the descendants of the Cliff Dwellers, and discover if the Grand Canyon was as spectacular as everyone said. He set out on November 4, 1891, with Al Wetherill and a pack-horse wrangler. They arrived on November 15 and stayed at a store at the foot of First Mesa operated by Tom Polacca (see Chapter 14). Nordenskiöld wrote: "Tom was a remarkable man. During his business trips among the different tribes . . . he had learned to speak many languages: English, Spanish, Navajo and several other Indian tongues."[12]

The party witnessed a dance at First Mesa; Nordenskiöld traded for various artifacts there and at Oraibi, then turned toward the Grand Canyon. After three days in the canyon bottom, just below the confluence of the Little Colorado, they headed for Mancos, several hundred bitterly cold miles away. Bedraggled, lice infested, barely shod, and nearly broke (they had two dollars), they struggled back on jaded horses across a snowy landscape, arriving at the Wetherill ranch on December 21, 1891.

Nordenskiöld returned to Sweden in early 1892 and immediately began writing up his excavation materials. The following summer he exhibited, by invitation, some fifty Mesa Verde artifacts and a number of his photographs at the 1892 Columbian Exposition in Madrid (see Chapter 17). There he met Mary Hemenway, accompanied by Jesse Walter Fewkes, who were exhibiting portions of the Thomas Keam collection that Fewkes had earlier purchased. Nordenskiöld and Mrs. Hemenway apparently hit it off, because she gave him twenty-three vessels from her collection and set aside others for the Swedish Ethnographic Museum. Nordenskiöld received the Order of Isabella Católica for his exhibit.[13]

The Cliff Dwellers of the Mesa Verde was published in 1893 in Swedish and soon after in English. At about the same time, Nordenskiöld married Anna Smitt. They moved into an apartment in Stockholm decorated with Hopi baskets and Nordenskiöld's photographs of Mesa Verde. Nordenskiöld kept in close touch with the Wetherills. His tuberculosis flared again in the spring of 1894, but he recovered somewhat by summer and was able to read a paper at the International Congress of Americanists, held in Stockholm (see below). He relapsed and by June 1895 was very weak. His father and Anna took him to the Jamtland mountains, where he had previously done much better. He died just as the train pulled into the station at Morsil. He was buried in the family plot at Vasterljunga; he was twenty-six.[14]

Nordenskiöld's *Cliff Dwellers* is unanimously regarded as the first scientific monograph in Southwestern archaeology. It set a standard not equaled for nearly twenty years. For most ruins, Nordenskiöld provides detailed discussions of setting, overall architecture, masonry details, and photographs and plan maps. In addition, he presents a detailed discussion of the pottery, using William Henry Holmes's classification of James Stevenson's general Southwestern collection as a base. The beginnings of systematic analysis of Southwestern ceramics lie in Holmes's and Nordenskiöld's work.[15]

Nordenskiöld was meticulous in his description of stone, bone, textile, and vegetal artifacts. His rationale for such close description is what makes his work so valuable: "Though in some respects the implements, weapons, and textile fabrics found in the cliff-dwellings are . . . a less interesting subject of description than the pottery, they are still of great importance. *Only by their aid we can picture to ourselves the life of the people.*"[16] In other words, it is the close analysis of *all* artifacts from archaeological sites and the careful noting of their *provenience* and relationships that makes a scientific understanding of past lifeways possible. The artifacts are *not* merely curios, Nordenskiöld is saying; they are *documents* which, when carefully analyzed, compared, and understood, collectively tell us about past lifeways. Nordenskiöld's analyses do just that. He compares several types of maize with modern Indian corn. He discusses how the fields were situated and irrigated on the mesa tops and (probably) on terraced slopes. He recognized and describes a large reservoir (Mummy Lake) on Chapin Mesa. He also notes beans, squashes, gourds, cotton cloth, and yucca fiber, with the latter used for textiles and cordage. He notes turkey droppings and bone implements made of turkey bones and speculates on the domestication of the bird. His descriptions of stone and bone implements are equally detailed and comparative.

In using ethnographic analogy, Nordenskiöld demonstrates a proper scientific caution. In Long House he found seven sticks, each broken on one end and carved on the other similar to sticks placed by Hopis in "secluded sacrificial shrines." The Long House and Hopi examples are, in form, the same. Therefore, the objects could have been "originally used in the same manner. But still it is not certain that among the cliff-dwellers these articles had merely a religious purpose."[17] Nordenskiöld's report is still used a century later. He was clearly enthralled by the Southwest, its archaeology and native peoples. Had he lived, he may well have returned and applied his sharp eye and analytical mind to further archaeological studies.

The Wetherills in Grand Gulch

Another early visitor to the Wetherill ranch was Charles B. Lang, a photographer and great enthusiast of the Four Corners region.[18] In 1890 Lang and a companion made their way into the "San Juan Triangle"— the area of southeastern Utah formed by the confluence of the San Juan and Colorado rivers (Map 7).

Lang's principal destination was Grand Gulch, where he took a number of photographs of rockshelters and cliff dwellings. The gulch is well named; it is a sinuous seventy-five miles from its headwaters to the San Juan River, with vertical or overhanging canyon walls and limited and difficult access. Lang's and others' reports of "untouched" cliff dwellings drew Charles McLoyd, an erstwhile Wetherill partner, and Charles Graham there in January 1891. They dug for three months, amassing a large collection that they exhibited in Durango. It was bought for three thou-

sand dollars by the Reverend Mr. Charles H. Green, a retired Baptist minister. Green financed another collecting trip by McLoyd to Grand Gulch in June 1891. Clearly there was money to be made in the "relics" business. McLoyd was back in the canyons of the Triangle in the winters of 1891–92 and 1892–93, accompanied on the second trip by John Wetherill.[19]

In the summer of 1893, Charles Lang and Richard Wetherill went into the photography business, advertising "Cliff Dwelling Views a Specialty!" It is unclear how much business they conducted, although photographs exist with a "Lang & Wetherill" stamp on them.[20] In September 1893, Richard went to the Chicago world's fair to be on hand to answer questions about the Mesa Verde collection exhibited there as part of the Colorado state exhibit. The collection was in the anthropology building (see Chapter 17). He was visited there by the Hyde brothers.

In the summer of 1892 Frederick E. Hyde, a prominent New York physician, and his two teen-age sons, Talbot and Fred, Jr., visited Alamo Ranch. They were headed west on the first leg of a world tour and stopped to see the Cliff Dwellings. The senior Hyde, together with the Duc de Loubat, for several years supported excavations in the Trenton gravels in the Delaware Valley in the futile search for American "Paleolithic Man"—a project overseen by Frederic Ward Putnam (see Chapter 18). The boys were later students of Putnam's at Harvard.[21] They were the grandsons and heirs of Benjamin Babbitt, founder of the soap company that produced BaBo. When Babbitt died in 1896, he left the two in quite comfortable circumstances. In Chicago, the Hyde brothers and Richard Wetherill agreed to form the Hyde Exploring Expedition to explore the Grand Gulch region. The agreement marked a new phase in Wetherill's archaeological experience. He probably had learned a fair amount about keeping site records and making maps and photographs from the youthful, but precise, Nordenskiöld. He may also have learned more about the importance of records and provenience data from the anthropologists frequenting the anthropological building at the fair. Most importantly, the Hyde brothers specified that all collections, notes, and records were to be deposited in the American Museum of Natural History in New York.

In December 1893, Richard, brothers Al and John, Charles Lang, and four others headed for the Grand Gulch region (Map 7). It was a mild winter and they stayed four months.[22] Early on, in Cottonwood Wash, Richard first noticed that there was an older cultural stratum beneath the Cliff Dweller level. On December 23, 1893, he wrote to Talbot Hyde:

> Our success has passed all expectations. . . . In the cave we are now working we have taken 28 skeletons . . . and curious to tell, and a thing that will surprise the archaeologists of the country, is the fact of our finding them at a depth of five and six feet in a cave in which there are cliff dwellings and we find the bodies *under the ruins, three feet below any cliff dweller sign.* They are a different race from anything I have ever seen. They had feather cloth and baskets, *no pottery*—six of the bodies had stone spearheads in them.[23]

Later, Wetherill referred to these new people as "basket people." They seemed to be both physically and culturally different than the Cliff Dwellers: they made many excellent baskets, but no pottery; they had no bows and arrows, but spears and *atlatls*; their sandals were different. Their heads were not flattened in the back like Cliff Dwellers, and "they are a larger race than the cliff dwellers." Wetherill suggested that Hyde pick a name, since he, Richard, had previously named the "Cliff Dwellers" (though this was not true). In response, Talbot Hyde suggested "Basket Makers." Richard didn't like the name, but it stuck; it was shortened in the 1940s to "Basketmakers."[24]

Wetherill sent some twelve hundred specimens to the American Museum of Natural History. He also sent several of the Basket Maker skulls to Nordenskiöld, together with information about his various excavations. Nordenskiöld's paper at the 1894 meeting of the International Congress of Americanists, noted above, summarized his own Cliff Dwellers work, as well as the Wetherills' finds in Grand Gulch.[25]

Nordenskiöld's paper, and especially the comments on it that followed, were very important over the next half-century in how Basket Maker and Cliff Dweller "populations" and relationships were interpreted. The comments were by Eduard Seler, the great nineteenth-century student of Mesoamerican cultures; Gustaf Retzius, a Swedish physical anthropologist and son of Anders Retzius, who in 1840 had coined the terms *dolichocephalic* and *brachycephalic*; and Rudolph Virchow, the famous German anatomist and archenemy of Darwinian evolution. Seler called attention to artifacts similar to Cliff Dweller artifacts from cave sites in northern Mexico, suggesting perhaps "an expansion of the 'cliff-dwellers' tribes toward the south."[26]

Retzius had analyzed the skulls brought back by Nordenskiöld and made a quick examination of those sent by Wetherill. He notes that the new skulls are not artificially deformed and are "exquisitely dolichocephalic, whereas skulls which were found otherwise in the cliff-dwellings, . . . certainly were brachycephalic for the most part. . . . It now seems . . . that these [new] skulls emanate from an even older period of this odd group of dwellings." Retzius notes that fifty years earlier his father proposed that there were two "groups" of North American Indians, "dolichocephals and brachycephals." However, subsequent work shows some "mixture of skull-types in some Indian tribes." He then defers to "Rudolph Virchow, the greatest living authority in this area," on the issue of whether or not the Grand Gulch skulls were artificially deformed. Virchow rambles on at length about how infant skulls may become deformed, but he comes to no substantive conclusion about the Basket Maker-Cliff Dweller problem.[27]

The issue of cranial deformation was critically important, given nineteenth-century assumptions about skull form as a primary "indicator" of racial and subracial types. Artificial deformation of dolichocephalics (long heads) could produce brachycephalics (round heads). If both round-headed and long-headed skulls were found, and the "rounded-headed-ness" was assumed to be natural, then two "races," or "sub-races" would be inferred. If, however, the round-headed-ness was due to artificial deformation, then only one, long-headed, population would be assumed, with individuals' skulls having been artificially deformed after birth. The long-head versus round-head issue remained in Southwestern archaeology for decades. In fact, Wetherill's Basket Maker "long heads," and his recognition that the long-headed Basket Makers were stratigraphically *earlier than* the round-headed Cliff Dwellers provided the basis for it.[28]

The Wetherills in Tsegi Canyon

In January 1895, Richard and Al Wetherill and Charlie Mason headed south across the San Juan River, skirted the east side of Monument Valley and entered Tsegi Canyon by way of Marsh Pass (Map 7). They camped in the main stem of Tsegi, where they noted a number of archaeological sites, but nothing really took their eye. A mule broke its hobbles and wandered away. Richard pursued the miscreant upcanyon, rounded a bend, looked up, and saw the ruin of Kiet Siel.

The setting of Kiet Siel in many ways is more spectacular than that of Cliff Palace. There are three structures up to three stories high. The rust red of the Navajo sandstone cliff rises high above the great arch of the rockshelter. Great tapestrylike streaks of manganese mark the routes of cascades down the cliff face when the rains come. From inside the rockshelter the falling water blurs the view of the cliffs across the canyon, adding a sense of unreality to the setting.

The Wetherills dug in Kiet Siel and elsewhere in Tsegi Canyon. The finds were rich. Richard wrote to Talbot Hyde: "We dug from one burial mound 400 pieces of pottery—very fine. . . . this is by all odds the finest collection of pottery I have seen."[29] Perhaps content with such a fine collection, or pressed for time, the Wetherills did not explore the Tsegi side canyons. Thus they missed the second great ruin, Betatakin. But John Wetherill would lead Byron Cummings, Neil Judd, and others there in 1909 (see Chapter 21).

In August 1895, Richard and Clayton Wetherill

were joined by T. Mitchell Prudden (see below), Herbert Cowing, and a local newsman, Muldoon Kelley, on a horseback trip to the Hopi Mesas to see the Snake Dance. They stayed with Tom Polacca. Cowing noted in his journal, "Our landlady makes the best pottery in town or in fact in any of the [Hopi] towns so far as I know."[30] This was Nampeyo, Tom Polacca's sister. Richard briefly met Jesse Walter Fewkes at some point during the dance at Walpi, but little else is known about the encounter. The group observed the ceremony, visited some of the other villages to trade, and headed back to Mancos.

"Proposal on the San Juan"

While Richard and the others were at the Snake Dance, a Quaker family, Sidney and Elizabeth Palmer, their eighteen-year-old daughter Marietta, and two younger children arrived at the Alamo Ranch.[31] The family owned a wheat farm in Burdett, Kansas, but were seldom there. For months at a time they traveled by wagon as far as Florida, and now, in 1895, to the Mancos Valley. They earned their way giving musical concerts and playing for dances in towns they visited. Their wagon, which Palmer designed, was fitted out for eating and sleeping. It also had cabinets for the various musical instruments and a photographic outfit. Sidney Palmer was much interested in both photography and archaeology, and had brought the family to see the ruins of the Mesa Verde.

When Richard Wetherill returned from the Snake Dance, he guided the Palmers to Cliff Palace and other ruins. The Palmers camped in Mancos Canyon for a couple of weeks; Richard visited often, mainly to see Marietta. During evenings around the campfire, talk turned to Chaco Canyon. A decade before, Palmer had tried to get there from Albuquerque, but had failed. Now the Palmer family and Richard decided to go.

In early October 1895, they set out and after six days' travel entered Chaco Canyon and camped in the shelter of Pueblo Bonito's back wall. For a very cold month, Wetherill and Palmer explored the canyon and

16.3. Frederic Ward Putnam at Chaco Canyon, 1899. Courtesy of the American Museum of Natural History.

the ruins as far east as Pueblo Pintado. Richard spent some time talking with the Navajos living nearby. He and Palmer dug in Pueblo Bonito and elsewhere. The finds piqued Richard's interest, and he wrote enthusiastically about them to the Hyde brothers.

In mid-November 1895, the group made their way to Jemez Pueblo, then to Cochiti and Santa Fe, and then turned south to Albuquerque and Socorro. From there they went west through the Mimbres country, down the Salt River and up the Verde Valley to explore Montezuma's Castle and other ruins. They then headed up Oak Creek Canyon to Flagstaff, then Tuba City, through Marsh Pass, thence to the San Juan River.

Richard and Marietta made a dangerous crossing of the river at a high water stage with the wagon floating and the mules swimming part of the time. On the far bank, Richard Wetherill, age thirty-seven, proposed to Marietta Palmer, age eighteen; she accepted.[32] It was now mid-April 1896. The archaeological-tour-by-wagon courtship had lasted nearly seven months. They parted company at Monticello, Utah, agreeing to marry that fall in California; they did so on December 12, 1896, in Sacramento. After a brief San Francisco honeymoon, they returned to Mancos.

Chaco Canyon

During the wagon tour, Richard had written in detail to the Hydes about Chaco Canyon and its archaeological potential. He and the Hydes had planned an expedition to the Marsh Pass region. But Richard's letters convinced the brothers that Chaco Canyon ought to be the location. Talbot Hyde wanted the expedition to be scientifically respectable and tried to persuade the venerable Frederic Ward Putnam to lead it. In 1894 Putnam had been appointed curator of anthropology at the American Museum of Natural History. He retained his curatorship at Harvard's Peabody Museum, and divided his time between the institutions (see Chapters 18, 19).

Putnam agreed to assume general oversight of the expedition, although he did not visit Chaco Canyon until 1899 (Fig. 16.3). He suggested his assistant at the American Museum, George Pepper, age twenty-three (Fig. 16.4). Hyde agreed to the appointment, perhaps because Pepper and he were the same age. Pepper arrived at the Alamo Ranch "with two cameras, a small trunk filled with stationery and notebooks, the kindly instructions of Professor Putnam, and his own determination to make a name for himself. . . . [H]e was

16.4. Hyde Expedition at Pueblo Bonito. Left to right: T. M. Prudden, George Pepper, Clayton Wetherill, Annie Wheeler (?) or Mary Phelps (?), baby Richard Wetherill II, Richard Wetherill, Marietta Wetherill. Courtesy of the American Museum of Natural History.

of slight frame, had a firm jaw and graceful, long-fingered hands. . . . His conversation was brisk, witty, and radiated optimism."[33]

George Hubbard Pepper (1873–1924) was born on Staten Island, New York. He was fascinated from boyhood by Indians and artifacts. After graduating from high school, he came into contact with Putnam and worked for several months in the Peabody Museum. In early 1896 Putnam arranged for his appointment as an assistant curator in the American Museum of Natural History. Pepper had never been to the West. His archaeological field experience consisted of collecting arrowheads as a youth on Staten Island. With these impressive credentials, he announced that he, not Richard, was in charge of the Hyde Expedition to Chaco Canyon.

Chaco Canyon, 1896 Season

In late April 1896, Richard Wetherill, George Pepper, Talbot Hyde, and three others set out from Mancos

for Chaco Canyon. Once there, a camp was established against the back wall of Pueblo Bonito (Fig. 16.4). Local Navajos were hired as laborers. Richard supervised excavations and ran the camp. Pepper observed, took notes, apparently cataloged artifacts, and complained mightily about having to sometimes do actual physical labor!

The search was for burials and associated grave goods. Two trash mounds associated with Pueblo Bonito were trenched, with few results. Operations were shifted across the canyon near Casa Rinconada and the Gap. Some thirty burials were found, but not the hoped-for treasure trove. Finally, attention was turned to Pueblo Bonito itself, and digging began in the north section of the ruin. A large cache of pottery vessels—114 jars and 22 bowls—were found near a kiva. Nearby were several high-status burials associated with effigy figures, carved wooden wands, and a basket covered with a 1,214 piece turquoise mosaic; it contained 2,150 disk-shaped turquoise beads, 152 small turquoise pendants, 22 large turquoise pendants, and

3,317 shell beads and pendants. By season's end some thirty-seven rooms had been cleared. A railroad freight car full of artifacts was shipped to the American Museum. Wetherill received 660 dollars for his season's work and said he lost money. There was friction between Wetherill and Pepper, and relations continued to be cool in the following years.[34]

Grand Gulch Again

When Richard Wetherill returned to Mancos, he heard a rumor from Charles Lang that the Field Columbian Museum of Chicago intended to send an expedition into the Grand Gulch area. He apparently felt that "his" territory was being invaded, and appealed to Talbot Hyde for funds to mount an immediate foray by the Hyde Exploring Expedition. Hyde was more sanguine and less territorial than Wetherill and declined. It turned out that the Field Museum was to explore elsewhere in the San Juan Triangle.

But an archaeological "angel" appeared at the Alamo Ranch in the person of a wealthy Harvard student, George Bowles, who was touring the Southwest with his tutor, C. E. Whitmore. Bowles agreed to fund a Grand Gulch expedition.[35] Wetherill then hastened off to Sacramento to marry Marietta. They returned to Mancos and immediately prepared for the Grand Gulch trip, which got underway in January 1897 (Fig. 16.5). The weather was bitterly cold and often stormy; travel was difficult. Ultimately, nine horses died, most in falls from the treacherous trails in and out of the canyon.

Wetherill concentrated on Basket Maker sites, digging in over thirty of them up and down the Gulch. He later split his party, sending a group to the vicinity of Navajo Mountain, and a second to Moqui Canyon, a tributary of the Colorado River. He led a third party into the Marsh Pass area, explored several ruins, and mapped and excavated further in Kiet Siel. The three groups finally rendezvoused at Marsh Pass. To

16.5. The Whitmore Exploring Expedition camp in Grand Gulch, 1897.
Left to right: Orian Buck, James Ethridge, George Hargrove, Levi Carson,
Marietta Wetherill, Teddy Whitmore, Charlie Mason, Hal Heaton.
Courtesy of the American Museum of Natural History.

add a final fillip of excitement and danger to their western trip, Bowles and Whitmore purportedly were kidnapped by some Navajos. They were held captive for four days atop Moqui Rock, a pinnacle with about one hundred square feet of flat space at the top, while a messenger rode frantically to Bluff City for a sack of several hundred silver dollars. The ransom was paid and the haggard captives released. Years later, Marietta Wetherill claimed that she and "Ben Bolton," one of the Whitmore-Bowles party, were kidnapped in Grand Gulch by Paiutes and held on a mesa top until Richard and Clayton Wetherill ransomed them for either fifteen hundred or nineteen hundred dollars and some horses. There is no record of a Ben Bolton with the Bowles-Whitmore party. On the other hand, there is no documentation of Bowles and Whitmore being kidnapped. Either way, it's a good yarn.[36]

The party returned to Alamo Ranch in April 1897. Bowles and Whitmore headed east and doubtless dined out for some time on their adventures in the wild Southwest. The expedition had recovered about two thousand artifacts, including numerous mummies. Talbot Hyde ultimately paid Bowles and Wetherill three thousand dollars for the collection and it was shipped to the American Museum. The collection and others from the Grand Gulch area remained largely unstudied until the 1990s.

Chaco Canyon, 1897 Season

Almost immediately after returning from Grand Gulch, Richard and Marietta prepared for a second season in Chaco Canyon. At some time during the season, the Navajo workers began calling Richard Wetherill "Anasazi"—he was, after all, digging up those whom the Navajo took to be "ancient ones"; they called Marietta "Asdzáni, Little Woman." Over time, Marietta developed good relations with the Navajo people. Her autobiography contains many stories, including one in which she and a woman were looking for dye plants on the mesa near Pueblo Alto and discovered the Chacoan road leading north from

the pueblo and other roads connecting to Pueblo Bonito and Chetro Ketl.[37]

Excavations were concentrated in Pueblo Bonito. Many rooms were cleared and artifacts recovered. Relations between Wetherill and Pepper continued to be cool. There was disagreement over excavation methods. In addition to loathing manual labor, Pepper was bored by having to keep proper financial records. Then too, Hyde was slow in keeping enough money in the bank in Durango. Supplies came from there; merchants were not happy about bounced checks and were constantly threatening to send the sheriff to collect.

Trading Post in Chaco Canyon

By October 1898, the Wetherills' financial troubles were reaching disastrous levels. The ranch was mortgaged to the "hubs of the last wagon," and many other debts had accumulated. The mortgage was finally foreclosed in 1902 and the ranch was sold at public auction. Richard decided to open a trading post in Chaco Canyon at Pueblo Bonito to serve the many Navajos in the area. He sent brothers Clayton and Al to Chaco to build the post. A small trading room was built against the rear wall of Pueblo Bonito; goods were stored inside some of the cleared rooms. Beams from the ruin were used in the roof. Business was brisk from the start.

In March 1898, Marietta Wetherill gave birth to a son. In early May, Richard, Marietta, infant son, and a nanny (Fig. 16.5) boarded a freight wagon and headed to Chaco Canyon. As soon as they arrived, Richard had a three-room structure built just to the west of Pueblo Bonito. One room was a large trading room, one was appropriated by Pepper, and one was for the Wetherills. Again, to the consternation of later archaeologists, beams from the Pueblo were "salvaged" and used in roof construction.

The trading post became part of the Hyde Exploring Expedition, with Wetherill as the managing, albeit minority, partner (he received 10 percent of the profits). Marietta did the trading most of the time, received on-the-job training in the "Trader Navajo" jargon and became an appreciative student of Navajo ways and ideas.[38] By 1899 the post was deep into the Navajo rug business.

By 1901 the Hyde Exploring Expedition's Indian trading enterprise had expanded to eight posts, a wholesale store in Albuquerque, and a retail store in New York City. There was also a dried-fruit processing plant and a harness shop in Farmington, New Mexico. In 1900, John and Louisa Wade Wetherill moved from Mancos to run the Ojo Alamo post north of Pueblo Bonito, the beginning of their long involvement in Indian trading.

Final Excavations at Pueblo Bonito

Wetherill and Pepper continued to excavate Pueblo Bonito in 1898 and 1899, but 1899 was the last season. In the eyes of the nascent professional archaeological community in the United States, and particularly in the eyes of Edgar Lee Hewett, by then president of New Mexico Normal University in Las Vegas (see Chapter 22), the Hyde Exploring Expedition, and particularly Richard Wetherill, were simply "professional pot hunters . . . vandalizing the ruins of the Chaco."[39] They had to be stopped, Hewett said, demanding a federal investigation, as did his fellow members of the Santa Fe Archaeological Society. J. Bradford Prince, governor of New Mexico Territory, added the weight of his office to the demands. Hewett had no more formal training in archaeology than did Wetherill and a lot less field experience, but he wanted to dig in Chaco Canyon. It took him twenty years to get there.

There were, in fact, two federal investigations in 1900 and 1901. Both exonerated the Hyde Exploring Expedition from charges of looting and selling artifacts, noting that the work was under the direction and sponsorship of the American Museum. But the political pressure was sufficient to lead the commissioner of the Public Lands Office, Binger Hermann,

to issue an order suspending further excavations. The order was made permanent in 1902.

In 1897, Warren K. Moorehead, editor of *The Archaeologist* magazine and head of the Archaeology Department at Ohio State University, had come to Chaco Canyon with a small party and dug in Pueblo Bonito elbow to elbow with the Hyde Expedition crew. Nothing could be done about it. Moorehead dug at various places in the Southwest over several years on behalf of several sponsors.[40] To prevent more of the same, in 1900 Wetherill filed a homestead entry on a 160-acre parcel that encompassed Pueblo Bonito, Pueblo del Arroyo, and Chetro Ketl, and the land on which the trading post was located. The second federal investigation determined that Wetherill had not satisfied the requirements of the Homestead Act and raised the suspicion that he was using the act to gain legal control of the ruins. In March 1902, the entry was suspended; Wetherill appealed. At about the same time, Talbot Hyde removed himself from active participation in the Hyde Exploring Expedition activities. He brought in a former Arizona cattleman and curio trader, J. W. Benham, as company manager. Benham seems to have systematically set about to push Wetherill out of the Hyde company affairs. He was apparently one source of the rumors that Wetherill continued to dig in Pueblo Bonito after the order to desist was issued. He strongly supported efforts by Hewett and the Santa Fe Archaeological Society to make Chaco Canyon a national park, since that would clearly put Wetherill out of business. By 1903 Benham had partly succeeded and Wetherill "was relieved of all connection with the company."[41] He did, however, retain ownership of the Pueblo Bonito post.

Wetherill's appeal of the suspension of his homestead entry was finally settled in his favor in April 1907. By agreement, he retained 113 acres, but none of the land on which the major ruins were located. But his entry was immediately protested, apparently by friends of Hewett, because the section contained coal deposits. Finally, in November 1912, matters were settled and a patent on the homestead was issued. By then Richard Wetherill had been dead for over two years.

Between 1902 and 1910, Wetherill built up a sizable ranching business, raising and trading horses and some cattle. He also had as many as five thousand sheep, most of them let to the Navajos on shares, grazing on the public domain for many miles around Chaco Canyon. In April 1903, William T. Shelton was appointed superintendent of the Navajo agency at Shiprock, New Mexico. According to Wetherill's biographer, Shelton took an intense dislike to him, and launched a venomous campaign to discredit him and drive him out of Chaco Canyon. The story is long and complex, unfolding in an atmosphere of mistrust and acrimony that finally involved a number of Navajos. On June 22, 1910, a young Navajo, Chiishch'ilin Biye, shot and killed Richard Wetherill. The subsequent trials, investigations, accusations, and counteraccusations served to thoroughly blacken Wetherill's name, at least officially. Chiishch'ilin Biye was convicted of voluntary manslaughter and served a three-year prison term. Paroled in 1915, he returned to the Chaco Canyon area and lived there until his death in 1950, his age approximately eighty. T. Mitchell Prudden, who had stuck with the Wetherills throughout the ordeal, tried to force an investigation of the whole matter by the Bureau of Indian Affairs. An investigation was conducted and all Bureau employees, including Shelton, were carefully exonerated before Prudden was notified that an investigation had been ordered.[42]

Richard Wetherill was thought to be rich. He died with $74.23 in the bank and about $10,000.00 in largely uncollectible debts owed him. Marietta and her five children managed to collect a few debts, but lost the Chaco Canyon ranch. Marietta, who said after Wetherill's murder, "I was a gypsy the rest of my life," moved several places and finally to Albuquerque, where she died in 1954. Her ashes were placed in Richard's grave behind Pueblo Bonito, in Chaco Canyon. When he was killed, the *Mancos Times* carried a brief obituary notice of the death of "Richard Witherill" [*sic*]. A front-page story in the same issue of the newspaper reported that Congress had appropri-

ated twenty thousand dollars to build a road from Mancos to the new Mesa Verde National Park. None of the Wetherills were mentioned in the story.[43]

The Hyde Expedition and Pueblo Bonito

The campaign to get a federal antiquities act passed, and to protect both Mesa Verde and Chaco Canyon centered, in part, on discrediting Richard Wetherill as a "professional pot hunter," who "vandalized" the great ruins of the Southwest for profit. The rumor-mongering by the Indian agent Shelton only added to poor Richard's bad press. The black archaeological legend was not confined to Richard. During the 1930s and 1940s, brochures distributed at Mesa Verde National Park and the text of talks given by the park rangers, labeled all the Wetherill brothers as vandals and pot hunters.[44] As archaeological techniques developed in the Southwest and archaeologists, National Park Service administrators, and others struggled often in vain to stem the ongoing pillaging of sites, Richard Wetherill became a kind of ogre figure, the arch looter of archaeological legend. There was a strong element of "presentism" in the stories; that is, a projection of current knowledge and attitudes onto the past: "He [Wetherill] didn't do archaeology" in 1897, according to the "proper standards" of 1917, or 1927, or 1967, when the present author first heard the legend at Mesa Verde. Gustaf Nordenskiöld set a high standard, and clearly Wetherill learned at least some things about careful observation, note taking, and recording from him.[45] He was a careful-enough observer to note the stratigraphic relationship between the earlier Basket Maker culture and the subsequent Cliff Dwellers in Grand Gulch. However, he was not generally believed until well after his death.

One reason perhaps that the archaeological black legend continued to hang over Richard Wetherill had to do with the bad blood between him and George Pepper. Pepper published only a few brief articles on Pueblo Bonito and finally an illustrated elaboration of his field notes in 1920.[46] The only mention of the Wetherills is in the preface by Clark Wissler. Part of the legend is that the excavation techniques used at Pueblo Bonito and elsewhere—which Richard as dig foreman was directly responsible for—were crude and sloppy, with little attention paid to provenience. The published and unpublished documentary records, notes, and photographs contradict that view.[47]

T. Mitchell Prudden

Theophil Mitchell Prudden (1849–1924) first arrived at the Wetherill's ranch in the summer of 1895. He had begun taking extended summer vacations in the Southwest a few years earlier. He would be a staunch friend of the Wetherills for the next twenty years. Prudden was born in Middlebury, Connecticut, graduated from Yale's Sheffield Scientific School in 1869 and the Yale Medical School in 1875. In the summer of 1873, he "occupied a sort of quartermaster position"[48] on one of O. C. Marsh's paleontological expeditions to Nebraska and Utah. In 1878 he began a long and distinguished career as a medical pathologist and ardent campaigner for improved public health laws, practices, and facilities in New York City. In 1892 he became professor of pathology at Columbia University. He had a graceful and wry writing style, which he used effectively in dozens of professional and popular magazine articles on public health. His popular articles and correspondence reveal a dry, sardonic, yet gentle wit, slightly self-mocking, but keenly alert. He was a tall, lanky, long-headed fellow; Gustaf Retzius might have called him "Dolichocephalic extremis" (Fig. 16.4).

Prudden made several contributions to Southwestern archaeology. He was the first to call attention in 1897 to Wetherill's Basket Maker culture, which underlay and preceded the Cliff Dweller culture. As he explored and mapped new portions of the Southwest each summer, he came to recognize the basic architectural unit of Pueblo society, which he named the "unit pueblo." A later paper called attention to small, circular kivas associated with unit pueblos. Both articles are still of use to Southwestern archaeology. In 1906, he published *On the Great American Plateau*, which reflects Prudden's exuberant fondness for the country, the archaeology, the Indian people, the traders, and the guides.[49]

In an 1897 article, "Elder Brother of the Cliff Dweller," Prudden pokes fun at Morgan's and Tylor's system of cultural evolutionary stages:

> Now if this old American did not know how to make pottery, he must, according to the widely accepted system of Morgan, be denied admission to the ranks of barbarism, and . . . be thrust sternly back among the savages. He might still be saved, however, by the creed of Tylor, if he knew how to till the soil; and though no agricultural implements were buried with him, as they often are with the Cliff-Dwellers, he was thoughtful enough to stow away in his excellent baskets some corn and seeds. So, as far as I can see, while he is damned to savagery by the American doctrine, he is saved to barbarism by that of the Englishman. May we not give him the benefit of the doubt?[50]

Prudden retired in 1909 as professor of pathology due to a "break in his long overtaxed physical and nervous strength."[51] His interest in the Southwest never flagged and he encouraged and supported new workers in the field. A. V. Kidder said in 1924:

> As a very young man going into the Southwestern field, I wrote to him asking his advice about outfitting and methods of travel; he at once replied most fully and cordially and invited me to come and see him in New York. He then gave us our first and, indeed, our only unsolicited contribution, and continued his financial support up to the year of his death. From that time on, I was always closely in touch with him, and his deep interest and his friendly advice were a great help and a stimulus.[52]

Harvard and the Hyde Expedition

Even though the Hyde Expedition was officially forbidden to continue excavations in Chaco Canyon, some digging continued under expedition auspices.[53]

In the summer of 1901, Frederic Ward Putnam and his wife were accompanied on a trip to the Southwest by Alfred M. Tozzer (1877–1954) and William C. Farabee (1865–1925), both graduate students at Harvard. The party stopped in Buffalo, New York, to visit the world's fair, then went to Chicago where they were joined by George Pepper and Talbot Hyde. The group arrived in Chaco Canyon on August 7. Putnam stayed for a couple of days to help excavate a site at the foot of Picture Cliff, west of Pueblo Bonito, and then left. Farabee and Tozzer set up a camp about eight miles west of Pueblo Bonito and proceeded over the next month to dig in some "burial mounds" and small ruins "previously selected" by Putnam and Richard Wetherill, with Farabee in charge. The first site was staked out in thirty ten-foot squares and totally excavated in four days by four laborers![54] The same careful technique was apparently applied to the other sites.

After Farabee left in September, Tozzer remained and moved into a house near the Wetherill trading post to do ethnography with the local Navajos. Tozzer seems to have appreciated Navajo humor and re-sponded with his own. In a letter to his parents he wrote, "I have been christened among them 'Turkey Boy' as my name is very similar to Navajo for turkey [*tazhii* in colloquial Navajo]. As I come around the corner to the store, the whole crowd set up a yelling of my name and then laugh as I hop along imitating a turkey and saying 'Gobble! Gobble!'"[55]

During October 1901, Tozzer witnessed a full Night Chant ceremony near Pueblo Bonito. His friendship with the Navajos apparently made it possible for him to photograph one sandpainting and sketch others. It may be that he was helped in gaining permission by Marietta Wetherill, although there is no proof of that. A model of at least one sandpainting was on display by 1909 in the Peabody Museum. In 1902 in his first professional paper, Tozzer systematically compares the ceremony and sandpaintings with Washington Matthews's descriptions in his *Night Chant,* which had just been published. He added more detail about Navajo beliefs and practices in two subsequent papers.[56] Tozzer, by then an instructor at Harvard, returned to the Southwest in 1908 (see Chapter 22).

CHAPTER 17

World's Fairs, Museums, and Modern Anthropology

THE PERIOD from about 1870 until 1910 marked the transition from ethnology to modern anthropology in America. It was also the time when positivist science gained ascendancy. Positivists assumed that there is a material universe independent of the observer, which is governed by discoverable sets of operating rules, natural laws of cause and effect. The universe can be apprehended and understood by proper scientific methods. The results are objective and true, when fully validated by other recognized knowledge makers, that is, other scientists: science is as science does.[1]

The Enlightenment hope for a "science of man" was carried into the nineteenth century and framed in positivist terms. Auguste Comte, Herbert Spencer, Karl Marx, Lewis Henry Morgan, and others asserted that positivist social sciences would objectively elucidate the laws governing human behavior.[2] Indeed, as far as Morgan was concerned, he had done that. His "laws" of social evolution were invariant: human soci-

eties marched lockstep through the several progressive stages of social development.

Science, technology, and industry were seen to operate synergistically, driving the engine of "Progress." By 1880, Europe and the United States were highly industrialized and great fortunes were accruing to those who owned the railroads and industries. By then Europe had colonized Africa, India, Southeast Asia, Australia, and the Pacific islands. More vast fortunes were accruing to those companies and governments controlling the flow of raw materials from the colonies back to the homelands. In the United States, until 1898 expansion was internal: ever further into the West. The Spanish-American War brought the United States external colonial possessions, Puerto Rico and the Philippines, as well as enormous influence in Latin America.

Three sets of institutions grew during this time and were funded by the great wealth generated through industrialism and colonialism: world's fairs, major museums, and research universities and institutes. World's fairs were ephemeral, yet institutionalized events consciously designed to celebrate the industrial progress and imperial expansion of northern Europe and Anglo America.[3] The fairs had enormous impacts on European and American lifeways and popular culture, including a further strengthening of stereotypical images of colonialized "native" peoples. Universities, research institutes, and museums were permanent, public institutions. They employed knowledge makers and purveyors—professors and curators, some of them anthropologists—who generated and displayed scientific, objective knowledge about the natural and human worlds.

There were particularly close links between world's fairs, natural history museums, and anthropologists. Museum-based anthropologists created exhibits for the fairs that presented and interpreted native peoples. All major fairs in Europe and North America from 1867 through 1933 had anthropological displays, sometimes including "living exhibits" of native peoples. Southwestern Indian people, and collections of ethnographic and archaeological artifacts from the region, were prominently featured in many of those fairs.

Modern world's fairs began with the 1851 Crystal Palace Exhibition in London. It was designed to show off, in "friendly" competition between nations, new technologies, machines, scientific advancements, and trade goods. There were also "fine arts" for the edification and uplifting of visitors. The exhibition set a precedent with the Crystal Palace itself—Joseph Paxton's great iron and glass enclosure that became a symbol of the new modern industrial age. As an aside, the terms *exhibition* and *exposition* were used interchangeably, with "exposition" finally winning out. The term *world's fair* was first used in 1876 in reference to the Philadelphia Exhibition, but only came into general usage in 1893 as a popular nickname for the Chicago World's Columbian Exposition and subsequent international expositions. The Crystal Palace Exhibition set the standard for the rest of the century. New York

City tried to meet it in 1853, but failed disastrously. Other cities soon stepped up; by 1900 more than two dozen expositions had been held in Europe, Australia and the United States, five in Paris alone.[4]

The fairs were short lived, but there was often a sentiment that permanent facilities of some sort ought to endure after they ended. The French used their expositions from 1867 on to build such facilities as the Trocadero museum complex, including a museum of ethnography. In 1876, Philadelphia built a permanent art museum; other cities followed suit.

Unofficial "side shows" sprang up outside the fairgrounds. In Paris in 1855, dancers, musicians, theater troops, circuses, jugglers, sword swallowers, fast-food vendors, cutpurses, and inhabitants of the demimonde set up shop. Philadelphia had a "Shantyville" offering fast-food eateries, con games, and such edifying exhibits as a "learned pig, a two-legged horse, a five legged cow," and a "gigantic fat woman." Shantyville mysteriously burned down during the fair and city officials did not allow it to be rebuilt.[5]

Thus, by 1876, the major elements of expositions were in place: first, if possible, official sponsorship by a national government, with funds to cover some construction and operating costs; second, the exhibition of new and ever-better industrial machinery, trade goods, and agricultural products; third, "cultural" exhibits and performances providing an "uplifting" element; fourth, in Europe there were usually individual "nation" buildings housing exhibits from participating nation states, and in the United States there were both nation buildings and "state" buildings. For those expositions aspiring to the status of "international," at least one major permanent building was designed for later use as a museum, library, or other public facility. Finally, to the despair of bluenose exposition managers, but in existence by popular demand, were the unofficial sideshows. Sideshow problems were resolved in Chicago in 1893 by bringing them onto the famous "Midway" inside the grounds and charging the concessionaires fees to help fund the fair; later expositions followed suit.

There was much that was of broad anthropological interest in both the sideshows and official exhibits. John Wesley Powell and Spencer Baird wanted an exhibit of living American Indians who would perform their "traditional activities" as part of the government exhibit at Philadelphia in 1876, but Congress refused the money. The idea did not die; the first of several official "ethnographic zoos," as they may uncharitably be called, was at the Amsterdam International Industrial Exposition of 1883. The Dutch government underwrote the development and display of model villages inhabited by "natives" from its Caribbean and Southeast Asia colonies. The villagers lived in "traditional" houses and worked at "traditional" activities while being gaped at by exposition visitors.[6] The French, planning the great Paris Universal Exposition of 1889, took careful note.

Otis T. Mason was a representative to the Paris Exposition from the Smithsonian Institution. After marveling at the four-hundred-meter-high tower built to symbolize the exposition by Alexandre Gustave Eiffel,[7] he reported: "On the Esplanade des Invalides *side by side with the latest inventions and with the whole civilized world as spectators* . . . [there were] twelve types of Africans, besides Javanese, Tonkinese, Chinese, Japanese, and other oriental peoples, living in native houses, wearing native costumes, eating native foods, [and] practicing native arts and rites . . . " Mason "spent many hours in these *savage enclosures and houses* studying the people and their arts and listening to their *rude music*."[8]

Mason saw replicas of a village and fort from Senegal, a Khmer pagoda from Cambodia, mosques from Algeria and Tunisia, tribal peoples from West Africa, a Madagascan village and a Javanese village, within a Park of Colonies and Protectorates. Nearby were separate Chinese and Japanese exhibits.[9] The people in their "savage enclosures," juxtaposed with the "latest inventions" for "the whole civilized world to see," were living affirmation of French colonial and imperial power. Finally, there was a new feature of great interest to Mason the scholar: some 120 scholarly congresses

were held, including those on criminal anthropology, prehistoric archaeology, and ethnography and popular traditions.[10]

In the United States, exhibits of native peoples went in two directions, one official and one unofficial. By the early 1880s, "Wild West" shows, the most famous being that of William Cody, "Buffalo Bill," were touring the country.[11] The dime novel and American popular theater had already created a pretend West of the imagination inhabited by stereotypical cowboys and Indians; Indians were still disguised as noble, ignoble, vanishing, and pathetic dusky heroine savages. For three decades these show-biz figures were living realities for millions of people in America, Canada, and Europe in Cody's and others' traveling shows. They then took on a new sort of reality in movies and television in the twentieth century.

The first officially sanctioned exhibit of Indian people in the United States was at a modest 1889 trade fair in St. Louis. An enterprising promoter, J. W. Crawford, gained permission from the Bureau of Indian Affairs (BIA) to bring a group of San Carlos Apaches, "in all their pride and strength," to the fair. They performed "their weird dances, ceremonies, and incantations, and exemplif[ied] their modes of savage warfare."[12] The Apaches were of great current interest, since the U.S. Army had finally prevailed over them only three years before.

The Apaches were the first of a long line of Southwestern Indians to find themselves willingly or unwillingly on exhibit at an exposition. The BIA agreed to their coming to St. Louis because they were to be juxtaposed with a group of Indian children from the Lawrence, Kansas, Indian School. By 1889, the BIA was desperately trying to implement its policy of assimilation of Indian people into American society. The BIA schools and missionaries on every reservation actively, indeed punitively, discouraged anything smacking of the "old tribal ways." There were, however, still thousands of traditional Indian people. The idea of contrasting the "savagery" of traditional people with the "progressive and civilized" manners and work habits of Indian children "properly" taught to act like Anglos held great appeal for bureaucrats, teachers, and missionaries.

The Smithsonian and World's Fairs

The federal government provided official sponsorship and funding for the Philadelphia Centennial Exhibition. Subsequent exposition promoters sought pork from the same barrel to insure that they would at least break even. Sponsorship also meant a government building in which the Smithsonian Institution and other federal agencies mounted exhibits.

The Smithsonian's annual reports for the period 1884 to 1904 reflect the enormous amount of work by the natural history, anthropology, and exhibits staffs of the National Museum and the Bureau of American Ethnology to design, build, ship, set up, tend, and tear down exhibits. For example, for the World's Industrial and Cotton Exposition in New Orleans in 1884, the museum and the bureau sent 176,000 pounds of exhibit, enough to fill seventeen railroad cars and cover 24,750 square feet of floor space.[13]

The Southwest in New Orleans

The central features of the Smithsonian's anthropology exhibit at the 1884 New Orleans fair were a relief map of the "Ancient Province of Tusayan," and Cosmos Mindeleff's models of the seven Hopi villages, as well as Acoma, Taos, and Zuni. The Zuni model was 1,425 square feet, "in the true colors of the village as well as all other details." Models of ruins included White House and Mummy Cave in Canyon de Chelly, Wejiji in Chaco Canyon, "Cliff Dwellings" in Mancos Canyon, and a Hovenweep tower. There were extensive artifact displays, especially the pottery collections made by James Stevenson. Variations of the models and artifact exhibits were shown at expositions in Louisville, Cincinnati, and Minneapolis in the later 1880s and at the St. Louis Exposition of 1904.[14]

There were no Indian people officially exhibited at New Orleans. But the Territory of Arizona, in con-

junction with the Atlantic and Pacific Railroad, sponsored an exhibit touting Arizona as "The Coming Empire of the Southwest." The central focus was Arizona's burgeoning minerals industry, but much was made of archaeological sites and the Hopi and Zuni, "whose villages, habits and customs are now attracting wide-spread attention." Navajo blankets adorned the displays.[15] This seemingly marks the beginning of the advertising of native cultures by Southwestern railroads (see Chapter 27).

The Columbian Expositions, 1892–1893

Celebrations of Columbus's "discovery of the New World" were planned by Spain and the United States for 1892. The Spanish celebration was relatively small, dignified, and scholarly. The American celebration was the sprawling, eclectic Chicago World's Columbian Exposition, or the Chicago world's fair, as it was popularly called. Both were important showcases for American anthropology, and Southwestern anthropological exhibits were featured at both venues.

In Madrid, the Spanish government constructed a new National Library and Museum and housed the exposition therein. The theme was arts and cultures of the Old and New worlds at or about 1492.[16] The Spanish royal decree proclaimed, with modest chauvinism, that the purpose of the exposition was to show "the elements of civilization with which . . . Europe was then equipped for the task of educating a daughter, courageous and untamed, but vigorous and beautiful, who had risen from the bosom of the seas, and who, in the course of a very few centuries, was to be transformed from a daughter into a sister — a sister proud in aspiration and in power." The New World exhibits focused on pre-Columbian history, "characteristics of American aborigines just prior to discovery, the period of discovery and conquest, and European influence up to the middle of the seventeenth century."[17]

Twenty-four nations contributed exhibits. Mexico's was very extensive, including examples of exquisite stone and mosaic work from Classic and post-Classic civilizations, as well as a 12 x 18 ft. model of the Templo Mayor of Cerupoala at Veracruz. The Smithsonian presented both pre- and post-Columbian North American materials. A 12 x 16 ft. copy of the Powell linguistic map of North American tribes was featured, together with Mindeleff's models of a "Mound Builders" site at Etowah, Georgia, the Fort Ancient site in Illinois, and the "Cliff Dwellers" White House in Canyon de Chelly. There was a set of colored engravings of prominent Indian leaders from Thomas McKenney and James Hall's *Indian Tribes of North America* of the 1830s, paintings by George Catlin and John Mix Stanley, and some thirteen hundred photographs and transparencies of Indians, many of them by Jack Hillers and William Henry Jackson.[18]

One exhibit, devoted entirely to the Hopi, was designed by Jesse Walter Fewkes and presented by the Hemenway Expedition; Mrs. Hemenway was in attendance. The exhibit showcased Fewkes's activities: "The collection . . . is intended chiefly to show the results of the operation during the past two years relative to the excavations and . . . publication of those results, *without any reference whatever to the operations prior to 1891,* nor to any except those . . . in the Province of Tusayan." So much for Frank Hamilton Cushing! There were also pottery vessels from the Thomas Keam collection (see Chapter 14).[19]

Fewkes also exhibited a "large collection of [kachina] dolls, . . . [which] naturally attracted attention, being a novelty in European museums," as well as "ceremonial objects—dress, paraphernalia, masks, and decorated head tablets, offerings to gods, photographs of shrines, and a few Tusayan musical instruments. . . . There were also, for the "first time in a museum or exposition, sacred pictures made of sand, called dry painting. An Indian altar with medicine bowl and corn, corresponding to the six cardinal points, were likewise shown. . . . The symbolic figures on the walls were copied from decorated objects made by the Indians and represented various gods of their mythology." Navajo rugs were scattered through the exhibit. Fewkes also exhibited bound volumes of Spanish documents, copied by hand by Adolph Ban-

delier (see Chapter 15).[20] Fewkes and Mrs. Hemenway received gold medals from the exposition judges. Finally, Gustav Nordenskiöld sent photographs, models, and specimens from his excavations at Mesa Verde.[21]

The Chicago World's Columbian Exposition

In 1871, Mrs. O'Leary's famous cow kicked over a lantern and burned down Chicago. Its roughly 300,000 inhabitants rallied and rebuilt the city, this time in iron, steel, stone, and brick, including the first "skyscrapers," Chicago's architectural gift to the world. Chicago flourished as a railroad, industrial, and meat-packing center. By 1880 there were 500,000 inhabitants; by 1890, 1,100,000-plus. Muckraking journalist Lincoln Steffens saw Chicago as "first in violence, deepest in dirt, loud, lawless, unlovely, ill-smelling, new; an overgrown gawk of a village, the teeming tough among cities."[22] Just so, but Chicagoans aspired to learning, culture, and respect; they were very tired of playing "Second City" fiddle to New York. By 1891 there was a growing Art Institute and a symphony orchestra. The proposed Columbian quatercentenary exposition was a chance to one-up the entire country. Chicago's business community went after it with a vengeance, and beat out New York, Philadelphia, Washington, and St. Louis. They formed a five-million-dollar stock company, later floated an additional five-million-dollar bond issue, and received government support. The complexities of organizing and launching an exposition of the magnitude envisioned were so immense that Congress slipped the opening date to May 1893. Then came the 1893 financial panic that badly crippled the country. But the World's Columbian Exposition opened on May 1, and despite rocky financial going early on, ultimately attracted 27 million people and turned a profit.[23]

The exposition buildings had 187 acres of floor space set on 686 acres of two tracts bordering Lake Michigan. The tracts were connected by the Midway Plaisance. Everything was on a grand scale; for example, in the agricultural building one could contemplate a twenty-two-thousand-pound Canadian cheese next to a thirty-eight-foot-high, thirty-three-thousand-pound "temple of chocolate," adjacent to a sixteen-foot-tall knight and charger made of prunes from the Santa Clara Valley in California.[24]

The Midway Plaisance was six hundred feet wide and a mile long. Dozens of concessionaires staged the sideshow *par excellence,* and paid 20 percent of their gross as rent. There were numerous ethnic or national "villages" said to be occupied by over three thousand people from forty-eight nations or dependent colonies. Multitudes thronged the Midway in the shadow of the giant 250-foot-high Ferris Wheel, Chicago's answer to the Eiffel Tower. They gaped mawkishly at Indian fakirs and strangely attired Javanese, Samoans, and Fijians, and stared nervously at "Dahomey cannibals" and their spouses, advertised as "Amazon warrior women." Most of all, they visited the Streets of Cairo, the Persian Palace of Eros, and the Algerian Village. There, hundreds of thousands of goggle-eyed country bumpkins and city slickers stared in fascination as Fahreda Mahzar, billed as "Little Egypt, the Darling of the Nile" (and four others), Fatima, and a "doe-eyed Algerian odalisque" performed the *danse du ventre.* The *danse* featured "a suggestively lascivious contorting of the abdominal muscles, which is extremely ungraceful and almost shockingly disgusting," said one commentator. Fatima, he went on, "was more lithesome, and executed the *danse* with a wild abandon that called for repression by the authorities."[25] Frederic Ward Putnam, director of the anthropology exhibits, took a loftier, tongue-in-cheek cross-cultural view: "What wonderful muscular movements the dancers make, and how strange the dance seems to us; but is it not probable that the waltz would seem equally strange to these dusky women of Egypt?"[26] Little Egypt and her compatriots performed *seriatim* from 10 A.M. to 10 P.M. daily. The Streets of Cairo exhibit took in more money than the Ferris wheel—nearly 800,000 dollars, versus 735,000 dollars.[27]

Fairgoers got a further look at other ethnic people

at Buffalo Bill's Wild West Show. By 1893 William Cody had been touring for a decade. Now he settled in for a six-month, 618-performance stand on fourteen acres outside the fairgrounds. Several million people (sources vary) saw the usual cowboys and cowgirls and seventy-four Lakota men and women from the Pine Ridge Reservation. There was also, for the first time in the United States, a coterie of English, French, German, Mexican, Argentine, Cossack, Syrian, Bedouin, and retired U.S. Sixth Cavalry, horsemen billed as the "Congress of Rough Riders of the World."[28]

Anthropology at the Fair

Frederic Ward Putnam, of Harvard, made the first appeal for official anthropological exhibits at the exposition.[29] In May 1890 he told the *Chicago Tribune* that the exposition was an opportunity to secure and display "a perfect ethnographic exhibition of the past and present peoples of America and thus make an important contribution to science . . . [It would] be the first bringing together on a grand scale of representatives of the peoples who were living on the continent when it was discovered by Columbus." In subsequent speeches and press releases, he also called for archaeological displays. The *Chicago Tribune* opined: "The [exposition] directors have no money to waste on the man of the ice sheet or stone monstrosities from serpents mounds—Professor Putnam, like all those dried-up prehistoric specialists, mistakes the purpose of the fair."[30] Dried up or not, in late 1891 the directors appointed Putnam as chief of the Division of Ethnology. He in turn appointed Franz Boas (see Chapter 18) as his principal assistant and head of the physical anthropology section, and one of his Harvard students, George O. Dorsey, as head of the section on archaeology. Marshall Saville was put in charge of Mexican and Middle American exhibits and Stewart Culin, of the University of Pennsylvania Museum, the section on religions, games, and folklore.[31] Culin's exhibit of games fascinated many who saw it, especially Frank Hamilton Cushing.

Putnam's vision was realized in the 161,000-square-foot anthropological building, built at a cost of 87,612 dollars. Costs of collecting and installing exhibits totaled 140,450 dollars.[32] While Putnam was chief of the Division of Ethnology, he insisted that the building be called the "anthropological building," and that the theme of the exhibits be "Anthropology—Man and His Works." His choice of "anthropology" gave a cachet to the term in the minds of the public, and helped establish "anthropology" as the "science of man" in American museums and universities, at future expositions and in the popular press.

The exhibits in the anthropology building were varied. Since Putnam had sent out a wide appeal for collections, he and Boas had to exhibit what they received in rather eclectic displays. An erroneous anthropological folktale is that "the concept of the culture area first took form in his [Boas's] arrangement on a geographical basis of the exhibits at the World's Fair, Chicago, 1893."[33] The American Indian ethnographic and archaeological exhibits were grouped together, but not in any ordered culture-area scheme; those in the separate Smithsonian exhibit were so grouped, however (see below).

The Indian Village and the School

Near the anthropology building was the Indian Village. The village initially was under the charge of the Bureau of Indian Affairs, but later fell under Putnam's aegis. The Bureau intended to again juxtapose a model Indian school and traditional people as in 1889, in St. Louis. But White reformers objected; they wanted only displays of "civilized" Indians. In the end, Cree, Haida, Kwakiutl, Iroquois, Sioux, Apaches, Navajos, Coahuillas, Papagos, and Yaquis lived in the village in traditional houses, and "made trinkets for sale."[34]

Because of the reformers' objections, the model Indian School was located away from the Indian Village. Again, its purpose was to show Indians abandoning "traditional ways," and becoming "civilized" under the beneficent tutelage of Anglo do-gooders. The school was supposed to be a model of the future, but was decorated with traditional Indian artifacts, including Navajo blankets and Pueblo pottery, provided by Thomas V. Keam.[35] Relatively few fairgoers found their way to the anthropology building, the village, or the school since they were tucked away in an almost secluded corner of the exposition grounds. Reflecting the growing romanticizing of traditional Indian people, the village and the "curios" in the anthropological building were much more interesting to visitors than the school.[36]

The Smithsonian Exhibit

In the government building, the Smithsonian anthropology exhibit centered around the giant enlargement of Powell's linguistic map used at Madrid in 1892. The exhibit was designed by Otis T. Mason, William Henry Holmes, and Frank Hamilton Cushing. Mason had moved away from glass-case displays of artifacts organized in assumed unilineal evolutionary sequences toward a life-group and culture-area approach. He selected "typical" tribal groups from the linguistic map and placed them within major North American biogeographic areas shown on another map published by the Department of Agriculture. He was able to demonstrate a close correlation between artifact types and biogeographic areas—an important link in the definition of culture areas. The linguistic map served to plainly show that language families were *not* correlated with biogeographic regions nor material culture.[37]

To help make his point, Mason used single mannequins and life groups. Many of the single mannequins were of prominent Indian leaders, the faces taken from "plaster casts from life," the clothing "his best war toggery." One commentator rhapsodized, "They have reproduced these chiefs exact in stature, features, complexion, dress. It is a work of the utmost value, the last true records of a dying race of men."[38] The Indians were still vanishing!

Southwest Anthropology at the Fair

Frank Hamilton Cushing designed and installed the Southwestern Indian groups in the Smithsonian exhibit. There was a Navajo silversmithing group of three men gathered around an "adobe forge and primitive goatskin bellows." Also included was a Navajo weaving group, one figure using a drop-spindle; a second, a mannequin "portrait" of a "woman-man . . . one of the most celebrated blanket-makers in the Navajo tribe weaving at an upright loom." This was probably Hosteen Klah (see Chapter 29), who was appearing live in the New Mexico building across the fairgrounds. The third group was of a Hopi kitchen, with figures of women parching and grinding corn and making *piki*, wafer bread, "on a baking-stone at the side-hearth." The fourth was a Zuni kiva in which three Zuni priests were "ceremonially reciting the Ritual-epic of Creation." There were also smaller-scale exhibits of a Zuni man making shell and turquoise beads, a Zuni woman using a back-strap loom, two Zuni women making pottery, and an unmarried Hopi "maiden of Oraibi, plaiting baskets of various kinds." Finally, there was a small display of Mindeleff's models of Acoma, Taos, and some of the Hopi villages.[39]

There were four Southwestern exhibits in the anthropology building. Gustaf Nordenskiöld sent a "model of an estufa and photographs of cliff dwellings of Colorado." There was the Wetherill collection from Mesa Verde, owned by the state of Colorado, with Richard Wetherill in attendance after September 1893 to answer questions; and a small "Cliff Dwellers" collection exhibited by Virginia McClurg, of Colorado Springs. McClurg was already playing a role in the creation of what would become Mesa Verde National Park (see Chapter 22). Finally, most of the Hemenway exhibit shown in Madrid was displayed by Fewkes.[40] Meanwhile, downtown at the Art Institute of Chicago, the Reverend C. H. Green, from Durango, Colorado, was exhibiting the archaeological collections from Grand Gulch, Utah, which he had purchased from the Wetherills and others.[41]

17.1. Cliff Dweller's exhibit, Chicago world's fair, 1893. Buel (1894).

The Cliff Dweller's Exhibit

The most popular anthropology exhibit was the Cliff Dwellers concession of the H. Jay Smith Exploring Company (Fig. 17.1). It was a seventy-foot-high cement reproduction of Battle Rock Mountain, "a weird and solitary landmark in the desert of Southwestern Colorado." For a quarter, visitors could see one-tenth scale models of Cliff Palace, Square Tower House, Balcony House, and "High House, one of the most inaccessible refuges of the persecuted Cliff Dweller," together with "panoramic paintings" of Long House, Spruce Tree House, and others. Full-size "estufas and living rooms" contained some two thousand artifacts, including numerous mummies, which Charles D. Hazzard had purchased from the Wetherills and C. M. Viets for Smith. The concession grossed 87,366 dollars, according to official records.[42] Smith had retained Frank Hamilton Cushing to advise on the exhibits, and Cushing spent a good deal of time during the fair talking with both Smith and Hazzard about his leading a new Cliff Dwellers expedition in the Southwest. Nothing came of the discussions.[43]

Members of the Anthropology Congress (see below) were antagonized "by the extraordinary and utterly unreliable teachings of the principal exhibitor of cliff dwellers' remains on the exposition grounds, through whose agency many erroneous notions respecting these remains have been disseminated among the people of the country."[44] Few who paid to get in knew the difference, and the concession did much to solidify the "Cliff Dweller" image in the popular imagination.

Most of the Southwestern Indian people at the fair were brought by one Antonio Apache, working with Putnam and Bureau of Indian Affairs staff. He was reputedly a Chiricahua Apache captured by the U.S. Army in 1877 and later sent to several schools in the East, including Harvard, where Putnam encountered him. Putnam sent him to the Southwest to collect artifacts and photographs for exhibits and recruits for the Indian Village. Among those recruited were Navajo Jake, a Fort Defiance silversmith. There were apparently a number of other Navajos, as well as Apache, Pueblo, and Papago people in the village. Antonio Apache went on to something of a career in exhibitions and tourism. In 1897, he developed an "Indian Village" exhibit at the New England Sportsman Show to which he shipped ten cases of Pueblo pottery and "bales" of Navajo blankets for sale. In 1900 he was hired by the Fred Harvey Company to guide tourist parties in the Southwest, to buy "curios," and to act as a general "goodwill ambassador."[45]

Finally, in the New Mexico building, there was an exhibit featuring several Pueblo and Navajo people, including Hosteen Klah, a Navajo who later became famous as a weaver, chanter, and collaborator with various Anglo students of the Navajo.[46]

The World's Congress Auxiliary

Following the Paris model of 1889, a World's Congress Auxiliary developed and held meetings on current major scholarly, social, technical, and economic concerns, under the slogan "Not Matter, But Mind." Some 225 divisions were established, ranging from agriculture to women. Between May 15 and October 28, there were 1,283 sessions in which 5,978 speeches or papers were given by 3,817 individuals, a veritable glut of verbiage.[47]

The two largest congresses were devoted to women and religion. The Women's Congress was a major forum for feminist concerns that would carry into the twentieth century (see Chapter 26). The "World's Parliament of Religions" lasted seventeen days, brought together hundreds of delegates representing most of the world's great, and many of its lesser, religions, and was thronged by thousands of listeners daily. It was perhaps the closest thing to a truly worldwide ecumenical conclave ever held, before or since. It is of interest that no American Indian delegates were invited, although Alice Fletcher (see Chapter 22) did read a paper on American Indian religion. There was an adjunct congress on evolution, at which papers by Thomas Henry Huxley, Herbert Spencer, and Ernst Haeckel were read.[48]

There were congresses on history, folklore, and anthropology. At the history congress, Frederick Jackson Turner read his now-famous paper "The Significance of the Frontier in American History."[49] By 1893 the study of folklore had become highly popular, and some scholars were bidding to make it an academic subject. There were papers on Cinderella, Northern European Trolls, Haitian Voodooism and House Ghosts in Pomerania, as well as "The Cliff Dwellers of Southwestern America," by Mrs. Palmer Henderson, and "How San Geronimo Came to Taos," by Virginia McClurg. A. M. Stephen, of "Keams, Arizona," read "Pigments in Ceremonials of the Hopi," and Washington Matthews, although ill, gave two papers on Night Chant symbolism and paraphernalia, and recordings of Navajo songs and prayers.[50] Matthews, Cushing, and John Gregory Bourke happily visited during the fair; it was the last time they were together.

The Congress of Anthropology was presided over by Daniel Brinton and had 255 attendees. Of those, about twenty Americans were professional anthropologists, in the sense of having essentially a full-time commitment to the doing of anthropology; some few even got paid. They included Franz Boas, J. G. Bourke, Daniel Brinton, Stewart Culin, F. H. Cushing, George Dorsey, J. W. Fewkes, Alice Fletcher, W. H. Holmes, Walter Hough, Carl Lumholtz, W J McGee, Zelia Nuttall, F. W. Putnam, Sara Yorke Stevenson, and C. Staniland Wake. Many of them were connected at some point with anthropological work in the Southwest. Delegates spent afternoons viewing and discussing exhibits in the anthropology and government buildings. Cushing discussed the Southwestern exhibits, his conclusions similar to those in his 1888 paper (see Chapter 13). A paper by Matilda Coxe Stevenson, "A Chapter in Zuni Mythology," was read for her. Cushing thought it "a poor effort, rambling, superficial, and in its differences from my own well known statements, really silly and somewhat venomous." It was business as usual in the ongoing Cushing-Stevenson feud. In Otis T. Mason's paper on "Aboriginal American Mechanics," he divided the continents of the New World into "culture or technogeographic areas," thus taking a major step toward the definition of "cultures areas," soon to be of central importance in Americanist anthropology.[51]

On the last evening, Cushing and many of the delegates visited the Streets of Cairo, to see "strange coarsely sensuous contortionate dances with head carried level, belly and hips extraordinarily jerked about and various plays with swords and vases of water."[52] The fair ended in November 1893. Before then a decision had been reached that one legacy ought to be a great natural history museum—the Chicago Columbian Museum (see Chapter 18).

Chicago's dazzling success prompted civic boosters in other American cities to develop their own expositions, some regional, some aspiring to be a "world's fair." Three are of interest because of their anthropological themes and exhibits of Southwestern Indian people: Omaha in 1898, Buffalo in 1901, and the grandest of them all, St. Louis in 1904.

The Trans-Mississippi and International Exposition

The Trans-Mississippi and International Exposition opened in Omaha, Nebraska, in 1898. On a site overlooking the Missouri River, progress was celebrated in

17.2. "Geronimo and Apaches." Geronimo in U.S. Cavalry uniform at Omaha world's fair, 1898. Photograph by Frank A. Rinehart. Courtesy of the Trans-Mississippi Exposition Collection, Omaha, Nebraska, Public Library.

a scaled-down version of Chicago's Great White City. The organizers decided that a central theme would be the Vanishing Savage giving way to Progress. They envisioned a grandiose "Last Congress of Red Indians" with representatives from "every tribe" in the United States. When fiscal reality set in, about 400 to 550 (individuals and groups came and went) prominent Indian leaders, elders, and their families from twenty, primarily Plains, tribes were recruited.

There was a small delegation from Santa Clara Pueblo, including the governor, Diego Naranjo, and previous governor, José de Jesus Naranjo, as well as a group of White Mountain Apache from San Carlos, Arizona, and a few Mohave people. There was also a small group of Chiricahua Apaches, then still technically prisoners of war at Fort Sill, Oklahoma Territory, including Geronimo. Geronimo was persuaded to don a U.S. Cavalry uniform and ride around the fairgrounds; it is not known how he saw the irony of the situation (Fig. 17.2). Soon after he was imprisoned in 1886, he began making and signing his name to bows and arrows that he sold to the army officers who guarded him. He continued the practice at Omaha and later fairs, and also sold autographs.[53]

At the Indian Congress camp fairgoers could watch Indian people acting out their "aboriginality," as the Omaha *Bee* put it.[54] James Mooney, from the Bureau of American Ethnology, had been hired to direct the Indian exhibits. He staged some "tribal ceremonies," including an Apache "devil dance . . . performed at night by the light of a fire, with a clown and other masked characters, after the manner of the Hopi," hardly ethnographically accurate. Mooney's classic study of the Ghost Dance of 1890 had been published the previous year and was widely known. He staged some performances of a Ghost Dance, using Cheyenne and Arapaho volunteers, but stopped "owing to an evident purpose to reduce everything to the level of a 'Midway' performance."[55]

The "Midway" aspect began when a local White business group, the Improved Order of Red Men, staged a sham battle against Indians from the congress. The battle quickly became a daily attraction,

usually with Sioux delegates battling other Indians. Amid much noise and gunsmoke, numerous people "bit the dust" and were "scalped by squaws" twice a day, until everyone ran out of blank ammunition.[56]

When President William McKinley visited, there was a special mock battle, with more shooting and scalping than usual, after which everyone shook hands with the president, beginning with Geronimo, who "doffed his head gear [an army cavalry hat] and a dignified smile passed over his wrinkled features." Some days later, Geronimo and General Nelson Miles, who had finally negotiated Geronimo's surrender in 1886, sat together in the grandstand to witness the sham battle. The pretend West was complete.[57]

At the end of the exposition, James Mooney wrote, "the general result was such—particularly from the practical standpoint of the ticket seller—that we may expect to see ethnology as a principal feature at future expositions so long as our aboriginal material holds out."[58] He was right in several senses: Indians, anthropologists, and show-biz impresarios had become partners. The fair continued the next year as the Greater American Exposition; battles of sham Indians versus real Indians and Indians versus cowboys were featured.

The Pan-American Exposition, Buffalo, New York, 1901

The Pan-American Exposition was held in Buffalo, New York, from May through November 1901. The developers planned to celebrate New World progress and U.S. influence in Latin America, hence the "Pan-American" theme. They ended with a 3-million-dollar debt and a dead president, William McKinley, who was shot on September 6 by an "anarchist" in the Temple of Music and died eight days later. The fair went on until November; concessionaires did a brisk trade in memorabilia related to McKinley and the Temple. The mind boggles at opportunistic fortunes unrealized because the "message" T-shirt was not yet invented!

The entire fair, the "Rainbow City," was conceived

as a metaphor of human evolutionary progress. The buildings were in a vague "Spanish Renaissance" style, in keeping with the Pan-American theme. As visitors moved along a central court, the coordinated color scheme of the buildings shifted from deep earth tones to whiter shades of pale, symbolizing the transition of humanity from nature to culture, from savagery to the ne plus ultra of White Anglo American high-tech engineers and entrepreneurs, 1901 style. At the far end of the court were the Temple of Music and the ethnology building. Beyond were the machinery buildings and a white, 391-ft. "Electric Tower" bathed in light hydroelectrically generated at nearby Niagara Falls—the symbol of Anglo achievement.[59]

The "Pan," also called the Midway, entertainment zone had concessions and exhibits of broad "anthropological" interest. These included the "original" Cardiff Giant, by then a known fake but exhibited nonetheless as "the fossil remains of a prehistoric man . . . dug up near Cardiff, New York in 1869, the remains being over 10 feet in length and weighing nearly 3,000 pounds." Nearby was the "Evolution of Man," illustrating "the Darwinian theory" by tracing the "genus Homo" from the "lowest type of Simian development to the missing link . . . [the] educated chimpanzee Esau, who all but talks, and from the lowest savage to the polished gentleman of today." There were the requisite belly dancers, a two-foot-tall Cuban midget woman who spoke seven languages, a "Darkest Africa" village made up of "a collection of some 35 different African native tribes," many of them apparently African-Americans who had hired on for the show, and various Eskimos, Hawaiians, Filipinos, and Gypsies.[60]

Finally, there was yet another "last great gathering of Red Men," assembled by impresario Frederick T. Cummins. The Buffalo edition had perhaps seven hundred people, among them "fifteen famous war chiefs," including Geronimo. Three times a day there was a "cavalcade of barbaric chieftains and their support," a grand entry of all the participants. Twice daily "five hundred Indians in [a] great sham battle," faked massacres and scalping. There was a "Stockade

of Six Nations," showcasing Iroquois history, and staffed, it was said, by actual Iroquois people. Outside the grounds Wild West shows featured more Indian people. Show-biz ethnography was in high gear, as Mooney had predicted, and "Show Indians," were gainfully employed therein.

Anthropology Exhibits

The ethnology building was supervised by one Dr. A. L. Benedict, a professor of physiology and digestive diseases in the Dental Department of the University of Buffalo. Benedict was both overwhelmed by his task and vastly underfunded by the fair organizers. The exhibits were a miscellany of archaeological and ethnographic artifacts, many of them for sale. Along an upper balcony were "plaques" showing oversize and flattened designs of Cliff Dweller pottery designs from Sikyatki, Gila, and Little Colorado, painted by a Miss Claire Shuttleworth. Despite its prominent placement in the center of the grounds, according to Benedict's report only 6 to 10 percent of the exposition visitors entered the ethnology building.[61]

Business was brisker in the government building, which housed the Smithsonian exhibit. William Henry Holmes and Otis T. Mason produced sixty life-sized figures "of types of tribes of our aborigines." Many of these were in life groups arranged by cultural "province." The "Pueblo" province included Zuni and Navajo life groups. There were also numerous glass cases stuffed with artifacts, including Pueblo pottery.[62]

The Louisiana Purchase Exposition

In 1904, St. Louis, Missouri, staged the Louisiana Purchase Exposition to celebrate the one-hundredth anniversary of Thomas Jefferson's real estate deal with Napoleon, and the subsequent "Opening of the Trans-Mississippi West." It was the most grandiose of world's fairs, covering 1,240 acres of Forest Park. The nineteen million visitors were dazzled by yet another ensemble of Classical and Renaissance revival buildings, called the "Ivory City," full of thousands of exhibits. Fairgoers tried new-fangled ice-cream cones and listened to the strolling brass bands playing the official fair song, "Meet Me in St. Louis, Louis," by Broadway songwriter Andrew Sterling, the stirring marches of John Phillips Sousa, and the elegant ragtime music of local composer Scott Joplin.[63]

Anthropological exhibits were prominently featured.[64] Frederick J. V. Skiff, the exposition's director of exhibits (on loan from his job as director of the Field Museum in Chicago), declared that "a universal exposition is a vast museum of anthropology and ethnology, of man and his works."[65] On August 27, 1901, "The most gigantic undertaking of science yet on record" was modestly announced by W J McGee, "director [sic] of the Smithsonian Institution," a "gathering, . . . a splendid and unique exhibit of all the earth's living tribes of primal humanity."[66] McGee was involved with the exposition long before his resignation from the Bureau of American Ethnology. He formally joined the staff the same day, July 31, 1903, he resigned (see Chapter 12).

Playing on the Smithsonian's motto, McGee hoped to "diffuse and incidentally increase knowledge of Man and his Works" at the fair. In his eyes, the assembled tribal peoples were living evidence for an apotheosis of Morgan's and Powell's theory of human culture history. The fair itself was a metaphorical drama of the culmination of human history in the Anglo technological and scientific society at the start of the new century. The "primal" peoples were the opening acts, as it were, of that drama.[67]

McGee's interpretation of the anthropology exhibits he arranged was a last major gasp of the racialist nineteenth-century ethnology he espoused: that there is a direct and determinative link between "race" and "stage" of social and cultural development; and that "lower races" are doomed to vanish, physically or culturally, in the face of Anglo progress. But before they go, their representatives should be shown at the fair.

Even with a large budget, McGee only managed to bring a few members of four tribal groups from outside the United States: nine Ainu from Japan, seven Teheulche from Patagonia, and four "Batwa Pygmies"

and a "small group" of "Red Africans," both from the Congo. The rest were American Indians. The groups lived in a compound in traditional houses and did traditional things. There was a second, and much larger, compound of Filipino people. The U.S. government was eager to show that it could manage the "savages and semi-civilized" peoples of the newly acquired Philippine Islands in the same "enlightened" manner that they managed American Indians. The Ethnological Survey for the Philippine Islands recruited a large contingent of Filipinos from different tribal and ethnic groups for the exhibit, as they had for the Buffalo Exposition.[68]

McGee arranged these various people in a sequence of "race-types" and "culture-grades" illustrating, he said, "human progress from the dark prime to the highest level of enlightenment, from savagery to civic organization, from egoism to altruism."[69] Skin color and level of traditional technology were the principal determinants of where he placed any group on his scale of progress:

A group of African pygmies, some of them of man-eating tribes [sic!], brought the collection of primitive races down to the lowest known human stage; the Ainus and Patagonians represented the semi-civilized savages still existing like our Indians in countries dominated by highly civilized races and like the Indians rapidly disappearing. . . . The exhibit . . . satisfied the intelligent observer that there is a course of progress running from lower to higher humanity and that all the physical and cultural types of man mark the stages in that course.[70]

Southwestern Indian people who lived in McGee's outdoor compound included Apaches, Cocopas, Maricopas, Navajos, Pimas, and people from Acoma, Santa Clara, and Laguna pueblos (Fig. 17.3). Many of them also participated in the Indian School exhibit next door. The Bureau of Indian Affairs continued its practice of displaying young Indian people in Anglo-run schools in juxtaposition with "traditional" people. This time, there was one large building with a wide

17.3. "Cocopa Indian Group Before Their Habitation," W J McGee in center. St. Louis world's fair, 1904. Courtesy of the Missouri Historical Society.

hallway. On one side were classes with students from five BIA schools demonstrating their skills in "domestic sciences." On the other side were "Blanket Indians," or "old Indians" (nearly three hundred people, eighty from the Southwest, during the course of the fair), making and selling traditional crafts, including "Pueblo women grinding corn and making wafer bread" and pottery, Pima and Jicarilla Apache basket weavers, Navajo "blanket weavers" and "celebrated silver smiths," numerous bead and buckskin workers from Plains tribes, and "Geronimo, working on bows and arrows, which he sells readily . . ."[71]

Geronimo later told his biographer, "I stayed in this place for six months. . . . I often made as much as two dollars a day, and when I returned I had plenty of

money—more than I had ever owned before." Geronimo was just as amazed by all the marvels of the fair as were most of the nineteen million paying visitors.[72]

The Pike, the exposition's entertainment zone, featured many old favorites including the great Ferris Wheel from Chicago, and Streets of Cairo belly dancers who, along with a troupe of French cancan dancers, once again stirred the ire of the bluenoses. The Wild West show is said to have included Will Rogers and Tom Mix in the cast.[73]

There was yet another "Cliff Dwellers" exhibit (Fig. 17.4). The promoter, W. Maurice Tobin, wanted to outdo the Cliff Dwellers exhibit in Chicago. Occupants were to be Zunis and Hopis, the latter to perform the Snake Dance several times daily. In the end,

"We talked in Spanish because we didn't know each others' Indian."[75]

The photographs of the Cliff Dwellers exhibit clearly demonstrate that it was all "show biz," despite the usual claims of "authenticity." Patrons paid a twenty-five-cent entrance fee, another twenty-five cents to witness a "snake dance" performed by Plains Indians with fake, or live (but rattle-less) snakes (Fig. 17.5), and another twenty-five cents for a performance of the "lighter side of Moki life: quaint bridal costumes, native dances, ancient chants, a native orchestra playing on stringed instruments made of dogs' ribs, sheeps' toes, tortoise shell rattles, and sun-baked squash." There was also an Eagle Dance, which at least was a Rio Grande Pueblo dance, although often not billed as such.[76]

the actual exhibit was much smaller than Tobin had hoped and the inhabitants were not Zunis or Hopis, but people from San Juan, Santa Clara, and San Ildefonso pueblos, including María and Julián Martínez on their honeymoon, and Ramos Archuleta, the governor of San Juan Pueblo. They were billed, however, as "Mokis" in the fair publicity.[74]

María Martínez told biographer Alice Marriott that she, Julián, and the others pretended to know little or no English and spoke Tewa. "The Indians pretended they did not understand what was said, and then they had something to laugh about when the white people had gone home and the Indians were alone on the fair grounds. . . . All María had to do was to sit and make pottery, and sometimes dance." María later told Susan Peterson that she met Geronimo in San Diego in 1915, but it had to have been St. Louis, since he had died in 1909. She liked him, she said.

Very little is known about what the people who participated in the fairs thought about their experiences, except for the brief statements by María Martínez and Geronimo. Some Anglos saw the exhibits as exploitative and denigrating, and doubtless many were. On the other hand, working in a Wild West show, especially William Cody's show, which paid relatively well, was better than life back on the rez as an unemployed "ward of the government." María Martínez seemingly found the world's fairs stimulating and lucrative; she participated not only in St. Louis, but in San Diego, in 1915 and 1916, Chicago in 1933, and both New York and San Francisco in 1939–40, as well as smaller expositions.[77]

The emerging trend in marketing Southwestern Indian arts and crafts (see Chapter 27) was reflected in exhibits in the anthropology building. There was "a specially notable display of Indian handiwork . . . by

Fred Harvey . . . a collection of Navajo and other native blankets with basketry, pottery and ceremonial objects." Another collection "designed to illustrate the preservation and improvement of aboriginal motives" was the "J. W. Benham exhibit of southwestern pottery, basketry and blanketry." Benefactors, such as Benham, said the fair publicity, "are engaged in the effort to make better Indians rather than . . . turning out counterfeit Caucasians; as a means to this end they are seeking to preserve and improve native arts and crafts."[78]

Finally, there was McGee. The "Anthropological exhibit," he averred, "represented the sum of human knowledge respecting races . . . a world's museum of human relics, and a congress of living examples of various human types, brought from the most remote parts of the globe." He then draws an idiosyncratic picture of world cultural history. In the chapter on "Mound Builders, Cliff Dwellers, Aztecs and Peruvians," he asserts that the Mound Builders were not

the ancestors of historic eastern tribes. Rather, they were "driven westward" by "such powerful nations as the Algonquians," and made their "last stand" as the Cliff Dwellers of the Southwest, then "finally perished at the hands of their [unspecified] enemies."[79]

"Pueblo Indians of New Mexico and Arizona are generally supposed to be descendants of the Aztecs," but McGee rejects the supposition because of their "remarkable degeneracy." Southwestern Puebloans, he says, "are among the lowest of humanity, with instincts, rather than reason, little above that of brutes." They exhibit a "dense ignorance associated with grossest superstition upon which rests a truly wondrous fanaticism. The Moki [Hopi] tribe are snake worshippers, . . . the Zunis are lazy beggars, and each branch of the Pueblos have their bloody witchcrafts [sic] and their tragic ceremonials, among which is self-torture [sic] . . . These people are not capable of building such large structures . . . [as] Casa Grande."[80]

McGee's improbable linking of Mound Builders

and Cliff Dwellers, and the outburst against the historic Pueblo peoples, must have startled and angered his former compatriots in the Bureau of American Ethnology and the anthropological community. Perhaps it was a parting shot; McGee never returned to anthropology after the exposition closed.

World's fairs had much to do with the development of American anthropology. The expositions from 1889 through 1904 took place during the time when literary, artistic, and touristic attention began to be focused on the Southwest and the commodification of the Indian "arts and crafts" market got under way. The various living exhibits, and the many anthropological and archaeological displays at the fairs, served to heighten public awareness of anthropology, while at the same time often reinforcing long-held stereotypes about Indian people in and outside the Southwest.

CHAPTER 18

Universities, Museums, and Anthropology

THE RELATIONSHIPS between philanthropy, universities, research institutes, museums, and anthropology were closely woven at the turn of the twentieth century. In 1892, the New York *Tribune* counted 4,047 persons in the United States thought to have a net worth of one million dollars or more. By that time, individuals with wealth far in excess of that figure—wealth derived from railroads, industry, and high finance—were being pilloried as "Robber Barons," and were seeking ways to change their images. Philanthropy on a large scale was one answer, including the creation and support of cultural institutions.[1] One of the first was Leland Stanford's chartering of Stanford University in 1885 (it opened in 1891), with endowments of unprecedented size. John D. Rockefeller responded with an endowment of 1,600,000 dollars to help found the new University of Chicago, and added more later. In 1889, Andrew Carnegie published his famous article "Wealth." He presented a moral justification for big-dollar philan-

thropy, reflecting the Protestant-ethic view that individuals are stewards of wealth, not simply consumers of it, and should use their money for the public good.[2] He practiced what he preached through the hundreds of Carnegie libraries and various educational and research institutions he created and funded.

But the problems of giving away money, especially large sums of money, are complex. There are many supplicants; sorting the worthy from the unworthy takes a great deal of time. By about 1899, businessman John D. Rockefeller hit upon a businesslike solution: "Let us erect a foundation, a trust, and engage directors who will make it a life work to manage, with our personal cooperation, this business of benevolence properly and effectively."[3] In the following decade, Rockefeller, Carnegie, and Russell Sage created and endowed several foundations: corporate institutions through which the "business of benevolence" was carried out. Other donors and foundations followed.

Some philanthropists also became trustees of institutions and channeled monies into them as part of their fiduciary responsibilities.

Much of this money went to "research universities" patterned on the model of German universities, which emphasized research and granted "higher" degrees: Master's degrees and doctorates of philosophy. After about 1810, Americans who could afford advanced training spent one or more years at one or more German universities. In 1869, Harvard made the transition from college to university on the German model. Johns Hopkins University, chartered in 1867, followed the pattern when it opened in 1876. By 1881 Columbia University and the University of Pennsylvania had followed suit. Clark University, in Worcester, Massachusetts, founded in 1889, was devoted solely to graduate work and science.[4] The state-chartered "land grant" universities, made possible by the 1862 Morrill Act, in time followed the German model.

Paralleling the emergence of research universities in the United States was the creation and growth of major museums. The period from about 1850 to 1920 is often called the "Age of Museums."[5] In the United States, several natural history and anthropology museums were founded between 1865 and 1915. The widespread support for natural history museums, zoos, and botanical gardens grew out of a popular natural history craze, with religious roots, that swept Europe and North America. Studying natural history to understand God's ways was socially acceptable, morally uplifting, and very popular. The pious invaded the countryside in droves to net butterflies and pick and press flowers. They compared notes on everything from algology to zoology at dozens of local and regional natural history societies, and flocked to natural history museums, zoos, and botanical gardens as they were created.[6]

Since natural man, in his various "savage" guises, was seen as part of nature, he fell in the province of natural history; therefore artifacts and information relating to him were deposited in natural history museums. As Frank Hamilton Cushing wrote to Stewart Culin (see below) in 1894: "Ours is a New World where things speak as in time primaeval, and our museums become books and histories or should become so, *for the History of Man in America is, thank heaven, a natural history and an unwritten one!*" Later critics saw the objects in natural history and anthropology museums as symbolic trophies of the domination of both nature and colonized peoples by imperialist nations.[7]

From its inception, the Smithsonian Institution was involved with anthropology, more so after the Bureau of Ethnology was sheltered under its wing in 1879 and John Wesley Powell began the long-term involvement with the Southwest. Other U.S. museums that developed major research and collecting programs in the Southwest between 1890 and about 1925 were the Peabody Museum of Archaeology and Ethnology at Harvard University, the Field Museum of Natural History in Chicago, the American Museum of Natural History in New York, the Brooklyn Museum in Brooklyn, and the Museum of the American Indian in New York.

Frederic Ward Putnam and the Harvard Peabody Museum

Frederic Ward Putnam (1839–1915) was a key figure in the development of both American anthropology museums and university anthropology departments for four decades. He was born in Salem, Massachusetts.[8] His youthful interest in natural history attracted the attention of Louis Agassiz, who invited Putnam to Harvard to study with him in 1856. Agassiz (1807–73) had come to the United States in 1846; in 1848 he was appointed professor of geology and zoology in the Lawrence Scientific School at Harvard. He was a powerful figure in American science, famed for his ability to raise money, for his careful research in comparative zoology, and for his unyielding opposition to the Darwinian theory of evolution. By 1856 he had put together state, university, and private funding for his great Museum of Comparative Zoology on the Harvard campus.[9] Putnam's years with Agassiz shaped his career as a natural historian and museum director. Museums, said Agassiz, were primarily institutions dedicated to field research, the amassing of collections for study, and the publication of results. That they might also be open to students and the public for educational purposes was secondary.

In 1866, O. C. Marsh, the prominent paleontologist, persuaded his wealthy uncle, George Peabody, to give Harvard a 150,000-dollar endowment toward a building, a collections fund, and a professorship for a museum of American archaeology. Harvard donated the building site for the Peabody Museum of American Archaeology and Ethnology. Peabody also endowed a museum of natural science at Yale University, and in 1867 gave 160,000 dollars for a Peabody Academy of Science and an associated museum in Salem. The latter focused on natural history collections and ethnological materials, much of it collected by Salem sea captains and merchants. In 1864, Putnam broke with Agassiz and retreated to Salem without finishing even a bachelor's degree. He was appointed director of the Salem Academy museum in 1867 at age twenty-eight.[10]

Jeffries Wyman, a well-known anatomy professor, was the first curator of the Peabody Museum at Harvard. He died in 1874; Putnam was appointed to replace him in 1876. Putnam and Wyman had spent much time together doing archaeology, and Putnam gradually shifted his interests from ichthyology to archaeology.[11]

In 1873, Putnam became the permanent secretary of the American Association for the Advancement of Science (AAAS), a position he held for twenty-five years. This put him at the center of the burgeoning science establishment, since he planned the programs and edited and published the annual reports. By 1876, Putnam was launched on his career as archaeologist, museum administrator, and association officer. He was not, however, appointed as the Peabody professor of archaeology and ethnology until 1887, owing to his lack of a doctorate and the enmity of Agassiz's son, Alexander, who sat on the Harvard Board of Overseers. Putnam's first students, beginning in 1890 were John Owens, who worked with Fewkes, and George A. Dorsey.[12]

Putnam's own fieldwork was primarily in Mound Builder archaeology. He was responsible for saving the Great Serpent Mound in southern Ohio by arranging for its purchase, and later turning it over to the Ohio State Archaeological and Historical Society.[13] His archaeological mentor, Jeffries Wyman, thought humans were likely of great antiquity in the New World and encouraged the search for evidence. Putnam continued that interest, which involved him for twenty-five years in "timorous support" for Charles C. Abbott, who was convinced he had found "Paleolithic" tools in the river gravels near his home in Trenton, New Jersey (see below).

Putnam's appointment at Harvard carried only a partial salary. He had no private income, but did have a family to support; hence, he was open to other opportunities. The first one was as head of the Ethnology Division of the Chicago world's fair, from 1891 until the end of 1893. Later, between 1896 and 1908, he played key roles in the development of anthropology programs at the American Museum in New York and at the University of California. There was, however, another position he coveted but did not get, in Chicago.

The Field Columbian Museum

The Chicago architect Daniel Burnham, who directed the design and construction of the world's fair buildings, had the motto "Make no small plans." Putnam agreed. On November 28, 1891, he addressed the Commercial Club of Chicago; many club members were involved in creating the fair. Playing on their competitiveness with New York, Putnam urged them to use the fair to develop a great natural history museum—to rival the American Museum of Natural History. C. Brown Goode, of the Smithsonian, was in Chicago at about the same time. He too declared that the fair provided the opportunity to establish a great museum.[14]

Wealthy and prominent Chicagoans agreed. While the fair was still under way, a museum board of trustees was formed and the Columbian Museum of Chicago was incorporated. Edward Ayer played a major role. Ayer had made his fortune providing wooden ties and telegraph poles to railroads. During the Civil War he was a lieutenant in Carleton's California Volunteers. While in Arizona, he chanced upon a copy of Prescott's *Conquest of Mexico*. Entranced, he became an avid student of Hispanic and American Indian history, ultimately amassing a huge collection of books, manuscripts, maps, prints, drawings, and artifacts. Ayer convinced Marshall Field, the dry-goods king, to put up 1 million dollars to get the museum started.[15] George M. Pullman, of Pullman Sleeping Car fame, put up 100,000 dollars, as did Harlow Higinbotham, a partner in Marshall Field company and president of the World's Fair Corporation. Ayer donated his artifact collection (his books, manuscripts, etc., were later given to the Newberry Library).

In keeping with world's fair precedent, a fine arts building was constructed as a permanent structure. After the fair closed, the anthropology and natural history collections were assembled there and Edward Ayer became museum president. In May 1894 it was renamed the Field Columbian Museum (in 1905 the name was changed to the Field Museum of Natural History). When Marshall Field died in 1906 he left eight million dollars to the museum, half for a building and half as an initial endowment. Between 1893 and 1943 the Field family gave over twenty million dollars to the museum. Construction began in 1915 and was finished in 1920.[16]

The early development of the museum was entangled with that of the new University of Chicago. The old University of Chicago opened in 1857 and closed in 1886. John D. Rockefeller put up 1,600,000 dollars to start the new University of Chicago in 1891. Marshall Field gave the land for the university, and there were other major donors, especially from the Chicago Jewish community. William Rainey Harper, who received a doctorate in Hebrew and linguistics from Yale when he was eighteen, became the first president. Harper had been active in the Chautauqua movement, where he had met Frederick Starr, a geologist turned anthropologist. Harper brought Starr, who was working at the American Museum in New York, to Chicago to start an anthropology program. He also brought in T. C. Chamberlin to head the Geology Department. Chamberlin had close ties in Washington, especially with Charles D. Walcott in the Geological Survey and William Henry Holmes in the Smithsonian.[17]

When the new museum was announced, there was much jockeying by Harper, Chamberlin, and Starr to have it be part of, or at least linked to, the University of Chicago. Starr wanted to control anthropology in both institutions; Chamberlin wanted a three-way linkage between the university, the museum, and the Washington science establishment. Frederic Ward Putnam wanted "his man," Franz Boas, to become head of the Anthropology Division. Boas had quit a permanent position at Clark University to take the world's fair job. As the museum became a reality, Boas wanted to be its curator of anthropology. Putnam wanted to become the museum's director, which would finally give him a full salary. But power politics, jealousy, mistrust, and back-room deals derailed the plans of Boas, Putnam, Harper, and Starr, and, in part, Chamberlin.[18]

The full story is very complex. In brief, Putnam had frequently clashed with Harlow Higinbotham, the president of the world's fair. Higinbotham, as president of the board of trustees, and Edward Ayer, as president of the museum, named Frederick J. V. Skiff as museum director. Skiff was a journalist who had been involved in staging expositions and trade fairs for several years. He was Higinbotham's deputy director for the fair. He remained as director of the museum until he died in 1921, although he frequently was on loan to various world's fairs, including St. Louis in 1904.[19] Skiff, Higinbotham, and the museum trustees did not want a link to the University of Chicago; exit Harper and Starr. Harper built a great university without a museum. Within the university, Starr became a deadwood anthropological appendage of the Department of Sociology. Albion Small, and later Robert Park and George Herbert Mead, built Chicago sociology into the premier department in the

United States.[20] Only after Starr retired in 1923, and Fay-Cooper Cole and Edward Sapir were brought in, did the University of Chicago begin to build an anthropology program.

Meanwhile, back at the Field Museum, Boas was hired temporarily to get the anthropology collections installed, but was not considered for a permanent position, despite his and Putnam's expectations and hopes. Chamberlin convinced Skiff, Ayer, and Higinbotham to hire Walcott and Holmes. John Wesley Powell resigned as director of the Geological Survey in 1894, and Walcott replaced him rather than go to Chicago. Powell moved back into the Bureau of Ethnology and needed a salary; Holmes's move to Chicago helped resolve that problem, but put Boas out of work in May 1894. Putnam did what he could to help, and W J McGee began buying manuscripts from Boas (see Chapter 12). Boas had two bleak years, and he never forgot nor forgave those he thought responsible, among them Holmes, who was the least involved of any in the machinations. But bad blood had been created, and would remain for decades.

Holmes was well rewarded at Chicago; his salary was four thousand dollars a year, second only to Skiff's, and considerably higher than Smithsonian salaries at the time. He threw himself into the work of the new museum. By December 1894 he was accompanying Allison V. Armour, scion of the meatpacking family, on his steam yacht *Ituna* to Yucatán and Mexico. Holmes collected roughly one thousand specimens at Palenque, Mitla, Monte Albán, Teotihuacán, and in the Valley of Mexico and made some stratigraphic test excavations.[21]

But things soon went awry. Holmes's relationship with Skiff deteriorated. Work and research standards were not up to Holmes's sense of scientific probity. A friend of Holmes, John Coulter, president of Lake Forest College in Chicago, had warned Holmes that taking the job presented a danger, "the common danger of Chicago, namely to make the Columbian Museum a big show instead of a center for scientific collections for study and work."[22] Holmes was not a showman. In 1897 he resigned, took a pay cut, and re-

treated back to the Smithsonian, where he remained until the end of his long and fruitful life and career.

In 1895, George A. Dorsey, having finished his Ph.D. at Harvard, became assistant curator of anthropology, despite being a "Putnam man."[23] Dorsey by temperament fit the Chicago style; he was aggressive and flamboyant, a showman. When Holmes resigned, Dorsey succeeded him as curator of anthropology. The Field Columbian Museum was the new institution on the museum scene in 1894. The anthropology collections remaining with the museum at the end of the world's fair totaled a relatively paltry fifty thousand specimens. When Dorsey took over, he launched an ambitious acquisitions program. He decided to focus first on North America, and began a hard-sell fund-raising campaign among the wealthy citizens of Chicago. He was successful, and for ten years he and various ethnographer-collectors scoured the various regions of North America. His collections documentation policy set a new standard by requiring sufficient documentation on each specimen to "make its use, history, origin, material, etc. available in a scientific journal," if required.[24]

H. R. Voth and the Hopi

One of Dorsey's principal ethnographer-collectors was Heinrich Richert Voth (1855–1931) (Fig. 18.1). Voth was born in a Mennonite village in southern Russia. He was baptized into the Mennonite church in 1873, intending to become a foreign missionary. His congregation emigrated to the United States in 1874, settling at Newton, Kansas. In 1877, Voth's aim of being a missionary was rekindled. He attended a Mennonite school and seminary and in 1881–82 took a two semester medical course at St. Louis Medical College.[25]

To the Mennonites, "foreign missions" could be any "heathen" group, including American Indians. Voth became a missionary among the Southern Arapahoes and Cheyennes at Darlington, Oklahoma, in 1882. His first wife died in 1889 and a daughter died in 1891. The distraught Voth toured Europe and the

18.1. H. R. Voth. Courtesy of Mennonite Library and Archives, Bethel College, North Newton, Kansas.

Middle East for several months. Returning, he remarried and, in July 1893, the couple moved to Arizona to establish a mission among the Hopi adjacent to Oraibi on Third Mesa. Oraibi was the most conservative of the Hopi villages and was already being riven by factionalism that led to a splitting of the village in 1906.

Voth spent two years learning Hopi; by 1894 he was proficient enough to become a government interpreter. He ministered to the sick, helped people when he could, and tried to win converts, although few heeded his message. He was well enough respected to gain admission to some kiva ceremonies. Once, it is said, he was allowed into a kiva, "but preached in Hopi throughout the rite, saying that the pagan cere-

mony was 'no good' and that all the participants would be burned in a big fire."[26] He was ambivalent about Hopi ritual and cosmology, feeling that it was his duty to record them, but at the same time suppress them by turning the Hopi into good Mennonite Christians. As he said, "What a pantheon, what a rich language, what traditions, and yet how utterly lacking in the elements to satisfy the longing of the soul and give peace to the heart for this life and hope for eternity." In the end, he made no converts.[27]

In 1897, George Dorsey came to Oraibi and stayed with Voth. Voth had begun collecting kachina dolls as a way to learn about the kachinas and their ceremonies and had made extensive notes and sketches of ceremonies. Dorsey enlisted Voth to collect for him and provided a camera and a typewriter. Voth soon forwarded some four hundred objects, including kachina dolls, stone tools, and masks. Dorsey pressured Voth to forego missionizing and become an ethnographer; Voth's wife and sister pressured him to do the opposite; his ambivalence increased. In 1901, Voth's wife died in childbirth. He moved his children and sister to Chicago. Dorsey had convinced Stanley Mc-Cormick to fund the Stanley McCormick Hopi Expedition. Voth worked in Chicago and later in Kansas, under its aegis. He reproduced several Hopi ceremonial altars and wrote a monograph on the Soyal ceremony, the first of several major monographs on Hopi ceremonials that remain as classics.[28]

In 1904 the Fred Harvey Company hired Voth to help design displays and purchase artifacts for Hopi House next to the El Tovar Hotel on the south rim of the Grand Canyon (see Chapter 27). The house included a Hopi altar and sandpainting. The extensive collection of artifacts that Voth made for Hopi House was sold to the American Museum of Natural History in 1910; Voth then made an even larger collection. By this time, the Fred Harvey Company was not only buying artifacts for its own collection and display, but for the tourist trade and for sale to museums. Voth was also supplying collections to others. In 1906 he sold 275 kachina dolls, "with detailed notes on each," to the Carnegie Museum in Pittsburgh.[29]

In 1913, Fred Harvey employed Voth and his son to reproduce three more Hopi altars for display in the Indian building in Albuquerque and at Hopi House. When the project was finished, Voth turned away from ethnography and collecting and went back to his church activities in Kansas and Oklahoma. He died in Newton, Kansas, in 1931. By that time, two young Mennonite boys born in Newton had left to study anthropology. One was Emil W. Haury, who was at the first Pecos Conference in 1927 as a student (see Chapters 25, 29), wrote up Cushing's los Muertos materials for his doctoral dissertation and became the dean of Southwestern archaeology. The other was Waldo Wedel, who wrote his dissertation on Kansas archaeology, then moved to the Smithsonian Institution, his base for a fifty-plus-year career as the dean of modern Plains archaeology.[30]

Voth's ethnographic and collecting career at Oraibi was unique, due to the factionalism of the time, his aggressiveness, and his contacts with Hopi people. No Anglo ever again had the access to ceremonies at Oraibi at the level that Voth did. At the request of the Hopi tribe, the models in the Field Museum and in the Harvey collection are no longer displayed.

Dorsey produced a popular book published by the Santa Fe Railway on Southwestern Indians in 1903 (see Chapter 27).[31] He continued at the Field Museum until 1915, became a U.S. Naval attaché in Spain during World War I, and later made his living as an independent scholar in New York City. His popular books, especially *Why We Behave Like Human Beings* (1925), which went through thirty-five reprintings in two years, were widely hailed when they were published, but have long since been forgotten.[32]

Archaeology and Philanthropy in Philadelphia

In 1888, leading Philadelphians formed the American Exploration Society to support archaeological work in Babylon, Egypt, Central America, Italy, and Greece. As was the practice, in return for its annual support, the society received a portion of the artifacts exca-

vated each year. The collections soon accumulated and there was a call for a museum.[33] Two prominent citizens who made the call were William Pepper and Sara Yorke Stevenson. In order to understand the development of anthropology in Philadelphia, and later in Brooklyn and Berkeley, it is necessary to introduce Pepper, Stevenson, and some of their friends. William Pepper (1843–1898), from an old Philadelphia family, was professor of medicine at the University of Pennsylvania, maintaining a private practice on the side. He also was university provost from 1880 until 1894. A person of great vision and enormous energy, said to require little or no sleep and to relax only "momentarily," he helped develop Penn into a major research university.[34]

Pepper apparently had an extraordinary bedside manner, especially with patients who were wealthy women; one such was Sara Yorke Stevenson (1847–1921) (Fig. 18.2). Sara Yorke was born in Paris, France,

18.2. *Sara Yorke Stevenson. Courtesy of the University of Pennsylvania Museum, Philadelphia.*

and lived there and in Mexico as a girl and young woman, then lived with an aunt and uncle in Philadelphia. She married Cornelius Stevenson in 1870. "Highly gifted, she possessed a magnetic personality, assured executive ability, and indomitable energy."[35] About 1891, Phoebe Apperson Hearst (1842–1919) and Zelia Nuttall came to Philadelphia at Stevenson's invitation. Hearst (see Fig. 19.3) was the widow of George Hearst who made, lost, and made several mining fortunes. He died in 1890 leaving Phoebe about eighteen million dollars; he also left a tidy sum and the San Francisco *Examiner* to their son, William Randolph Hearst.[36]

By 1880 Phoebe Hearst was an active philanthropist. Two trips to Europe sharpened her interest in Classical antiquity and European art. One of her close confidantes was Zelia Nuttall (1857–1933), whom she met and befriended about 1876, when Nuttall returned to San Francisco after living in Europe for eleven years with her family.

Nuttall was the daughter of a wealthy San Francisco doctor, Robert K. Nuttall, and Magdalena Parrott Nuttall, of a prominent San Francisco banking family. As a child, Zelia received from her mother a copy of Lord Kingsborough's work on Mexican antiquities; the gift led to a lifelong fascination with Mexican archaeology and history. In 1880 Zelia married the dashing and peripatetic French explorer, anthropologist, linguist, and bibliographer Alphonse Louis Pinart (1852–1911). But the marriage soon foundered, after Pinart went through much of Nuttall's money, having spent his own inherited fortune on his travels and publications.[37] They separated in 1884 and divorced in 1888. Zelia assumed the name "Mrs. Nuttall," and began serious study of Mexican archaeology, settling near Mexico City, where for many years she hosted visiting anthropologists and many others. About 1895 Frederic Ward Putnam made Nuttall an honorary assistant in archaeology at the Peabody Museum at Harvard, a position she retained for forty-seven years. Her discovery of the "Codex Nuttall," and rediscovery of the Codex Magliabecchiano were major contributions to Mesoamerican stud-

ies, along with numerous papers on Mexican archaeology, ethnobotany, and ethnohistory.[38] Soon after their arrival, William Pepper added Mrs. Hearst and Mrs. Nuttall to his list of private patients.

Pepper and Sara Stevenson were key actors in the development of the university museum, starting in 1889. For twenty years, Stevenson was simultaneously the unpaid curator of the Babylonian, Egyptian, and Mediterranean sections of the museum, and secretary (and later president) of the board of managers. Daniel Brinton, a native Philadelphian, by 1890 recognized as the senior scholar in American anthropology, was appointed professor of American linguistics and archaeology, in both the university and the museum. It was "a signal honor [which, however] carried no pecuniary rewards for the incumbent"; he also never had any students.[39]

Late in 1889, with the strong support of Putnam, Pepper and Stevenson hired Charles C. Abbott as curator of archaeology. Abbott had received an M.D. degree from the University of Pennsylvania in 1854, but had unwisely chosen to make a living as a popular-science writer and archaeologist. He had been in correspondence with Putnam since 1870, and Putnam had funded portions of Abbott's fieldwork. In 1872 Abbott published "The Stone Age in New Jersey," which started a three-decade-long, clamorous debate over the antiquity of humans in the Western Hemisphere. Abbott and his supporters were convinced that chipped stone tools found in the Trenton gravel deposits were not only typologically similar to those of the Old Stone Age in Europe, but were of equivalent age. His detractors, led by William Henry Holmes, vociferously disagreed. In the meantime, Putnam's support helped Abbott became the first paid curator of the nascent museum.[40] The second curator hired was Stewart Culin.

Robert Stewart Culin (1858–1929) was one of the more interesting and colorful of American museum anthropologists (Fig. 18.3). Born and reared in Philadelphia, after high school he entered his father's mercantile business. Little is known about him until the 1880s, when he became an officer in the local

18.3. Stuart Culin. Courtesy of the University of Pennsylvania Museum Archives, Philadelphia.

Numismatic and Antiquarian Society and began publishing papers on Chinese-American culture and society, especially religion, secret societies, medicine, and games. Culin later said that his interest in Chinese culture began when he sought the origins of mahjongg, a game popular in the U.S. from the 1880s to the 1930s. He had lived in Philadelphia's Chinatown, learned Chinese, and began his studies.[41] Through local scholarly groups, he met Daniel Brinton and William Pepper.

In 1890 both Culin and Brinton were elected to the museum's board of managers. In 1892 Culin became curator of general ethnology and the American section, and was named director of the museum, except for Sara Stevenson's Babylonian, Egyptian, and Mediterranean fiefdoms within it.[42] His first task was to take charge of the museum's exhibit at the 1892 expo-

sition in Madrid. His second was to fire Charles C. Abbott, who had no curatorial skills and whose "Paleolithic" monomania dominated his actions.[43] Culin also agreed to head the Folk-Lore and Primitive Religions section of the 1893 Chicago world's fair.

When Cushing's health took yet another downturn, he turned to Pepper for treatment on the advice of Stevenson, Nuttall, and Culin. Pepper prescribed a working vacation in Florida, and he and Phoebe Hearst funded the joint, and ill-fated, University of Pennsylvania and Bureau of American Ethnology-sponsored, Pepper-Hearst Expedition of 1895–96 (see Chapter 13).

Hearst began to support other archaeological research through the American Exploration Society. On Cushing's recommendation, she purchased, for 14,500 dollars, the combined Hazzard-Green collections that had been exhibited in Chicago and donated them to the university museum, thus beginning its Southwestern collection.[44] In 1900, funded by John Wanamaker, the department-store magnate, Culin made a whirlwind tour of Indian reservations with George Dorsey, who mentored Culin on how to collect artifacts. In 1901 Wanamaker supported additional collecting trips, during which Culin purchased collections from Thomas Keam, H. R. Voth, and others.[45]

Meanwhile, Culin continued and expanded his interest in games. Culin and his wife Helen had formed a close personal and intellectual friendship with Emily and Frank Hamilton Cushing during their months together at the Chicago world's fair. Cushing was fascinated by Culin's games and their implications for culture history, especially the "remarkable analogies . . . between oriental and modern European games . . . and those of the American Indian."[46] They planned a comprehensive joint study of games worldwide, but Cushing's health problems interfered. Culin, however, proceeded. He put together another exhibit of games for an exposition in Atlanta in 1896, which stimulated the interest of George Dorsey at the Field Museum. Dorsey had all his collectors seek out gaming implements. He turned the collections and notes over to Culin, who combined them with others into a massive annotated catalog published in 1907 by the Bureau of American Ethnology, the famous *Games of North American Indians.*[47]

Cushing had participated in a divinatory dice game, *sho-li-we,* at Zuni. This led him to convince Culin that "games . . . must be regarded not as conscious inventions, but as survivals from primitive conditions, under which they originated in magical rites, and chiefly as a means of divination."[48] Culin's continued study of parallels between Old and New World games led him to speculate that divination, and indeed, civilization, originated in America, perhaps at Zuni(!), and diffused to the Old World via Asia. He later retracted the assertion that all New World games derive from divination, but continued to explore interhemispheric cultural connections throughout his career.[49] His studies of Asian and North American games remain as classics and major reference works.

Finally, as a coda, Culin was well acquainted with Philadelphia artist Thomas Eakins. Eakins painted both Culin's and Cushing's (see Fig. 8.1) portraits in 1895 and exhibited them in 1901. Culin's portrait was called "The Archaeologist." It apparently was stolen in 1930 and never recovered.[50]

The Brooklyn Museum

Brinton and Culin tried to broaden the scope of the university museum to general anthropology. Sara Stevenson had a different view, focused on Old World civilizations; she won. Brinton retreated to the university. Culin lasted until 1903 and then left—in a cloud of acrimony and threatened lawsuits—for the calm of The Brooklyn Museum.[51]

Brooklyn was chartered as an independent city in 1834. Its citizens strongly supported the development of cultural institutions. One such was the Brooklyn Institute, founded in 1840, upgraded to the Brooklyn Institute of Arts and Sciences in 1890. Institute members planned a combined natural history and art museum for the "education, refinement, elevation, and pleasure of all the people," to rival the American Museum and the Metropolitan Museum across the

river in Manhattan. Designed by the premier architectural firm of McKim, Mead and White, construction of what is now The Brooklyn Museum of Art began in 1897–98, the same year Brooklyn became a borough of New York City. A Department of Ethnology was created in February 1903, when Stewart Culin was appointed curator.[52]

Culin in the Southwest

When Culin moved to Brooklyn, the threnody of the vanishing savage was being sung by every anthropologist and museum collector. He took up the refrain. If he was going to fill his exhibits with authentic traditional material culture, he had to scramble. He told his trustees, "The Indian-as-savage [is] soon to disappear"; soonest, he thought, in the Southwest, hence best to start there.[53]

But what was "authentic traditional material culture"? James Stevenson had shipped railcars of heirloom material from Zuni, Hopi, and the Rio Grande pueblos to the National Museum. The dealings of Thomas Keam, the Wetherills, and Tom Polacca with museum collectors had not gone unnoticed by Indian traders. They rapidly bought up whatever "traditional" items they could for eventual sale to museum collectors or to the burgeoning tourist market. A lively hogan/pueblo "cottage" industry in the manufacture of new "authentic ancient and traditional" items sprang up, encouraged by the traders.

In 1904 Matilda Coxe Stevenson wrote of Zuni that "the less orthodox [Indian] men will manufacture almost anything the collector may desire. Spurious ancient fetishes are made by the sackful and passed off as genuine. So it is also with the masks and altars. Any number of fraudulent objects may be obtained at the prices set by the clever Indians."[54] By 1903, Andrew Vanderwagen, a missionary turned trader at Zuni, had acquired the "entire contents of three shrines" and had three Zuni artisans secretly making ceremonial masks and kachina dolls to order in his basement. Culin bought the shrine objects and a large collection of newly made masks and dolls from Vanderwagen for 1,028 dollars. He was not able to acquire any Zuni masks that had actually been used in a ceremony.[55]

Culin wanted "complete" collections, examples of all the material culture items in "traditional" use by a tribe or pueblo. If he could not acquire an heirloom or an implement still in use, he commissioned a replica or bought one from the traders. He had Zunis make replicas of games, prayer sticks, dance paraphernalia, jewelry, farming implements, tools, and costumes. He even provided the "correct" material, if needed. For example, he wanted to reproduce Cushing's Zuni costume. He found a blue woolen shirt at Zuni, but the leggings were a problem. He had to order Indian-tanned buckskin from a Denver department store and have it dyed. He had to find a Zuni tailor and supply him with sinew and a bone awl. The silver buttons on the leggings, which had led the Zunis to call Cushing "Many Buttons," were a major problem. In order to get a Zuni silversmith to make the buttons, Culin had to buy the man's ancient forge, seemingly the same one Sitgreaves had illustrated in 1853 (see Fig. 2.5), and buy him a new forge before he would consent to make the buttons.[56] The forge was for ironworking; the smith simply saw the opportunity to upgrade his shop at the Brooklyn Museum's expense.

All this raises the issue of "authenticity" that haunts the art, antique, and artifact collecting world. Thomas Hoving's wonderful chronicle of his years as director of the Metropolitan Museum in New York is filled with stories and lessons about fake artworks, antiques, and artifacts, as are hundreds of scholarly articles and sensational newspaper stories.[57] At the turn of the millennium, it is still a sticky and burning issue. If an object is made by a Zuni person, in what senses is it "spurious," or "fraudulent"? Does a dance mask made by a Zuni only become "authentic" by being used in a ceremony? In the 1990s, the state of New Mexico passed legislation saying that a person must be legally certified as an "authentic Indian" in order to sell "authentic Indian jewelry" in New Mexico. But is a legally certified authentic Indian the same as a "real Indian"?

Culin took a pragmatic approach. He co-opted the authenticity issue by asserting the expertise of the anthropologist: "the intelligent collector who knows what he wants. The Indians themselves do not know." An anthropologist "must learn the language of things unprejudiced by their apparent age or the place where he may happen to find them."[58] This is the posture of the positivist expert who, by training and experience, knows the "truth"—or the "authentic artifact"—when s/he sees it.

For Culin, knowing the "language of things" allows the expert collector to tell the story of the "authentic Indian" in exhibits. As Diana Fane comments, "Such a collector could also distinguish the fake from the real, conjure up lost arts, and make fragments whole again. . . . The concept of the language of things allowed Culin to assume authorship as well as ownership of the Indian past and to restore the bits and pieces to their fullness of meaning in the exhibits case."[59]

For his Southwestern exhibits, Culin focused on Zuni and Navajo; Zuni as a memorial to Cushing, and because Dorsey and Voth at the Chicago Field Museum had "done" the Hopi; and Navajo because they hadn't yet been "done." He also wanted archaeological materials to provide time depth. He bought an extensive collection from Mummy Cave in Canyon de Chelly from Indian trader Charles L. Day of Chinle, Arizona, for four thousand dollars, outbidding the National Museum.[60] Day also sold him a very large collection of Navajo items, including unredeemed pawn and articles from caves in Canyon del Muerto, "relics of a band of Navajo who were killed by Mexicans in the cañon about 100 years ago, the tragedy giving the cañon its name." This was the slaughter of "hundreds" of Navajo women and children killed by ricocheting bullets fired by Spanish soldiers and auxiliaries into rockshelters high in the ledges of the canyon where the victims were hiding. J. Lorenzo Hubbell, of the Ganado trading post, helped Culin acquire a set of Navajo Yeibichei masks, which, he claimed, were "the very set which Dr. Matthews had tried unsuccessfully to obtain."[61] Authenticity in another form!

Culin sought help wherever he could. At Cochiti Pueblo he acquired carved stone images, masks, and fetishes from the Catholic missionary Father Noel Dumarest, as well as a vocabulary and "an extensive unpublished account of the ceremonies" of Cochiti, written by Dumarest. He also managed to acquire A. M. Stephen's Hopi journal. Elsie Clews Parsons edited and published both the Stephen and Dumarest manuscripts (see Chapter 26).[62]

Culin's Southwest Exhibits

Culin's close friendship with Cushing led him "to go to Zuni and complete the work" that Cushing had begun before he died. In 1905 he presented a temporary Zuni exhibit centered around Thomas Eakins's portrait of Cushing, which Emily Cushing had loaned to the museum.[63] In 1906 Culin opened a large hall, with one side "devoted to Zuni, especially Zuni masks and ceremonial objects." The opposite side was devoted to Apaches, Navajos, Hopis, and Cliff Dwellers. "A large collection of material from the cliff dwellings in Cañon de Chelly, obtained by Mr. Culin in 1903, is an important feature of the exhibit." There were "many recent Navaho and Hopi objects, intermingled with the remains of the cliff-dwellings proper," and a "set of old masks for the Yebichei dance. All together one hundred thirty three different masks of the Southwestern Indians are exhibited in this hall."[64] Culin's hall was widely acclaimed by the press and critics when it opened. In the 1920s he re-did his Southwest exhibit and incorporated parts of it into a large, multicultural "Rainbow Room" exhibit, also widely praised.[65]

Culin at St. Michaels Mission

Culin was greatly aided in his collecting by missionaries. In the late 1890s, the Franciscans established a mission station on the Navajo Reservation at Cienega, Arizona. Soon renamed St. Michaels, the mission was a few miles south of Fort Defiance, along the road from Gallup, New Mexico, to Ganado and Keams Canyon. In 1900, Fr. Anselm Weber was named mission superior, and two young priests, Frs. Leopold Ostermann and Berard Haile, were sent as assistants. The three remained on the Navajo Reservation for the rest of their lives. Father Haile (1874–1961) was born Jacob Haile in Ohio. Orphaned at an early age, he grew up in Catholic schools and a seminary. In 1891, he took the Franciscan habit and a new name, Friar Berard, as was the custom. He was ordained a priest in 1898.[66]

In 1902, during his last collecting trip for the university museum, Stewart Culin arrived at St. Michaels to find the three priests and a lay brother, Simeon Schwemberger, living in an "old Indian trading store," with a new school and residence being built. Brother Schwemberger cooked and kept house, "without skill or grace," according to Culin.[67] The three young priests had begun studying Navajo language and culture. Like their illustrious Franciscan predecessor Bernardino Sahagún, in sixteenth-century Mexico, they felt they had to understand the language and traditional ways of the people in order to properly convert them.

According to Father Berard's recollections, Culin asked them to help him collect Navajo games, which they did, as well as other ethnographic and linguistic data with the idea of creating some sort of Navajo dictionary. Culin helped them acquire a printing press and type fonts. A retired newspaper compositor from Cincinnati, George Connolly, came west for his health and became the resident printer. Thus began the St. Michaels Press. In 1910, the press issued the 536-page *An Ethnologic Dictionary of the Navaho Language,* containing materials collected by Frs. Haile, Ostermann, and Marcellus Troester. Culin helped by selling subscriptions and having Brooklyn Museum artist Herbert Judy do sketches for the dictionary, which is rich in descriptive detail relating to the words and phrases. With the work of Washington Matthews, the *Ethnologic Dictionary* conveyed to the world the subtlety and complexity of Navajo life and thought. Father Berard became particularly proficient in Navajo language, society, and ritual, capped by his great treatise on the Blessingway, not published until after his death.[68]

Stewart Culin died in 1929. Like Otis T. Mason and William Henry Holmes, he was a quintessential "museum man," rooted in the study of material culture and what it can be made to tell when properly documented. His contributions to Southwestern anthropology were the collections he amassed and used in his exhibits in The Brooklyn Museum, seen over the years by hundreds of thousands of schoolchildren and adults until they were dismantled in the 1930s. On another level, stimulated by Frank Hamilton Cushing, Culin produced the two great works on Asian and American games, for which he is best remembered.

CHAPTER 19

Building a New American Anthropology

The American Museum of Natural History

The American Museum of Natural History, that vast and venerable architecturally eclectic pile on Central Park West at Seventy-ninth Street in New York City, founded in 1869, is the oldest major U.S. museum of natural history.[1] There was no clear vision of what the museum should be until after Moris Jesup (1830–1908) became president in 1881. Jesup was a wealthy railroad developer who retired from business in 1880. At first the museum simply exhibited stuffed animals and birds. Coached along by a small staff, primarily trained by Agassiz at Harvard, Jesup was ultimately convinced, and then convinced his fellow trustees, that the museum should do research as well as have exhibits.

In 1891 Jesup and Seth Low, the new president of Columbia University, began an arrangement of joint faculty-curator appointments. The first was Henry Fairfield Osborn, a brilliant vertebrate paleontologist,

lured from Princeton. He was wealthy and well connected—his father was president of the Illinois Central Railroad; his maternal uncle by marriage was J. Pierpont Morgan.

Frederick Starr had been hired about 1890, but soon left to join the faculty at the new University of Chicago. In April 1894, Jesup asked Frederic Ward Putnam to become curator of archaeology and ethnology and build a program. The appointment was half-time, allowing him to keep his position at Harvard. Putnam hired George Hubbard Pepper (see Chapter 16) and Marshall Saville (1867–1935), a specialist in pre-Columbian Mexico. He also hired Franz Boas (see Fig. 26.6), who was looking for work. Jesup, Putnam, and Low arranged a joint appointment for Boas at a combined salary of three thousand dollars a year.

Franz Boas (1858–1942) was born in Prussia "into a family whose Jewish identity seems to have been more a matter of tradition and family loyalty than faith."[2]

He studied medicine, then mathematics and physics, and finally geography. His dissertation research on the physics of light in water led him to an interest in human perception, and his concern with geography led to an increasing preoccupation with human perceptions of landscapes. That led him to Baffinland in 1883–84 to study Eskimos' "dependence on the knowledge of the land and the range of wandering peoples on the configuration of the land."[3] Before he left he received anthropology training from Adolph Bastian and Rudolph Virchow. His trip was a success and he shifted his interests to anthropology.

Boas came to the attention of Edward B. Tylor, then chair of the Northwest Coast committee of the British Association for the Advancement of Science (BAAS). Under BAAS sponsorship, in 1886 Boas made the first of many trips to the "Northwest Coast": the Pacific coast of the United States and Canada from about the Oregon-California border to southern Alaska, as seen from the East Coast.[4]

Boas married, and emigrated to the United States in 1887. He had met Frederic Ward Putnam the previous year. Putnam, as secretary of the American Association for the Advancement of Science, helped Boas get a job as the geography editor of *Science,* the association's journal. Boas immediately started a debate with Holmes, Mason, and Powell at the Smithsonian about "proper" museum exhibits (see below).[5] In 1888 he moved to Clark University and there granted the first American Ph.D. in anthropology to Alexander Chamberlain in 1892. He left Clark to join Putnam at the Chicago world's fair.

Putnam and his staff began to develop exhibits and a research program. That meant cultivating donors to support fieldwork and buy collections. The museum's endowment and its operating funds from the city of New York did not provide such support; that came from trustees or outside philanthropists. The trick was to find donors who were interested, then keep them involved over the several years that most projects required. Some projects envisioned by Boas had no end dates—at least in his mind—which irked donors.

During Putnam's tenure, from 1894 to 1904, the principal donors to the Anthropology Department were the president of the museum, Moris Jesup and his wife, three members of the Huntington family—Collis, his wife Arabella, and her son Archer—and the Duc de Loubat. Joseph Florimond Loubat (1831–1927) was born in New York in 1831 and educated in Paris and Jena. He used his inherited fortune to collect books, race yachts, dabble in scholarship and diplomacy, live well, and indulge in philanthropy. Frequent and large donations to the Roman Catholic Church earned him the papal title of Duc de Loubat from Leo XIII in 1893. He funded archaeological excavations in Greece, and the great German scholar Eduard Seler's Mexico-Guatemala Expedition of 1895–97, then created a chair in Mexican archaeology for him at the University of Berlin. Between 1896 and 1909 he supported the high-quality publication of a number of major Mesoamerican codices, including the Borgia, Vaticanus B, and Magliabecchiano. Loubat became Marshall Saville's patron, supported his work in Mexico for about ten years, and created the Loubat Chair in Archaeology at Columbia University for him.[6]

Collis Huntington was one of the "Big Four," who, along with Mark Hopkins, Charles Crocker, and Leland Stanford, Jr., built the Central Pacific and Southern Pacific railroads. In 1884, Collis, age sixty-three, took a trophy wife, Arabella, a beautiful, ambitious, thirty-something, vague-about-her-background woman, in New York City, with the fashionable Reverend Henry Ward Beecher officiating. Arabella had a fourteen-year-old son, Archer, whom Collis adopted. When Collis died in 1900, he left his estate to his nephew and longtime business associate, Henry E. Huntington (1850–1927), and to Arabella and Archer. As an aside, in 1913, Henry married Aunt Arabella; they moved to southern California and founded the great Huntington Library and Art Gallery on their estate in San Marino.[7]

Archer Huntington (1870–1955), in his mature years a ruggedly handsome six-foot-four (Fig. 19.1), traveled extensively in Iberia and became fascinated

19.1. Archer Huntington, ca. 1905. Courtesy of the Hispanic Society of America, New York.

with its peoples and history. He learned Spanish, Portuguese, and Arabic. He began seriously collecting manuscripts, rare books, and artworks relating to Spain and Portugal and their colonial possessions. In 1904, he founded the Hispanic Society of America, donating land in upper west-side Manhattan, funding a building, and conveying his forty-thousand-volume library. Over time, Archer and his mother provided the land and most of the money for the Renaissance Revival complex of buildings at 155th and Broadway called the Audubon Terrace Museum group—the Hispanic Society, the American Numismatic Society, the American Geographical Society, the American Academy of Arts and Letters, and the Museum of

the American Indian. The Huntingtons' gifts to the American Museum in support of anthropology were modest, but critical.

Putnam and the Southwest

Putnam arrived at the American Museum just as the Hyde brothers linked the museum to the Wetherill's Chaco Canyon excavations (see Chapter 16). In 1890, the Norwegian explorer Carl Lumholtz (1851–1922) arrived in the United States on a lecture tour. Lumholtz, like John Lloyd Stephens, Sir Richard Burton, and later, Hiram Bingham and Roy Chapman Andrews (the collective prototypes for Indiana Jones of the movies), was an explorer-raconteur. They were daring, dashing off to far-off exotic climes to bring back data and collections "in the interests of science," despite great personal danger and hardships. They had the ability to convince wealthy patrons and high government officials to support their adventures. Lumholtz claimed to have had a vision directing him to northwest Mexico to seek the "lost remnants of the Cliff Dwellers." He soon had thirty-eight "private subscribers" funding the trip, including Andrew Carnegie, Mrs. Joseph Drexel, Archer Huntington, Frederick E. Hyde (Senior), J. Pierpont Morgan, the Duc de Loubat, and William C. Whitney in New York, Allison Armour in Chicago, Phoebe Apperson Hearst in San Francisco, and Adolphus Busch in St. Louis. He also received one thousand dollars and formal sponsorship from the American Geographical Society. Putnam made him part of the Hyde Expedition; hence giving him American Museum sponsorship. Lumholtz spent several years in northern Mexico and produced some good ethnographic and natural history data, engagingly presented in his highly popular *Unknown Mexico*.[8]

Meanwhile, Putnam began a physical anthropology project in the Southwest, led by Aleš Hrdlička (Fig. 19.2). Hrdlička (1869–1943) was born in Humpolec, Bohemia, and emigrated with his family to New York in 1882.[9] Between 1889 and 1894, he

19.2. Aleš Hrdlička. Courtesy of the National Anthropological Archives, Smithsonian Institution.

color-coded races: black (Ethiopian), brown (Malay), yellow (Mongolian), red (American), and white (Caucasian). Blumenbach averred that the form of the skull, metrically defined, is a clear indicator of "racial type," and suggested that brain size (cranial capacity) is a direct indicator of intelligence. He coined the term *Caucasian* because he was enamored of "a most beautiful skull of a young Georgian female" from the Caucasus Mountains.[11]

Between 1820 and 1851, Samuel George Morton (1799–1851), a prominent Philadelphia physician and natural historian, followed Blumenbach's lead, studying cranial capacity as *the* indicator of intelligence, and skull form as *the* indicator of "racial type." He measured the cranial capacity of his collection of one thousand skulls by filling them with white mustard seed. His averaged results "proved" that Whites had the highest cranial capacity (87 in.^{3}), with Indians second (83 in.^{3}), and Blacks last (78 in.^{3}). Here, said Morton, were "real" numerical data, providing a "scientific basis" for *ranking* races! In 1977, Stephen Jay Gould recalculated Morton's figures and found no significant differences when all the data were taken into account.[12] It has long since been known that cranial capacity bears no relationship to intelligence.

By the 1860s "craniometry" was a highly respectable science, especially in France under the guidance of Paul Broca (1824–1880) and his students. Broca invented the "cephalic index," a numerical ratio of the length of the skull in relation to its width. The Swedish anatomist Anders Retzius then added the terms *dolichocephalic,* long heads, those with an index less than 75, and *brachycephalic,* round heads, those with an index greater than 75.[13] The measuring of living individuals, anthropometry, also became a major endeavor. Measurements grew increasingly complex between 1870 and 1900. The manipulation of all those data was a major factor that led Lambert Jacques Quetelet, and later, Francis Galton and others to develop modern statistics.[14] There were various spin-offs, such as the Bertillon System in France used to metrically classify criminals, and attempts to correlate "physical types" with specific forms of insanity.

graduated from the Eclectic Medical College and the Homeopathic Medical College, both in New York. He subsequently spent four months in Europe, studying anthropometry in Paris and visiting leading research hospitals in Europe and Britain. He returned to New York fired with anthropometrical enthusiasm.

Nineteenth-century ethnologists were concerned with the "place" of the various "races" in the scheme of things. Racial definitions had always been vague, often based on visible physical features, with skin color being predominant.[10] But scholars wanted a more "scientific racial indicator," preferably one that was metrically based. Enter Johann Friedrich Blumenbach (1752–1840), a German anatomist and natural historian at Göttingen University. His scheme had five

Hrdlička embraced all this as his life's work. He took a position with the Pathological Institute of the New York State Hospitals. He formulated a grandiose research plan to measure and make observations "on about 40,000 of the abnormals of all classes" then languishing in New York state institutions, and to collect autopsy specimens and skeletons. But there was a serious problem: there were no comparable data from "normal people" on which to base a "standard."[15]

Hrdlička's definition of "normal, standard people" was WASPs—White Anglo Saxon Protestants, or "Old Americans," as he called them. This led him on a twenty-five-year odyssey, from the halls of the Ivy League to the backwoods of Tennessee, to measure and observe individuals whose ancestors had been in North America for four generations (later reduced to three, to increase his sample). He finally concluded that persons of Anglo (English, Irish, and Scottish) ancestry were tending toward a "common American type." Non-WASPs from southern Europe, like Hrdlička himself, were "tending" in the same direction; a metrical verification of the American melting pot, he thought.[16]

To increase his database, Hrdlička contacted Frederic Ward Putnam. Putnam gave him access to the museum's skeletal collections, and introduced him to the Duc de Loubat. Loubat paid Hrdlička's expenses to accompany Carl Lumholtz to northern Mexico for three months in 1898. There he found "normal [Indian] people" among the Tarahumara, Huichols, and Tepehuanes of northern Mexico who could, literally, be measured against his developing standard of White people. In 1899, Putnam arranged for the Hyde brothers to fund Hrdlička's continued work in the Southwest, including Chaco Canyon, where he measured and observed various Navajo and Ute people (see Chapter 16). According to Putnam, "The objects of this investigation are: first, to definitely settle the racial geography of the region; . . . this must be accurately known before trustworthy inferences can be made as to the origin and history of the various tribes; second, to discover the relationship between these surviving tribes and the extinct peoples of the region."[17]

The Hydes continued their support through 1902. During a final eight-months trip, Hrdlička ranged as far south as Puebla, Mexico. He measured and observed every Indian who could be coerced into sitting still. He collected skulls and skeletons wherever he could, including twelve Yaqui skulls. Of the latter, "eleven were obtained, along with some ethnological specimens, from the recent Yaqui-Mexican battlefield in the Sierra of Mazatlan, . . . and one is that of an executed and then half-cremated Yaqui prisoner from the Yaqui river."[18] Science uber alles! Hrdlička later reported that he had visited "all" the Indian tribes, except the "dangerous Seri" in the Southwest and into Mexico as far as the "Aztecs" of Puebla and Morelos. He measured and observed nearly 3,000 individuals, took 1,500 photographs, and acquired 300 skulls and skeletons, 120 facial casts, and 3,000 ethnological and archaeological specimens.[19]

Putnam introduced Hrdlička to Washington Matthews, William Henry Holmes, and Otis T. Mason. Holmes, Mason, and Smithsonian secretary Langley found the funds to form a Division of Physical Anthropology in the National Museum and hired Hrdlička. He remained there until his death.[20] Smithsonian and U.S. Army Museum skeletal collections were consolidated as the basis of the enormous collection Hrdlička amassed over the years, occupying hundreds of drawers in a very long, high-ceiling hallway and adjacent bays in the National Museum of Natural History.

Hrdlička's Southwest

Hrdlička made one additional trip through the Southwest in 1905. He ultimately produced two major studies of the anthropometry of living Southwestern Indians and osteology of skeletal collections.[21] His "Physiological and Medical Observations" on three thousand Indian people contains dozens of tables of anthropometric measurements—height, weight, cephalic index, etc. Many of them seem rather odd a century later; for example: "Pulse-respiration ratios, in relation to stature" for pubescent girls; "Teeth [number of molars], size of breasts, [and elapsed time since] onset of menstruation." Finally, there is a table of "various pathological conditions" containing data from 101 Indian agencies on "albinism, goiter, cretinism, insanity, all forms, idiocy, all grades, monstrosities, all varieties," and the prevalence and types of tuberculosis.[22]

While the tables appear odd, they must be seen in context. Some data were collected for public health purposes. From 1870 to 1925 physicians and health officials were struggling to cope with endemic and epidemic diseases, ranging from typhoid to tuberculosis, and to develop adequate sewage systems and water supplies. Problems were particularly acute on Indian reservations, hence Hrdlička's survey. Then current systems of medical practice—allopathy, homeopathy, and eclectic—assumed some correlations between anthropometrically defined physical or racial types, and various physiological conditions, medical problems, forms of insanity and criminality, and intelligence.

Hrdlička's catalog of crania contains data on 645 Pueblo and Basketmaker, and 18 Navajo skulls. All the Basketmaker skulls were from the 1897 Hyde Expedition to Grand Gulch, and all are dolichocephalic, as Richard Wetherill had observed (see Chapter 16). Detailed measurements and observations are presented in a bewildering ninety-page table. He concludes that the Pueblos differ significantly from the Californians and Shoshoneans of the Great Basin, as well as the Apache, Walapai. and Havasupai. Furthermore,

> The dolichoid pueblo crania, in all their important relative dimensions, resemble the Algonkin, while the brachyoid Pueblo skulls are practically identical with the mound crania of Arkansas, Louisiana. . . . [T]he Navaho, though speaking Athapaskan, are . . . not Apache, but essentially Pueblo. They are a mixture evidently of various old pueblo elements, dolicho, as well as brachycranic, with traces of the Apache.[23]

In "The Origin and Antiquity of the American Indian" (1925), Hrdlička presents his conclusions on the "origins" issue,[24] based on all the craniological and anthropometric data then available: Humans first reached the Western Hemisphere across the Bering Strait and/or along the Aleutian Island chain and down the coast. Second, American Indians are "practically identical with a type" found in Siberia, the northeast coast of continental Asia, parts of Tibet, China, Japan, Mongolia, and in "much of Malaysia and even Polynesia." But they are *not* Mongoloid like the majority of the Chinese and Japanese. Third, Indians of both North and South America of are of the same "type" because they have very similar features, among them, hair, eyes, skin color, nasal bridge and "shovel-shaped" upper incisors, "deeply and peculiarly concave, with marked borders surrounding the concavity" on the lingual side of the teeth.[25]

In popular histories of American anthropology, Hrdlička is seen as stubbornly opposing any significant time depth for the peopling of the Western Hemisphere. In fact, he opposed assertions of human occupation in deep time unsupported by solid geological evidence. Given the distribution of early human forms and archaeological cultures in Eurasia, and current knowledge of Pleistocene geology, he suggested "somewhere between possibly ten or at most fifteen thousands of years ago" for the initial peopling of the Western Hemisphere.[26]

Hrdlička's model of the peopling of the Western Hemisphere is very similar to all subsequent models: a movement of hunter gatherers across the Bering Strait, or along the Aleutian Island chain and Pacific Coast (the concept of Beringia—the land bridge—was not well established in the 1920s). Groups would "follow the game, spread rapidly and multiply rapidly, and under favoring conditions it would not have taken many centuries to people both North America and South America."[27]

The first emigrants were dolichocephalic people "represented in North America today by the great Algonquian, Iroquois, Siouan, and Shoshonean stocks; farther south by the Piman-Aztec Tribes; and in South America by many branches extending over large parts of that continent." Next came brachycephalic "Toltec types," who settled "along the northwest coast, the central and eastern mound region, the Antilles, Mexico (including Yucatan), in the Gulf States, over much of Central America, reaching finally the coast of Peru and other parts of northern South America." Finally came the Athapascans, "a virile brachycephalic type," and then the Eskimo. Most Athapascans remain(ed) in Alaska and northwestern Canada; "but some contingents moved along the west coast into California, "where they left the Hupa." Others moved to the Southwest, by an unspecified route, "where we know them as the Apache. This seems to be the story of the genesis of the American Indians as derived from the present and generally acceptable anthropological evidence."[28]

Hrdlička's view of the peopling of the Southwest is ambiguous. He implies that the Pueblos derived from two different "stocks," the long-headed "Algonquian . . . Pima-Aztec" stock and the rounded-headed "Toltec . . . Gulf" stock. One implication is that ancestral Puebloans came to the Southwest from different directions. Another reading, in light of Morgan's hypothesis (see Chapter 6) that the Mound Builders and those who peopled Mesoamerica and South America derived from the San Juan Basin, could be that both long heads and round heads originated in the Southwest and radiated out from there. Whether or not he is "correct" is not at issue. He was presenting a genetic model—trying to plausibly account for cultural history by linking physical types, cultures, and languages. His assertion that the Navajos are physically Pueblos, but linguistically Apachean, is an example. As long as cephalic indices were seen as valid indicators of physical type, then all of the genetic models had some plausibility. If cephalic indices were seen as spurious, then the plausibility became evanescent.

Finally, Hrdlička's metrical demonstration that Wetherill's Basket Makers are, indeed, long headed, lent support to an idea that rattled around in Southwestern archaeology until the mid-1940s before finally being discarded: that Pueblo round heads and Basket-

maker long heads were different "races," with the former replacing the latter (see Chapter 25).[29]

Boas and the Jesup Expedition

While Lumholtz and Hrdlička were knocking about the Southwest, Boas and Putnam proposed, and Morris Jesup agreed to, the Jesup North Pacific Expedition. A full summary of the six-year expedition is beyond our scope, but some aspects of it are crucial to understanding later developments in American anthropology. The Hemenway Expedition was the first large-scale research program in anthropology; the Jesup Expedition was the second; and the Torres Strait Expedition carried out in 1898–99 by British scholars, including Alfred Cort Haddon, was the third.[30]

The Hemenway Expedition brought together researchers in archaeology, physical anthropology, ethnohistory, and ethnography. The Jesup Expedition had all these, plus linguists. Both expeditions were "problem oriented"—asking specific research questions within the larger anthropological agenda of the day, especially "the problem of the earliest history of the native races of our continent and their relations to the races of the Old World."[31] In short, the venerable "origins issue." Boas proposed the Northwest Coast and eastern Siberia, with their "multiplicity of languages" and cultures and "great variety" of physical types, some seemingly linked and some not, as the places to sort out the origins issue.[32]

Jesup put up about forty thousand dollars a year. Field-workers amassed extensive collections, including the great war canoe, totem poles, and other spectacular items that still grace the Northwest Coast hall of the American Museum. Research projects were carried out, often under great hardships, in both northwest North America and Siberia.

Boas concluded that the Jesup Expedition was a success. It demonstrated, he said, "that the isolated tribes of eastern Siberia and those of the northwest coast of America form one race, similar in type, and with many elements of culture in common." There were later "invaders" who inserted themselves in and among the original tribes—Athapascans, Salish, and Eskimos in America and Yakut and Tungus in Siberia.[33] The Jesup Expedition was not the final word on the origins question, just as Hrdlička's model was not; the issues still continue to be investigated at the turn of the millennium.

Reorganizing American Anthropology

It was Franz Boas's aim to reorganize American anthropology, in terms of theory, method, and training. There was an Anthropological Congress at the St. Louis world's fair in 1904. There, major addresses were given. One was by W J McGee, full of racialist bombast and platitudes (see Chapter 17). The second was by Alfred Cort Haddon, in 1904 the new leading light in British anthropology. Haddon tried very hard to define what anthropology and its subdivisions are all about, part of a much larger discussion then ongoing (see below). The third was by Boas, his famous "History of Anthropology" paper in which he swept aside the developmentalism of Morgan, Powell, and McGee in favor of his own vision of what anthropology was about.[34]

Boas's plans reflected the so-called four-field approach. That is, anthropology necessarily includes archaeology, linguistics, cultural anthropology, and physical anthropology. Priority one in Boas's plan was the development of a cadre of "trained men"—schooled in rigorous research methods in both university and museum settings around the country, with himself as master of the dance, as it were. His situation at the American Museum and Columbia University was one such setting. Harvard University and the Peabody Museum was another. Boas planned to train students in cultural anthropology and linguistics; Putnam would train the archaeologists. The physical anthropologists would get trained between the two. Boas had produced the first "trained man" in Alexander Chamberlain. The second, George A. Dorsey (previously introduced), trained by Putnam, received his doctorate in 1894. Over the next six years, Roland

B. Dixon, William C. Farabee, John R. Swanton, and Frank Russell also received doctorates at Harvard.[35] By 1901 Boas had turned out his first Ph.D. at Columbia, Alfred Lewis Kroeber.

In 1902, George Grant McCurdy reported to Section H, the anthropology section of the American Association for the Advancement of Science, that at least one anthropology, or anthropology-related course, was being taught at thirty-one institutions. Most were taught by individuals trained in other fields. Some, as at Yale, featured "Philosophical anthropology, an outline study of man, his body and mind in their relations, his relations to nature, to his fellows, and to God," offered by Professor E. Hershey Sneath. Only Columbia and Harvard universities offered advanced degrees. An extensive review of the status of anthropological organizations published in the *American Anthropologist* in 1906 added the University of California. Aside from the Smithsonian Institution, the review listed the Peabody Museum at Harvard, the American Museum of Natural History, the Brooklyn Museum, the Field Museum of Natural History in Chicago, and the Anthropology Museum at the University of California as being involved in collections and research relating to American Indians, including the Southwest.[36] Boas's vision of a cadre of "trained men" in anthropology had a long way to go, but it was under way.

Boas's own university-museum nexus was not to last; trouble was brewing within the museum. Jesup was unhappy with Boas's handling of expedition publications; Boas bridled at his scientific judgment being questioned by anyone, even the president of the museum. When Hermon Bumpus was appointed museum director, he and Boas immediately clashed over many issues. Boas finally withdrew in a huff to Columbia University, where he had received tenure in 1899.

Boas slowly built a graduate program at Columbia. He concentrated on training ethnographers and linguists and further developing his vision of what anthropology was about. He contributed greatly to the infrastructure of anthropology by his activities in professional organizations and his support of scholarly journals. He made major contributions to the study of American Indian languages, especially in the *Handbook of American Indian Languages,* published by the Bureau of American Ethnology.[37]

Boas also became active in social issues, including the debate over emigration quotas and the push for eugenics. His 1911 study of the malleability of immigrants' head forms and its implications for the ongoing nature versus nurture debate was the death knell for craniometry as a "sure indicator of race," although skulls continued to be measured for thirty years. He and many of his students were actively involved in the swirling mélange of left-wing and humanitarian organizations, causes, and programs that animated the country, and especially New York City, in the early part of the twentieth century (see Chapter 26).[38]

Between 1901 and 1912 Boas trained A. L. Kroeber, Robert H. Lowie, Edward Sapir, Alexander Goldenweiser, and Clark Wissler, although Wissler did not write his doctoral dissertation under his direction. They were sent out to wherever Boas could find jobs for them to continue and expand his program for American anthropology. The first major expansion node was the University of California, Berkeley.

19.3. Phoebe Apperson Hearst. Photograph by George Prince. Courtesy of the California Historical Society.

West Coast Anthropology

In 1898, William Pepper died quite suddenly, at age fifty-five, perhaps of exhaustion, thus severing Phoebe Hearst's major tie to the Philadelphia intellectual community. In 1897 she had traveled to Egypt, where she met George Reisner, excavating under American Exploration Society sponsorship. Reisner was impatient with Sara Stevenson's "meddling." Hearst and Reisner agreed on a personal-services contract for him to excavate in Egypt for five years, with the artifacts to go to the University of California at Berkeley. When

Hearst did not renew Reisner's contract in 1904, the Boston Museum of Fine Arts and Harvard University picked up his support, which continued until his death in 1942. Hearst had met the German scholar Max Uhle in Philadelphia in 1897. His work in Peru was supported by the American Exploration Society as well. Hearst financed Uhle's Peruvian work between 1900 and 1905, with the collections again going to California. By 1900 she was also purchasing Greco-Roman antiquities in Europe, and funding some California archaeology by Philip Mills Jones.[39]

Phoebe Hearst's (Fig. 19.3) heart was in California. In 1896, she commissioned architect Julia Morgan to design and build her famous mansion, Hacienda de Pozo de Verona, in the Alameda Hills. She began plans for a School of Mines building at the University of California. She loved the campus setting in the Berkeley Hills, but loathed the university's "unsightly, badly-kept buildings in the worst taste of the U.S. Grant period of American architecture."[40] Those viewing Grant's tomb in New York City, or other architectural hodgepodges from the 1870s and 1880s, will instantly understand. The university developed a plan for major campus improvements. Hearst offered to finance these improvements and was appointed as the first woman regent of a university in California.

By 1901 Zelia Nuttall and Frederic Ward Putnam were urging Hearst to fund an anthropology program at the University of California.[41] In September 1901, Hearst invited Alice Fletcher, Zelia Nuttall, Frederic Ward Putnam, Franz Boas, and Benjamin Ide Wheeler, the president of the university, to her estate; Boas could not come. The group agreed to the establishment of a Department of Anthropology, funded by Mrs. Hearst, hence "free of all expense to the University," as Wheeler reported to the regents.[42]

The department was to have an advisory committee consisting of Fletcher, Hearst, Nuttall, Putnam, and Wheeler, as well as Boas and John C. Merriam, a University of California paleontologist and, later, president of the Carnegie Institution of Washington. Nuttall pressed Boas to take up work in California under the Hearst auspices. Boas declined, proposing instead that his envisioned nationwide program for the development of "trained men" be implemented by Mrs. Hearst's funding of four fellowships in ethnology at Columbia and two at Harvard in archaeology, under his direction and control. At the end of five years the fellowships, by then attached to trained men, would be transferred to California. "Give me the opportunity to direct the operations and . . . a strong department . . . could be formed without any further cooperation." Mrs. Hearst and the committee declined, much to Boas's displeasure, since, he pouted, it thwarted "all that . . . [I have] tried to build

over the years." Boas was dropped from the advisory committee.[43]

Putnam was appointed professor and chairman of the Anthropology Department in 1902, resigning his American Museum position but keeping his Harvard post. He spent about one-quarter of his time in California, primarily during summers. The "department" was, in fact, a mélange of all of Mrs. Hearst's interests, including Reisner's Egyptian and Uhle's Peruvian collections. There was to be a museum to house the various collections, therefore a curator was needed. Boas recommended Alfred Lewis Kroeber (1876–1960).[44]

Kroeber was twenty-four years old. Born in Hoboken, he grew up in New York City in an upper middle-class German family filled with intellectuals and professional people, such as the distinguished historian Herbert Muller and the geneticist Hermann Muller, who won a Nobel Prize in 1946. He entered Columbia College at age sixteen, taking a B.A. and M.A. in English, and then began work on a doctorate. In 1896 he signed up for Boas's language seminar, repeating it in 1897–98, and switched to anthropology.

In 1899, Boas arranged with Mrs. Jesup to send Kroeber to the Southern Arapaho in Oklahoma, and the following year to the Northern Arapaho at Wind River, Wyoming, and the Bannock and Shoshone in Idaho. In 1900, the California Academy of Sciences offered a fellowship in California ethnology. Boas recommended Roland Dixon, who declined; the fellowship then went to Kroeber. This was Kroeber's credential for California experience when he was hired by the University of California.

To house the Hearst collections, the university built a 60 by 80 ft. corrugated iron building on campus. But the weight of the collections threatened the foundations, so they were moved to space in the Affiliated Colleges buildings in San Francisco. The iron building, however, housed the Anthropology Department until 1952.[45] Kroeber commuted back and forth across the bay. He settled in and began a systematic survey of California Indian tribes, which finally culminated in his monumental one-thousand-plus-page

Handbook of the Indians of California in 1925.[46] The department grew slowly. Kroeber's first doctoral student was Samuel A. Barrett, in 1908; his second was William Duncan Strong in 1926.[47]

Two early Berkeley students came to play major roles in Southwestern anthropology: Pliny Earle Goddard (1869–1928) and Nels C. Nelson (1875–1964). Goddard was a Quaker from Maine.[48] He attended college in Indiana, graduated in 1892, and married Alice Rockwell. In 1897, the Goddards and their seventeen-month-old daughter rode horseback into the remote Hupa Indian country along the Trinity River in northwestern California. They were lay missionaries, sponsored by the interdenominational Woman's Indian Aid Association of Philadelphia.

Goddard rapidly learned the Hupa language and began recording Hupa culture. By chance, he encountered Stewart Culin, who was collecting Indian games. Culin encouraged Goddard to further his education. In midsummer 1900, the Goddards, and now two daughters, rode out of the Trinity Valley. Goddard entered the University of California as a graduate student under Benjamin Ide Wheeler, a Classicist and university president.

In 1901 Goddard became an assistant in anthropology. He took his doctorate under Wheeler in 1904, and was promoted to assistant professor in 1906. Frederic Ward Putnam had arranged with the Hyde brothers to fund the publication of Washington Matthews's great Navajo *Night Chant* in 1902. In the same year Phoebe Hearst purchased Matthews's papers with the understanding that Goddard would work on them after Matthews's death, and he began to do so in 1905.

Goddard was a popular lecturer. One of his students was Nels C. Nelson, six years younger than Goddard; they became close friends. Nels Christian Nelson (Fig. 19.4) was born in Denmark. The oldest of numerous children in a poor family, he was bound out to a farmer and later sent to an uncle in Minnesota. There he finally started the first grade at age seventeen in 1892, graduating from high school in 1901. He rode a cattle car to California, saved his money from odd

19.4. Nels C. Nelson, ca. 1922. Photograph by H. S. Rice. Courtesy of the American Museum of Natural History.

jobs, and entered Stanford University, working his way as a janitor in a bank. In 1905, he moved to the University of California, intending to study philosophy, but discovered anthropology and was hooked. He soon was working with John C. Merriam, the paleontologist who had archaeological interests as well. San Francisco Bay was ringed with deep middens, large mounds of shells, artifacts, and living debris deposited over many centuries by Indian people harvesting the rich food resources of the bay and adjacent lands. Merriam had started Max Uhle on the excavation of the Emeryville Shellmound in 1902–3. He put Nelson to work surveying for additional sites along the California coast; Nelson later estimated that he walked three thousand miles during the survey. He also excavated at various sites, including the Ellis Landing site where he used teams of horses and Fresno scrapers to dig out some twenty-five hundred cubic yards of fill in two weeks.[49] Nelson took courses from Kroeber and Goddard, receiving a B.L. in 1907 and an M.L. in 1908. He was then hired as an assistant in the Anthropology Museum and to do some teaching.

In 1908 Phoebe Hearst effectively withdrew her support from the Anthropology Department, cutting it from twenty thousand dollars a year to two thousand dollars, the latter earmarked for the museum. Many of her properties in San Francisco had been destroyed in the 1906 earthquake, creating severe financial problems for her for several years and forcing a retrenchment in her philanthropic interests.[50] Kroeber's and Goddard's salaries were picked up by the university. Putnam formally retired in 1909, having acted as titular head from the outset. Times were hard for Kroeber and his still nascent department.

Meanwhile, at the American Museum in New York, Clark Wissler was rebuilding the Anthropology Department after the departures of Putnam and Boas. He was negotiating with Archer Huntington to fund a long-term research and collecting program in the Southwest. Prospects at Berkeley seemed bleak, and when Wissler offered Goddard a position in 1909 as assistant curator of ethnology, he accepted. Nelson assumed some of Goddard's teaching responsibilities at Berkeley. But the possibilities of advancement seemed dim. In April 1911, Nelson wrote Goddard noting that T. T. Waterman, who had recently joined the department, "has married and is prospering in every way on $83.00 per month! The step has wrought a most salutary change in him—so wonderful that I sometimes wish I could marry too; but life seems so short and there are so many things I'd like to do—travel, work in the Southwest, Mexico and Peru, etc."[51]

The timing of Nelson's letter was opportune. Huntington had funded Wissler's Southwest project. Nelson went to New York to discuss a job in August 1911. He was favorably received, and steps were taken to get him hired. Goddard encouraged him to accept, saying "there is no other institution that can give you better opportunities for work . . . Chicago has the drawback of Dorsey; Washington that of politics.

Here, one has a free hand to do his best, money for field work, and proper appreciation of what he accomplishes."[52]

Nelson was encouraged enough to return to Berkeley and propose marriage to Ethelyn Hobbs Field (Fig. 19.5), Kroeber's secretary; she accepted. Nelson was offered a job at the American Museum at sixteen hundred dollars a year, plus field money, to begin work in the Southwest as soon as possible. Ethelyn Nelson would accompany him to the field as a paid part-time helper. As soon as the 1911–12 academic year was over, the Nelsons left for the Southwest.[53]

Kroeber carried on at Berkeley. With Goddard and Nelson gone, he was able to hire T. T. Waterman. In 1916–17, Robert H. Lowie came as a visiting faculty member, then joined the department full time in 1921, after being pushed out of the American Museum.

19.5. Ethelyn Hobbs Nelson, ca. 1922. Photograph by H. S. Rice. Courtesy of the American Museum of Natural History.

The Museum of the American Indian

In Manhattan, one can take the subway from downtown to the American Museum of Natural History at Seventy-ninth Street and Central Park West. If one stays on board, rides to 157th and Broadway and walks two blocks back to 155th Street, one finds the Audubon Terrace Museum group, previously noted. The buildings are there due to the passions, interests, and money of Archer M. Huntington, and George Gustav Heye (1874–1957).

Hubert Howe Bancroft's and Archer Huntington's addiction for books led them to found major cultural institutions, the Bancroft Library and the Hispanic Society. George Heye was also passionately addicted —to amassing an ever-larger collection of Indian artifacts.[54] The end result was the Museum of the American Indian, founded in 1916, and, after a long and complex history, transferred to the Smithsonian Institution in 1987 as the National Museum of the American Indian.

George Heye was born in New York City, the son of Gustav and Maria Lawrence Heye. Gustav made a fortune in Standard Oil, which George inherited. George graduated in 1896 from Columbia University and began a career as an engineer, but soon moved into finance and became a partner in the banking firm of Battles, Heye and Harrison. Heye began his interests in Indians as a youthful casual collector of artifacts. The official story is that he became interested in artifacts while conducting field surveys for an electrical line in northern Arizona in 1896, and "in 1903 he acquired his first large group of prehistoric pottery from New Mexico."[55]

The hobby soon became an obsession. The ever-increasing collection was stored in various warehouses and lofts in New York; parts of it for some years were on loan to the University of Pennsylvania Museum. In 1909, Heye turned full time to his passion. By 1913 his first wife, Blanche Williams Heye, apparently had enough of living among tens of thousands of artifacts, and divorced him in a well-publicized action in which she sought seventy-eight-thousand dollars a year alimony, but settled for twenty thousand dollars. In 1915, Heye married Thea Kowne Page, a woman of means who also collected Indian artifacts. In their twenty years together, George and Thea were very much partners in developing the collections and the museum.

Heye relentlessly pursued artifacts. In 1914, he and three of his employees were convicted of desecrating a historic Munsee Indian cemetery, the Minisink Burying Ground, in Sandyston Township, New Jersey. Heye was fined one hundred dollars and his men ten dollars each. Heye threatened to appeal on the grounds that the judge had placed "a damper on scientific investigation and research," but paid the fines instead. A museum legend is that Heye fought the case through to the New Jersey Supreme Court, and won.[56] Heye sought respectability for his collection, much of it—both archaeological and ethnographic —acquired under circumstances ranging from more or less legitimate to very dubious, such as the cemetery excavation.

By 1915, Heye and Archer Huntington were discussing the development of a museum as part of Huntington's cultural park at Audubon Terrace. Huntington donated land, said to be valued at 140,000 dollars, and Heye and his friends put up 350,000 dollars for equipment and a building, the latter designed by Charles P. Huntington, Archer's nephew. Heye provided an endowment for salaries and operating costs and deeded his collection, estimated at 400,000 objects, to the Museum of American Indian, Heye Foundation. The founding trustees were Archer M. Huntington, Harmon W. Hendricks, James Bishop Ford, Minor Keith, and Heye as chairman.

The museum officially opened on November 15, 1922, and by then was said to contain 1,800,000 objects. Anthropological luminaries at the opening included Jesse Walter Fewkes of the Bureau of American Ethnology, Walter Hough of the U.S. National Museum, Frank Speck from the University of Pennsylvania, Samuel K. Lothrop from the Harvard Peabody Museum, and Elsie Clews Parsons. No anthropologists from Columbia University or the American Museum of Natural History are listed. Heye's relationships with them, especially Franz Boas, were frosty. When the museum was announced in 1916, Boas had written to Heye saying "nobody can deny that you have the right to do with your money as you please," but urging that Heye's collections be merged with those of the American Museum. Heye acknowledged that it was indeed his money, that he would build his own museum, and therefore "the discussion is ended."[57] A highlight of the opening was provided by "a delegation of ten Indians from different tribes [who] arrived at the reception as a surprise . . . to convey their appreciation for what was being done to preserve the records of their race. The unexpected guests came in full native costume, and included Red Eagle, Sheet Lightening, Canoe, White Swan, and her daughter Chickadee."[58] It is highly probable that the "surprise" delegation was arranged by Heye. An indication of Heye's legitimacy problems appears in the *New York Times* account of the opening:

> Members of the diplomatic corps from Washington and the resident Consuls found in the collection many specimens which had been brought from their countries. It was whispered that certain international complications might arise if the exact places from which some of the treasures came were known. For this reason some of the cards describing objects gave only a general hint as to the original finding place.[59]

Before the museum opened it was already out of storage space. In late 1924, Archer Huntington donated a six-acre plot of land in the Pelham Bay section of the Bronx, and on it Heye built what began as a branch museum but ended as a storage facility, "the Annex." Subsequently, an ethnobotanical garden, concrete replicas of tipis and other Indian dwellings, and two real Northwest Coast totem poles, were placed on the grounds, known in the neighborhood as "the Reservation."[60]

With the creation of the Heye Foundation in 1915, Heye shifted his operation into high gear. One of his major collectors, and later an employee, was Mark Raymond Harrington. By 1908 Harrington was a partner in a company (perhaps aptly) called "Covert and Harrington Commercial Ethnologists, Collections Illustrating American Indian Life for Schools, Colleges and Museum Supplied with Authentic Materials."[61] As early as 1907, Marshall H. Saville and George Pepper, their ties with the American Museum growing increasingly tenuous, were excavating in Ecuador for Heye, and both ultimately joined his staff. Other prominent anthropologists who excavated or collected ethnographic materials for Heye included Samuel Barrett, Alanson Skinner, Frank Speck, T. T. Waterman, Warren King Moorehead, Samuel K. Lothrop, and Junius Bird.

Heye's principal backers were Minor Keith and Harmon Hendricks. Keith built railroads in Central America, was a founder of the United Fruit Company, owned coffee plantations and ranches in Central and South America and various mining interests throughout the Western Hemisphere, and was married to the daughter of the president of Costa Rica. He was an avid collector of pre-Columbian antiquities, especially Costa Rican and Nicaraguan ceramics and gold. Harmon W. Hendricks (??–1928), a partner in a metals manufacturing and wholesaling firm, was especially interested in North America. He funded the museum's excavations at Haiwikuh (see Chapter 24) and gave the museum 250,000 dollars in his will.[62] Another donor was Joseph (Udo) Keppler, Jr. (1872–1956), a prominent political cartoonist, who succeeded his father, Joseph Keppler, as the owner and principal cartoonist of *Puck,* one of the great magazines of scathing political satire in the United States from 1877 to 1918. Joseph, Jr., was a collector of Indian artifacts and a prominent Indian rights activist; during Theodore Roosevelt's presidency, he turned down an offer to become commissioner of Indian Affairs.[63]

When the museum was founded, Heye named Marshall Saville as director, but it was not a happy choice. In 1918, Heye lured Frederick Webb Hodge away from his position as ethnologist-in-charge at the Bureau of American Ethnology. Hodge gave the Heye Foundation credibility. Jesse Nusbaum (see Chapter 22) joined Hodge after he finished his World War I military service.

CHAPTER 20

The Western Scholar-Entrepreneurs

SOUTHWESTERN ANTHROPOLOGY came of age between 1900 and 1930. Part of that growing up was an ongoing sectional rivalry between eastern and western institutions, and those who created and used them, for control of Southwestern anthropology. Three individuals, whom we call western scholar-entrepreneurs, were centrally involved in the rivalry and contributed greatly to the development of Southwestern anthropology. They were Charles F. Lummis, Byron Cummings, and Edgar Lee Hewett.

Charles Lummis

Charles Fletcher Lummis (1859–1928) was born in Lynn, Massachusetts.[1] His father was an administrator in Methodist women's seminaries, where young Lummis was privately tutored. He entered Harvard with a thorough grasp of Latin, Greek, Hebrew, and Classical history. Among his classmates was Theodore Roosevelt. Lummis devoted his college career largely to poetry, athletics, and poker, although he did learn something about natural history and archaeology. In the summer of 1878, while working at a resort hotel in the White Mountains of New Hampshire, he fathered a daughter with a "New Hampshire Schoolma'm," although he claimed not to have known of the child until she turned up on his doorstep in Los Angeles in 1906.

In 1880 Lummis secretly married a medical student, Dorothea Roads.[2] Just before graduation, he contracted "brain fever," and withdrew from Harvard. The "attack," perhaps brought on by failing grades, was the first of several instances in which Lummis seemingly suffered a debilitating illness as a means of escaping a personal difficulty.

Lummis and Dorothea moved to her parents' home in Scioto, Ohio. By 1882 he was editing the Scioto *Gazette*. For recreation, he dug in nearby archaeological sites, now known as the Mound City group. In 1884, he made a deal with the flamboyant owner of the Los Angeles *Times,* Colonel Harrison Gray Otis. Lummis would become city editor of the paper. But, he would *walk* to Los Angeles from Ohio, following railroad lines, sending weekly travelog dispatches to the *Times* (and to the Chillicothe *Leader,* back in Ohio). The revised sketches became *A Tramp across the Continent,* published in 1892.[3] During the "tramp" he fell in love with the Southwest. The trip took Lummis 112 days of actual walking, over a 143-day period (Fig. 20.1). His pedometer recorded 3,507 miles—6,513,541 steps, according to his estimate.[4] His route was to Denver, then south to Alamosa, Colorado, down the Rio Grande Valley to Isleta Pueblo, west to Cajon Pass, and into the Los Angeles Basin. From Alamosa onward Lummis tried to pick up Spanish, with poor results at first: "It would start your ribs to hear me talk Spanish. I have sworn in a posse of about twenty words, and handle them with the easy grace of a cow shinnying up an apple tree tail first." At San Ildefonso Pueblo he learned more Spanish and entertained his hosts with "a down-at-the-heel mouth harp, which I play like a cat with false teeth."[5]

Lummis was heartily welcomed in Santa Fe, and he became entranced with the community and its mixture of peoples. He visited Tesuque Pueblo, noting the corner fireplaces where " you may see sundry rude images baking. . . . Some very excellent but still green people who come out here from the East, buy these fantastic images and take them home as 'Indian idols.' Thereby they become a laughing stock."[6] These were the famed "Tesuque War Gods."

Lummis moved on to Albuquerque, then to Isleta. The Isletans seem to have contributed to his admiration of Pueblo people in general: "the Pueblos have uncommon merits. I do not believe there is a christian American community in the world, which can approach in morality one of these little towns of adobe. . . . The Pueblos are sharp but honest traders, good neighbors to each other and hospitable . . . to the strangers who come among them. I wish they would send out missionaries to their American brothers." His opinion of the Navajos was quite different: "dirty, thievish, treacherous and revoltingly licentious."[7]

20.1. *Charles Fletcher Lummis, 1880s. Courtesy of the Southwest Museum.*

During the final stages of his trek, Lummis suffered a broken arm—which he set himself. He struggled across the Mojave Desert and finally entered the Los Angeles Basin on January 31, 1885. Otis drove out to San Gabriel Mission to meet him. The two then walked together "in the brilliant moonlight" the last ten miles into Los Angeles. The next day he began his editorial duties with the *Times.* Lummis only worked for Otis a few years, but the two remained devoted to a major cause, the promotion of the Southwest and particularly Los Angeles. Lummis's devotion was enthusiastic and romantic. Otis's was calculated to enhance his power and line his pockets; he succeeded admirably at both.

Harrison Gray Otis (1837–1917) was a major figure in southern California. Born in Ohio, he learned the printing trade, went to school when he could, and became active in Republican-party politics. He served in the Civil War and was discharged with the brevet rank of lieutenant colonel. After the war he continued dabbling in politics and worked at various patronage jobs. In 1876 he became editor of the Santa Barbara, California, *Press,* then, for a change of pace, worked for three years as a treasury agent on the Seal Islands, two storm-swept dots in the Bering Sea. He fled back to sunny California as soon as he could.

In 1882 Otis bought an interest in the Los Angeles *Times,* which had recently absorbed the *Weekly Mirror.* He would dominate the Times-Mirror Company—and through the *Times,* southern California—for three decades. In the Broadway play *Lil Abner,* based on Al Capp's comic strip, there is a satirical song about General Bullmoose, the epitome of the powerful capitalist entrepreneur: "What's Good for General Bullmoose is Good for the U.S.A." In Otis's view, what was good for Colonel Otis was good for southern California. He was an arch conservative, fanatically committed to laissez-faire capitalism and the open shop. His battles with the printers' unions were vicious and unending, culminating in the *Times* building being blown up in 1910.

Otis was a central figure in the great boom-and-bust land speculation schemes of the 1880s and 1890s in the Los Angeles Basin. He was a member of the behind-the-scenes "oligarchy" that acquired the rights to the water of Owens Valley, California, brought to Los Angeles via the great aqueduct project built by William Mulholland in the early 1900s. In the late 1880s, a young New Hampshireite moved to southern California to cure his tuberculosis, and became circulation manager for Otis's *Times.* His name was Harry Chandler; he later married Otis's daughter. In 1914 he assumed control of the newspaper and, ultimately, the Chandler family financial empire.[8]

The late 1880s was a time of boom and bust in Los Angeles. Lummis, the "bantam cock of paradox," was in the thick of it for three years as *Times* city editor—"years of coffee, cigarettes, whiskey, compulsive womanizing, and twenty-hour work days."[9] It ended with a paralytic stroke of his left side. In February 1888, he went to Isleta Pueblo to recuperate. He suffered two more strokes, or so he claimed. The third left him

without speech, apparently after receiving a letter from Dorothea demanding a divorce.

Whatever the realities of Lummis's paralysis, he was aided in his recovery by Eva Douglas, sister-in-law of the Indian trader at Isleta Pueblo. The two were married at ex-wife Dorothea's house in San Bernardino, in March 1891. The second aid to recovery was Lummis's meeting with Adolph Bandelier in August 1888, when the latter walked into his camp at Los Alamitos. The two later traveled to South America together (see Chapter 15).

Lummis the Arch-Mythmaker

A central theme of this book is that the Southwest is an idea invented by Anglo-Americans, an invention they have come to believe is reality. Charles F. Lummis was one of the principal inventors. Lummis's Southwest was flexible; sometimes it included southern California, sometimes not, depending on his purpose. If he was promoting the interests of Otis's oligarchy, he actively promoted the "California Dream," as Kevin Starr so aptly calls it.[10] Lummis's "core" Southwest region is essentially the one portrayed here.

During the 1890s Lummis produced ten books, including *A Tramp across the Continent.* Three are important for present purposes: *Some Strange Corners of Our Country: the Wonderland of the Southwest* (1892); *The Land of Poco Tiempo* (1893), and *The Man Who Married the Moon* (1894). *Some Strange Corners* was radically revised and enlarged in 1925, and renamed *Mesa, Canyon and Pueblo.* It represents Lummis's mature view of the history, archaeology, and folklore of the Southwest. *The Land of Poco Tiempo* contains vignettes of Southwestern life. *The Man Who Married the Moon* presents thirty-two folktales collected by Lummis at Isleta Pueblo. When it appeared, some critics likened it to Kipling's *Jungle Book,* and Joel Chandler Harris's Uncle Remus stories.[11]

When Lummis returned from his trip to Peru with Bandelier in 1893, he became editor of *Land of Sunshine.* He devoted the next twelve years to the magazine, later changing its name to *Out West, a Magazine of the Old Pacific and the New.* He made the magazine an instrument for boosting the Southwest and California. California was a veritable Eden, yea even Paradise, according to Lummis, his writers, and his poets. The core Southwest was, he said, a place in which gentle and wise natural women and men—both Indian and Hispanic—live idyllic, gracious, and dignified, if poor, lives in an enchanting desert landscape.

The Mission Myth

Lummis fostered the myth of the California Spanish missions and their denizens, the Franciscan friars and the so-called Mission Indians. The latter were various southern and central California Indian bands rounded up by friars and soldiers and forced to live and work at the missions. The myth depicted the missions as havens, and the friars and Indians as their happy inhabitants. The documented historical realities of Mission Indians' lives is very different. They were totally under the control of the Franciscans and the soldiers and crowded into unhealthy mission barracks. They were often whipped, raped, mutilated, branded, and placed in stocks or hobbles for minor infractions.[12]

The central figure in mission mythmaking was Helen Hunt Jackson (1830–1885).[13] Orphaned as a teenager, she married, but lost her husband and two children. She remarried in 1875 and moved to Colorado Springs, Colorado. She traveled widely, usually without her husband, supporting herself as a travel writer for magazines. In 1879 she became interested in Indian rights. She plunged into research and assembled a 450-page work on broken treaties and mistreatment of Indians, *A Century of Dishonor,* published in 1881. In the same year she went to southern California to do a series of magazine articles and became enamored of California's Spanish past and the missions. She met the friars at Santa Barbara, the only still-functioning mission. She met people of Spanish ancestry struggling to maintain some of the old ways in the face of the massive changes being wrought by the Anglo newcomers.

Jackson was commissioned in 1882 by the Department of the Interior to investigate the condition and plight of the Mission Indians. Her 1883 recommendations for securing Indian lands, and providing educational and medical aid, were ignored.[14] Outraged, she decided to write the *Uncle Tom's Cabin* of the Mission Indians. Like Harriet Beecher Stowe, she hoped to generate sympathy for the downtrodden. *Ramona,* a classic example of the pathetic dusky heroine stereotype, appeared in 1884. By 1893 it had sold over eighty thousand copies. The story of the star-crossed half-white, half-Mission Indian Ramona, her Indian husband Allesandro, her Spanish husband Felipe, and their travails in Anglo-dominated California was meant to generate sympathy for the Mission Indians and the disappearing Spanish way of life. Instead, *Ramona* became the canonical text for a romantic, mythical, mission-period Arcadia, an enchanted place and time, "a garden of earthly delight which in truth had never existed with such sensuousness and imaginative fullness," as Jackson had painted it.[15] It gave the recent Anglo emigrants a golden past, "a past made appropriate," a past in which southern California chambers of commerce could revel.[16] The myth was neatly summarized fifty years ago by Franklin Walker:

> The kindhearted industrious Franciscans, led
> by the saintly Serra, had brought civilization and
> temporary affluence to the docile and grateful
> California Indians. The great ranchos soon covered
> the land; they were lavish in their hospitality and
> were peopled with brightly dressed and beautiful,
> fine-tempered señoritas. Everyone took it easy in
> that Arcadia, and there was nothing of the push and
> shove of modern commercial life. The adobe houses
> were cool and comfortable; the tinkling guitars and
> the lovely mission bells brought music to a quiet
> land; and everywhere courtesy, generosity, and
> lightheartedness reigned supreme.[17]

Ramona later provided grist for the Hollywood dream factory. There were three silent versions, the first by D. W. Griffith in 1910, with Mary Pickford. The fourth, in 1936, featured a nice Mormon girl of Anglo derivation, Loretta Young, as the dusky pathetic heroine, Ramona.

The Landmarks Club

While Jackson's *Ramona* sparked an interest in California missions, it did little to preserve the actual historical missions. Some interest waxed in 1892, but soon waned.[18] Lummis took up the cause. In a December 1895 editorial he called for the preservation of the missions as historical monuments, architectural set pieces, and tourist attractions. He used the magazine to report the doings of the Landmarks Club, a group dedicated to mission preservation.[19]

The club focused on four missions that were in dire straits: San Diego, San Juan Capistrano, San Fernando, and Pala, an *asistencia* of San Luis Rey. By 1903 the club could report expenditures of over seven thousand dollars, and its satisfaction that the four missions were stabilized and protected.[20] When Lummis became head of the Los Angeles Public Library in 1905, the club began to lose its impetus; it expired during World War I. Later mission-preservation efforts took other forms, very much in the idealized, historically inaccurate restoration mode that Lummis had feared.

The mission-preservation campaign had other side effects, particularly as the major stimulus for the development of the Spanish or Mission Revival architectural style. California gave a major boost to the style with its state buildings at the Chicago world's fair and subsequent expositions. The style was soon adopted by the Santa Fe Railway for its hotels and stations, along with the equally made-up Santa Fe style (see Chapter 27).[21] The epitome of the style was Frank Miller's Mission Inn, in Riverside, California, a "Spanish Revival Oz" structure that underwent its own restoration in the 1980s. Miller also commissioned one John Steven McGroarty, a Los Angeles *Times* reporter, to produce a suitable southern California pageant. Between 1912 and 1929, McGroarty's *The Mission Play* was seen by 2.5 million people in a specially built Mission Revival style playhouse in San Gabriel. In recognition of his mythmaking, "McGroarty was named poet laureate of California, knighted by the Pope and the King of Spain, and twice elected to Congress."[22] Where else but California?

The Sequoya League

In 1899, Lummis inserted himself and his magazine into the roiling political cauldron of Indian rights issues.[23] He began with a series of articles entitled "My Brother's Keeper." He subjected Indian education to scathing criticism, especially the practice of forcibly putting Indian children in boarding schools far from home. Although Lummis fulminated vigorously, his tirades had little immediate effect.

Lummis was a naive, noisy, and bumptious latecomer in the arena of Indian rights, part of the larger realms of Indian-White relations and Indian-government relations that had begun before there was a United States. Eurocolonials and Euroamericans had been centrally concerned with the "managed savage" for over two centuries.[24] Many individuals and organizations long before Lummis had proposed, and sometimes implemented, often contradictory plans and programs to allow them to be "My [Indian] Sister's and Brother's Keeper," under the taken-for-granted premise that "Big [White] Sisters and Brothers Know Best."[25] New Englanders, continuing a long-standing tradition of defining the nation's moral character, whether or not the nation wanted them to, were prominent in the movement. After the Civil War many abolitionists turned their attention to Indian rights.

There was no doubt about the suffering, genocide, indignities, and travails that Indian people had undergone—there was a century's worth of horror stories for all to see. The issues centered on whose remedies should be adopted. No one asked the Indian people what *they* wanted. The basic government policy from Thomas Jefferson's time on was Removal—move all Indian people onto reservations; it didn't work. After the Civil War the policy shifted to turning managed savages into "civilized" Christian farmers in overalls who would own 160-acre plots of private property allotted to them from their commonly held reservation lands. Once they were farmers and property owners, and learned to read and write English, so ran the theory, Indians could then become citizens—and would meld into the general population, thus resolving the "Indian problem." That didn't work either. The only Indian citizens before the 1920s were the Pueblos of the Southwest, who were given that status, at the insistence of the Mexican government, in the treaties settling the U.S.-Mexican war in 1848 and 1853.

Indian people in California were particularly devastated by the influx of Anglos after 1846.[26] By 1900 most of them in Southern California lived in small, poverty-stricken enclaves, remnants of earlier Mission Indian groups. In 1901, Lummis took up the problems of Mission Indians, some of whom were being forced to move from their homes, much against their will. He and fifty others formed the Sequoya League to help Indian people, to cooperate with the Indian Bureau in shaping policy, and to stimulate a revival of Indian arts and crafts to generate income. The scope of concern was national, although the immediate problem was the Mission Indians.

Lummis was able to invoke his old Harvard tie with Theodore Roosevelt. He had kept in touch with Roosevelt, and taken it upon himself to advise him on a variety of national and international policy issues, whether or not Roosevelt wanted it, and whether or not Lummis knew anything about the issues. Now he got himself appointed to a commission to study the Mission Indian problems. The study was done; it said the Indians should move. When they refused, Lummis found himself in the untenable position of advocating the use of federal troops to force them to move. He emerged with much egg on his face, to the delight of the commissioner of Indian Affairs, William A. Jones, and many eastern Indian rights advocates. One of the latter, Samuel Brosius, raised questions about Lummis's sexual escapades (a matter of apparently well-founded rumors over many years), and, even worse, complained that he was "working with the Ethnological people to keep Indians what they are, so as to be a

study for future generations."[27] The latter complaint was probably directed at the recently deceased John Gregory Bourke, and James Mooney, of the Bureau of American Ethnology. Both were attacked for advocating that Indian people should be able to determine their own lives and live in their own traditional ways, if they chose to do so.[28] It was a complaint that Cushing had heard in the 1880s; other "ethnological people" in the Southwest and elsewhere would hear it again from Anglo reformers.

Bullying the Moqui

In January 1902, Indian commissioner Jones sent a letter to Indian agents and school superintendents identifying "a few customs among the Indians which . . . should be modified or discontinued." These included long hair for men, body paint, traditional dress, dances, and feasts. He suggested persuasion, but if that didn't work then withholding jobs and rations or even a "short confinement in the guard house at hard labor, with shorn locks."[29] It was a serious blunder and Jones was widely lambasted by both reformers and Indians. But he only partially retreated, and various zealous agents went ahead.

One such was Superintendent Charles E. Burton, in charge of the Hopi training school at Keams Canyon, day schools at Polacca, Second Mesa, and Oraibi, and a Navajo school at Blue Canyon. According to Burton, "Their long hair is the last tie that binds them to their old customs of savagery, and the sooner it is cut, Gordian like, the better it will be for them."[30] The Hopi and Navajo people were outraged. They were even more outraged by the policy of forcibly sending their children to Bureau of Indian Affairs boarding schools, no matter how enlightened the schools were made to seem at world's fairs. Often children were literally kidnapped and did not return home for several years.

The problem was particularly critical among the Hopi.[31] At Oraibi, on Third Mesa, some people, called "the Friendlies" by the Anglos, wanted their children to go to school; others, called "the Hostiles," did not. Rancorous bickering had begun in the 1880s, exacerbated by drought, low food supplies, and the continued incursions of Navajos onto Hopi lands. In 1891, leaders of both factions were arrested. By 1896–97, there was a major split over control and conduct of rituals. In 1901, there was a smallpox epidemic. The forced haircutting was a major outrage to both sides. H. R. Voth wrote to George Dorsey, late in 1902, that the "Hopis . . . hair has grown wonderfully since last winter's shearing time," adding, "The Oraibis are still very much embittered over that hair cut affair."[32] The Oraibi split became spatially real on September 6, 1906, when the leader of the Hostiles literally drew a line in the sand, and declared that whichever side got pushed across it had to leave. The Hostiles lost, and moved to Hotevilla, about seven miles from Oraibi.[33]

Sometime after the "shearing," Lummis sent Gertrude Gates, who knew something of the Hopi, to investigate; Burton ordered her off the reservation. In April 1903, Lummis launched an attack on Burton in a series of articles in *Out West,* called "Bullying the Moqui."[34] There, his wordsmithing reached new heights. Lummis later compared Burton to Spanish Inquisitors and New England witch burners, calling him "Barber-in-Chief to the People of Peace," whose regime needed something "more modern, a little more rational than Suasion by Six-shooter, Civilization by Scissors, and Education with a Club."[35] Lummis and the Sequoya League filed charges against Burton. A BIA investigator and a League observer went to Hopi to investigate; Burton was exonerated. Theodore Roosevelt called on the League and Lummis to fully retract the charges. In the end Lummis could only bring himself to write, "To Mr. Burton, the League frankly tenders its direct apology for whatever injustices have been done to him personally," then spilled the blame

" . . . if the American public could look down all at once through some magic focus . . . we should all see, on this God-forsaken desert, the dry, hungry, cliff-nesting towns of the Hopi, . . . the People of Peace; the gentlest, most tractable and most inoffensive of American Indians; the first Quakers of America. . . . Among and over these people . . . we should all see a reign of terror in the name of Education. We should see the reservation schools . . . filled only by raids of armed Navajos, the dreaded and immemorial foes of the Moquis, . . . and who are therefore the natural "police" of the new regime. . . .

We should see a father clinging to his five-year-old boy, who, in mortal terror because this Gentle Evangel of Civilization [a White teacher] had flogged him, dared not go to school again. We should see the father and child torn asunder by violence; the child lugged off sobbing to school; the father forcibly hustled down off the cliff to the school house, his hands bound behind him with baling wire, and his hair sheared off roughly and publicly as a punishment. . . .

We should see this oppressor [Burton] and his be-pistoled Navajos . . . herding the men into a Council Chamber under threat of shooting, and there handling them and forcibly shearing them as they were so many sheep, sometimes leaving the scars of the shears on their faces. While we should *not* see it, there would be someone to remind us that cutting off the hair of these Indians as a punishment was absolutely forbidden by the King of Spain in 1621, who sternly rebuked a few misguided blockheads of *his* day who had so little sense. The King of Spain knew enough to know (and said) that for Indians this "was the greatest possible disgrace and degradation," and absolutely forbade any further such "cruelty," as he termed it. . . . Chas. E. Burton, the Superintendent and Disbursing Agent of the Moquis and the Navajos . . . is the man responsible for, and actively operating, the state of affairs hereinbefore inadequately outlined."[36]

onto Burton's subordinates.[37] Lummis lost face with Roosevelt, but would continue to interact with him on other issues.

Lummis, the AIA, and the Southwest Museum

As previously noted, the Archaeological Institute of America (AIA) was founded in 1879. In the following two decades, affiliated societies were slowly established across the country: New York in 1884; Detroit, Wisconsin, and Chicago in 1889; Cleveland in 1895. By 1900 the AIA needed new blood and new money and there was a push for new affiliate chapters and members. Between 1900 and 1903, affiliate societies were formed in Washington, D.C., Missouri (principally St. Louis), Iowa, Pittsburgh, San Francisco, and Los Angeles. As in Philadelphia and Boston, it was now fashionable to be interested in archaeology—especially Classical archaeology and mysterious Egypt.

The San Francisco society began with Phoebe A. Hearst as president, David Starr Jordan and Benjamin Ide Wheeler as vice presidents, and Frederic Ward Putnam on the executive committee.[38] The Los Angeles chapter became the Southwest Society, with J. S. Slauson, a Los Angeles financier, as president; Harrison Gray Otis, George F. Bovard, president of USC, and J. A. Foshay, superintendent of the Los Angeles school system, as vice presidents; and Lummis as secretary.

Members of the other AIA affiliates had their own interests and energy on which to draw. The Southwest Society had Charles Lummis, and he had his magazine *Out West.* He used it to support the causes of the AIA, the Southwest Society, and a proposed Southwest Museum, just as he already was using it in support of the Landmarks Club and the Sequoya League.

Early in 1904, Lummis laid out the society's (read *his*) program. The ruins of Greece, Rome, and Palestine are all well and good, he wrote, but "in California, Arizona, New Mexico and Mexico there is an almost incomparable treasure-house for the archaeologist—with the enormous advantage that side by side, we can study the antiquities and the almost exact ethnologic conditions under which they were produced. That is, we have the human, as well as the antiquarian documents. But both are disappearing with a rapidity that is astounding and literally alarming." Therefore immediate action was needed.[39]

The charter of the Southwest Society stated that its objects were to "stimulate and prosecute study and exploration of the American Southwest; to assemble and preserve the fruits of such research. . . . to conduct excavations, to gather, acquire and have charge of, archaeological, ethnological and other collections, to record folk-lore, folk-songs, vocabularies and the like."[40] Finally, all these collections and data should be properly housed. "We want a Museum in Los Angeles," wrote Lummis, "not an Old Curiosity Shop of jumbles from God-knows-where, but a Museum which can compare with any in the world in everything but bulk."[41] A museum is needed because "Southwestern archaeology, . . . is being gophered by everyone but Southwesterners. . . . Specimens go East and abroad by the literal carload. It is about time that some of these collections were saved to the section where they really belong."[42] Similar regionally chauvinist sentiments were abroad in New Mexico and Arizona as well.

Lummis made membership competition with other affiliate societies into an explicit rivalry, and began printing a membership scorecard. In April 1904 he could gleefully report that membership had grown to sixty-six; by early 1906 there were over four hundred, nearly twice as many as any other affiliate society.[43] He also began recruiting women's clubs as organizational members of the society, recognizing the importance of such groups, as would Edgar Lee Hewett in Santa Fe. Lummis was very clear about the uses of the burgeoning membership: "it gives the Southwest Society stronger representation and voice in the Council of the Institute. Representation in this council is in proportion to membership. In a short time this young Western member will out-vote any other society."[44]

Lummis and the society used their membership votes to press for additional research in the Southwest and Mesoamerica. Finally, Lummis crowed, "[The society] has secured (perhaps most important of all) a concession long denied to Harvard College and all the other universities and museums of the East—the right to explore and to excavate on the Indian reservations and Forest reserves of the Southwest; and it has been granted an official status with the scientific bureaus of the government."[45] The "concession" was pure nonsense, but it seemed to give a special cachet to the Southwest Society in its competition with other AIA affiliates.

The Southwest Museum

Lummis first proposed the idea of a museum of the Southwest, located in Los Angeles, about 1895. By 1903 his plan was for a central museum in Los Angeles with branch regional museums in the smaller Southwestern cities. In 1904, he reported that a museum foundation committee was formed. The committee envisioned a building that "shall be an architectural monument . . . of the historic 'Mission' plan; that it shall occupy a sightly and commanding eminence . . . that the museum shall adhere to the strictest scientific standards both in history, in art and in archaeology . . . [which will] command the respect of scholars everywhere."[46]

By early 1906 Lummis could report that "Mr. Henry E. Huntington has offered the Southwest Society its choice of four magnificent hill-sites, of which the largest is worth at least $100,000 in the market."[47] The museum committee finally settled on a site in Highland Park and paid about twenty-three thousand dollars for it. In 1907 the Southwest Museum Foundation was established. The site plan and elevations were started in May 1911.

At that point, Lummis went blind—the result, he said, of Guatemalan "jungle fever." In 1913, his eyesight was "stewed" back by the salubrity of New Mexico scenery, and he was able to supervise museum construction for two years. But, in 1915, he came to cross-purposes with his board, partly over finances and partly over the issue of the "tributary" museums.

He resigned as secretary of the museum in March 1915, although he remained on the museum board until his term ended in 1919. Some restitution came in 1923, when he was officially recognized as founder of the Southwest Museum at the dedication of the Lummis Caracol Tower, which gives the museum its distinctive appearance high on its hill above Arroyo Seco.

By late January 1914 construction of the museum had advanced far enough that collections were moved in. The museum opened "without fanfare or ceremony" on August 3, 1914. Over time its collection grew into one of the greatest of American Southwest materials, despite the ongoing financial travails well known to all museums.[48]

Lummis in Later Years

After his forced departure from the Southwest Museum, Lummis's health problems multiplied. He and Eva divorced in 1910. He continued to live at El Alisal, the pastiche of Spanish American and Indian architecture he had begun in the 1890s in Arroyo Seco, with the help of Pueblo Indian artisans. There, for over two decades, he conducted a salon and dinner gatherings, which he called "noises." Dressed in a wide-wale corduroy suit, soft-collar shirt, wide sash, and moccasins, Lummis entertained, and usually dominated, "the great, the near-great, the merely colorful, and assorted hangers-on," including John Burroughs, Helena Modjeska, Joaquin Miller, Mary Austin, the Duke of Alba, John Muir, Sarah Bernhardt, Maynard Dixon, Douglas Fairbanks, Will Rogers, Nora May French, and many others.[49]

Lummis's last years were spent revising *Some Strange Corners of Our Country* into *Mesa, Canyon and Pueblo,* and preparing a new edition of *The Spanish Pioneers*. The preparation of the latter and a book of verse, *A Bronco Pegasus,* became a race against advancing brain cancer. He lived to see the publication of both volumes. On November 24, 1928, he received a telegram confirming acceptance of another book, *Flowers of Our Lost Romance.* He died the next day.

CHAPTER 21

Byron Cummings

THE SECOND western scholar-entrepreneur was Byron Cummings (1861–1954).[1] Cummings was the youngest of eight children born to Moses and Roxanne Cummings, in upstate New York. He received bachelor's and master's degrees from Rutgers College, and in 1893 became an instructor in Latin, Greek, and English at the University of Utah in Salt Lake City. By 1895, he was professor of Ancient Languages and Literatures and head of the Classics Department.

In 1905–6, Edgar Lee Hewett (see below) was touring various cities on behalf of the AIA, drumming up interest in local archaeology and helping form new chapters. Cummings's interest was piqued. In the summer of 1906, he made a brief horse-and-buggy trip through Nine Mile Canyon in east-central Utah. The canyon has several cliff dwellings and some large and very striking rock-art panels. He was intrigued enough to plan an extended visit to White Canyon in 1907. By then he had been instrumental in helping

form the Utah chapter of the AIA and planning, at least on paper, a university museum. He also found a backer, one Colonel E. A. Wall, who funded his archeology trips in 1907–9. Under the just-passed Antiquities Act of 1906, the government issued a permit to the AIA to be administered on behalf of its various chapters by Hewett, who had become the Institute's director of research. Thus, Cummings, sponsored by the Utah chapter and ultimately the AIA, nominally reported to Hewett.

The large natural bridges in White Canyon had been known to Indian people for centuries and local cattlemen since the 1870s, but had received national attention only since 1903. Cummings took along a newspaperman and four students, one of them his nephew, Neil M. Judd. He planned to map the bridges and ruins in the canyon. The maps were later part of the documentation for President Roosevelt declaring the Natural Bridges National Monument under the Antiquities Act in 1908.[2]

While Cummings was working in White Canyon, Hewett was introducing three Harvard undergraduates to archaeological surveying some miles to the east. (Their saga is recounted in Chapter 22.) At the end of the summer, one of them, A. V. Kidder, met Neil Judd briefly in Bluff City, the beginning of a long friendship that would have major consequences for Southwestern archaeology.[3]

In 1908, Cummings excavated in sites dotting Alkali Ridge near the town of Grayson (later Blanding), Utah (Map 7). The sites were later determined to be Basketmaker III and Pueblo I in age, but in 1908 it was only apparent that there were both pithouses and unit pueblo structures.[4] Cummings had raised funds through the Utah AIA chapter for the excavation and apparently expected to be in charge. But Hewett had declared Kidder to be in joint charge without Cummings's knowledge. Kidder apparently was forced to exercise the diplomatic skills for which he later became famous.[5] Neil Judd was on the crew, and Hewett had sent along Jesse Nusbaum, his photographer and handy person of all trades. Nusbaum became part of the Judd-Kidder cohort.

After the work at Alkali Ridge ended, Cummings and Judd returned to Bluff, Utah, to meet John Wetherill. In 1906, John and Louisa Wade Wetherill, and a partner, Clyde Colville, opened a trading post at Oljeto in Monument Valley, just inside the Utah line; in 1910, they moved south to Kayenta, in Arizona. There was major trouble brewing among the Navajo, primarily over the continuing issue of Indian children being forcibly sent to Bureau of Indian Affairs schools. The U.S. Army had been called in. When Wetherill, Cummings, and Judd arrived at Oljeto, they found six troops of cavalry, a machine-gun platoon, a wagon train, a pack train and numerous packers, guides, interpreters, and cooks. Through the good offices of Louisa Wetherill, who was fluent in Navajo and trusted by the people, and with help from John Wetherill and Colonel Hugh L. Scott, an expert in Indian sign language and the army's designated troubleshooter in Indian disputes, matters were settled, and the army and the Navajos dispersed.[6] Wetherill was supposed to guide Cummings and company into the Tsegi Canyon area (Map 7), but because of the crisis and the press of other business could not, so they explored on their own.

When Cummings stopped at Oljeto on his way back to Utah, Louisa Wetherill reported that a Navajo had asked her what Cummings was doing in the country. She mentioned that he was exploring, and had seen three natural bridges in Utah the previous year. That reminded the Navajo of a bridge somewhere toward Navajo Mountain, "shaped like a rainbow." He, like others she asked, had heard of but not seen the great bridge. She promised to keep asking about the bridge, and Cummings determined to spend the following summer searching for it. But by the time Cummings, Judd, and Wetherill reached Bluff, Utah, the word was out, and all the locals were abuzz about the mysterious great bridge.

Tsegi Canyon and Rainbow Bridge, 1909

Cummings, accompanied by son Malcolm, nephew Neil Judd, and two other University of Utah students, Donald Beauregard, a budding artist who had spent two years in Paris, 1906–8, and Stuart Young, a photographer, arrived at the Wetherills early in the summer of 1909. The good Colonel Wall had again provided one thousand dollars, and Cummings received a few hundred dollars from his university. The sources are not clear, but apparently Hewett and Nusbaum rendezvoused with the Cummings group at Bluff on the San Juan River at the beginning of the field season (Fig. 21.1).[7]

With John Wetherill guiding, the group penetrated further into the Tsegi Canyon area. John and Richard Wetherill had dug in the great cliff-ruin site of Keet Seel in the 1890s. From Marsh Pass, they had gone up Tsegi Canyon and turned right into Dowozsheibito Canyon; Richard had tracked the wayward mule into Keet Seel Canyon (see Chapter 16). They had not explored a side canyon that entered Tsegi Canyon from the left, opposite Dowozsheibito. Now in 1909, Wetherill and Cummings did turn up the left-hand

21.1. Cummings Party at San Juan River, Utah, 1909. Back row, left to right: Neil M. Judd, Donald Beauregard, John Wetherill, Jesse Nusbaum. Front row, left to right: Byron Cummings, Malcolm Cummings, Edgar Lee Hewett. Photograph by Stewart Young. Courtesy of the Arizona Historical Society.

canyon, and found Betatakin, the second of the great cliff houses in the Tsegi drainage. They did some digging and determined to return.

They then struck westward to the headwaters of Navajo Creek, which drains into the Colorado River, and recorded Inscription House. The site is named for an inscription on an interior wall thought to read "1661 Anno Domini," and therefore to indicate a visit by an unknown Spanish traveler. According to Judd, the inscription was first spotted by the Wetherill twins, Ben and Ida, and Malcolm Cummings.

The foregoing is the official version of the trip. There is good evidence that John Wetherill had already "discovered" Betatakin and Inscription House, but liked to let his clients think they were the first to make discoveries. Wetherill was a modest, self-effacing man with a great private sense of humor. There is also fair evidence that the Inscription House date is "1861," probably placed there by Mormon missionaries known to have been in the area at that time.[8]

The Rainbow Bridge

Louisa Wetherill had located two San Juan Southern Paiutes, father and son, who lived in Piute [*sic*] Canyon and who had seen the great bridge while hunting stray horses. The son, Noscha (or Nasja) Begay, was engaged as a guide. The San Juan Southern Paiute band's traditional territory centers on the slopes of Navajo Mountain. The mountain is a great, 10,400-

foot-high laccolithic dome extruded upward through the sedimentary Navajo and Wingate sandstones of the Rainbow Plateau; it lies just south of the confluence of the Colorado and San Juan rivers. The flanks of the mountain and the surrounding sandstones are cut by an incredibly labyrinthine maze of deep, often sawcut, canyons. In 1909 the only feasible route was overland by horseback from the Monument Valley area.

Learning that a government surveyor, William Boone Douglass, and his party were also seeking the bridge, Cummings waited for them, perhaps persuaded to do so by John Wetherill, although it meant sharing discovery of the bridge. The joint Cummings-Douglass party finally reached the "Rainbow Bridge" on August 14, 1909 (Map 7). There are various accounts of the trip. There was a great deal of later wrangling, extending over more than fifty years, as to who first reached the bridge, Cummings or Douglass. The argument is compounded by much evidence that many Indians and numerous Whites had visited the bridge long before 1909—the Whites perhaps as early as 1880 or even before. There is also circumstantial evidence that John and Louisa Wetherill had found their way to the bridge in 1908, but John, again, let his client, Cummings, claim the credit of at least being the first to *see* the bridge.[9]

In later years, the bridge became a destination for numerous individuals, many of them guided by John Wetherill. By November 1910, Wetherill could report to Cummings that "I have made four trips to the Bridge, three of them took in the top of Navajo Mt. and the ruins," His customers included Herbert Gregory, the famed geologist, and a "Mrs. Sargent, a globe trotter."[10]

As an aside, John Wetherill placed a register book at the bridge during the Cummings-Douglass trip, and all the members of the party signed it, as did most everyone who visited on later trips. It contains the names of Theodore Roosevelt, Zane Grey (three trips), Byron Cummings again in 1920, and Charles Bernheimer and Earl H. Morris (see Chapter 24). An entry for October 19, 1921, contains the names of

the U.S. Geological Survey team mapping the Colorado and San Juan rivers in preparation for building dams on them. A second entry for September 12, 1922, contains the names of a large party of engineers and bureaucrats, including Arthur Powell Davis, John Wesley Powell's nephew and head of the U.S. Reclamation Service (now the Bureau of Reclamation), who were planning the dams. Hoover Dam was built in the 1930s. The dam on the San Juan, creating Navajo Reservoir, and Glen Canyon Dam, creating Lake Powell, were built between 1957 and 1963.[11]

When the parties returned to Oljeto, Cummings, who was on sabbatical leave, stayed on to excavate in the Betatakin Ruin. In a letter to Hewett, he wrote:

We have made a trip to Navajo Mountain; visited a large bridge, or rather a great natural arch on the north side of the mountain. . . . Since visiting "Keetseel," I do not care to take hold of it even if we have all the money necessary in hand. It has been dug into too much. Let the govt. handle that. . . . In another canyon about ten miles from . . . Keetseel we discovered a large house [Betatakin], nearly as extensive . . . It contained about 120 rooms I should judge. Why can't the Utah Society have the privilege of clearing that out and saving the material for its museum? I am winning over some of the Navajos and I am sure we can do it well and *scientifically* with the means at our disposal.[12]

Later, Cummings wrote Hewett from Bluff, Utah: "We arrived here from Oljato tonight. We have cleared out all the rooms in Betatakin except those in the extreme . . . southeast [section of the site]." He also dug in Keet Seel and two other sites.[13]

Cummings returned to the Tsegi drainage and dug in several other sites in 1911 and 1913. He never got around to writing reports on this work and the materials lay unreported in the University of Utah Museum until 1969.[14] Between 1913 and 1944, with the exception of 1918, and 1922 and 1925 (when he worked at the Cuicuilco ruin in the Valley of Mexico), Cummings made at least one archaeological field trip into the Four Corners area after 1919, calling the trip "a summer course among the Cliff Dwellers."[15]

Cummings Moves to Arizona

Cummings was very active during his years at the University of Utah. He organized the university's first football team in 1893—there ultimately was a Cummings Field on campus. He served concurrently as dean of men (1904–15), dean of the School of Arts and Sciences (1906–15), and did triple duty as dean of the Medical School in 1910. He was a very popular teacher and administrator and enjoyed strong support within the community. But in early 1915 he was faced with a crisis that led to his resignation and ultimate move to Arizona.

In February 1915, the class valedictorian, one Milton Sevy, gave a speech that was mildly critical of the Utah state legislature and the Mormon Church, a risky thing to do in Utah where the separation of church and state was not thought necessary by those in power. Cummings knew of the speech and supported the student's right of free expression. The subsequent brouhaha led to the dismissal of three faculty members by the Board of Regents. One was fired for "uttering in a private conversation with a colleague" his dissatisfaction with the Board of Regents and the university president, John T. Kingsbury (later memorialized by a grandiose Renaissance Revival administration building named for him). The dismissed faculty member was not allowed to know who his accusers were; he was simply sacked. In a subsequent policy directive, the Board of Regents stated that "in cases of such serious disagreement as the President reported to exist between himself and certain professors, 'the Board is not concerned to know who is right and who is wrong in this disagreement,' but only to determine the relative value of the services of those concerned, and to eliminate from the University those whose services it believes to be less valuable."[16]

The Board thought the president had more value. In another statement, the Board said that faculty members, the president, and board members "have an equal right to free thought, free speech and free action," but if a faculty member disagreed with the president and the board, "he may . . . find an institution and state where . . . [his] sentiments . . . may be approved. If so, that is where he belongs."[17] All attempts by alumni and others to infuse some due process, fairness, or even public discussion into the mess were stonewalled by the regents. It was far too much for Byron Cummings and he resigned on March 15, 1915, along with seventeen (or twenty-four—sources vary) other faculty members.

The case had immediate national significance, especially for the young American Association of University Professors, which sent a committee to investigate. Its members were E. A. Seligman and John Dewey, from Columbia University; Frank Fetter and H. C. Warren, from Princeton; and Arthur O. Lovejoy, of Johns Hopkins—all major figures in American higher education at the time. The Association, then as now, was centrally concerned with academic freedom and tenure, and due process in faculty-administrative relations.[18]

On June 22, 1915, Cummings was offered a "three-fifths" time appointment as professor of archaeology "at a salary of $1,400 per year" by the president of the University of Arizona, Rufus Bernhard von Klinschmidt. The rest of his time was to be devoted "to the organizing and building up of our University Museum," apparently with the remainder of his salary coming from a museum-related fund.[19] Cummings had found his niche. Over time, he created a Department of Archaeology (later the Department of Anthropology), and the Arizona State Museum, and played a major role in forming the Arizona Archaeological and Historical Society. He dug at the famous site of Cuicuilco, in the southern end of the Valley of Mexico. In 1925 he took an interested undergraduate along, Emil Haury (previously mentioned). At various times in the 1920s, Cummings was a dean, acting president, and president of the University of Arizona. He retired from the department and the museum in 1937–38, and was known affectionately as "The Dean."[21]

CHAPTER 22

Edgar Lee Hewett

THE THIRD western scholar-entrepreneur was Edgar Lee Hewett (1865–1946), a key figure in Southwestern anthropology for forty years (Fig. 22.1).[1] From 1909 until the 1940s he directed both the Museum of New Mexico and the School of American Research. From 1911 to 1915 he also directed the exhibits at the San Diego Panama-California Exposition. From 1915 to 1928 he was director of the San Diego Museum of Man, and professor of anthropology at San Diego State Teachers College, while keeping both New Mexico positions. In 1929 he became professor of anthropology at the University of New Mexico and in 1934 helped found the Anthropology Department at the University of Southern California.

Between 1904 and 1930 Hewett often clashed bitterly with members of the "eastern establishment" over policies, professional standards, and control of key institutions and the funds to operate them. Although he was formally sponsored by the Archaeological Institute of America and, in part, the Smithsonian

Institution, he was not *of* the eastern establishment. He was, and saw himself as, a westerner. He was vilified and slandered by his enemies, both in the East and the clamorous, bared-claw hotbed of Santa Fe public life. He usually managed to publicly ignore them. He was also widely admired nationally, and in Santa Fe and southern California.

Hewett, together with Byron Cummings, were the last of the nineteenth-century American anthropologists, even though they worked in the twentieth century. Like John Wesley Powell and Frederic Ward Putnam, they were self-taught. Hewett did acquire a doctorate—in sociology from the University of Geneva in Switzerland. His detractors, however, regarded the degree as little more than the product of a diploma mill.[2]

Whatever else he was, Edgar Lee Hewett was stubborn and contentious; adversaries called him *El Toro*. A key to his personality and actions is found in his autobiography. He was taught to box at an early age:

"Only a few times through life have I had occasion to use my instruction in boxing, but to this day, on provocation my hands and feet snap into position."[3] Throughout his several careers, Hewett was often provoked; he provoked others. On balance, he won more rounds than he lost.

Hewett grew up on a farm in the Midwest and became a schoolteacher. In 1890 he began teaching school in Florence, Colorado. He and his wife spent their summers in a horse-drawn campwagon touring the West, hoping the open air and sunlight would cure her tuberculosis. Hewett became intrigued by the archaeological ruins on the Pajarito Plateau, west of Santa Fe. He read voraciously in archaeology, and began to lecture on the subject.

In 1897 Hewett met a prominent citizen and attorney of Las Vegas, New Mexico, Frank Springer, and the two became fast friends. Soon after, through Springer's influence, Hewett was appointed president of the newly created New Mexico Normal School (now New Mexico Highlands University) in Las Vegas. In addition to administrative duties, he taught anthro-

pology and archaeology. He took students on frequent field trips and spent weekends and summers at Pecos Ruin, on the Pajarito Plateau, and, in 1902, in Chaco Canyon.

Hewett made his first trip to Washington, D.C., in 1900, where he met John Wesley Powell and Frederic Ward Putnam, who happened to be in town. He also met and became close friends with Alice Cunningham Fletcher (Fig. 22.2) and William Henry Holmes.[4] In 1898, he helped form the Archaeological Society of New Mexico. Soon the society was petitioning the U.S. General Land Office to investigate the activities of the Hyde Expedition and Richard Wetherill in Chaco Canyon (see Chapter 16). Hewett had been pushing for a national cultural park on the Pajarito Plateau; now he added Chaco Canyon as a second possibility. He wrote a major report on New Mexico antiquities in 1903, part of the annual report of the governor of the New Mexico Territory.[5]

But there was trouble in Las Vegas. While well liked by students and faculty, local opinion makers disliked Hewett's unconventional teaching methods and his refusal to court them. His persistent efforts to get large tracts of public land set aside for national parks angered powerful ranchers and landowners.[6] His contract was not renewed by the university regents for 1903–4. Frank Springer, however, remained his ardent champion. His firing was a major turning point. At age thirty-nine Hewett decided to become an archaeologist. But he needed an advanced degree if he was to be taken seriously within the emerging American anthropology community. He sold his possessions and used the money to go to the University of Geneva to get a doctorate and make an archaeological tour of the Near East. He returned to Washington, D.C., taking whatever odd-job anthropological work was available. His wife died in 1905, and while mourning her, Hewett threw himself into the fight for passage of a federal antiquities act.

The 1906 Antiquities Act

The 1906 Antiquities Act was the culmination of efforts for over a century to achieve some protection and conservation for American antiquities.[7] Earlier efforts were mixed: the failed petition of 1882 and the successful 1889 attempt to set aside Casa Grande (see Chapter 13). Rampant looting of Southwestern sites continued throughout the 1890s, stimulating concern in many quarters. By 1899 a coordinated effort was under way. The American Association for the Advancement of Science appointed a Committee on the Protection and Preservation of Objects of Archaeological Interest; the Archaeological Institute of America created a Standing Committee on American Archaeology. Frederic Ward Putnam sat on both committees and thus linked the two. Bills began to be drafted, and in their wording, institutional jockeying for control of archaeological resources on public lands began.

Bills were introduced in 1904 and again in 1905; all had fatal flaws in the eyes of one or another group wishing to control the public lands sites.[8] Enter Hewett, stage right. In the spring of 1903, Congressman John F. Lacey of Iowa, chairman of the House Com-

mittee on Public Lands, spent two weeks on a horseback trip with Hewett, probably arranged by Frank Springer, an Iowa native. They looked at various ruins in Colorado and New Mexico, and discussed the problems of vandalism and site protection around evening campfires. Lacey's interest was quickened.[9] In 1904 General Land Office Commissioner W. A. Richards asked Hewett to review the problems of protecting archaeological sites on public lands in the Southwest. Hewett's report was comprehensive, and allowed the Congress to get a firm grasp of the problem for the first time.[10]

In 1905 Hewett was appointed to the American Anthropological Association (AAA) committee on antiquities and became the committee's secretary and spokesperson in Washington. At a joint AAA/AIA meeting in Ithaca, New York, in December 1905, he presented a draft bill that, he said, would resolve conflicts in earlier bills and be politically feasible in Congress. For Hewett, "politically feasible" meant a bill that would *not* give control of western archaeology to eastern archaeologists. The draft was unanimously endorsed.[11]

In January 1906 Congressman Lacey introduced the bill in the House; a companion bill was introduced in the Senate. The flamboyant Charles F. Lummis came to town to help lobby for the bill. In their haste to get the bill passed and fend off weakening amendments, Lummis's and Hewett's rough-and-tumble tactics offended a number of eastern sensibilities; some remained offended for the next three decades. The fact that they succeeded in getting their bill passed, and blocking control of western archaeology by eastern universities and the Smithsonian, made matters worse. On June 8, 1906, President Theodore Roosevelt signed into law the "Lacey Bill,"—the 1906 Antiquities Act, as it has come to be known. The wording is Hewett's.[12]

As part of its campaign to develop new chapters, in 1899 the AIA appointed an Americanist committee consisting of Frederic Ward Putnam, Franz Boas, and Charles P. Bowditch. Bowditch was a prominent Boston businessman and major donor to the Peabody

Museum at Harvard. He had become entranced with the Maya in the late 1880s and began funding expeditions to Central America.[13] In 1899, he created a fellowship in American archaeology at Harvard; the first recipient was Alfred Tozzer.

In 1905, Jesse Walter Fewkes, Francis Kelsey, Alice Fletcher, and Charles Lummis were added to the committee. The committee awarded a six-hundred-dollar fellowship to Hewett. His instructions were to help stimulate and develop western chapters of the Institute and conduct an archaeological survey of the Mesa Verde, in anticipation of its becoming a national park. He was also instructed to "make a comparative study of the culture,—especially of the art and architecture,—of the ancient Pueblo peoples with that of the ancient Mexicans, with the object of ascertaining whether there was any ethnical connection between the two regions." Having done that, he could then "make a preliminary survey of the region from the pueblos to ancient Mexico, carrying on . . . studies tending toward the solution of the problem of the connection between ancient Mexico and the ancient pueblos and between ancient Mexico and ancient Central America."[14]

From January to June 1906, Hewett saw to the first two tasks (including sparking Byron Cummings's interest), while lobbying for the antiquities act. In June, he set out on horseback from Casas Grandes, Chihuahua, surveying along the flanks of the Sierra Madre to the Valley of Mexico.[15] When he reached Mexico City, he visited with Alice Fletcher, who was a guest of Zelia Nuttall. They had long talks about the direction American archaeology ought to take.[16]

Alice Cunningham Fletcher (1838–1923) played many major roles in American anthropology and Indian affairs for nearly four decades, from about 1880 to 1910.[17] While teaching in New York City, she was active in feminist and temperance movements. At some point she became interested in anthropology; by 1879 she was lecturing on "Ancient America," and had become a protégé of Frederic Ward Putnam. She was a founding member of the Archaeological Institute of America in 1879.

Fletcher became involved in Indian affairs in 1880 and was active in seeking passage of the Dawes allotment act of 1885, and then in its administration—the ill-conceived law that divided tribally held Indian lands into 160-acre individually owned parcels in yet another attempt to force Indians to become farmers and, thus, civilized.

In 1886, Putnam made Fletcher an (unpaid) assistant in ethnology at the Peabody Museum at Harvard. In 1890, Mary Copley Thaw, of Pittsburgh, created a lifetime fellowship for Fletcher, administered through the Peabody Museum. Nationally known and highly respected, she settled in Washington, D.C., and continued to play major roles in American anthropology and Indian affairs.

In December 1906, Fletcher presented a plan to the AIA Americanist Committee designed to stimulate work in the New World and to strengthen AIA ties with its burgeoning western chapters. It called for "preparation of a map of the culture areas of the American continent [to] facilitate the task of correlating work . . . in progress, . . . [and] make it possible to direct the efforts of the various Societies of the Institute which desire to support active field work in our own country . . . A preparatory step . . . would be the appointment of an officer to be known as Director of American Archaeology, whose immediate duty would be to direct and coordinate all work undertaken by the affiliated societies . . . This should be followed by the establishment of a School of American Archaeology, in which graduate students should be received for instruction and employment in field research . . ." The committee accepted Fletcher's plan and recommended Hewett as Director of American Archaeology. He was elected two days later and made a member of the committee.[18] Some in the AIA welcomed Hewett's appointment; others withheld judgment.

Santa Fe and the School of American Archaeology

Hewett settled in Santa Fe in 1906. His local network, led by Frank Springer, Judge John R. McFie, and Paul

A. F. Walter, all prominent in Republican politics, agreed that the venerable Palace of the Governors would be a splendid home for the proposed archaeology school and for a museum. They moved to convince the New Mexico territorial legislature to let the AIA use the Palace for the school, and to convince the AIA that there should *be* a school and that it should be in Santa Fe.

"Throw 'Em Off da Pier"

Hewett advertised his first archaeological field school through a circular. Three Harvard students, Alfred Vincent Kidder, Sylvanus Griswold Morley, and John Gould Fletcher, signed on for the summer of 1907. Their adventures and misadventures are one of the primal legends of Southwestern archaeology.[19]

Alfred Vincent ("Ted") Kidder (1885–1963) was from an old New England family.[20] His mining-engineer father had broad interests, read widely, and knew Louis Agassiz and Lewis Henry Morgan. His library contained Bureau of American Ethnology and Smithsonian reports which young Kidder browsed avidly. After private schooling in Massachusetts and Switzerland, he entered Harvard in 1904 with vague thoughts of a medical career, but came to grief in the chemistry courses. He enrolled in a course taught by Roland B. Dixon, met Frederic Ward Putnam, and became interested in anthropology. He heard of Hewett's field school, went to Alfred Tozzer's office to apply, and met Sylvanus Griswold Morley and John Gould Fletcher.

Sylvanus Griswold Morley (1883–1948), "Vay" to all who knew him, was born in Pennsylvania.[21] He was fascinated by archaeology and lost civilizations. A family friend put him in touch with Frederic Ward Putnam. Putnam patiently answered Morley's questions and set him to reading. But Morley's father concluded that there was no future in archaeology, and sent him off to military school. He dutifully graduated in 1904. His father had been killed in a mine accident in 1903. Morley felt freer to pursue archaeology and entered Harvard in 1904. Putnam was his mentor, al-though Morley took no formal classes with him. Roland Dixon stimulated his interest in general anthropology and Charles Bowditch and Alfred Tozzer quickened his fascination with Maya civilization. He received a fellowship to go to Yucatán for four months early in 1907. He toured numerous sites, sketched, measured, and photographed, and was entranced by the ruins. He hated the climate, the rain forest, the difficulties, and the diseases, and continued to do so for four decades, but he had found his life's work.

Morley returned to Harvard, learned of Hewett's field school, and persuaded a friend, John Gould Fletcher, to come along. Fletcher (1886–1950) was from Arkansas, the only son of a well-to-do banker.[22] He grew up awkward and shy. He went to Phillips Academy and then to Harvard, with law school to follow. The writer Van Wyck Brooks, a fellow student at Harvard, recalled Fletcher's "queer white skull-like face peering out through the crimson curtains of the Harvard Union . . . an old man's son, he seemed to have been born old himself, stiff-jointed, with big angular bones and stooping shoulders; and, as a stranger from the South, he had been, as he wrote, 'the most forlorn and hopeless individual at Harvard.'"[23]

Kidder, Morley and Fletcher traveled by train to Mancos, Colorado, with Kidder a day ahead of the others. From Mancos, Kidder rode with the local mail carrier to Bluff City, Utah, and met Hewett on July 2, 1907. The next day, they rode horseback to McElmo Creek to a small ranch run by the Holley family, which was to be headquarters, and then on up the canyon to meet Morley and Fletcher. By nightfall, Fletcher remembered, "Both Morley and I limped exhaustedly out of our saddles . . . and onto the camp beds, without bothering about supper. Kidder, who had suffered the most, rolled out of his saddle . . . and slept on the ground."[24]

The next day, Hewett took them to the confluence of McElmo and Yellow Jacket canyons. He spent a few hours showing them some ruins. Then, according to Kidder, Hewett "waved an arm, taking in it seemed, about half the world, 'I want you boys to make an archaeological survey of this country. I'll be back in three weeks.' "[25] Offering no further advice or training, Hewett rode away, leaving them to their own devices.

Hewett later wrote that he had learned this pedagogical technique from a young waterfront ruffian in Chicago who taught kids to swim by "throwing 'em off da pier." The three had many misadventures, including run-ins with ill-tempered horses, putting plaster of paris in the biscuit dough, and spreading their bedrolls in irrigation ditches and on anthills. The stuff of legends, true or no.[26]

Only Morley had any useful training for their assignment. He could make maps, and had some idea about site recording from his trip to the Maya country. Hewett had given them a fifty-foot tape measure. Kidder had the foresight to bring a pocket compass, and both he and Morley had brought Kodak cameras.[27]

They had to make a general map of the region, for Hewett had supplied none and probably none existed. They rode, searched out ruins, and measured and described them as best they could. Morley was very nearsighted and Kidder feared he would tumble off a cliff at any moment. Slight of build and high-voiced, Morley was neverendingly cheerful and the group leader. The three grew better at their task as they proceeded. It was monotonous, but they came to appreciate the stark beauty and subtleties of the desert. Among the sites they recorded was Cannonball Ruin, which Morley tested the following year.[28]

Hewett returned on July 25. He had contracted to map the major ruins in the newly created Mesa Verde National Park. The four rode to Cortez, Colorado, where they met Jesse Nusbaum and moved up to the mesa.[29] Kidder later recalled that "mapping, without transit or plane table and alidade, of large structures built on many levels, as well as adapted to irregular and often sloping surfaces, was not easy. It took five days for Fletcher and me to do our part of the work on Sprucetree House, two more for Morley to wind up his note taking."[30]

The mapping was finished about mid-August. Hewett had received six hundred dollars from the Southwest Society to excavate on the Pajarito Plateau

in a ruin on Puyé Mesa.[31] Although Hewett was there part of the time, he gave no instruction in excavation techniques, probably because he knew little more than his students. They removed fallen walls and cleared rooms, aided now and then by workmen from San Ildefonso Pueblo. Kidder and Morley found the work tedious but worthwhile. Fletcher hated it; he thought the country was magnificent, but the work and his companions palled.[32] He fled to Europe and became a poet, remaining there for twenty years.

In 1927 Fletcher returned to Arkansas. He married the novelist Charlie May Simon, led an active literary life, and received the Pulitzer Prize for poetry in 1939. In his later years he began to suffer periodic bouts of depression, and finally took his own life in 1950.[33] He produced a few poems drawn from the "furtive scribblings" of his Southwest experience, such as *Cliff Dwelling*:

The canyon is choked with stones and undergrowth;
The heat falls from the sky
Beats at the walls, slides and reverberates
Down in a wave of grey dust and white fire;
Stinging the mouth and eyes.

The ponies struggle and scramble,
Half way up, along the canyon wall;
Their listless riders seldom lift
A weary hand to guide their feet;
Stones are loosened and clatter
Down to the sunbaked depths.

Nothing has ever lived here,
Nothing could ever live here;
Two hawks, screaming and wheeling,
Rouse the eye to look aloft.
Boldly poised in a shelf of stone,
Tiny walls peer down on us;
Towers with little square windows.

When we plod up to them,
And dismounting, fasten our horses;
Suddenly a blue-grey flock of doves,
Burst in a flutter of wings from the shadows.

Shards of pots and shreds of straw,
Empty brush-roofed rooms in darkness;
And the sound of water tinkling,
A clock that ticks the centuries off to silence.[34]

While Fletcher sought his muse in London, Kidder and Morley had found archaeology in the Southwest.

The School of American Archaeology

In the summer of 1907, Hewett brought Alice Fletcher to see Santa Fe and the Pajarito country; she was enthralled. They continued to plan a School of American Archaeology. But discontent was rife in Cambridge. Charles Bowditch resigned as chair of the AIA Americanist committee, weary of the bumptious Hewett and Lummis. He thought Alice Fletcher could keep them in check, since he thought Frederic Ward Putnam could keep *her* in check. But Putnam's "protégé" was nearing seventy and had ideas of her own that coincided with Hewett's. In December 1907 she pushed a resolution through the AIA annual meeting to create a School of American Archaeology "to conduct the researches of the Institute in the American field and afford opportunities for field work and training to students of archaeology." The location was to be determined, but likely in the western United States.[35]

A managing committee was created with Fletcher as chair and Franz Boas, Jesse Walter Fewkes, Francis W. Kelsey, Charles Lummis, and Frederic Ward Putnam as members. On December 31, 1907, Hewett was appointed director of the school. After a brief period to get things organized, he left for Europe and the Near East for eighteen weeks, one or two of which were spent finishing his doctorate at the University of Geneva.

Formal approval of the school helped Hewett and his allies acquire the Palace of the Governors and establish the school in Santa Fe. But there were other viewpoints. Franz Boas had been nurturing plans for an International School of American Archaeology and Ethnology in Mexico City. He hoped to include the

AIA, and its funds, within the consortium of universities, research institutions, and governments he was putting together to support his school. Placing the school in Santa Fe would cripple that support. Boas, Tozzer, and others did manage to get the school in Mexico City underway, but it fell victim to Mexican revolutionary and World War I turmoil and ceased operation in 1915–16.[36]

In 1908 Kidder came back for a second season; Hewett sent him off to work with Byron Cummings at Alkali Ridge (see above). Later in the summer, Kidder and Jesse Nusbaum returned to Mesa Verde for more mapping, supported by 1,250 dollars that Hewett had raised from Colorado State University, the Colorado Historical Society, and private subscriptions.[37]

In 1908 Hewett held another field school, this time in Canyon de los Frijoles, where he began work on the large ruin of Tyuonyi. The Peabody Museum of Harvard put up 500 dollars, as did the New Mexico Archaeological Society; 250 dollars came from private subscriptions, most likely Frank Springer. The field assistants were Sylvanus Morley and John Peabody Harrington. Roland B. Dixon and Alfred Tozzer represented Harvard. Tozzer and Dixon did *not* hit it off with Hewett. They thought him and his field methods crude. Whatever Hewett did, by omission or commission (one legend is that it began when Hewett, ever frugal, denied Tozzer a second helping of bacon at breakfast), he made a lifetime enemy of Tozzer, who became famous for his deeply felt and long-lasting enmities toward those he disliked. In 1912, Tozzer wrote to Frederick Webb Hodge, "I . . . consider Hewett's influence over the young men under him bad, his methods of work unscientific and too extended, his methods of scattering propaganda undignified, and his assumption of omnipotence unexampled."[38]

In November 1908, Bowditch, Boas, Putnam, Fletcher, and Hewett met in Cambridge to select a site for the School of American Archaeology. Bowditch, Putnam, and Boas were against Santa Fe; Fletcher and Hewett were for it. But Fletcher sent mail ballots to the four absentee members. The recount made it six to three in favor of Santa Fe. Boas was apoplectic. Bowditch and Putnam sent Tozzer to the annual AIA meeting in Toronto in December in an attempt to get the committee vote overturned; he failed.[39]

Hewett's Santa Fe allies now moved forward. They convinced the 1909 New Mexico legislature to establish the Museum of New Mexico. The legislation stipulated that the museum and the school would be housed in the Palace of the Governors, and that the school would operate the museum. Hewett was appointed director of the museum. The legislation provided operating expenses for the museum but the director's position carried no salary, a provision Hewett had requested.

The museum would be controlled by a board of regents, appointed by the governor of New Mexico. The school would be controlled by a managing committee, appointed by the AIA. The chairman of the regents would sit on the school's managing committee. Hewett recommended the membership for both groups. He had learned his lesson about governing boards in Las Vegas: the majority of the members should, if possible, be handpicked by him. The museum's board of regents was stacked with prominent New Mexicans favorable to Hewett. The AIA committee was chaired by Alice Fletcher. Members included Hermon C. Bumpus of the American Museum, Byron Cummings, Jesse Walter Fewkes, Frederick Webb Hodge, William Henry Holmes, Charles Lummis, Congressman John Lacey, and two AIA officers. Frank Springer represented the museum's board of regents.[40]

Thus, by the late spring of 1909, Hewett was well positioned. His salary came from the AIA, supplemented by lecture fees and monies made now and then from Santa Fe real estate and other investments. Taking no salary as museum director was a master stroke, since it removed the position from political pork-barreling, and allowed him to maintain a posture of altruism. He carried on a relentless schedule of lecturing around the country for the AIA, continually widening his networks. His carefully managed image made him seem to be "Doctor Archaeology," at least in the West and Midwest.

All this incensed the eastern anthropologists. Bowditch, Putnam, and Boas launched a counterattack. There was much talk of how "poor Alice" had been "deceived," and "hoodwinked" by horrible Hewett. She was not personally criticized; it would have been extraordinarily impolitic to attack someone regarded by many as a living saint. Francis Kelsey totally disagreed that Fletcher was duped by Hewett, calling her "one of the most clear-headed and capable administrators that I have met."[41] Putnam, Boas, and Bowditch carried their fight to the December 1909 annual meeting of the AIA. They lost again, and thereupon resigned from the Institute, but not from the fight.

With the school and the museum now realities, Hewett moved ahead. He hired Jesse Nusbaum and Kenneth Chapman (see Figs. 22.3, 24.6, and 24.7) on the staff of the museum, and Sylvanus G. Morley and John Peabody Harrington (see below) on the staff of the school. Hewett had known Chapman for ten years.[42] Kenneth Milton Chapman (1875–1968) was born in Indiana, studied at the Art Institute of Chicago in 1893–94, and worked as an engraver and commercial artist. But he developed a cough, perhaps tuberculosis, and went to Las Vegas, New Mexico, for a year to recover; he never went back. Hewett hired him as an art instructor at the Normal School and introduced him to Pueblo pottery designs—the start of a lifetime's fascination for Chapman. Frank Springer's very serious hobby was paleontology, especially crinoids. In 1902, he hired Chapman to do the exacting drawings of hundreds of crinoids for his publications, issued through Harvard, the Smithsonian, and Cambridge University.[43] Chapman's association with Springer, as friend and part-time artist, continued until Springer died in 1927. In 1909 Hewett hired Chapman as "Executive Secretary" for the museum, but his duties included artist, mapmaker, archaeologist, lecturer, receptionist, and sometimes janitor.

Jesse Nusbaum (1887–1961) was born in the farming cooperative and temperance society founded by Horace Greeley in Colorado.[44] Jesse worked as an apprentice to his father, a master brick mason and building contractor. He taught himself photography and became interested in archaeology by reading Nordenskiöld's *Cliff Dwellers of the Mesa Verde*. In 1907 he graduated from Colorado Normal School in manual arts and science and was hired as an instructor in the same subjects at the New Mexico Normal School in Las Vegas. Hewett hired him for the summers of 1907 and 1908, then for the museum. Jesse Nusbaum was six feet, four inches tall, laconic, and a great storyteller in a deep, vibrant voice. He could design and build whatever was asked for; he made excellent maps and extraordinary photographs. Like Chapman, he did whatever was needed to make the museum function.

In the summer of 1909, Hewett continued work in Frijoles Canyon, and went back to Puyé. Nusbaum and Chapman supervised various Tewa workers from San Ildefonso and Santa Clara pueblos. Morley

22.3. *School of American Archaeology field school at Frijoles Canyon, 1910. Back row, left to right: Wilfred Robbins, Donald Beauregard, John P. Harrington, Frederick Webb Hodge, Edgar Lee Hewett, Neil M. Judd, Maude Woy, Barbara Freire-Marreco. Front row, left to right: Sylvanus G. Morley, Kenneth Chapman, J. P. Adams, Jesse Nusbaum, Nathan Goldsmith, Junius Henderson. Courtesy of the Museum of New Mexico Photographic Archives.*

visited often; his size and demeanor led the Tewa to nickname him "hummingbird." Under Hewett's guidance, the Museum of New Mexico began acquiring major archaeological sites, including Pecos, Quarai, and Gran Quivira. He also found funds for Adolph Bandelier to write up his Southwestern materials.[45] Hewett's plans were that Nusbaum and Chapman would take care of the museum. Morley represented Hewett's first step toward a program of Maya research. Harrington would be used in yet another project.

The School and the BAE

In 1910, Hewett and Frederick Webb Hodge, just appointed to head the Bureau of American Ethnology, announced a joint School of American Archaeology, Bureau of American Ethnology (SAA-BAE) program for an interdisciplinary study of the Upper Rio Grande Valley. There were to be linguistic and ethnographic studies of Rio Grande pueblos, including material culture, sociology, mythology, religion, and environment, continued ethnohistoric research, a comprehensive program of archaeological research focusing on the Pajarito Plateau, and studies of the climate, vegetation, fauna, "and all other physiographic conditions, with their effects upon the life and cultures of both ancient and recent inhabitants."[46]

Hewett put together a team for the 1910 season, based at Frijoles Canyon (Fig. 22.3). He brought in Junius Henderson, a geologist and curator of the natural history museum at the University of Colorado, and Wilfred W. Robbins, a biologist from the same institution. J. P. Adams, whom Nusbaum knew from Greeley, did topographic mapping. He was assisted by Nathan Goldsmith, a student from Cornell University. Neil Judd and Donald Beauregard, Cummings's students from Utah, helped supervise the continuing clearing of Tyuonyi. Jesse Nusbaum and Sylvanus Morley, who had spent the spring in Guatemala and Honduras, were at Frijoles part time. The two women at the field school were Maud Woy, a history teacher from Denver, and Barbara Freire-Marreco, a graduate student in anthropology at Oxford University.[47]

Advent of the "Angry God"

John Peabody Harrington (1884–1961) was one of the oddest ducks ever to work in American anthropology.[48] He exasperated everyone by his quixotic behavior, but all agreed that he was a genius. Harrington was obsessed with his self-appointed mission to record American Indian languages before they died out, which he pursued from 1907 until his death in 1961. He left an estimated 800,000 pages of notes squirreled away in trunks and boxes in warehouses and peoples' attics until he needed them. He usually never returned, although he always planned to do so. The National Anthropological Archives at the Smithsonian Institution after many years collected the bulk of them.

Harrington feared his own death because he could no longer work nor think. But he feared the death of his Indian consultants even more: they might inconsiderately die before he could record their languages. He suffered lifelong chronic gastroenteritis, occasional ulcers, and "terminal paranoia."[49] He avoided anything that might keep him away from fieldwork, or force him into the office to write, although he published over 150 items, most of them brief.

There are many legends about Harrington. A. V. Kidder once encountered him somewhere in New Mexico nose to nose with a billy goat, tugging on its beard; the goat was protesting vociferously. When Kidder asked why, Harrington demanded silence, and again pulled the goat's beard. There was another bleat of protest. Said Harrington, "That's the most perfect umlauted A I've ever heard."[50]

Harrington grew up in Santa Barbara, California. He enrolled in Stanford University in 1902 to study classic and modern languages. He took summer classes from A. L. Kroeber and Pliny Earle Goddard at the University of California. This allowed him to graduate first in his class in two and one-half years. He declined a Rhodes scholarship, electing to study anthropology and linguistics in Germany, including a final semester at the University of Berlin. Harrington

did not complete his doctorate; he was in a hurry to get back to California and start recording Indian languages. In 1907 he began working with the Mohave people along the lower Colorado River. Harrington's approach to his work is reflected in an early letter discussing his work with the Mohave:

> [I collected a] . . . valise full of notebooks filled with Mohave word forms. . . . I succeeded . . . in gaining the entire confidence of one man about my age. . . . I collected a lot of material on the Mohave verb from him. . . . His patience, insistence upon accuracy and love of detail astonished me. . . . In almost every "camp" people were to be found sick or dying with measles, smallpox, syphilis, consumption or unknown ailments—an excellent opportunity for me to study the various kinds of Mohave doctoring.[51]

Early in 1908, Harrington met Edgar Lee Hewett. Hewett invited Harrington, at his own expense, to New Mexico to begin work on Tewa languages, and introduced him to Matilda Coxe Stevenson, then living near San Ildefonso. She became an ardent supporter of his work; he later appropriated her linguistic materials without crediting her. Hewett offered Harrington a small salary and expenses. His assignment was to begin a linguistic and ethnographic survey of Southwestern Indian peoples, especially the Rio Grande pueblos.[52]

In June 1909, Harrington plunged in, moving almost frantically from group to group. His peripatetic style was now established. He immediately invaded A. L. Kroeber's turf, who regarded California as his personal domain. No anthropologist "invaded" another's tribe(s) without permission. Harrington ignored such niceties. His compulsion to record, and his paranoia, led him to go wherever he could, secretly if possible. He irritated everyone, but all agreed that his genius "shouldn't be double hobbled," and hoped that in the end the results would be worth it.[53]

Harrington's compulsion to record dying languages is reflected in a letter and poem he sent to Hodge, probably in 1928:

"Candelaria Leiva, the last surviving Ventura [Ventureño Chumash] Indian woman, died recently . . . Although the regret expressed in this sonnet may seem almost too strong, *it is not strong enough to show how badly I really feel over the loss of old Candelaria before she had been interviewed to any extent.*

> The year has turned and with it pass the flowers.
> And she who knew their ancient names is gone.
> Outliving a dead age she lingered on
> By miracle of God with curious dowers
> To lend assistance in this work of ours.
> And we were chained, but fretted. And anon,
> Just as we thought our freeing struggle won,
> Hideous fate snatched her from us. My mind sours.
> My spirit rancors at the dismal thought
> That grief, sheer grief, shall be our only gain;
> That grief alone shall of our dream remain;
> That we heard clear but answered not the call,
> Saw the condition plain but heeded not,
> While money-gaining held us in its thrall."[54]

This, then, was the person Hewett hired in 1909. He wanted Harrington because he needed a linguist for the joint SAA-BAE research program. The program's most successful results were Harrington's collaboration with Robbins, Henderson, and Barbara Freire-Marreco on studies of Tewa ethnogeography and ethnobiology.

The magnum opus was Harrington's "Ethnogeography of the Tewa Indians," a six-hundred-page compilation of information, from a Tewa perspective, on the geography, topography, and related features of the Rio Grande region, its environs, and its products. It was reviewed by A. L. Kroeber, who called it a "scholarly work, whose size and detail approximate the monumental . . ." But, Kroeber went on, here are all these data, and no synthesis to tell us what they mean; hopefully, Harrington would produce one. He never did.[55]

Frederick Webb Hodge was very impressed with Harrington and hired him into the Bureau in February 1915. Harrington did not appear right away; he was busy in California with exhibits at the San Diego world's fair. When he finally arrived in Washington, he had a new wife with him, Carobeth Tucker (1895–1983), whom he had met in a summer-school class he was teaching at San Diego Normal School in the summer of 1916. She was nineteen and fascinated by science, particularly evolution and anthropology.

She had signed up for an archaeology course with Hewett: "the Doctor himself came in with a mixture of pomposity and condescension, straightened a picture on the wall, and, adapting himself to my limited female intellect, told me to remember that museum work was not very different from housework. (I loathed housework and experienced instant disenchantment.)" Her linguistic course was taught by Harrington: "I silently and romantically exclaimed that he looked 'like an angry god!' I had not hoped to encounter one of those mythical creatures, a scholar, a scientist, who was also young and beautiful."[56]

Soon Tucker was staying after class—to discuss phonetic transcription. Matters progressed to an understanding. They were married in the spring of 1916 and immediately plunged into intense fieldwork, living penuriously at the best of times, traveling in a Model T Ford from one Indian settlement to another. The new Mrs. Harrington became chauffeur, typist, transcriber, and fearful nursemaid to her spouse's giant, fragile ego. From Harrington's perspective the marriage "will enable us practically to double our output of work," as Harrington wrote to Charles Lummis.[57]

Carobeth Tucker Harrington divorced her "angry god" in 1923 and married George Laird, a Chemehuevi Paiute man she met through Harrington. Much later, when she was over eighty, she produced the story of her relationship with Harrington and two classic works on Chemehuevi culture and mythology, based on what she learned with and from Laird.[58] Harrington continued to career around the country until he died, often passing through the Southwest, always pursuing speakers of dying languages, always stashing his data in hiding places, in the end producing much, yet little.

Hewett and the San Diego Exposition

Hewett's reputation as "Doctor Archaeology" and expert organizer led to a dramatic opportunity in 1911. At the urging of Charles Lummis, Hewett was asked to become Director of Exhibits for the proposed Panama-California Exposition in San Diego in 1915 to celebrate the opening of the Panama Canal. The "official" exposition, the Panama-Pacific Exposition, would be in San Francisco, but the boosters of little San Diego (population eighty thousand) decided to stage their own, to "put San Diego on the map." The exposition theme was to be anthropological in a broad sense.

Many thought Hewett was already overextended with two directorships. Frederick Webb Hodge wrote to Mitchell Carroll, the AIA secretary, that Hewett was not paying attention to their joint project, and if allowed to take on the San Diego job, he would terminate their agreement.[59] The AIA gave its approval and Hodge ended the project; Hewett forged ahead.

Hewett and Boas

While Hewett was agreeing to take on the San Diego directorship, another attempt to discredit him came from the East Coast. This time Franz Boas provided the ammunition. The issue went back to the investigation of the Bureau of American Ethnology in 1903 and the payments made to Boas for linguistic manuscripts (see Chapter 12). In November 1911 Boas sent a typeset "Open Letter" to Hewett asking him to affirm or deny statements he was said to have made about Boas receiving "double or triple" payments from the Bureau of American Ethnology for manuscripts.

The gist of Boas's lengthy letter was: one, Hewett had publicly alleged that Boas was guilty of double- or triple-dipping; two, Hewett had denied the allegations, but Roland Dixon, Alfred Tozzer, Joseph Spinden, Francis Kelsey, and Sylvanus Morley had, at various times, affirmed Hewett's statements; therefore, Boas considered Hewett's denial "at least a prevarica-

tion." Since suing Hewett in New Mexico would be expensive for Boas, he "begged to ask" that Hewett agree to a trial in an eastern state. "If you will not, I must be content with making public the facts.—Franz Boas." Boas attached copies of earlier letters he had written to the AIA, resigning in protest over Hewett's winning control of the School of American Archaeology, and impugning Hewett's work as unscientific and hasty, hence "little short of criminal [and the] publications which he produces . . . insignificant, or premature."[60] In his self-righteous omniscient umbrage, it seemingly never occurred to Boas that he was slandering Hewett.

Boas's letters were published in *The New Mexican* and widely gossiped over. Hewett was silent. His supporters gained a good deal of sympathy for him by appealing to regional chauvinism: us western good guys versus those eastern snobs telling us what to do. In the end, Boas remained enraged and Hewett said and did nothing.

The next uproar came in 1913. In 1912, the city of Santa Fe, its chamber of commerce, and the Santa Fe Railway began touting Santa Fe as a tourist destination (see Chapter 27). The chamber, against Hewett's advice, declared that Santa Fe was the oldest city in the United States, and had some sixty thousand mailing envelopes printed stating the claim in a logo. Hewett, citing Hodge and Bandelier, publicly disagreed. Soon after, he evicted the chamber of commerce from the Palace of the Governors, where it had maintained an office at Hewett's sufferance. This was too much for Henry H. Dorman, president of the chamber and an ally of Bronson Cutting, who owned *The New Mexican* newspaper and was an avowed Hewett enemy. Not only was Dorman stuck with sixty thousand historically inaccurate envelopes, but he had no office. The resulting brouhaha, carefully nurtured by Cutting, was truly marvelous. Letters from Alfred Tozzer to Dorman, gleefully printed in *The New Mexican,* said (among other things): "I rejoice that Santa Fe has at last . . . placed Hewett where he belongs. His methods of work serve as a laughing stock for a great many of us. . . . I think, with the exception of a few people in Washington, there is not an American archaeologist who stands for him. . . . HIS SCIENTIFIC REPUTATION IS OF NO VALUE."[61]

The hoopla grew during October and November 1913. Hewett stayed in San Diego; his local supporters handled the infighting. Cutting stated "that he did not consider Dr. Hewett capable of being a director in the School of American Archaeology, nor did he consider the managing committee of the Institute capable of selecting a director for this school or any other school."[62] In response, sixteen organizations, ranging from the New Mexico Archaeological Society to the Ladies Aid Society of the Methodist Church, and the governor of New Mexico, issued formal resolutions of support for Hewett. Even the Santa Fe Chamber of Commerce passed a resolution, by a 79 to 6 vote, repudiating its own director and supporting Hewett.[63]

Undaunted, Cutting and Dorman decided to develop their *own* plan of reorganization for the school and carry it to the AIA annual meeting in Montreal. Dorman appeared there on January 2, 1914, with a reorganization plan signed by fifteen Santa Feans. A telegram of support was sent by Roland B. Dixon, Pliny Earle Goddard, and Franz Boas saying "we know such plan to have approval of many serious anthropologists in Cambridge, New York, Chicago, California and urge you support it." The school's managing committee thoroughly grilled Dorman; he retreated in confusion. The committee sent a resolution to the Santa Fe Chamber of Commerce. It acknowledged Dorman's appearance and the allegations against Hewett made in the reorganization plan. Then:

WHEREAS, the aforesaid H. H. Dorman, upon request, stated that he was unable to furnish data and evidence upon which the statements in the communication were based; THEREFORE, Be it Resolved that this communication be laid upon the table.[64]

Hewett, the Maya, the Southwest, and the San Diego Exposition

Hewett was given an initial budget of 100,000 dollars for the anthropology exhibits at the San Diego exposition. He brought in Aleš Hrdlička to develop a major exhibit on human evolution. He created a position for J. P. Harrington to study the Indian people of California and develop an exhibit. And he began to develop a plan to get his Maya program under way and make it part of the exposition. In 1912, he received a grant of three thousand dollars from the St. Louis AIA chapter and additional funds from the exposition. With no knowledge of Mayan archaeology, he chose the first site he encountered, Quiriguá in Guatemala. Conveniently, the site was on land belonging to the United Fruit Company, which supported his work and later turned the site into an archaeological park. Hewett brought along Jesse Nusbaum and Sylvanus Morley, later hired Earl H. Morris (see Chapter 24), and in 1914 Neil Judd joined the team for a season to help make the papier-mâché squeezes used to produce replicas of the Quiriguá stelae for the exposition.[65]

In January 1912, Hewett was in New York. In a *Times* interview he stated that Quiriguá "is believed to be the oldest city on the two American continents." He promised to have the Maya glyphic system deciphered by June 1912, and said that no one had been to Quiriguá from the time of Stephen's and Catherwood's visit in the 1840s until Hewett "rediscovered" it. He also posited some connections between the Maya and the Zuni, and drew an analogy between Maya glyphs and Southwestern dry paintings. Alfred Tozzer was outraged by such flummery, and vented his spleen to the *Times*. He wrote to Hodge, "We all feel here [Harvard] that something should be done, but what?"[66] Hewett blithely sailed for Guatemala.

Hewett and others did get the Panama-California Exposition opened in Balboa Park. It was a great success. Anthropology had central billing. Aleš Hrdlička had spent nearly 100,000 dollars and three years traveling in Europe, Siberia, Mongolia, Alaska, Africa, and the Philippines to collect skulls, casts of fossil humans, and make measurements and life masks for his human evolution exhibit.[67] The exhibit included an evolutionary sequence of "Primal Man," beginning with "Java Man," through "Neanderthal Man," and ending with "Cro-Magnon Man." There were also fifteen male and fifteen female busts, modeled from life masks, of each of the "three main races—the white, yellow-brown and black." These were arranged in a sequence—Negritos, Pygmies, Bushmen, Zulus, Asians, American Indians, and Whites—making it quite clear that the "darker" races were seen as lower in the "scale of evolution" than the Whites. "The series of the white race include casts of living representatives of eminent American families"; that is, Hrdlička's "Old Americans" (see Chapter 18), seen by him as the epitome of human evolution.[68]

Southwestern anthropology was amply displayed. In the Indian arts building, there were models of houses "to show the manner of living of the different Indian races up and down the Pacific Coast," the work of J. P. Harrington. There were "booths in which living descendants of the early races are showing the arts and crafts as they are still practiced," and an "extraordinary display" of some five thousand pieces of pottery, "most of it dug up in New Mexico and Arizona."[69] Beyond the "Isthmus," San Diego's version of the Midway, lay the Painted Desert, a mini-theme park funded by the Santa Fe Railway to promote Southwest tourism (see Chapter 27). It was designed by Kenneth Chapman, and built by Jesse Nusbaum and a crew of San Ildefonso Pueblo workers, led by Julián Martínez. There were replicas of Taos Pueblo and a San Ildefonso kiva, as well as "Cliff Dwellings," occupied by pretend "Cliff Dwellers." There were hogans, wickiups, corrals, and sheep and goat pens. Living cacti, yuccas, and juniper trees, transplanted from Arizona, dotted the compound. Here lived Hopis, Zunis, Rio Grande Puebloans, Navajos, Apaches, and Havasupais. They staged daily ceremonies and dances, did chores, wove blankets, and made baskets and pots. One of the potters was María Martínez, by 1915 an old hand at the world's fairs.

As planned, the anthropology exhibits, including the Maya stelae replicas and murals of reconstructed Mayan cities painted by Carlos Vierra, remained as permanent exhibits in the exposition's California building, which became the San Diego Museum of Man, with Hewett as director.[70] He also began teaching anthropology at San Diego Normal School (hence the classes taken by Carobeth Tucker), spending winters in San Diego and summers in Santa Fe. His various boards of directors acquiesced to all this and he continued the pattern for the next thirteen years, meanwhile being involved in many other activities (see Chapters 27, 29).

CHAPTER 23

A "New Archaeology" in the Southwest

VERY SOON AFTER he became the geography editor of *Science,* Franz Boas published a brief article in the magazine, "The Occurrence of Similar Inventions in Areas Widely Apart." He criticized Otis T. Mason's anthropology exhibits in the U.S. National Museum: glass cases filled with look-alike artifacts arranged in (presumed) "evolutionary sequences." The article announced that twenty-nine year-old Herr Doktor Boas was now in America and ready to be noticed. It also marked the beginning of a sea change in American anthropology, from the older evolutionism of Morgan and Powell to twentieth-century historical particularism, as it came to be called. The immediate issue was the design of museum exhibits, but there were larger questions about constructing the anthropological universe, proper methods for its study and presentation, indeed, the very goals of anthropology.[1] The structure and context of the archaeological and ethnographic research in the Southwest beginning in 1909–10 was formed by the Boas-Mason debate and its consequences.

The social evolutionism promulgated by Morgan and Powell hinged on the premise of universal psychic unity: human minds and reason were the same everywhere. It followed that as the elementary ideas in human minds unfolded, societies and cultures (including material cultures) would evolve through the same stages of development in the lock-step fashion envisioned by Morgan (see Chapter 6). Some societies would proceed more slowly than others, due to environmental limitations or historical accident. But at any one stage, the social forms, ideologies, *and forms of material culture would be the same everywhere.*

German cultural historians and philosophers of history, beginning with Johann Gottfried Herder (1744–1803), thought otherwise.[2] Herder insisted that human reason is not universal, but contingent and linked to specific historical forms. He rejected psychic unity and lock-step stage-development of human societies. Rather, he said, each "Volk" (read "ethnic group," "tribe," "race," or "nation") embodies a unique "Volk-Geist" (read "genius" or "worldview," or "group psyche"); each interacts in a synergistic way with its environment to produce a unique, organic whole with its own social forms and ideologies. Each Volk is the product of its *Bildung*, its own unique historical development, and must be understood in its own terms, not as a product of humanity-wide historical "forces."

These ideas were embraced by Wilhelm von Humboldt, who, in 1795–97, proposed a "Plan for a Comparative Anthropology." The proper task of anthropology, he said, is the study of "historical trajectories" of "nations." The trajectories result from arbitrary and accidental happenings within the synergistic interactions of a Volk, its Geist and its environment, and the interactions of various Volk with one another. Herder's and Humboldt's ideas had an enormous impact on German historiography, geography, and anthropology throughout the nineteenth century.

This viewpoint leads to cultural relativism: each sociocultural entity must be understood in its own terms and in its own environmental and historical contexts. Psychic unity cannot be assumed to be panhuman, but is a question to be investigated. And patterned expressions of culture—tools, implements, even institutions—don't necessarily have the same origins or arise from the same causes.

Nineteenth-century cultural historians and museum curators in the United States, Britain, France, and Germany were dealing with the same data sets: patterned expressions of human behavior embodied in material culture—tens of thousands of moccasins, shields, canoes, bows and arrows, baskets, pots, drums, etc.—and nonmaterial culture—bewildering arrays of differing marriage practices, kinship systems, myths, legends, and so on. How to "make sense" of all these data? Classify them; create typologies. The basic assumption in typology is, "look alikes are alike." In other words, a rose is a rose. But is it? There is an epistemological quagmire awaiting the unwary. As George

Stocking deftly demonstrates, Franz Boas and Otis T. Mason waded into this bog in their debate.[3]

The key issue was, while look-alikes look alike, did they have the "same functions"—or not? Did they arise from the "same causes," have the "same origins" —or not? Mason argued that artifacts can be classified *as if* they are biological specimens. "In human culture, as in nature elsewhere, *like causes produce like effects.* Under the same stress and resources the same inventions will arise."[4] Psychic unity will operate; hence, look-alikes *are* alike.

Boas disagreed. Mason, he said, omitted one cause of similar inventions "which overthrows the whole system: *unlike causes produce like effects.*" Because "the elements affecting the human mind are so complicated; and their influence is so utterly unknown, . . . *an[y] attempt to find like causes must fail. . . .* Though like causes have like effects, like effects have not like causes."[5] Further, "each ethnological specimen" must be understood in its own historical, sociocultural, technological, and environmental contexts; otherwise, "we cannot understand its meanings."

Finally, he argued, rows of glass cases filled with disparate artifacts arranged in presumed evolutionary sequences negate the principle that "in ethnology all is individuality." What museums should do is illustrate "the historical development of tribes, the influence of neighbors and surroundings, etc." Exhibits should demonstrate "the fact that civilization is not something absolute, but that it is relative, and that our ideas and conceptions are true only so far as our civilization goes. . . . this . . . can be accomplished only by the tribal arrangement of collections."[6]

The debate took place in 1887. By 1893 the Smithsonian exhibits at the Chicago world's fair, designed by Mason, reflected "the idea of the ethnic [tribal] unit."[7] In 1896 Mason defined "eighteen American Indian environments or culture areas," for the Western Hemisphere, in which, "natural conditions [were] diversified enough to bring into prominence arts adapted to each culture area and obtrusively different from those of other areas." For each culture area, Mason described the climate, topography, house forms, modes of transport, and major classes of tools and implements. He called the Southwest the "Pueblo" area, with "arid climate, elevated mesas, irrigable valleys, . . . Pueblos, either underground, cave, . . . cliff, mesa . . . ; towers." Characteristic implements include "pottery in great profusion, . . . mealing stones in sets; sandpainting, irrigation."[8]

In 1897, Mason and Holmes began reorganizing the National Museum exhibits by culture areas, or "geo-ethnic provinces." In 1902, Holmes presented a map of nineteen Western Hemisphere "provinces," including the "Colorado-Rio Grande arid area (Pueblo, Apache)." In 1904, in his "History of Anthropology" address at the St. Louis world's fair, Boas effectively laid the ghost of nineteenth-century evolutionism.[9] The tide had turned.

But if evolutionism was defunct, what was culture history about? One answer came from Germany in the work of Friederich Ratzel and his students. For them, culture history consisted in tracing points of origin and distributions of culturally patterned forms through space, and then accounting for the distributions by migrations, or diffusion through trade and culture contact. Ratzel and his students focused on "classes" of patterned forms. Classes were analyzed into subunits called "traits," or "culture elements." A "trait" was whatever an analyst said it was. In time, *all* patterned forms or expressions of human behavior, material or non-material, were seen as "traits" or "culture elements." The next step was to define "trait complexes" that clustered together within a defined region.

Writing culture history became an exercise in determining presumed points of origin for traits and trait complexes and plausibly accounting for their spatial distributions. It followed that a specific culture —for example, Hopi—was not seen as an organic whole, but as an *agglomeration of traits and complexes,* a "thing of shreds and patches," as Robert Lowie would later say. Writing Hopi culture history consisted of determining the origins of all the traits and complexes

comprising Hopi culture, and tracing how they got to the Hopis.

Between 1914 and 1917, Clark Wissler formed culture areas and the distributions of cultural traits and complexes therein into a culture-history approach called "historical particularism." He modified Holmes's 1902 map, reducing the number of culture areas to fifteen, one of which is coeval with our Southwest. He, and others who followed his lead, never defined "trait"—it was whatever an analyst said it was. A "trait" could be a bowl-shaped basket, its technique of manufacture, or a design element on it.[10]

Boas's key question remained: do unlike causes produce like effects (or vice-versa), and how can you tell? The question was usually stated as: "if look-alikes having the same function are found in different places are they independently invented or diffused from a point of common origin?" There was the residual question of psychic unity: if look-alikes having the same function are found in areas widely apart, but not in between, are they evidence for psychic unity? The question segued into unending and unresolved debates over "convergence versus parallelism" as cultural processes.[11]

Ratzel and Wissler were concerned with the distribution of traits across space. But what about distributions through time? This brings up the same three problems that bedeviled Isaac Newton and led him to wander in the chronological wilderness for forty years (see the Introduction). First, how to develop a chronology for a specific culture and tie that chronology to the "absolute" B.C.E./C.E. time scale? Second, how to link one culture to another; and third, how to establish the *direction* of the linkage? Newton used and misused historical documents to develop a chronology and demonstrate that all other world civilizations were linked to, and derived from, biblical Israel. But for cultures with no documents, how are links established, and which cultures derive from which? To return to the Southwest, do the civilizations of Mesoamerica derive from the Pueblo cultures of the Southwest, as Lewis Henry Morgan had it, or is the reverse true? The second question is, in lieu of dated documents, how do you establish a *relative chronology* ("older than/younger than") that can be tied, at some future point, to an "absolute" time scale to date the ruins dotting the Southwestern landscape?

In 1916, the linguist Edward Sapir published "Time Perspective in Aboriginal American Culture: A Study in Method," in which he reviewed, rationalized, and critiqued all the then-current methods in American anthropology and archaeology for establishing relative chronologies. One was stratigraphy, and Sapir wondered why American archaeologists had made so little use of it, saying, "I am convinced that the stratigraphic method will in the future enable archaeology to throw more light on the history of American culture than it has done in the past." Sapir also discussed "seriation of cultural elements" (he used "element" and "trait" synonymously), pointing to three assumptions of this method. One is that "simpler forms of a cultural element [are] of greater age than more complex ones"; two, "the larger the territory covered by a culture trait, the older the trait itself"; three, "as a rule," a culture complex (a cluster of related traits) "is oldest in the tribe in which it has received the greatest elaboration."[12]

In the 1920s, Clark Wissler folded these ideas into an "Age-area" concept or hypothesis. The third idea, that the center of greatest elaboration of any cultural complex is the presumed locus of origin of that complex, is a form of "center-periphery model" used since Newton's time to account for the origins and diffusions of numerous natural and cultural phenomena. Ultimately, in the 1930s, A. L. Kroeber took up these ideas, applied them in detail to all culture areas north of the Isthmus of Panama, and brought them to culmination in his magisterial *Cultural and Natural Areas of Native North America.*[13]

These several concepts—traits, types, culture areas, age-areas, loci of origin, and so on—were the basic assumptions underlying the "historical particularist," or "culture history" approach that dominated American ethnography until about 1940, and American archae-

ology until 1960.[14] It provided a means to establish relative chronologies, cultural linkages, and directions of those linkages, especially for archaeologists. The first applications were in the Southwest by those whom Clark Wissler in 1917 called "New Archaeologists."

The American Museum in the Southwest, 1905–1929

Frederic Ward Putnam had developed an anthropology program at the American Museum of Natural History, and hired Franz Boas to make it work.[15] Putnam left in 1902 for the University of California. By then things had begun to go awry. There was some friction between Putnam and Boas. Morris Jesup expressed displeasure with the pace of the publications program of the Jesup Expedition, to which Boas took umbrage. Boas's judgment as a scientist was to him self-evident. When that judgment was successfully challenged by Hermon Bumpus (see below), he responded by resigning from the American Museum and moving full time to Columbia University in 1905.

There were other internal stresses and strains. The stress points are reflected in internal museum correspondence and the shifting departmental names in the museum's annual reports. Putnam founded a Department of Anthropology. In 1903, after he left, there suddenly was a Department of Archaeology, housing Marshall Saville, Harlan Smith, and George Pepper, with Putnam as "Advisory Curator"; and a Department of Ethnology, housing Boas, Livingston Farrand, and Clark Wissler (Fig. 23.1), newly hired as "Assistant in Ethnology." In 1905, after Boas left, there was once again a Department of Anthropology housing everyone on the staff. In 1906, there were again Departments of Ethnology and Archaeology, the former in the charge of Clark Wissler as "Acting Curator," the latter housing only Saville. By 1908, the Duc de Loubat had created the Loubat Chair in Archaeology for Saville at Columbia, and thereafter Saville was "Honorary Curator of Mexican Archaeology" at the museum. By 1909 Pepper and Harlan Smith had left

23.1. Clark Wissler, ca. 1918. Photograph by Julius Kirschner. Courtesy of the American Museum of Natural History.

and there was once more a Department of Anthropology, with Clark Wissler as curator, and a new addition, Robert H. Lowie, as assistant curator.

Wissler was faced with building a long-range anthropology program. It was an uphill battle for resources and staff with an unsympathetic museum president. Henry Fairfield Osborn joined the museum in the 1890s, and soon became an advisor to Jesup. In 1901 he was elected to the board of trustees and named second vice president. In 1903, he convinced Jesup and the board to bring in Hermon C. Bumpus, from Brown University; Bumpus soon became director of the museum. He clashed with Boas and finally drove him out. Jesup died in 1908, and Osborn became president of the museum, to no one's surprise.

Bumpus, it is said, was jealous of Osborn and foolishly accused him of "fiscal mismanagement and subtle dishonesty." Osborn was exonerated and Bumpus was summarily fired in 1910.[16]

Osborn was very conscious of properly manipulated publicity. He sent out frequent press releases hailing the American Museum's "naturalist-explorers" and their adventures in the "wild places of the world." The public, and a new suite of trustees Osborn had brought in, loved it. Osborn was also acutely conscious of his place, and that of other wealthy WASPs, in American society—at the top, running things. He actively supported the eugenics movement throughout the 1910s and 1920s, as did his friend Madison Grant, author of *The Passing of the Great Race,* a book which supported the idea that WASPs were the epitome of biological and social evolution. Osborn told Grant in 1909 that the American Museum should become a "positive engine" for the "propagation of socially desirable views."[17]

Osborn saw to it that money poured into his Vertebrate Paleontology program, which was "the most important in the Museum, [because there] the evidence and great questions of evolution are most plainly studied . . ." He had little use for anthropology, writing to a friend: "Between ourselves, much anthropology is merely opinion, or gossip of the natives. It is many years away from being a science. Jesup and the Museum spent far too much money on anthropology."[18] In this rather chilly climate, Clark Wissler began to rebuild anthropology.

Clark Wissler (1870–1947) was born and raised in Indiana, attended Indiana University and in 1901 earned a Ph.D. in experimental psychology at Columbia University under James M. Cattell.[19] He also took anthropology classes from Franz Boas and Livingston Farrand. In 1902 he became assistant in ethnology at the American Museum. When Boas left in 1905, Wissler remained, becoming curator of anthropology in 1909, a position he held until he retired in 1942. Wissler's own fieldwork was with the Plains Indians, especially the Blackfeet people, beginning in 1902. He parlayed the Plains work into a major anthropological research program in the museum, especially after Robert H. Lowie, hired in 1909, began his longtime work with the Crow people.[20]

The A. M. Huntington Southwest Program

The Jesup Expedition provided the museum with spectacular collections from the Northwest Coast. The Indian people there were and are superb artists, especially wood carvers—from small boxes through the intricate dance masks to great totem poles and war canoes. Those collected by the expedition remain on display a century later. Great Plains Indian people were seen by most Anglos as "real Indians" thanks to Wild West shows, world's fairs, dime novels, and the movies. Hence, the collections made by Wissler and Lowie, of tipis and war bonnets, intricately beaded clothing and moccasins, were widely appreciated by the museum-going public. Now Wissler turned his attention to a third area from which crowd-pleasing collections could be obtained—the Southwest. At the same time, he wanted to advance anthropology as a science and strengthen the position of his department within the museum.

Wissler's search for funds led one trustee to write to Osborn: "I firmly believe in the fiduciary responsibility of the owners of capital, so here is my check. Only I do wish those Indians had not made so many pots."[21] Collis and Arabella Huntington, and then Archer Huntington, had funded much of the ethnography and collecting done by Roland B. Dixon in California. In 1904, Archer Huntington diverted his funds to the Hispanic Society he was building in upper Manhattan, but remained interested in anthropology and American Indian studies. In 1909, he began a ten-year program of support, at five thousand dollars per year, for Wissler's Southwest program. The program, together with Wissler's own theoretical position, led to a new orientation and research agenda in Southwestern ethnography and archaeology.

To staff his new program, Wissler hired Pliny Earle

Goddard and Herbert J. ("Joe") Spinden in 1909, and Nels Nelson in 1912. Spinden was born in 1879 and apparently raised in South Dakota (he was notoriously closed-mouth about biographical details). He finished a Ph.D. at Harvard in 1909 and came to work for the American Museum. Spinden was a "great bear of a man," with deep blue, "Siamese cat" eyes, and, in later years, a shock of white hair. He deeply distrusted authority in any form, and had an ardent taste for ribaldry, wine, women, and song. Wissler assigned Goddard to work with Apaches and later Navajos. Spinden's principal assignment was to work in Central America, but Wissler wanted an ethnographic survey of the Rio Grande and Western Pueblos. Spinden made some preliminary reports on dances and pottery, and collected a number of song texts (not published until 1933), but by 1915 was shifted again to Central America and the West Indies.[22]

A "New Archaeology" in the Southwest

Wissler's original focus was on ethnographic Southwestern cultures. He wanted data and objects for a new Southwestern hall, which he installed between about 1912 and 1920, using the latest ideas in "life group" exhibits (Fig. 23.2). In 1912 he began shifting his emphasis to archaeology. By 1917, four individuals associated with the museum—Nels Nelson, Leslie Spier, A. L. Kroeber, and Earl Morris, together with A. V. Kidder—had developed some new chronological methods using stratigraphy and seriation. Wissler called these methods the "New Archaeology," to set it apart from the "old, unscientific" archaeology being done by the likes of Edgar Lee Hewett, Byron Cummings, Jesse Walter Fewkes, and Walter Hough. He announced this "new archaeology" in 1917 in the *Museum Journal*.[23] The announcement and related publicity were carefully crafted to give the impression, at least to Archer Huntington, of a scientific breakthrough by the museum staff and their peers in the Southwest.

Fewkes, Hewett, and Cummings paid little or no attention to stratigraphy. To them, archaeological de-

23.2. *Hopi Life Group, Southwest Hall, American Museum of Natural History, 1915.*
Courtesy of the American Museum of Natural History.

posits, no matter how deep, represented an unknown but brief period of time. They worked within the older framework propounded by Morgan and Powell: archaeology is another way to do ethnology; the historic present is an all-the-same continuation of the past, and the American past was relatively brief. While they paid some attention to provenience, where artifacts came from within a site, the emphasis was still on displayable items—whole pots, baskets, and so on. There was no attempt to systematically establish chronologies, and the determination of culture-to-culture linkages was based on the interpretation of indigenous legends and some attention to "look-alike" artifact forms, especially whole pottery vessels.

To the new archaeologists, archaeology as ethnology was unfruitful. They also asserted that intercultural linkages had to be demonstrated, not assumed. Indeed, for some decades prehistoric Southwestern cultures came to be seen as home-grown, indigenous developments, owing nothing, except perhaps corn, beans, and squash, to Mesoamerica.

The "new" archaeologists applied methods long known and used in Europe and Egypt: paying close attention to stratigraphy within sites and applying some form of seriation to classes of artifacts, especially broken pottery sherds. The term *seriation* was in use by 1658, to mean "serial succession," as in the sequential succession of rulers to office. By the late 1800s it was being used in chemistry, as in the table of elements. The general archaeological definition is "the action or result of arranging items in a sequence according to prescribed criteria."[24] Seriation depends on the fluctuations of fad and fashion over some period of time —from years to millennia—and the application of simple counting and statistical measures to arrange material traits in sequences thought to reflect those fluctuations.

The "Ceramic Bacillus"

Untold millions of potsherds repose in museums throughout the world. Many of them have been sorted, classified, counted, and arranged into "types" and "wares." To lay persons, archaeologists' obsession with sherds is somewhat mystifying. Why all the fuss over busted crockery? Because, properly studied, potsherds provide a means to establish chronologies and determine cultural linkages and derivations; they are excellent "index artifacts."

Pottery appeared in both hemispheres soon after settled, farming-based societies came into existence. The plasticity of the clay allows for elaboration of forms; incised and painted designs are common.[25] Vessel forms and decorations on them are culturally specific, and change over time as intracultural fads and fashions wax and wane. Such changes attracted the attention of archaeologists in the Old World after about 1850. They observed that new forms and decorations came into existence and coexisted with older forms and decorations. Over time, the older forms diminished and died out. It is precisely this waxing and waning of elements of style and form through time that makes pottery especially useful as index artifacts to establish relative time sequences. And their spatial distributions also make them useful for establishing culture-to-culture linkages. Pottery seriation seemingly began in Egypt in the 1890s. Sir Flinders Petrie arranged pottery collections from particular sites according to stylistic changes in shape, color, painted designs, etc. He then determined their percentage frequencies to arrive at a proxy measure of relative time. George Reisner, also working in Egypt, used similar techniques.[26]

New Archaeologists at Work

The new archaeology began when Nels and Ethelyn Nelson arrived in El Paso, Texas, in June 1912 to start an extensive archaeological survey up the Rio Grande Valley. They joined Clark Wissler in Santa Fe in July. Wissler, ever the diplomat, immediately met with Edgar Lee Hewett at the School of American Archaeology to head off any potential turf war; Hewett seems to have okayed the project. Nelson and Wissler decided to focus on the large pueblo sites in the Galisteo Basin, south of Santa Fe, that were abandoned after the Pueblo Revolt of 1680 (Map 4). Nelson began work at San Cristóbal. He had no experience in excavating superimposed architectural features, but muddled through. His workmen cleared 262 rooms in six weeks.

Both Nelson and Wissler issued brief reports rejecting the older archaeology-as-ethnology approach. Nelson wrote:

> It is felt that many problems relating to the *origin and distribution of peoples and to cultural traits* now observable in the Southwest cannot be solved in their entirety by the examination of present-day conditions or even by consulting Spanish documentary history . . . By a tolerably exhaustive study of the thousands of ruins and other archaeological features characteristic of the region, we may hope in time to gain not only an idea of prehistoric conditions but perhaps also an *adequate explanation of the origin, the antiquity and the course of development leading up to a better understanding of the present status of aboriginal life in the region.*[27]

Wissler wrote that Nelson would "take up the historical problem in the Southwest *to determine if possible* the relations between the prehistoric and historical peoples." To that end, the Galisteo Basin was chosen because it "seemed most likely to have been the *chief center of Pueblo culture* as we now know it."[28] The origin, antiquity, prehistoric conditions, and course of development of Pueblo cultures are matters of investigation, not simply taken-for-granted projections back through time from the present. And Wissler is making an assumption that Galisteo is a *center* of Pueblo culture within a center-periphery model.

In 1912–13, Henry Fairfield Osborn visited Europe. He toured a number of Upper Paleolithic cave sites in France and Spain guided by Emile Cartailhac, Otto Obermaier, and Henri Breuil, all well-known archaeologists. They were using stratigraphic methods in their excavations. Osborn decided that the American Museum needed an exhibit on the evolution of humans in the Old World and that he should inform the American public about life and times in Paleolithic Eurasia. He sent Nels Nelson to Europe to observe the excavations and to study museum collections. Nelson participated in the excavation of Castillo Cave in Spain and observed firsthand the stratigraphic techniques being used. When he returned, he was assigned to ghostwrite most of Osborn's *Men of the Old Stone Age* (1914), which subsequently ran through three editions and many reprintings, the last in 1948. The American Museum opened a "Hall of the Age of Man" in 1925.[29]

In 1914 Nelson returned to the Galisteo Basin, searching for a place to make some stratigraphic cuts. He selected San Cristóbal (Fig. 23.3). "A visibly stratified section of the refuse exposure showing no evidence of disturbance was selected and a block of this measuring 3 by 6 feet on the horizontal and nearly 10 feet deep was excavated. . . . The potsherds from each separate foot of debris were kept apart." Nelson counted the numbers of different types of sherds, not-

ing that black-on-white sherds were heavily represented in lower levels but died out in upper levels. Conversely, various painted types had different distributions within the stratigraphic column, starting in middle levels, becoming common and then petering out in upper levels; and so on.[30] He thus verified stratigraphically his intuitive sense of the temporal sequence of pottery types in the Rio Grande area. Wissler perceived the importance of the effort and shifted the emphasis of the Huntington Expedition to archaeology. The attempt to establish a chronology for the Southwest prior to 1540 C.E. was under way. In 1915, Nelson returned to the Galisteo and dug at La Bajada, assisted by Earl H. Morris (see below). In 1916, Nelson was at Zuni with Leslie Spier, before he and Morris dug in the trash mounds in Chaco Canyon to try to establish further stratigraphic controls for Chacoan sites, which was only partly successful.

Nels Nelson's last Southwestern field season was 1916. While others had major field projects, Nelson was swamped by curatorial duties. He finally vented his frustration to Henry Fairfield Osborn in June 1924. Perhaps because Nelson had ghostwritten Osborn's *Men of the Stone Age,* he responded by sending

23.3. San Cristóbal Pueblo, Galisteo Basin, New Mexico; under excavation, 1914. Photograph by Nels C. Nelson. Courtesy of the American Museum of Natural History.

Nelson to Mongolia: "Palaeolithic man in central Asia is eagerly awaiting your arrival. Against the heretical teachings of Hrdlicka that the Garden of Eden was in France and not in central Asia, your mission is to hunt our ancestors in their original lair, to prove that their sojourn in France was after a long preliminary period of primary education on the vast roof of the world . . ."[31] Osborn had long held that Central Asia was the birthplace of humankind, hence his instructions to Nelson.

The Nelsons were sent to join the flamboyant cowboy of science Roy Chapman Andrews's Third Asiatic Expedition to the Gobi Desert, billed as a search for the "birthplace of man." Instead, Andrews had found new mammalian and reptilian fossils, and, in 1923, the famed fossilized dinosaur eggs. Nels and Ethelyn Nelson joined Chapman in 1925; they found neither birthplace nor cradle of humanity, but rather some prosaic stone tools in a series of stratified late Pleistocene and early Holocene sand dunes.[32]

The Gobi Desert expedition was Nelson's last field trip. He retired from the American Museum in 1943 and died in 1964, at eighty-nine, a long way in years and experience from the Danish immigrant who began the first grade at age seventeen in Minnesota and later started the chronological revolution in Southwestern archaeology.

23.4. A. V. Kidder, 1912. Photograph by Jesse L. Nusbaum. Courtesy of the Museum of New Mexico.

Kidder at Pecos

After Hewett's 1907 field school, John Fletcher fled to his poetic muse, but Kidder and Morley came back for more. In 1908 Morley finished his master's degree at Harvard, writing a thesis on Maya glyphs, a topic he pursued assiduously for the rest of his life. In February 1908, Hewett offered Morley a job with the School of American Archaeology, at six hundred dollars the first year and twelve hundred dollars a year thereafter. It was enough to allow Morley to marry his fiancée, Alice Williams, and move to Santa Fe (the couple were divorced in 1915). Morley worked rather unhappily for Hewett through 1914, when he managed to escape to the Carnegie Institution of Washington,

where he spent the rest of his career, living in Santa Fe when he was not in Maya country.[33] Kidder (Fig. 23.4) graduated from Harvard in 1908 and came back to work that summer for Hewett, first at Alkali Ridge in Utah with Cummings, and then to Mesa Verde to continue mapping the ruins with Jesse Nusbaum. His first archaeological publication was on Alkali Ridge.[34]

In the winter of 1908–9 Kidder toured the ruins of Greece and Egypt with his family and their friends the Appletons, including daughter Madeleine. The romance of the ruins worked its charms. Madeleine Appleton and "Ted" Kidder were married in 1910. Madeleine Kidder (1891-1981) (Fig. 23.5) was a partner in Kidder's archaeology work throughout their lives.

*23.5. Madeleine Kidder, ca. 1918. J. O. Brew Collection. Courtesy
of the Peabody Museum, Harvard University.*

Largo Canyon areas. In his memoirs, written in the 1950s, Kidder reports:

> I, having been incurably infected by the ceramic bacillus on my first exposure in the McElmo country, took the greatest pleasure in several new types I saw at Puyé. . . . I gave one of them a specific designation; a thick gray ware . . . with decorations in dull black. I called it Biscuit, and it became, I believe, the first of countless hundreds of named ceramic types resulting from the taxonomic orgy that has spread, like the Black Death in the Middle Ages, over both Americas and has resulted in so hopeless a situation that only recently have attempts been made to haul our archaeological heads out of the still rising floods of nomenclature that threatens to engulf us.[37]

"Taxonomic orgy" is apt. By the 1950s there *were* "countless hundreds" of named pottery types in the Southwest, as well as various "family trees" of pottery "wares" and types "descendant" from those wares. With reference to ceramic nomenclature, Kidder said, "when I came back to Southwestern archaeology [after years of work as a Mayanist] I felt like an elderly rabbit returning to his native briar patch to find it overrun by a thousand descendants."[38]

Edgar Lee Hewett, in his 1908 dissertation, briefly sorted pottery types from the Pajarito Plateau (Map 7) into three major wares and noted that sherd distributions demonstrated that glazed wares were prehistoric and not Spanish introductions. Like Fewkes and others at the time, Hewett saw ceramics as indicators of cultural affiliation, but, excepting glaze wares, not as chronological indicators.[39] In Kidder's 1914 dissertation on Southwestern ceramics, he presented a detailed seriation of the various types defined on the

In 1909 Kidder started graduate school at Harvard. One teacher was the Egyptologist George A. Reisner (1867–1942). Reisner, who discovered the royal cemetery of Cheops near the Giza pyramids, was the leading American Egyptologist, widely known and respected for his "advanced" and modern field methods. Kidder was very fortunate, since Reisner rarely left Egypt to visit his sponsors at Harvard and the Boston Museum of Fine Arts. In a field-methods course, according to Kidder, Reisner "explained the aims of archaeology and how to attack a problem, how to determine a culture's chronological relations to other cultures and its trade contacts with its contemporaries, gave a lot of stratigraphic theory, . . . taught a classification of various kinds of debris, described details of cataloging and discussed the house-keeping problems of organization."[35] Kidder also took a course from George Chase, an expert on Greek painted ceramics; he later adopted Chase's analytical techniques, and applied them to his own ceramic analyses in the Southwest.[36]

Kidder returned to the Southwest in 1912 to investigate historic pueblo sites in the Gobernador and

basis of form and decoration, and provided a guide for naming types. He understood the uses of pottery as indicators of relative time and cultural linkages.[40] He noted that little attention had been paid to stratigraphy in Southwestern archaeology, and made it clear that he needed sites with good, deep stratigraphy to verify his typology.

Kidder spent the 1914 field season with Samuel Guernsey in the Kayenta area of Arizona (see below). He was in touch with Nels Nelson about the latter's stratigraphic tests at San Cristóbal. The pueblo was abandoned in 1680. Nelson's sherd sequence thus extended back from 1680 for an unknown length of time. His stratigraphic sequence of sherds was generally the same as Kidder had defined on stylistic grounds for the northern Rio Grande region. Kidder had visited Pecos Pueblo in 1910, with Kenneth Chapman, and made a large surface collection of sherds. Now he saw an opportunity for a stratigraphic test. Pecos had been abandoned in 1838; it was known to have been occupied in 1540 when Coronado passed through. The sherds Kidder picked up in 1910 suggested a much longer time depth. It was the perfect test case.

Kidder and the Phillips Academy

In 1901 Mr. and Mrs. Robert Singleton Peabody of Philadelphia established a Department of Archaeology at Phillips Academy, Andover, Massachusetts. By 1906, there was "an artistic building, a collection of thirty thousand specimens," a curator, Warren King Moorehead, and an honorary director, Dr. Charles Peabody. The purpose was to teach archaeology in a secondary prep school; classes were voluntary. "While the department is too young [1906] to judge of ultimate results, one thing is made certain, namely, that no one of the four hundred students at Andover leaves school without knowing there is such a science as American archaeology, a fact not even yet of universal or even general knowledge. . . . The department is self-supporting, and hopes to continue to be of service to the archaeological interests of anthropology." In 1915, on the recommendation of Roland B. Dixon, of Harvard, and Hiram Bingham, of Yale, A. V. Kidder was hired to develop a new archaeology program.[41] He proposed that the program begin at Pecos Pueblo; the trustees agreed.

Kidder gained Edgar Lee Hewett's approval, since

23.6. A. V. Kidder excavations at Pecos Pueblo, 1915. Courtesy of the Museum of New Mexico Photographic Archives.

the Museum of New Mexico controlled the site. Madeleine Kidder and Samuel and Rachel Lothrop came along as assistants in 1915. Samuel Lothrop went on to a long and distinguished career in Caribbean and Latin American archaeology. Hewett sent Jesse Nusbaum to stabilize the ruins of the church (one story is that he used Model T Ford frames inside the buttresses), and J. B. Adams to help with the mapping.

Kidder excavated at Pecos Pueblo (Fig. 23.6) in 1915 and 1916, was in the U.S. Army in 1917–19, and returned in 1920. In 1916 he hired Harvard student Carl Guthe as an assistant. Guthe (1893–1974) completed his Ph.D. the next year. He worked on the Pecos project in 1916, 1917, 1920, and 1921. In 1917, he made an extensive survey of the Pecos Valley, and northward along the Rio Grande into the San Luis Valley in Colorado, tracing out the northern limits of pueblo cultures. He also dug in Rowe Ruin, downriver from Pecos, an early black-on-white pottery site. In 1921 he worked with María Martínez and other potters at San Ildefonso, studying pottery manufacture the better to classify the ceramics from Pecos and elsewhere.[42] Guthe moved to the University of Michigan in 1922, where he played a central role in the founding of the University of Michigan Museum of Anthropology and was a prominent archaeologist for four decades.

In 1920 Kidder brought Ernest A. Hooton (1887–1954) from Harvard to Pecos to study the burials. By 1920 Hooton was well on the way to becoming a dominant figure in American physical anthropology of the old school of osteology and anthropometry. A man of idiosyncratic humor (he named his children Newton and Emma, and was given to bad puns and doggerel verse), he produced a major study of the Pecos skeletal material. His analyses kept alive the long head/round head problem in Southwestern archaeology (see below).[43]

In 1920 Kidder brought another Harvard student, George C. Vaillant, as assistant. Vaillant (1901–45) worked at Pecos again in 1924 and 1925 and was with Kidder and Earl Morris during their Canyon de Chelly trip in 1925. In 1927, Vaillant finished his doctorate under Alfred Tozzer and was hired by the

American Museum of Natural History. Over the next decade, he applied the "new archaeology" principles to the Valley of Mexico and produced the first complete stratigraphic and seriation sequences there. This culminated in his famous *The Aztecs of Mexico* in 1941, written for a popular audience. After service in World War II, he became director of the University of Pennsylvania Museum; he took his own life in 1945.[44]

Pecos and Its Pottery

The main sections of Pecos Pueblo sit on a narrow mesa top. For centuries the occupants threw their trash over the east edge of the mesa and it accumulated on the talus slope below. Kidder dug trenches into this rubbish heap (see Fig. 23.6), peeling away the deposits in "natural," that is, visibly different layers and keeping track of the potsherds and other artifacts from each layer. He noted that Pecos was known to have been occupied from 1540 to 1838, but that the "potsherds scattered about the ruins [comprised] . . . practically all the types of prehistoric wares known to occur in the upper Rio Grande district." He therefore believed "that the site had been settled in very early times and that people had lived there, presumably continuously, through all the intervening centuries." This seemingly unique situation would yield, he hoped, "remains . . . so stratified as to make clear the development of the various Pueblo arts" and thus allow a "proper chronological order[ing of] numerous . . . ruins whose culture has long been known but whose relation to one another has been entirely problematical."[45]

Kidder's hopes were realized. The pottery types he found fell stratigraphically into the sequence he had previously arranged stylistically. The "earliest or [stratigraphically] lowest type was the black-and-white," followed by a "long series of wares with glazed ornamentation," the last of the series found with European objects, and finally, "a yellowish pottery excellently finished and tastefully decorated with dull black pigment." There was also historic period pottery from the Hopi villages, Acoma, Zuni, and Jemez, and prehistoric wares from the Little Colorado, the San Juan, and possibly the Lower Gila, drainages. There were trade items from the Great Plains and possibly Mexico. "We may thus hope to learn, from trade objects found at Pecos and in the chronologically arranged one-culture ruins, the relative age of many other groups, not only in the Southwest but even well beyond its borders."[46]

In 1917, the Kidders proposed a nine-period chronology for the Rio Grande Valley and adjacent areas. The first six periods were each relatively younger, the last three "absolute," that is, tied to the Western calendar and hence to Newton's time scale: "Early Historic (1540–1680), Late Period (1680–1840), Present (1840–1917)." They noted that the glaze wares appeared and superseded black-on-white wares before the shift toward the large multistory pueblos, as Bandelier had earlier observed (see Chapter 15).[47]

The goals of chronology and cultural connections seemed within reach. For the first time, there was a chronology that could be used to order, at least in relative time, hundreds of ruins. There was also a systematic method of analysis through which cultural linkages, and the direction of those linkages, could be established. Because groups of sites could be dated relative to other groups, it was possible to begin estimating population size through time, something that had been a puzzle since Anglos began speculating about the ruins.

Kroeber at Zuni

While Kidder was searching for chronological order at Pecos, Alfred L. Kroeber was seeking it at Zuni Pueblo. He was there studying kinship and family life (see Chapter 26). But he also made some observations on Zuni potsherds that had far-reaching implications for archaeology.

Kroeber returned to Zuni in the summer of 1916, where he was joined by Leslie Spier (1893–1961), an assistant at the American Museum and first-year graduate student at Columbia. Wissler arranged for Robert Lowie to teach at Berkeley during the 1916–17 aca-

demic year while Kroeber remained in New York to write. In *Zuni Potsherds,* Kroeber says he "recorded the native names of ancient villages in and near Zuni Valley," visited during the course of his afternoon walks. At each he filled his pockets full with sherds, took them back to his lodgings, and sorted them by color and style patterns. Some ruins were known to have been occupied when Coronado came in 1540; others were known to have been abandoned in 1680. The latter usually had standing walls or remnants of walls. Some sites had no standing walls and had melted down, appearing to be older. On the historic sites Kroeber found that nearly all the sherds had "striking black on red and black on yellow patterns." On the oldest-appearing sites, the sherds were entirely white slip with black designs, "in general of the familiar Cliff-Dweller type." Two sites had some black on white sherds and a "fair proportion of red ware." Kroeber ended up with ten types. By seriating them according to stylistic features, and calculating simple frequency percentages of each sample, he arrived at a relative chronology for ruins within the valley, which he divided into seven "periods" ranging back through time from 1915. "I have not turned a spadeful of earth in the Zuni country," he wrote. "But the outlines of a thousand years' civilizational changes which the surface reveals are so clear, that there is no question of the wealth of knowledge that the ground holds for the critical but not over timid excavator."[48]

Finally, Kroeber dismissed earlier archaeology and the current work of Fewkes, Hewett, and Cummings:

The problems of prehistoric Zuni and of the earliest Southwest will be solved only by determined limitation of attention. There has been treasure hunting . . . for fifty years, some with the accompaniment of most painstaking recording, measuring, and photographing; but these dozens or hundreds of efforts, some of them costly, have produced scarcely a rudiment of true history. It is fatal for the investigator to exhume pottery in the morning, note architectural construction at noon, plot rooms in the afternoon and by evening become excited over a find of turquoise or amulets. . . . The fine bowls, precious jewelry, and beautiful axes that already cumber our museums, will find their use, but [only] at the end of study. . . . At present five thousand sherds can tell us more than a hundred whole vessels.[49]

He concluded by saying that only when the chronologies of "Zuni, of the Hopi country, of the Rio Grande, of the San Juan, and of the Gila" are worked out independently can any valid conclusions be drawn. And, he added, the resolution of the chronological issues was "surely . . . one of the most promisingly productive of scientific problems."[50] Here was a call to action.

With Kidder and Kroeber showing the way, the "new" Southwestern archaeology shifted into high gear. Leslie Spier joined the team. Spier (1893–1961) was born and grew up in New York City and took an engineering degree before finding his way into anthropology with Boas at Columbia.[51] He spent the summer of 1916 with Kroeber at Zuni and portions of 1917 doing stratigraphic test excavations and extensive surveying along the Little Colorado River and as far west as the Verde Valley. He collected hundreds of sherds, sorted them into types, and calculated percentages of occurrence for each site. His few stratigraphic tests confirmed his seriation rankings and his "wares, series, and types" of pottery seemed to form a relative chronological sequence that generally confirmed Kroeber's. Spier also noted that his various types were associated with a sequential development of architectural styles—from simple, single-unit "slab structures" to the large multistory pueblos in existence at some point before historic times.[52]

By 1920 Kidder's "ceramic bacillus" and stratigraphic excavation techniques had thoroughly infected the younger Southwestern archaeologists and were the tools for honing and refining relative chronologies and establishing linkages between groups. The archaeological agenda for the next four decades was now set and would be followed almost slavishly.

Back to the Basket Makers

Two other archaeological projects of major importance to Southwestern archaeology also began in the watershed years of 1914–15 in the Marsh Pass area and at Aztec Ruin. His doctoral dissertation finished, A. V. Kidder in 1914 headed to the Kayenta country of northeastern Arizona, which Byron Cummings had begun exploring in 1908. He was accompanied by Samuel Guernsey, an artist and archaeological curator of the Peabody Museum at Harvard. There is a brass-headed nail in the basement floor of the Peabody Museum at Harvard, where, legend has it, Kidder and Guernsey shook hands and said, "Let's do the Southwest." In 1915 and thereafter, Guernsey was in charge of the Kayenta work, while Kidder worked at Pecos Pueblo. Those who funded Guernsey's work included Augustus Hemenway, who had installed Fewkes as head of the Hemenway Expedition in 1889. The expedition headquartered at John and Louisa Wetherill's Kayenta Trading Post.[53]

Kidder and Guernsey focused on the Tsegi Canyon region (Map 7), digging several sites, most of them dry rockshelters. Their report, published by the Bureau of American Ethnology in 1919, is regarded as a founding document of the new Southwestern archaeology.[54] Aside from the careful excavation, analysis, and description of sites and artifacts, the report is important because it cautiously verified and gave credence to Richard Wetherill's distinction between the older Basket Maker and younger Cliff-Dweller cultures. But what were their relationships? "Was the Basket Maker culture the product of a people inhabiting the region before the coming of the Cliff-dwellers, and later displaced by them; or was the Basket Maker the prototype of the Cliff-dweller, and did gradual growth take place in the region from the Basket Maker . . . to the Cliff-dweller?"[55] Kidder and Guernsey weren't sure, but the hypotheses were now clearly on the table and would be pursued for the next two decades. Finally, they equated Cliff-dweller/Cliff-house with "Pueblo," establishing the term in archaeology; "Cliff-Dweller" continued for a time in popular literature and poetry.

Earl Morris at Aztec Ruin

Clark Wissler's Huntington Southwestern project included excavation and stabilization of the well-known Aztec Ruins by Earl H. Morris (Fig. 23.7). Morris was in the eyes of his peers the consummate "dirt archaeologist," that is, one who is in the trenches doing the digging (the fun part), and doing the lab work and writing the reports (the drudgery part, which often lags many years behind the fieldwork). Earl Halstead Morris (1889–1956) was born in Chama, New Mexico, to Scott and Juliette Halstead Morris.[56] His father was a teamster who rented out himself and his teams and wagons for whatever work was to be done at mines, sawmills, and construction sites. He supplemented the family income by digging for artifacts to sell to collectors. In later years, Earl Morris said that when he was three, his father gave him a short-handled pick and showed him how to dig for artifacts.

In 1891–92 the family moved to Farmington, New Mexico, but soon moved to various other places between 1894 and 1904, when they returned to Farmington. Scott Morris was killed that year in an argument over a business deal. Embittered by his father's murder, Earl grew up in Farmington. He entered the University of Colorado in 1908. There, he volunteered in

the university museum with Junius Henderson, who would later work with Edgar Lee Hewett in Frijoles Canyon (see Chapter 22).

Earl Morris's Southwestern archaeology falls into two major parts: first, the excavation and stabilization of the Aztec Ruins; second, his dogged pursuit of Basket Maker culture from 1913 until 1940. His archaeological, in contrast to his pothunting, career began in the spring of 1911, when he happened to meet Edgar Lee Hewett on a train. Hewett brought him to Frijoles Canyon to excavate that summer. In 1912 and 1914, Hewett sent him to Guatemala to work at Quiriguá with Morley. But Morris and Hewett had a falling out. Morley, meanwhile, had fled to the Carnegie Institution. In between Guatemala trips, Morris continued digging in the Southwest. He received his B.A. in 1914 and M.A. in 1915 from the University of Colorado. Livingston Farrand had gone from Columbia University to be president of the University of Colorado. He recommended Morris to Clark Wissler, who was looking for an additional archaeologist for the Huntington program. In 1915 Morris worked in the Galisteo Basin with Nels Nelson, learning stratigraphy and seriation, and in 1916 with Nelson in Chaco Canyon.

The Aztec Ruins are situated on the northeast bank of the Animas River, several miles upstream from its confluence with the San Juan River at Farmington, New Mexico (Map 7). In 1776, Domínguez and Escalante noted the ruins; they were later described by J. S. Newberry in 1859, Lewis Henry Morgan in 1878, and T. Mitchell Prudden in 1903. Prudden wrote that "here one of the most promising of the old pueblos lies waiting for the trained and authorized explorer."[57] Many untrained and unauthorized people had dug there over the years.

In 1916, with two thousand dollars of J. P. Morgan's money, Clark Wissler obtained rights from the site's owner to dig in the ruins, and hired Earl for the job. That fall Morris shipped his artifacts and himself to

23.7. E. H. Morris excavations at Aztec Ruin, 1917. Courtesy of the American Museum of Natural History.

New York, where he entered the graduate anthropology program at Columbia University; he did not finish. When Archer Huntington contributed an additional seventy-five hundred dollars for further work at Aztec in 1917, Morris was hired as a staff member of the museum and put in charge of the excavation. In 1918, the museum contributed five thousand dollars to continue the work; Huntington added five thousand dollars more, plus sixty-five hundred dollars to buy the site. In 1923 part of the site was turned over to the National Park Service as a national monument; the rest of it came later. In 1918 Wissler offered Morris twelve hundred dollars a year to be the museum's agent at Aztec, with the proviso that he could work elsewhere as well. Morris built a small house for himself and his mother on the site and lived there until 1934.[58]

The site consists of a dozen ruins and mounds. The largest, the West Ruin, is over 300 by 400 feet in size. It proved to have as many as 350 rooms, in places three stories high; a large plaza and great kiva. Despite decades of looting there were still roofed rooms with intact artifact assemblages. Morris excavated about three-quarters of the West Ruin between 1916 and 1921. By 1921 he had enough stratigraphic data to see that there had been two occupations. The first was Chacoan in architecture and artifacts, very like the large village sites of Chaco Canyon proper. At some point the Chacoans had gone away and a layer of sterile wind-blown sand and dust had covered the site. Later, people from the Mesa Verde area moved in, did some remodeling and adding on, lived there for some time, and then went away. In 1921 there was only the stratigraphy and the seriated artifacts to establish these two sequential occupations in relative time—but it was a major addition to Southwest culture history. The same pattern of Chacoan construction, occupation, and abandonment, followed by later Mesa Verde-ian reoccupation, remodeling, and abandonment, Morris thought, occurred at other large sites in the San Juan Basin.[59]

Morris and the Basket Makers

In 1913 Morris began working in an area between the La Plata and Mancos rivers in southern Colorado (Map 7); he would return there off and on for many years. Most of the archaeological sites were very different than the nearby Cliff Dweller sites. There were small, circular, semisubterranean houses, some with adobe and pole superstructures, different ceramics, and burials of individuals with long heads. There were no round heads as there were among the Cliff Dwellers. Morris called them "Pre Pueblo."[60] In 1920 he found similar sites south of Shiprock, New Mexico, in an area he called Cemetery Ridge. Meanwhile, Kidder and Guernsey had begun working in the Tsegi area, where they clearly distinguished Basket Maker from Cliff Dweller/Pueblo strata. In some rockshelters there were small vertical slab-lined "cists," apparently food-storage structures. Other shelters had slab-lined pits big enough to live in, such as Dupont Cave in southwest Utah, which Jesse Nusbaum excavated for the Museum of the American Indian in 1920.[61] Similar "slab houses" were found in open sites on mesa tops. In 1919 Kidder and Guernsey wondered whether there had been "a gradual growth . . . from the Basket Maker through the Slab House to the Cliff Dweller?" Development "from the Basket Maker cist to the Slab-house semisubterranean room seems a logical development, . . . The masonry cliff-house or pueblo room, with its square corners would be but another step . . . the kiva perhaps being a ceremonial reminiscence of the earlier subterranean type of dwelling."[62] Morris's "Pre Pueblo" more or less equaled Kidder and Guernsey's "Slab-house," and "Post Basket Maker," as they later called it, and in his own thinking the sequence made sense. But it was not demonstrated to anyone's satisfaction in 1920. Morris devoted much of the next decade to the problem.

The Bernheimer Expeditions

In 1920, a slender, middle-aged, well-to-do cotton broker from New York City, Charles L. Bernheimer, hired John Wetherill and his men for a pack-horse trip to Rainbow Bridge. Bernheimer, who styled himself a "tenderfoot and cliff dweller from Manhattan," had spent much time in the Southwest, but had not made any extended pack-horse trips.[63] Wetherill's people at first thought him a true dude greenhorn, with his insistence on wearing pajamas and a wool skiing cap at night, and his large medicine chest full of unguents and balms. But he quickly won their respect by the way he handled himself and his horses.

In 1921, Bernheimer asked Clark Wissler if there might be an archaeologist available to go along on a second trip to Rainbow Bridge. Earl Morris was the man. As earlier noted, when John Wetherill guided the Cummings-Douglass party to Rainbow Bridge in 1909, he took along a ledger book that he and all the party signed and left at the base of the bridge. Later parties, most guided by the Wetherills, signed the register; for example, Theodore Roosevelt and others in 1913, Zane Grey and others on three occasions, and Bernheimer and company on four. On July 10, 1921, Bernheimer wrote, "A sense of homesickness brought me here on a second visit to the Arch and the wonders of the journey"; Wetherill wrote, "Everytime I see new beauties. It improves with acquaintance"; Earl Morris, "ANMH NY" wrote, "Here hath the Master Builder wrought with consummate skill."[64] There was a third trip in 1922, and a fourth in 1929 to Natural Bridges and into Moqui and Lake canyons, which drain into Glen Canyon.

Morris found very little archaeology on the trips, but he did convince Bernheimer that searching for the "Old People," as he styled the Pre-Pueblo/Basket Makers, could be interesting. In June 1923, Bernheimer funded a brief survey into the rugged Carrizo Mountains on the Navajo Reservation, then into Canyon del Muerto to look at Mummy Cave, and finally back to Cemetery Ridge.[65] Bernheimer was sufficiently impressed to support additional work in Canyon del Muerto in the fall of 1923.

In August 1923 Morris, age thirty-five, married Ann Axtell, age twenty-three (Fig. 23.8). Ann had decided that the best way to become an archaeologist in the

23.8. Ann Axtell Morris and Earl H. Morris, 1920s. Courtesy of the University of Colorado Museum.

male-chauvinist 1920s was to marry one. She had met Morris a few years earlier. Like Frank Hamilton Cushing and other young Anglos, Ann Axtell was smitten by images of Indians. She discovered archaeology in college and spent a season working for the American School of Prehistoric Archaeology in France. Then, as she later wrote, "an Archaeological Husband . . . tumbled headlong into my life . . . He is a very excellent archaeologist and a most excellent husband . . . who is named Earl Halstead Morris."[66] The newlyweds spent their honeymoon in a small gray tent in Canyon del Muerto, while they dug in Mummy Cave.

For several years after joining the Carnegie Institution, Sylvanus Morley had planned an extensive project at the great Mayan site of Chichén Itzá. Late in 1923, to better support himself and his wife, Morris hired on as archaeological supervisor, while Morley handled his ongoing studies of the Maya glyphs. Part of the year Morris continued to work in the Southwest. But his situation in Yucatán became an unhappy one, although not with Morley. When A. V. Kidder became head of the Division of Historical Research of the Carnegie Institution in 1929, he quietly created a Southwest section and set Morris to work full time, with the proviso that he could collaborate with the American Museum and the University of Colorado.[67]

Meanwhile, when not in Yucatán, the Morrises, funded by Bernheimer and Ogden Mills, an American Museum trustee who was later Secretary of the Treasury, pursued the Basket Makers in Mummy Cave and adjacent sites. In 1925, Wissler hired A. V. Kidder to work at Mummy Cave so Morris could catch up on report writing; Kidder promptly placed Morris in charge of the fieldwork. Morris's final work at Mummy Cave was in 1931, the year Canyon de Chelly was declared a national monument to preserve Mummy Cave, White House, Antelope Cave, and other sites. The tower in Mummy Cave threatened to collapse; Morris and a team of specialists undertook stabilization work. Behind the tower wall they found several calling cards and notes. One read "M.D. Jer Sullivan and Alex M. Stepen [*sic*], A.M, September 2,

1885."[68] Jeremiah Sullivan, the Indian Service physician, and Alexander M. Stephen, from Keams Canyon (see Chapter 10), had visited the site.

In 1930, Bernheimer funded excavations in an area that Morris called the Prayer Rock district between the Carrizo and Lukachukai mountains in northeastern Arizona. The next year the Carnegie Institution funded the work. There, especially in the deep dry deposits of Broken Flute and Obelisk caves (Map 7), Morris recovered some of the richest collections of Basket Maker materials ever found, especially textiles. As an aside, they were finally reported in daughter Elizabeth Ann Morris's doctoral dissertation of 1959 and her excellent monograph of 1980. Morris continued fieldwork in the La Plata area until 1939. In the early 1930s, the Morrises began an intensive study of the over two hundred complexly woven and well-made Basket Maker sandals from the Prayer Rock area. Ann's declining health after 1934 and death in 1945, and Earl's health problems, precluded its completion. The study appeared in 1998, authored by Elizabeth Morris and two colleagues. Morris did his last fieldwork in 1940; he retired from the Carnegie Institution in 1955 and died the following year.[69]

CHAPTER 24

Expanding the New Archaeology

PRIOR TO World War I, the major new archaeology projects were those run by Nels Nelson in the Galisteo Basin, Earl Morris at Aztec Ruin, Guernsey in the Tsegi area, and Kidder at Pecos Pueblo. Morris continued through the war years. In 1920 Kidder returned to Pecos and Frederick Webb Hodge launched a major project at Zuni sponsored by the Museum of the American Indian. In Arizona, Byron Cummings conducted "informal trips among the Cliff Dwellers" for interested amateurs and students. A survey and excavation program was begun in Colorado. After the creation of the National Park Service in 1916, archaeology became one of its major functions, especially at Mesa Verde National Park and various national monuments. And Chaco Canyon once again became a focal point as young turk New Archaeologists used the Park Service, the National Geographic Society, and the Smithsonian Institution as leverage to invade Edgar Lee Hewett's domain.

The Battle for Chaco Canyon

Hewett tried, but could not keep the Southwest as a private reserve for western archaeologists. He managed to gain control of several ruins, including Pecos, Quarai, and Gran Quivira. He cooperated with others, as with Kidder, when it was advantageous to him and the Museum of New Mexico to do so. But the continued influx of eastern archaeologists was troublesome. In 1920, some of them invaded Chaco Canyon, which Hewett had long regarded as his private preserve. The invasion was doubly offensive because it was engineered by Hewett's former students or employees, Neil M. Judd, Sylvanus Griswold Morley, and Earl H. Morris, with Kidder playing the diplomat, as he often did. Worse, in 1916 Hewett had signed an elaborate cooperative agreement with the Smithsonian Institution and the Royal Ontario Museum of Toronto, Canada, to jointly work in Chaco

24.1. *Chaco Canyon Reconaissance, 1920. Left to right: Neil M. Judd, Jack Martin, Charles Martin, unknown; seated on wagon: Sylvanus G. Morley. Judd Collection. Courtesy of the National Anthropological Archives, Smithsonian Institution.*

Canyon.[1] The plan was delayed by World War I, but was still essentially in place. The invasion by the young turks scuttled it.

The ring leader was Neil Judd, who had known Hewett since 1908 and attended Hewett's field school in 1910. In 1911, Judd was hired by the U.S. National Museum at the Smithsonian; he remained there for forty-three years. In 1915–16 he launched his own research program by returning to Utah to dig "mound" sites along the west flank of the Wasatch Mountains, especially at Paragonah and Fillmore.[2] The sites contained pottery and architecture similar to, yet distinct from, the Puebloan sites of Arizona and New Mexico. Kidder, in his 1924 summary (see below) saw such sites as culturally "peripheral" to the core Southwest; Noel Morss, who worked in Utah as part of the Claflin-Emerson expeditions of 1928–31, labeled them "Fremont," for the Fremont River in east central Utah.[3]

Judd wanted to be in the center, not on the periphery, of the Puebloan Southwest. In 1917 he supervised the stabilization of Betatakin Ruin in the Tsegi Canyon area, which he and Cummings recorded in 1909, and which, together with Kiet Siel and Inscription House, became parts of Navajo National Monument

the same year. In 1918 he surveyed in the Colorado River drainage in southern Utah.

By 1919 Judd was a full curator in the National Museum and ready for bigger things. He sought the aid of Kidder, Morley, and Morris. They were well aware that Hewett planned to restart his cooperative agreement, now only with the Royal Ontario Museum, and had ample funds to do so. Judd had no money and heavy curatorial duties at the National Museum. But he was part of the Washington science establishment. Morley sat on the National Geographic Society's (NGS) Research Committee, created to support exploration and research and provide fodder for the *National Geographic* magazine.[4]

In April 1920 Judd was given an NGS grant to conduct a reconnaissance of Southwestern ruins and Pueblo villages. With Kidder and Morris along part of the time, Judd and Morley made a grand tour, including a visit to Hodge at Hawikuh, and a trip into Chaco Canyon (see Fig. 24.1). There they encountered one of Hewett's crews digging in Chetro Ketl.[5] On September 7, 1920, Judd was interviewed in Santa Fe for *The New Mexican* newspaper. He described the tour, then threw a gauntlet at Hewett's feet: "several days were devoted to an examination of house remains within Chaco Canyon National Monument *where the National Geographic Society is contemplating the inauguration of intensive archaeological research.*"[6]

But Judd had problems. Hewett held two permits from the Secretary of the Interior to "explore and excavate" in Chaco Canyon.[7] Protocol normally precluded one archaeologist invading another's domain. Worse, Judd wanted to work on Chetro Ketl; Hewett was already digging there. Morley and Judd concluded that seeking a permit to *literally* invade Hewett's archaeological space was poor politics, at best; better to go after Pueblo Bonito and Pueblo del Arroyo (Map 8).[8]

Judd applied for a permit to excavate in both sites, and submitted a proposal to the NGS research committee for a multi-year program similar to that developed by Hewett and Hodge for the Rio Grande: studying culture history in relation to physiographic and ecological settings. Writing to Stephen T. Mather, director of the National Park Service, Judd stressed the "inestimable value . . . to science" of the Chaco ruins. In a swipe at Hewett, he continued, "promiscuous collecting of specimens and haphazard excavations [should] be prohibited . . . Only research institutions of unquestioned standing, represented in the field by archaeologists of merited reputation, should be permitted to undertake investigations . . ."[9]

Hearing that Judd might succeed, Hewett counterattacked. He published a suite of profusely illustrated articles on his Chaco Canyon program in the January 1921 issue of *Art and Archaeology* magazine, noting that it had been underway since 1916, thus asserting turf rights.[10] There was also the critical matter of the Wetherills' stone house immediately behind Pueblo Bonito. It was owned by Mrs. H. B. Sammons of Farmington; she leased the house and land to a sheep rancher, who in turn sublet it.[11] Hewett had arranged to use the house as a laboratory and living quarters; Judd wanted it for the same purposes. Earl Morris convinced Mrs. Sammons to lease the house to Judd. Hewett managed to raise a legal question as to whether Mrs. Sammons had clear title, thus effectively

blocking Judd. In the end, Judd had to build a tent camp and dig a well in the arroyo of Chaco Wash.[12]

In January 1921, the NGS committee approved Judd's proposal. He applied for an antiquities permit and asked the Smithsonian to grant him several months' leave each year to direct the project. Hewett persevered; through his Washington contacts, he tried to block the permit. He argued that since the Smithsonian, as a public agency, should never engage in anything "controversial," it should not let Judd participate in the project. Hewett ignored the fact that the same argument might apply to him in New Mexico. It was rumored that Hewett had a bill introduced in Congress giving control of key sites on federal lands to state institutions.[13] Meanwhile, Hewett suffered a reverse in Santa Fe: the New Mexico legislature learned of Judd's grant and cut the four thousand dollars from his budget that he had requested to continue at Chetro Ketl.[14]

Judd arrived in Chaco Canyon in May 1921, built a tent camp, dug a well, and proceeded to begin work at Pueblo Bonito. On August 3 he wrote to Morris, "El Toro has yet to put in an appearance. He recently spent several weeks in Washington trying to convince those there that our dependency upon his water supply and especially the dust from our excavations rendered it absolutely impossible for him to proceed," but no one in Washington agreed.[15]

After Judd left for the season, Hewett sent a crew to Chetro Ketl for a few weeks, but he did not return again until 1929. In his 1922 annual report, he rationalized his withdrawal: given Judd's and Morris's projects, "probably an undue amount of attention is being paid to this section of the Southwest. It is not, therefore, . . . a serious loss if we reduce our activities in the Chaco Canyon for the present and increase in other sections equally important and less known."[16] With these sour grapes, Hewett moved to Gran Quivira, to begin excavations in cooperation with the National Park Service.

Judd finished the excavation and stabilization of Pueblo Bonito in 1926 (Fig. 24.2). In 1927 he followed

24.2 (above). Excavation of Pueblo Bonito, 1926. Judd Collection. Courtesy of the National Anthropological Archives, Smithsonian Institution.

24.3 (right). 1925 Agriculture Conference in Chaco Canyon. Back row, left to right: Karl Ruppert, Frank A. Thackery, L. C. Hammond, Frank H. H. Roberts, Jr.; front row, left to right: Kirk Bryan, William Henry Jackson, Neil M. Judd, C. S. Schofield, Monroe Amsden. Courtesy of the National Anthropological Archives, Smithsonian Institution.

out the roads radiating from the canyon for short distances, speculating they were used to transport logs for the thousands of roof beams in the ruins. He also held two or three field seminars at his Chaco camp, with a small group focusing on current topics, such as the origins of Southwestern agriculture (Fig. 24.3).

Judd's Interpretation of Pueblo Bonito

Judd's massive technical reports on Chacoan architecture and material culture did not appear until 1954–1964, after he retired, although he wrote various short summaries for the National Museum. He also wrote articles for the *National Geographic Magazine,* heavily edited to conform to the magazine's style: breezy, romantic, with a breathless excitement of discovery, hyperbole, emphasizing bare-breasted cheesecake and beefcake, and the "mysterious" in nature, the past, and human activities while glorifying science, Americanism, and upper-class Anglo values.[17] There was a marked male chauvinism and a benevolent racism toward non-Whites. The 1921 article announcing Judd's Chaco project has a gratuitous photograph of a (clothed) Zuni woman holding a large decorated olla, and captioned, "Two Beauties of the Zuni. The Zuni women are attractive Indian types when young; the Zuni pottery still is made according to aboriginal methods and patterns."[18]

Chaco Canyon, said the editors, had once been a "populous island in a sea of sand," set in a "giant [but] unwatered, canal carved by nature." The canyon's "isolation . . . adds another mystery to the bygone metropolis of the canyon's maw: Whence came the lumber to build and whence the water to cultivate the corn, beans, and squash of the . . . aboriginal farms?" Judd's interdisciplinary team hoped "to patch from a crazy-quilt of half-submerged ruins a complete picture of the lives, customs, and culture of these early Americans."[19]

In later articles, Judd speculated that Chaco Canyon was the source for the Seven Cities of Cibola legend; in 1925 he estimated that "a hundred thousand tons of earth and stone and blown sand have been carted away" in the excavation of Pueblo Bonito and stressed the enormous size of the ruin. "No other apartment house of comparable size was known in America or in the Old World until the Spanish Flats were erected in 1882 at 59th and Seventh Ave, New York City."[20]

Life was good at Pueblo Bonito, Judd averred; "colorful clan ceremonies [were] periodically performed . . . their fundamental purpose the propitiation of tribal gods . . . [for] more bountiful harvests." But wandering "human wolves crept in through the autumn shadows to prey upon the village and steal all that could be carried away. . . . hunters by instinct

and rovers by preference." To keep them out, the single gateway to Pueblo Bonito "was reduced to a narrow door and this was subsequently and permanently closed in the interest of still greater security. Thereafter, access to the great house was gained by a ladder which could be drawn up."[21]

Sherds of characteristic pottery vessels from regions peripheral to Chaco Canyon were found in the excavations. To Judd, this meant that Pueblo Bonito was "a monument to the cooperative efforts of peoples physically related, though culturally distinct, who were drawn together, through mutuality of interest, from widely separated localities. . . . Cliff-dwellers from the picturesque cave villages of . . . Mesa Verde were welcomed by the Bonitians, together with migrating clans from the . . . Little Colorado River in Arizona. Relics peculiar to each of these distinctive cultures abound in Pueblo Bonito . . . "[22]

Judd's assertions reflect common, but undemonstrated, assumptions made by the new archaeologists. One is the use of ethnographic analogy: current Pueblos have "colorful" clan ceremonies designed to attract rain; therefore the Chacoans must have done so too. Following A. V. Kidder's lead (see below), Judd conjured up wandering, skulking nomads to account for evidence of conflict, even if there was no clear archaeological evidence for such folk. Finally, Judd fell prey to the common archaeological fallacy that pots equal people. He did not consider a more parsimonious explanation: that the pots were simply trade items; their presence did not automatically demonstrate "migrating clans."[23]

The "Talkative Tree Rings"

While Judd speculated about the nature of Chacoan society, he shared the central concern of his New Archaeology compatriots: how old, in "absolute" years, were the ruins they were digging? The answer came from A. E. Douglass, of the University of Arizona, an astronomer who studied tree rings in an attempt to understand the influence (if any) of sun spots on world weather patterns. In 1923, Judd announced that the NGS research committee had authorized seventy-five hundred dollars for a "subsidiary expedition" (usually called the "beam expedition") to collect wood from archaeological sites to be used by Douglass in his dendrochronology studies. The ultimate aim was to establish an absolute chronology of Chacoan and other ruins on the Colorado Plateau.[24]

Andrew Ellicott Douglass (1867–1962) was New England born, the son of an Episcopalian minister and a mother who encouraged his active interest in science, especially astronomy, from an early age.[25] After graduating from Trinity College in Connecticut, he became an assistant at the Harvard Observatory. In 1894, he became associated with Percival Lowell, of the Boston Lowells, a wealthy businessperson and avid amateur astronomer. Douglass helped him establish the Lowell Observatory in Flagstaff, Arizona. In 1906 Douglass moved to the University of Arizona, where he remained for over fifty years.

Douglass became interested in the annular growth of tree rings about 1901. Many species of deciduous and coniferous trees put on an annual growth ring— the cambial wood just beneath the bark. It had long been known that tree rings are indicators of age. By the 1890s there was speculation about relationships between climatic factors and tree rings. Douglass took up the question from both astronomical and meteorological perspectives. By 1900 astrophysicists were studying the structure of the sun and fluctuations in solar radiation, including the 11.3-year cycle of the enigmatic sunspots. Some thought there were relationships between the sunspot cycle and variations in global weather patterns; others disagreed.

Douglass saw the issue as a hypothesis to be tested. He reasoned that since the heat of the sun causes the evaporation of ocean water and is the ultimate "heat engine" driving the winds that carry the water over and onto land, variations in solar activity could affect weather patterns, including annual precipitation. He noted that throughout the Desert West annual precipitation, not ground water, affects tree growth; therefore a year of abundant precipitation should produce a wider annular ring in trees than a drought year.[26]

If there were consistent correlations between variations in tree-ring widths and the sunspot cycle, then he could hypothesize that there is a relationship between fluctuations of solar radiation and world weather patterns. He pursued this hypothesis and the tree-ring evidence for it, for nearly sixty years. As a by-product, he provided Southwestern archaeologists and, subsequently, archaeologists in many world areas with a means of telling "absolute" time.

Dendrochronology is not simply counting rings, but developing a thorough knowledge of the patterning of ring growth from many specimens of each usable species in a given region. In years of abundant precipitation, rings may be quite wide (sometimes even double); less precipitation produces narrower rings; hard drought years may produce no rings at all. Ultimately a master chart of the patterning for a region is developed, beginning with trees cut at a known date, for example, 1900 C.E. Specimens are moved along the chart until their ring pattern is matched, and are thus "cross-dated."[27]

Douglass began collecting tree-ring samples in 1904, from timber cut that year in the San Francisco Mountains near Flagstaff. He also collected samples from living trees elsewhere on the Colorado Plateau and in the sequoia and redwood forests of California. By 1909 he was able to demonstrate that differential ring-width patterning could be traced generally in trees across the Desert West, and had developed a master chart for the Colorado Plateau. By 1915 he had a chronology from 1900 back to about 1400.

In May 1914, Clark Wissler read Douglass's paper on estimating rainfall from tree rings.[28] He wrote to Douglass suggesting that samples from roof beams in archaeological sites might be used to extend the chronology back in time, and wondered if the sites themselves might be dated by correlating the rings from their beams with Douglass's chronology. Wissler sensed the potential for making a major contribution to the nascent "new" archaeology he was nurturing, and committed some Huntington Survey funds to support Douglass. Earl Morris, who had just joined the American Museum, sent specimens from the

Gobernador region and Johnson Canyon, Colorado, in 1916. Morris became an ardent beam collector, contributing hundreds of specimens over the next decades (Fig. 24.4). In 1918, Morris collected samples from Aztec Ruin and Pueblo Bonito. Douglass was able to cross-date the two sites, showing that the Aztec samples were cut within two years of each other and that construction of Aztec minimally began forty to forty-five years after that of Pueblo Bonito. It was a major breakthrough. As Nash says, "Douglass had, for the first time, calibrated the temporal relationship of two prehistoric sites against an annual, if not yet common-era, calendar."[29] In 1919 Douglass visited Morris at Aztec Ruin and collected more samples. Douglass, Morris, and others also began to recognize not only that the ruins might be dated, but that "hard" evidence might be developed for prehistoric climatic variations and the impact of those variations on ancient lifeways and settlement patterns.[30]

Archer Huntington terminated his funding of the American Museum's Southwestern project in 1920, hence Wissler could no longer support Douglass.[31] But Neil Judd was getting his Chaco Canyon project under way and Wissler contacted him. In 1922, Judd was able to convince the NGS committee that a successful tree-ring chronology would allow him to closely date the construction sequence of Pueblo Bonito and other sites in the canyon. The committee provided twenty-five hundred dollars for the first of three "Beam Expeditions" (1923, 1928, and 1929), during which teams collected hundreds of samples from archaeological sites, historic Pueblos, and churches.

By 1928 Douglass had a prehistoric "floating" chronology of several hundred years duration. Many of the major ruins—in Chaco Canyon, at Mesa Verde, Wupatki, and elsewhere could be cross-dated. A beam collected by Morris from the Kawaiku site in the Jeddito Valley, Arizona, extended the historic sequence back to 1357. But there was a "Gap," of X years between 1357 and the chronologically younger end of the floating chronology.

Early in 1929, the NGS committee provided an additional five thousand dollars to support work to close the Gap. Douglass hired University of Arizona students Lyndon Hargrave and Emil W. Haury to help. The key to closing the gap was pottery seriation. Using a seriation sequence developed by Hargrave, the team focused on ruins on the Mogollon Plateau in Arizona. On June 22, 1929, Hargrave and Haury excavated a beam (labeled HH-39) from the Whipple Ruin near Show Low. Douglass and Judd arrived just in time to take pictures. Douglass spent several hours analyzing the beam and cross-checking against his charts, then finally turned to Hargrave, Haury, and Judd (who were waiting breathlessly) and said, "I think we have it." Sample HH-39 closed the Gap, its rings overlapping the historic and floating chronologies.[32] In fact, Douglass had already closed the Gap by using fragmentary specimens; being supercautious he wanted incontrovertible confirmation; he now had it. Suddenly, the chronology of what would come to be called the Anasazi cultures of the Colorado Plateau and the Rio Grande drainage was tied to the "absolute" time scale of the

24.4. Earl H. Morris wrapping dendrochronology samples. Courtesy of the University of Colorado Museum.

current-era calendar. It was a triumph for Douglass's brilliance and tenacity and Wissler's foresight. The Gap closure was kept secret until the *National Geographic* could make a suitable publicity splash with the announcement.[33] There were one or two naysayers. Harold Gladwin, who founded the Gila Pueblo research center in 1928 (see Chapter 29), tried for years to disprove Douglass's methods, but failed.[34] There were also chronological surprises: sites thought to be contemporary proved not to be (see below).

Tree-ring chronology continued to be refined in the decades to follow in the Southwest and elsewhere. In 1937 Douglass finally achieved a long-held dream, the establishment of the Tree Ring Laboratory at the University of Arizona, where he pursued dendrochronology and climatic change until his death at age ninety-five.[35] He was also responsible for helping create an astronomical observatory at the University of Arizona; he lived to see and be honored at the establishment of the Kitt Peak National Observatory near Tucson in 1960.

Hodge, Heye, Hendricks, and Hawikuh

By 1916, when ground was broken at the Audubon Terrace site next to Archer Huntington's Hispanic Society and Numismatic Society buildings, George Heye and his Museum of the American Indian were on the way to the big time in the museum world. But Heye had a problem: lack of credibility, respect, and prestige, despite the support of Huntington and Keith. Many of Heye's acquisitions were suspect, even under the laissez-faire collecting rules of the day. The historic cemetery incident was one example; the lack of specific provenience for pieces from Latin America, hinted in the newspaper reports of the museum's opening, was another. There were out-of-joint noses and jealousy within the museum community as well.

Heye wanted his museum to have the respect, credibility, and prestige of the American Museum, the Field Museum, and even the Smithsonian. He had acquired that "good stuff" through covert wheeling and dealing. True to type, he went after prestige and

respectability in the same way. In early 1915, he began quietly courting Frederick Webb Hodge. A joint excavation project was arranged, digging a mound at Nacoochee, in Georgia. Hodge and Heye had long talks. By 1915 Hodge was a leading figure in American anthropology, a highly capable administrator, and superb editor. He had edited many of the Bureau of American Ethnology reports; he saw the *Handbook of North American Indians* into print, thus finally completing the task set for American anthropology by Lewis Cass in 1826. He was editing Edward Curtis's monumental *The North American Indian* (see Chapter 26), and had put the *American Anthropologist* on a firm footing as its editor between 1903 and 1916. In 1910 he succeeded William Henry Holmes as ethnologist-in-charge of the Bureau. He had continued to work in the Southwest when he could, and edited several major historical documents.[36]

But there was another side to Hodge—he was a born raconteur and he relished the high life, partying, ardent spirits, women, and laughter induced by scatological, sexual, or practical jokes; and he loved fast cars, especially a Mercedes roadster that he drove with verve at high speeds. His tastes were very much those of George Heye, and Heye correctly concluded they would come to a meeting of like minds. The Nacoochee dig was simply the opening gambit; now the question was, what would it take to move Hodge to New York? While the Bureau did not have the panache of Powell's day, still Hodge had good connections within the Smithsonian and had lived with Margaret Magill Hodge and their family in Washington for nearly thirty years. But he had never run a major field project of his own. He had been Cushing's factotum; he had occasionally gone to the field with Fewkes. He had edited hundreds of thousands of other peoples' words about *their* field projects, but had never organized, directed, collected, analyzed, and published a major project to call his own. And he was fifty years old. If Heye found the money, where might he do such a project? Hodge chose Hawikuh, the ruins of the village where the Zunis had killed Fray Marcos de Niza's erstwhile companion Esteban in

May 1539; the village that first confronted Coronado in 1540—certainly one of the most historic places in the Southwest.

The Franciscans established a mission at Hawikuh in 1628 and began building a church; a *visita* was established soon after at Halona. In 1632, the Zunis rose in revolt, killed a priest, burned the church, and retreated to Corn Mountain, where they remained until 1635 or 1636. The church and friary were rebuilt sometime after 1642, burned and sacked by Apaches in 1672, apparently rebuilt, and then burned again in the 1680 Pueblo Revolt; the pueblo was not reoccupied thereafter.[37]

Hodge moved cautiously. Either he or Heye proposed a joint Bureau of American Ethnology-Museum of the American Indian expedition. There was precedent in the recent Bureau-School of American Archaeology joint effort with Hewett. Hodge and Heye tried to get the project underway in 1916, but there were antiquities permit problems and the Zunis raised some objections. Meanwhile, both George and Thea Heye were actively courting Hodge; rumors began to circulate.[38]

Hodge solved the permit problems and the issues with the Zunis, and began fieldwork at Hawikuh in June 1917 (Map 7). His staff included Jesse Nusbaum, whom Heye had easily lured away from Hewett when the former returned from military service. Heye's financial angel, Harmon Hendricks, donated over thirty-five hundred dollars to get the project going, and continued to support it for the next five years. Heye dubbed the project the Hendricks-Hodge Expedition; Hodge preferred the Hendricks-Heye Expedition.[39]

On September 25, 1917, Heye sent Hodge a personal handwritten letter, with a cover note that said, "Dear Fred—If this does not suit, send me a draft of one you want. Best wishes, George." The letter read, in part, "In confirmation of my conversation with you of several months back, I take pleasure in offering you a position in this institution. The excavations at Hawikuh have indicated that it is a large & most important problem, and I feel to do this work thoroughly

you should devote the major part of your time to it. Hoping you will do us the great honor of accepting a position on our staff . . ."[40] Hodge accepted privately, but no public statement was made until January 12, 1918, when Heye wrote to Hodge:

> I was delighted to get your letter of January 9th which gave me permission to free the good news. Every member of the staff . . . has come to me personally to congratulate the Museum on your acquisition. Of course, I kept my face straight and accepted their congratulations for they little know what a lazy and drunken beast you are. Do not worry, your secret is safe with me. . . . I really want to tell you how sincerely glad I am that you are coming to us, not alone for personal reasons but also for the added prestige it will give our Institution. The only person who insisted all along that you were coming with us was Hewitt [*sic*] of Santa Fe. He told Jesse, nearly two years ago, that you would come with us.[41]

Later, they celebrated in style at Thea Heye's birthday party at a swank New York hotel (Fig. 24.5).

When Franz Boas heard that Hodge might move, he wrote urging him to stay with the Bureau. Hodge replied that indeed he was moving: "The opportunity for getting away from a desk and doing some intensive archeological work which has been a dream ever since the Hemenway days, was presented some time ago by Mr. Heye, and I have embraced it." Boas replied, welcoming Hodge to New York City, but hoping that someone other than Jesse Fewkes would succeed him: "It seems . . . that the best move . . . would be to put Kroeber into your place. . . . there is no doubt that he [is] the broadest among the group of younger men . . . I feel very certain that he would make an excellent administrator."[42] Smithsonian Secretary Charles Wolcott appointed Fewkes.

The Hendricks-Hodge Expedition worked in the Zuni area for six seasons, from 1917 to 1923, with the exception of 1922. Hodge wanted to be sure that the expedition was up to date. He adopted the stratigraphic and seriation methods of Kidder and Nelson;

24.5. Thea Heye's birthday party, May 12, 1919, New York City. Left to right: George Heye, Thea Heye, Harmon Hendricks, Frederick Webb Hodge, Jesse Nusbaum, George Dorsey, George Pepper, Joseph Keppler. Courtesy of the Southwest Museum.

24.6. Group at Hawikuh excavation camp, 1920. Back row, left to right: Sylvanus G. Morley, Edwin Coffin, Jesse Nusbaum, Aileen O'Bryan Nusbaum, Eleanor Hope Johnson, Neil Judd, Earl Morris. Front row, left to right: Frederick W. Hodge, A. V. Kidder, Deric O'Bryan Nusbaum (young boy). Courtesy of the Southwest Museum.

he and his staff made meticulous notes, maps, and photographs. His methods met the approval of Kidder, Morris, Judd, and Morley when they visited (Fig. 24.6) during their tour in 1920. The excavation of Hawikuh was on a larger scale than Kidder's work at Pecos. The trash mound was sectioned, some 370 rooms of the native village were cleared, the mission church and friary were almost completely excavated,

and about one thousand burials were excavated and recorded.[43] In 1919 and again in 1923, the adjacent site of Kechipauan was partly excavated by Hodge's team and a team from Cambridge University, and the collections shared. The latter excavations were seemingly never reported.

Hodge was interested only in the historic section of Hawikuh, that is, the native pueblo after 1539, and the church and associated friary. The church, the friary, and the historic village overlay deep earlier deposits, representing possibly several hundred years of occupation before 1539. To the dismay of later archaeologists, Hodge did not penetrate into those layers, and they remain unexcavated. Hodge managed to do some artifact analysis, and in 1937 published a documentary history of Hawikuh, but it remained for Watson Smith and Richard and Nathalie Woodbury to complete Hodge's excavation report in 1966, a decade after he died and forty-three years after the fieldwork ended.[44]

There was also a photographic component to the Hendricks-Hodge Expedition. Hodge was on good terms with many Zuni people. In the 1880s, they had given him the affectionate name of Téluli. He employed about forty Zuni men as excavators during the course of the work at Hawikuh, which added a tidy sum each year to the Zuni economy. Hodge wanted to document, in still and motion pictures, his excavations of Hawikuh, perhaps to demonstrate that his methods were state of the art. But he also wanted to document Zuni daily life, and the ceremonies. He and his staff produced more than 1,250 stills and about ten thousand feet of motion picture film in both efforts. Many conservative Zunis were upset by the filming, especially of the ceremonies. In the summer of 1923, motion pictures were made of a "rain dance" and some other public ceremonies. But later in the year, when Hodge's staff attempted to film the Shalako ceremony, many Zunis objected, and the priests confiscated the camera and film in a highly charged confrontation. The camera and film were later returned by the Indian agent, and not "smashed" as legend has it. The political fallout kept Hodge from returning, and affected the work of two ethnographers, Ruth Benedict and Ruth Bunzel, who came to Zuni in the summer of 1924 (see Chapter 26). Photographing Zuni ceremonies has been banned ever since.[45]

Hodge remained at the Museum of the American Indian until 1932, when he became director of the Southwest Museum in Los Angeles, remaining there until 1956. In his final years he lived in Santa Fe, where

he died at age ninety-two—the last of the ethnologists John Wesley Powell sent to the Southwest.

The Colorado Connection

During the 1910s and 1920s, four archaeologists from, or associated with, Colorado worked in the Southwest. The first was Jean Allard Jeançon (1874–1936), born in Newport, Kentucky.[46] After high school, he studied music in Kentucky, Cincinnati, and New York. He moved to Colorado in 1894. He was self-taught in archaeology and ethnography; educated, he said, by Smithsonian and Bureau of American Ethnology publications. He claimed to have spent much time at various Tewa pueblos in New Mexico and became a self-acknowledged expert on them. He met and apparently impressed Jesse Walter Fewkes and was hired by the Bureau of American Ethnology from 1919 to 1921. Under Bureau auspices, he excavated in the late period pueblo site Poshuouinge in the Chama Valley (Fig. 24.7) earlier described by Escalante and Newberry (see Chapter 3).[47] In 1921 he became director and curator of the Department of Archaeology and Ethnology of the State Historical and Natural History Society of Colorado, the predecessor of the Colorado Historical Society. In June 1923, he was hired by Neil Judd for the first Beam Expedition. But he almost immediately got into trouble with Jesse Nusbaum for sawing into beams in archaeological sites, instead of using the prescribed boring tool. He then had an attack of appendicitis, and left the expedition.[48]

Jeançon had an affiliation with the University of Denver, where by May 1924 he was directing an "authentic" Hopi pageant, probably modeled after those staged at Mesa Verde by Virginia McClurg and Aileen O'Bryan Nusbaum (see below). He told Frederick Hodge that he wished to "convince people that an Indian pageant can be something besides a lot of yipping and yelling, and bloody scalps, etc. It was based on an old Hopi corn legend; I had real Hopi songs and dances and the costumes were copies of robes and dresses in my own collection."[49]

24.7. J. A. Jeançon (left) and Kenneth M. Chapman at Poshuouinge Pueblo, Chama Valley, New Mexico, 1919. Photograph by Wesley Bradfield. Courtesy of the Museum of New Mexico.

Jeançon parted company with the Historical Society in 1927 for "health" reasons, and by February 1928 was manager of the Nateso Pueblo in Indian Hills, west of Denver, another "authentic" exhibit of Indian culture. "The pueblo consists of 13 houses with a total of 45 rooms built around an oblong square . . . all erected by Indians from San Ildefonso, Tesuque and Santa Clara of 'dobe bricks and it resembles, in every way, a real pueblo." The complex included a small museum with "about 1500 very choice objects," a "ceremonial house with two Zuni and Hopi altars and an excellent Navajo sandpainting," as well as a "suite of rooms fitted up in the old style Pueblo fashion with store rooms, living room and mealing room." Some thirty-five to forty Indians lived there in the summer; on Sundays they staged "Indian dances and games . . . no wild west features, only a simple, honest portrayal of Pueblo life. During the week the Indians live and act as they do at home. It is a strictly educational proposition and appears to have a good future." By January 1929 the company funding the pretend-Pueblo was bankrupt and in receivership, and Jeançon was "again out of a job."[50] He apparently remained in the Denver area until his death in 1936.

Jeançon's link to the University of Denver was through Etienne Bernardeau Renaud (1880–1973). Born in France, Renaud studied at the University of Paris and Catholic University in Washington, D.C. He took a master's degree and later a doctorate from the University of Colorado. Beginning in 1916, he taught Romance languages and anthropology at the University of Denver and was Anthropology Department head for twenty-eight years. He directed an archaeological survey on the High Plains and, like Charles Abbott in New Jersey, found abundant "paleoliths." His survey is charitably summarized by Cassells: "Great difficulty is encountered when relocation of his numerous sites is attempted."[51] Renaud's real contribution to archaeology was the training and encouragement he gave to students, especially John J. Cotter (1911–1999), H. Marie Wormington (1914–1994), and Frank H. H. Roberts, Jr. (1897–1966). Both Cotter and Wormington made major contributions to Paleo-Indian studies, beginning in the 1930s, and Cotter was a pioneer in the development of historical archaeology as well.

Frank H. H. Roberts, Jr., was born in Ohio and grew up in Laramie, Wyoming, and in Denver.[52] In 1910 his father became president of New Mexico Normal University in Las Vegas, where E. L. Hewett had been the founding president (see Chapter 22). Roberts took degrees in English, history, and political science at Denver University, but Renaud and Jeançon stimulated his interest in archaeology. In 1924 he entered Harvard to study anthropology, along with fellow students Oliver La Farge, Harry Shapiro, George Vaillant, and Franz Blom. He went to work for Neil Judd at Pueblo Bonito in the summer of 1926 (his doctoral dissertation was on Chacoan pottery). That fall he was hired by the Bureau of American Ethnology. He remained with the Bureau until he retired as its last director in 1964, after which the Bureau was merged with the anthropology divisions of the National Museum of American History.

In the summer of 1927, Frank and Linda Butchart Roberts spent their honeymoon digging an archaeological site: Shabik'eschee Village on a mesa top just south of Chaco Canyon. It was the first "pure" single phase Basket Maker site dug in the Southwest and provided a key to the Pecos Classification developed later that summer (see Chapter 25). From 1928 through 1933, Roberts dug other very important Pueblo sites, especially Kiatuthlanna in eastern Arizona, and the Village of the Great Kivas on the Zuni Reservation.[53] Thereafter, he turned to the emerging problem of "early man" (see Chapter 25).

Finally, the Colorado connection must include Paul Sydney Martin (1899–1974). Martin was born in Chicago and took his bachelor's and doctoral degrees at the University of Chicago. He wanted to be a Mayanist, and worked with Sylvanus Morley at Chichén Itzá in 1926 and 1928. But major bouts with malaria and amoebic dysentery convinced him to move to more xeric climes. In 1928 he succeeded Jeançon at the Colorado Historical Society and began work on sites north of Cortez, Colorado, especially the Ackman-Lowry Ruin, which continued for a decade. In 1929, he moved to the Chicago Field Museum where he remained until he retired in 1973.[54] Another Colorado product, previously introduced, was Jesse Nusbaum. It is useful to consider his contributions to Southwestern anthropology in relation to the development of the National Park Service.

National Monuments and the National Park Service

In the 1906 Antiquities Act, Congress gave the president the power to set aside national monuments by executive order, but retained the creation of larger national parks for itself. Between 1906 and 1916, twelve national monuments containing major archaeological-site complexes were created in the Southwest. They include Bandelier, Chaco Canyon, El Morro (Inscription Rock), Gila Cliff Dwellers, and Gran Quivira in New Mexico; Aztec Ruin was added in 1923 when the American Museum of Natural History turned it over to the National Park Service. In Arizona there was Casa Grande in 1892, as well as Montezuma's Castle, Navajo (Betatakin, Kiet Siel, and In-

scription House), Petrified Forest, and Tonto; Canyon de Chelly was added in 1931. In Colorado, there was Mesa Verde National Park and part of Hovenweep, added in 1923; in Utah there was Natural Bridges, and the rest of Hovenweep.

But there was no systematic way to fund the maintenance of parks and monuments, to protect them from looters, or to provide for visitors. Some had caretakers, often on a part-time basis at minimal salaries; others were looked after by federal employees from various agencies on a catch-as-catch-can basis. After long and complex maneuvering and negotiations, the National Park Service was created in 1916, under the directorship of Stephen Mather and his extremely able assistant (and later director), Horace Albright. The general story of the National Park Service is told elsewhere.[55] Here the concern is with monuments and parks in the Southwest, especially Mesa Verde because events took place there that had larger impacts on Southwestern anthropology.

Mesa Verde, McClurg, and the Colorado Cliff Dwellings Association

The campaign to make Mesa Verde a national park had a long history. The Hayden Survey in the 1870s introduced the "Cliff Dwellers" to the scholarly world and the public. The exhibits and Cliff Dwellers concessions at the 1893 Chicago, 1898 Omaha, and 1904 St. Louis world's fairs, together with numerous popular magazine articles, fixed the idea of the Cliff Dwellers in the public imagination.

The central character in the Mesa Verde campaign was Virginia Donaghe McClurg (?–1932).[56] Little is known about Virginia Donaghe before she arrived in Colorado in 1877. In Colorado Springs she worked for newspapers and then opened a private school, which she conducted until her marriage to Gilbert McClurg in 1889. In 1882 she decided to visit the cliff dwellings in the Mancos Canyon area, despite a contretemps between the U.S. Army and the Southern Utes ongoing at the time. She returned in 1886, later claiming to have discovered Balcony House during the trip. In the intervening period she had begun collecting artifacts and lecturing about cliff dwellers.[57]

The Wetherills' activities and Nordenskiöld's removal of artifacts to Sweden created a stir, which McClurg helped create. In 1893, she arranged to be officially sponsored by the state of Colorado at the Chicago world's fair. There, she exhibited a small collection of Cliff Dweller artifacts in the anthropology building, and presented a paper at the Folklore Congress (see Chapter 17).

In the 1890s, suffrage and other political issues were the focus of women's clubs, organized into state and national federations; McClurg was active therein. She gave lectures on "The Prehistoric Southwest" and pressed for petitions to Congress to preserve the ruins of the Mesa Verde. In 1897, at her behest, the Colorado State Federation of Women's Clubs appointed a fourteen-person (later increased to twenty) committee to seek action on the Cliff Dwellings. The leaders were McClurg and Lucy Elizabeth Peabody, of Denver, who had worked for the Bureau of American Ethnology before her marriage.

In 1899 McClurg wangled an appointment as a special commissioner to the Southern Ute tribe. She negotiated a lease with Ignacio, a Southern Ute leader, which gave the Colorado Federated Women's Clubs control over the cliff houses on Wetherill and Chapin mesas for ten years at three hundred dollars per year. The lease was not approved by the Secretary of the Interior, despite McClurg's assertions otherwise.[58] The Colorado congressional delegation told her that no action would be possible until there was an accurate map to distinguish public and Indian lands. In March 1900, the women's clubs put up the money, and a map was made.

In May 1900, the Colorado Cliff Dwellings Association was incorporated for the purposes of "the restoration and preservation of the Cliff and Pueblo ruins in the State of Colorado; the dissemination of knowledge concerning these prehistoric people; the collection of relics; and the acquiring of such property as is necessary to attain such objects."[59] Virginia McClurg became Regent General; Lucy Peabody was

First Vice-Regent. The association logo, designed by McClurg, was a swastika from a Mesa Verde bowl over which was inscribed "*Dux Femina Facti*"—"the women lead the way."

McClurg envisioned a national organization, but there were chapters only in Colorado, Utah, California, and New York, with a membership, according to McClurg, of some two hundred "prominent women" (Peabody counted only eighty-seven dues-paying members).[60] McClurg campaigned widely for the Cliff Dwellings cause. She claimed to have given "993 lectures on Colorado Cliff Dwellings from Portland, Maine to Portland, Oregon" between 1893 and about 1915. In 1901 she sent a watercolor of Cliff Palace, a bowl from one of the ruins, and a sonnet to Theodore Roosevelt, soliciting his support. According to McClurg, Roosevelt thanked her for the bowl and the poem, "for it said what I had often felt about this strange, simple, dead semi-civilization. Oh! how the romance and golden mystery of the west that has gone, of the west that has vanished with vanished sunsets, must strike chords in the hearts of all who have, themselves, the lift-upward within them."[61]

In September 1901, the American Association for the Advancement of Science met in Denver. After the meeting, McClurg arranged for a visit to Mesa Verde by various anthropologists. The junketeers included McClurg, Peabody, Jesse Walter Fewkes and his wife, George Grant McCurdy, Frank and Theresa Russell (see Chapter 26), and about ten others. Leaving the train in Mancos, the party traveled by wagon to the mouth of Soda Canyon, and then by horseback up the canyon to Cliff Palace. Along the way, Fewkes named a small ruin "Hemenway House," for Mary Hemenway.[62]

Between 1901 and 1905 several bills "Creating the Colorado Cliff Dwellings National Park" were introduced in Congress, but died in committee. By 1905–6 it looked as if Congress would act favorably on both Mesa Verde and an antiquities act. Edgar Lee Hewett was active in working on both bills. But a major schism rent the Cliff Dwellings Association over control and administration of Mesa Verde once it was set aside. Virginia McClurg wanted a state park controlled and administered by the Cliff Dwellings Association, with her as superintendent. She planned "to have the proposed park policed by Indians, who would on no account disturb the dwellings for fear of setting loose evil spirits. And so the superstition of the past is made to co-operate with the Twentieth Century enfranchised woman — clear-eyed, calm browed and unafraid."[63]

But the majority of McClurg's clear-eyed, calm-browed compatriots, led by Lucy Peabody, had a different view and were not afraid of expressing it — there should be a national park administered by the Department of the Interior. Association members lined up behind either Peabody or McClurg. So did the Colorado congressional delegation, to its members' obvious discomfort, and two bills were introduced. The controversy generated numerous newspaper articles and editorials; for example, the Denver *Daily News* noted that McClurg's prestige was what was really at stake.[64] McClurg responded by correctly pointing out that Peabody's bill left the major ruins outside the proposed park boundaries. In the end, Teddy Roosevelt signed the Mesa Verde National Park bill into law on June 29, 1906. The ruins did indeed lie outside the original boundaries, but the error was corrected.

Most Cliff Dwellings Association members now resigned — their task completed — but not McClurg. Having failed to get the park she wanted, she tried to be appointed as superintendent. When that failed, and Hans M. Randolph was appointed, she tried to force the Secretary of the Interior to appoint her faction of the association as official advisers to Randolph. That too failed, due in part to behind-the-scenes maneuvering by Lucy Peabody and Edgar Lee Hewett, although Hewett tried to appear neutral.[65]

Lucy Peabody's revenge was to have two articles on Mesa Verde, written by her Denver allies, published in a national feminist magazine, *The Modern World*. McClurg is not mentioned, Hewett is praised, and Peabody is extolled as "the Mother of the Mesa Verde National Park." She also received a public vote of thanks from the American Anthropological Association in 1907. Virginia McClurg's response was to throw her support behind construction of the fake cliff dwellings at Manitou Springs, west of Colorado Springs. Real sites were dismantled and reconstructed to look like parts of Cliff Palace, Balcony House, Square Tower House, and Spruce Tree House. The place is a still-functioning tourist trap, at which it is implied that the ruins are for real.[66]

The battle continued long after the antagonists were dead. In the 1940s, Jesse Nusbaum (see below) was fending off attempts by supporters to rename Square Tower House "Peabody House," and to place a marble plaque in Balcony House memorializing Virginia McClurg. There was a precedent: in mapping Mesa Verde in 1907–8, Hewett had renamed Square Tower House "Peabody House," and followed Fewkes's naming of "Hemenway House" in Soda Canyon. The names were not adopted.[67]

McClurg tried again in 1913. For a number of years, her husband had headed the Colorado Springs Chamber of Commerce. The Reclamation Service was created by Congress in 1903 and was busily developing irrigation projects and "reclaiming" the West. Gilbert McClurg was a great booster of western reclamation. He made many national lecture tours for the cause, and threw in "Cliff Dwellings, [and] Spanish, Indian, Pioneer Tales, Legends, Romance and Folklore" for added interest. By 1913 he sought a change. Mrs. McClurg sought the Mesa Verde superintendency for him, including a personal appeal to an old friend, U.S. Supreme Court Justice Mahlon Pitney; but it was not to be.[68]

In 1917 McClurg wrote, dramatized, set to music, designed the costumes for, and conducted a "Pageant of the Marriage of the Dawn and the Moon, a Cliff Dwelling Legend." This extravaganza, with twenty-four actor/singers, mostly teenage girls, was presented on September 8, 1917, in Spruce Tree House at Mesa Verde (Fig. 24.8). It was followed by a "huge barbecue" at which foods "similar to those consumed by the ancient cliff dwellers" were served, including "baked ears of maize, squash, beans, roast beef and mutton."[69] No ancient cliff dweller dined on beef or mutton; both

24.8. Virginia McClurg's "Pageant" in Spruce Tree House, Mesa Verde National Park, 1917. Courtesy of the Colorado Historical Society.

came to the Southwest with the Spanish. McClurg reported that several hundred spectators, "from near and far," were "most appreciative." The pageant set a precedent for similar spectacles presented in the 1920s by Aileen O'Bryan Nusbaum (see below).

After about 1915, the McClurgs divided their time between Colorado and Connecticut, active to the end in historical matters. Virginia McClurg died in 1932. The following year a collection of her poems (which she had selected) were published.[70] They are paeans of praise to the natural wonders of Colorado and the Rockies. Curiously, there is no mention of Cliff Dwellers.

Jesse Nusbaum and Mesa Verde

When Hans M. Randolph was appointed the first superintendent of Mesa Verde National Park in 1907, he set up headquarters in Mancos. A trail, and later a road, of sorts, was built up onto the mesa; no attempt was made to keep it open in winter. The first automobiles made the trip in 1913. Randolphe was succeeded by several superintendents who headquartered in Mancos and continued in the general relaxed manner that he had established. Usually their relatives ran

the concessions in the park, including young boys who "car-hopped" onto running boards and offered to guide tourists to the ruins for a fee or a tip. There were no signs directing visitors to the ruins.

Soon after Casa Grande National Monument was created, the Department of the Interior contracted with the Bureau of American Ethnology, through the Smithsonian, for work to stabilize, restore, and protect the site. Jesse Walter Fewkes took up the task. After the Mesa Verde park was created, Fewkes did similar work there in 1908–9, 1915–16, and 1919–22 on at least sixteen ruins.[71] Ruins restoration and stabilization were nascent arts, at best, and much of Fewkes's work, and his interpretations of specific ruins, were questioned by later restorers and archaeologists. But the ruins were stabilized to hopefully withstand the patter of tourist feet.

By 1920, there were serious problems on the Mesa Verde. Some superintendents and their relatives were looting ruins and treating the park as a personal fiefdom. In October 1920, Stephen Mather made an inspection tour and was appalled by what he saw. On the advice of several people, Mather recruited Jesse Nusbaum to become superintendent of Mesa Verde in May 1921. Mather faced down a U.S. senator from Colorado, L. C. Phipps, and made it clear that Nusbaum's and all future appointments in all National Park Service facilities would be made by him, not from the congressional pork barrel, although it didn't hurt that Nusbaum was a Colorado native.[72]

Jesse Nusbaum had first gone onto the Mesa Verde in 1907, with Kidder, Morley, and Fletcher. He worked there again in 1908, and in 1911 repaired and stabilized Balcony House, using funds provided by the Cliff Dwellings Association funneled through the Archaeological Institute of America to Hewett.[73] In

1920 Nusbaum married Aileen O'Bryan, who had a son, Deric, by a previous marriage. The new family was together with Frederick Webb Hodge at Hawikuh (see Fig. 24.6).

Jesse, Aileen, and Deric lived year-round on the mesa, not in Mancos. Nusbaum's management style was hands-on and blunt; he weathered numerous political attacks stirred up by disgruntled locals. He improved the road up the mesa to make it fully accessible to automobiles. Many of the programs and procedures he started—well-marked trails, uniformed ranger-guides, a visitor's center and museum, evening fireside lectures—became standard Park Service practice. He began a program of restoration and stabilization of additional ruins, in some cases quietly correcting obvious errors by Fewkes. In the winter, he conducted a research program:

24.9. John D. Rockefeller, Jr., party at Cliff Palace, Mesa Verde National Park, 1924. Photograph by Jesse Nusbaum. Courtesy of the Colorado Historical Society.

Our excavations here take place in the dead of winter as that is the only time when I am free . . . and it is the only time when we can count on snowbanks all over the park to supply us with water for camp purposes. . . . We only work in protected caves so snowfall never halts the work, once we are established on the ground. Our force is composed of . . . two rangers, my boy Deric, and three Navajo Indians I have trained for the work. The man who runs the pack and saddle business in the park is free in the winter, and I use him for packing, etc.[74]

Nusbaum also excavated in a variety of ruins between 1924 and 1928, including Step House Cave in which he demonstrated the presence of Basket Maker pit houses and associated artifacts.[75]

Nusbaum's winter program was supported by John D. Rockefeller, Jr. In 1924, Rockefeller and his three oldest sons, John III, Nelson, and Laurance, made an automobile tour of the Southwest, and of Yellowstone and Glacier national parks.[76] They were accompanied by Rockefeller employees Bert Mattison and R. W. Corwin, company physician for the Rockefeller-owned Colorado Fuel and Iron Company. Corwin was a Greeley, Colorado, native and longtime friend of Jesse Nusbaum; he was also on the managing committee of the School of American Research.

The Rockefeller party first visited Santa Fe, touring the Palace of the Governors and meeting briefly with Hewett, a meeting discussed in more detail in Chapter 29. They moved on to Taos and then Mesa Verde. The Nusbaums entertained them with personal tours of the ruins (Fig. 24.9), a steak fry, and a pageant.

The pageant (Fig. 24.10), written and staged by Aileen Nusbaum, "brought together in a scientific way a story of the ancient cliff dwellers, based on tradition, folklore, present-day sacred ceremonies, and archaeological facts." Aileen used the Navajo workmen from the park staff to play Cliff Dwellers; son Deric "was one of the two palefaces to take part— the two undersized corn maidens." The pageant was staged at night in Spruce Tree House, illuminated by red flares. The Rockefellers and other visitors were

The Rockefellers invited the Nusbaums to visit them in New York. The consequences of that visit are discussed in Chapter 29.

Aileen's son Deric lived a life that many young boys would envy—he had the run of the mesa and its ruins. He was schooled at home, hence stayed on the mesa year-round. He published two books by age fourteen, *Deric in Mesa Verde* and *Deric with the Indians,* issued by the major New York house of G. P. Putnam's Sons in a series for and by young authors. Aileen Nusbaum published a children's book, *The Seven Cities of Cibola,* retelling Zuni legends taken from Cushing's works. All three books were written during the long winters atop the mesa.[79] The Nusbaums were divorced in 1932. Deric O'Bryan went on to become a Rhodes scholar and earn a doctorate in archaeology from Cambridge University, working in the Southwest before and after World War II, before settling in England.[80]

Jesse Nusbaum got his museum built and continued as superintendent until 1928, when he went on leave to become director of the Laboratory of Anthropology in Santa Fe (see Chapter 29). He returned to Mesa Verde from 1936 to 1939 and again from 1942 to 1946. He was appointed by the Secretary of the Interior as Departmental Consulting Archaeologist in 1927, a position he held until he retired in 1956. That position became increasingly important after the reorganization of the National Park Service in 1933 and the passage of the federal Historic Sites Act in 1935,

seated on the opposite canyon rim, six hundred feet away; the acoustics were excellent, due to the bandshell shape of the ruin's alcove. In subsequent summers, Aileen Nusbaum's pageants became more complex, including a "Fire Ceremony," with a cast of forty, and an "Eagle Ceremony," of about equal size. Some ended with a curtain call "Yeibechei Ceremony" by the Navajo actors.[77]

Rockefeller was taken by the park and the Nusbaums. He donated two thousand dollars to match another five thousand dollars given by Stella M. Leviston, a frequent park visitor, to build a museum as well as providing support for Nusbaum's winter excavation program.[78] Rockefeller returned to Mesa Verde in 1926 with his wife, Abby, and their younger sons, Laurance, Winthrop, and David. They were again entertained by the Nusbaums, including a new pageant.

which gave the Park Service "lead agency" responsibilities in all phases of federal historic preservation, including archaeology.[81]

Jesse Nusbaum's counterpart as a highly capable, hands-on Park Service administrator was Frank Pinkley (1881–1940). Pinkley arrived in Phoenix in 1900, to get over a mild case of tuberculosis. In 1901 he became caretaker of Casa Grande. He lived in a tent on the site and managed to get a roof over the ruin. In 1906–8, he helped Jesse Walter Fewkes excavate and stabilize the ruin. In 1918 he became custodian of Casa Grande and Tumacacori, a Spanish mission south of Tucson. By 1924 he was superintendent of the Southwest National Monuments office in charge of fourteen monuments; when he retired in 1940, he was administering twenty-seven monuments in four states. In Pinkley's eyes, the monuments were always the stepchildren of the Park Service: they never received the staff nor funding they needed. Nonetheless, Pinkley ran his show with a gruff élan and a great deal of caring and is one of the legendary figures in the Park Service.[82]

Mesa Verde and the several national monuments played an important role in educating the public about Southwestern archaeology. Following Jesse Nusbaum's model, Mather and Albright turned Park Service personnel from caretakers to professionals concerned with proper preservation, and public interpretation and education.

CHAPTER 25

A. V. Kidder and
Southwestern Archaeology

IN 1924 A. V. Kidder pulled together all the results of the new Southwestern archaeology and relevant earlier work in a tour de force he modestly titled *An Introduction to the Study of Southwestern Archaeology*.[1] Therein he presented a summary of his excavations at Pecos Pueblo and what was known or conjectured about the archaeology of the San Juan, Rio Grande, Little Colorado, Upper Gila, Mimbres, and Lower Gila river basins and the internally draining Chihuahua Basin. The book, together with the 1927 Pecos Classification (see below), examined a number of assumptions and guiding ideas in Southwest culture history, including the Southwest-Mexican connection, Morgan's hypotheses of the San Juan Basin as a center from which cultures radiated into adjacent regions, and his postulated evolution of house types, as well as the uses of pottery and stratigraphy to construct relative chronologies. At the same time, Kidder's conclusions and the Pecos Classification set or stimulated

new research agendas pursued for the following three decades and longer.

The first Southwest inhabitants, Kidder thought, were hunter gatherers, "a more or less nomadic people, thinly scattered over the country, ignorant of agriculture and pottery making," living in a manner analogous to the ethnographic Great Basin peoples. They may have been Uto-Aztecan speakers. These "Basket Makers" learned to grow maize and "took up farming in a more or less haphazard way," in perhaps 1500 to 2000 B.C.E. Over time there were "fuller harvests." Surpluses led to an increased population and provided leisure time for the production of "elaborate sandals, fine basketry, and carefully made implements," but no pottery. "Such were the Basket Makers" who reached their highest level of development in the San Juan Basin.[2]

At a later time, the Basket Makers learned to make pottery, probably "from tribes to the south." They enlarged their storage cists into roofed semisubterranean pit houses. These "advances" characterize the "post-Basket Maker period." The people were the same, characterized physically by dolichocephalic skulls.[3]

The introduction of the bow and arrow and "particularly the practice of skull deformation," probably by a new "race" of round-headed folk, begins the "pre-Pueblo period." Kidder admits that the use of "hard bedded cradles," which deform infants' skulls, could have made brachycephalics of dolichocephalics. But his "feeling" is that "the pre-Pueblo [people] were actually of a different physical type, naturally brachycephalic . . . their broad-headedness . . . merely accentuated by deformation." He was following the advice of Hooton, who persisted in thinking that skull form was a biological indicator of "race." The notion that the round-headed Pueblo people were different from the long-headed Basketmakers was not laid to rest until a major restudy of numerous Southwestern skeletal remains from Hawikuh, Pecos, and elsewhere by Carl Seltzer, was published in 1944.[4]

This "new people, if such they were," occupied all of the San Juan Basin, and spilled out into the Little Colorado, Upper Rio Grande, and Upper Gila regions. They clustered in "more or less permanent settlements" of small above-ground houses, and made black-on-white pottery. They developed a "rudimentary type of kiva, a ceremonial survival of the . . . semi-subterranean dwelling of former days." The San Juan remained the center of cultural development.[5]

In the succeeding "early Pueblo period . . . little ruins of . . . coursed masonry or adobe, with closely grouped rectangular rooms . . . corrugated and black-on-white pottery" and proto-kivas are found widely across a huge area from northern Utah into and across much of Arizona and New Mexico. Here were Morgan and Bandelier's small-house ruins, and, "late in the period," Prudden's "unit pueblos." Villages were in open, unprotected locations. Again, the San Juan Basin was the probable center of origin. Kidder thought the spread was due to some increase in population, but mainly "a taking over of the culture by tribes who were already semi-agricultural, and there-

fore ready to embrace the manifest advantages of the new form of life." Who these "tribes" may have been is left unsaid.[6]

Perhaps these unknown tribes were among the "forces . . . [which subsequently] tended to break up this early wide-spread population, and concentrate it into more compact groups." Hewett and his colleagues in the joint School of American Archaeology-Bureau of American Ethnology project of a decade earlier saw the principal "force" of Southwest population movements and cultural waxings and wanings as climatic change, as did Ellsworth Huntington.[7] Kidder thought that climate change may have been a contributing factor, but favored "strife between the farmers and hunting tribes" of the Plains, Rockies, and Great Basin for food resources. He saw this not as a "great incursion of nomads," but probably at the scale of "a few bands working in here and there and adopting a semi-parasitic existence." Over time, this created a domino effect. "The nomad," having "sack[ed] . . . frontier settlements," had to push farther in to gratify his new tastes. Ruined farmers, too, their crops destroyed or stolen, might themselves have turned hunter-raiders and so increased the inward pressure. Wars between village and village . . . may have also occurred . . ."[8]

As the northern peripheral areas were abandoned, in the San Juan and Mesa Verde core, "unit-type villages began to bunch together . . . [in] somewhat larger aggregations." Ultimately, small towns were abandoned and people gathered in large communities "more or less isolated from each other." Thus the Pueblos were forced "into that very form of life which, by fostering communal effort, was to permit them to attain their highest achievements."[9] This was the "Great Period" when the Chacoan towns, the large cliff houses of Mesa Verde and Kayenta, and the Rio Grande and Little Colorado "compact pueblos" were formed. On the Lower Gila and in Chihuahua, there were the "casas grandes," built by an "amalgamation of Mexican Indians forced northward [for unspecified reasons], with Pueblos forced or strayed south."[10]

Kidder saw the Great Period as a culmination, a

time when "life was not too easy, not too hard . . . when opportunity and necessity were evenly balanced." Out of this came the "highest developments" in Pueblo "architecture, arts, and probably . . . in social and religious organization." But it didn't last. The "strongly fortified" later Great Period sites, and the Hovenweep watch towers testify to the "hard fight" the Pueblos made of it before the Chaco, Mesa Verde, and Kayenta regions were abandoned.[11] When was the abandonment? "Toltecan" pottery was found at Pueblo Bonito. In a 1922 summary of Mesoamerican archaeology, Herbert Spinden placed the end of the Toltec empire at 1070 B.C.E.; hence Kidder concluded that the abandonment of Chaco began before or about 1100. The Upper and Lower Gila drainage and the Chihuahua Basin were abandoned later, due to "pressure by nomads."[12]

Although chary of attributing "any great degree of historical accuracy [to] the Hopi and Zuni clan migration stories," Kidder thought they correlated with a new amalgamation of "increments of population" from north and south into the large, late pueblos "in and near [the Hopi-Zuni] center," and along the Rio Grande, by a process of "infiltration rather than migration." New pottery styles, especially Kidder's beloved Glaze and Biscuit wares, appeared sometime between the end of Chaco and the advent of the Spanish. Finally, by 1540 there was yet another "shrinkage," due to unspecified causes, into the sixty or seventy historic Rio Grande pueblos and those of Acoma, Zuni and Hopi.[13]

The First Pecos Conference

Kidder wrote most of his archaeological summary in 1922. He continued work at Pecos in subsequent years, and there was the concurrent surge of research in other sites and regions previously noted. Kidder was not happy with his sequence of chronological names for the Basket Makers and Pueblos. Although the "pottery bacillus" was now nearly pandemic, there was no agreed-upon pottery typology nor any system of naming types. By 1927 he felt a general conclave

was in order. Neil Judd had held several small "field conferences" at his Chaco Canyon camp in 1921, 1923, and 1925, where a few knowledgeable individuals had gathered to discuss specific issues, such as the origins of Southwestern agriculture. The agriculture conference included agronomists F. A. Thackery and C. S. Schofield and photographer William Henry Jackson, making his first visit to Chaco Canyon since 1875 (see Fig. 24.3).[14]

Kidder adopted the field-conference idea, but envisioned a larger group. He sent out letters and postcards inviting people to come to Pecos, camp with him and Madeleine, and talk over a number of issues. Most letters said he had been discussing "Southwestern matters" with Earl Morris, Neil Judd, and Frank Roberts. They agreed it was time to "arrive at an understanding in regard to the underlying problems, the methods of accumulating and presenting data, and (last, but in some ways most important) a standardized nomenclature for artifacts, decorative motifs, and periods of culture."[15]

There were about forty participants (Fig. 25.1). Table 5 lists those discussed herein.

The conference began on August 29, 1927. The day before, Kidder, Chapman, Morley, and Judd met in Santa Fe and incorporated the Laboratory of Anthropology (see Chapter 29). Now they turned to the issues outlined in Kidder's letters. The end result was the "Pecos Classification," a congeries of levels loosely based on house forms and pottery types ordered into eight relative time units.

In 1948 Kidder credited T. T. Waterman—last encountered recently married and living happily in Berkeley on eighty-three dollars a month (see Chapter 18)—with creating the classification.[16] Waterman's circumstances had improved somewhat over the years. At Berkeley he had taken courses and done fieldwork with Pliny Earle Goddard, which convinced him to switch from studying for the ministry to anthropology (perhaps Goddard served as a role model through his own switch from missionizing to linguistics). Thomas Talbot Waterman took his Ph.D. from Columbia under Boas in 1913, then knocked around the

25.1. Pecos Conference 1927. Courtesy of the Museum of New Mexico Photographic Archives.

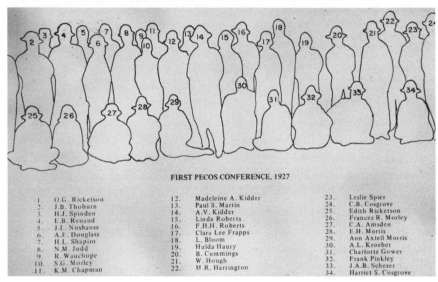

FIRST PECOS CONFERENCE, 1927

1.	O.G. Ricketson	12.	Madeleine A. Kidder	23.	Leslie Spier
2.	J.B. Thoburn	13.	Paul S. Martin	24.	C.B. Cosgrove
3.	H.J. Spinden	14.	A.V. Kidder	25.	Edith Ricketson
4.	E.B. Renaud	15.	Linda Roberts	26.	Frances R. Morley
5.	J.L. Nusbaum	16.	F.H.H. Roberts	27.	C.A. Amsden
6.	A.E. Douglass	17.	Clara Lee Frapps	28.	E.H. Morris
7.	H.L. Shapiro	18.	L. Bloom	29.	Ann Axtell Morris
8.	N.M. Judd	19.	Hulda Haury	30.	A.L. Kroeber
9.	R. Wauchope	20.	B. Cummings	31.	Charlotte Gower
10.	S.G. Morley	21.	W. Hough	32.	Frank Pinkley
11.	K.M. Chapman	22.	M.R. Harrington	33.	J.A.B. Scherer
				34.	Harriet S. Cosgrove

Table 5   Participants in 1927 Pecos Conference

"Active Southwesternists":
Kenneth M. Chapman, Harold S. Colton and Mary-Russell Ferrell Colton, C. Burton Cosgrove and Harriet S. Cosgrove, Byron Cummings, Andrew E. Douglass, Mark R. Harrington, Edgar L. Hewett, Walter Hough, Neil Judd, Alfred V. Kidder and Madeleine Kidder, Ann Axtell Morris and Earl H. Morris, Jesse Nusbaum, Frank Pinkley, Etienne B. Renaud, Frank H. H. Roberts, Jr., and Linda B. Roberts.

"Other Interests":
Lancing B. Bloom, Erna Gunther (Spier), Alfred L. Kroeber, Frances R. Morley and Sylvanus G. Morley, Edith Bayles Ricketson and Oliver G. Ricketson, Jr., Leslie Spier, Herbert J. Spinden, and Thomas T. Waterman.

"Students":
Clara Lee Fraps (Tanner), Emil W. Haury, Hulda Penner (Haury), Paul S. Martin, Robert Wauchope.[17]

Table 6   The Pecos Classification

Basket Maker I, or Early Basket Maker—a postulated (and perhaps recently discovered) stage, preagricultural yet adumbrating later developments.

Basket Maker II, or Basket Maker—the agricultural, atlatl-using, non-pottery making stage . . .

Late Basket Maker, Basket Maker III, or Post-Basket Maker—the pit- or slab-house-building, pottery-making stage; [all] Basket Maker stages are characterized by long-headed population . . .

Pueblo I, or Proto-Pueblo—the first stage during which cranial deformation was practiced, vessel neck corrugation was introduced, and villages composed of rectangular living rooms of true masonry were developed . . .

Pueblo II—the stage marked by widespread geographical extension of life in small villages; . . . [elaborate corrugated decoration of] cooking vessels . . .

Pueblo III, or Great Period—the stage of large communities, great development of the arts, and growth of intensive local specialization.

Pueblo IV, or Proto-Historic—the stage characterized by contraction of area occupied; by the gradual disappearance of corrugated wares; and, in general, by decline from the preceding cultural peak.

Pueblo V, or Historic—the period from 1600 A.D. to the present.

---

university and museum world, holding various positions. He was visiting professor at the University of Arizona in 1927–28. He was widely known as a brilliant and incisive thinker with a broad knowledge of anthropology, who "loved concrete facts and sharply defined findings."[18]

The Pecos Classification was in fact a committee effort involving many compromises (Table 6), based on Kidder's system from 1924.[19]

As in any gathering of academic and museum people, there was much diversity of opinion about the utility and applicability of the classification (college administrators often say that getting academics to agree on anything is like herding cats). Nonetheless, the classification was a major accomplishment of the new archaeology. Its architects regarded it as provisional, subject to modification and change.

In 1929, Waterman, who had finally settled at the University of Hawaii, published "Culture Horizons in the Southwest" as a lead article in the *American Anthropologist*. Therein, his "love of concrete facts and sharply defined findings" and his impatience with sloppy research and thinking was clearly evident in a carefully reasoned, yet jocular and satirical, analysis of

archaeological classifications and opinions about intraregional differences and Southwest-Mexican connections by Cushing, Morris, Kidder, Fewkes, Prudden, Mindeleff, and others. He pointed out that all the authors, but especially Fewkes and Cushing, often contradict themselves, sometimes in the same article or monograph. He tried to impose order on the perceived chaos by suggesting a sequence of thirteen cultural "horizons," based on house forms and pottery types. But the horizons were to be seen only as heuristic devices; indeed "these horizons do not really exist. Most horizons merge into adjacent horizons" when the archaeological materials are closely examined. But that's okay. "Investigators may never agree upon names for these horizons. Meanwhile the terms in common use seem remarkably awkward, and those worked out at the Pecos conference no better. The names selected, whatever they may be, are of little moment as long as one of us knows what the others of us mean."[20] The "knowing" was the crux of the matter. Archaeologists would spend all of the 1930s and 1940s trying to sort out what each other meant in their various classificatory schemes (see the Epilogue). Meanwhile, the Pecos Classification took on canonical status, even though no one seemingly liked it. As for Waterman, he was widely ignored. Frank H. H. Roberts, Jr., in a major summary of Southwestern archeology in 1935, also a lead article in the *American Anthropologist,* does not mention him.[21]

Kidder sent a telegram to Jesse Walter Fewkes informing him of the conference deliberations and expressing the good wishes of all attendees. Kidder and Fewkes had maintained a frequent and cordial correspondence since they met at Mesa Verde in about 1915. Fewkes was regarded by Kidder's New Archaeology compatriots as the archetypical "Old Archaeology" practitioner for his disregard of stratigraphy and his refusal to adopt their system of pottery classification. Fewkes was in Washington confined to bed by the infirmities of age, and was unable to reply until two weeks after the conference:

> A conference in the Southwest by archaeologists from different institutions is to my mind one of the most important indications of the most novel school of American archaeology. . . . The fundamental ideas now underlying the determination of our Southwest ruins by stratigraphy is one that this generation of young archaeologists is better able to decide than any other, and the eyes of all the older school are looking at the work to be accomplished by this conference. May it act wisely and well, not only to shed light on this direction of research in the determining of time but likewise on similar questions upon which the chronology of the Southwest depends.[22]

The wand was passed. The "old school" archaeology had ordained the "new" archaeology as the establishment archaeology. It would remain so until challenged by yet another "new archaeology" in the 1960s. But that's another story.[23]

The Second Pecos Conference

Kidder hosted the second Pecos Conference in August 1929. By then the dendrochronology "Gap" had been closed and most of the discussion centered on the chronological implications and rewriting of culture history required by the new-found ability to link the chronology to Newton's time scale. A second and major discussion centered on whether or not the classification developed in 1927 really "fit," or even made sense, when applied to the ruins in the Mogollon Rim country, the Lower Gila River Basin, and the Basin and Range country of southeastern New Mexico, especially the region drained by the Mimbres River.[24]

There was also the excitement of looking at the first-ever aerial photographs of Pecos, Chaco Canyon, the Hopi country, Canyon de Chelly, and the Pajarito Plateau. The potential of aerial photography for archaeology had been recognized in Europe during World War I and began to be widely used in the 1920s. Early in 1929, Charles Lindbergh had observed Maya ruins during his flights across the Yucatán Peninsula for Pan American Airways. He contacted the Carnegie Institution, Kidder's new employer, about the potential for aerial exploration of the Yucatán. Kidder arranged for a test in the Southwest. Charles and Ann Morrow Lindbergh landed on a "more or less cleared bit of brush land" near Pecos, to the great delight of the Kidder children. They stayed overnight, and the next day flew off to take photographs. In October 1929, Kidder and the Lindberghs did make an aerial reconnaissance of numerous Maya ruins.[25]

Soon after the conference ended, the Kidders left Pecos for the last time, ending a fifteen-year involvement with the ruin and a twenty-plus-year involvement with the Southwest. In that time A. V. Kidder had become a national leader of the New Archaeology. He published major reports on Pecos between 1936 and 1958, but there was never a major final synthesis.[26] His new and very demanding job interfered: for the next two decades, he would direct the Division of Historical Research of the Carnegie Institution of Washington. Programs he initiated in 1929–31 led to the development of modern studies of Maya ethnography and acculturation, especially Robert Redfield's famous *Folk Culture of Yucatán,* and, ultimately, to the decipherment of the Maya glyphs, to which Morley devoted his professional life.[27] Kidder used the resources of the Carnegie to further archaeological involvement with the "ceramic bacillus" by supporting the research over many years of Anna O. Shepard in the intricacies of ceramic technology.[28] He also arranged for the Institution to support Earl Morris's work in the Southwest. Ted Kidder died in 1963, the acknowledged dean of Americanist archaeology. Soon after, the Kidder Medal was created. It is awarded periodically by the American Anthropological Association to individuals who, like Kidder, have made major contributions to the field.

Origins, Once Again

One central theme of this book is the origin and antiquity of humans in the Americas. The origins question arose by 1500 C.E. (see the Introduction). Prior to acceptance of the idea of "deep time"—that the earth is far older than Ussher's chronology—most writers, such as Albert Gallatin, argued for a long, if unspecified time for the advent of humans in the Western Hemisphere. By the 1890s both the origins and antiquity issues became tangled in typological debates, such as Charles Abbott's purported paleoliths, and arguments over geological contexts of artifacts and purportedly ancient skeletal remains. William Henry Holmes battled for decades against Abbott's paleoliths, and he and Aleš Hrdlička rejected any and all claims of great antiquity for humans in the Western Hemisphere based on less than incontrovertible evidence. Holmes occasionally became somewhat manic about the issue.[29]

But in 1924, in a cutbank of Lone Wolf Creek near Colorado City in west-central Texas, the articulated bones of an extinct form of bison were found seven feet below the ground surface. Paleontologist Harold L. Cook encased the matrix containing the bones in plaster-soaked burlap (a standard paleontological procedure) and took the material to his laboratory. As the matrix was being cleaned away, two whole and one partial projectile points were found with the bones.[30] In early 1926, as the story goes, a cowboy riding down an arroyo near Folsom, New Mexico, noticed some large bones eroding from the arroyo wall. Word got to J. D. Figgins, a paleontologist at the Denver Museum of Natural History, who came to investigate, accompanied by Cook. They found beautifully crafted projectile points in immediate association with the bones of an extinct form of bison.[31] Also in 1926, children from the Double Adobe school in Cochise County, thirteen miles northwest of Douglas, Arizona, found fossil ivory protruding from a cutbank of nearby Whitewater Draw. Word got to Byron Cummings at the University of Arizona, who brought his students, Lyndon Hargrave and Emil Haury, to investigate.[32] They found a partial mammoth skull in a marl deposit in the arroyo wall. Under the marl was a sandy layer containing fossil bison and horse bones and stone-grinding tools similar to those used historically to process seeds and bulbs. Cummings made a brief report published in the *Tombstone Epitaph,* and went on to other things.[33]

Figgins and Cook notified various scientists, who were skeptical. Figgins went back to Folsom in 1927 (Fig. 25.2) and found a projectile point in undoubted association with the bison bones. He stopped work and sent telegrams to the Smithsonian, the American Museum, and other eastern institutions. The Smithsonian telegraphed Frank Roberts at the Pecos Conference and instructed him to investigate. He did so, and was joined by A. V. Kidder and by Barnum Brown from the American Museum of Natural History. They concurred with Figgins: there was no doubt of the association of the point with the bones—bones of an extinct form of bison of late Pleistocene age.[34] Geological studies in Europe had placed the end of the last Ice Age at around ten thousand years ago, and paleontological evidence in both hemispheres indicated a major die-off (from unknown causes) of large Ice Age mammals at about the same time. Within a three year span, 1925–27, archaeological and geological evidence was discovered in the Southwest and seen as

*25.2. "Site of the Latest Artifact and Bison Association, Folsom, New Mexico"; J. D. Figgins
(right). Courtesy of the Peabody Museum, Harvard University.*

evidence of humans being in the Americas for ten millennia, possibly more. After four centuries of speculation, there was suddenly a plausible deep time frame for humans in the Americas. The search for "early man" became a major project in the Southwest and elsewhere during the following decades, reframing the origins issue in new ways (see the Epilogue).

CHAPTER 26

Ethnography in the Southwest

Prelude

Modern ethnographic fieldwork in the Southwest began when Frank Hamilton Cushing rode his mule into Zuni Pueblo on September 18, 1879 (see Chapter 7). By 1900 Cushing and Stevenson at Zuni, Stevenson at Zia, Bandelier at Cochiti, Voth and Fewkes at Hopi, Matthews with the Navajo, and Bourke with the Apache had collected and published much useful information, but many groups were totally unstudied, and there was not a "full" ethnography of any pueblo or tribe. W J McGee had bumbled through two disastrous trips to the Seri in 1894 and 1895, during which he managed less than a week of ethnographic work. Undeterred, he produced 330 pages of bluster, signifying little.[1]

A potential bright new star appeared in 1898 in the person of Frank Russell (1868–1903). He had graduated in 1892 from the University of Iowa, joined a natural history expedition to northwestern Canada, and spent much of the next three years collecting natural history specimens and ethnographic artifacts. He entered Harvard in 1895 to study anthropology with Putnam, and received a Ph.D. in 1898. That summer he was at Dulce, New Mexico, with the Jicarilla Apache; here, he compiled an extensive dictionary and collected the only known data on Jicarilla ethnobotany. He apparently then moved on to the Pima, returning there in 1899 (Fig. 26.2).[2]

Russell married Frances Theresa Peet (1873–1936) in June, 1900 (Fig. 26.1). Their honeymoon trip was by train from Iowa to Gallup, New Mexico, and then by horse and wagon (with the first thirty miles to St. Michaels Mission by bicycle!) to Keams Canyon, Ganado, Awatovi, the Hopi Mesas, and the Little Colorado River to conduct an extensive archaeological survey.[3]

In April 1901, Russell was hired by Powell and McGee at the Bureau of American Ethnology. They managed this by furloughing Matilda Stevenson and using

26.1. *Frances Theresa Russell, ca. 1915. Courtesy of Stanford University Libraries Special Collections.*

26.2. *Frank Russell on Pima Indian Reservation, Arizona, 1901 or 1902. Photograph by Frances Theresa Russell. Courtesy of Stanford University Libraries Special Collections.*

her salary for Russell. It was a serious mistake, as they learned (see Chapter 12). The Russells went back to Arizona for an archaeological survey and to work with the Pima from November 1901 through June 1902. Back in Washington, Frank Russell completed what is still the basic ethnography of the Pima. He also established the term *Hohokam* in Southwestern archaeology: "Hohokam, 'That which has perished,' is used by the Pimas to designate the race [*sic*] that occupied the pueblos that are now rounded heaps of ruins in the Salt and Gila river valleys."[4]

Unfortunately, Russell had contracted tuberculosis. He died in Kingman, Arizona, in November 1903.[5] Theresa had graduated from Iowa University in 1895 and studied at Radcliffe in 1898–99. In 1906 she went to Stanford University as a graduate student in philosophy, but remained as an instructor of English. She received a Ph.D. from Columbia University

in 1920 and became a well-known professor of English at Stanford, the author of many poems, and numerous books and articles on nineteenth-century literature. She died in 1936.[6]

Barbara Freire-Marreco (1879–1967) was the first English woman anthropologist. In 1908, she and two men received the first anthropology degrees awarded by Oxford University. She attended Hewett's Frijoles Canyon field school in 1910 and did ethnobiology work with J. P. Harrington (see Chapter 22). She worked at Santa Clara and Hano for varying intervals between 1910 and 1913, and with the Yavapai in 1913. In England, after 1913, she lectured at the London School of Economics, did fieldwork in Spain and edited *Notes and Queries in Anthropology,* the standard British field guide. Her papers on Southwestern ethnography were useful additions on which others built.[7]

Edward S. Curtis:
Imaging the "Vanishing Indian"

If Russell and Freire-Marreco can be said to represent scientific ethnography, as it was understood in 1900, the photographer/ethnographer Edward Sheriff Curtis (1868–1952) represents arch-romanticism. Moving to the Puget Sound area as a young man, he started a photography business in Seattle and was soon making photographs of local Indian people.[8] In 1898, on Mt. Rainier he rescued a lost climbing party: C. Hart Merriam, chief of the U.S. Biological Survey; George Bird Grinnell, editor of *Field and Stream* magazine and an expert on Plains Indians; and Gifford Pinchot, later head of the U.S. Forest Service. They were most grateful and became his mentors and sponsors.

In 1899, Merriam and Grinnell arranged for Curtis to become the photographer for an Alaskan expedition. Edward H. Harriman, president of the Union Pacific Railroad, funded a large-scale multidisciplinary study cruise along the Alaskan coast in the summer of 1899. Curtis's photographs illustrated the thirteen volumes of published data.[9]

Grinnell urged Curtis to continue photographing Indian people "before they vanished." Through Grinnell and Harriman, Curtis was invited to photograph Theodore Roosevelt's children in New York; Roosevelt became a patron. In 1905, Curtis exhibited his work in Washington and New York City and received much publicity. Encouraged by his high-powered patrons, Curtis formulated a grandiose "life's work": a photographic *and* textual documentation of *all* the "vanishing Indians" of the United States and Alaska. In January 1906, he met with J. Pierpont Morgan, who made him a deal. Morgan would provide fifteen thousand dollars a year for five years and underwrite publication of the results. There would be a grand set of twenty volumes of illustrated text and twenty folios of photographs in five hundred sets, published at three thousand dollars each. Curtis would have to raise additional monies as needed elsewhere. Frederick Webb Hodge agreed to edit the series.

With Morgan's first fifteen thousand dollars in hand, Curtis formed a traveling ethnographic team, including W. E. Myers, a newspaper reporter who apparently had a good ear for Indian languages. They began with the San Carlos Apache in June 1906, soon moving on to Canyon de Chelly and the Navajo. By August they were at Hopi for a Snake Dance, then surveyed the Pima, Papago, Mohave, and Walapai. They then "retired to obscure rooms," a cabin on Puget Sound, and worked on manuscripts seventeen hours a day, seven days a week. The photographs were developed and printed in Curtis's Seattle studio. By February 1907 the first two volumes of manuscript and prints were finished and sent off to the printers.

Curtis and his team continued this pattern of intense, hit-and-run fieldwork and marathon writing bouts for the next twenty-four years. Curtis's obsession with the project ended his marriage in 1920. The twenty-volume set of *The North American Indian,* when finally completed, probably cost the Morgan family over 400,000 dollars; the total cost was somewhere between 800,000 dollars and 1 million dollars. Only 291 of the planned 500 sets were actually distributed.[10]

Curtis died in Hollywood in 1952, essentially forgotten. His magnificently printed *The North American Indian,* infrequently consulted, reposed quietly in library rare-book rooms. But after 1964, a biographical film and books and exhibits of his work began to appear, and his Indian photographs (Fig. 26.3) began to command increasingly larger prices.[11]

Curtis in the Southwest

Curtis's work is a classic example of the vanishing savage syndrome. Theodore Roosevelt's foreword to the first volume reiterates the centuries-old theme: "Our generation offers the last chance for doing what Mr. Curtis has done. The Indian as he has hitherto been is on the point of passing away. . . . It would be a veritable calamity if a vivid and truthful record of these conditions were not kept. . . ." Curtis said he wanted to produce such a record of all the tribes "that still retain to a considerable degree their primitive customs

26.3. "Canyon de Chelly, Navajo"; photograph by Edward S. Curtis. Don Fowler collection.

and traditions. . . . the Indians as a race, already shorn of their tribal strength and stripped of their primitive dress, are passing into the darkness of an unknown future."[12]

Curtis used his photographic skills to create romantic images of what he thought Indians *should have been like* before they started to vanish. He retouched photographs to remove objects of Anglo manufacture, including wagons, parasols, hats, clocks, suspenders, and product labels. He added pots, or other "Indian" objects. He carried Indian clothing from tribe to tribe, to "properly" dress his subjects "as Indians," if need be.[13] He used soft focus, lighting, and the sepia tones

of the plates to give a mood of romanticism to his subjects.

In 1904, Curtis shot both still photographs and motion pictures of a Navajo "Yabichei dance," part of the Night Chant. A Seattle newspaper reported:

Ed. Curtis makes photographs of secret rites of Navajoes. Scientists from Smithsonian Institution said this could not be done. . . . [But Curtis accomplished] that which Uncle Sam, with all his power and authority, had tried for two decades to do and failed. . . . In addition to individual pictures of the masked dancers . . . Curtis brought back a "moving picture" of the dance itself . . . [which] will convey to the onlooker the exact and lifelike picture of a dance that, *in its reality*, had never been seen by the light of day, or had been looked upon by the eyes of a white man.[14]

The dance was, in fact, staged with the aid of Sam and Charlie Day, Anglo traders at Chinle, Arizona. With the Days' help, Curtis convinced three Navajo men to hide out in a "closed room over Charlie's store," where Curtis made the Yeibichei masks under their direction. Fourteen men were then recruited to perform the "dance" in a secluded ravine, while Curtis's cameras whirred and clicked. Among the masked participants, as Fringed Mouth God and Humpbacked God, were Charlie and Sam Day.[15] Knowledgeable Navajos who have seen the movie footage suggest that the performers were not very familiar with the dance, and danced it clumsily and *backwards,* perhaps to secularize it. It seems that the film was, in fact, *printed* backwards (the dancing, nonetheless, was clumsy).[16]

Curtis's written description of the ceremony is an unacknowledged paraphrase of Washington Matthews's *Night Chant* of 1902. The Night Chant myth was dictated to Curtis by Charlie Day. While Curtis does not claim that he or his team ever saw an *actual* Night Chant ceremony, the tone of the writing *implies* firsthand observation of a "real" ceremony. Thus, Curtis's oft-repeated claim that he recorded *authentic, traditional Indian ways* becomes more than problematic.[17]

Curtis also filmed a Hopi Snake Dance at Oraibi in 1904. He later claimed that in either 1906 or 1912 (sources vary) he participated in an Oraibi Snake Dance after being "initiated into the Snake Order as a priest," for a "full sixteen days of the ceremony." This included gathering the snakes, and dancing "dressed in a G-string and snake dance costume and with the regulation snake in my mouth . . . while spectators witnessed the dance and did not know that a white man was one of the wild dancers."[18] It is highly unlikely that this ever happened.

When the first volumes appeared in 1907, they were criticized by Franz Boas and other anthropologists. Theodore Roosevelt appointed a committee of inquiry consisting of Henry Fairfield Osborn, William Henry Holmes, and Charles D. Walcott. Curtis submitted his notes and wax cylinders of recorded music. The committee signed a letter endorsing and praising Curtis's work. So much for ethnographic veracity, Boas style.[19]

Some, at least, of the 291 twenty-volume sets and 20 accompanying folios of *The North American Indian* remain intact in research libraries, the texts largely unread. Other sets have been torn apart, their photographic plates sold and resold for increasingly higher prices, as have "original" Curtis prints made by his studio to generate income to keep the project afloat. In his photographs, captions, and texts, Curtis is the epitome of the yearner, earnestly questing after, by creating, an imagined "authentic reality" of the ever-vanishing savage (see Fig. 26.3).

Elsie Clews Parsons and Southwestern Anthropology

Boasian-style ethnography flourished in the Southwest between about 1918 and 1940, driven by the quiet determination—and checkbook—of Elsie Clews Parsons (1875–1941). Her own scholarly contributions to both ethnography and folklore studies during that time were enormous.[20]

Elsie Clews was born in 1874 in New York City, the daughter of an English emigrant banker, Henry Clews, who made his fortune in the Civil War, and Lucy Madison Worthington, a socialite from a Southern family ruined by the war. Elsie grew up as a "rebel," to her mother's never-ending despair. She hated white gloves and veils, paying meaningless social calls, shopping in Paris, and all the false bother of being "a lady." The family summer home in Newport, Rhode Island, afforded her the pleasures of riding and sailing, which she loved. Winter and summer she kept to a regular regime of studying a great variety of subjects on her own. She entered Barnard College in 1892. She went on to earn a Ph.D. in sociology in 1899 at Columbia University; Franz Boas served on her doctoral oral examination committee.[21] As in Chicago, New York sociologists plunged into the "settlement movement." Young, educated middle- and upper-class Anglo idealists, most of them women, moved into the immigrant ghettos and working-class neighborhoods of American cities to effect positive social change and "furnish a common meeting ground for all classes for their mutual benefit and education."[22]

These individuals were also in the forefront of a new feminism, which by 1900 had a much more sweeping agenda than the earlier suffragettes—nothing less than de facto gender equity and equality in all areas of life, including sex and marriage.[23] Elsie Clews became an acknowledged spokesperson for this movement. She married Herbert Parsons in 1900 in an agreed-upon "experimental marriage" based on their mutual ideals of gender equity and personal equality. In 1902, Herbert was elected to Congress, serving three terms before returning to New York to become a highly successful attorney.

Their experimental marriage survived, despite numerous tribulations, primarily because of their basic honesty and respect for one another. By about 1913 they had worked out an arrangement to jointly care for their four children and live together for parts of the year, but with both free to have other relationships. This enabled Elsie to travel widely, often with a companion-lover. For several years her companion was Christopher Grant La Farge, a prominent architect and artist, and father of Oliver La Farge (see Chapter 28).

In the years 1900–16, Parsons became a well-known critic of American mores and social forms. Her incisive books and articles on the family, chastity, social freedom, and women and sex were ethnographies of her own "tribe"—upper-class eastern Anglos—with comparative data from other cultures to highlight important points. *The Old Fashioned Woman: Primitive Fancies about Sex* was particularly reviled, and appreciated. In it, Parsons used ethnographic data from around the world in "an extended feminist joke," a satire on Anglos' assumptions about "woman."[24]

Parsons first visited the Southwest in 1910. She met Clara True (Matilda Coxe Stevenson's nemesis) who invited her to stay at her ranch. With a Santa Clara guide, Parsons rode onto the Pajarito Plateau. She was hooked; the mix of Anglo, Hispanic, and Indian cultures intrigued her.

In New York, Parsons visited the American Museum of Natural History where she met Clark Wissler and Pliny Earl Goddard. Goddard introduced her to a group of Franz Boas's students—particularly Robert Lowie, Alexander Goldenweiser, and Paul Radin. The "Boasians" encouraged her to work in the Southwest. She also met Mabel Dodge, holding court at her salon near Greenwich Village, and the two became close and lifelong friends.

The years 1910–15 were heady times for Greenwich Village bohemianism and social activism. At Mabel Dodge's "evenings," Parsons met Emma Goldman, "Big Bill" Heywood, Sigmund Freud, Lincoln Steffens, John Reed (Dodge's lover before his ill-fated trip to Russia), Max Eastman, Walter Lippmann, and numerous other artists, journalists, anthropologists, social activists, feminists, socialists, and anarchists— "movers and shakers," as Mabel called them,—who mingled and talked the good talk.[25] They were consciously attempting the creation of the "modern" world, as they dreamed it.

It was to be a world of liberalism, tolerance, rationality, social and sexual equality, universal civil rights and suffrage, and personal freedom. Then came World War I and with it heightened racism, war hysteria, the abridgment of civil rights and liberties, the suppression of dissent and academic freedom in universities, the demonization of German-Americans into "Huns," and the rattling of sabers by superpatriots humming George M. Cohan's "Over There."[26] Some liberals fought back, but were silenced or jailed. Parsons adopted a strict pacifism in articles such as "War and the Elders" and "Ideal-Less Pacifism," and was shunned or ridiculed by most members of her Anglo "tribe."[27] She retreated into the rationality of anthropological science and humanistic folklore, as she defined them, and remained there for the rest of her life.

Anthropology in New York City

By 1918–19 Parsons was aware that anthropology, as practiced by the Boasians, was in danger. At the American Museum, Archer Huntington had begun to lose interest in funding the Southwest project. There were few other sources of funds. Never a fan of anthropology, Henry Fairfield Osborn used the tight times as an excuse to trim Clark Wissler's staff. On January 28, 1920, Wissler was given the Department of Anthropology's budget for the calendar year 1920, listing his salary at 5,000 dollars, Pliny Goddard's at 4,800 dollars, Robert Lowie's at 3,000 dollars, and Herbert Spinden's and Nels Nelson's at 2,750 dollars each. Three days later, he received letters from Museum Director F. A. Lucas stating that "in view of financial conditions," Lowie and Spinden would be terminated, as would Talbot Hyde, who had been paid 1,800 dollars per year for "special services."[28] Leslie Spier had already been put on notice and was shown in the budget for only three months. Spinden had not published much of anything, and his garrulous and antiauthoritarian behavior irritated Osborn. Lowie had made major collections in the Great Plains and published a good deal, but was viewed as a radical for his popular articles opposing the racialist ideas of Osborn and his associate Madison Grant, author of *The Passing of the Great Race*. Lowie, like Parsons, used ethnographic data from other cultures to attack and ridicule these ideas.[29] Lowie taught for a year the New School of Social Research (see below) until Kroeber managed to hire him at the University of California, where he remained for nearly four decades. Spier finished up his Havasupai fieldwork, supported by Parsons, and took a position at the University of Washington. Spinden moved to the Harvard Peabody Museum until 1926; to the Buffalo, New York, Museum until 1929; and then to the Brooklyn Museum until his retirement in 1951.

Parsons thought that one way to help anthropology was to make it better known to the general public. To this end, she supported and began teaching at the Free School for Political Science, later called the New School for Social Research, which opened in 1919. The school grew out of the dissatisfactions of prominent feminists, educators, and others with the suppression of intellectual freedom, especially in Columbia University, both before and during the world war. Caroline Bacon, a former professor at Smith College, Emily Putnam, a dean at Barnard, and James Harvey Robinson, Charles Beard, John Dewey, Parsons, and others planned a cooperative school and research institute for adults, with no formal curricula or degrees. The founding faculty included economists Wesley Mitchell and Thorstein Veblen, political scientist Harold Laski, and, thanks to Parsons's influence and funds, anthropologist Alexander Goldenweiser, who had been fired from Columbia. "Goldy," always in trouble over women, money, and "radical ideas," was the intellectual star of the Boasian group. He came from a well-to-do Russian Jewish immigrant family, and was "by nature and nurture . . . a cosmopolitan citizen of the world of letters and scholarship that encompassed many fields and extended far beyond the bounds of his specialty." The Free School/New School was his kind of milieu, quickly becoming, as Margaret Mead put it, a place "in a ferment of ideas taught by brilliant people."[30] Parsons taught a course during the school's first year; one of her students was Ruth Benedict (see below).

Parsons tried to popularize anthropology in other ways. This led to her *American Indian Life* project in 1921–22. She asked twenty-seven anthropologists to write short stories from the perspective of an individual within a culture they knew well. The idea was to show the common humanity of Indians and Anglos, yet point out why people in different cultures do things differently. The project provoked joking and protest from the participants, but cajoled by Parsons, they proceeded. The elaborate book appeared in 1922, complete with drawings by Grant La Farge.[31] The stories by Pliny Goddard about an Apache girl, by Leslie Spier about a Havasupai boy, and by Alfred Kroeber about a Mohave boy are told very much from the insider's perspective that Parsons wanted. Her own story about the life cycle of a Zuni woman is told from Parsons's perspective, not the woman's, and fails to do what she wanted the stories to do. Fortunately, her colleagues did as she said, not as she did. The book was widely and favorably reviewed.[32]

Parsons's Research Agenda and the Southwest Society

In early 1918, Parsons proposed to Clark Wissler a "plan of cooperative work and a general research program" for Southwestern ethnography and linguistics. She foresaw an encyclopedia of cultures to be developed over several years with individual scholars being given definite assignments. Their work was to be financed "privately or by the institution to which they are already attached."[33] Wissler encouraged the idea, but had no financial assistance to offer. He hoped that Parsons would "take up the question of ritualistic pattern among the Pueblos, beginning with . . . Zunis and gradually extend your studies to a comparative view of ritualism in the Southwest."[34] She did so.

Parsons handled the private funding by creating the Southwest Society, which was talked into existence at a luncheon of New York anthropologists. On December 9, 1918, a formal constitution was adopted, with Pliny Goddard as director and Parsons as secretary-treasurer. Parsons had "high hopes . . . [for] cooperation in Southwestern research." She saw the society as "something of a syndicalist experiment in the research workers running their own machinery and controlling their own funds."[35]

The society ledger book in Parsons's papers shows that for 1918, Goddard, Hodge, Talbot Hyde, Nelson, Lowie, Wissler, Fewkes, Culin, Learned Hand (the famous judge who was a close friend of Parsons), Clarence Day, and Parsons each donated one dollar. There was also an "anonymous" donation of four hundred dollars. In 1919, additional one-dollar donors included George Heye, Jesse Nusbaum, M. R. Harrington, Tozzer, Kroeber, Prudden, and Sapir. Anonymous donations totaled 750 dollars; 200 dollars of that went to Leslie Spier for work at Havasupai and 350 dollars to support Boas at Laguna Pueblo. In 1920

there were twenty-one $1.00 donors and $465.69 spent on "Keresan language field work," that is, on Boas. In 1921, there were twenty 1-dollar donors and 951 dollars spent on Boas and Schiff at Laguna and Cochiti, and 275 dollars on Spier and Erna Gunther at Havasupai.[36]

There are no ledger entries after 1922. However, Parsons continued supporting fieldwork and publications through her fictive society until her death. The total amount of her support is unclear. It is known that she provided over forty-two thousand dollars in publication support for the American Folklore Society between 1916 and 1940, and probably an equal amount for anthropology publications. Her generosity elicited some humor. In 1923, Nels Nelson wrote to J. Alden Mason, "Mrs. Parsons seems to be shelling out a little money for work right along. It is said she sold some of her jewels three or four years ago to get more money for Southwest work, but whether the jewelry was useless, or she was trying to outdo Queen Isabella, I don't know."[37]

Those Parsons supported headed to the Southwest to fill in knowledge of pueblos and tribes and pursue new questions. The British anthropologist W. H. R. Rivers had revived kinship studies and placed kinship in relation to family organization, residence patterns, and economic behavior at the forefront of studies of tribal societies. Kroeber and Lowie went to Zuni and Hopi in 1915 and 1916, in part to collect data to verify or refute Rivers's ideas.[38] Boas's insistence on seeing tribal groups in their historical and ecological settings added new questions. The Southwest once again was seen as a "laboratory" in which many questions could be posed and "tested."

Parsons had her own research agenda. She wanted to "survey" all the Pueblos to gain a better understanding of the range and variety of social, economic, and ritual forms and practices. These data were critical for her major interest, acculturation, part of her general "passion for cultural overlays."[39] She relished, and sought to untangle, the historical blending, the overlays, of Pueblo, Hispanic, and Anglo elements of culture in contemporary social and religious forms and practices. Given her intense participant observation experience with her own upper-crust Anglo "tribe," she also was very interested in the role of individual psychology in culture change.

Parsons in the Field

Parsons spent some months of each year in the field (Fig. 26.4), in the Southwest, the American South, and the Caribbean. The rest of the year was spent at one or another of her family homes—writing. At home, "mornings were sacred. She tolerated no interruptions of her work between breakfast and lunch, day in and day out, weekday or weekend." A full-time secretary assisted. Her scholarly output was staggering: in the three-year period 1915–17 she produced eighty-five publications, including two books.[40]

In the summer of 1915 Parsons became friends with Margaret Lewis, a woman of Cherokee ancestry who taught school at Zuni. Lewis's home was Parsons's base of operations for several years. She struck up a similar friendship at Laguna Pueblo with Margaret Eckerman, the daughter of an Anglo man and a Pueblo woman. At Hopi she was adopted into the family of Sihtaime, a religious leader of the Patki clan, by the traditional hair-washing with yucca suds, and stayed in the pueblo with the family. During her years of studying the Rio Grande pueblos, she stayed with Mabel

26.4. Elsie Clews Parsons, 1928, at Dude Ranch in New Mexico. Courtesy of the American Philosophical Society.

26.5. Anthropology picnic, ca. 1920. Left to right: Ruth Benedict, Franz Boas, A. L. Kroeber. Photograph by Esther Schiff (Goldfrank). Courtesy of the National Anthropological Archives, Smithsonian Institution.

Dodge Luhan at Taos, or at a dude ranch near San Juan Pueblo, and later on her own ranch near Santa Clara Pueblo.[41]

Parsons and Kroeber

Alfred Kroeber (Fig. 26.5) was at Zuni Pueblo in the summer of 1915, partly to study kinship and family life, partly to escape depression from the death of his first wife from tuberculosis, and partly to recover from a continuing inner-ear problem that affected his balance. Then, Ishi, the Yana Indian man whom Kroeber had rescued from the California foothills in 1911 and was very close to, died of tuberculosis in March 1916. Ishi's death threw Kroeber further into the doldrums.[42] He spent the first half of 1916 at the American Museum; Parsons was often there and they became close friends. The friendship deepened over

time; there were long visits to one or another of Parsons's summer homes in 1916, and again in 1918 when Kroeber spent six months in New York to undergo a course of psychoanalysis.

In the fall of 1918, Parsons and Kroeber worked together at Zuni, he on language and she on ceremonies. The Zunis later remembered their joint visit and speculated whether or not they were lovers, because they often went together to Towayalane (Corn Mountain). Flora Zuni, who knew them both, thought they went there "to have a nice time"; Margaret Lewis thought "it might have been true," but "who knows?"[43] Whatever else happened, they quietly stole prayer sticks from the shrines on the mountain. Parsons wanted an ongoing collaborative fieldwork relationship with Kroeber, but after 1918 it didn't work, apparently because Kroeber wanted more than that, writing to her, "I got the sense that you wanted nothing between us but shop."[44] Pliny Goddard, the arch-gossip of the Boasian crowd, wrote in an undated (but probably 1920) letter to Parsons that Kroeber "wanted you very much this summer. He should have known that there are others, but he looks upon you as a goddess unfettered by human ties. . . . I am rather sorry for Kroeber. He doesn't know how to sip his wine."[45] Whatever the dimensions of their relationship, Parsons clearly helped Kroeber get through his psychological funk between 1916 and 1922. Kroeber got through his problems partly by becoming a lay analyst in the early 1920s. An undated engraved announcement in F. W. Hodge's papers reads: "A. L. Kroeber, Ph.D., has opened an office for the practice of psychoanalysis in the Physicians' Building, 516 Sutter Street, San Francisco. Hours by appointment." Kroeber and Parsons remained close personal friends, colleagues, and correspondents until Parsons's death in 1941. Kroeber wrote a warm and moving obituary.[46]

Folklore and Mexico

When Parsons turned to Southwestern ethnography, she also began studying African-American folklore. She started with Portuguese-speaking Blacks from the Cape Verde Islands who were laborers and domestics in Newport, Rhode Island, where Parsons summered.[47] Her interest in folk tales, riddles, and proverbs was stimulated by her interest in acculturation, the mixing of oral traditions. As she wrote to Boas, "I have 26 tales of the European type, told completely and excellently and 27 tales of the African type together with a number of obvious hybrids."[48]

She worked her way down the eastern seaboard, visiting Black schools in North and South Carolina and the Hampton Institute in Virginia, then on to the Sea Islands of South Carolina and Georgia, and finally, over the years, across the Caribbean. She often chartered boats to small islands and collected riddles or tales from anyone who would talk with her. She ultimately followed a trail of tales, so to say, to the Mediterranean and on into Egypt and the Sudan. In 1926 from Luxor, Egypt, she wrote that she had heard "the origin stories of those . . . [I] once heard in the Bahamas or the Sea Islands & wondered where they came from, knowing they were not European."[49]

Parsons funded, through her Southwest Society, the work of Aurelio Espinosa in Spain and New Mexico, Harold Courlander in Haiti and Santo Domingo, Zora Neale Hurston in Florida and Alabama, and Arthur Huff Fauset in Nova Scotia, as well as the initial work of Melville and Frances Herskovits in the Caribbean and Dahomey, West Africa.[50]

In 1929, Parsons began visiting Mexico. This resulted, in the early 1930s, in a collaboration with graduate student Ralph Beals on studies of social and cultural parallels between the Huichol, Mayo, and Yaqui in northern Mexico and the Southwestern Pueblos.[51] Parsons also spent many months, between 1930 and 1933, living in the town of Mitla in Oaxaca. There she did not have be a "high grade detective" (see below); she was very much a part of the community, but kept a detached view, the participant-observer in the best sense, "one who is willing to be part of what she sees," as Parsons's biographer Desley Deacon puts it. In Mitla, Parsons found a cultural "filigree" of Zapotec, Aztec, Mixtec, Spanish, and Anglo threads. Rather than portraying the people as anonymous consultants, she presents them in all the intertwined complexities of their lives. Deacon rightly calls *Mitla: Town of Souls,* published in 1936, "a modernist tour de force."[52]

In between trips to Mexico and the Caribbean, Parsons brought together the strands of her own Southwestern work, the works of those she supported, and earlier ethnographies and ethnohistories. In the 1920s, she purchased Alexander Stephen's Hopi Journal from Stewart Culin for five hundred dollars. The journal itself was a monumental accomplishment on Stephen's part. Edited by Parsons, and published in 1936, it became a major document on Hopi life and culture, all 1,400 pages of it. While working on Mitla and the Hopi Journal, Parsons was also finishing her own masterwork, *Pueblo Religion,* published in 1939, all 1,250 pages of it.[53]

Parsons's passion for detail, for historical connections, for the sources of ceremonial practices and ideas, both Indian and Hispanic, boggle the mind. She describes both traditional Pueblo and Catholic ceremonies practiced at the various pueblos in detail. In the penultimate chapter, "Variation and Borrowing," she is very much the historical particularist, tracing out which ceremonial practices and regalia may have been borrowed from one pueblo by another, or which moved from the Spanish to the pueblos. She is especially good on the intermingling of dozens of Pueblo and Catholic practices and beliefs, including the syncretism of Jesus with Poseyemu-Montezuma (see Chapter 3).[54]

Finally, Parsons considers processes of culture change, especially why certain practices, beliefs, and ceremonies are or are not adopted, giving hundreds of specific examples. In a larger framework, she ruminates on the comparative impacts of Hispanics and Anglos on Pueblo religion:

> Catholicism has by and large enriched Pueblo religion, contributing God and the saints to the pantheon, fiestas to the calendar, candles and who knows how many other details to ritual. Protestant sects contribute nothing to Pueblo religion but dissension and apostasy. . . . Protestantism as it combines with modernized economy . . . may not only break down the old culture very rapidly but impede the general tendency to social integration or unity.[55]

Parsons's prime example of this process is the split at Oraibi in 1906, which had many related causes (see Chapter 18). She worries as well about the overall impact of Anglo schooling (in which children are taught that traditional ceremonies are "merely superstitious," or "obscene") as well as the market economy: "The wage system produces new economic needs as well as the means of satisfying them, even illicitly, through commercializing ceremonial." That includes selling ceremonial pottery and paraphernalia and dancing in the Anglo-created ceremonies in Santa Fe and Gallup.[56] As anthropologist, Parsons is aware that processes of change are always ongoing in all cultures:

Pueblo Religion contains twelve hundred pages of supporting data. As yearner anthropologist, she wishes it were not so; that somehow her own capitalist Anglo tribe would leave the Pueblos as she thought them to be in 1912.

With *Mitla* and *Pueblo Religion* published, in 1940 and 1941 Parsons turned to Ecuador. She returned to New York in November 1941 to finish her inaugural speech as incoming president of the American Anthropological Association (AAA), the first woman to hold that office. But suddenly she was gone. After an emergency operation for appendicitis, she died of kidney failure on December 18, 1941. Gladys Reichard (see below) read Parsons's presidential address before the AAA membership on December 29.[57] Like everything Elsie Clews Parsons had done, it was forward looking, charting a new course for anthropology, and the contributions it could and should make to a better, more rational, saner existence for humanity—hopeful words as the world plunged headlong into the maelstrom of World War II. In her will, Elsie Clews Parsons instructed that her remains be cremated and not buried anywhere, that there be no funeral, and the family not wear mourning clothes; they honored her wishes.[58]

The Boasians in the Southwest

In 1918, Franz Boas was sixty years old. He had finished his major research work by about 1911 and had turned out a number of Ph.D.s. During the war when he had few students, the university cut his budget, including his secretarial help, and he had a bout with cancer. One of his favorite students, Herman Karl Haeberlin, died soon after finishing his dissertation, leaving Boas shaken.[59]

Boas had been vocally pro-German during the war, and for years had actively fought racism, the eugenics movement, and the misuse of science for racialist purposes. In 1919, he published an article in *The Nation*, condemning unnamed anthropologists for spying in Central America. Sylvanus G. Morley, Herbert Spinden, and probably Samuel Lothrop were those

26.6. *Franz Boas at Mt. Taylor, New Mexico, 1919.*
Courtesy of the American Museum of Natural History.

tics. Who better than Boas, editor of the *Handbook of American Indian Languages*?[61] Parsons had briefly considered the anal-retentive and paranoid J. P. Harrington, but thought better of it. When Boas began work, an alarmed Harrington wrote to Hewett, "Do not be blind to what Boas is scheming in New Mexico. His motto is 'to hell' with you and me, and I want to act quickly and get ahead of him."[62] Boas spent portions of three summers in the Southwest. Parsons's rejuvenation plan worked; Boas wrote to her, "It is not too much to say that the new work has made me younger & reborn a good deal of my energy and enterprise, and for that I have to thank you." He produced a two-part monograph on Keresan linguistic texts; Parsons paid for its publication.[63]

Part of Boas's rejuvenation was from new students. Gladys Reichard and Erna Gunther entered the doctoral program in 1919. Melville Herskovits arrived in 1920, Ruth Benedict in 1921. The next year, Esther Schiff became a graduate student; Ruth Bunzel replaced her as Boas's secretary, and then became a graduate student herself in 1924. Margaret Mead arrived in 1923. All these individuals, except Mead and Herskovits, did Southwestern fieldwork in the 1920s and 1930s.

Boas's work only partly accomplished what Parsons wanted. But his new graduate students produced a good deal of what she had in mind, and more. Between 1920 and 1930, Esther Schiff (Goldfrank), Ruth Bunzel, Gladys Reichard, and Ruth Benedict, were in the Southwest for varying periods. Collectively, they brought a new "ethnographic sensibility," as George Stocking calls it, to American anthropology.[64]

Esther Schiff Goldfrank

Esther Schiff (1897–1997) grew up in New York and graduated in 1918 from Barnard College.[65] In her senior year, she took an introductory anthropology class from Boas. Soon after, Boas contacted her and asked her to become his secretary. She learned only later that her twenty-five-dollar-a-week salary was paid by Parsons. In the spring of 1920, Schiff coaxed Boas into

not named. William Henry Holmes and the "Washington Crowd" were furious. At the December 1919 meeting of the American Anthropological Association, Boas was censured and expelled from the association.[60] He emerged battered, but not bowed; he was later reinstated, and by 1923 the "Boasians" had regained control of the association and its journal, the *American Anthropologist*.

Parsons began her own program of rehabilitating Boas. Early in 1919, she arranged to pay Esther Schiff's salary as Boas's secretary. She also convinced Boas to begin a study of the Keresan languages, starting with Laguna Pueblo (Fig. 26.6), heeding Kroeber's dictum that an understanding of Pueblo cultural interconnections requires an understanding of Pueblo linguis-

letting her join him in the field for a short period. Parsons agreed to pay her expenses if she worked with consultants or helped Boas.

At Laguna, Boas introduced Schiff to Jennie Day. The two started their mutual ethnographic endeavor by recording cooking recipes and methods. When Parsons arrived, she and Schiff worked with several women on medicinal plants and their uses. Thus did Esther Schiff begin her anthropological career.[66] After ten days at Laguna, Boas and Schiff met Parsons and Grant La Farge at San Felipe Pueblo. They tried to work there, but no one would talk with them; they had the same experience at Santa Ana and Santo Domingo. By July 6 they called it quits for the summer. The next year, Schiff again accompanied Boas to Laguna, doing more work on her own, while Boas gathered his texts. They then moved on to Cochiti for a brief time (Fig. 26.7). Schiff began taking anthropology classes that fall. Both returned to Cochiti again in 1922 for several weeks. Schiff was befriended by Isabel Diaz, a Cochiti woman. With Diaz's female relatives, they explored the complexities of Cochiti kinship and clanship and observed some ceremonies.

In the fall of 1922, Schiff renewed her acquaintance with a widower with three sons named Walter Goldfrank; they were married the following December. While awaiting the birth of her daughter in 1924, Esther Schiff Goldfrank wrote *The Social and Ceremonial Organization of Cochiti*.[67] Later in 1924, Parsons lured Goldfrank back to the Southwest to work at Isleta Pueblo, south of Albuquerque (the baby was left in the charge of a "good nanny"). Parsons was enlisting people to collect myths and folk tales, and that was Goldfrank's assignment. But the people of Isleta were unfriendly, so Goldfrank wound up working with an Isletan elder, Juan Abeita, a pseudonym, at the Alvarado Hotel in Albuquerque. Parsons later worked with Abeita as well and incorporated Goldfrank's data into a monograph on Isleta.[68]

Goldfrank's monograph on Cochiti appeared in 1927. Soon after, she reports, at an anthropology picnic Pliny Goddard pointed at her three-year-old daughter Susan, "turned to me and said with special emphasis on the first word, '*That* is the best thing you ever produced.' I thought he was right then and I think he was right now."[69] Goldfrank's husband died in 1935. She returned to anthropology for a time, then married Carl Wittfogel, the great Marxist culture historian, in 1940, and began to work with him on his theories of the origins of state-level societies in relation to the control of irrigation systems in arid environments.[70]

There is a coda to Goldfrank's and Parsons's involvement with Isleta Pueblo. Between 1935 and 1941, Parsons acquired a series of watercolors depicting ceremonies and daily activities, and letters describing them, from a young Isleta artist, Joe Lente. Parsons had written a study of them, dedicated to Goldfrank, "to whom I owe the opening of Isleta,"

26.7. Esther Schiff (Goldfrank) at Cochiti, 1922. Courtesy of the National Anthropological Archives, Smithsonian Institution.

but she died before it was finished. Ultimately, Goldfrank edited the manuscript, and it and the paintings were published in a special edition of a Bureau of American Ethnology bulletin in 1962.[71] Esther Schiff Goldfrank died on April 23, 1997, at age one hundred, the last of "the Boasians."[72]

Ruth Bunzel

Ruth Bunzel (1898–1990) was born in New York City of German and Czech parents.[73] She graduated from Barnard College in 1918. She became Franz Boas's secretary in 1922, replacing Esther Goldfrank. In 1924, she planned a summer vacation to visit Ruth Benedict at Zuni, but Boas had other ideas. According to Bunzel, Boas told her, "Do a project of your own." When she protested that she was not an anthropologist, he retorted: "You're interested in art. They make pottery there. Go do a project on the relationship of the artist to her work." "So," said Bunzel, "I had a problem to work on." She began reading, went to the American Museum to study and photograph Zuni pots, and "three weeks later I was on the train to Zuni," in the company of Ruth Benedict, both funded by Parsons.[74]

The two found Zuni in a political uproar over Frederick Webb Hodge's attempt to film the Shalako ceremony the previous winter (see Chapter 24). The conservative faction in the pueblo had protested vociferously, and the filming was stopped. Parson's friend Margaret Lewis, one of the "liberals," with whom Benedict and Bunzel hoped to stay, had moved to Dulce, New Mexico, until things cooled down. The two found accommodations with Flora Zuni, whose family was in the conservative faction, and whose mother, Catalina, was an accomplished potter.[75] Bunzel had found a home. She lived with Flora for five summers and two winters, was formally adopted into the family, was made a member of the Badger clan, and was given the name *Maiatitsa*, "Blue Bird," for the blue smock she wore when making pottery, but also *Hopaanso*, "Grandmother Bunzel."[76] According

to Flora Zuni, she and Bunzel got on well; "she was just like a sister to me," she said, although in later years she complained that Bunzel forgot her kinship obligations to the family.[77]

Catalina Zuni and other women were Bunzel's mentors in pottery making. Once established, she was able to begin serious inquiry into Zuni ceremonialism while continuing her pottery study. Her five summers and two winters at Zuni enabled her to witness the entire ceremonial year. She learned the Zuni language, and her grasp of Zuni ceremonialism was probably equal to Cushing's. Unlike Cushing, Bunzel published what she learned.

Her *Pueblo Potter* was the first of numerous studies of Zuni pottery, and remains an important reference for contemporary Zuni potters.[78] It appeared in 1929, two years after her mentor Franz Boas's *Primitive Art*. The period from 1910 to 1930 was a time when "primitive art," including Southwestern art, was "discovered" by, and was rapidly being incorporated into, the modern art world (see Chapter 27). Aesthetes, art critics, and anthropologists argued the "sources of artistic creativity and expression," and "the role of the artist in traditional society."[79] Bunzel's contribution was the assertion that Zuni potters "operate within the limits of established style," that is, within culturally defined patterns. Zuni and Acoma potters in the 1920s were still making pottery primarily for domestic use; they were not yet incorporated into the art market, as were the Rio Grande and Hopi potters. There, "commercial success has stimulated new and interesting developments," that is, conscious creativity. Zuni and Acoma potters still made "traditional" pots.[80]

Bunzel's publications on Zuni ceremonialism, kachinas, and ritual poetry are classics on which subsequent students of Zuni life, ceremony, and ideology have built.[81] In 1930 she began working in the Guatemalan Highlands, at first as a Guggenheim fellow, and later as part of a much larger Mayan studies project funded by the Carnegie Institution, begun by A. V. Kidder and Robert Redfield when Kidder took over the Carnegie's History Division. Having designed and laid the groundwork for the project, she was told by Kidder in 1933 that there was no money to continue. He then hired Sol Tax, one of Redfield's graduate students at the University of Chicago, and expanded the project. Although regarded by many as one of the best and brightest anthropologists of the day, Bunzel never regained the ground she lost in 1933. She never held a tenured job, although she taught part time at Columbia University for many years. She died in 1990. Her answer to the male chauvinism of Kidder and Redfield was her classic study of the Guatemalan village of Chichicastenango, a fitting companion to her mentor and patroness Parsons's *Mitla,* but hardly recompense for a lost career.[82]

Gladys Reichard

Gladys Amanda Reichard (1893–1955) was born of Quaker parents in Pennsylvania (Fig. 26.8).[83] She taught elementary school for about five years before starting college. At Swarthmore she majored in clas-

26.8. Gladys Reichard, 1930s. Courtesy of the Museum of Northern Arizona.

sics, but became interested in anthropology. In 1919, she went to Columbia University to study with Boas. She soon moved into the Boas household, where she remained for some years. Boas sent her to study the Wiyot of California, and her dissertation was on Wiyot grammar.[84] Boas arranged a teaching position for her at Barnard in 1923, and she remained there until her death in 1955.

In 1923, Parsons started Reichard working with the Navajo by providing seven hundred dollars for her to team up with Pliny Earl Goddard for the summer. Parsons's own fieldwork with Kroeber, and her traveling with Grant La Farge, was a precedent. From Parsons's gender-equity perspective, men and women ought to be able to work together as professionals in the office or in the field. If a love affair developed, it was no one's business except the participants'. Parsons supported their work for three years, and Reichard's work periodically thereafter. In July 1928, Goddard died suddenly of an undiagnosed stomach cancer at a summer home that Reichard and he had just established. Later, Reichard finished his last manuscript on Navajo texts.[85]

Kroeber's "Zuni Clan and Kin," his theoretical articles, and Lowie's *Primitive Society* (1920) had focused renewed interest on social organization and kinship.[86] In 1920, very little was known in detail about the social organization and kinship systems of the Pueblos, Navajos, Apaches, or other Southwestern groups. Part of Parsons's research agenda was to collect such data. Reichard's assignment was Navajo social organization. Her *Social Life of the Navajo Indians,* which appeared in 1928, was a tour de force.[87] She collected genealogies of some thirty-five hundred individuals, presenting her data in numerous mind-numbing charts and appendices. But from those data, for the first time, anthropologists understood the full extent of some fifty Navajo matrilineal clans and their functions in the regulation of marriage, economic life, and ceremonialism. Reichard demonstrated the normal structure of a Navajo extended family centered on a senior female, her daughters, granddaughters and possibly great-granddaughters, with their spouses and children. She also made clear that property was controlled by both males and females, and that Navajo gender equity, which so puzzled U.S. Army officers in the nineteenth century (see Chapter 4), did exist.

Learning to Weave

Reichard was aware of Ruth Bunzel's success in studying Zuni by becoming an apprentice potter, and sought to emulate her: "I decided that learning to weave would be a way of developing the trust of the women. . . . By weaving, I could observe the daily round as a participant, rather than as a mere onlooker."[88] By becoming a member of a family, she was also in a much better position to learn about Navajo religion. Elsie Parsons provided fifteen hundred dollars to get her started in 1930.[89]

Reichard asked Roman Hubbell at the Ganado trading post for help. He introduced her to the family of Red-Point, or Miguelito, a prominent singer whose wife and daughters, especially Marie and Atlnaba, were expert weavers. Reichard was welcomed into the family, given a large and comfortable hoganlike storage structure in which to live, and began her apprenticeship. Weaving on the upright Navajo loom is an exact and difficult art. In *Spider Woman*, Reichard chronicles her slow and painful progress under the watchful eyes of her mentors.[90] By the end of her third season, she was able to produce a respectable saddle blanket. In the process she learned much about native vegetable dyes, shepherding, the production of wool, and the economy of sheep and weaving. All this she presented in *Navaho Shepherd and Weaver*.[91] She also learned the Navajo language, which gave her greater access to religion and ritual. Miguelito was the first of several singers who taught her about the chants and their meanings. As an adopted daughter, she was able to observe numerous chants, except those parts not to be seen by women. Ultimately, in 1950, she produced her magnum opus, *Navaho Religion*.[92]

What comes through most clearly in all her work is Reichard's warm and humane regard for the Navajo people. Her description of Roman Hubbell introducing her to Red-Point's family reflects this:

> Here is a white woman [Hubbell said], peculiar in many ways, who wants to learn to weave. As he tells the weaver this, she darts at me a pleased but quizzical look. Furthermore this white woman wants to live right here with the Indians. She wants to have a shade like theirs. She wants a loom anchored to the ground at which she can sit as they sit, on the ground. She wants to learn to weave as Navajo women weave. This particular Navajo woman is interested, but she cannot help being amused. The white woman has shown she liked the weaver from the moment she saw her, the weaver has reciprocated.[93]

Reichard's long association with Navajo people and her admiration for them is reflected in her novel, *Dezba, Woman of the Desert,* published in 1939.[94] The book was one of a series written by anthropologists in the 1930s to present in an accessible fashion the lives and cultures of Indian peoples—an expansion of Parsons's effort in the 1920s. Dezba is a composite of many senior heads-of-family women Reichard knew. Reichard skillfully conveys the richness of Navajo culture, beliefs, and practices, and how the people found their way in the Anglo world of the 1920s and 1930s, when their traditional expectations and practices came increasingly into conflict with Anglo society and the usually befuddled policies of the Bureau of Indian Affairs.

Reichard continued to work with the Navajo people until her death. In the 1930s and 1940s, her work was often denigrated as "old fashioned, Boasian" by Clyde Kluckhohn, at Harvard, who saw himself as the premier Navajo scholar. But times change. The generation of Navajo scholars of the 1980s and 1990s—Sam Gill, Louise Lamphere, and Gary Witherspoon—see Reichard's work as being ahead of its time, the foundation for their own work; to them, it's Kluckhohn who seems dated.[95] *Sic transit gloria mundi.*

Ruth Benedict: Patterning the Pueblos

Ruth Fulton (1887–1948) (see Fig. 26.5) was born in New York City. She was shy, made more so by partial deafness resulting from measles as an infant. She grew up in Buffalo, attended a private girl's school and graduated from Vassar in 1909.[96] She spent a year in Europe, taught and did social work for three years, and then married Stanley R. Benedict, a biochemist at the Cornell Medical School in New York City. She soon felt constrained as "the wife" in suburbia; matters worsened when she discovered she could not have children. Seeking direction and coherence in her life, she studied with John Dewey at Columbia University in 1918–19. In the fall of 1919 she signed up for Elsie Clews Parsons's "Women and the Social Order," or "Sex in Ethnology," course at the New School for Social Research. Parsons steered her to Alexander Goldenweiser, whom Benedict considered "a rare teacher" and who stimulated her and other "neophytes."[97] She considered a career in anthropology. Parsons took her to see Boas; Goldenweiser gave her a strong recommendation. She had found an intellectual nesting place.[98]

Benedict plunged into graduate work, although Boas waived most credit requirements for her. She gave her first professional paper, "The Vision in Plains Culture," at the 1921 meeting of the American Anthropological Association. It was published as a lead article in the *American Anthropologist,* a distinct honor for a graduate student. She then turned to a related area for her doctoral dissertation, "The Concept of the Guardian Spirit in North America."[99]

By spring 1922 she was Dr. Ruth Fulton Benedict, but was not a member of the club: she had not "gone to the field." That summer she did some memory ethnography with a Serrano elder in southern California. She returned to become Boas's teaching assistant at Barnard. But there were no steady jobs. Parsons hired her for one thousand dollars to do more library work on a concordance of Southwestern folklore—Pueblos, non-Pueblos, and Hispanic. She worked unhappily but assiduously at this for a year.

In the summer of 1924, Parsons funded Benedict to study folklore at Zuni and Cochiti. In 1925, she returned to Zuni and Cochiti, and was back at Cochiti again in 1927. Her major publications were on Zuni and Cochiti folklore, and she edited the *Journal of American Folk-Lore* from 1925 through 1939.[100]

While Benedict was becoming an anthropologist, her personal life was in turmoil. Although her marriage did not formally end until 1930, it had come unraveled by about 1919. An intensely personal individual, Benedict's search for meaning in her life is reflected in her poetry. She often exchanged poems with Edward Sapir, and published her own as "Anne Singleton." She also began to cope with her sexuality. An intense affair with Margaret Mead during the mid-1920s allowed her to begin to come to terms with herself.[101]

Benedict's importance in Southwestern anthropology lies in her search for personal meaning, and in her interpretations of Indian cultures as part of that search. A central issue of commensurability, investigated from many perspectives, has long been "nature versus nurture"; how much of human nature (including individual "personality") is innate, and how much is shaped by one's social and cultural milieu? At the end of the millennium, the argument continues in battles over "sociobiology."[102] From the 1910s to the 1930s, in psychology the argument was between the behaviorists on the nature side, led by J. B. Watson and the Nobel laureate Ivan Pavlov, and the Gestalt psychologists on the nurture side, led by Wolfgang Köhler and Kurt Koffka. Various schools of psychoanalysis, centered around Sigmund Freud and Carl Jung, thought some of each might be involved. Cultural relativists, such as the Boasians and most liberals, argued that nurture—culture—was determinate. Margaret Mead's famous *Coming of Age in Samoa* investigated aspects of the issue.[103]

For Ruth Benedict the determinants and definitions of "normal" and "abnormal" personalities in every society were the critical issues. Were "normal" and "abnormal" culturally defined, or naturally determined, especially in relation to sexuality? She began a cross-cultural investigation of the question and turned to her own and others' data on Southwestern Pueblos.

The issue comes back again to natural man in Western thought, in his several guises. The Enlightenment's noble savage was seen as uncorrupted by civilization, an exemplar of morality and ethics in a "properly constructed" society. But for the Counter-Enlightenment Romantics, who conceived not a clockwork universe but one that was organic and sentient, there was another side to the noble savage. Nature was seen as fecund and sublime, embodying a dark and amoral force; possessing a "blood consciousness," to use D. H. Lawrence's term, opposed to rational order and efficiency, the ultimate creative force, which can be good or destructive, but is always beautiful.

Being a part of nature, savages *naturally* have more of this life force. Many Romantics, such as Percy and Mary Shelley and their sometime house guest Lord Byron, explored the possibilities of this force, which could wreak good or evil. In Mary Shelley's classic tale, Frankenstein's monster, infused with the life force, runs amok, strewing terror and destruction. Friedrich Nietzsche puzzled over—and reified—the force. Sigmund Freud pursued it through levels of humans' conscious and unconscious minds. For some, the force exists only in nature on earth. For others, it is inherent in the cosmos, and contests to control it are fought in George Lucas's *Star Wars* galaxies. In the Southwest, Pueblo and Navajo myths tell of the dangers of wrongly directed uses of similar life forces. It is a powerful and pervasive metaphor.[104]

Benedict had read Walter Pater and Nietzsche. Both used the Greek god Dionysus, the Romantic god of fecund sublime chaos, and Apollo, an Enlightenmentlike god of order and rationality, as symbols of the dichotomy of human psychological forces.[105] In 1928 Benedict read a paper, "Psychological Types in the Cultures of the Southwest," at the International Congress of Americanists meetings in New York. "There is," she said, among the Pueblos, "a difference in psychological type fundamentally to be distinguished from that of surrounding regions." She drew from Nietzsche and Pater the "two psychological types, . . . Apollonian and Dionysian." The Dionysian seeks illumination, she said, through "the annihilation of the ordinary bounds and limits of existence. . . . With [William] Blake, he believes 'the path of excess leads to the palace of wisdom.'" The Apollonian distrusts all this, and outlaws such experience from his conscious life. He "knows but one law, measure in the Hellenic sense. He keeps to the middle of the road, stays within the known map, maintains his control over all disruptive psychological states." As Nietzsche said, "even in the exaltation of the dance, he remains what he is, and retains his civic name."[106] To Benedict, the Pueblos, particularly Zuni and Hopi, are arch-Apollonians; other North American Indians are Dionysian. The self-torture and fasting of the vision quest, the Sun Dance, and other religious experiences filled with "ecstasy and orgy" are central to all of them. Surrounded by Dionysian cultures, the Apollonian Pueblos have "an *ethos* distinguished by sobriety, by its distrust of excess, that minimizes to the last possible vanishing point any challenging or dangerous experiences. They have a religion of fertility without orgy, an absorption in the dance without using it to arrive at ecstasy. . . . They have even stripped sex of its mystic danger. They allow to the individual no disruptive role in their social order."[107]

It is true, says Benedict, that Pueblos share various cultural traits and practices with adjacent tribes. Yet these are reworked by the Apollonian "bent." There is, she thinks, "a fundamental psychological set which has undoubtedly been established for centuries, . . . and which has bent to its own uses any . . . [traits taken] from surrounding peoples and has created an intricate cultural pattern to express its own preferences."[108]

The "intricate cultural *pattern*" was the key; "without it the cultural dynamics of [the Southwest] are unintelligible. For the typical choices of the Apollonian have been creative in the formation of this culture, they have excluded what was displeasing, revamped what they took, and brought into being endless demonstrations of the Apollonian delight in formality, in the intricacies and elaborations of organization."[109]

Rather than seeing a culture as a cluster of randomly agglomerated traits, as in Wissler's and Lowie's particularism, Benedict argued that "psychological sets" operated as filters in the *selection and reworking* of cultural traits into "intricate cultural patterns" that form *holistic configurations.*

Benedict wrote to Margaret Mead about the reception of her paper: "Kroeber's question was just, 'How does the old man [Boas] take a paper like that?' Edward [Sapir] said it was a good lecture, . . . and Kidder came up to say it was illustrated just as much by the pueblo art and material culture as by their religion. Wissler scowled through a great deal of it . . . Elsie [Clews Parsons] was speechless and rose to make all sorts of pointless addenda when she recovered her breath. Professor Danzel . . . said it was the most important paper of the Congress . . . the same from [Hortense] Powdermaker."[110] In light of the subsequent history of American anthropology, Danzel was correct. Benedict, Mead, and Sapir were launching the culture and personality school that dominated American cultural anthropology until the late 1950s. Benedict's paper was the linchpin.

Benedict added another dimension in the early 1930s: that psychological abnormality is culturally relative. She tried to defuse the stigma of homosexuality in American society by attempting to demonstrate that categories of abnormality are culturally defined. In "Anthropology and the Abnormal," published in 1934, she pointed to the stigmatized roles of homosexuals in American society and the definition of their sexual orientations as "abnormal." But "wherever homosexuality has been given an honorable place in any society, those to whom it is congenial have filled adequately the honorable roles society assigns to them."[111] As, for example, We'wha, the Zuni berdache, consultant and friend to Matilda Stevenson (see Chapter 7).

Benedict's concern to show that sexual abnormality is culturally relative was carried over, along with the concepts of psychological types and of cultures as holistic configurations of patterned elements, into her magnum opus, *Patterns of Culture,* also published in 1934.[112] *Patterns of Culture* is the largest-selling anthropology book of all time, having been continuously in print from 1934 into the new millennium. The sections on the Southwest derive from her own and Ruth Bunzel's studies at Zuni, and of others with the Hopi. Benedict's Hopis and Zunis are the supreme noble savages in Apollonian dress. She saw in them everything she wanted: moral rectitude, stability, order, stasis, boundedness, meaning, and a tolerance for the "abnormal." As the ultimate Southwestern yearner anthropologist, she made them into everything she wished them to be, and drew from them intellectual sustenance and emotional solace.

In the process, Benedict, Sapir, and Mead refocused anthropology on people as acting, caring humans, weaving and living the intricate patterns of their lives, rather than simply passive carriers of randomly accumulated complexes of traits. Benedict also did more than any other anthropologist to convey the message of cultural relativity, of respect and understanding for the values of others. She died in September 1949, by then a major figure in American anthropology, as well as in the wider world. She is the only American anthropologist to have a postage stamp issued in her honor, a 46¢ stamp in 1995. At her memorial service, Alfred Kroeber read from her work:

> For what is the meaning of life except that by the discipline of thought and emotion, by living life to its fullest, we shall make of it always a more flexible instrument, accepting new relativities, divesting ourselves of traditional absolutes? To this end we need . . . something of respect for the epic of our own culture, something of fine tolerance for the values that have been elaborated in other cultures than our own.[113]

Leslie White

Leslie A. White (1900–1975) was born in Colorado and grew up in rural Kansas and Louisiana (see Fig. 29.1). After World War I navy service, he attended Louisiana State University for two years and then transferred to Columbia University where he took a

B.A. and M.A. in psychology. He did not take any anthropology classes at Columbia, but did take courses from Alexander Goldenweiser at the New School. Through Goldenweiser, he met Elsie Parsons. In 1924, White entered the Sociology Department at the University of Chicago, but was drawn to anthropology and the Southwest. His doctoral dissertation, "Medicine Societies in the Southwest," was rejected by Ellsworth Faris, chair of the department, for its "lack of theory." The ensuing uproar contributed to a separate Anthropology Department under Fay-Cooper Cole in 1927.[114]

White took a joint position at the University of Buffalo and the Buffalo Museum of Science in 1927, where he became very much interested in Lewis Henry Morgan, ultimately editing many of his papers. In 1930, he moved to the University of Michigan, where he remained for forty years, an iconoclastic, often controversial figure. He devoted himself to the rehabilitation of Morgan's reputation, to cultural evolutionism and the reification of culture as "superorganic," and, after 1939, to lambasting Boas, the Boasians, and other anthropologists for their intellectual cliquishness and shortcomings, as White perceived them.[115]

Parsons began supporting White's fieldwork at Acoma Pueblo in 1926, and continued that support, including publication of his monographs, through the 1930s. He ultimately produced major works on the Keresan-speaking pueblos of Acoma, San Felipe, Santo Domingo, Santa Ana, and Zia.[116] Since the religious leaders in all five pueblos were (and remain) adamantly secretive about their social and religious practices, White had clandestine contact with his consultants, as did Parsons and others who studied the Rio Grande pueblos. While Parsons understood the secrecy intellectually, it was a source of irritation. In her introduction to Alexander Stephen's *Hopi Journal*, she wrote, "He had opportunities for observation that, one fears, will never again be afforded. The exclusive spirit of the eastern Pueblos has spread to the Hopi to render the work of the ethnologist among them, too, that of high grade detective. What we may call their abiding and characteristic evasiveness was a

source of perplexity—and irritation—even to Stephen."[117] In his Santo Domingo report of 1935, White wrote:

> To the reader unfamiliar with the pueblos of New Mexico it should be said that in most of them it is utterly impossible to do ethnological work in the open. . . . These pueblos are very strongly opposed to telling outsiders anything pertaining to their customs and beliefs. . . . Strict watch is kept over all that none may betray the pueblo's secrets. Santo Domingo is one of the most conservative of all the pueblos and is bitterly opposed to telling white people, ethnologists above all, anything.[118]

In the foreword to his San Felipe report, White wrote, "I was assisted by several people. Some assisted me knowing well my mission. . . . They were kind to me; I enjoyed their hospitality. I sincerely hope that no harm or unpleasantness will come to them because of my acquaintance."[119]

All students of the Pueblos, and the Navajos and Apaches, from Cushing and Stevenson to White and Parsons and others, assumed the role of "ethnologist . . . as high grade detective" to greater or lesser degrees. All saw themselves as "scientists," committed to the idea that all knowledge should be part of the human commons. They were aware, at a romantic level, that "esoteric" knowledge and paraphernalia are protected for many reasons. But, at a scientific level, the people, the knowledge, and the paraphernalia were seen as objects, like all else to be investigated and made public for the "greater good." If such investigations could not be made openly, then "detective work" was warranted.

White's studies suffered from his inability to observe or participate in pueblo activities, except public performances, such as the summer Corn Dance at Santo Domingo Pueblo. But he managed to collect much information reflecting the rich social, economic, and ceremonial lives of the occupants of the five pueblos—far more than the leaders of the pueblos wanted any outsider to know. His tenacity is reflected in the fact that his reports on Santa Ana, San Felipe, Santo Domingo, and Zia pueblos are regarded as "the only source," or "the only major source" by those who summarized knowledge of those pueblos for the Smithsonian's *Handbook of North American Indians.*[120]

The point-counterpoint of science and romanticism is clearly evident in the ethnographies of Parsons, Boas, Benedict, Bunzel, Reichard, and White. Parsons and Benedict represent the extremes. Parsons saw herself as an inductive scientist, compiling reams of "facts" from which generalizations about cultural process and culture history might be extracted. In the end, she extracted few generalizations in her magisterial *Pueblo Religion,* but much of humanistic interest comes through, as it does in her classic study of Mitla. In Benedict's work, the romanticism is patent: cultures, and personalities shaped by them, are patterned, yet unique, and must be judged in relative terms. Generalizations in the usual scientific sense are not important, perhaps not possible. What is important is the solace both the Pueblos themselves—and those who study them—find in the Apollonian middle way.

CHAPTER 27

Inventing the Southwest, 1890–1930

A PERVASIVE THEME in American mythography is "the West." The mythical pretend West contains many wondrous, often harsh, and terrifying places where deeds heroic and dastardly were played out by good men and bad—railroad builders, miners, ranchers, cowboys, Indian fighters (civilian and military), tin horn gamblers, and gunslingers. There were good women and bad—pioneer mothers, school marms, dance hall floozies, and hookers with golden hearts. In the pretend West noble whites battled nature, the elements, savage indians, and each other on and beyond the ever-moving frontier. In song, story, poem, dime novel, melodrama, Wild West show, and later, movies and television, epochal doings took place in epochal landscapes.

Integral to the myth were natural man and woman in their savage guises. On the frontier they were generally ignoble. The transmutation from ignoble to noble savages trailed some hundreds of miles behind the advancing frontier—the further east the Anglo viewer,

the nobler Indian people were seen to be. After 1890 with the imprisonment of Geronimo and his fellow Apaches and the massacre at Wounded Knee, Indian people were no longer a threat and could be marginalized out of sight onto reservations while being romanticized into the pretend West.

Noble savage and pathetic dusky heroine legends proliferated, led by Helen Hunt Jackson's *Ramona*. An editorial in *The Independent* magazine in 1903 opined that "good Indian legends can be grown in almost any locality with a little care and attention; . . . it adds an interest to a very ordinary cliff to know that a persecuted and necessarily beautiful Indian maiden leaped thence to her death." The Denver and Rio Grande Western Railway publicity department located one such precipice in Dolores Canyon in western Colorado, where "the remarkable daughter of the high priest of Montezuma, who had fled from Mexico after the conquest, and died to escape from Coronado," leapt to her death for obscure reasons.[1] By 1900 even the shade of "Montezuma" was so ensconced in Anglo mythography that it did not need explanation.

The Southwest of the Santa Fe Railway

Railroads were the great high-tech achievement of the nineteenth century, moving people and goods across vast distances at high speeds. Railroads were in fierce competition for routes and passengers. A part of the competition came to center on tourism. In seeking to attract tourists, the railroads helped create and amplify the pretend West. It was one thing to read about it, to look at paintings and photographs, and applaud its denizens in the Wild West shows; it was another to go see it for oneself—in comfort on the California Limited.

The Southwest was not fully incorporated into the pretend West until after 1890.[2] Before that, its natural wonders were seen not as sublime, but quite fearful, rude places. In 1886, Santa Fe Railway publicity promised that the deserts of Arizona and southeastern California were no worse than the six hundred miles of Utah and Nevada desert that had to be crossed on a competing transcontinental line. Indeed, the Arizona/California desert was "the narrowest and cleanest of all those howling wildernesses which, by a peculiar dispensation of Providence, every transcontinental line must cross."[3]

The Atchison and Topeka Railroad had begun humbly in Kansas in the early 1860s. In a bid for government land grants it became, in name, an interstate railroad, the Atchison, Topeka and Santa Fe, known generally thereafter as "the Santa Fe." Despite its name, only a branch line reached Santa Fe in February 1880, to be greeted by a fiesta, with the last spike driven by Governor Lew Wallace.[4]

To reach the West Coast, the Santa Fe became embroiled in rough-and-tumble economic and legal battles for rights-of-way and access with the Southern Pacific Railroad, which finally ended in 1895 and a name change to "Railway." Part of the strategy during the rail wars was to increase tourist traffic. By about 1890, the Santa Fe, and the associated Fred Harvey Company, decided that the Southwest should *not* be a wilderness to be crossed posthaste, "narrow and clean" though it might be, but marketed as a "Land of Enchantment"—a picturesque place to safely and comfortably enjoy a "weekend exposure to the primitive world."[5]

The Santa Fe Railway publicity department created a favorable tourist image in many ways. It brought several Southwestern artists to prominence by putting their paintings on as many as 300,000 calendars distributed annually.[6] It commissioned articles and books filled with hyperbole. One of the more egregious examples was Lilian Whiting's *The Land of Enchantment: From Pike's Peak to the Pacific,* published in 1906. Whiting, a self-proclaimed aesthete, champion of the feminist novelist Kate Field, and descendant of Cotton Mather, seems to have been the first to use the slogan "Land of Enchantment." The phrase was not adopted by the State of New Mexico Highway Department until the 1930s.

According to Whiting, New Mexico was a place of mystery: "The ancient Indian pueblos are still largely inhabited, and strange ruins of unknown civilization add their atmosphere of mystery," such as "the mouldering ruins of old Pecos . . . the fabled site of the ancient Aztec city where tradition says Montezuma was born." The state abounds in "cliff and communal buildings . . . older than any other ruins on the American continent, and probably in the world. . . . Where else on earth is there so much of the beautiful in scenery, of romance, of historic monuments, of prehistoric remains, of the ancient, the unique, the picturesque, the sublime . . . " In Arizona one could visit "Assamanida, the Country of the Departed Spirits," a poetic name "the Iroquois [*sic!*] Indians gave to the Painted Desert."[7]

Whiting's effusion was followed by Agnes C. Laut's *Through Our Unknown Southwest,* published in 1913 and often thereafter. Purportedly a guidebook, it is full of romantic misinformation. The "natives" are uniformly quaint, curious, and poor but happy. There is a mixture of bad history about the Spanish and inaccurate ethnography about the Indians.[8]

The guidebooks produced by the railway were somewhat better; for example, one by Charles A. Higgins, an assistant passenger agent. A revised edition of 274,000 copies of *To California over the Santa Fe Trail* was published in 1905, complete with numerous pen-and-ink illustrations. Higgins saw the Pueblos as "an intelligent, complex, industrious and independent race," that "has absolutely maintained the integrity of . . . [their] individuality, self-respecting and self-sufficient. . . . He [*sic*] is a true pagan, . . . rich in fanciful legend, and profoundly ceremonious in religion. . . . [yet possesses a] purity of well-being of his communities."[9]

For those wanting more ethnographic detail, the Santa Fe commissioned George A. Dorsey, of the Chicago Field Columbian Museum, to write *Indians of the Southwest,* first published in 1903. Its chief purpose was to sell Indian arts and crafts in the Fred Harvey shops (see below). Since the shops sold Plains and California Indian items, Dorsey described some tribes from those areas as well. The longest section is on the Hopi, incorporating materials collected by Heinrich Voth (see Chapter 18).[10]

Indians, Anthropologists, Fred Harvey, and the Santa Fe

The history of the Fred Harvey Company and its handshake relationship with the Santa Fe Railway is well known in the lore of the Southwest. The lore includes an otherwise forgettable 1946 movie starring Judy Garland, Angela Lansbury, and Cyd Charisse as typical "Harvey Girls." The film is enlightened only by the theme song, "On the Atchison, Topeka and Santa Fe," which won an Oscar.[11] Both Fred Harvey and the railway adopted California Mission Revival and "Santa Fe style" architecture for stations, hotels, and restaurants and became deeply involved in the Indian arts and crafts market.

Dozens of anthropologists and art historians have written hundreds of publications on the history of Southwestern arts and crafts.[12] The key points are that between about 1880 and 1900 the Indian traders deal-ing with Navajo, Hopi, and Zuni, such as Thomas Keam, Lorenzo Hubbell, and J. B. Moore, had integrated both silver jewelry making and Navajo weaving into the world market. The traders largely dictated designs of both weaving and jewelry. Navajo wearing and saddle blankets became Navajo rugs. "Traditional" rug designs, such as Ganado, Wide Ruin, and Two Gray Hills, were those favored by traders at those locations. Navajo rugs were wholesaled by the bale and sold by the pound; only the "better examples" were sold individually. "Sikyatki revival" pottery, produced by Nampeyo and others at Hopi, was at first largely controlled by Thomas Keam, but other traders were soon involved. By 1900, the production of Hopi kachina dolls had became commodified as well.[13]

The Rio Grande pueblos were already producing "curios" when the first train reached Santa Fe in 1880. Tesuque and Cochiti pueblos made a variety of pottery bowls, ollas, and effigy pots and figures, especially "authentic Tesuque rain gods." These, as well as archaeological pieces "taken from recent excavations in New Mexico," were sold by Aaron and Jake Gold and others from 1880 on in Santa Fe. By the mid-1880s Santa Fe curio dealers were buying pottery vessels and figures by the wagon load and shipping them east by the barrelful.[14]

Fred Harvey entered the Indian arts and crafts market in the late 1890s. The flagship Mission Revival style Alvarado Hotel in Albuquerque, opened in 1901, "the first building in New Mexico to revive Spanish tradition and thereby make the whole Southwest history-conscious," was connected to the depot by an arcade containing the Indian building. John Frederick Huckel had created an Indian department, which Herman Schweizer, a longtime Santa Fe/Harvey employee, managed. Schweizer acquired most of the best pieces brought into the Fred Harvey Fine Arts Collection, as well as the items sold in the shops. The Indian building had a shop and museum of Indian artifacts, including a replica of a Hopi altar designed by Heinrich Voth. There were also Indian craftspersons at work: "See patient Navajo squaws weaving blankets, their men engaged in fashioning showy bracelets, rings and trinkets; Indians from Acoma and Laguna making pottery; skillful squaws plaiting blankets; . . . Undisturbed by the eager gaze of the tourist, the stoic works on as unconcernedly as though in his reservation home."[15]

Other outlets included Hopi House adjacent to El Tovar Hotel on the south rim of the Grand Canyon. Designed by Mary Colter, it was a terraced, three-story stone structure with exposed vigas patterned after houses at Oraibi on Third Mesa. One room contained part of the Harvey collection of Navajo blankets, which won a prize at the 1904 St. Louis world's fair (see Chapter 17). A Totem Room had replicas of sandpaintings and another of Voth's Hopi altars. Hopi and other Indian artisans lived in the upper floors. During the day they wove blankets and baskets, carved kachina dolls, made pottery and jewelry, and at 5:00 P.M. danced on the patio for the edification of the tourists.[16]

Fred Harvey's El Navajo Hotel (opened 1923, demolished 1957) in Gallup was publicized as a "tribute to American Indians." Under architect and designer Mary Colter's direction, the interior was decorated with replicas of Navajo sandpaintings. This was a very controversial act for many Navajos, since sandpaint-

ings are sacred and supposed to be destroyed at the end of each night's ceremony in which they are used. But for the railway's *Santa Fe Magazine,* "the sand paintings [are] authentic copies . . . of these profoundly interesting examples of Indian art, tradition and religious faith, which, for the first time, have been brought out of the inaccessible byways of the Navajo country into the highways of the tourist travel."[17]

The sandpainting decorations were copied from a collection of eighty-four watercolor reproductions collected by Sam and Charlie Day, the traders at Chinle, Arizona, who had starred in Edward Curtis's ersatz Yeibichei film (see Chapter 26). The railway invited two thousand Navajos to the ceremony, including a number of well-known singers. "The building was dedicated . . . with a House Blessing rite from Blessingway sung by . . . Little Singer and Little Warrior, with Mr. and Mrs. Sam Day, Jr., as sponsors."[18]

The next step in the Santa Fe/Harvey tourism campaign was the development of side trips. Under the direction of R. Hunter Clarkson, luxury motor coach and car services were developed. In 1925 Clarkson purchased Koshare Tours from Erna Fergusson to create the Harvey Detours (Figs. 27.1, 27.2). Fergusson was a well-known New Mexico native and sister

27.1. Harvey Detours at Santa Clara Pueblo, New Mexico. Charles F. Lummis Collection. Courtesy of the Southwest Museum.

of Harvey Fergusson, newspaperman, novelist, and historian. She was hired to train the tour guides—well-educated young women called Couriers.[19]

The Couriers received crash courses in Southwestern anthropology and history from Edgar Lee Hewett, A. V. Kidder, Sylvanus Griswold Morley, Charles Lummis, and Frederick Webb Hodge, among others. Subsequent training courses were conducted by Hewett and his Museum of New Mexico staff. When a Detours contingent stopped at the La Fonda Hotel in Santa Fe, an evening lecture at the museum by Hewett, Kenneth Chapman, or other museum staff members was often part of the tour. The tours visited various pueblos, as well as archaeological sites, such as Puyé west of San Ildefonso. Thousands of "dudes" learned their Southwestern anthropology from the tours and the guidebooks provided by the railway and the Fred Harvey Company.

The Santa Fe Style

When New Mexico and Arizona were finally admitted to statehood in 1912, forward-looking citizens began considering ways of attracting new business and capital to their states. The Santa Fe Railway was already deeply and profitably involved in tourism. Another rapidly growing "industry" was respiratory recuperation. The dry, sunshiny climates of Colorado, New Mexico, and Arizona offered help and possible cure for sufferers of "consumption," phthisis, or tuberculosis, as it was called after the tubercle bacillus was isolated in 1882. The crowded, humid, unhygienic nineteenth- and early twentieth-century industrial cities of the East were major breeding grounds for the disease. The Southwest offered a dry climate thought to promote remission and even a cure. Sanitoria sprung up at Colorado Springs, Albuquerque, Phoenix, and Santa Fe. Sunmount, operated by Dr. Frank Mera, was the fashionable sanitorium in Santa Fe. Often those who came seeking a cure found it, and remained to play active roles in the political and cultural affairs of the states and the region.

The City Different

The city of Santa Fe began to reinvent itself for the tourist trade in March 1912, when a City Council Planning Board was created. H. H. Dorman was the chairman, Bronson Cutting was in charge of publicity, and Edgar Lee Hewett was chair of the committee on nomenclature. What was needed, it was agreed, were ways to make the town seem to be a unique place. Hewett and his committee set about changing the names of the streets from English to Spanish; for example, Telegraph Road became Camino del Monte Sol.[20] The chamber of commerce began claiming that Santa Fe was the oldest town in the United States, a brouhaha noted earlier. But being the oldest (or second oldest) town in the United States with made-up Spanish street names did little to make Santa Fe the "City Different." Perhaps changing its look would help. Between 1880 and 1910, various buildings and houses in the several eclectic styles of the day—Second Empire, Queen Anne, Carpenter Gothic, Bungalow—had become common. They were in jarring contrast to the older buildings standing next to them. Santa Fe was beginning to look like every other western town.

What was needed was a plan to preserve the existing adobe buildings and develop a style for new construction appropriate to the Hispanic and Pueblo heritage of the town and the region. Frank Springer,

Hewett, Morley, Nusbaum, and others agreed that the Hispanic and Pueblo architectural heritage ought to be emphasized and preserved. Sylvanis Morley jumped into the work of the planning board and chaired a committee on architectural style. At a "New-Old Santa Fe" exhibit in November 1912, Morley exhibited a ten-foot scale model, built by Jesse Nusbaum and Percy Adams, of a "Hispanic portal . . . as it might have looked in the mid-1770s" on the Palace of the Governors. The following year, Nusbaum removed the gingerbread-style portal and replaced it with the model's design (Figs. 27.3, 27.4). Morley had purchased an old adobe house and began remodeling it in the new style. Nusbaum had also designed a building for the U.S. Forest Service embodying a flat roof, external vigas, and a portal with columns.[21]

But what was the "Santa Fe style" to be? By 1907 the fledgling University of New Mexico had begun to build its campus buildings in the "pueblo" style, a program that continued by fits and starts until the late 1920s, when the style was officially adopted by the

27.3. Palace of the Governors, Santa Fe, 1905. Courtesy of the Museum of New Mexico Photographic Archives.

27.4. Palace of the Governors, Santa Fe, 1922. Courtesy of the
Museum of New Mexico Photographic Archives.

university.[22] The Santa Fe Railway and Fred Harvey were building Mission Revival hotels and depots, appropriate perhaps for California, but not for Santa Fe.

The next step was taken by brother architects Isaac H. and William M. Rapp. They had designed the New Mexico Territorial Capitol, a building very much in the Roman Revival style of capitol buildings in other states (later vastly modified into the Bataan Memorial Building) and other public buildings in Santa Fe. A client of the Rapps admired the Franciscan church of San Esteban del Rey at Acoma Pueblo and asked them to design a warehouse in Morley, Colorado, "as nearly as possible" like it. The building, completed in 1908, was in a highly visible location alongside the Santa Fe Railway tracks. Sylvanus Morley and his committee decided that the Rapps' design embodied much of what they were seeking in their Santa Fe style.[23] In 1913, Rapp, Rapp and Hendrickson (a new partner) received the commission to design the New Mexico building for the 1915 Panama-California

Exposition in San Diego. The San Esteban design was reworked slightly; Jesse Nusbaum supervised construction. The building, greatly modified, still stands in Balboa Park.

Hewett and his colleagues felt that another way to develop Santa Fe was to stimulate an art colony similar to the one coalescing in Taos (see Chapter 28). Hewett offered studio facilities in the Palace of the Governors and held exhibits there; he and others began talking about building an art museum. The 1915 state legislature appropriated thirty thousand dollars on condition that an equal amount of non-state funds be raised; ultimately, Frank Springer provided the funds.

The Rapps' design for the Museum of Fine Arts facade is patterned after the six Franciscan mission churches at Acoma, San Felipe, Cochiti, Laguna, Santa Ana, and Pecos pueblos. Jesse Nusbaum again supervised construction, which was completed in 1917. The State School for the Deaf, built in 1917; the La Fonda Hotel, remodeled for the Fred Harvey

Company by Rapp, Rapp and Hendrickson in 1921; and the Federal Building, constructed from 1921 to 1926, gave great cachet to the style.[24]

The artists, writers, and others who began moving to Santa Fe adopted the style in their dwellings. Amelia Elizabeth White and her sister Martha arrived in 1922, to remain for the rest of their lives. They commissioned William Penhallow Henderson (see below) to design a compound for them on Garcia Street—some fifteen structures in the Santa Fe style, which they called El Delirio.[25] Years later Elizabeth White gave El Delirio to the School of American Research for its campus. A Santa Fe city ordinance in the 1950s declared the "pueblo" and "territorial" as the only proper (and legal) variants of the Santa Fe style within the city's historic district.

Anthropologists and Indian Painters

Although information is scanty, it is clear that individuals in various pueblos by the early 1880s were drawing pictures based on their own experience, using whatever materials were at hand. In 1881, John Gregory Bourke bought from a young Jemez boy "a couple of pictures, cleverly done, representing the Zuni or Moqui Coyamases dancing."[26] Jesse Walter Fewkes had a number of Hopi men make colored pictures of kachinas in the 1890s. By the mid-1880s a number of young Navajos were drawing various scenes, including ceremonies, often using colored pencils on wrapping paper obtained at trading posts. Like Plains Indian people and their "ledger drawings," both Pueblo and Navajo people were using Anglo implements and paper to make pictures based on their own ideas and cultural backgrounds.

The focal point for "early modern" Southwest Indian painters was San Ildefonso Pueblo. Edgar Lee Hewett began his field schools in the Pajarito Plateau region in 1907, and over several years employed a number of men from San Ildefonso as shovel hands. One such was Alfredo Montoya. According to Tonita Peña, she, her sister Alfonsita, and Alfredo Montoya were encouraged to draw and paint by a teacher in the San Ildefonso day school, Ester B. Hoyt. Montoya sold some of his drawings of dances to a couple attending the field school. Stylistically, his paintings are regarded as precursors of later San Ildefonso painters. Montoya died in 1913. He was married to Tonita Martínez, a sister of Crescencio Martínez. Crescencio, in turn, was married to Maximiliana Montoya, a sister of María Montoya. María married Julian Martínez in 1904. Julián Martínez apparently began doing crayon drawings around 1908. Others seem to have been working in adjacent pueblos soon after.[27]

By 1916, Crescencio Martínez was selling paintings to Alice Corbin Henderson; in 1917 she began buying from Alfonso Roybal, Crescencio's sister's son, better known as Awa Tsireh. Martínez began working for Hewett in the Pajarito archaeological excavations and showed Hewett some of his paintings. Impressed, Hewett gave him paper and water colors, and commissioned him to "produce . . . pictures of all the characters that appear in the [nonsecret] summer and winter ceremonies." Martínez did twenty-two of a planned twenty-three paintings before he died during the influenza epidemic of 1918. He sold very similar paintings to Alice Corbin Henderson and Mary Austin. Hewett and his staff were also encouraging others, including Julian Martínez, Abel Sanchez, and Romando Vigil, and Tonita Peña.[28]

The Santa Fe Indian School

As interest in Indian painters grew, Hewett and others began looking around for other potential Indian artists. One source of talent proved to be the Santa Fe Indian School, founded in 1890 by the Bureau of Indian Affairs, along the lines that it tried to portray in the various world's fairs (see Chapter 17). The Santa Fe school did not have an art department, possibly subscribing to the then-current government dictum that *any* Indian culture should be discouraged in the process of remaking Indian children into Anglolike farmers, artisans, and domestics. However, in 1915 when a new superintendent, John De Huff, and his wife Elizabeth, arrived at the school, they began encouraging student artwork. Four students were particularly active: Alfonso Roybal from San Ildefonso, Fred Kabotie and Otis Polelonema from Hopi, and Velino Shije Herrera from Zia.

By 1919, the Indian artists began to be caught up in the network of patronage, publicity, museum and gallery exhibits, published criticism, and money that makes up the Euroamerican "art world." Members of the Santa Fe art colony moved to call attention to Pueblo artists, to bring them within the network. In 1920, modernist painter Marsden Hartley wrote effusively about "the" Indian artist: "Science looks upon him as a phenomenon; esthetics looks upon him as a giant of masterful expression in our midst. The redman is poet and artist of the very first order among the geniuses of time."[29]

In 1922, Hewett appeared before the American Federation of the Arts in Washington to trumpet a "great revival" of Indian painting. John De Huff, speaking before a group of Indian Service teachers at Flagstaff, Arizona, declared as one of his major aims "to foster and preserve the Indians' native culture. . . . The Indian as a rule, has an unusual artistic instinct. . . . There is no reason why a potentially great painter or illustrator or decorator should be made a fourth or fifth class blacksmith or starving agriculturalist. . . . As well might one consent to the razing of some great architectural monument as to sanction the notion of letting the decorative art of the Indian die out."[30]

In addition to publicity, the Museum of New Mexico provided close guidance for many of the Pueblo painters. Studio space was provided in the Palace of the Governors, as was paper, paints, and encouragement. For example, the Hewett papers contain extensive correspondence between Lancing Bloom and various Pueblo painters, such as Velion Herrera and Tonita Peña. Peña was born at San Ildefonso, but moved to Cochiti as a young girl. Bloom often criticized the paintings, suggesting colors and the number and placement of figures. The museum also acted as agent for the painters and sold paintings by mail. A 1921 receipt shows that one Wheeler J. Bailey purchased four paintings: Mountain Sheep

Ceremony, by Fred Kabotie, twelve dollars; Buffalo Dance, by Awa Tsireh eight dollars; Eagle Dance, no name given, eight dollars; Deer Dance, by Tonita Peña, five dollars.[31]

The artists, in turn, wrote to Bloom about their paintings, their problems, and their need for money. In January 1921, Tonita Peña wrote to Bloom: "It is better [for me] to paint all this month all you want until March because I can't paint in April, too many flys [sic]. . . . And I will tell you Mr. L. B. Bloom I want you to send me some money about $20 or $25. I got the $10 but I haven't got enough to buy flour . . ." Bloom replied, sent her some money and more paints.[32]

In 1919, the Museum of Fine Arts in Santa Fe had two exhibitions of the works of young Pueblo painters. In 1920, John Sloan arranged for their works to be shown as a feature of the Society of Independent Artists annual exhibition at the Waldorf Astoria in New York. They were so well received that the painters were featured again in 1921. Also in 1920, Mary Austin arranged for a showing of the San Ildefonso painters at the American Museum of Natural History in New York, and Alice Corbin Henderson saw to an exhibit of Awa Tsireh's paintings at the Chicago Art Club. Exhibitions followed in other cities in succeeding years, including Denver, San Francisco, Madrid, and Prague, culminating in a major Indian arts exhibit in New York City in 1931. The painters were now deeply enmeshed in the patronage-publicity-museum-criticism network.[33]

Pueblo Pottery

The relationships between Nampeyo, Thomas Keam, and Jesse Walter Fewkes in stimulating the Hopi pottery revival in the 1890s were noted earlier. Hewett's excavations at Frijoles Canyon provided a similar stimulus for the Eastern Pueblos. At Puyé, excavations turned up blackware pottery sherds, some with exterior polish. Hewett sought Tewa potters who might duplicate the blackware, including Julián and María Martínez of San Ildefonso. María Montoya was born about 1887. She learned to make polychrome pottery from her aunt and grandmother. María and Julián were married in 1904 and spent their honeymoon at the St. Louis world's fair (see Chapter 17). They created an excellent blackware and began experimenting with polishing techniques, determining that a polished background with a matte finish design painted on was easiest to handle. By 1920, the blackware had become very popular. The Martínezes showed others at San Ildefonso how to fire the blackware. Santa Clara potters were firing blackware before María and Julián began their experiments. As blackware grew in popularity, Santa Clara potters began producing carved or pressed-in, rather than painted, designs.[34]

Hewett employed María and Julián to demonstrate pottery making and decoration at the Palace of the Governors. Julián also continued watercolor painting. In between, he worked as a museum janitor, and on the restoration of archaeological sites in Frijoles Canyon for the Museum of New Mexico and the National Park Service.

Indian Arts Fund

As interest in Pueblo pottery quickened, collectors and museums outside New Mexico rapidly began acquiring older historical pieces; in Santa Fe there was an increasing concern that such pieces would disappear locally. Legend has it that one night in 1922 the writer Elizabeth Shepley Sergeant held a dinner party at her home in Tesuque.[35] Those present lamented with Sergeant over a just-broken Zuni pot. Talk turned to the rapidly disappearing older pieces, the need to have good examples as models for the revivalist potters, and what should be done about it. The upshot was the formation of the Pueblo Pottery Fund, managed by Wesley Bradfield, Harry P. Mera, and Elizabeth Sergeant, with Kenneth Chapman in the lead. Donations of funds and pots were quietly solicited. The first acquisitions were Sergeant's mended Zuni pot and four pieces from Acoma. By 1923 the fund had 20 pieces. By 1925 over 450 pieces were stored in Mera's house and the basement of the Fine Arts Museum, and John D.

Rockefeller, Jr., was quietly supporting the fund (see Chapter 29).

Soon the scope of the fund was broadened to include other arts and crafts, and the Indian Arts Fund, Inc., came into existence. It had a twenty-five-person board that included Chapman, Mera, Samuel Guernsey, Frederick Webb Hodge, Alfred Kidder, and Sylvanus Morley, as well as writers Mary Austin and Elizabeth Sergeant, artists Frank Applegate, Andrew Dasburg and B. J. O. Nordfeldt, and Mabel Dodge Luhan and Amelia Elizabeth White. The collection, premier in the world, is now held by the School of American Research and the Laboratory of Anthropology.

Kenneth Chapman had more than a sentimental interest in Pueblo pottery. By 1919 he had worked for ten years at the Museum of New Mexico, doing all jobs from factotum to acting director while Hewett was away. Chapman had worked for years doing the exacting drawings for Frank Springer's fossil crinoid monographs. Now Chapman appealed to Springer to help him get half his time designated for research; Springer convinced Hewett to allow it. Chapman was thus launched on what became a life's work: his outstanding studies of historic Southwest Indian arts, but especially Pueblo pottery designs.[36]

According to Chapman's unpublished memoirs, his interest in Pueblo pottery designs and the pottery fund was kindled by María Martínez. One day in 1920 he was discussing San Ildefonso designs with her. In reply to his question about older design combinations, she responded:

> "Why, Mr. Chapman, you ought to do better than we can, because you have been taking all our old pottery away from us and making pictures of it, and then sending it away, and we can't remember any of the old designs." That gave me food for considerable thought. There was no money in sight for a purchase fund, but some way must be found to collect and preserve the fine old crafts where they could be studied by the Indians themselves.

Chapman began studying San Ildefonso designs and mounted a display in the museum, which aroused interest in

> the decorative arts of the then little known pueblo of San Ildefonso and, two years later, it led to the organization of the little group who began soliciting contributions toward a Pueblo Pottery Fund for purchase of desirable pieces to be held forever in Santa Fe. . . . [Later,] the group then known and incorporated as the Indian Arts Fund, had won Mr. John D. Rockefeller, Jr.'s support and later played its part in the organization of the Laboratory of Anthropology, where more than three thousand specimens are housed. Maria's chance remark had worked wonders![37]

The Indians Arts Fund and the efforts by Anglo artists to involve Indian painters in the art network were partly outgrowths of Anglo ideas about primitivism and natural man. The arts and crafts movement in the United States, stimulated by William Morris and others in England, was at its peak from about 1900 to 1920. The principal tenet was the celebration of individual, authentic "folk" craftsmanship, as a counterfoil to machine-age industrial production. Working with one's hands was seen as uplifting. Therefore, preservation and encouragement of well-made handicrafts of any sort was a good thing, with potentially positive social and moral consequences. This ideal is reflected in a 1907 article in *The Craftsman*, the movement's U.S. journal, about Frederick Monsen, who spent much time at Hopi between about 1890 and 1910 (see the section on photographers in Chapter 28). Monsen's "long experience with Indian capabilities and characteristics" led him to oppose "the destruction of the ancient crafts and the attempt to replace them by modern commercial work that is practically valueless as well as hideous and commonplace." In Monsen's view, the "Government" should "exercise some intelligence in reviving and preserving the wonderful old handicrafts of the peaceful tribes, instead of giving the children instruction in the trades and industries of the white man," thus

making it "a great deal easier" for Indian people to earn a living. Further, Monsen "holds that in the preservation of the Indian crafts, as well as Indian traditions, games, ethics, morals, and religion, there lies a strong influence for good that ultimately would affect our modern art and life."[38]

A central tenet of the modernist art movement was the rejection of effete academic representational art as a corrupt product of a decadent civilization. Some modernists saw "primitive art"—from African and Melanesian wood carvings to Pueblo paintings and pots—as "real art" since it was produced by real, natural (and not artificial civilized) people. Those who did so sought to connect their own art with this real art, thus bypassing the effete and other kinds of art they detested. D. H. Lawrence went seeking a generic "life force" in the Pueblos and in Mexico (see Chapter 28). Modernist painters went looking for an ideological wall plug somewhere in Santa Fe or Taos to connect their art to the life force of the art produced by Indian natural men and women. As Kenneth Dauber has cogently argued, it was this "connection" which, in part, led the modernists to support the exhibits of the Pueblo painters in New York, Chicago, and elsewhere. Tom Wolfe pointed out, in *The Painted Word,* that art is not art until the critics say so. When the Pueblo painters gained "critical acceptance" in the exhibits, they were made part of the art network, thus legitimizing them and, in a real sense, their modernist patrons.[39]

The Indian Fairs

A fiesta has been celebrated sporadically in Santa Fe since the 1700s. During the reinvention of Santa Fe after 1912, Fiesta was resuscitated partly as a tourist attraction and partly so that the locals could dress up in Hispanic and medieval costumes and have a parade and a party. It culminated in burning a large wooden figure "Zozobra—Old Man Gloom." In 1922, a Southwest Indian Fair and Arts and Crafts Exhibition was made part of Fiesta.

In addition to encouraging the revival of Pueblo

pottery, Hewett and Chapman actively sought to ensure that the potters were given a fair price for their wares. The local curio traders were loath to do this, preferring the old system of buying pots by the wagon load and paying minimal amounts for what they did buy. In 1921, Hewett and Chapman had a museum employee selling high-quality pots for the potters, at much higher prices than what the traders were charging. The traders threatened to have Hewett arrested. Undaunted, he persisted and the traders changed their buying policies. By 1922 Hewett, Chapman, and others had developed the Indian Market in a bazaar setting: outdoor booths with the artists and craftspersons selling their own products.[40]

As a part of the Indian Market, a "summer Santa Fean," Rose Dougan, established a two-thousand-dollar endowment to provide annual prizes for a San Ildefonso pottery competition. Chapman convinced her that the competition should be more general and the prizes would be awarded at the Indian Fair. Chapman took the lead in organizing the exhibition, held in the Santa Fe armory (Fig. 27.5).

It was also decided to hold competitive Indian dances as part of Fiesta (Fig. 27.6). At the conclusion of the 1922 Fiesta, Hewett wrote to Juan Gonzales, governor of San Ildefonso. "My dear Juan: I am sending you . . . some checks that are due your people for prizes at the Fiesta and Indian Fair. The $40.00 prize, should, I think, go to the dancers who took part in the Basket Dance and Eagle Dance. Your dancers and those of Tesuque were so nearly equal that the cash prize of $80.00 was divided equally between them. If among yourselves you think it best to put the $40.00 in general funds belonging to the whole pueblo, that will be all right with us."[41] In later years, Indian Market became a separate event from Fiesta. By 1999 Indian Market was infusing an estimated 215 million dollars yearly into the economy of northern New Mexico.

While Santa Feans focused on Pueblo art and dances as part of Fiesta, other New Mexico towns began to see the economic possibilities of gatherings of Indians. Gallup was the first, establishing the Gallup Inter-Tribal Indian Ceremonial in 1922 (Fig. 27.7). Gallup did not have a deep historical past, as did Santa Fe. There was some nearby coal mining and

27.5. Indian Fair, Santa Fe, New Mexico, 1922. Courtesy of the Museum of New Mexico Photographic Archives.

27.6 (above). Basket
Dance at Santa Fe
Amphitheater, 1922.
Courtesy of the San
Diego Museum of Man.

27.7 (left). Gallup, New
Mexico, Inter-Tribal
Ceremonial 1926.
Photograph by Charles
F. Lummis. Courtesy of
the Southwest Museum.

in the 1880s a division point was established for the railroad. Subsequently, the famed "Route 66" came through town.

The boosters of the Gallup Ceremonial proposed to erect a 250-foot-high statue of "The Indian," rivaling the 302-foot-high Statue of Liberty on its base. This monument to generic Indianness would stand on the east edge of Gallup as a permanent sign for the Inter-Tribal Ceremonials. The aesthetes of Santa Fe were horrified; others were merely bemused. The statue was not erected; seemingly it never got beyond the publicity and saloon-talk stage.

However, the Ceremonial promoters forged ahead, and the event quickly grew quite large. Its focus was spectacle: what has come to be called "fancy dancing" performed by groups from different tribes and pueblos. The 1926 *Official Program of Events* lists a variety of foot and horse races in the afternoons, including a standard-length marathon.[42] Evenings were devoted to a variety of "tribal" dances performed by Apache, Navajo and Pueblo teams. There were also twice-daily concerts by "Princess Tsianina, Cherokee-Creek mezzo-soprano, America's own prima donna, and Hoske Noswood, Navajo baritone in a selection of Indian songs by Cadman, Grunn and Leurence."

Not to be outdone, in about 1925 Albuquerque, according to Harvey Fergusson, "built a grandstand and put on an Indian show, known as the 'First American,' which drew a good crowd and was a truly astonishing mixture of banality, absurdity, and really impressive primitive spectacle. Here 'Indian' tenors and sopranos, with much white blood and Broadway training [probably Tsianina and Noswood], sang sentimental ditties. Conquistadores paraded in linoleum boots and armor, carrying stage property spears and swords. Genuine cowboys got drunk and did a lot of wild shooting. The Navajos danced their fire dance and lifted up the shrill unearthly chants of the Yebechi." [43] What more could a tourist dude want from the pretend Southwest?

CHAPTER 28

Literary and Pictorial Ethnography

In chapter 26 the flip sides of the noble savage image—Apollonian and Dionysian—and how they were used by Ruth Benedict were noted. Many Anglos who came to the Southwest sought one or both of these images; either was preferable to the corrupt denizens of civilization. Others came seeking only nature, and found surcease in the aridity of the landscapes and the luminosity of the light. Following Oliver La Farge (see below), all such are called "yearners," be they tourists, artists, poets, novelists, essayists, or their groupies and hangers-on of all genders. Claude Lévi-Strauss, who has sought to define the European and Euroamerican fascination with "the Other," claims that all anthropologists are yearners; perhaps so.[1] What is clear is that many Anglos, anthropologists or not, came variously seeking artifacts, art, knowledge, inspiration, curiosity satisfaction, and the psychic energy—sometimes defined as "life forces"—thought to emanate from "natural" people. Whether they saw the people they found, Indians and

Hispanics, as Apollonian or Dionysian, or some combination thereof, depended on the expectations and images that they brought along. Much of this was expressed in novels, poems, short stories, essays, paintings, and photographs. Here, some examples most closely tied to anthropology are reviewed.

Writing Popular Southwestern Ethnography

In 1934, Elizabeth Shepley Sergeant wrote: "In this unindustrialized New Mexico, even science is largely the science of archaeologist, ethnologist, anthropologist—the sort of science that unconsciously feeds the novelist, the poet. . . . Science produced the first Southwest classics: Bandelier, Cushing, Lummis were scientists in whom the story telling instinct ran strong."[2] The "instinct ran strong" in later ethnographers as well, especially in Benedict, Bunzel, and Reichard. There were many others—writers, novelists, and poets—who drew on the work of the academic ethnographers, or were excellent ethnographic observers in their own right.

Ethnography is the most difficult of the humanistic arts; transcultural insight and empathy and an eye for nuance are key requirements. The numbers of writers, novelists and poets who wrote in an ethnographic framework between 1880 and 1930 are legion. Among the first such was the poet Alice Corbin, who arrived in Santa Fe in 1916 with her husband, William Penhallow Henderson. The same year, Mabel Ganson Evans Dodge Sterne abandoned her salon in Greenwich Village and moved to Santa Fe. She quickly found it "quite tiresome," perhaps because Alice Corbin was already the queen bee, and moved on to Taos. There, Mabel's world-weariness fell away, she said, as she discovered the "spiritual qualities" of the Taos Indians, especially Tony Luhan, whose drumming she found particularly compelling. She shed her current husband, Maurice Sterne, pensioned off Tony's Taosian wife, and settled down as Mabel Dodge Luhan, artist, writer and self-appointed doyen and publicist for the literary and art colony of Taos.

Luhan sought to bring leading literary lights to Taos, especially D. H. Lawrence. Lawrence was only in New Mexico about eighteen months during two trips between 1922 and 1925. But he "amply repaid his daunting hostess by providing a lifetime of gossip, innuendo and anecdote—not only for Mabel but for self-made and occasional *Taoseños* through many years to come."[3]

By the early 1920s the artists' and writers' colonies were burgeoning in both Taos and Santa Fe. Poet and sinologist Witter Bynner arrived in 1922; his longtime secretary-companion, Spud Johnson, soon after. Mary Austin came to visit in 1918, but did not settle in Santa Fe until 1924.[4] They and others came for one or more of the reasons previously cataloged; others came because it was fashionable to be part of the scene.

In New Mexico native Harvey Fergusson's 1930 satire of Taos and Santa Fe *Footloose McGarnigal,* an artist tells the hero, "He [the Indian] can't come into your world and you can't go into his. Here in Taos, we paint them and patronize them, and crowd around all their sacred ceremonies like boys watching a dog fight, and to them we simply aren't there except to the extent that we're a minor nuisance." As for his fellow Anglos, "The place is a museum of misfits . . . except for a few . . . painters who really paint. Nearly all of them piddle in some art or other, but only a few really work. If they can't do anything else, they always go in for saving the Indians. That's the latest fad. . . . All these queer lost souls that hang around the Indians. . . . What really fascinates them is the perfect peaceful rhythm of the Indian life, going on as it has for a thousand years without missing a beat."[5]

Whatever it was they sought, many artists, writers, and ethnographers found it. There was first of all the setting: the "howling desert" transformed by Santa Fe Railway flacks and yearners' wishes into an enchanted land filled with luminous light. Within this sublimity, close to its harsh but nurturing naturalness, lived groups of Indian and Hispanic people, seen as having romantic, noble, and enriching, although sometimes tragic, lives.

One of the first writers in this vein was Charles Francis Saunders (1859–1941), a Quaker businessman and editor who visited the Southwest between 1902 and 1910. His *The Indians of the Terraced Houses* (1912) presents a personal and romanticized description and history of the Pueblos. Saunders was strongly opposed to any government attempt to assimilate the Pueblos into Anglo culture; he preferred them in their "natural" state.[6]

In contrast, there was Leo Crane's *Indians of the Enchanted Desert,* in 1925, and *Desert Drums,* in 1928. Crane (1881–1958?) was an Indian agent "who fought mostly losing battles against an inefficient government for a lot of Indians he thoroughly understood but never really liked very much."[7] Nor did he like the "do-gooder" yearners any better; in fact, he liked them less. In 1910 he was appointed Indian agent at Keams Canyon, Arizona, transferring in 1919 to Albuquerque in charge of the Pueblos. His opposition to the chicanery of Interior Secretary Albert Fall and the Bursum Bill got him transferred in 1922 to a reservation in

South Dakota; soon thereafter he left the Indian Service. Crane was outraged over the treatment the Pueblos had received from the Spanish, Mexicans and Anglos alike. *Indians of the Enchanted Desert* is a summary of Navajo and Hopi cultures and a chronicle of wrongs they suffered at the hands of the others. *Desert Drums* is a summary of the Rio Grande pueblos and a chronicle of their mistreatment, together with satirical and scathing observations on the shenanigans of Fall, Bursum, their cronies, and various do-gooder yearners.[8]

Other popular ethnographic and ethnohistoric summaries that appeared between 1926 and 1930 included works by Mary Roberts Coolidge and her writer husband Dane Coolidge. Mary Coolidge (1860–1945) was a well-known sociologist; she received a doctorate from Stanford in 1896 and taught there until 1903. Her 1909 book on Chinese immigration was the first major scholarly analysis of the long-festering "Chinese problem" in the American West. Her *Why Women Are So* (1912) was, like Elsie Clews Parsons's *The Old Fashioned Woman* (1913), a major statement of "cultural feminism" in American society.[9] The couple spent part of each year in the Southwest. In 1929 Mary Coolidge published *The Rain-Makers,* which she dedicated to Edgar Lee Hewett. It is a popular yet thorough summary of archaeology and ethnography based on then-current academic and museum publications. In 1930 both Coolidges produced *The Navajo,* which was again, a popular summary of Navajo mythology, chants, art, and social life, based on available scholarly sources.[10]

One of the best known novelist-ethnographers was Laura Adams Armer (1874–1963), a San Francisco artist and photographer. In 1923 she began visiting the Southwest to study Navajo and Hopi mythology. She developed a close rapport with a Navajo chanter. A sandpainting was made for her and she was permitted to photograph sandpainters working. She copied a number of other sandpaintings in oils for Mary Cabot Wheelwright; one hundred of them were exhibited in the 1930s at the Laboratory of Anthropology. She also exhibited paintings of Indian lifeways across the country. With the help of Roman Hubbell, at Ganado, Armer produced the first Native American motion picture directed in an Indian language—Navajo. The film, *The Mountain Chant,* was shown at the American Museum of Natural History in the fall of 1928.[11]

Her first book, *Waterless Mountain,* with a foreword by Oliver La Farge, appeared in 1931. The story is about a young Navajo boy destined to become a chanter. There are good portrayals of herding, of daily life, of chant rituals, weddings, and Navajo perceptions of the White man's world. Armer continued to write for many years, primarily juvenile fiction about the Navajos and the Southwest, which she and her husband illustrated.[12]

Several novels for teens were produced between about 1890 and 1930 in which ethnography and ethnohistory are used. Most have some sort of love interest, often across tribal boundaries, and are set against some contemporary or historical problem. They include Alida Sims Malkus's *The Dragon Fly of Zuni* and Dama Margaret Smith's 1931 *Hopi Girl.* Children's books include Cornelia James Cannon's *The Pueblo Boy* and *Pueblo Girl,* both set against the Spanish invasion of Zuni and the Rio Grande pueblos in 1540–42, and Grace Moon's *Chi-Wee: The Adventures of a Little Indian Girl,* a series of vignettes.[13]

Among the major novelists associated with the anthropological Southwest during the 1910s and 1920s were Willa Cather, Oliver La Farge, D. H. Lawrence, and Aldous Huxley. All produced classics that remained in print for decades. In the mid-1920s, Willa Cather published *The Professor's House* and *Death Comes for the Archbishop.* The latter is Cather's most famous work, her fictionalized, somewhat biased and racialist account of the French priest John Baptist Lamy, archbishop of Santa Fe from 1851 until his death in 1888. *The Professor's House* contains a section, "Tom Outland's Story," which reflects Cather's view of Richard Wetherill at Mesa Verde, together with her own experiences there, and her reading of Nordenskiöld's *Cliff Dwellers.*[14]

Oliver La Farge (1901–1962) was born in New York

City.[15] His father, artist and architect Christopher Grant La Farge, was a companion and lover of Elsie Clews Parsons (see Chapter 26). After an unhappy schooling at Groton, La Farge entered Harvard in 1920, determined to become an expert in European Paleolithic archaeology, inspired by Henry Fairfield Osborn's *Men of the Old Stone Age.* He rowed, high jumped, helped edit the *Lampoon,* was senior class poet, and studied some anthropology.

In 1921, 1922, and 1924, La Farge did archaeology with Samuel Guernsey in Arizona (see Chapter 24).[16] When he was preparing for his first field trip in 1921, his father "brought me a message from Doctor [Elsie Clews] Parsons, worded in mild scorn of archaeology and hoping that I would become an ethnologist. With this she sent me reprints of some of her articles. Her interests derived from the belief that I might have some of my father's qualities, in itself a compliment, and here was a little secret to have by myself, the suggestion that my official occupation was not the very highest one and that I could privately prepare myself for the higher."[17] The Navajo people La Farge encountered around the Wetherill trading post at Kayenta fascinated him, and he began to study them seriously. He ultimately wrote a Master's thesis on the Navajo.

At the end of the 1924 field season, La Farge and two classmates, Bartlett H. Hayes, Jr., and Douglas S. Byers, made a horseback trip from Lukachukai, where they met Father Berard Haile, across the Navajo and Hopi reservations. Along the way they met Lorenzo Hubbell, saw a Hopi Snake Dance, and met Laura Adams Armer at Oraibi. They rode northwestward across Black Mesa to the Wetherills' trading post at Kayenta. By this time, La Farge wrote, "The Indians had got me," and he turned ethnographer, as Parsons had hoped. La Farge explains himself (and others) as anthropologist and yearner:

> There are some people, such as traders and governents officials, whose acquaintance with Indians and resultant fondness for them is solidly founded on the realities of life. Most of the rest

of us, scientists (it's highly noticeable in them), serious amateurs, and the broad group that is known in the West as "yearners," are escapists. How escapism operated in my case is clear by now, I think. As one goes deeper in after having succumbed to the initial attraction and the well established glamour, the appeals to the escapist become ever stronger. As a result Indians are surrounded by a cult with a series of degrees of initiation, elaborated and maintained by people with an instinct for avoiding reality.

> Apart from their picturesqueness and the fact that being one who 'knows the Indians' has been elevated into a distinction like a sort of Ph.D. which one partly awards to one's self, partly receives by acclamation from one's friends, about the most powerful abiding pull they exert lies in the simplicity of their native way of life.[18]

In the fall of 1924 La Farge received the Hemenway fellowship in anthropology at Harvard. But he "got in bad with the powers that were in Southwestern research" and left after one semester.[19] He joined the staff of the Department of Middle American Research (later the Middle American Research Institute) at Tulane University at the invitation of Frans Blom.

Blom (1893–1963) was a polyglot bon vivant from Denmark who wound up doing exploration for an oil company in Central America, where he became interested in the Maya. His drawings of stelae brought him to the attention of Sylvanus Morley. Soon Blom was working with Manuel Gamio at Palenque and for the Carnegie Institution at Uaxactun. Realizing a need for formal training, he went to Harvard to study with Alfred Tozzer and there met La Farge.[20] In 1925 Blom was hired at Tulane and he recruited La Farge for an expedition to Veracruz, Tabasco, and Chiapas in Mexico and on into Guatemala: a survey conducted partly by sloop along the coast of Tabasco, but primarily by horseback, covering some twelve hundred miles. Blom and La Farge described the now-famous great Olmec stone heads at Tres Zapotes and discovered another famous Olmec site, La Venta. The report of their survey, *Tribes and Temples,* is a fascinating mixture of archaeology and ethnography.[21]

La Farge became an assistant in ethnology at Tulane in 1926, and in 1928 came up for promotion. Instead of being promoted, he was fired; apparently he had insulted the son and daughter of a Tulane trustee at a New Orleans masked ball. He had anguished for some years about becoming a writer. Spurred by the necessity of eating after his dismissal, La Farge plunged ahead. *Laughing Boy* appeared in November 1929. In 1930 it was awarded the Pulitzer Prize, beating Ernest Hemingway's *A Farewell to Arms,* Sinclair Lewis's *Dodworth,* and Thomas Wolfe's *Look Homeward Angel.*[22]

Laughing Boy is a deeply moving story of a young traditional Navajo jeweler who marries a Navajo woman, Slim Girl, who earlier had spent six years in BIA boarding school and later became a prostitute. She is torn between wanting a traditional Navajo life and taking what she can from the White world. In the end, she is killed by a Navajo man trying to kill Laughing Boy. The book reflects La Farge's view of the corrupting impact of White culture on the Navajos and other Indian people, a theme he pursued in a number of short stories throughout the 1930s.[23] *Laughing Boy* was translated into several languages and continues in print into the third millennium.

The critical and popular acceptance of *Laughing Boy* thrust La Farge into a career as a writer, and ultimately into a lifetime involvement as an Indian rights activist. He lived in Santa Fe for many years with his second wife, Consuelo Otille Baca de La Farge. He died in 1963, fighting for Indian rights to the end.[24]

D. H. Lawrence and Aldous Huxley

In several senses, the romantic Dionysian savage reached very different kinds of apotheosis in D. H. Lawrence's *The Plumed Serpent* and in Aldous Huxley's *Brave New World,* both of which drew on anthropological sources. The two were compatriots and friendly critics who spent much time together following Lawrence's sojourns in New Mexico. The character Mark Rampion in Huxley's *Point Counter Point* is a somewhat satirical sketch of Lawrence; some critics maintain that the Savage in *Brave New World* is partly Lawrence.[25]

Lawrence did not produce a Southwest novel, but he was deeply influenced by the country and the Indian people. His posthumously published essay "New Mexico" makes that clear: "New Mexico, one of the United States. . . . New Mexico, the picturesque reservation and playground of the eastern states, very romantic, old Spanish, Red Indian, desert mesas, pueblos, cowboys, penitentes, all that film stuff. Very nice, the great South West, put on a sombrero and knot a red kerchief around your neck, to go out into the great free spaces! That is New Mexico wrapped in the absolutely hygienic and shiny mucous-paper of our trite civilization. . . . But break through the shiny sterilized wrapping, and actually *touch* the country, and you will never be the same again. . . . Curious as it may sound, it was New Mexico that liberated me from the present era of civilization, the great era of material and mechanical development. . . . the moment I saw the brilliant, proud morning shine high up over the deserts of Santa Fé, something stood still in my soul and I started to attend."[26]

Lawrence's novel *The Plumed Serpent* has puzzled readers and scholars since its publication in 1926; there is a sizable, and contradictory, critical literature. The novel stems from a trip to Mexico he made with Frieda Lawrence and Witter Bynner in 1922. Lawrence drew on the ancient Mesoamerican deity Quetzalcóatl, myths of other Aztec deities, and his own observations of Southwestern Indian rituals and dances. The central theme seems to be the principal female character's quest for the Dionysian life force of the savage. Lawrence was strongly influenced by anthropological writings on "primitive" religion: Tylor's *Primitive Culture* and especially James George Frazer's *The Golden Bough,* which has to do with the myth of a reviving god and his worship in a cyclical universe. Ideas from them are incorporated into the novel.[27]

Aldous Huxley (1894–1963) was an English essayist and novelist and grandson of Thomas Henry Huxley. The central character in his brilliant dystopian novel *Brave New World* (1932) is "the Savage."[28] The setting is in the future, six hundred years "After Ford." There is a world society in which science and technology are used to achieve social stability. Babies are grown in bottles; individuals are genetically engineered and socially conditioned to happily occupy specific social categories from Alpha Pluses to Epsilon Minuses. Unlimited sex, mind-soothing but physiologically harmless drugs, especially "soma", large amounts of leisure time, "feely" motion pictures, and compulsory communal ritual orgies keep everyone content. No one grows visibly old; all are kept young by hormones and chemicals. Ultimately people die, happily, stoned on soma; their bodily chemicals are recycled. The past, and all the great human thought in literature and philosophy from the past, are blotted out.

An Alpha Plus couple from London visit "the Reservation," a tourist attraction in New Mexico where Indians are kept behind high-powered electrical fences. Indian women give birth to children who grow up and grow old; everyone lives "close to nature." At "Malpais" Pueblo, the couple encounter the son of a Beta Minus woman and an Alpha Plus man. Years before, the woman had visited the Reservation with her male companion. Despite her rigorous adherence to prescribed contraceptive practice, the "Malthusian Drill," as Huxley drolly calls it, she became pregnant. She was injured and separated from the man, who returned to London without her. Found by the Indians and, in her eyes, in utter disgrace because of her pregnancy, she remained on the reservation. She bore the child and raised him, teaching him to read from a manual on the care of bottle-babies, and later, the works of William Shakespeare. The latter came from an Indian lover, Popé, who found it in an old box in a kiva. The blond, blue-eyed young boy was not accepted by young Indians, yet managed to learn much traditional culture from the elders. The culture, as Huxley imagines it, is a combination of Pueblo and Penitente elements, for example, snake dances combined with flagellation ceremonies. The boy put all this together with the ideas he derived from Shakespeare.

The Alpha Plus couple take "John Savage" and his mother, Linda, to London, where they create a sensation. No one has seen a physically old person nor someone who has given actual birth to a child, nor such a child, unless they have visited the Reservation. Huxley uses the Savage's reactions to the super-scientific Fordian civilization, as well as talks between him and Mustapha Mond, one of the "World Controllers," to discuss human freedom, pain, suffering, and free will versus happiness and social stability. One theme is the conflict between romanticism and science writ large, and Huxley uses his protagonists to mercilessly examine both sides. The post-Fordian world provides a manufactured yet ultimately meaningless happiness. This is contrasted with a longed-for culture in which apparent freedom, emotion, truth, beauty and pain, suffering and death, and life close to nature exist and in which the ultimate romantic quest for meaning is possible. In the end, the Savage, seduced by sex, soma, and ritual orgies, kills himself.

Huxley's descriptions of New Mexico, the Reservation and the lives and culture of the Indians are graphic, the more so since when he wrote the novel he had yet to visit the Southwest (he was later a guest of Mabel Dodge Luhan in Taos). He drew his imagery from discussions with Lawrence in 1927–28, from Lawrence's essays, and from Smithsonian and other ethnographic reports on the Pueblos. He took names and bits of stories from Frank Hamilton Cushing's *Zuni Folk Tales*. The name of Linda's lover, Popé, is, of course, that of the leader of the 1680 Pueblo Revolt. Malpais, the vast volcanic badlands south of Mt. Taylor, in New Mexico, is the name Huxley gives to the pueblo, which is clearly Acoma.[29]

Paintings and Drawings

In addition to scores of literary images of Southwestern peoples, there are literally thousands of pictorial images: paintings, drawings, and photographs, beginning with the military drawings of the 1840s. Collectively, they have contributed significantly to the romantic image of the place and its peoples, even those striving for "ethnographic reality." There are dozens of histories of Anglo Southwest painting and the topic is not reviewed further here.[30]

Photography

Photography was very important in Southwestern anthropology in conveying images of the country and the people. The work of Timothy O'Sullivan, William Henry Jackson, and Jack Hillers in the Southwest with the Wheeler, Hayden, and Powell surveys (respectively) during the 1870s has been discussed. Their photographs were distributed in government publications, were seen by millions at world's fairs, and were widely available in stereopticon "views."[31] But there were many other photographs and views of Southwestern Indian people and scenery available, especially after about 1875. Richard Rudisill's invaluable catalog lists dozens of obscure and well-known men and women photographers who worked in Colorado, Arizona, and New Mexico from the 1850s through 1912.[32] Many produced photographs and views that were wholesaled for general distribution.

After the demise of the Hayden Survey, William Henry Jackson opened a studio in Denver, and he and his various assistants photographed widely in the Southwest. In 1899 Jackson leased his negatives and his services to the Detroit Photography Company. He and assistants took photographs at Acoma, Laguna, and elsewhere in 1899 and later.[33] Others, such as Charles Lummis, George Wharton James, Sumner Matteson, Louis C. McClure, Karl Moon, and Frederick Monsen used their own photographs in books and articles or sold them to magazines.[34] Monsen (1865–1929) worked for various geological surveys in the West and Alaska and later explored widely in the Southwest, Mexico, and Central and South America. He spent much time at Hopi and made a large series of photographs. A number of them were used in his articles in *The Craftsman,* a magazine devoted to the promotion of the arts and crafts movement in the United

States.[35] Charles Lummis was an excellent photographer. He made several series of photographs of the Pueblos and was the first to photograph the cross-bearing and mock-crucifixion of the Penitentes.[36]

Edward S. Curtis's carefully posed, composed, and retouched photographs of Hopi, Acoma, Navajo, and others were integral to his "Vanishing Indian" project. There was a similarly romantic, although smaller scale, project funded for several years by Rodman Wanamaker, the Philadelphia department-store magnate. He sponsored three western expeditions between 1908 and 1913 to photograph and make movies of Indians and produced a large-format book, *The Vanishing Race,* in 1913.[37]

Two other photographers who produced major bodies of work on Southwestern Indians were George Ben Wittick (1845–1903), who had various photography businesses in Santa Fe, Albuquerque, Gallup, and Fort Wingate between 1878 and 1903, and Adam Clark Vroman (1856–1916), based in Pasadena, who made several major photographic trips to Arizona and New Mexico between 1894 and 1904.[38]

Some collections of ethnographically important photographs were made around the turn of the twentieth century, but only became generally known as late as the 1980s. One such is the remarkable collection by Kate Cory (1861–1958), who apparently came to the Southwest to paint, but wound up living on the Hopi Mesas for several years. She afterward lived in Prescott, Arizona, until her death.[39]

The advent of the Kodak hand-held camera and roll film in 1888, and a viable process of enlarging photographs from negatives, after about 1885, made photography generally available to the public. Tourists, professional photographers, and anthropologists alike could now take snapshots of Southwestern Indians and scenery, and did so at every opportunity, rudely intruding into Pueblo ceremonies and dances until the various pueblos permanently banned all photography beginning about 1917.

Some professional photographers and anthropologists continued to photograph Indian people when and where they were allowed to do so, producing

several distinguished bodies of work. Certainly the best known is Laura Gilpin (1891–1979), who began photographing in the Southwest in 1917, at first landscapes, then archaeological ruins, and finally Indian people (see Fig. 24.10 and Fig. 28.1). She had a long and rich relationship with the Navajo people beginning in 1930, capped by her magnum opus, *The Enduring Navaho,* published in 1968.[40]

The Cinema

Somewhat less known are images of Southwestern Indian people in motion pictures. They first appeared in "documentaries" in 1898, the *Eagle Dance, Pueblo Indians,* and *War Dance, Pueblo Indians,* followed by *Moki Snake Dance by Wolpi [sic] Indians* in 1901. Edward Curtis filmed his pseudodocumentary of a Navajo Yeibichei Dance in 1904 (see Chapter 26).

Between 1903 and 1930, several hundred movies were produced in which Indians figured in the plots. All the "savage" images and stereotypes previously discussed were presented and magnified. Only about forty films featured Southwestern Indians: Apaches in twenty, beginning with *Apache Gold* (1910); Navajos in nine, starting with *The Navajo's Bride* (1910). Hopis were featured in seven, the first being *The Rights of a Savage* (1912); Zunis were depicted only in *The Sacred Turquoise of the Zuni* (1910). Rio Grande pueblos were featured in four films, from *A Pueblo Legend* (1912) to *The Secret of the Pueblo* (1923). In early films the actors all were Anglos. Mary Pickford was a winsome Indian maid more than once.

A favorite plot was some variation on a happy-ending Romeo and Juliet, for example *Redskin* (1929), in which a Navajo man educated in the East loves his classmate, a Pueblo girl. While fleeing from her people, the boy improbably discovers oil in the desert and stops a Pueblo attack on his family's hogan where the girl is staying, by an offer of oil rights. He then marries the girl.[41]

The most notable film to portray Southwestern Indians before 1930 was *The Vanishing American.* The popular western novelist Zane Grey first serialized the story in 1922 in *The Ladies' Home Journal.* There, Nophaie, a young Navajo, falls in love with a White schoolteacher, goes away to the First World War, returns to the reservation, fights a corrupt, land-grabbing Indian agent, and wins the schoolteacher. In the book version of 1924, Nophaie dies from influenza and does not consummate his love for the White teacher.[42]

28.2. Still from movie "Vanishing American," 1925. Courtesy of Paramount Pictures.

The movie version was filmed in 1925, partly on location in Monument Valley; John Wetherill was in charge of logistics. The film has a long prologue, beginning with a quote from Herbert Spencer about the survival of the fittest. Nophaie is a recurring character—the noble but doomed warrior-savage. He appears first as leader of the Navajos as they conquer the Cliff Dwellers (Fig. 28.2), an idea given credence by the authority of A. V. Kidder's *Introduction to Southwestern Archaeology* of 1924.[43] A dying Cliff Dweller predicts that a stronger race will appear and conquer the Navajos. The Spanish come; Nophaie, now a Pueblo warrior, is killed again, and the Pueblos submit to the Spaniards. Finally, Kit Carson and his men conquer the Navajos and the symbolic Nophaie dies once more. The Navajos wind up on the reservation. There, Nophaie number four confronts a corrupt Indian agent—and falls for the White schoolteacher. She teaches him about Christianity and gives him a small Bible. Nophaie saves his White rival for the teacher during the First World War. Later, as he tries to stop fighting between Navajos and corrupt Whites, he is killed by a bullet in the chest that goes through the Bible. His death as a Christian martyr brings peace. "The final scene is an extreme long shot of a lengthy procession of Indians vanishing over the horizon as they carry the body of Nophaie away."[44]

CHAPTER 29

New Institutions, New Directions

SEVERAL NEW SOUTHWESTERN anthropological organizations were begun in the late 1920s—the Laboratory of Anthropology in Santa Fe, the Museum of Northern Arizona in Flagstaff, Gila Pueblo in Globe, Arizona, the Museum of Navajo Ceremonial Art in Santa Fe, and the Heard Museum in Phoenix. All were brought into existence by private philanthropy.

The Laboratory of Anthropology

The creation of the Laboratory of Anthropology in 1928 was a unique event in American anthropology. It was also another major defeat for Edgar Lee Hewett, following the Chaco Canyon coup by Judd, Morley and Morris (see Chapter 24).[1] The origins of "the Lab," as it was and is known, turned on the visits to the Southwest in 1924 and 1926 by John D. Rockefeller, Jr., Abby Aldrich Rockefeller (in 1926), and their sons. The key was a friendship that grew up be-

tween the Rockfellers and Jesse and Aileen Nusbaum during visits to the ruins of Mesa Verde on both trips.

During the 1924 trip, Rockefeller and his three oldest sons visited Santa Fe. As previously noted, they were accompanied by R. W. Corwin, a friend of Jesse Nusbaum and member of the managing committee of the School of American Research. Corwin introduced Rockefeller to Hewett (see Fig. 29.1). Rockefeller suggested to Hewett that the Palace of the Governors ought to be restored and furnished as a historic building. The museum collections and research areas, he suggested, ought to be placed in a new facility. He also thought that a major library might be built that would house the collections of the School of American Research, the museum, and possibly the city and state libraries. Rockefeller told Hewett that "he would appreciate receiving a report on the cost of carrying out such a program of proposals as he made and would give such a report very careful consideration."[2] Amazingly, Hewett did nothing.

29.1. John D. Rockefeller, Jr. (left), and Edgar Lee Hewett outside Museum of Fine Arts, Santa Fe, 1924. Courtesy of the Museum of New Mexico Photographic Archives.

The Rockefellers moved on to Taos and thence to Mesa Verde, where they met Jesse and Aileen Nusbaum, who entertained them with personal tours of the ruins, a steak fry, and one of Aileen's pageants (see Chapter 24). Rockefeller returned to Mesa Verde in 1926 with Abby and their three younger sons, Laurance, Winthrop, and David. They were again entertained by the Nusbaums. The Rockefellers invited the Nusbaums to visit them in New York: "They said of the thousands of people they met—sooner or later most of them asked for money—they actually had few true friends—those that never asked them for anything material—we were among those and they

wanted to see more of us—have us in their home, etc."[3]

Rockefeller told Nusbaum about Hewett ignoring his earlier request. Nusbaum suggested that the Rockefellers see Kenneth Chapman in Santa Fe, who would show them the Indian Arts Fund collection (see Chapter 27). Chapman gave them a tour of the collection, housed, at Hewett's sufferance, in the basement of the Fine Arts Museum. Hewett managed to be out of town, although he knew the Rockefellers were coming. The Rockefellers were very impressed with Chapman, the collection, and its purposes. On the spot, Rockefeller promised Chapman a minimum of twenty-five hundred dollars for future acquisitions. Chapman put the funds in an Albuquerque bank and made no mention of the source, to keep prices from going up.[4] Rockefeller asked Chapman to write the sort of report he had previously requested from Hewett—how to further develop and support anthropological and historical organizations in Santa Fe. Chapman, with some help from Nusbaum, produced a report and proposal.[5] When Hewett found out, he averred that *he* would submit the report. Chapman countered that *he also* would submit a report, because Rockefeller had specifically asked him to so do.

Hewett's document was a major proposal to undertake massive anthropological research programs in Siberia and Latin America, but not in the Southwest. He also proposed to acquire the rest of the city block behind the Palace of the Governors for new laboratories and a library. With a cover letter in which Rockefeller's interest in Hewett's scheme was greatly magnified, Hewett channeled the proposal through the president of the AIA, Ralph Magoffin, of New York University. Magoffin seems to have taken Hewett's hyperbole about Rockefeller's interest to mean possible general support for the AIA. Apparently, additional proposals for support of the Institute's overseas schools were prepared to be submitted with, or following, Hewett's proposal.

Hewett and a "strong committee" of prominent AIA board members tried to make a presentation to Rockefeller in New York City. But Rockefeller was unavailable, or so said his staff. Probably Hewett and Magoffin, through ignorance of Rockefeller's manner of doing business, badly misplayed their hand. Rockefeller made small donations on a personal basis, as with Nusbaum and Chapman; larger grants were subjected to thorough staff review. At the same time he was considering Southwest matters, his staff was planning the program to support Colonial Williamsburg, to which the Rockefeller family and foundations ultimately donated over 65 million dollars.[6] Even if Rockefeller were available, it is unlikely that he would have agreed to a hard-sell presentation by a committee of strangers.

Apparently, the entire AIA proposal package was missent to the Laura Spelman Rockefeller Foundation, not to J. D., Jr.'s office, and was summarily rejected. Meanwhile, Rockefeller received two proposals from Chapman, but not Hewett's. After much searching, the latter was found at the Foundation. Hewett's proposal was reviewed by Rockefeller and his staff, and Hewett was informed that "Mr. Rockefeller would not be inclined . . . to contribute toward the project."[7]

Rockefeller was still interested in doing something in Santa Fe; he turned to Chapman's proposals, for he had submitted two. One outlined an umbrella organization that would consolidate the Museum of New Mexico, the School of American Research, the New Mexico Historical Society, state and city libraries, and the Indian Arts Fund—a truly mixed bag. It also requested funds to acquire land for expansion around the Palace of the Governors. The second proposal requested an endowment to establish a museum for exhibiting the Indian Arts Fund collection, as well as funds for related fieldwork and collections. The museum was to be located on a choice piece of donated land south of Santa Fe.

Rockefeller called Jesse and Aileen Nusbaum to New York to review the entire matter in early December 1926.[8] The next day, Jesse sent a coded telegram to Chapman: "El Toro fell in crowding fence. Your big horse highly commended. Interests have selected trained man to thoroughly study situation. Your pet

colt will receive separate consideration if big horse fails. Had most interesting conference. Mums the word . . . Jesse L. Nusbaum."[9] The "trained man" was Hermon C. Bumpus, who after being fired by Henry Fairfield Osborn at the American Museum, had gone on to be president of Tufts College and, for a time, a member of Hewett's AIA managing committee. Since 1924, Bumpus had served with Rockefeller on the Board of Trustees of Brown University. He was also a former president of the American Association of Museums (AAM) and in 1926 was chair of its committee on "Outdoor Education." Rockefeller supported the committee and had helped fund the development of interpretive programs at Yosemite, the Grand Canyon, and elsewhere; hence his contribution to Nusbaum's museum at Mesa Verde.

After the demise of the Boas international school in Mexico, there had been talk among university-based anthropologists of the need for field schools to train students in both archaeology and ethnography. By 1925 the discussion had turned to an "intercollegiate" field school. Since field schools were clearly a form of "outdoor education," Clark Wissler, A. V. Kidder, and Bumpus saw a way of promoting, through the AAM program, an intercollegiate field school, preferably in the Southwest. In the spring of 1926, a proposal for the support of graduate anthropological field training "at some suitable spot in the pueblo area of the Southwest" was submitted to the Laura Spelman Rockefeller Memorial Foundation.[10] John D. Rockefeller, Jr., had read that proposal. Having heard the Nusbaums' views on the Chapman and Hewett proposals, and reviewing them in detail, Rockefeller now asked Bumpus to evaluate all the proposals and travel to Santa Fe to investigate the situation and make a recommendation. Rockefeller wrote to Kenneth Chapman at length, discussing the proposals and saying that Bumpus was on his way.[11]

Bumpus set out for Santa Fe via Cambridge, New York, Washington, and Chicago where he consulted "informally with anthropologists and other men of science . . ." He arrived in Santa Fe in early February 1927. There, he was wined and dined by Hewett's allies, and less ostentatiously hosted by Chapman and the Nusbaums. Bumpus met "many of those who might be classified as the local intelligentsia," but spent most of his time "very largely in examining the surrounding country."[12]

Bumpus and Hewett agreed, in principle, that the Palace of the Governors should become a "historical museum"; that land behind the palace should be acquired and a library placed there; and "that, if a new and comprehensive Archaeological Laboratory and Museum should be constructed at Santa Fe . . . ," Hewett would cooperate, but that there should be no "unfriendly rivalry" for collections and sites. Finally, they agreed that if proper facilities were built, the Indian Arts Fund would place its collection there.[13] From Chapman and Nusbaum, Bumpus learned that land for a *new* facility, *not* tied to Hewett's organizations, would be donated if needed. The donors were Amelia and Martha White, assisted by Francis Wilson and Hewett's old nemesis, Bronson Cutting.[14]

Bumpus returned to New York and submitted his report to Rockefeller. He recommended that Rockefeller support a new entity: a "Museum and Laboratory of Anthropology" that would incorporate the Indian Arts Fund collection and be placed on the donated land in Santa Fe. It would not be affiliated with the School of American Research nor with the Museum of New Mexico.[15]

Hewett made one final bid for control: he called a meeting of interested parties at the Cosmos Club in Washington, D.C. Kidder reported to Chapman:

> I am in a state of complete nervous and physical collapse, following two days of more or less acrimonious sessions with Hewett, Bumpus, et al. How these blighters manage to sail through weeks on end of this sort of stuff, I cannot understand. Wednesday morning at the Cosmos Club reminded one of the lobby of a convention hall. Hewett was buzzing with Hrdlicka and Magoffin in corners; Bumpus with Hodge and Holmes in other corners. We met at two—the Executive Committee of the Museum Association, the members of Hewett's board who

could be in Washington, Magoffin, and certain innocent bystanders, like Judd and myself. [After much vituperation and posturing, there was] a sort of dog fight, which led nowhere but which eventually resulted in the appointment of a small conference group to attempt to get together on fundamentals. This group consisted of Bumpus, Hewett, Judd and myself; and we put in yesterday afternoon drawing up a declaration of principles, which is very sugary.[16]

The declaration said that if a new entity came into existence, everyone would cooperate; in short, it was a truce.

Bumpus reported back to Rockefeller, again recommending an independent Museum and Laboratory of Anthropology. Rockefeller responded that he had requested information on existing institutions, but was now confronted with a "new situation." He remained interested, but "could only consider a request tendered by an organization perfected and already in operation."[17] Kidder and Bumpus called a meeting. On June 6, 1927, "there was held at the Yale Club, New York City, a meeting to organize an anthropological laboratory, museum and field station in Santa Fe, New Mexico." On a motion by Franz Boas, those present, including Kenneth Chapman, Roland B. Dixon, Pliny Earle Goddard, Frederick Webb Hodge, A. V. Kidder, Herbert J. Spinden, and Clark Wissler, became "the Committee on Organization of the Anthropological Laboratory." Kidder became temporary chair, with the power to appoint an executive committee, "of which K. M. Chapman shall be secretary," and the executive committee was charged to proceed to organize the laboratory. The executive committee was Kidder, Chapman, Wissler, Dixon, Hodge, Morley, and Judd.[18] A quorum of the committee met in Santa Fe at the end of August 1927, formally incorporated a "Museum and Laboratory of Anthropology" in Santa Fe, and named a founding board of trustees. The next day, they moved to Pecos to attend the first Pecos Conference (see Chapter 25). There were thirty founding trustees including anthropologists from most universities with graduate programs, various museum representatives, Hewett, Magoffin, Byron Cummings, and J. F. Zimmerman, president of the University of New Mexico. There were two women—Elsie Clews Parsons and Amelia White.[19]

Things moved quickly. On December 19, 1927, Kidder sent a lengthy letter and a proposal to Rockefeller. Both John D. Rockefeller, Jr., and the Rockefeller Foundation provided funds during 1928 and the "Museum and Laboratory of Anthropology" became a reality. In 1931, "Museum" was dropped from the title.[20] There was much behind-the-scenes scuffling over who would be the director—the academics wanted one of their own. But wiser political heads recognized Jesse Nusbaum's administrative talents and connection with the Rockefellers; Nusbaum went on leave from the National Park Service and was named director. Plans were drawn up for a building in the Santa Fe style, designed by John Gaw Meem; it opened in 1931, and its inaugural event was the third Pecos Conference.[21]

Hewett did not give up. There was much skirmishing and rumormongering on both sides in 1928 and 1929. The central issue, as George Stocking points out, remained regional chauvinism. Both Hewett and Byron Cummings strongly felt that local research and collecting should be done by local scholars, and that local collections should remain in local institutions. In 1927, Cummings pushed a law through the Arizona legislature mandating that archaeological collections made by anyone remain in Arizona. A federal court declared the law unconstitutional, and the U.S. Attorney General's office ruled that antiquities on federal lands were exclusively federal property. Hewett got a similar law through the New Mexico legislature in 1929, but the Lab's lobbyist convinced the governor to veto it.[22] Hewett wanted the Lab to be part of the Museum of New Mexico. This would allow him and J. F. Zimmerman, president of the University of New Mexico, to integrate the Lab into an Anthropology Department at the university. In the end Zimmerman and Hewett were forced to go their own way. Hewett

was appointed to found the department in 1929. Among his first acts was to reactivate his long-delayed excavation program in Chaco Canyon.

The halcyon days of the Lab were 1929–34. Rockefeller's funding was on a diminishing sliding scale, with the expectation that additional support would be generated from other sources. But the onset of the Depression made that impossible. The vision that the founding trustees had for the Lab was as a research and training center where graduate students would receive training in all four subfields of anthropology: archaeology, ethnography, physical anthropology, and linguistics. Each summer an instructor took three to five students on a two- to three-month field project. In the six years of field schools, 1929–34, there were fifty-eight students, many of whom became prominent anthropologists over the next three to four decades.

Those who focused their subsequent work on the Southwest included Isabel Kelly, Harry Hoijer, and Father Berard Haile in 1929. The latter two were taught by Edward Sapir and worked on Navajo linguistics, with Hoijer becoming the leading authority on Athapaskan languages from the 1940s to the 1960s. Father Haile has already been introduced (see Chapter 18). Isabel Kelly attended the archaeology field school, but Kidder and Kroeber thought women should be ethnographers and discouraged her. Kelly took her Ph.D. from the University of California in 1932, then received a three-year fellowship from the National Research Council administered through the Lab to do major ethnographic work with various Southern Paiute groups. She then moved to Mexico, where she had a long and productive career as an archaeologist.[23]

The 1930 class included John Otis Brew, who would subsequently excavate the great Hopi site of Awatovi and serve for many years as director of the Peabody Museum at Harvard; Morris Swadesh and Carl Voegelin, both of whom made major contributions to Southwestern Indian linguistics; Walter Dyk, whose biography of a Navajo man, *Son of Old Man Hat,* is one of the classic Southwestern works; and Harold E. Driver, a student of Kroeber's, who took historical particularism to its ultimate conclusion in his comparative studies of North American Indian cultures. The ethnology class of 1931, taught by Ruth Benedict, included Morris E. Opler, who became the major authority on the Apache. The 1932 ethnology class, taught by Leslie White, included Fred Eggan, Edward A. Kennard, and Mischa Titiev and was held on the Hopi Reservation (Fig. 29.2). All three subsequently made major contributions to Hopi ethnography and acculturation studies. (Ed Kennard supervised the present author's dissertation in the 1960s.) The 1933 archaeology class, taught by Frank Roberts, included Erik K. Reed, who became a prominent Southwestern archaeologist from the 1940s to the 1970s and had a long career in the National Park Service, based in Santa Fe. The ethnology class, taught by Ralph Linton, included Waldo R. Wedel, who became the leading authority on Great Plains archaeology over a fifty-year career at the U.S. National Museum; and E. Adamson Hoebel, whose studies of Plains Indian "law ways" are classics.[24]

The Museum of Northern Arizona

At the turn of the twentieth century, well-to-do and highly capable women were centrally responsible for the creation of two major anthropological institutions—Sara Yorke Stevenson and the University of Pennsylvania Museum, and Phoebe Apperson Hearst and the Museum and Department of Anthropology at the University of California. In the Southwest of the 1920s, four other well-to-do and equally capable women played central roles in the creation of four unique institutions—the Museum of Northern Arizona, Gila Pueblo, the Heard Museum, and the Wheelwright Museum of the American Indian.[25]

In 1925–26, Harold S. Colton and Mary-Russell Ferrell Colton, of Philadelphia, moved onto one hundred acres of pine forest along Fort Valley Road just west of Flagstaff, Arizona, purchased for 19,500 dollars.[26] Colton, from a well-to-do Philadelphia Main Line family, was a professor of zoology at the

University of Pennsylvania, where he had gone to school. Mary-Russell Colton, from eastern Pennsylvania, was an artist and art restorer. Married in 1912, the couple spent their honeymoon on an extensive camping trip through Arizona and New Mexico, and were particularly taken by the area around Flagstaff. In the following years, they made extensive trips through the Southwest, focusing on Flagstaff and the Navajo and Hopi reservations. In 1913, they sat with Theodore Roosevelt on a Walpi rooftop to witness the Snake Dance, a trip arranged by Lorenzo Hubbell. In 1916, they rode by mule team and wagon from Flagstaff to Tuba City to Oraibi and back to Flagstaff. At Oraibi for the Snake Dance, they met Byron Cummings, an important connection for all three in the following years.[27]

The same summer, the Coltons found their first archaeological site when their son picked up some potsherds at a picnic area just east of Flagstaff. Thus began their fifty-year engagement with the

29.2. Laboratory of Anthropology ethnographic field school at Hopi Mesas, Arizona, 1932. Left to right: Edward A. Kennard, Jesse Spirer, Leslie A. White, Fred Eggan, Mischa Titiev. Don Fowler collection; gift of Edward A. Kennard.

archaeology of the Colorado Plateau. They began a systematic site survey and by 1928 had recorded and published information on 1,250 sites. The central focus of Southwestern archaeology in the 1920s was chronology, and seriation of potsherds seemed to be the key. Harold Colton was increasingly infected by Kidder's "ceramic bacillus" and its implication for studying archaeology in a way that appealed to his scientific training.[28]

By 1922 Colton and various northern Arizona residents began discussing a regional museum. Like Hewett and Cummings, they were distressed that Jesse Walter Fewkes, from the Smithsonian, and others from "large Eastern museums" were digging in local sites and sending the artifacts away: "members of expeditions [arrived] almost every year . . . [and drove] into the . . . back country. Later in the season . . . these members, now dusty and bearded, return[ed], accompanied by boxes of specimens which were shipped away to Eastern centers."[29] An attempt to establish a museum languished at first, but after the Coltons settled in Flagstaff in 1926, the idea was revived; community leaders rallied in support. Harold Colton happened to meet the ubiquitous Hermon Bumpus, who was at the Grand Canyon on yet another errand for John D. Rockefeller, Jr., and Bumpus was able to give Colton and his group much sage advice. The Coltons attended the 1927 Pecos Conference, where Harold actively participated in the discussions and was further stimulated to increase his development of an archaeology program in the Flagstaff region.

The Northern Arizona Society of Science and Art was incorporated in late 1927; trustees were elected in May 1928. The museum began in the Flagstaff Women's Club, used for exhibits and offices, and whatever donated space in downtown Flagstaff could be found. Harold Colton became president of the society and director of the Museum of Northern Arizona. In 1929, Lyndon Hargrave, Byron Cummings's student who had worked on the Beam Expedition, became assistant director. In 1930 Katherine Bartlett was hired as curator of anthropology and John C. McGregor as curator of archaeology. Mary-Russell Colton

became curator of art and began a program of collecting, studying, and encouraging the development of Navajo and Hopi arts and crafts.[30] The museum's archaeology program in the 1930s is touched on in the Epilogue.

Gila Pueblo

The third organization created in 1927–28 was the Gila Pueblo Archaeological Foundation, founded by Harold S. Gladwin and Winifred Jones McCurdy (Gladwin). Harold Sterling Gladwin (1883–1976) was born in New York City and attended college in England. In 1904 he became a stock broker, purchasing a seat on the New York Stock Exchange in 1908. In 1922, he sold his seat, retired from business, and moved to the West Coast to pursue avocational interests, including archaeology. He was accorded a courtesy affiliation with the Southwest Museum in Los Angeles and began a serious study of Southwestern archaeology, along with a companion, Winifred Jones McCurdy (they were married in 1932). By the mid-1920s they were in touch with A. V. Kidder, who encouraged them to focus on the Mogollon Rim area and the Gila River drainage. In 1926 Gladwin purchased a Pueblo ruin near Globe, Arizona, and rebuilt it into a private research center, Gila Pueblo. Over the years of its existence, 1928–50, the Gladwins provided all the funding for Gila Pueblo staff, research projects, and publications. In 1950 the collections and related materials were transferred to the Arizona State Museum. The principal activities of Gila Pueblo took place in the 1930s (see the Epilogue).[31]

The Heard Museum and Pueblo Grande

Dwight B. Heard and Maie Bartlett Heard moved to Phoenix in 1895, seeking relief for Dwight's respiratory problems. They prospered in business and as publishers of *The Arizona Republic*. Maie Heard began collecting Indian and other ethnic arts and crafts as house decorations, but soon was filling storage areas in various buildings. In 1928–29, the Heards created and endowed what became the Heard Museum. Dwight Heard died in 1929, but Maie Heard carried on, fully involved in the development of the museum until her death in 1951. The Heard Museum did not develop a research program, but concentrated on ethnic arts, finally settling on American Indian, especially Southwestern, art. It has grown into a major regional museum with an unparalleled collection.[32]

Across town from the Heard Museum lies the ruin of Pueblo Grande, which Bandelier noted and Cushing partially excavated during the Hemenway years. By the 1920s most of the other major ruins in the Phoenix area had succumbed to streets, buildings, and large-scale farming. Pueblo Grande survived, although subjected to various excavations and vandalism. In 1924, the city of Phoenix bought a major portion of the ruin, and in 1929 hired Odd Halseth, who had previously worked for Edgar Lee Hewett as city archaeologist. The complex history of Pueblo Grande, before and after 1930, is artfully chronicled by the papers in a volume edited by Christian Downum and Todd Bostwick.[33]

Navajo Museum of Ceremonial Art

In 1918, a "tall angular daughter" of Boston Brahmin background, Mary Cabot Wheelwright (1878–1958), came to Santa Fe. She divided her time thereafter between sailing in Maine, living at the Cosmopolitan Club in New York City, and a pied-à-terre hacienda near Alcalde, New Mexico.[34] She traveled widely across the Southwest, searching, as she did elsewhere, for the deeper, especially the religious, meaning of life; seemingly a true yearner. In the 1920s, at a trading post owned by Arthur and Franc Newcomb, she met the Navajo singer Hosteen (or Hastiin) Klah. Then in his fifties, Klah was recognized as a preeminent ceremonial practitioner, having mastered four major chantways.[35] Klah was a *nadle,* the Navajo equivalent of the Zuni We'wha, and an accomplished weaver (after 1931 he began weaving rugs with sandpainting motifs). By all accounts he was a remarkably wise and prescient individual in whose philosophy Wheel-

wright found the meaning she sought. She began a serious and far-ranging study of Navajo ceremony and religion with Klah and others.

As Wheelwright's and Klah's relationship deepened, she conceived the idea of a museum focused on Navajo ceremony and religion. She first offered her collection of materials and a building to house them to the Laboratory of Anthropology as it was being developed in 1927–28. But her plan to have an octagonal structure patterned after the traditional Navajo hogan was rejected by architect John Gaw Meem as inappropriate next to his Santa Fe style Lab. Morley, Kidder, and the building committee also rejected the plan because a scientific institution (after all, they were building a *Laboratory* of Anthropology) should not include a museum "conceived upon an emotional, rather than scientific basis."[36] No romantic yearners need apply at the Laboratory of Scientism!

After five years of Santa Fe style acrimony, Wheelwright built her own museum adjacent to the Lab on land donated by Amelia White. Elegantly designed in the octagonal hogan form by William Penhollow Henderson with active input from Hosteen Klah, the museum opened in 1937 as the House of Religion, becoming the next year the Museum of Navajo Ceremonial Art, and in 1976, the Wheelwright Museum of the American Indian.

Most of the major institutions that would continue to define the anthropological Southwest until the end of the millennium were in place by 1940. In New Mexico there were the Museum of New Mexico, School of American Research, Laboratory of Anthropology, and the Museum of Navajo Ceremonial Art in Santa Fe. Hewett created a museum at the University of New Mexico in Albuquerque in 1932. It became the Maxwell Museum of Anthropology in 1971. The Millicent Rogers Museum in Taos was founded in 1952.

In Arizona there was the Arizona State Museum in Tucson, the Heard Museum and Pueblo Grande Museum in Phoenix, and the Museum of Northern Arizona in Flagstaff. In Los Angeles there was the Southwest Museum, and in San Diego the San Diego Museum of Man. Southwestern halls or exhibits were also found in various museums great and small in Colorado, Utah, in the Midwest, along the East Coast, in Europe, and even in New Zealand. The anthropology of the Southwest had indeed become global.

Conclusion

One theme of this book is that the American Southwest is an Anglo invention, a place "seen from" and "seen as." A second theme is that the invention of American ethnology was closely intertwined with the invention of the Southwest. Ethnology then metamorphosed into anthropology, and anthropology fissioned into ethnography, archaeology, linguistics, physical anthropology, and folklore—"different hairs on the same dog," as the late folklorist Blanton Owen put it.[37] The third theme is that the Southwest was a central place in which the metamorphosis occurred: a place *seen as* a laboratory for anthropology when *seen from* the central intellectual axis of the Anglo world: Boston/New York/Washington.

A fourth theme is that European assumptions and questions about the origins, commensurability, nature, and cultural histories of the people Columbus called "Indians" became Anglo assumptions and questions. Origins questions were posed by 1500: where did these people come from and how did they get here? In 2000 those same questions are still on the table, still debated. One difference is the time frame and concern with chronology. Isaac Newton gave the world "absolute time," a concern with chronologies linked to it, and posed the general question of cultural linkage: which culture spawned which other cultures? Bishop Ussher gave him about 5,700 years to work with. Darwin and the nineteenth-century geologists gave the world "deep time" to work with, eons more than the bishop thought possible. But, as of 2000, those focused on the origins issue use only about three times as much time: 15,000 years for the advent of people into the Western Hemisphere.

The French and British traders and colonists of North America invented the "savage." Enlightenment philosophers, romantics, and those actually in contact with Indian people fissioned the savage into noble, ignoble, vanishing, and managed images. Enlightenment savants studied savages to determine the nature of "human nature," and thus commensurability. By the 1850s, such savants began to be called ethnographers. Romantics immersed them in the formula of natural equals both good and authentic: artificial (civilized) equals bad or corrupt. Therefore, since "the savage" lives "naturally" or "close to nature," she/he, by definition, is "authentic" and morally good. Anglos seeking palliation from the artificialities of their own civilization studied, admired the work of, or hung out with the natural women/men of the Southwest; following Oliver La Farge the seekers are called yearners.

One legacy of the Enlightenment is the point of view called "science": seeing the universe as governed by unknown causes and processes. The task of the scientist is to transform those unknowns into knowns by following specific sets of rules and procedures collectively called "the scientific method." In the sixteenth century, Francis Bacon saw this as a never-ending process: transforming an unknown into a known creates new unknowns. In Southwestern archaeology, indeed in archaeology generally, this became routinized. Nearly every excavation report ends with the conundrum "more work needs to be done."

By about 1850 science was mystified (in Ludwig Feuerbach's sense) into Science, or positivism, as the intellectual historians call it. Scientists saw the universe and all it contains as governed by natural laws, which they would discover in an impartial and objective, hence truthful, manner. In post-1870 American anthropology this translated into the essentialist stage theory of social and cultural development espoused by Lewis Henry Morgan and his disciple, John Wesley Powell. They sent Adolph Bandelier, Frank Hamilton Cushing, and others to the laboratory of the Southwest to investigate its culture history and demonstrate the validity of Morgan's general scheme and his model of how the Southwest fit within it. But Franz Boas introduced a form of German romanticism to America, which in the works of Clark Wissler and others was transformed into the approach called historical particularism. Wissler and his followers kept the cachet of Scientist, while rejecting the scientism of Morgan and Powell. As New Archaeologists, they took up the same task Isaac Newton spent forty years on—attempting to develop and tie chronologies to absolute time. By 1930 they found that tree rings gave them part of the chronology they sought; it then became a matter of working out the cultural linkages.

In ethnography, Elsie Clews Parsons saw herself as a scientist within the particularist approach: gather a multitude of "facts" and look for patterns, which might (someday) allow guesses about cultural processes. Those she funded, especially Ruth Benedict, took other ideas from German romanticism, princi-

pally that cultures are organic wholes, to be understood in their own terms and not agglomerations of shreds and patches to be understood in a universal scientific framework. Benedict's patterns were very different from Parsons' patterns. They allowed her to declare the principle of cultural relativity and the fluidity of personality formation: it's okay that, in other societies at least, more than two genders are condoned.

Finally, all this took place within those peculiar institutions devoted to knowledge making and knowledge display and dissemination called universities and museums. They provided the money and home-base facilities that allowed American anthropologists to go to the Southwest in search of science or romanticism. Some found both.

CHAPTER 30

Epilogue

THE YEARS 1930 and 1931 were transitional years for Southwestern anthropology, as they were for the larger American society sliding into the Depression. The Boas decade was over. By 1931 the only Boas student actively working in the Southwest was Gladys Reichard. Bunzel and Parsons had turned to Guatemala and Mexico; Ruth Benedict was exploring cultural patterning and culture and personality studies; Esther Schiff Walters was busy with matronly duties. Leslie White, who was not a Boasian but was supported by Parsons, continued to do ethnography. At the University of Chicago, the recently founded anthropology department had hired Edward Sapir, regarded as Boas's most brilliant student.[1] Sapir had spent a decade in Ottawa as an anthropologist attached to the Geological Survey of Canada, during which time he had studied Athapaskan languages. Now he began to train students at Chicago; two of them, Fred Eggan and Harry Hoijer, would do seminal work in the Southwest.

Another emerging ethnographer was Clyde Kluckhohn. In 1927 and 1928, young Kluckhohn made long pack-horse trips crisscrossing the Colorado Plateau. He was fascinated by the Navajo people. He took a Ph.D. at Harvard, joined the faculty there, and became the leading authority on Navajo.[2]

Historical particularism reached its peak in Clark Wissler's works of the 1920s and A. L. Kroeber's attempt to use the method to arrive at generalizations about cultural process. Kroeber directed the so-called culture element distribution studies throughout the 1930s. This culminated in his classic *Cultural and Natural Areas of Native North America* of 1939, in which cultural traits, culture areas, and center-periphery models were brought together. In some senses it marked the end of what began as the Boas-Mason debate.[3]

The hot topics in 1930s cultural anthropology were cultural patterning, culture and personality, and acculturation. Ruth Benedict, Margaret Mead, Ralph Linton, and Clyde Kluckhohn emerged as the leaders of cultural patterning and culture and personality studies. Acculturation is the study of the interactive relationships between two (or more) cultures when they come into contact. Earlier American anthropologists, seeking the authentic savage, had ignored the facts of several hundred years of acculturation between English, French, and Spanish, on the one hand, and Indians, on the other, in their quest for the faux-authenticity of the "ethnographic present." Elsie Clews Parsons had recognized the fact of acculturation from the outset and sought to understand it within the historical particularist framework. Parsons, Bunzel, and others who began to study Indian cultures in Latin America, and Melville and Frances Herskovits who began studying Black communities in the Caribbean and the American South, recognized they were dealing with colonial acculturation situations. Acculturation was also dominant in what began to be called "applied anthropology"—using ethnographic and linguistic knowledge to aid native communities. This became a major theme during the reorganization of Bureau of Indian Affairs policies under John Collier in the 1930s.[4]

Southwestern archaeology remained rooted in the culture history approach of Wissler's new archaeology. Kidder's 1924 summary and the Pecos Classification of 1927 continued and reified Morgan's center-periphery model of culture history: that the San Juan Basin was the origin point, the source of Puebloan culture; all else was "peripheral." There was the northern periphery in the upper reaches of the Colorado River drainage, and beyond in the eastern Great Basin where the ruins and pots were Pueblolike. To the south, in the mountains along the Arizona-New Mexico border and the hot desert of the Lower Gila River basin, the ruins were seen collectively as Pueblo South. To the west, beyond the Little Colorado River, it looked like Pueblo West all the way to the Virgin River in southwestern Utah and southern Nevada. This was a classic case of the "view from" syndrome—seeing the archaeology in adjacent regions from the perspective of your own site or area and seeing what's there as simply variations of the archaeology of your area, which you assume is the center. Others, standing on different sites or in different areas, assume *they* are at the center.[5]

Some archaeologists didn't like the San Juan-center view-shed, among them Harold Gladwin, who had created the Gila Pueblo foundation in 1928. Encouraged by Kidder, he and his staff concentrated on broad surveys of the southern desert. The more they looked, the less San Juan-Pueblolike the ruins and the ceramics seemed to be. They called what they saw Hohokam, following Frank Russell's lead.[6]

In 1930 Gladwin hired Emil Haury and then funded him to spend two academic years at Harvard to get a Ph.D. Encouraged by Alfred Tozzer and Roland Dixon, Haury exhumed Cushing's Los Muertos collections from the basement of the Peabody Museum and studied them for his dissertation, thus resurrecting Cushing and the original Hemenway Expedition in the process. Frederick Webb Hodge told Haury that Cushing had made few notes, maps, etc., and Haury, having no reason to doubt the senior man in the field, said so. It would not be until the 1990s that David Wilcox and Curtis Hinsley found Cushing's materials tucked away in the Huntington Library in the Bronx and exonerated Cushing's reputation. Cushing's Los Muertos materials looked very Hohokamlike to Haury. His subsequent excavations in the site of Snaketown, south of Phoenix, confirmed that Hohokam was indeed different.[7]

The ruins and ceramics in the mountains along the Arizona-New Mexico border and on the Mogollon Rim looked different from either Hohokam or Pueblo, and the Gladwins called the culture there Mogollon. Haury's excavations of the Harris site confirmed that view.[8] Other ruins lay to the east in the Mimbres Valley and adjacent areas. The sites had long been vandalized for the wondrous pottery bowls decorated with anthropomorphic, zoomorphic, and fantastic figures that brought high prices in the antiquities market. Kidder had encouraged two local avocational archaeologists, Harriet and Cornelius Burton (Hattie and Burt) Cosgrove, in their careful excavations of sites in the Mimbres valley. Wesley Bradfield, the associate director of the San Diego Museum of Man during Hewett's tenure there, excavated Cameron Creek Village in the late 1920s.[9] As the Gila Pueblo work proceeded in the 1930s, Mimbres came to be seen as a branch of Mogollon. Mimbres and its ceramic art would be a focal point for Southwestern archaeologists and art historians for the next seven decades.[10]

In 1936, Kidder suggested that Basket Maker and Pueblo be collectively renamed *Anasazi,* a Navajo term for "ancient ones," he said, drawing a parallel with the Pima term *Hohokam.* Harold Colton and Lyndon Hargrave, meanwhile, focused on the region around Flagstaff and ultimately concluded that they saw two different patterns named Sinagua and Coconino. Having been infected by the strains of Kidder's "ceramic bacillus," Southwestern archaeologists spent three decades after 1930 in sorting and classifying potsherds and warring over ceramic nomenclature and the delineation of regional variations on the theme of pottery-making farmers in the Southwest.[11]

In the process they became rather isolationist, perhaps in keeping with the political temper of the times. Except for maize, some attempted to see all cultural developments within the three regional traditions, including the invention of pottery, as homegrown. It would not be until Emil Haury published an article in 1945, admitting that more than maize had come north across a border that did not exist until the 1850s, that discussion of the Southwestern-Mexican connection was again reopened.[12]

The venerable origins issue was given a new dimension in 1927 by the discovery of the Folsom site. In the 1930s and 1940s there were major efforts to discover more about "Early Man," or "Paleoindian." There was the excavation of the Lindenmeier site in northwestern Colorado by Frank Roberts, a second "Folsom Complex" site, and of the stratigraphically earlier Clovis site by John Cotter. There was also the excavation of Gypsum Cave, near Las Vegas, Nevada, by Mark R. Harrington, which seemingly revealed wooden artifacts and projectile points under Pleis-tocene sloth dung. But it proved illusory due to Harrington's sloppy excavation methods.[13]

There was still the problem of what cultural traditions existed in the several thousand years between "Late Pleistocene Man," characterized by the Clovis and Folsom complexes, and the beginnings of the three regional farming traditions. The key work was by E. B. Sayles, who defined the so-called Cochise culture and its variants as the "in-between" cultures. They were verified stratigraphically by Emil Haury in his excavation of Ventana Cave in 1940–41.[14]

In the year 2000, as in 1930, the consensus with regard to the origins issue is that Clavigero, Humboldt, Jefferson, Gallatin, Boas, and Hrdlička were right—the first humans in the Western Hemisphere derived from Northeast Asia. The matters of contention, then as now, have to do with routes of travel and timing. In 1930, ten thousand years seemed possible; at millennium's end, ten thousand to fifteen thousand seem probable.[15]

Although it did not appear so at the time, 1930–31 was also a transition point in the East-West battle for control of Southwestern archaeology. When the Laboratory of Anthropology opened in 1931, it seemed to be a permanent monument to eastern dominance of the Southwest. But by 1934 the Lab was nearly bankrupt and its eastern supporters were unable to help in keeping it afloat. It limped along until it was absorbed into the Museum of New Mexico in 1947.

There was a Harvard presence throughout the 1930s: J. O. Brew's excavations at Alkali Ridge and later at Awatovi.[16] The last Bernheimer expedition in 1931 marked the end of the American Museum's archaeology program in the Southwest. With the exception of Paul Martin's forty-year archaeology program out of the Chicago Field Museum into the Mogollon country, subsequent Southwestern archaeology was conducted by regional institutions—universities and museums in Utah, Colorado, New Mexico, Arizona, California, and occasionally Texas, and by the National Park Service.[17]

Between 1929 and 1940, Edgar Lee Hewett finally

was able to rule Chaco Canyon through his University of New Mexico summer field schools. Among Hewett's graduate students were Florence Hawley (Ellis), Margery Ferguson (Lambert), Paul Reiter, Anna O. Shepard, Stanley Stubbs, and Gordon Vivian, all of whom made significant contributions to Southwestern archaeology.[18]

Hewett failed to see that a final Chaco Canyon report was produced. It had been, and would continue to be, something of a tradition in Southwestern archaeology to never quite get that final report out, or get it out ten to forty to eighty years late. Unfortunately, the tradition continues in the year 2000.

In the seven decades since 1930, a staggering number of anthropological research projects have been undertaken in the American Southwest, adding to what was already done. It truly has been a "laboratory for anthropology" in a broad sense, the most studied region in the world. The number of paintings, drawings, photographs, novels, short stories, and popular articles produced about Southwestern landscapes and native peoples before and after 1930 is equally astounding.

Science and romanticism were brought by Anglos to the place they called the Southwest beginning in 1846. The cumulative verbal and pictorial images are the (invented) Anglo Southwest; or, to borrow and modify a felicitous phrase from William Goetzmann, the Southwest of the Imagination.[19] But there are other "Southwests," seen not as peripheral to the Anglo East, but central by those studied for 150 years in the Anglo laboratory and place of romantic yearning. Zunis, Hopis, Navajos, Hispanics, and other "native peoples" of the Anglo Southwest now use those tools of archaeology, ethnography, and ethnohistory that they find appropriate, together with their own cultural knowledge and understanding, to further define who they are and where they came from. Such knowledge can enrich everyone, no matter how they define "the Southwest."

Abbreviations

ALAB Archives, Laboratory of Anthropology, Museum of New Mexico, Santa Fe.

BEC/BAEC Bureau of (American) Ethnology Collection, National Anthropological Archives, Smithsonian Institution, Washington, D.C.

CHP Cushing and Hodge Papers, Southwest Museum Library, Los Angeles.

CWP Clark Wissler Papers, American Museum of Natural History Archives, New York City.

DAB *Dictionary of American Biography*, 1928–90, under the auspices of the American Council of Learned Societies, 20 vols. and 8 supplements, edited by A. Johnson, D. Malone, and others. Charles Scribner's Sons, New York.

ECPP Elsie Clews Parsons Papers, American Philosophical Society Library, Philadelphia.

EHMP Earl H. Morris Papers, Department of Anthropology Archives, American Museum of Natural History, New York.

ELHP Edgar Lee Hewett Papers, Division of History, Museum of New Mexico, Santa Fe.

GVMP Gilbert and Virginia McClurg Papers, Pioneers Museum, Colorado Springs, Colorado.

KMCP Kenneth M. Chapman Papers, Indian Arts Collection, School of American Research, Santa Fe.

MVRCA Archives of the Research Center, Mesa Verde National Park, Colorado.

NAA National Anthropological Archives, Smithsonian Institution, Washington, D.C.

NCAB *National Cyclopedia of American Biography*, 1898–1984, 69 vols., James T. White Co., Clifton, NJ.

NMJP Neil M. Judd Papers, National Anthropological Archives, Smithsonian Institution, Washington D.C.

NNP Nels Nelson Papers, Department of Anthropology Archives, American Museum of Natural History, New York.

OED **1971** *The Compact Edition of the Oxford English Dictionary*, 2 vols. Oxford University Press, Oxford.

OED **1989** *The Oxford English Dictionary*, 2d ed., 20 vols. Clarendon Press, Oxford.

RMSC Correspondence of the Geographical and Geological Survey of the Rocky Mountain Region, J. W. Powell in Charge, National Archives, Washington, D.C.

WMP Washington Matthews Papers, Wheelwright Museum of the American Indian, Santa Fe.

Notes

Preface

1. O'Gorman (1942: 7), paraphrased by Phelan (1970: 76).

2. Wittgenstein (1961).

3. The idea of "the Other" has been developed by Johannes Fabian (1983, 1991) and a host of writers following his lead.

4. For Zuni, see Cushing (1896); for the Tewa Pueblos, see Ortiz (1969); for the Navajo, see Farella (1984), Levy (1998), and Zolbrod (1984).

5. For example, Fowler and Fowler, eds. (1971).

Prologue

1. Lummis (1893, 1925, 1969, 1989).

2. Reed (1951: 428). On various delineations of the anthropological Southwest, see Beals (1943), Fontana (1990: 453), Kroeber (1928), León-Portilla (1972: 83), Spicer (1962), and Waterman (1929). Byrkit (1992) provides an exhaustive review of various criteria by which the Southwest has been defined.

3. Hunt (1967), Bender (1982), Brown (1982), and Shelford (1963: 260–305, 373–94).

4. Henige (1998); see also Reff (1992), and Stodder and Martin (1992).

5. From "Consensus Classification of Native Languages of North America" in Goddard (1996a: table 3).

6. From Goddard (1996a: table 3). See also Miller (1983), Stanislawski (1979), Eggan (1979a), and Hale and Harris (1979).

7. For the synonymic miasma of Apachean names, see Opler (1983: 385–92).

8. Young (1983: 393), Gunnerson (1979), Hale and Harris (1979: 171–72). See also Reed and Reed (1992: 69–136), and Towner (1996).

9. Hunt, Gallagher, and Orr (1984: 254).

10. Bahr (1983), Ezell (1983), and Fontana (1983).

11. Alvarez de Williams (1983), Bee (1983), McGuire (1983), Schwartz (1983), and Stewart (1983).

12. Kelly and Fowler (1986), Callaway, Janetski, and Stewart (1986).

13. For an overview of the impacts of horses on North American Indian cultures, see Ewers (1955).

14. The following section is drawn from Gibson (1966), Haring (1963), and the updated synthesis of Riley (1999).

15. Anderson and Dibble (1950–82, 13:31).

16. On the Spanish in the Caribbean and eastern North America, see Clissold (1961: 24–26) and Howe and Harrer (1947: 130–31, 182). For South America, see Bandelier (1893: 1–112) and Shields (1945).

17. Hodge (1907: 3–126), Sauer (1971: 108–125 and fig. 10).

18. F. Bandelier (1905: 229–30); see also A. Bandelier (1981: 85–101). Many historical questions about the Marcos-Esteban trek have been hotly debated (Rodack 1985), and some still remain open.

19. The following account is based on Winship (1896: 488–512).

20. Bannon (1974: 28–71), Kessell (1979: 32–46), and Naylor and Polzer (1986).

21. This section draws on Bolton (1916), Gutiérrez (1991), Kessell (1979), and Simmons (1991).

22. On the Pueblo Revolt, see Hackett (1942), Kessell (1979: 229–97), and the popular synopsis by Silverberg (1994).

23. Stanislawski (1979: 600).

24. Brew (1979: 519–22), Gutiérrez (1991: 39–174), Kessell (1979: 111–228).

25. Simmons (1988).

26. On the Apaches, see Moorhead (1968) and Gunnerson (1974); on Navajo-Spanish-Pueblo relations, see Reeve (1957, 1958, 1959, 1960); on Comanche-Spanish-Pueblo relations, see Kessell (1989: 357–410); on Southern Ute raiding activities, see Schroeder (1965).

27. Thomas (1941).

28. Gerhard (1993: 3–19 and maps 1–8).

29. From Gutiérrez (1991: 103–7, 167–75, and tables 2.1, 4.2, 4.4, and 4.6). Upham (1992: 227 and table 3) derives somewhat different estimates for the period 1793–1821.

30. Jeter and Juelke (1978), Mera (1987).

31. On the roles of the missions and presidios in Spanish foreign and expansionist policy, see Bolton (1917, 1930), Bannon (1974), Hennessy (1978: 28–48, 54–57), Kessell (1976: 3–26), and Polzer (1976).

32. Mitchell (1981), Fülöp-Miller (1963).

33. Bolton (1919, 1936).

34. Burrus (1971).

35. Bolton (1919 1:66, 128–29).

36. Donohue (1969), Dunne (1955), Ives (1939), Pradeau and Rasmussen (1980), and Treutlein (1949).

37. Kessell (1976: 13–25, 127, 159, 186–87, 202).

38. Bolton (1930 1:v), Bannon (1974: 153–60), Bolton (1930, 1933), Galvin (1965).

39. Galvin (1965: 65).

40. Galvin (1965: 73–75).

41. Galvin (1965: v-ix).

42. Adams and Chavez (1975: xiv-xix).

43. Adams and Chavez (1975: xvi).

44. Chavez and Warner (1976: 113–14).

45. Sánchez (1997).

46. The Vargas quote is in Kessell (1989: 168); for the "Rim of Christendom," see Bolton (1936); on "misery" in New Mexico colonial life, see Simmons (1988).

Introduction

1. Huddleston (1967: 114–21).

2. Hodgen (1964: 53).

3. Bandelier (1893), Clissold (1961), Shields (1945).

4. Deacon (1966).

5. The following section draws on Arciniegas (1986), Berkhofer (1979), Chaplin (1997), Fowler (1990), Hanke (1959), Hodgen (1964), Pagden (1982, 1993), Seed (1993), and Vaughan (1965, 1982).

6. Berkhofer (1979: 71).

7. Fowler (1990).

8. Lovejoy (1948), Lovejoy and Boas (1935: 8–13, 447); for contrary views, see Krech (1999) and Redman (1999).

9. Cantwell (1996), Deloria (1998).

10. Fülöp-Miller (1963: 227–302), Dickason (1984).

11. Montaigne (1947: 66, 68, 71–72).

12. Thwaites (1896–1901), Berkhofer (1979: 74), Liebersohn (1998: 13–38), Dickason (1984: 251–78).

13. Colin (1987), Honour (1975), Moffitt and Sebastián (1996).

14. Seed (1995).

15. Jennings (1975), Vaughan (1982).

16. Hodgen (1964: 111–12), Honour (1975: 64), Fowler and Fowler (1991: 52–53).

17. Shakespeare (1978: 81).

18. Dryden (1978: 30).

19. Dryden (1962, 1966).

20. Fowler and Fowler (1991: 52–56), Stedman (1982: 105–252), Turnbaugh (1980: 11).

21. Grotius (1964), Hobbes (1965), Montesquieu (1949, 1985).

22. Locke (1960, 2:§49, 1; §108, 1–2).

23. This discussion is based principally on Meek (1976).

24. Hobbes (1965: 84–85).

25. Locke (1960, II:§22, 1–4; §34, 1–7; §45, 20–24).

26. Arneil (1996: 69).

27. Peckham and Gibson (1969).

28. The following draws on Becker (1932), Crosby (1997), Manuel (1959, 1963), McGrane (1989), Toulmin (1990), and D. J. Wilcox (1987).

29. Barrow (1988: 27–85), Milton (1981).

30. Manuel (1959, 1963), D. J. Wilcox (1987).

31. D. J. Wilcox (1987: 8–9). In the more politically correct multicultural time from the 1970s into the 1990s, B.C./A.D. increasingly was transmuted into the nonsectarian B.C.E./C.E., "before current era/current era," used herein.

32. Manuel (1963: 89).

33. Coe (1968: 83). An English edition of Ussher's great work appeared in 1658 (Ussher 1658). Lightfoot's amendment apparently appeared in post-1650s editions of his "A Few, and New, Observations upon the Booke of Genesis . . . ," first published in 1642 (cited by Coe 1968: 85).

34. Newton (1728).

35. On periodization in geology, see Albritton (1986); for archaeology, see Grayson (1983: 27–54).

36. Albritton (1986); see also Toulmin and Goodfield (1966).

37. This section draws heavily on McGrane (1989).

38. Lafitau (1974–77).

39. McGrane (1989: 68).

40. Harris (1968).

41. For discussions of the French Enlightenment uses of the analogical savage, see Hampson (1983), Liebersohn (1998: 13–38), and Kafker (1996).

42. Stafford (1984).

43. Ferguson (1966), Millar (1779); see Lehmann (1979) and Meek (1976).

44. Cited by Meek (1976: 164).

45. Toulmin and Goodfield (1966) and Harris (1968) provide general historical overviews and discussions of theories of social and cultural change. See also Wilson (1998).

46. Bettinger (1991), Kelly (1995).

47. Vaughan (1965: 260–308).

48. Williams (1973).

49. Carter (1993), Greene (1984: 37–126).

50. Gerbi (1973) contains an excellent history and analysis of the dispute.

51. Pearce (1965: 55).

52. Bonfante (1954).

53. Jefferson (1944: 220–27), Greene (1984: 376–408).

54. Fowler (1975: 20–22).

55. Jefferson (1944: 225–26).

56. Barton (1797).

57. Jefferson (1944: 226).

58. Silverberg (1968), Kennedy (1994).

59. Jefferson (1944: 223).

60. Jefferson et al. (1799), Chinard (1943: 270), Hallowell (1960: 16–18), Wissler (1942: 18), Carter (1993: 26).

61. Du Ponceau (1838: 89), cited by Campbell (1997: 38); see also Goddard (1996b: 28).

62. Pickering (1820).

63. Haas (1969), Swiggers (1998: 23–40).

64. Fowler (1975), Stafford (1984).

65. Jefferson's instructions are in Jackson, ed. (1978, 1: 57–66); see also Jackson (1981).

66. Du Ponceau et al. (1819); see also Long (1823), Dillon (1967), Conklin (1940), and Tyler (1988).

67. Adams (1879) and Walters (1957).

68. Gallatin (1836); see also Adams (1960, 2:525–26).

69. Thomas (1820: 1).

70. Atwater (1820).

71. Reprinted in Adams (1960, 2:625).

72. Wallace (1959: 21). Stephens's (1837, 1843) travel books were best-sellers in the United States and Europe.

73. Bartlett (1848).

74. Stocking (1971: 372).

75. Ethnological Society of Paris (1841), Degérando (1883, 1969), Fowler (1975), and Urry (1972).

76. American Ethnological Society (1845: iii-iv).

77. Cass (1823).

78. Cass (1826).

79. Brown (1979: 275–77).

80. The following sketch is drawn from Bremer (1987).

81. Schoolcraft (1847).

82. Schoolcraft (1851–57), Bremer (1987: 281–84, 293–301, 323–25). Many who tried to use the volumes were frustrated by the disorganization and the layers of Schoolcraft's verbal dross, all made worse by the lack of an index. The Bureau of American Ethnology finally prepared an index a century later (Nichols 1954).

83. See Brodie (1966: 34–82), and Brooke (1994: 184–208).

Chapter 1

1. Bannon (1974: 5).

2. For Sahagún, see d'Olwer (1987) and the masterful translation of Sahagún's great *Florentine Codex* by Arthur J. O. Anderson and Charles E. Dibble (1950–82).

3. Wagner (1937), Cline (1973).

4. Franch (1973), León-Portilla (1979), and Wagner (1937: 200–208).

5. Anderson (1973).

6. Clavigero (1979), Ronan (1973: 273, 293–94). Another major work, the *History of Baja California*, appeared after Clavigero's death in 1789 (Lake and Gray 1937).

7. Keen (1971: 293–350), Mitchell (1981: 204), Phelan (1970).

8. Clavigero (1979, 1:213–21).

9. Clavigero (1979, 1:85–90, 107, 112, 114–15). Clavigero continues with a detailed description of Casa Grande derived from the descriptions by Kino and Anza (Bolton 1919, 1936).

10. Robertson (1840, 4:715–16, 800–851).

11. Humboldt (1814, 1:169–72; 2:248–54).

12. Kingsborough (1830–48), Ternaux-Compans (1837–41); see also Graham (1977), Wagner (1954: 189–93), and Willey and Sabloff (1993: 30).

13. Prescott (1837, 1843).

14. Bustamante and Simmons (1995: 18 and n. 8), Lamar (1965: 34), Connor and Skaggs (1977: 28–33).

15. Merk (1963: 24). For the Mexican perspective on American Manifest Destiny, see Brack (1975).

16. Schroeder (1973).

17. Lamar (1965: 36–82), Estergreen (1962: 152–85).

18. Connor and Faulk (1971).

19. Hollon (1949), Hardy (1920), Gregg (1954).

20. Hollon (1949: 3–29, 128–29).

21. Ruxton (1950, 1951), Garrard (1938), Wislizenus (1848).

22. Ruxton (1950: 105, 177, 180).

23. Ruxton (1950: 183, 185).

24. Ruxton (1950: 183–86).

25. Garrard (1937: 257–58).

26. Wislizenus (1912: 6).

27. Wislizenus (1912: 9).

28. Wislizenus (1848: 20, 24–25).

Chapter 2

1. Horgan (1979: 45).

2. Goetzmann (1959: 17).

3. Frémont (1845).

4. Galvin (1970).

5. Jackson and Spence (1970–84).

6. Lamar (1966: 68–70). Both Garrard (1938) and Ruxton (1950) provide contemporary accounts of the rebellion and its aftermath.

7. Roessel (1983: 506), Bailey (1966: 180–82).

8. Carvalho (1857), Goetzmann (1959: 40).

9. See Goetzmann (1959: 65–374; 1966: 231–352), Hine (1968, 1982), Wallace (1955), and Weber (1985).

10. Galvin (1966: 3).

11. Abert (1847), Galvin (1966: 3–4).

12. Connor and Skaggs (1977: 129–30), *DAB* (6:153–54), Cullum (1868 1:387–88).

13. Emory (1848, 1854).

14. Cullum (1868 1:409).

15. Hine (1982: 1–47). Ned Kern, age twenty-two, was entranced by Frémont's charisma. In California, Frémont named a river after him.

16. On Polk and Frémont, see Schroeder (1973: 51–53).

17. Hine (1982: 48–66), Weber (1985: 17–50), Hafen and Hafen (1960).

18. Cullum (1868 2:328–29), *DAB* (14: 212–13). For Kern's activities with Sitgreaves, see Weber (1985: 143–86).

19. Sitgreaves (1853: 4, 20).

20. On Stephens's consulship, see *DAB* (17: 579); see also Squier (1852).

21. Cited by Goetzmann (1959: 168).

22. Hine (1968: 71–80).

23. Goetzmann (1959: 183–95), Hine (1968: 81–93).

24. Bartlett (1854).

25. Bartlett (1889); the first edition was published in 1848.

26. Goetzmann (1966: 265).

27. Goetzmann (1959: 262–377).

28. A route roughly along the Thirty-second Parallel across Texas and down the Gila River at first was considered already known through the work of Emory and others. However, late in 1853, Lt. John Pope was ordered to survey across the Llano Estacado and Lt. John G. Parke

was ordered to survey along the Gila River and connect with Pope's route (Goetzmann 1959: 289–92).

29. Goetzmann (1959: 287).
30. Humboldt (1858: xxii).
31. Möllhausen (1858).
32. Möllhausen (1858, 1:v-xviii).
33. Whipple, Ewbank, and Turner (1856).
34. Cullum (1868 2:7–8).
35. Frazer (1968: 138).
36. DeLeon (1907: 116).
37. Thompson (1983: 1–123), Starr (1985: 21–29).
38. Huseman (1995).
39. Ives (1861: 110).
40. Cullum (1868, 2:307), DeLeon (1890: 357–58; 1907: 116–20), *DAB* (9: 520–21).
41. Newberry (1861, 1876), Powell (1875a).

Chapter 3

1. Cordell (1997).
2. *OED* (1971: 1599).
3. Williams (1979).
4. Kessell (1979), Schroeder (1979: 432, and table 1).
5. Fagan (1984: 23).
6. Bandelier (1892b), Prem (1997: 21–24).
7. Parmentier (1979).
8. Gregg (1844: 144–45).
9. Sunder (1960: 247–51).
10. Parsons (1939b: passim).
11. Möllhausen (1858, 1:337), Domenech (1860 1:164–65).
12. Emory (1848: 62).
13. Quotes from G. Williams (1979: 39–42); G. Williams (1979, 1985: 124–25, 170–71) and Deacon (1966) are the principal sources on the Madoc legend. As Seed (1995: 16–40) points out, for the English, to take formal possession of a foreign land meant establishing food-production facilities: "plantings," or "plantations," hence, the deliberate use of the term by Peckham.
14. G. Williams (1979: 42–43).
15. Deacon (1966: 197), Catlin (1857, 2:appendix A).
16. Domenech (1860 1:210), Ten Broeck (1854: 74).
17. Bailey (1948), Leone (1979: 43–147).
18. Goodman (1969: 12).
19. Stegner (1942: 148–52).
20. G. Williams (1979: fig. 8), Deacon (1966: 10).
21. Abert (1847: 71–73).
22. Carleton (1854: 296).
23. Carleton (1854: 309–10).
24. Carleton (1854: 313–14), Vivian (1964: 31–33).
25. Schroeder (1979: 237–42) summarizes the available ethnohistoric data on the Salinas pueblos.
26. Bushnell (1925: 508).
27. Emory (1848: 63–64, 66–71).
28. Emory (1848: 79, 81–83).
29. Bartlett (1854: 278–84). Bartlett had copied Font's manuscript in San Francisco during his visit earlier in 1852.
30. Hammond and Rey (1928: 205–6), cited by DiPeso (1974, 1:14–15).
31. Bartlett (1854: 350–51, 357).
32. Bartlett (1854: 361–62).
33. DiPeso (1974).
34. Lister and Lister (1981: 5–6), Gregg (1844: 152).
35. McNitt (1964: xliv-xlv, lxx-lxxix).
36. Simpson (1964: 35).
37. Simpson (1964: 36).
38. Simpson (1964: 44).
39. Simpson (1964: 39–41, 43).
40. Simpson (1964: 45).
41. Simpson (1964: 45–49).
42. Simpson (1964: 49–50, 52 and n. 54).
43. Lekson (1999).
44. Simpson (1964: 62–69, 92–93).
45. Simpson (1964: 113).
46. Sitgreaves (1853: 8–9).
47. Newberry (1876).
48. Newberry (1876: 67) and Museum of New Mexico, Laboratory of Anthropology archaeological site records; Hewett (1938: 26).
49. Newberry (1876: 80).
50. Newberry (1876: 87–88).
51. Newberry (1876: 88–89) and Museum of New Mexico, Laboratory of Anthropology archaeological site records.
52. Prescott (1843), Ternaux-Compans (1838–41), Kingsborough (1831–48). This section is based on Fowler and Wilcox (1999).

53. Gallatin (1848a, 1848b), Squier (1848), Tyler (1988). Emory (1848: appendix 1) published both Gallatin's letter and his reply to it in his report. See also Tyler (1988).

54. Gallatin (1836: 142, 160; 1845: 2, 10–11, 174–77; 1848b: 25).

55. Blumenbach (1865: 273–74), Greenberg (1987), Campbell (1997: 95–106).

56. Gallatin (1845: 49–115, 177–78, 181).

57. Gallatin (1845: 195–96).

58. Gallatin (1845: 200–201, 203).

59. Gallatin (1848a: lxxxvi–lxxxvii).

60. Meltzer (1993).

61. For a comprehensive review, see Jett (1983).

62. See Mathien and McGuire (1986) and Riley and Hedrick (1978) for summaries of specific issues.

63. Möllhausen (1858, 2:64–86), Buschmann (1853). Sydney Lamb (1964: 113–16) points out that Buschmann (1853, 1859) had, in fact, produced evidence for the connections, but it was not accepted by Powell (1892a) and others owing to Buschmann's obscure and crabbed writing style. See also Campbell (1979; 1997: 133–39, 156–69).

64. Atwater (1820: 246), Meltzer (1998: 47), citing Squier and Davis (1848: 119).

65. Squier (1848: 525).

66. Domenech (1860).

67. Domenech (1860, 1:xii). The abbé thus acknowledges his sources in the preface. His colored engraved illustrations are fair, but unacknowledged, copies of those by Möllhausen, the Kern brothers, Stanley, Catlin, Eastman, and various other artists.

68. Huddleston (1967: 31), Domenech (1860, 1:6).

69. Whipple (1855: 37), Domenech (1860, 1:61–62).

Chapter 4

1. Gibson (1971), Powell (1971).

2. Quoted by Weber (1979: 296).

3. Emory (1857: 68, 70).

4. White (1935: 20–21), Möllhausen (1858, 1:331–37).

5. Ten Broeck (1854: 81–88), Ives (1861: 61).

6. Ten Broeck (1854: 82).

7. Ten Broeck (1854: 83–85). His description closely matches the Hemis Kachina dance of the Niman ceremony as described by Earle and Kennard (1971: 41–45 and plates 14–15). The identification of the dance as a Hemis Kachina performance is by Barton Wright (personal communication, 3/23/1987): "To the best of my knowledge this is the first description of a Hopi dance. . . . The dance is quite clearly a performance of the Hemis Kachina coming in April rather than July as they do now. . . . The personnel in the dance with Hemis are the Kachin' Mana and two Avachhoya or Kokosori. The sound the kachinas make and the dance movement are characteristic of Hemis as well. Being presented in April, the Hemis are accompanied by the usual Tcuku. The warriors against the clowns are Chaveyo (I think) and the two Kokosori. Probably there were others but all are lumped under "horrible looking figures." . . . It is of great interest to me that in the course of less than fifty years the Hemis kachina becomes an integral part of the Niman ceremony and is now given only in July, except for individual appearances during the Powamu."

8. Ten Broeck (1854: 85), Eggan (1950).

9. Ten Broeck (1854: 85–88).

10. Ten Broeck is not cited in the articles on the Hopi in the Smithsonian *Handbook of North American Indians*, vol. 9 (Ortiz 1979).

11. Emory (1848: 87).

12. Emory (1848: 101).

13. Schoolcraft (1851–57, 5:205–11). Bartlett's (1854, 2: 325–29) description of Apaches is derived in large part from Henry's report.

14. Quoted by Twitchell (1909: 99).

15. Emory (1848: 47).

16. Letterman (1856), *DAB* (11: 194).

17. Schoolcraft (1851–57, 5:80–91, 209–20, 416–31);

18. Schoolcraft (1851–57, 5: 218).

19. Letterman (1856: 288).

20. Letterman (1856: 294).

21. Letterman (1856: 288), Schoolcraft (1851–57, 5:90).

22. Ives (1861: 97, 108).

23. Emory (1848: 82–85) seems to have been the first to use the term *Maricopa*, an abbreviation of *Cocomaricopa*, which the Spanish had used since the time of Father Kino in the 1690s (Harwell and Kelly 1983: 83; Ezell 1983: 152–55).

24. Bartlett (1854, 2:213–57).

25. Schoolcraft (1851–57, 5:689).

26. Dall (1896).

27. Turner (1852), Whipple, Ewbank, and Turner (1855: 84), Shipley (1978: 87), Campbell (1997: 206–329).

Chapter 5

1. Rhees (1880: 1–25).

2. Rhees (1901: 277–95, 343–46).

3. Rhees (1901, 1:330–34).

4. Rhees (1901, 1:343–46).

5. McKelvey (1991: xx–xxiii).

6. Bieder (1986), Berkhofer (1978: 113–94).

7. This section draws on Bartlett (1962), Goetzmann (1966), Hinsley (1981), Stegner (1954), and Wilkins (1958).

8. King (1872).

9. Wilkins (1958: 95–96).

10. Horan (1966).

11. King's reports were capped by his *Systematic Geology* (1878), a brilliant yet archaic work, the last major exegesis of catastrophism in American geology. It was applauded politely and then ignored by King's scientific friends of Darwinian and uniformitarian persuasions (Goetzmann 1966: 461–66).

12. The following sketch is based on White (1893) and Goetzmann (1966: 490–97).

13. Goetzmann (1966: 492–94).

14. Jackson's life, nearly one hundred years long, is covered in C. S. Jackson (1947) and W. H. Jackson (1940).

15. Goetzmann (1966: 409, 504–8).

16. Mark (1980: 131–71).

17. Bartlett (1962: 63).

18. Jackson (1875).

19. C. Jackson (1947: 224).

20. Jackson (1876), Holmes (1876).

21. Jackson (1940: 31).

22. Kincaid (1983).

23. Goetzmann (1966: 467). This section draws on Goetzmann (1966: 390–429, 467–88) and Dawdy (1993).

24. Wheeler (1872: 11–12).

25. Goetzmann (1966: 475).

26. Dawdy (1993: 29–36).

27. Goetzmann (1966: 479–81).

28. See Schmeckbier (1904: 44–66) for complete citations.

29. Putnam (1879).

30. Cope (1879).

31. Gatschet (1879).

32. Gilbert (1877, 1890), Pyne (1980).

33. The standard interpretive biographies on Powell are by Darrah (1951), Stegner (1954), and Worster (2000).

34. Joseph Henry, *Diary*, Apr. 23, 1867. Smithsonian Institution Archives.

35. Fowler and Fowler (1969a: 154).

36. The documentation on the 1869 river trip is extensive. See Darrah (1951: 108–43), and Powell (1875d).

37. U.S. *Statutes* 16:242.

38. Powell (1875c).

39. On Hillers, see Fowler (1972, 1989). On the second river trip, see Dellenbaugh (1962), and Fowler and Fowler (1969b).

40. Powell and Ingalls (1874), reprinted in Fowler and Fowler (1971: 97–119).

41. Powell and Ingalls (1874), Powell (1875a–d); Powell's field notes on the Numic peoples are in Fowler and Fowler (1971); descriptions of his material culture collections are in Fowler and Matley (1979).

42. Fowler (1989: 60–80).

43. Ingram (1876: 151); see also Trennert (1974).

44. Ingram (1876: 151).

45. Ingram (1876: 147–52), Fowler (1989: 77–79).

46. Kohlstedt (1980).

47. Eight major volumes were published between 1877 and 1893. See Schmeckbier (1904: 43) for full citations.

48. J. W. Powell to J. H. Trumbull, 2/6/1877; J. W. Powell to A. Gatschet, 3/12/1877, RMSC; Gatschet (1879), Mooney (1907).

49. J. W. Powell to J. Q. Smith, 6/3/1877, RMSC; Powell (1881a: xiii); J. W. Powell to J. G. Swan, 12/18/1877, RMSC.

50. Hewitt (1895).

51. See Bureau of American Ethnology (1971) for a list of Pilling's bibliographies.

52. Powell (1877).

53. J. W. Powell to C. King, 1/23/1877; Powell to J. S. Newberry, 1/25/1877; Newberry to J. Garfield, 1/20/1877, RMSC.

54. Powell (1878a).

55. Wilkins (1958: 230–43).

56. Powell to Atkins, 2/20/1879, RMSC.

57. U.S. *Statutes* 20:397.

Chapter 6

1. Powell (1881a: xxxiii).
2. S. F. Baird to J. W. Powell, 7/9/1879; C. Schurz to J. W. Powell, 7/22/1879, BEC.
3. Baird to Powell, 7/8/1882; Powell to Baird, 8/10/1882; Baird to Powell, 7/7/1883; Powell to Baird, 11/23/1883; Baird to Powell, 10/4/1884; Baird to Powell, 6/29/1886, BEC.
4. Powell to Baird, 4/4/1880; Powell to H. G. Davis, 6/2/1880, BEC.
5. On Bureau appropriations, see Rhees (1901, 1:932–33, 1045; 2:1541).
6. Scott (1968: 21–42), Census Office (1883: xviii–xix).
7. Powell to F. A. Walker, 2/7/1880, BEC; Powell to Baird, 1/13/1883, 1/15/1883, 1/16/1883, 1/26/1883; Baird to Powell, 1/29/1883; Fowler and Fowler (1971: 13).
8. Wilkins (1958: 317–22, 354–56).
9. Stegner (1954: 248); see also Wilkins (1958: 262–63).
10. Stegner (1954: 248–49).
11. This section is drawn from Resek (1960), and White (1959).
12. Tocqueville (1945: 106–10); Morgan to Powell 9/10/1880, 9/22/1880, BEC.
13. Snow (1994: 158–82), Tooker (1978a, 1978c).
14. Quoted by Resek (1960: 25).
15. Morgan (1954), Tooker (1978b: 440, 1994), Fenton (1951: 296–310), Powell (1881b: 114).
16. Morgan (1954, 1:79–80). Morgan was unaware that Father Lafitau (1974, 1:69–70) had described the system in his great work of 1724. By the 1850s Lafitau had fallen into deep obscurity and there is no indication that Morgan knew his work (Resek 1960: 70n; Fenton and Moore 1974–77, 1:lxxxiii–iv). Lafitau's work is not listed among the holdings in Morgan's personal library (Trautman and Kabelac 1994).
17. Quoted by Resek (1960: 74).
18. Resek (1960: 75), Riggs (1852), Morgan (1959).
19. Morgan (1871: 5), Resek (1960: 79).
20. Morgan (1871).
21. Toulmin and Goodfield (1966: 233–34).
22. Resek (1960: 121–26), White (1937).
23. Lubbock (1865).
24. Morgan (1877: v–vii).
25. Morgan (1876a, 1876b: 66, 71, emphasis in original).
26. The mania for kinship studies in anthropology seems to have peaked in 1949 (Murdock 1949, Lévi-Strauss 1949).
27. Resek (1960: 133).
28. White (1942: 3–9), Hollcroft (1953).
29. White (1942: 10, 14), Morgan (1880b).
30. Hollcroft (1953: 125–26), W. F. Morgan (1879).
31. White (1942: 22–23).
32. White (1942: 24).
33. Bandelier (1879); see also Hollcroft (1953: 127), and Lange and Riley (1996: 27).
34. Powell to Morgan, 5/23/1877, 7/18,1877, RMSC; Morgan to Powell, 10/6/1880, BEC.
35. Darrah (1951: 226–36), Powell (1878b).
36. Adams to Morgan, 7/14/1877, in Cater (1947: 83).
37. Morgan to Powell 11/13/1880; Morgan to J. C. Pilling 3/26/1881, BEC.
38. The following sketch is derived primarily from Lange and Riley's (1996) excellent biography of Bandelier. Bandelier's first name is variously spelled by his biographers: Adolphe, Adolph, and Adolf. Hereafter, Adolph is used since it seems to be the most common usage. There are several errors of fact in earlier biographies of Bandelier, for example, in Hodge (1932); see Lange and Riley (1996: 15–16) and Lange, Riley, and Lange (1984: 7–8, 217–19) for corrections.
39. For the Morgan-Bandelier correspondence, see White (1940).
40. White (1940, 1:55).
41. Bandelier (1877, 1878, 1879, 1880).
42. Norton and Howe (1913, 2:97).
43. Norton and Howe (1913: passim).
44. Putnam to Morgan, 1/31/1880, quoted by Resek (1960: 148).
45. Norton to Thomas Carlyle, 7/23/1880; quoted in Norton and Howe (1913, 2:111–12).
46. Lange and Riley (1996: 34–37).
47. Morgan (1880a).
48. Minutes of AIA Executive Committee meeting for Jan. 17, 1880, quoted in Lange, Riley, and Lange (1984: 20).
49. Morgan to Powell, 1/24/1880, BEC.
50. Powell to Morgan, 2/25/1880, Morgan to Powell, 3/14/1880, BEC. White (1940, 2:165–76).

51. Minutes of AIA Annual Meeting for May 15, 1880, quoted and excerpted in Lange, Riley, and Lange (1984: 27–29); Parkman to Powell, 6/4/1880, Morgan to Powell, 6/8/1880, BEC.

52. Powell to Parkman, 6/11/1880; Powell to Bandelier, 6/11/1880; Powell to Parkman, 6/26/1880; Norton to Powell, 6/29/1880; Powell to Norton, 7/7/1880, 7/8/1880; Putnam to Powell, 7/17/1880; Norton to Powell, 7/19/1880, BEC.

53. Bandelier to Norton, 7/29/1880, printed in Lange, Riley, and Lange (1984: 245, n. 75).

54. Powell to Parkman, 4/11/1882, BEC.

55. Morgan (1880a: 30, emphasis added).

56. Morgan (1880a: 46).

57. Morgan (1880a: 77).

58. Morgan (1881: 221–23).

59. Morgan to Powell, 6/16/1880, BEC.

60. Resek (1960: 151).

Chapter 7

1. U.S. *Statutes* 21:275, 443; Powell to Baird, 4/4/1880; Powell to H. G. Davis, 6/2/1881, BEC.

2. Crossette (1966).

3. Flack (1975: 86).

4. Quoted by Flack (1975: 84).

5. Stegner (1954: 294–328).

6. Darrah (1951: 336–49), Stegner (1954: 269–345), Worster (2000).

7. See Bureau of American Ethnology (1971) for a list of relevant publications by these individuals.

8. Thomas (1894).

9. The published and archival documentation on Cushing and the Stevensons is quite large. Key sources on their artifact collecting activities are Hinsley (1992a) and Parezo (1986, 1987). For Hillers, see Fowler (1972, 1989).

10. J. W. Powell to James Stevenson, 8/4/1880, BEC.

11. Cushing letter in Green (1990: 35).

12. J. Stevenson to J. Pilling, 10/17/1879, BEC.

13. J. Stevenson to J. Pilling, 12/17/1879, 11/21/1879, BEC.

14. T. E. Stevenson (1881: 1), M. C. Stevenson (1904: 16–17).

15. T. E. Stevenson (1881: 9–10).

16. Bandelier, 2/23/1883, in Lange, Riley, and Lange (1970–84, 2:40).

17. Cushing (1896: 337).

18. M. C. Stevenson (1904: 17).

19. Domínguez (1956: 198), Merrill and Ahlborn (1997: 178–81 and figs. 9.1, 9.2).

20. J. Stevenson (1881a: 334–74), Merrill and Ahlborn (1997: 191–92 and figs. 9.8, 9.10).

21. Stevenson (1884: 90–91 and plate 16).

22. Powell (1889: xxix).

23. Cushing (1896: 417–24), Parsons (1918).

24. Merrill and Ahlborn (1997: 181–84), Merrill, Ladd, and Ferguson (1993).

25. This section draws on Parezo (1993) and the Stevensons' correspondence files in BEC.

26. Cited by Parezo (1993: 40).

27. J. Stevenson (1881a: 330–31, 1881b: 431).

28. Cited by Brandes (1965: 6).

29. Stevenson (1887).

30. This section is based on the annual summaries of field work in the Bureau of Ethnology annual reports and on correspondence in BEC.

31. Fowler (1989: 131).

32. Anonymous (1886) reproduced in Babcock and Parezo (1988: 10–11).

33. J. Stevenson (1891).

34. Powell (1889: xliv).

35. T. E. Stevenson (1888).

36. Parezo (1993: 43–44).

37. Parezo (1993: 52–53, 61).

38. Stevenson (1915).

39. Roscoe (1991: 28–29); see also Roscoe (1987) for an extensive bibliography on Indian "berdaches." On Zuni terminology and practices, see Parsons (1916b, 1939).

40. Stevenson (1904: 380).

41. Viola (1981).

42. Roscoe (1991: 56).

43. Parezo (1993: 55–56).

44. Cited by Roscoe (1991: 61).

45. Mason (1886: 24), cited by Roscoe (1991: 61 and figs. 15–20).

46. Roscoe (1991: 70).

47. Stevenson (1904: 312–13).

48. Parezo (1993: 57).

Chapter 8

1. Van Gennep (1960; original 1909).

2. On the phenomenon of anthropologists beginning field work as graduate students and ending as "elder of tribes," see the papers in Fowler and Hardesty (1994).

3. V. Deloria (1969).

4. The following sketch of Cushing is based on Brandes (1965), Green (1979, 1990), Hinsley (1999), Hinsley and Wilcox (1995, 1996), Hodge (1900), Mark (1980: 96–130), Pandey (1972), and on Cushing's voluminous correspondence in the National Anthropological Archives and the Southwest Museum Library.

5. Cushing (1875).

6. Cushing (1970: 13). The quote is from Cushing's "My Adventures in Zuni," first published in *Century Illustrated Monthly Magazine* in 1882–83.

7. Cushing to Baird, 7/18/1880, BAEC, emphasis in original; reprinted in Green (1990: 116–17).

8. Green (1990: 178–80).

9. Brandes (1965: 61–64).

10. Hinsley (1996: 21).

11. From Baxter (1881); reprinted in Hinsley and Wilcox (1996: 45–47).

12. From Baxter (1881); reprinted in Hinsley and Wilcox (1996: 54).

13. C. Fowler (1978: 37–38).

14. Baird to Powell, 1/23/1882; Baird to Cushing, 01/24/1882, BAEC.

15. Brandes (1965: 96–107).

16. Quoted in Bender (1984: 84).

17. Quoted in Bender (1984: 121).

18. Quoted in Bender (1984: 124).

19. S. Jackson to Baird, 12/22/1882; C. H. Howard to Powell, 12/26/1882, BAEC.

20. Bender (1984: 166–67).

21. Bender (1984: 169).

22. J. C. Pilling to Cushing, 1/19/1884; Cushing to Powell, 1/29/1884, 3/30/1884; Powell to Cushing, 3/21/1884, BAEC.

23. Quoted in Green (1990: 41).

24. Cushing (1970: 77–78).

25. See Quaife (1921: 103–14 and 155 n. 66), Thoreau (1980: 342–44), Cooper (1954), Berger (1964), Blake and Costner (1990), Penn and Willingham (1970).

26. Powell (1875c).

27. Cushing (1970), Baxter (1882a, 1882b), the latter reprinted in Hinsley and Wilcox (1996: 63–96).

28. Carter (1978: 23).

29. For Price and Coues at Havasupai, see Cutright and Brodhead (1981: 220–25). Coues later became the editor of several journals of western exploration that included those of Lewis and Clark, Zebulon Pike, and Father Garcés.

30. Brandes (1965: 70–71).

31. Cushing (1965), Euler (1965: 4–5), Schwartz (1983).

32. On ten Kate and the Snake Dance, see McIntire and Gordon (1968); on Sullivan see Bourke (1884: 83); see also Hovens (1995).

33. Overviews of Southwestern religions may be found in several articles in Sullivan (1989).

34. Cushing (1883).

35. Benedict (1935), Bunzel (1932a-d), Stevenson (1904), B. Tedlock (1992), D. Tedlock (1979).

36. Cushing (1884–85).

37. Hughte (1994).

Chapter 9

1. This biographical sketch is based on Mooney (1905), Wedel (1969), Poor (1975), and the papers in Halpern and McGreevy (1997).

Data on Matthews's relationship with the Hidatsa woman are equivocal. Matthews apparently supported the child, Berthold Matthews, who remained in his native village, for many years, including sending him to Oberlin College when he grew up (Poor 1975: 11–12). Caroline Matthews is never mentioned by her husband in any of his publications or papers, although she traveled with him as a dutiful army wife, and was eulogized by James Mooney (1905: 514), a close friend of the couple, as "his closest companion, his most helpful and interested assistant, his best inspiration, and his tender nurse at the end." See Matthews (1873, 1877) for his Hidatsa work.

2. Darwin (1873: 22); Mallery to Matthews, 11/28/1879; Matthews to Mallery, 11/6/1879, 11/27/1879, 12/19/1879, BEC.

3. Matthews to Powell, 2/7/1881; Powell to General

Pope, 10/9/1880; Pope to Powell, 10/20/1880; Pilling to Matthews, 11/6/1880; Powell to Matthews, 1/8/1881; Telegram, Matthews to Pilling, 9/1/1882; Pope to Powell, 12/8/1882, BEC.

4. Frink and Barthelmess (1965: 28–35); Matthews to Powell, field report for October 1884, Washington Matthews Papers, Archives, Wheelwright Museum of the American Indian, Santa Fe (hereafter cited as WMP).

5. Matthews (1887).

6. U.S. Army, Special Order, no. 100, 4/28/1894; Special Order no. 226, 10/7/1895, WMP.

7. Matthews (1902a).

8. Putnam to Matthews, 12/30/1902, 1/1/1903, 1/24/1903, WMP. A copy of the contract and letters transmitting monthly payments from Mrs. Hearst's business agent are in the Matthews papers; Matthews (1907). In 1951 the Matthews papers were transferred from the University of California to the Museum of Navajo Ceremonial Art, now the Wheelwright Museum of the American Indian, in Santa Fe.

9. Witherspoon (1977: 10).

10. Roessel (1983: 506, 510–20 and fig. 16), Frazer (1965: 104–8), Brugge (1994).

11. Witherspoon (1983: 525).

12. Adair (1944: 3–5, 124).

13. Matthews (1883: 178; 1897: 11–12). In 1894, as Jake the Silversmith, Nigehani apparently accompanied a circus through the eastern United States with his workshop as a sideshow attraction.

14. Matthews (1884), Kent (1985: 8), Brugge (1983: 491–93), Blomberg (1988: 4).

15. Matthews (1884: 387).

16. See Farella (1984), Faris (1990), Haile (1981), Levy (1998), McNeley (1981), Reichard (1950b), Wyman (1970, 1975, 1983), and Zolbrod (1984).

17. Wyman (1975: 4).

18. Wyman (1975: 4–5).

19. Wyman (1975: 9).

20. Wyman (1983: 20).

21. Wyman (1970: xix, 4; 1983: 19–24 and table 1; 1975: 8–9); see also Haile (1938a: 639, 1938b: 10).

22. Matthews (1885a, 1885b, 1887).

23. Stevenson (1891).

24. Faris (1990: 8, 40–41).

25. Matthews (1902a).

26. Matthews (1897: 36; 1902a: 5, 25, 222–26; 1907: 26–46).

27. Farella (1984), Faris (1990), Levy (1998), Zolbrod (1984).

Chapter 10

1. The following sketch is drawn from Bloom (1933–38), Hodge (1896), Porter (1986), Richardson (1958), and Sutherland (1964).

2. Porter (1986: 2).

3. Porter (1986: 2–4). Bourke never mentioned the details of his actions that gained him the Medal of Honor, but his daughter, Anna Bourke Richardson (1958: 7), reported that the family learned it was due to his rallying the troops and leading the charge at Stones River after all the officers were killed.

4. Cited by Bloom (1933–38, 9:283).

5. Porter (1986: 12–13); see also Bourke (1886, 1891a) and Crook (1946).

6. Bourke (1891a).

7. Bourke (1980) is a microfilm copy of the diaries. The originals are in the library at West Point; extensive excerpts are reprinted in Bloom (1933–38), Casanova (1968), and Sutherland (1964), and form much of the basis for Porter's (1986) biography of Bourke.

8. Sutherland (1964: 173–96).

9. Porter (1986: 69–72), Sutherland (1964: 12).

10. Dorsey to Powell, 1/18/1881; Powell to Bourke, 1/20/1881, BEC; Bloom (1933–38, 10:377–78).

11. Richardson (1958: 8); Bourke to Powell, 2/28/1881, Powell to Bourke, 3/3/1881, Pilling to Bourke, 3/24/1881, BEC; Bloom (1933–38, 10:378); Sutherland (1964: 173); Porter (1986: 88).

12. Bourke never published a description of the Sun Dance, although his notes take up two volumes of his diary-notebooks; Porter (1986: 89–94) provides a summary.

13. Porter (1986: 98–99).

14. Porter (1986: 100–106).

15. Bourke, Diary 52: 20–21, cited by Porter (1986: 105–6).

16. Bourke (1884), Keam (1883).

17. Sutherland (1964: 1283–99).

18. See Bourke (1886), Porter's (1986: 141–209) sum-

mary based on Bourke's diaries, Thrapp (1967), and the historical and cultural summaries in Basso (1983) and Opler (1983).

19. Casanova (1968).

20. Bourke to Pilling, 9/13/1885, Pilling to Bourke, 10/1/1885, BEC; Porter (1986: 268).

21. Bourke (1891a, 1892).

22. Bourke (1888: 5).

23. Bourke (1891b).

24. Powell to the Secretary of the Interior, 4/1/1891, BEC; Porter (1986: 210–66).

25. Porter (1986: 291).

26. Porter (1986: 292–306).

27. This section is based on Graves (1998).

28. Article in *Daily Alta California,* quoted by Graves (1998: 27–28).

29. Graves (1998: 109–38).

30. Graves (1998: 139–70).

31. The basic source on Stephen is a brief sketch by Elsie Clews Parsons (1936b: xx–xxiv). Additional details and corrections are added by Graves (1998: 145–46).

32. Bourke (1884: 80).

Chapter 11

1. J. P. Knott to J. W. Powell, 8/15/1882, Longacre (1999), BEC. The following biographical sketches are based on Nabakov (1989) and the Mindeleff brothers' correspondence in BEC.

2. J. W. Powell to J. Stevenson, 7/3/1881.

3. V. Mindeleff (1891: 14).

4. V. Mindeleff (1891: 16–41).

5. Powell (1894: xxxvi–xxxvii).

6. Bureau of American Ethnology (1971: 4).

7. Powell (1897: xlvii), C. Mindeleff (1897, 1898, 1900).

Chapter 12

1. Powell to Langley 6/30/1893; Langley to McGee 7/11/1893, BAEC.

2. Darrah (1951: 279, n. 12).

3. E. McGee (1915: 61–62), *NCAB* (10: 350).

4. McGee to G. B. Goode 9/1/1893, BAEC.

5. S. P. Langley, Two confidential memoranda re-

garding the Bureau of American Ethnology, 2/19/1902, BAEC.

6. S. P. Langley, Confidential memorandum regarding the Bureau of American Ethnology, 10/11/1902, BAEC.

7. McGee (1898).

8. Records Relating to the Investigation of the Bureau of American Ethnology, 1903, BAEC; hereafter cited as "Records (1903)."

9. Records (1903: 125).

10. C. B. Dinwiddie to M. C. Stevenson, 2/21/1902, copy in Records (1903).

11. Records (1903: 248, 250).

12. American Anthropological Association, Articles of Incorporation, copy in Records (1903).

13. Records (1903: 620).

14. Powell (1892b, 1895, 1898a, 1898b, 1900).

15. Records (1903: 824).

16. McGee to W. H. Holmes, 7/31/1903; R. Rathbun to McGee, 8/1/1903, copies in Records.

17. E. McGee (1915), Hodge (1912).

18. McGee (1912).

19. Spitzka (1903, 1913). The wager is described by Darrah (1951: 390–91) and Stegner (1954: 349, 416 n. 9). It is part of the vast body of oral folklore of the Smithsonian Institution. The present author first heard various versions of it in the late 1960s.

20. Hodge (1907–10).

Chapter 13

1. This section is based on Brandes (1965: 119–33), the materials in Hinsley and Wilcox (1995), and the Cushing/Hodge papers (CHP) in the Southwest Museum Library, Los Angeles.

2. Jackson (1881, 1884).

3. Hinsley and Wilcox (1995: 550–52), *DAB* (8: 518–19).

4. Dewey (1995: 562–63).

5. Cushing (1901); see Green (1979: 332).

6. Hinsley and Wilcox (1995: 521), Brandes (1965: 128–29).

7. Brandes (1965: 130), Hinsley and Wilcox (1995: 566); on Morse, see *DAB* (13: 242–43).

8. Hovens (1995: 639).

9. Brandes (1965: 126–31), Hinsley and Wilcox (1995: xx).

10. F. W. Hodge, Diary, 12/8/1886, CHP; on Hodge's life, see Judd, Harrington, and Lothrop (1957).

11. H. C. ten Kate to F. W. Hodge, 4/11/1930, CHP; Heÿink and Hodge (1931), Hovens (1995: 635–43).

12. Darrah (1951: 321).

13. This section is based on Wilcox (1993).

14. Wilcox (1993: 44, 49–55), Bandelier (1883, 1890–92: 444–45).

15. Downum and Bostwick (1993), Wilcox, Howard, and Nelson (1990).

16. Brandes (1965: 137–40); the earthquake incident is related by Hodge (1945: viii).

17. Matthews (1902b: 144).

18. For Cushing's and Baxter's trip to Casa Grande, see Cushing (1995) and Brandes (1965: 138–41); on the petition to Congress, see Lee (1970: 31–33).

19. Hinsley and Wilcox (1996).

20. ten Kate (1892: 119), Hovens (1995: 661–66).

21. Hinsley and Wilcox (1995: 531–33), Brandes (1965: 152).

22. Telegram, A. Hemenway to F. C. Cushing, 6/15/1889, CHP.

23. Hinsley and Wilcox (1995).

24. Matthews, Wortman and Billings (1893), ten Kate (1892), Bandelier (1892a).

25. Haury (1945b, 1995).

26. Cushing (1890).

27. Cushing (1890: 181–82).

28. Tylor (1958), Hodgen (1977).

29. Cushing (1890: 162).

30. Fowler (1992).

31. Koepping (1983).

32. The quotes in this and the following six paragraphs are taken from throughout Cushing's (1890) article; the emphases in phrasing are added.

33. Cushing (1896: 321–66).

34. Ferguson and Hart (1985: 22).

35. Cushing (1896), Stevenson (1904), Bunzel (1932b).

36. Quoted by Ferguson and Hart (1985: 23).

37. Tylor (1958: 1).

38. Herder (1966).

39. Baxter (1882b: 73), Cushing (1884–85: 18).

40. Haeberlin (1916), Benedict (1930, 1932).

41. Kroeber and Kluckhohn (1952), Williams (1976).

42. Lummis (1900: 11); Cushing quoted by Brandes (1965: 158).

43. Brandes (1965: 159).

44. Hinsley and Wilcox (1995: 533).

45. Brandes (1965: 165).

46. Brandes (1965: 166).

47. Gilliland (1975).

48. Gilliland (1975: 47–246, and plates 10–144).

49. Mark (1980: 118–19).

50. Haury (1945), Gilliland (1975).

51. F. H. Cushing to S. Culin, 4/5/1900. Culin Archival Collection, Cushing Collection: correspondence [6.1.005], 1899–1900, Brooklyn Museum of Art Archives. I am indebted to Diana Fane and Deborah Wythe, of The Brooklyn Museum of Art, for calling my attention to this very important letter. The Cushing legend says: "On Wednesday evening, April 10, 1900, he and his wife sat at dinner in their Washington home. Their talk was animated. As they discussed his developing plans for the summer expedition to Maine, Frank Hamilton Cushing choked on a fishbone, hemorrhaged, and died before help could be summoned" (Brandes 1965: 204).

52. Hodge (1900: 367).

Chapter 14

1. This section draws from Swanton and Roberts (1931), Hinsley (1983), and Hough (1931, 1932).

2. Swanton and Roberts (1931: 609).

3. S. Baxter to F. H. Cushing, 9/16/1891, CHP; Hinsley (1983: 63).

4. Fewkes (1890a). In the 1960s, the National Anthropological Archives launched a diligent, but unsuccessful, search in Boston and Washington for Fewkes's thirty-five wax cylinders from his Maine and Southwest work.

5. Hinsley (1983).

6. Hinsley (1983: 63); F. H. Cushing to S. Baxter, 6/16/1891, CHP.

7. Hinsley (1992a: 134).

8. J. G. Owens to D. Stratton, 4/24/1891, CHP; cited by Hinsley (1983: 65; 1992a: 127).

9. W. Matthews to F. H. Cushing, 1/7/1891, CHP; cited by Hinsley (1983: 163–64).

10. Fewkes and Stephen (1892, 1893); see also Wade and McChesney (1980: 8), and Graves (1998: 161 and n. 60).

11. Wade and McChesney (1980).

12. See Fewkes (1919b) for a listing.

13. Owens (1892: 165).

14. Fewkes (1890c, 1891, 1892a).

15. Fewkes (1890a, 1890b, 1910).

16. Gilman (1891, 1908), Gilman and Stone (1908), Roberts (1927), Stocking (1995: 109), Fewkes and Harrington (1925).

17. Powell to Fewkes, 3/14/1895; Langley to Powell 5/21/1895, 5/24/1895; Langley to McGee 5/22/1895; McGee to Fewkes 5/24/1895. BEC

18. Fewkes (1896a: 558–59).

19. Fewkes (1896a: 559).

20. Fewkes (1896a, 1898a, 1898b, 1900a, 1904).

21. Lomatuway'ma, Lomatuway'ma, and Namingha (1993), Fewkes (1896a: 566–69).

22. Lomatuway'ma, Lomatuway'ma, and Namingha (1993: 117–47).

23. Fewkes (1900a).

24. Fewkes (1900a: 633).

25. Cordell (1997: 416–28), Schaafsma (1994: 35–137).

26. See Frisbie (1973), Graves (1998: 160–70), Kramer (1996), and Wade and McChesney (1980).

27. Swanton and Roberts (1931: 611).

28. Fewkes (1896a: 577; 1898a: 660; 1919a: 218).

29. Hough (1917: 322; 1931, 1932), Fewkes (1919a), Frisbie (1973: 238–39).

30. This section draws from Graves (1998), Kramer (1996), Wade (1980, 1985), and Wade and McChesney (1980, 1981).

31. Fewkes (1898a: 632–728; 1919a, combined in Fewkes 1973). Stephen's notes and drawings of Hopi pottery symbols are presented in Patterson (1994).

32. Bourke (1884), Fewkes (1897), Fewkes, Stephen, and Owens (1894).

33. Fewkes (1896b, 1897a, 1897b, 1900b, 1903), Fewkes and Stephen (1892, 1893), Fewkes, Stephen and Owens (1894). For Voth, see Chapter 18.

34. Stephen (1936); On Hopi kachina ceremonies and the associated "dolls," see Bradfield (1973, 2:46–305), Colton (1959), Earle and Kennard (1971), Frigout (1979), Hieb (1979), and Schaafsma (1994).

35. Hieb (1979: 577) first paragraph; Tyler (1979) second paragraph.

36. Hieb (1979: 577), Frigout (1979: 564).

37. Earle and Kennard (1971: 7).

38. Colton (1959), Fewkes (1894, 1897a, 1903).

39. Brody (1991: 154, 155).

40. Fewkes (1915).

41. Fewkes (1892a, 1907, 1909a, 1909b, 1919c).

42. Judd (1967: 28–29).

43. Fewkes (1914).

Chapter 15

1. The definitive biography of Bandelier is by Lange and Riley (1996) based on their editing of Bandelier's journals of his years in the Southwest (Lange and Riley 1966; Lange, Riley, and Lange 1970, 1975, 1984). They have corrected a number of errors in the earlier biographies, for example, those in Goad (1939) and Hodge (1932). Other major sources on Bandelier's life include his correspondence with Lewis Henry Morgan (White 1940) and the Mexican historian and bibliographer Joaquín García Icazbalceta (White and Bernal 1960), as well as miscellaneous correspondence in Hammond and Goad (1949) and Radin (1942). Bandelier was probably christened "Adolphe"; in the edited journals, Lange and Riley use "Adolph," the most common usage by Bandelier and others, but "Adolf" in the title of their biography.

2. Wilson (1997: 63–70).

3. Keleher (1957: xii); see also Horn (1963: 177–209).

4. Susan Wallace is quoted in Horn (1963: 208). On the Wallaces' life in New Mexico, see L. Wallace (1906: 913–45), S. Wallace (1888) and Horn (1963: 199–219). For *Ben Hur,* see Wallace (1880).

5. Rudisill (1973: 13–14, 17, 51, 62).

6. Bandelier (1890b).

7. Lange and Riley (1966: 88–90, 145, 178, 193); Lange, Riley, and Lange (1970: 45, 154).

8. Bandelier to Norton, 11/18/1880, cited in Lange, Riley, and Lange (1984: 252 n. 85).

9. White (1940, 2:161–62).

10. Quoted by Hammond and Goad (1949: 3).

11. Bandelier (1890–92, 2:163–68).

12. Davis (1981).

13. Lange and Riley (1996: 55–59).

14. Lange, Riley and Lange (1984: 263–64 n. 96). Bandelier's conversion is discussed in Lange and Riley (1996: 59–66).

15. Bandelier (1884a); see also White (1940, 2:234–44).

16. White (1940, 2:249).

17. One such letter to García Icazbalceta (White and Bernal 1960: 271) is translated and cited in Lange, Riley,

and Lange (1970: 386, n. 240); see also Lange and Riley (1996: 88–89).

18. Lange and Riley (1996: 101).

19. Lange and Riley (1996: 106–7).

20. This painful period in Bandelier's life is described by Lange and Riley (1996: 103–11).

21. Archaeological Institute of America (1885: 40–41).

22. Archaeological Institute of America (1885: 27–29).

23. Harvey (1988: 68–69).

24. Bandelier (1890b); the encyclopedia articles are listed in White (1940, 1:98).

25. In 1969 the late Ernest J. Burrus, S.J., published an index of the 502 illustrations as well as color reproductions of 30 of the watercolors and maps (Burrus 1969a, 1969b). A portion of the "Histoire" was published in English translation in 1988 (Bandelier 1988, Rodack 1988).

26. On his Hemenway work, see Bandelier (1890c).

27. Lange, Riley, and Lange (1984: 175–76).

28. Lange and Riley (1996: 151–82).

29. Lange and Riley (1996: 183–201).

30. Sahagún (1932). Fanny Bandelier translated the first four books of the Codex on the Aztec gods, ceremonies, and soothsayers. Her final years are discussed by Lange and Riley (1996: 215–34).

31. The scattering was quietly conducted by Douglas Schwartz, president of the School of American Research (SAR), Jeton Brown, of the SAR staff, Charles Lange, coeditor of Bandelier's Southwestern journals, and John Hunter, Kevin McKibbin, and Dan Murphy of the National Park Service (Lange and Riley 1996: 237).

32. Bandelier (1890–92, 2:591).

33. Morgan (1880a: 30).

34. Bandelier (1890–92, 1:127).

35. Bandelier (1881b: 92–97, 104–7; 1884b: 62, 78, 84).

36. Fowler and Wilcox (1999: 215).

37. Bandelier (1890–2, 1:128–29, 131–32 n. 2; 2:258–59, 273); see also Schroeder (1979: 236–42).

38. Bandelier (1890–92, 1:136); see also Schroeder (1979: 254).

39. Bandelier (1890–92, 2:577, 584–85 and 585 n. 1).

40. Bandelier (1890–92, 2:583).

41. Crown (1994), Washburn and Crowe (1988).

42. Bandelier (1890–92, 2:122–31, 1:585).

43. Bandelier (1890–92, 2:589).

44. Lange and Riley (1996: 139), Fewkes (1895a, 1895b).

45. Comparato (1979: 110–12).

46. The following sketch is based on Caughey (1946) and Clark (1973), as well as Bancroft's (1890) literary autobiography.

47. Bancroft (1890: 295–96).

48. Cline (1973) discusses the actual authorship of Bancroft's works.

49. Bancroft (1883, 4:682–86).

50. Bancroft (1883, 1:471–75).

51. Bancroft (1883, 1:502–4, 507–8, 511–12, 514, 524–25).

52. Bancroft (1883, 1:537–38, 555).

53. Bancroft (1883, 3:660–61, 680).

54. Bancroft (1890, 39:326–64), Cline (1973: 333–34).

55. Bancroft (1883, 2:133–629).

56. Bancroft (1883, 2:171–73, 175 n. 34).

57. Morgan (1876a: 265, 267), White (1940, 1:164, 216, 224); see also Gibson (1947: 82–84).

58. Bancroft (1890, 38:38).

59. Caughey (1946: 349–65).

60. The following sketch is drawn from Bannon (1964, 1978) and Weber (1988).

61. Turner (1894). On the impact of Turner's thesis on the writing of Southwestern history, see Weber (1988).

62. Bannon (1978: 45–46, 277), Hodge (1907–10). Encouraged by William Henry Holmes, who was then head of the Bureau of American Ethnology, Bolton developed an extensive ethnohistorical study of various Caddoan tribes in Texas, but he put it aside and it was not published until 1987 (see Bolton 1987).

63. Bolton (1913).

64. Jameson (1907: 189). The Carnegie Institution remained involved in producing guides, culminating in Charles Hackett's (1937) guide to documents on New Mexico and Nueva Vizcaya.

65. Bolton (1936: viii–ix).

66. See Bolton (1949, 1950).

67. Sauer (1971). A. L. Kroeber, like most ethnographers, spent as much time as possible "in the field." His monumental, thousand-page *Handbook of the Indians of California* (1925) was the result of incessant travel to the dozens of "tribelets" in California over a period of twenty years.

68. Bolton (1917, 1930), Bannon (1964).

69. Winship (1896), *DAB* Supplement (5: 755–56).

70. The following section draws on McLaughlin (1905, 1906), Jameson (1907), and Kidder (1930).

71. Hodge and Lewis (1907), Bolton (1916).

72. Bannon (1974).

73. Spicer (1962), John (1975), Kessell (1979).

74. See especially Weber's (1992) magisterial *The Spanish Frontier in North America.*

Chapter 16

1. On the Wetherill family in Mancos, see McNitt (1966) and Wetherill (1977).

2. McNitt (1966: 22).

3. Wetherill (1977: 110–11).

4. Blackburn and Williamson (1997: 22–23).

5. Wetherill (1977: 180–81).

6. Chapin (1889, 1892).

7. Biographical information on Nordenskiöld comes from Arrhenius (1984), and Wetherill (1977: 214–32).

8. In 1918 Carl Gustaf Mannerheim led the conservative Finns in their successful war against Finnish Bolsheviks and some twenty thousand Russian troops. He again successfully led the Finns against the Russians in 1939–44 and served as president of Finland, 1944–46.

9. Nordenskiöld (1991: 27–35). On Alice Eastwood (1859–1953) and her botanical career in Colorado and California, see B. Wetherill (1977: 195–213) and Wilson (1955: 39–49, 145–68, 208–9).

10. Nordenskiöld (1991: 14).

11. Cited by Lister and Lister (1984: 82).

12. Cited by Lister and Lister (1984: 49); see also Stanislawski (1979: 587–88).

13. Lister and Lister (1984: 87).

14. Stolpe (1897: 248), Arrhenius (1984: 12).

15. Nordenskiöld (1893: 76–92), Holmes (1886a, 1886b, 1888).

16. Nordenskiöld (1893: 93, emphasis added).

17. Nordenskiöld (1893: 100–101).

18. This section draws on McNitt (1966: 53–75), B. Wetherill (1977: 136–43), M. Wetherill (1992: 64–69), Atkins (1993), and Blackburn and Williamson (1997).

19. Blackburn and Williamson (1997: 26–28), McNitt (1966: 55), 23.

20. Advertisement in *The Mancos Times,* Summer 1893, cited by McNitt (1966: 55); Blackburn and Williamson (1997: 47).

21. Putnam (1905: xli).

22. This section is based on the excellent restudy of the work and collections of the Wetherills and others in Grand Gulch (Atkins 1993; Blackburn and Williamson 1997).

23. Cited by McNitt (1966: 65), emphasis added).

24. R. Wetherill to T. Hyde, 12/23/1893, cited by McNitt (1966: 65); R. Wetherill to T. Hyde, 2/4/1894, 3/1894, cited by Blackburn and Williamson (1997: 51). The correspondence is in the archives of the American Museum of Natural History, New York. The change from "Basket Maker" to "Basketmaker" was proposed by Charles Amsden (1949: 44).

25. Nordenskiöld (1897). Unfortunately, in the events surrounding Nordenskiöld's death, the paper was lost and only an abstract and the discussion following the paper were printed.

26. Remarks by E. Selers in Nordenskiöld (1897: 24–28).

27. Remarks by G. Retzius and R. Virchow in Nordenskiöld (1897: 24–28).

28. Kidder (1962: 329–30), Seltzer (1944).

29. Cited by McNitt (1966: 83).

30. Cited by McNitt (1966: 89).

31. The following is based on M. Wetherill (1992: 39–57) and McNitt (1966: 99–117, 151).

32. M. Wetherill (1992: 53–54).

33. McNitt (1966: 140–41).

34. Pepper (1920: 173), McNitt (1966: 150–51), Snead (1999).

35. This section draws from Blackburn and Williamson (1997: 59–67) and McNitt (1966: 154–63).

36. McNitt (1966: 162), M. Wetherill (1992: 79–83), Blackburn and Williamson (1997: 62).

37. M. Wetherill (1992: 45–46).

38. M. Wetherill (1992: 85–182).

39. McNitt (1966: 188).

40. McNitt (1966: 178).

41. McNitt (1966: 187–90, 208).

42. McNitt (1966: 263–303), M. Wetherill (1992: 209–29).

43. McNitt (1966: 313–18), M. Wetherill (1992: 230–37).

44. B. Wetherill (1977: 285–89).

45. Lister and Lister (1984: 73).

46. Pepper (1905, 1909, 1920)

47. Most of the Hyde Expedition materials are in the archives of the American Museum of Natural History archives. George Pepper's notes and papers relating to Chaco Canyon are in the archives of Tulane University, New Orleans.

48. L. Prudden (1927: 19); see also Hektoen (1929).

49. Prudden (1896, 1903, 1918).

50. Prudden (1897: 61).

51. L. Prudden (1927: 157).

52. A. V. Kidder to L. Prudden, dated only "1924"; in Prudden (1927: 179).

53. This section is drawn from Andrews (1970) and Phillips (1955).

54. Andrews (1970: 4). Andrews presents Farabee's notes of the excavations and a summary analysis of the artifacts; both artifacts and notes are in the Peabody Museum at Harvard.

55. Cited by Andrews (1970: 5).

56. Tozzer (1905, 1908, 1909).

Chapter 17

1. Gosden (1994: 10).

2. See Harris (1968) for an overview of nineteenth-century positivist social science.

3. The following discussion is drawn from Benedict (1983), Findling and Pelle (1990), Greenhalgh (1991), and Rydell (1984, 1989, 1992, 1993).

4. Findling and Pelle (1990).

5. Philadelphia Inquirer (1876: 2).

6. Findling and Pelle (1990: 79).

7. Mathieu (1989).

8. Mason (1891: 35).

9. Gautier (1889).

10. Mason (1890: 31).

11. On the origins and history of Wild West shows, see Moses (1996) and Blackstone (1986).

12. Quoted from exposition publicity by Trennert (1987a: 132–33).

13. Hough (1893: 270).

14. Hough (1893: 271), McVicker (1993).

15. Trennert (1987a: 133).

16. Luce (1895: 12).

17. Quoted by Luce (1895: 12).

18. Hough (1892: 3–113), Luce (1895: 12).

19. Fewkes (1895a: 279, 293, emphasis added).

20. Fewkes (1895a: 293; 1895b), Luce (1895: 13–14, 17).

21. Luce (1895: 17), Hough (1893: 276).

22. Cited by Bulmer (1984: 13–14).

23. Higinbotham (1898: 11).

24. Truman (1893: 9), Burg (1976: 198).

25. Buel (1894: 200, 221–23), McCullough (1976: 41).

26. Quoted by Collier (1969: 5).

27. Higinbotham (1898: 482–91).

28. Moses (1996: 106–41), Blackstone (1986: 26–27).

29. The literature on anthropology and native peoples at the Chicago fair is very extensive. Sources followed here include Fagin (1984), Fogelson (1991), Fowler and Fowler (1991), Hoxie (1979), Jacknis (1991a), Moses (1996: 129–67), and Trennert (1987a, 1987b).

30. Both cited by Collier (1972: 4, 7).

31. Handy (1893: 1091).

32. Higinbotham (1898: 350–52, 482–91).

33. Spier (1959: 151), cited by Fagin (1984: 260).

34. Flinn (1893: 70).

35. Trennert (1987b: 205–7).

36. Trennert (1987b: 207–11).

37. Fagin (1984: 255), Mason (1894: 206).

38. Truman (1893: 404).

39. Cushing (1893b: 1–3; 1893a: passim).

40. Holmes (1893b: 432).

41. Green (1893).

42. Smith Company (1893: 13–19), Higinbotham (1898: 482).

43. Cushing (1893a: passim).

44. Holmes (1893: 432).

45. Trennert (1987a: 136, 141–42), Bryant (1974: 118–20).

46. Newcomb (1964: 113).

47. Truman (1893: 235–50).

48. Barrows (1893), Ziolkowski (1990), Burg (1976: 262).

49. Turner (1894).

50. Bassett and Starr (1898: 3–13, 260–65), Poor (1975: 52).

51. Cushing (1893a: 50, 52–53), Mason (1894), Holmes (1893b: 432).

52. Cushing (1893a: 53).

53. Mooney (1899: 146–47), Opler (1983b: 409 and fig. 6).

54. Cited by Rydell (1984: 221).

55. Mooney (1896, 1899: 146–47).

56. Rydell (1984: 221–24).

57. Haynes (1910: 232).

58. Mooney (1899: 127).

59. Pan-American Exposition (1901: 11–14).

60. Pan-American Exposition (1901: 47, 53), Williams (1991: 89).

61. Benedict (1901: 99; 1901–2: 44), Pan-American Exposition (1901: 177).

62. True, Holmes, and Merrill (1903).

63. Buel (1905), Francis (1913).

64. The following is based on the St. Louis exposition archives and publications in the Missouri Historical Society, and on Breitbart (1997), McVicker (1993), and Troutman and Parezo (1998).

65. Skiff (1905: x).

66. St. Louis Republic (1901), St. Louis Post-Dispatch (1901).

67. St. Louis Globe-Democrat (1903), McGee (1905a: 1).

68. McGee (1904a, 1904b), Swarthout (1904), Hanson (1905: 465–80).

69. McGee (1903: 29).

70. Francis (1913, 1:522, 534).

71. McCown (1904: 40–41).

72. Barrett (1915: 197–206), Debo (1976: 388–90).

73. McCullough (1976: 64–70).

74. Breitbart (1997: 70–83).

75. Marriott (1948: 119–20), Peterson (1981: 109).

76. Hanson (1905: 121).

77. Blackstone (1986: 87–88), Peterson (1981: 109).

78. Francis (1913, 1:530).

79. McGee (1905b: 1569–70, 1588–94).

80. McGee (1905b: 1589–90).

Chapter 18

1. Bremner (1988: 223).

2. Carnegie (1889).

3. Cited by Bremner (1988: 111).

4. Diehl (1978).

5. Barber (1980: 13–26), Fowler and Fowler (1991: 45–52).

6. Barber (1980: 13–26), Sheets-Pyenson (1988: 3–23).

7. F. H. Cushing to S. Culin, 10/1894, quoted by Fane (1991a: 21), emphasis added; Harris (1962, 1981).

8. This section draws on Mark (1980: 14–61) and Hinsley (1985, 1992b).

9. Lurie (1960).

10. Mark (1980: 19).

11. Appel (1992: 109).

12. Hinsley (1992b: 133–34).

13. Dexter (1965: 113), Hinsley (1985: 59–61).

14. On the origins of the museum, see Collier (1969, 1972), Field (1943) and Rabineau (1981).

15. Lockwood (1929: 189–90).

16. Field (1943).

17. Diner (1980: 15), Miller (1975); on Harper, see DAB (8: 287–92).

18. McVicker (1999), Miller (1975).

19. NCAB (12: 29).

20. Bulmer (1984: 33–40).

21. Holmes (1895–97).

22. Quoted by McVicker (1999: 22).

23. NCAB (22: 200–201).

24. G. A. Dorsey to J. W. Hudson, 3/5/1901, quoted by Rabineau (1981: 34).

25. Kaufman (1973: 326–31); see also Parezo (1999), Titiev (1972), and the archives of the Field Museum of Natural History, Chicago.

26. Titiev (1972: 361).

27. Eggan (1979: 2).

28. Parezo (1999: 8–9), Voth (1901, 1903a, 1903b, 1905, 1912a, 1912b), Dorsey and Voth (1901, 1902).

29. Jacobs (1980: 11).

30. Haury (1945b, 1995), Wedel (1959, 1961).

31. Dorsey (1903).

32. Dorsey (1925, 1931).

33. Madeira (1964: 17); see also Darnell (1970, 1988) and Winegrad (1993).

34. DAB (14: 453–56).

35. DAB (17: 635–36).

36. DAB (8: 488–89), Bonfils (1928), Swanberg (1961).

37. Parmenter (1966).

38. Tozzer (1933: 478).

39. Darnell (1970: 82–83).

40. Abbott (1872), Dexter (1971), Holmes (1893a, 1894), Hinsley (1985: 66), Meltzer and Dunnell (1992).

41. Fane (1991a: 14–15).

42. Darnell (1970: 82).

43. Hinsley (1985: 67–68).

44. Allen (1990: 62–70).

45. Allen (1990: 70–78), Fane (1991a: 17–18), Washburn (1995).

46. Cushing (1893a), Culin (1907: 29).

47. Culin (1907).

48. Culin (1958: xviii); see also Cushing (1895).

49. Culin (1903, 1907: 35), Lyman (1982).

50. Fane (1991a: 15, 308 n. 12).

51. Darnell (1970: 80–83).

52. Fane (1991a, 1991b, 1992).

53. Quoted by Fane (1991a: 20).

54. Stevenson (1904: 381), cited by Fane (1991a: 23).

55. Fane (1992: 74, 79).

56. Fane (1992: 75–77).

57. Hoving (1993: 135–40, 352–53).

58. Quoted by Fane (1991a: 24).

59. Fane (1991a: 25).

60. Fane (1991b: 48–49).

61. Culin quoted by Fane (1991b: 52); on the Canyon del Muerto massacre, see Reeve (1971: 111–13).

62. Fane (1991b: 54).

63. Quoted by Fane (1992: 69); the painting remained on loan until 1928, when the museum purchased it. In 1947 it was deaccessioned to the Gilcrease Art Institute in Tulsa, Oklahoma, where it remains (Fane 1992: 85 n. 51).

64. Hodge (1906: 473).

65. Jacknis (1991b: 37–41).

66. Bodo (1998: xix).

67. Fane (1991b: 53–54).

68. Bodo (1998: 17–27), Franciscan Fathers (1910).

Chapter 19

1. This section is based on Kennedy (1968).

2. Liss (1996: 157). Boas is the subject of a large biographical and critical literature, for which see the bibliographies in Stocking (1974). The following section and later materials on Boas are drawn from Bunzl (1996), Herskovits (1953), Liss (1995, 1996), and Stocking (1968, 1974). Darnell (1998) came to hand after this chapter was written; it adds greatly to the understanding of Boas and his role in American anthropology.

3. Boas in a letter to his uncle, Abraham Jacobi, 5/2/1883, quoted by Liss (1996: 175).

4. On Boas's Northwest Coast work, which extended over many years, see Berman (1996), Jacknis (1996), and Rohner and Rohner (1969).

5. Boas (1887a). The importance of the Boas-Mason-Powell exchange is generally recognized by historians of American anthropology. See especially Jacknis (1985), Stocking (1974), Gruber (1986: 178–79), Hinsley (1981: 98–100), and Mark (1980: 32–36).

6. Nicholson (1973: 353), McVicker (1992: 148–58).

7. The sketch of the Huntingtons is drawn from Lavender (1970: 343–77), Thorpe (1994: 306–464), and the Hispanic Society (1954).

8. Lumholtz (1987: vii–xviii); William Merrill, personal communication, 10/15/1998.

9. This sketch is drawn from Stewart (1940) and Spencer (1979).

10. Shoemaker (1997).

11. Blumenbach (1865: 235–43, 264–69, 298–300). His several treatises on physical anthropology appeared between 1776 and 1795. They were translated from Latin and widely disseminated in Europe throughout the nineteenth century.

12. Morton (1839, 1849), Gould (1981: 54–69).

13. Garson (1886–87: 11), Gould (1981: 99).

14. Gould (1981: 73–112), Haller (1971: 19–34).

15. Stewart (1940: 9), Spencer (1979: 76–206).

16. Hrdlička (1925a: 408, 412).

17. Putnam (1900: 45).

18. Hrdlička (1902: 71).

19. Hrdlička (1909: 406).

20. Stewart (1940: 12), Spencer (1979: 252–88).

21. Hrdlička (1908, 1931, 1935).

22. Hrdlička (1908: 101–406 and tables 1–9).

23. Hrdlička (1931: 94–95).

24. Hrdlička (1917a, 1925b: 484–94); see also Spencer (1979: 289–476).

25. Hrdlička (1925b: 484).

26. Hrdlička (1925b: 487, 490, 491).

27. Hrdlička (1925b: 490–94).

28. Hrdlička (1925b: 490–92).

29. Seltzer (1944).

30. Stocking (1995: 98–115).

31. Boas (1903: 73).

32. Boas (1903: 73–74), Freed, Freed and Williamson (1988).

33. Boas (1903: 115).

34. Boas (1904, 1906), Haddon (1906), McGee (1906).

35. Hinsley (1992b: 134–35).

36. MacCurdy (1902: 216), Hodge (1906).

37. Boas (1911b), Mithun (1996: 43).

38. On Boas as social activist, see Herskovits (1953: 102–22), Hyatt (1990), and Stocking (1974: 307–40).

39. Thoresen (1975: 259), Rowe (1954: 6–7).

40. Bonfils (1928: 96).

41. Thoresen (1975: 260–61), Freeman (1965: 84–87).

42. Quoted by Thoresen (1975: 265).

43. Freeman (1965: 86). The quotes are from letters from Boas to Zelia Nuttall, 5/16/1901, and F. W. Putnam 4/4/1902, the latter apparently never mailed; quoted by Freeman from the Boas correspondence in the American Philosophical Society Library.

44. Steward (1961, 1973).

45. Steward (1961: 1045).

46. Kroeber (1925).

47. Steward (1973: 7–14).

48. Kroeber (1929).

49. Nelson (1910: 373).

50. Bonfils (1928: 115).

51. Nelson to Goddard, 4/24/1911, NNP

52. Goddard to Nelson, 9/12/1911, NNP

53. Nelson to Goddard, 9/22/1911; Wissler to Goddard, 10/23/1911; Wissler to Nelson 10/25/1911, NNP.

54. Heye and his museum received a good deal of press over the years. The following sketch is based on New York Times (1914–28) and on Force (1999: 3–24).

55. Museum of the American Indian (1956: 3).

56. New York Times (1914–28: 7/22/1914: 18:4). In the official history of the Museum of the American Indian (1956: 8) and in Heye's biography in *NCAB* (1958, 43: 634–35) the incident is given a positive spin. On the legend, see Force (1999: 6).

57. New York Times (1914–28: 11/16/1922: 12:1). Speck and Lothrop had collected for Heye in New England and South America, respectively. Fewkes had directed a joint BAE-Heye Foundation program in the Caribbean. The Boas-Heye exchange is quoted by Force (1999: 9).

58. New York Times (1914–28: 11/16/1922: 12: 1).

59. New York Times (1914–28: 11/16/1922: 12: 1).

60. By 1930, the museum library had outgrown space at the Audubon Terrace facility. Archer Huntington again came to the rescue, by adding a section to the Huntington Free Library at 9 Westchester Square in the central Bronx. Researchers using the library and the collections faced interesting, sometimes challenging, subway or bus trips from Manhattan to the two Bronx facilities.

61. Harrington (1985: 44–45).

62. New York Times (1914–28: 5/19/1928: 7: 3).

63. *DAB* (10: 352–53), West (1988: 340).

Chapter 20

1. Biographical sources on Lummis include Bingham (1955), Fiske and Lummis (1975), and Houlihan and Houlihan (1986).

2. One biographer, Bingham (1955), has the name as "Rhodes."

3. Lummis (1969, 1989).

4. Lummis (1989: 293).

5. Lummis (1989: 118, 120).

6. Lummis (1989: 133).

7. Lummis (1982: 140–53; 1989: 186–87, 192).

8. On Otis, see *DAB* (14: 100–101); on Chandler, see *DAB* (Supp. 3, 154–57).

9. Starr (1985: 76).

10. Starr (1973, 1985, 1990).

11. Bingham (1955: 15).

12. Castillo (1978: 101–2), Cook and Marino (1988: 474–77).

13. This section follows Starr (1985: 55–63) and Thomas (1991).

14. The report was printed as an appendix to the second, and subsequent, editions of Jackson's *A Century of Dishonor* (1885: 458–514).

15. Starr (1985: 62).

16. Thomas (1991: 119).

17. Walker (1950: 121–23), cited by Thomas (1991: 124–25).

18. Bingham (1955: 104–5).

19. Lummis (1895: 44).

20. Bingham (1955: 120).

21. Thomas (1991: 125–32), Gratten (1980).

22. Starr (1985: 86, 88).

23. Bingham (1955: 111–28).

24. Works on the history of Indian-White relations are legion. This section is based on articles in Washburn (1988), as well as Berkhofer (1979: 113–94), Hagan (1997: 120–38), and Mardock (1971).

25. Mardock (1971: 1–7).

26. Castillo (1978), Shipek (1978).

27. Quoted by Hagan (1997: 128).

28. Moses (1984: 128–54).

29. Quoted by Hagan (1997: 129).

30. Quoted by Hagan (1997: 131).

31. This section is drawn from Titiev (1944).

32. H. R. Voth to G. A. Dorsey, 11/25/1902, 12/15/ 1902, Field Museum Archives.

33. Titiev (1944: 86).

34. The articles are reprinted in Lummis (1968).

35. Lummis (1968: 35, 37).

36. Lummis (1968: 16–18, 20).

37. Lummis (1968: 87).

38. Lummis (1904a: 173).

39. Lummis (1904a: 174–75).

40. Lummis (1904a: 175, 177; 1904b: 372).

41. Lummis (1905a: 86).

42. Lummis (1905c: 343–44).

43. Lummis (1904d: 596).

44. Cited by Bingham (1955: 25).

45. Lummis (1905b: 344).

46. Lummis (1905d: 285).

47. Lummis (1906a: 238).

48. Robinson (1960: 17).

49. Starr (1985: 84).

Chapter 21

1. Biographical materials are from Judd (1950, 1968: 3–45) and Tanner (1954).

2. Judd (1950: 14–15).

3. Judd (1968: 16).

4. Kidder (1910), Brew (1946).

5. Judd (1950: 19).

6. Judd (1968: 27–28), Gillmor and Wetherill (1953: 155–60).

7. Judd (1968: 44).

8. Judd (1968: 36). Wetherill's prior finding of the two sites is discussed by Jett (1992: 41–42). Evidence for the Inscription House inscription reading "1861," rather than "1661," is in Ward (1975: 1–17), cited by Jett (1992: 48 n. 24).

9. Cummings (1910), Gillmor and Wetherill (1953: 161–71), Cummings Publication Council (1959), Richardson (1986: 61–62). For a judicious review of the claims

and counterclaims of "first" discovery, see Jett (1992) and Rothman (1993).

10. J. Wetherill to B. Cummings 11/6/1910. Byron Cummings Papers, Arizona Historical Society, Tucson.

11. The Rainbow Bridge register book was removed by the National Park Service in 1965. It is in the archives of the Glen Canyon National Recreation Area office, Page, Arizona, where it was reviewed by the present author in September 1998.

12. B. Cummings to E. L. Hewett 9/3/1909, ELHP.

13. B. Cummings to E. L. Hewett 11/5/1909, ELHP.

14. On Cummings's Tsegi work, see Anderson (1969).

15. On Cummings's Southwestern field trips, see Turner (1962) and Wilcox (1997).

16. Quoted by Seligman et al. (1915: 4).

17. Quoted by Seligman et al. (1915: 5–6).

18. Hofstadter and Metzer (1955).

19. R. B. von Kleinschmidt to B. Cummings, 6/22/ 1915. Byron Cummings Papers, Arizona Historical Society, Tucson.

20. Cummings (1926, 1933).

21. Reed and King (1950).

Chapter 22

1. This section is adapted from Fowler (1999) and draws also from Elliott (1987), Chauvenet (1983: 33–96), Hinsley (1986), and Stocking (1981, 1982).

2. Hewett's dissertation, written by him in English, then rendered into excellent French by an unknown translator, was published in Geneva in 1908 in a small edition, as was the common practice in European universities. His course work at Geneva and his dissertation were for decades rather mysterious. According to the Documents Librarian at the University of Geneva in 1985:

Mr. Hewett only stayed briefly in Geneva. He registered for the summer session of 1904 in the Faculty of Letters, probably in order to make the necessary contacts for the preparation of his dissertation. The matter of his doctorate was brought up again during the session of March 10, 1907 when the Faculty Council decided to dispense with the preliminary examination for the doctorate and named the committee for the defence of his dissertation.

The discussion that took place in the Faculty Council on May 23, 1908, concerning the language in which the dissertation should be defended, shows the difficulties with which Mr. Hewett handled French. I quote: "Mr. Hewett did not seem to be able to defend the dissertation in French." It was suggested that he be authorized to express himself in English. This favor was denied him, but in view of the exceptional quality of the dissertation, the council made the decision to dispense with the defence of the dissertation. . . .

To my knowledge, none of the three members of the committee for the defence of the dissertation was particularly interested in the archaeology of the Southwestern United States. (Josette Wagner to Madeleine T. Rodack, 2/1/1985, cited in Schroeder [1993: xiii]. Madeleine Turrell Rodack retranslated Hewett's dissertation and it was published in 1993.)

3. Hewett (1946: 6).
4. Chauvenet (1983: 42); Mark (1988: 303–5).
5. Hewett (1903).
6. Ferdon (1993: 14).
7. Fowler (1986), Lee (1970).
8. Hewett (1904a), Lee (1970: 66–67).
9. Chauvenet (1983: 42).
10. Hewett (1904a, 1905).
11. Hewett (1906: 113).
12. Lee (1970: 77).
13. Mark (1988: 299).
14. F. W. Putnam to E. L. Hewett, 2/8/1906, ELHP.
15. E. L. Hewett to W. H. Holmes, 8/1/1906; E. L. Hewett to C. Bowditch, 10/26/1906, ELHP.
16. Mark (1988: 296–98, 305–7).
17. The following sketch is based on Mark (1980: 62–95; 1988: 203–77). See also Chauvenet (1983: 42).
18. Bowditch (1907: 47–48), Mark (1988: 306–7).
19. Givens (1992: 11–24).
20. The major biographical sources on Kidder are Givens (1987, 1992) and Woodbury (1973).
21. Brunhouse (1971) is the principal biographical source on Morley.
22. Fletcher's (1988) autobiography is the main source on his life.
23. Brooks (1955: 227).

24. Fletcher (1988: 32).
25. Kidder (1957, 3:39), quoted by Givens (1987: 100).
26. Hewett (1943: 149–51).
27. Kidder (1957, 3:35), quoted by Givens (1987: 107–8).
28. Fletcher (1988: 32); Morley (1908).
29. Fletcher (1988: 33).
30. Kidder (1957, 2:60), cited by Givens (1987: 121).
31. Hewett (1907–18: 33).
32. Fletcher (1988: 34–35).
33. Simon (1953).
34. Reprinted in Henderson (1928: 38–39).
35. Hewett (1907–18: 25–26).
36. Boas (1912, 1915), Godoy (1977), Tozzer (1915), Stocking (1974: 285).
37. Hewett (1908).
38. A. M. Tozzer to F. W. Hodge, 2/10/1912, CHP. According to Tozzer's obituary:

In the summer of 1907 [sic], Tozzer, along with Dixon, Kidder, and Morley took part in a joint expedition of the Peabody Museum and the Archaeological Institute in the Rito de los Frijoles, New Mexico, under the direction of E. L. Hewitt [sic]. This collaboration with Hewitt marks the beginning of another cycle of Peabody Museum folklore. Tozzer's personal relationships were invariably characterized by an absolute and clear-cut integrity that resulted in the warmest kind of friendship or, less often, the exact reverse. . . . His loyalty, both to friendships and enmities, has become traditional in the Peabody Museum. (Phillips 1955: 74, 76)

39. Mark (1988: 320).
40. Fletcher (1910: 1–3, 14–27).
41. Cited by Mark (1988: 321).
42. This sketch of Chapman is drawn from Ellis (1969) and Chapman's unpublished memoirs (Chapman n.d.).
43. Springer (1901, 1911, 1926).
44. Biographical information on J. Nusbaum is taken from R. Nusbaum (1980).
45. Hewett (1907–18: 64).
46. Hewett (1907–18: 80–81).
47. Hewett (1907–18: 94–95).
48. Biographical information on Harrington is found in Laird (1975) and Stirling and Glemser (1963).

49. Walsh (1976: 13).

50. Quoted by Walsh (1976: 9).

51. J. P. Harrington to H. R. Fairclough, 1/24/1908. Copy in ELHP.

52. E. L. Hewett to J. P. Harrington, 1/28/1909; J. P. Harrington to E. L. Hewett, 2/20/1909, ELHP.

53. A. L. Kroeber to E. L. Hewett, 9/29/1909, ELHP; Kroeber to F. W. Hodge, 1/27/1916, Hodge to Kroeber, 1/29/1916, CHP.

54. Undated letter from J. P. Harrington to F. W. Hodge, CHP, emphasis added.

55. Henderson and Harrington (1914), Robbins, Harrington, and Freire-Marreco (1916), Harrington (1916), Kroeber (1918: 450–51).

56. Laird (1975: 2, 15).

57. J. P. Harrington to C. Lummis, 6/9/1916, CHP.

58. Laird (1976, 1984).

59. F. W. Hodge to M. Carroll, 12/8/1911, CHP.

60. F. Boas, Open Letter to E. L. Hewett, 11/10/1911, ELHP.

61. A. M. Tozzer to H. H. Dorman, 10/11/1913, 10/24/1913, copies in ELHP.

62. New Mexican (1913).

63. Lowitt (1992: 46–47), Resolutions (1913), Santa Fe Chamber of Commerce (1913).

64. A. Peabody to Santa Fe Chamber of Commerce, 1/3/1914, copy in ELHP.

65. Judd (1968: 146–53), Brunhouse (1971: 52–62).

66. New York Times (1912), Tozzer (1912), A. M. Tozzer to F. W. Hodge, 2/10/1912, CHP.

67. Hrdlička (1917b).

68. San Diego Union (1915: n.p.).

69. Panama-California Exposition (1915: 10).

70. Wright (1980).

Chapter 23

1. Boas (1887a), Mason (1887), Powell (1887).

2. Bunzl (1996), Herder (1966).

3. Stocking (1974: 1–5).

4. Mason (1887: 534), Hough (1908: 662).

5. Boas (1887b: 587).

6. Boas (1887b: 589).

7. Hough (1908: 662)

8. Mason (1896: 646, 651).

9. Holmes (1902, 1903), see also Holmes (1914); Boas (1904).

10. Wissler (1914, 1916a, 1917a), Kroeber (1931).

11. The best summary is still Goldenweiser (1933: 35–58); see also Boas (1911c).

12. Sapir (1949: 398, 401, 409, 412); on Sapir's roles in Americanist anthropology, see Darnell (1990).

13. Wissler (1923, 1926); Blaut (1993), Kroeber (1931: 255, 1939), Snead (2001).

14. Lyman, O'Brien, and Dunnell (1997a, 1997b).

15. Much of this section is based on the voluminous correspondence in the library archives and the Department of Anthropology archives at the American Museum, as well as unsigned brief summaries of anthropology activities that appeared annually in the *American Museum Journal* between 1900 and 1919. In 1920, the *Journal* was renamed *Natural History*, the title it still enjoys.

16. Hellman (1969: 112), Kennedy (1968: 171).

17. Kennedy (1968: 157–58); H. F. Osborn to Madison Grant, 2/10/1909, quoted by Kennedy (1968: 154).

18. H. F. Osborn to H. Bumpus, 7/17/1908, quoted by Kennedy (1968: 162); H. F. Osborn to W. B. Scott, 5/22/1909, quoted by Kennedy (1968: 162–63).

19. This sketch of Clark Wissler is derived from Freed and Freed (1983) and Nelson (1948), as well as the Wissler correspondence files in the archives of the American Museum.

20. Wissler (1910, 1912, 1913). For Lowie's many years of work with the Crow, see Lowie (1956, 1959).

21. C. H. Dodge to H. F. Osborn, 10/8/1914; cited by Kennedy (1968: 162).

22. Spinden (1915, 1933).

23. Wissler (1917).

24. *OED* (1989: 15:12); Webster's Dictionary (1974: 1225); see also Browman and Givens (1996) and Brainerd (1951).

25. See Rice (1987) for a definitive statement on the uses and importance of ceramics in archeology and world cultural history.

26. Petrie (1899: 297); see also Brainerd (1951).

27. Nelson (1913: 63, emphasis added).

28. Wissler (1915: 397, emphasis added).

29. Osborn (1914, 1925), Hellman (1969: 203).

30. Nelson (1916: 165–66); see also Woodbury (1960a: 400–401, 1960b: 98–99), Spier (1931).

31. N. C. Nelson to H. F. Osborn, 6/10/1924; H. F. Osborn to N. C. Nelson, 2/18/1925, NNP.

32. Hellman (1969: 171–79).

33. Brunhouse (1971: 49, 63–94).

34. Kidder (1910).

35. Quoted by Wauchope (1965: 151).

36. Wauchope (1965: 152).

37. Kidder (1957, 2:82), cited by Givens (1987: 22).

38. Kidder (1957, 2:82), cited by Givens (1987: 22).

39. Hewett (1993: 83–84, 89–90).

40. Kidder (1914); a portion of the dissertation was published the next year (Kidder 1915).

41. Hodge (1906: 497–98), Givens (1992: 38–39).

42. Guthe (1925).

43. Hooton (1930).

44. Kidder (1945).

45. Kidder (1915: 120).

46. Kidder (1915: 122–23).

47. Kidder (1917), M. A. Kidder and A. V. Kidder (1917: 360).

48. Kroeber (1916b: 7, 11, 14).

49. Kroeber (1916b: 21).

50. Kroeber (1916b: 21).

51. Basehart and Hill (1965: 1259).

52. Spier (1917a, 1917b, 1918, 1919).

53. Kidder and Guernsey (1919: 14), Lister and Lister (1968: 19).

54. Woodbury (1973: 24–27), Taylor (1948: 49).

55. Kidder and Guernsey (1919: 210).

56. The following section draws heavily on Lister and Lister (1968).

57. On Domínguez, Escalante, Newberry, and Morgan, see Prologue and chapters 2, 6; Prudden (1903: 254).

58. Morris (1919b, 1921b, 1924, 1928); see also Lister and Lister (1968: 24–56; 1987).

59. Cordell (1997: 365–97), Elliott (1995: 53–77).

60. Morris (1919a, 1921a).

61. Nusbaum (1922).

62. Kidder and Guernsey (1919: 210).

63. Bernheimer (1924: xi), Leake and Topping (1987).

64. Rainbow Bridge Register, 1909–1963. Document HQSTO FCAB 5, Archives, National Park Service, Glen Canyon National Recreation Area, Page, Arizona.

65. Bernheimer (1924: 147–72), Lister and Lister (1968: 111–14).

66. A. Morris (1934: 15), Lister and Lister (1968: 115).

67. Lister and Lister (1968: 168–80).

68. Lister and Lister (1968: 143–44).

69. E. A. Morris (1959, 1980), E. H. Morris (1939), Morris and Burgh (1941), Hays-Gilpin, Deegan, and Morris (1998).

Chapter 24

1. Hewett (1907–18: 101–3).

2. Judd (1926).

3. Morss (1931); see also Gunnerson (1969), Janetski (1997: 112–13).

4. Abramson (1987: 143).

5. Hewett (1921a: 13).

6. New Mexican (1920: 2, emphasis added).

7. S. T. Mather to N. M. Judd, 12/10/1920, 12/22/1920. NMJP.

8. S. G. Morley to N. M. Judd, 9/9/1920, NMJP.

9. N. M. Judd to S. M. Mather, 10/18/1920: 3–4; S. T. Mather to N. M. Judd, 12/10/1920, 12/22/1920. NMJP.

10. Bloom (1921), Bradfield (1921), Chapman (1921), Hewett (1921a, 1921b).

11. Hewett (1922: 116).

12. N. M. Judd to E. H. Morris, 10/15/1920, 4/6/1921, 5/30/1921; N. M. Judd to Mrs. H. B. Sammons, 10/14/1920; E. H. Morris to Mrs. H. B. Sammons, 3/31/1921, NMJP.

13. N. M. Judd to E. H. Morris, 5/30/1921.

14. E. H. Morris to N. M. Judd, 2/8/1921, 3/31/1921, NMJP.

15. N. M. Judd to E. H. Morris, 8/3/1921, NMJP.

16. Hewett (1919–29: 77–78).

17. Judd (1922, 1954, 1959, 1964).

18. National Geographic Magazine (1921: 640).

19. National Geographic Magazine (1921: 637).

20. Judd (1923: 101; 1925: 227).

21. Judd (1925: 231–32).

22. Judd (1923: 108).

23. Lekson (1999), Sebastian (1992).

24. Judd (1923: 103–8).

25. This section draws on Webb (1983: 1–100) and Nash (1999).

26. Douglass (1914: 101).

27. Nash (1999: 11–13).

28. Douglass (1914).

29. Nash (1999: 27).

30. Lister and Lister (1968: 39), Nash (1999: 28).

31. Douglass (1921), Wissler (1921).

32. Haury (1986: 58–59).

33. Douglass (1929: 764–70).

34. Webb (1983: 161–71).

35. Bannister and Robinson (1986: 53).

36. Hodge and Lewis (1907).

37. Hodge (1937: 6–41, 78–107).

38. G. Heye to F. W. Hodge, 8/9/1916, 8/28/1916, CHP.

39. Smith, Woodbury and Woodbury (1966: 2).

40. G. Heye to F. W. Hodge, 9/17/1917, CHP.

41. G. Heye to F. W. Hodge, 1/12/1918, CHP.

42. F. Boas to F. W. Hodge, 1/15/1918, 1/19/1918; F. W. Hodge to F. Boas, 1/17/1918, CHP.

43. Smith, Woodbury, and Woodbury (1966: 2–3).

44. Smith, Woodbury, and Woodbury (1966), Elliott (1995: 79–101).

45. Hodge (1924), Johnson (1998: 100–105), Pandey (1972: 331–32).

46. The following sketch is based on Cassells (1983: 233) and a series of letters from Jeançon to F. W. Hodge in CHP.

47. Jeançon (1923).

48. Nash (1999: 40–41).

49. J. A. Jeançon to F. W. Hodge, 5/20/1924, CHP.

50. J. A. Jeançon to F. W. Hodge, 2/4/1928, 1/3/1929, CHP.

51. Cassells (1983: 243).

52. Stephenson (1967).

53. Roberts (1929, 1931, 1932).

54. Martin (1929), Martin, Roy, and von Bonin (1936).

55. Albright and Cann (1985), Altherr (1985), National Park Service (1991).

56. This section is based on the Gilbert and Virginia McClurg Papers (GVMP) in the Pioneers Museum, Colorado Springs, Colorado; various unpublished materials in the archives of the Research Center, Mesa Verde National Park (MVRCA); letters from Virginia McClurg and Lucy Peabody to Edgar Lee Hewett, and he to them (in ELHP); and Hoben (1966).

57. McClurg (1930: 216–19); undated (post-1917) biographical sketch of Virginia McClurg, GVMP.

58. McClurg (1930: 217). Extensive records searches by National Park Service staff determined that the lease was not approved (McClurg files, Mesa Verde National Park Research Center).

59. Articles of Incorporation, Colorado Cliff Dwellings Association, 4/2000, GVMP.

60. L. Peabody to E. L. Hewett, 8/6/1907, ELHP.

61. Hoben (1966: 38–39); annual meeting of Colorado Cliff Dwellings Association, 1901; Aug. 18, 1901, newspaper clipping in GVMP.

62. Nusbaum (1980: 65).

63. Meredith (1906: 208).

64. Various newspaper clippings in V. McClurg scrapbook, GVMP.

65. L. Peabody to E. L. Hewett, 8/6/1907, 8/12/1907, ELHP.

66. Frowe (1906: 12), Keating (1907: 149); Hoben (1966: 66–67).

67. J. Nusbaum to Region Three Director, 12/6/1945, 7/26/1946, MVRCA.

68. Printed flier (ca. 1910), V. McClurg to M. Pitney, 10/17/1913, GVMP.

69. Baggs (1918: 306–7).

70. McClurg (1933).

71. For example, Fewkes (1909a, 1909b).

72. Nusbaum (1980: 72–73).

73. Nusbaum (1980: 72).

74. J. Nusbaum to W. Burr, 2/16/1927, copy in ELHP.

75. Smith (1985: 11).

76. Harr and Johnson (1988: 199–212).

77. Nusbaum (1925: 41–42, 1926: 110–11), D. O'Bryan to R. C. Heyder, 4/22/1986, MVRCA.

78. "Museum Building #13," undated document, MVRCA.

79. A. Nusbaum (1926), D. Nusbaum (1925, 1926).

80. D. O'Bryan to R. C. Heyder, 4/22/1986, MVRCA.

81. Nusbaum (1980).

82. Pinkley (1925), National Park Service (1991: 32–33).

Chapter 25

1. Kidder (1924).

2. Kidder (1924: 323).

3. Kidder (1924: 324–26).

4. Kidder (1924: 329–30), Hooton (1930), Seltzer (1944).

5. Kidder (1924: 330–32).

6. Kidder (1924: 334–35).

7. Kidder (1924: 335), Hewett, Henderson, and Robbins (1913), Huntington (1912).

8. Kidder (1924: 336).

9. Kidder (1924: 337).

10. Kidder (1924: 338).

11. Kidder (1924: 339–40).

12. Kidder (1924: 341), Spinden (1922: 155).

13. Kidder (1924: 341, 343).

14. Judd (1968: 129–30).

15. A. V. Kidder to C. Wissler 1/28/1927, cited by Woodbury (1993: 15).

16. Woodbury (1993: 92).

17. From Woodbury (1993: 20).

18. Kroeber (1937), Woodbury (1993: 65–66).

19. Kidder (1927).

20. Waterman (1929: 394).

21. Roberts (1935).

22. J. W. Fewkes to A. V. Kidder, 9/15/1927, copy in J. W. Fewkes Papers, National Anthropological Archives

23. Sabloff (1998).

24. Woodbury (1993: 100–110).

25. Aldana (1983: 249).

26. Givens (1992: 77–117).

27. Kidder (1930), Redfield (1941), Coe (1993).

28. Bishop and Lange (1991).

29. Meltzer (1983: 34–35).

30. Cook (1925).

31. Figgins (1927).

32. Haury (1976b: 158).

33. Cummings (1927), Hallman (1999).

34. Figgins (1927), Meltzer (1983: 35).

Chapter 26

1. McGee (1898), Bowen (1983: 248).

2. Russell (1898). My thanks to Richard I. Ford (personal communication, 4/6/1999) for calling attention to Russell's Jicarilla Apache work.

3. T. Russell (1906).

4. T. Russell (1901), F. Russell (1908: 24). Ellsworth Huntington, the climatologist who worked in southern Arizona in 1910–15, used the term more generally for Southwestern ruins, but his usage was not adopted (Huntington 1912; Martin 1973: 97).

5. Hodge (1903).

6. For example, T. Russell (1920, 1932).

7. Babcock and Parezo (1988: 20–21), Freire-Marreco (1914, 1930, 1931), Robbins, Harrington, and Freire-Marreco (1916).

8. Davis (1985: 19).

9. Goetzmann and Sloan (1982), Merriam (1900–1910).

10. Davis (1985: 75, 78, 253 n. 23).

11. Boesen and Graybill (1977), Coleman and McCluhan (1972), Davis (1985), Fowler (1972), Gidley (1998), Graybill and Boesen (1976), McCluhan (1975).

12. Roosevelt (1907: xi), Curtis (1907–30, 1:xiii–xiv; folio 1, plate 1); see also Curtis (1906, 1909a, 1909b).

13. Lyman (1982: 70–94).

14. Seattle Sunday Times, 5/22/1904, cited by Davis (1985: 36, emphasis added); on Tonelili, see Matthews (1902: 29, 129, 150–51).

15. Faris (1990: 50–54, 72 n. 39).

16. The footage is included in McCluhan's (1975) film "The Shadow Catcher." See also Lyman (1982: 65–69) and Faris (1990: 50–54, 71–72, nn. 38–39).

17. Boesen and Graybill (1977: 58–66), Davis (1985: 33).

18. See McCluhan's (1975) film "The Shadow Catcher"; Boesen and Graybill (1977: 136).

19. Boesen and Graybill (1977: 28, 40–41).

20. The following is based on the biographies of Parsons by Deacon (1997), Hare (1985), and Zumwalt (1992), as well as Hieb (1993), Kroeber (1943), Lamphere (1989), and the E. C. Parsons Papers in the American Philosophical Society Library (ECPP).

21. Deacon (1997: 1–2, 406 n. 40).

22. Robbins (1901: 1081) cited by Deacon (1997: 31).

23. Rosenberg (1982: 147–77), Early (1997).

24. Parsons (1907, 1913a, 1913b, 1915a), Deacon (1997: 123).

25. Luhan (1936).

26. Hollinger (1975), Kennedy (1980).

27. Parsons (1915b, 1916a).

28. F. A. Lucas to C. Wissler, 1/28/1920, 1/31/1920, CWP.

29. Grant (1916), Lowie (1914a, 1914b, 1914c).

30. Wallis (141: 250), Deacon (1997: 233–34), Johnson (1952: 272–88).

31. Parsons (1922).

32. Marrett (1923: 266), Deacon (1997: 237–38).

33. E. C. Parsons to C. Wissler, 1/3/1918, ECPP.

34. C. Wissler to E. C. Parsons, 1/21/1918, ECPP.

35. E. C. Parsons to H. Parsons, 12/28/1918, quoted by Hare (1985: 148).

36. Southwest Society Ledger Book, in ECPP.

37. N. C. Nelson to J. A. Mason, 11/14/1923, NNP; Zumwalt (1988: 89).

38. Kroeber (1909, 1917b), Lowie (1915, 1959: 67–75), Rivers (1907, 1910), Tylor (1888). On the context of this debate, see Stocking (1995: 184–208).

39. Quoted by Zumwalt (1992: 210).

40. Hare (1985: 139).

41. Parsons (1920: 179), Hare (1985: 123–33), Deacon (1997: 230).

42. T. Kroeber (1959, 1970: 76–93).

43. Pandey (1972: 330).

44. A. Kroeber to E. Parsons, 5/4/1920, ECPP, quoted by Deacon (1997: 212).

45. P. Goddard to E. Parsons, summer, 1920, ECPP.

46. Deacon (1997: 201–13), Kroeber (1943). A copy of Kroeber's business card is in CHP.

47. Parsons (1923: xi).

48. E. Parsons to F. Boas, 7/15/1916, ECPP.

49. Quoted by Zumwalt (1992: 195).

50. Zumwalt (1988: 84–85, 1992: 191).

51. Parsons and Beals (1934).

52. Parsons (1936a), Deacon (1997: 345).

53. Parsons, ed. (1936), Parsons (1939b).

54. Parsons (1939b: 1078).

55. Parsons (1939b: 1132–33).

56. Parsons (1939b: 1142).

57. Parsons (1942).

58. Deacon (1997: 379–81).

59. Haeberlin (1916).

60. Boas (1919); on the expulsion and its larger context, see Stocking (1968: 270–307).

61. Kroeber (1916c), Boas (1911–22).

62. J. P. Harrington to E. L. Hewett, 8/6/1920, ELHP.

63. F. Boas to E. Parsons, 7/9/1920, ECPP, quoted by Deacon (1997: 51), Boas (1925–28).

64. Stocking (1989).

65. The following is based on Goldfrank's (1977) autobiography.

66. Goldfrank (1977: 46–47).

67. Goldfrank (1927).

68. Goldfrank (1977: 94–97), Parsons (1932).

69. Goldfrank (1977: 97).

70. Wittfogel (1957).

71. Goldfrank (1962, 1967, 1977: 208–20).

72. New York Times, 5/25/1997.

73. This section draws from Hardin (1993), and Fawcett and McLuhan (1988).

74. Bunzel (1985), quoted by Hardin (1993: 260); Bunzel quoted by Mead, editor (1959: 34).

75. Hardin (1993: 261–62).

76. Fawcett and McLuhan (1988: 30), Tedlock (1992: 301).

77. Pandey (1972: 333).

78. Bunzel (1929), Hardin (1983, 1993: 260), Nahohai and Phelps (1995).

79. Boas (1927), Cahill (1933), Berlo (1992).

80. Bunzel (1929: 1, 5).

81. Bunzel (1932a-d), Tedlock (1992: 300–304).

82. Deacon (1997: 268–72), Bunzel (1952).

83. This section draws from Smith (1956), Lamphere (1993), and Lyon (1989).

84. Reichard (1925).

85. Deacon (1997: 309), Lamphere (1993: 163), Goddard (1933).

86. Kroeber (1909, 1917b), Lowie (1915, 1920, 1959: 67–75).

87. Reichard (1928).

88. Reichard (1950a: n.p.), cited by Babcock and Parezo (1988: 49).

89. G. Reichard to E. Parsons, 7/6/1930, 8/13/1930, ECPP.

90. Reichard (1934).

91. Reichard (1936).

92. Reichard (1950b).

93. Reichard (1934: 4).

94. Reichard (1939).

95. Gill (1981), Lamphere (1993: 157–59), Witherspoon (1977, 1980).

96. The following is based on Babcock (1993), Briscoe (1979), Caffrey (1989), Mead, editor (1959), Modell (1983), and Stocking (1989: 208–28).

97. Caffrey (1989: 97).

98. Benedict, unpublished autobiographical fragment, cited by Caffrey (1989: 98).

99. Benedict (1922, 1923).

100. Benedict (1931, 1935), Briscoe (1979: 467–68).

101. Caffrey (1989: 169–82, 185–96), Darnell (1990: 159–64).

102. For example, E. O. Wilson (1996, 1998).

103. Mead (1928).

104. Thorslev (1984: 84–125).

105. Nietzsche (1927), Pater (1899); see also Benedict (1932).

106. Benedict (1930: 572).

107. Benedict (1930: 572–73, 1934b: 78–80).

108. Benedict (1930: 581).

109. Benedict (1930: 581).

110. R. Benedict to M. Mead, 9/21/1928, quoted in Mead (1959: 308).

111. Benedict (1934a: 63).

112. Benedict (1934b).

113. Quoted by A. L. Kroeber in Kroeber et al. (1949: 11).

114. Service, Beardsley, and Dillingham (1976: 612).

115. White (1949, 1963).

116. White (1928, 1932a, 1932b, 1935, 1942, 1962).

117. Stephen (1936: xxi).

118. White (1932a: 28).

119. White (1932b: 4).

120. For example, Strong (1979).

Chapter 27

1. Cited by Pomeroy (1975: 38–39, 175–76).

2. This section draws on Berlo (1992), Blue (2000), Bryant (1974), Howard and Pardue (1996), McCluhan (1985), Poling-Kempes (1989), Thomas (1978), Weigle and Babcock (1996), and Weigle (1988).

3. Cited by Pomeroy (1975: 63).

4. Bryant (1974: 33–34, 62–63).

5. Bryant (1974: 173–212).

6. Wade and Chase (1996: 150).

7. Whiting (1906: 183–266).

8. Laut (1913).

9. Higgins (1905: 39–40).

10. Dorsey (1903).

11. Poling-Kempes (1989).

12. Among the first, and still highly useful, general surveys is Tanner (1968).

13. Wade (1976: 50–87).

14. Batkin (1998: 188).

15. Cited by Grattan (1980: 12–13).

16. Grattan (1980: 14).

17. Parezo (1983: 22–62), Santa Fe Magazine (1923: 19).

18. Wyman (1960: 27).

19. Thomas (1978).

20. Sheppard (1988: 65).

21. Brunhouse (1971: 60–62), Sheppard (1988: 75), Wilson (1997: 123–26 and fig. 75).

22. Hughes (1939: 25–35).

23. Sheppard (1988: 43–44, 57–58 and figs. 6, 43–44, 52–55).

24. Morley (1915: 278–301), Sheppard (1988: 59–60, 73–78 and figs. 56, 73–82), Shishkin (1968), Wilson (1997: 129–31 and figs. 81–82).

25. Stark and Rayne (1998).

26. Bloom (1933–38: 13:228).

27. Dunn (1968: 189–90, 195).

28. Dunn (1968: 197, 203), Peterson (1977: 288).

29. Hartley (1920: 7), cited by Dauber (1993: 76).

30. Hewett (1922a: 124), DeHuff (1922: 61–62).

31. Miscellaneous receipts by Lansing Bloom, ELHP.

32. T. Peña to L. Bloom, 1/22/1921; L. Bloom to T. Peña, 2/15/1921, ELHP.

33. Tanner (1973), Dauber (1993).

34. Peterson (1977: 71–100).

35. This section is drawn from Clark (1964) and Chapman (n.d.); see also Dauber (1993).

36. Chapman (1922, 1933–36, 1938, 1970).

37. Chapman (n.d.: 4).

38. Akins (1907: 5).

39. Dauber (1993), Wolfe (1975).

40. Wade (1976: 79–83).

41. E. L. Hewett to J. Gonzales, 9/15/1922, ELHP.

42. Gallup Intertribal Ceremonial (1926).

43. Fergusson (1930: 130).

Chapter 28

1. Lévi-Strauss (1973).

2. Sergeant (1934: 352), cited in Weigle and Fiore (1982: 129–35). The framework for this section is based on Weigle and Fiore's chronicle of writers in Santa Fe, on Dilworth (1996: 9–20), and on Wilson (1997: 131–35).

3. Weigle and Fiore (1982: 18).

4. Weigle and Fiore (1982: 13).

5. Fergusson (1930: 103, 107, 115, 150).

6. Saunders (1912).

7. Farington (1972: xi).

8. Crane (1925, 1928).

9. Deegan (1991), Coolidge (1912), Parsons (1913b).

10. Coolidge (1929), Coolidge and Coolidge (1930).

11. Dicker (1977: 135–36), Babcock and Parezo (1988: 208–11).

12. Armer (1931, 1935).

13. Malkus (1928), Smith (1931), Cannon (1926, 1929), Moon (1925).

14. Cather (1925, 1927), Fryer (1987), Harrell (1992).

15. This section draws on Byers (1965), McNickle (1971), and Hecht (1991).

16. La Farge (1945: 76).

17. La Farge (1945: 151).

18. La Farge (1945: 153).

19. La Farge (1945: 76–77).

20. Byers (1965: 406).

21. Blom and La Farge (1927).

22. Caffey (1988: 11–22), Hecht (1991: 46).

23. Caffey (1988: 23–105).

24. Hecht (1991: 326–31).

25. Meckier (1969: 78–123).

26. Lawrence (1972: 141–47).

27. Lawrence (1926), Clark (1964: 143), Kessler (1959: 260), Vickery (1973: 323).

28. Huxley (1932).

29. Firchow (1984: 57–76), Meckier (1969: 78–82, 112–16).

30. Udall (1996), and Eldredge, Schimmel, and Truettner (1986) provide excellent overviews.

31. Fowler (1989: 19).

32. Rudisill (1973).

33. Hales (1988: 145–46).

34. Rudisill (1973: passim).

35. Rudisill (1979).

36. Houlihan and Houlihan (1986).

37. Dixon (1913), Rudisill (1973: 24, 60).

38. Mahood (1961), Packard and Packard (1970), Broder (1990).

39. Wright, Gaede, and Gaede (1986).

40. Babcock and Parezo (1988: 186–89), Pitts (1981), Gilpin (1926, 1927, 1968).

41. Hilger (1986: 49–50).

42. Grey (1925), Stedman (1982: 176–78).

43. Kidder (1924: 337).

44. Hilger (1986: 7–8).

Chapter 29

1. This section is based on Fowler (1999), Stocking (1981, 1982), Toulouse (1981a, 1981b), Peckham, Fox, and Lambert (1981), Nusbaum (1934), and the unpublished papers of Kenneth Chapman (KMCP), Frederick Webb Hodge (CHP), E. L. Hewett (ELHP), Jesse Nusbaum (MVRCA), and the archives of the Laboratory of Anthropology (ALAB).

2. Nusbaum (1954: 11), Nusbaum (1946).

3. Nusbaum (1954: 11).

4. K. M. Chapman to J. D. Rockefeller, Jr., 9/19/1926; Chapman (n.d.), KMCP.

5. K. M. Chapman to J. D. Rockefeller, Jr., 10/4/1926, KMCP.

6. Hosmer (1981, 1:11–73), Harr and Johnson (1988: 13–197).

7. T. B. Appelget to E. L. Hewett, 11/16/1926, ELHP.

8. Nusbaum (1980: 22).

9. Copy of telegram in Chapman (n.d.: 22).

10. H. C. Bumpus to Executive Committee, American Association of Museums, 2/11/1927, p. 1, copy in ALAB.

11. J. D. Rockefeller, Jr., to K. M. Chapman, 12/10/1926, KMCP.

12. H. C. Bumpus to Executive Committee, American Association of Museums, 2/11/1927, pp. 1–2, copy in ALAB.

13. H. C. Bumpus to Executive Committee, American Association of Museums, 2/11/1927, pp. 7–8, copy in ALAB.

14. Chapman (n.d.: 11), McGreevy (1993: 90).

15. H. C. Bumpus to J. D. Rockefeller, Jr., 3/21/1927, copy in ALAB.

16. A. V. Kidder to K. M. Chapman, 4/22/1927, KMCP.

17. Quoted in Bumpus and Kidder (1927: 4).

18. Bumpus and Kidder (1927); A. V. Kidder to F. W. Hodge, 8/3/1927, CHP.

19. Kidder (1927), Woodbury (1993: 19–100), Nusbaum (1934).

20. Kidder et al. (1927); A. V. Kidder to J. D. Rockefeller, Jr., 12/19/1927, copy in ALAB.

21. Woodbury (1993: 115–25).

22. B. Cummings to E. L. Hewett, 12/18/1927, ELHP; Hewett (1929), Stocking (1982).

23. Kelly and Fowler (1986), Hoijer (1938, 1956).

24. Brew (1946), Swadesh (1967), Voegelin and Voegelin (1957), Dyk (1938), Driver and Kroeber (1932), Driver and Massey (1957), Opler (1983a), Eggan (1950), Earle and Kennard (1971), Titiev (1944, 1972), Llewellyn and Hoebel (1941), Wedel (1961), Reed (1951).

25. McGreevy (1993), Woodbury and Woodbury (1988).

26. This section is based on Bartlett (1953), Colton (1953a), and Miller (1991).

27. Miller (1991: 60–67).

28. Colton (1918, 1938, 1953b), Colton and Colton (1918).

29. Colton (1953a: 1).

30. Colton (1953a: 2–4).

31. There is little information on Harold Gladwin. The foregoing was pieced together from *Who Was Who in America* (7:224) and Haury (1995).

32. McGreevy (1993: 78–80).

33. Downum and Bostwick (1993).

34. McGreevy (1993: 83–89).

35. Newcomb (1964: 157).

36. Laboratory of Anthropology (1931), cited by McGreevy (1993: 87).

37. Glaser, Graham, and Mackey (1999).

Chapter 30

1. Darnell (1990).

2. Kluckhohn (1927), Kluckhohn and Leighton (1946).

3. Kroeber (1939).

4. Kelly (1988).

5. Fowler (1978).

6. Gladwin and Gladwin (1934).

7. Haury (1945a, 1995), Hinsley and Wilcox (1995), Gladwin et al. (1937), Elliott (1995: 133–61).

8. Haury (1936).

9. Cosgrove and Cosgrove (1932), Davis (1995), Bradfield (1931).

10. LeBlanc (1983). Works on Mimbres ceramics are voluminous; for elegant examples, see Brody, Scott, and LeBlanc (1983) and Brody and Swentzell (1996).

11. Kidder (1936), Colton (1938, 1939).

12. Roberts (1935), Haury (1945a).

13. Cotter (1937), Roberts (1937), Harrington (1933).

14. Sayles (1983), Haury (1950).

15. Dillehay and Meltzer (1991).

16. Brew (1941, 1946).

17. Martin (1979).

18. Ferdon (1993).

19. Goetzmann and Goetzmann (1986).

Bibliography

Abbott, Charles C.

1872   The Stone Age in New Jersey. *American Naturalist* 6: 144–60, 199–229.

Abert, James W.

1847   *Report of Lt. J. W. Abert of his Examination of New Mexico in the Years 1846–'47.* 30th Cong., 1st sess. Senate Executive Doc. 23, House Executive Doc. 41.

Abramson, Howard S.

1987   *National Geographic: Behind America's Lens on the World.* New York: Crown.

Adair, John

1944   *The Navajo and Pueblo Silversmiths.* Norman: University of Oklahoma Press.

Adams, Eleanor, and Fray Angelico Chavez

1975   *The Missions of New Mexico, 1776: a Description by Fray Francisco Atanasio Domínguez with Other Contemporary Documents.* Albuquerque: University of New Mexico Press.

Adams, Henry

1879   *The Life of Albert Gallatin.* New York: P. Smith.

Adams, Henry, ed.

1960   *Writings.* 3 vols. New York: Antiquarian Press. Originally published 1879.

Akin, Louis

1907   Frederick Monsen of the Desert: The Man Who Began Eighteen Years Ago to Live and Record the Life of Hopiland. *The Craftsman* 11: 678–82.

Albright, Horace M., and Robert Cahn

1985   *The Birth of the National Park Service: The Founding Years, 1913–33.* Salt Lake City and Chicago: Howe Brothers.

Albritton, Claude C., Jr.

1986   *The Abyss of Time. Changing Conceptions of the Earth's Antiquity after the Sixteenth Century.* San Francisco: Freeman, Cooper Co.

Aldana, Barbara Kidder

1983   The Kidder Pecos Expedition, 1924–1929: A Personal Memoir. *The Kiva* 48(4): 243–50.

Allen, Rebecca

1990   The History of the University Museum's Southwestern Pottery Collection. In J. J. Brody, *Beauty from the Earth: Pueblo Indian Pottery from the University Museum of Archaeology and Anthropology.* Pp. 61–87. Philadelphia: University Museum, University of Pennsylvania.

Altherr, Thomas L.

1985   The Pajarito or Cliff Dwellers' National Park Proposal, 1900–1920. *New Mexico Historical Review* 60(3): 271–294.

American Ethnological Society

1845   Constitution of the American Ethnological Society. *Transactions of the American Ethnological Society* 1: iii–iv.

Amsden, Charles

1949   *Prehistoric Southwesterners from Basketmaker to Pueblo.* Los Angeles: Southwest Museum.

Anderson, Arthur J. O., trans.

1973   *Rules of the Aztec Language: Classical Nahuatl Grammar, A Translation with Modifications of Francis Xavier Clavigero's "Reglas de la lengua mexicana."* Salt Lake City: University of Utah Press.

Anderson, Arthur J. O., and Charles E. Dibble, trans. and eds.

1950–82. *General History of the Things of New Spain; Florentine Codex by Fray Bernardino de Sahagún.* Monographs of the School of American Research no. 14, pts. 1–13. Santa Fe: School of American Research, and Salt Lake City: University of Utah Press.

Anderson, Keith M.

1969   Tsegi Phase Technology. Ph.D. diss., University of Washington, Seattle. Ann Arbor, Mich.: University Microfilms 69–18, 269.

Andrews, Anthony

1970   The 1901 Expedition to Chaco Canyon, New Mexico: Account of the Expedition and Analysis of the Material. Chaco Center Manuscript 2128J. Albuquerque: University of New Mexico.

Appel, Toby A.

1992   A Scientific Career in the Age of Character: Jeffrey Wyman and Natural History at Harvard. In *Science at Harvard University, Historical Perspectives* C. A. Elliott and M. A. Rossiter, eds. Pp. 96–120. Bethlehem, Pa.: Lehigh University Press.

Archaeological Institute of America

1885   *Sixth Annual Report, 1884–85.* Boston: Archaeological Institute of America.

Arciniegas, Germán

1986   *America in Europe. A History of the New World in Reverse.* San Diego: Harcourt, Brace Jovanovich.

Armer, Laura A.

1931   *Waterless Mountain.* New York and Toronto: Longmans, Green and Co.

1935   *Southwest.* London, New York, and Toronto: Longmans, Green and Co.

Arneil, Barbara

1996   *John Locke and America: The Defence of English Colonialism.* Oxford: Clarendon Press.

Arrhenius, Olof W.

1984   *Stones Speak and Waters Sing: The Life and Works of Gustaf Nordenskiöld.* R. H. and F. C. Lister, eds. Mesa Verde, Colo.: Mesa Verde Museum Association.

Atkins, Victoria M., ed.

1993   *Anasazi Basketmaker: Papers from the 1990 Wetherill-Grand Gulch Symposium.* Cultural Resources Series no. 24. Salt Lake City: Bureau of Land Management.

Atwater, Caleb

1820   Description of the Antiquities Discovered in the State of Ohio and Other Western States. *Archaeologica Americana: Transactions and Collections of the American Antiquarian Society* 1: 105–267.

Babcock, Barbara

1993   "Not in the Absolute Singular": Rereading Ruth Benedict. In *Hidden Scholars: Women Anthropologists and the Native American Southwest.* N. J. Parezo, ed. Pp. 107–28. Albuquerque: University of New Mexico Press.

Babcock, Barbara A., and Nancy J. Parezo, eds.

1988   *Daughters of the Desert: Women Anthropologists and the Native American Southwest, 1880–1980.* Albuquerque: University of New Mexico Press.

Bachofen, Johann J.

1861   *Das Mutterrecht.* Basel: Benno Schwabe.

Baggs, Mae L.

1918   *Colorado; The Queen Jewel of the Rockies.* Boston: Page Co.

Bahr, Donald M.

1983   Pima and Papago Social Organization. *Handbook of North American Indians, vol. 10, Southwest.* Pp. 193–200. Washington, D.C.: Smithsonian Institution.

Bailey, Lynn R.

1966   *Indian Slave Trade in the Southwest; A Study of Slave-taking and the Traffic of Indian Captives.* Los Angeles: Westernlore Press.

Bailey, Paul D.

1948   *Jacob Hamblin, Buckskin Apostle.* Los Angeles: Westernlore Press.

Bancroft, Hubert H.

1883   *The Works of Hubert Howe Bancroft: The Native Races, vol. I, Wild Tribes; vol. II, Civilized Nations; vol. III, Myths and Languages; vol. IV, Antiquities; vol. 5, Primitive History.* 2d ed. San Francisco: A. L. Bancroft and Co.

1890   *The Works of Hubert Howe Bancroft, vol. XXXVIII, Essays and Miscellany; vol. XXXIX, Literary Industries.* San Francisco: A. L. Bancroft and Co.

Bandelier, Adolph F.

1877   On the Art of War and Mode of Warfare of the Ancient Mexicans. *Tenth Annual Report of the*

Peabody Museum of American Archaeology and Ethnology. Pp. 95–161.

1878 On the Distribution and Tenure of Lands and the Customs with Respect to Inheritance among the Ancient Mexicans. *Eleventh Annual Report of the Peabody Museum of American Archaeology and Ethnology.* Pp. 365–448.

1879 On the Sources of Aboriginal History of Spanish America. *Proceedings of the American Association for the Advancement of Science for 1878.* Pp. 315–37.

1880 On the Social Organization and Mode of Government of the Ancient Mexicans. *Twelfth Annual Report of the Peabody Museum of American Archaeology and Ethnology.* Pp. 557–699.

1881a Historical Introduction to Studies among the Sedentary Indians of New Mexico. *Papers of the Archaeological Institute of America, American Series* 1(1): 1–33.

1881b A Visit to the Aboriginal Ruins in the Valley of the Rio Pecos. *Papers of the Archaeological Institute of America, American Series* 1(2): 34–133.

1883 Report by A. F. Bandelier on his Investigations in New Mexico in the Spring and Summer of 1882. *Bulletin of the Archaeological Institute of America* I: 13–33.

1884a Report of an Archaeological Tour in Mexico in 1881. *Papers of the Archaeological Institute of America, American Series* II. Boston: University Press.

1884b Reports by A. F. Bandelier on His Investigations in New Mexico during the Years 1883–1884. Appendix to *Fifth Annual Report of the Executive Committee, Archaeological Institute of America, Cambridge.* Pp. 55–98.

1890a Contributions to the History of the Southwestern Portion of the United States. *Papers of the Archaeological Institute of America, American Series* V. Cambridge.

1890b *The Delight Makers.* New York: Dodd, Mead, and Co.

1890c The Historical Archives of the Hemenway Southwestern Archaeological Expedition. *Proceedings of the Seventh Annual Meeting of the International Congress of Americanists (1888), Berlin.* Pp. 450–59.

1890d Sketch of the Knowledge which the Spaniards of Mexico Possessed of the Countries North of New Galicia, Previous to the Return of Cabeza de Vaca, in the Year 1536. *In* Contributions to the History of the Southwestern Portion of the United States. Pp. 3–23. *Papers of the Archaeologi-cal Institute of America, American Series* V. Cambridge.

1890–92 Final Report of Investigations among the Indians of the Southwestern United States, Carried on Mainly in the Years from 1880 to 1885, Part I–II. *Papers of the Archaeological Institute of America, American Series* III-IV. Cambridge.

1892a An Outline of the Documentary History of the Zuñi Tribe. *Journal of American Ethnology and Archaeology* 3(4): 1–115. Cambridge.

1892b The "Montezuma" of the Pueblo Indians. *American Anthropologist,* o.s. 5: 319–26.

1893 *The Gilded Man (El Dorado) and Other Pictures of the Spanish Occupancy of America.* New York: D. Appleton and Co.

1910 Documentary History of the Rio Grande Pueblos of New Mexico. I. Bibliographic Introduction. *Archaeological Institute of America. Papers of the School of American Archaeology* 13: 1–28.

1981 *The Discovery of New Mexico by the Franciscan Monk Friar Marcos de Niza in 1539.* M. T. Rodack, trans. Tucson: University of Arizona Press.

1988 History of the Colonization and Missions of Sonora, Chihuahua, New Mexico and Arizona to the Year 1700. M. T. Rodack, trans. *Journal of the Southwest* 30(1): 48–120.

Bandelier, Fanny, trans.

1905 *The Journey of Alvar Nuñez Cabeza de Vaca.* New York: A. S. Barnes and Co.

Bannister, Bryant, and William J. Robinson

1986 Archaeology and Dendrochronology. In *Emil W. Haury's Prehistory of the American Southwest.* J. J. Reid and D. E. Doyel, eds. Pp. 49–54. Tucson: University of Arizona Press.

Bannon, John F.

1970 *The Spanish Borderlands Frontier, 1513–1821.* New York: Holt, Rinehart, Winston.

1978 *Herbert Eugene Bolton: the Historian and the Man, 1870–1953.* Tucson: University of Arizona Press.

Bannon, John F., ed.

1964 *Bolton and the Spanish Borderlands.* Norman: University of Oklahoma Press.

Barber, Lynn

1980 *The Heyday of Natural History, 1820–1870.* Garden City, N.Y.: Doubleday.

Barrett, Stephen M.

1915 *Geronimo's Story of His Life.* New York: Duffield and Co. Originally published 1906.

Barrow, John D.
1988   *The World Within the World*. Oxford: Clarendon Press.

Barrows, John H., ed.
1893   *The World's Parliament of Religions*. 2 vols. Chicago: Parliament Publishing Co.

Bartlett, John Russell
1848   The Progress of Ethnology and Geography. *Transactions of the American Ethnological Society* II, Appendix. Pp. 1–151.
1854   *Personal Narrative of Explorations and Incidents in Texas, New Mexico, California, Sonora and Chihuahua . . . in 1850–53*. 2 vols. New York: D. Appleton and Co.
1889   *Dictionary of Americanisms: A Glossary of Words and Phrases Usually Regarded as Peculiar to the United States*. 4th ed. Boston: Little, Brown and Co. First edition 1848.

Bartlett, Katherine
1953   Twenty-Five Years of Anthropology. *Plateau* 26(1): 38–60.

Bartlett, Richard H.
1962   *Great Surveys of the American West*. Norman: University of Oklahoma Press.

Barton, Benjamin S.
1797   *New Views on the Origins of the Tribes and Nations of America*. Printed for the author by John Bioren, Philadelphia.

Basehart, Harry W., and W. W. Hill
1965   Leslie Spier, 1893–1961 *American Anthropologist* 67(6): 1258–77.

Bassett, Henry W., and Frederick Starr, eds.
1898   *The International Folk-Lore Congress of the World's Columbian Exposition*. Chicago: I. C. H. Sergel Co.

Basso, Keith H.
1983   Western Apache. *Handbook of North American Indians, vol. 10, Southwest*. Pp. 462–88. Washington, D.C.: Smithsonian Institution.

Batkin, Jonathan
1998   Some Early Curio Dealers of New Mexico. *American Indian Art* 23(3): 68–81.
1999   Tourism Is Overrated: Pueblo Pottery and the Early Curio Trade. In *Unpacking Culture. Art and Commodity in Colonial and Postcolonial Worlds*. R. B. Phillips and C. B. Steiner, eds. Pp. 282–97. Berkeley: University of California Press.

Baxter, Sylvester
1881   Solved at Last: Mysteries of Ancient Aztec History Unveiled by an Explorer from the Smithsonian Institution. Wonderful Achievements of Frank H. Cushing. *Boston Herald* June 16, 1881. Reprinted in *The Southwest in the American Imagination. The Writings of Sylvester Baxter, 1881–1889*. C. M. Hinsley and D. R. Wilcox, eds. Pp. 45–54. Tucson: University of Arizona Press.
1882a An Aboriginal Pilgrimage. *Century Illustrated Monthly Magazine* 24 (n.s. 2): 526–36.
1882b The Father of the Pueblos. *Harper's New Monthly Magazine* 65: 72–91. Reprinted in *The Southwest in the American Imagination. The Writings of Sylvester Baxter, 1881–1889*. C. M. Hinsley and D. R. Wilcox, eds. Pp. 63–96. Tucson: University of Arizona Press.

Beals, Ralph L.
1943   Northern Mexico and the Southwest. In *El Norte de México y el sur de los Estados Unidos*. Pp. 191–99. Mexico City: Mexican Society of Anthropology.

Becker, Carl
1932   *The Heavenly City of the Eighteenth Century Philosophers*. New Haven, Conn.: Yale University Press.

Bee, Robert L.
1983   Quechan. *Handbook of North American Indian Languages, vol. 10, Southwest*. Pp. 86–98. Washington, D.C.: Smithsonian Institution.

Berlo, Janet C.
1992   The Formative Years in Native American Art History. In *The Early Years of Native American Art History*. J. C. Berlo, ed. Pp. 1–21. Seattle: University of Washington Press, and Vancouver: UBC Press.

Bender, Gordon L., ed.
1982   *Reference Handbook on the Deserts of North America*. Westport, Conn.: Greenwood Press.

Bender, Norman J.
1984   *Missionaries, Outlaws, and Indians: Taylor F. Ealy at Lincoln and Zuñi, 1878–1881*. Albuquerque: University of New Mexico Press.

Benedict, A. L.
1901–2 Official Correspondence of the Division of Ethnology. Papers of the Pan-American Exposition, Buffalo, New York, 1901. Buffalo, N.Y.: Buffalo and Erie County Historical Society.

Benedict, Burton
1983   *The Anthropology of World's Fairs: San Francisco's Panama Pacific Exposition of 1915*. Berkeley: Lowie

Museum of Anthropology, and London: Scholar
Press.

Benedict, Ruth

1922   The Vision in Plains Culture. *American Anthro-
        pologist* 24: 1–23.

1923   The Concept of the Guardian Spirit in North
        America. *American Anthropological Association
        Memoirs* 29.

1930   Psychological Types in the Cultures of the South-
        west. *Proceedings of the International Congress of
        Americanists* 23: 572–81.

1931   Tales of the Cochiti Indians. *Bureau of American
        Ethnology Bulletin* 98.

1932   Configurations of Culture in North America.
        American Anthropologist 34: 1–27.

1934a   Anthropology and the Abnormal. *Journal of Gen-
        eral Psychology* 10: 59–82.

1934b   *Patterns of Culture.* Boston and New York:
        Houghton Mifflin.

1935   *Zuñi Mythology.* 2 vols. New York: Columbia Uni-
        versity Contributions to Anthropology 21.

Berger, Thomas

1964   *Little Big Man.* New York: Dial Press.

Berkhofer, Robert F., Jr.

1978   *The White Man's Indian: Images of the American
        Indian from Columbus to the Present.* New York:
        Vintage Books.

Berman, Judith

1996   "The Culture as It Appears to the Indian Him-
        self": Boas, George Hunt, and the Methods of
        Ethnography. In *Volkgeist as Method and Ethic:
        Essays on Boasian Ethnography and the German
        Anthropological Tradition.* G. W. Stocking, Jr.,
        ed. Pp. 215–56. History of Anthropology, vol. 8.
        Madison: University of Wisconsin Press.

Bernheimer, Charles L.

1924   *Rainbow Bridge.* New York: Doubleday, Page and
        Co.

Bettinger, Robert L.

1991   *Hunter-Gatherers: Archaeological and Evolutionary
        Theory.* New York: Plenum Press.

Bieder, Robert E.

1986   *Science Encounters the American Indian, 1820–1880:
        The Early Years of American Ethnology.* Norman:
        University of Oklahoma Press.

Bingham, Edwin R.

1955   *Charles F. Lummis, Editor of the Southwest.* San
        Marino, Calif.: Huntington Library.

Bishop, Ronald L., and Frederick W. Lange, eds.

1991   *The Ceramic Legacy of Anna O. Shepard.* Niwot,
        Colo.: University Press of Colorado.

Blackburn, Fred M., and Ray A. Williamson

1997   *Cowboys & Cave Dwellers: Basketmaker Archaeol-
        ogy in Utah's Grand Gulch.* Santa Fe: School of
        American Research Press.

Blackstone, Sarah J.

1986   *Buckskin, Bullets and Business: A History of Buffalo
        Bill's Wild West.* Westport, Conn.: Greenwood
        Press.

Blake, Michael, writer, and Kevin Costner, director

1990   *Dances With Wolves.* Film. Los Angeles: Guild/
        Tig Productions.

Blaut, James M.

1993   *The Colonizer's Model of the World: Geographical
        Diffusionism and Eurocentric History.* New York:
        Guilford Press.

Blom, Frans, and Oliver La Farge

1927   *Tribes and Temples; A Record of the Expedition to
        Middle America conducted by the Tulane University
        of Louisiana.* 2 vols. New Orleans: Tulane
        University.

Blomberg, Nancy J.

1988   *Navajo Textiles: The William Randolph Hearst Col-
        lection.* Tucson: University of Arizona Press.

Bloom, Lansing B.

1921   The Emergence of Chaco Canyon in History. *Art
        and Archaeology* 11(1–2): 29–35.

Bloom, Lansing B., ed.

1933–38 Bourke on the Southwest. *New Mexico Histori-
        cal Review* 8: 1–30; 9: 33–77, 159–83, 273–89,
        375–435; 10: 1–35, 271–322; 11: 77–122, 188–207,
        217–82; 12: 41–77, 337–79; 13: 192–238.

Blue, Martha

2000   *Indian Trader: the Life and Times of J. L. Hubbell.*
        Walnut Creek, Calif.: Kiva Pub. Co.

Blumenbach, Johann F.

1865   *The Anthropological Treatises of Johann Friedrich
        Blumenbach.* T. Bendyshe, trans. Anthropological
        Society of London. London: Longman, Green,
        Longman, Roberts, and Green. Originally
        published 1775–1786.

Boas, Franz

1887a   The Occurrence of Similar Inventions in Areas
        Widely Apart. *Science* 9: 485–86.

1887b   Museums of Ethnology and Their Classification.
        Science 9: 587–89.

1896 The Limitations of the Comparative Method in Anthropology. *Science* 4: 901–8.

1903 The Jesup North Pacific Expedition. *American Museum Journal* 3(3): 73–115.

1904 The History of Anthropology. *Science* 20: 513–24.

1906 The History of Anthropology. In *Congress of Arts and Science, Universal Exposition, St. Louis, 1904.* H. J. Rogers, ed. Vol. 5: 468–82. Boston: Houghton Mifflin.

1911a *Changes in the Bodily Form of the Descendants of Immigrants.* 61st Cong., 2d sess., Senate Doc. no. 208. Washington, D.C.

1911b Introduction. *In* Handbook of American Indian Languages, Pt. 1. F. Boas, ed. Pp. 5–83. *Bureau of American Ethnology Bulletin* 40.

1911c *The Mind of Primitive Man.* New York: Macmillan.

1912 International School of American Archaeology and Ethnology in Mexico. *American Anthropologist* 14: 192–94.

1915 Summary of the Work of the International School of American Archeology and Ethnology in Mexico, 1910–1914. *American Anthropologist* 17(2): 384–91.

1919 Scientists as Spies. *The Nation*, Dec. 20, 1919: 797.

1925–28 *Keresan Texts.* American Ethnological Society Publication 8 (1–2).

1927 *Primitive Art.* Cambridge, Mass.: Harvard University Press.

Boas, Franz, ed.

1911–22 Handbook of American Indian Languages. 2 vols. *Bureau of American Ethnology Bulletin* 40.

Bodo, Murray, ed.

1998 *Tales of an Endishodi: Father Berard Haile and the Navajos, 1900–1961.* Albuquerque: University of New Mexico Press.

Boesen, Victor, and Florence Curtis Graybill

1977 *Edward S. Curtis, Photographer of the North American Indian.* New York: Dodd, Mead and Co.

Bolton, Herbert E.

1913 *Guide to Materials for the History of the United States in the Principal Archives of Mexico.* Carnegie Institution of Washington Publication no. 163.

1917 The Mission as a Frontier Institution in the Spanish-American Colonies. *American Historical Review* 23: 42–61.

1930 Defensive Spanish Expansion and the Significance of the Borderlands. In *The Trans-Mississippi West.* J. F. Willard and C. B. Goodykoontz, eds. Pp. 1–42. Boulder: University of Colorado.

1936 *Rim of Christendom. A Biography of Eusebio Francisco Kino, Pacific Coast Pioneer.* New York: Macmillan Co.

1950 *Pageant in the Wilderness: The Story of the Escalante Expedition to the Interior Basin, 1776.* Salt Lake City: Utah Historical Quarterly, vol. 18.

1987 *The Hasinais: Southern Caddoans as Seen by the Earliest Europeans.* R. M. Magnaghi, ed. Norman: University of Oklahoma Press.

1990 *Coronado on the Turquoise Trail, Knight of Pueblos and Plains.* Albuquerque: University of New Mexico Press.

Bolton, Herbert E., ed.

1916 *Spanish Exploration in the Southwest, 1542–1706.* New York: Charles Scribner's Sons.

1919 *Kino's Historical Memoir of Pimeria Alta . . . 1683–1711.* 2 vols. Cleveland: Arthur H. Clark Co.

1930 *Anza's California Expeditions.* 5 vols. Berkeley: University of California Press.

Bonfante, Giuliano

1954 Ideas on the Kinship of European Languages from 1200 to 1800. *Journal of World History* 1: 679–99.

Bourke, John G.

1884 *The Snake Dance of the Moquis of Arizona.* New York: C. Scribner's Sons.

1886 *An Apache Campaign in the Sierra Madre. An Account of the Expedition in Pursuit of the Hostile Chiricahua Apaches in the Spring of 1883.* New York: C Scribner's Sons.

1888 *Compilation of Notes and Memoranda Bearing upon the Use of Human Ordure and Human Urine in Rites of a Religious or Semi-Religious Character among Various Nations.* Washington, D.C.: War Department.

1891a *On the Border with Crook.* New York: C. Scribner's Sons.

1891b *Scatalogic Rites of All Nations: A Dissertation upon the Employment of Excrementitious Remedial Agents in Religion, Therapeutics, Divination, Witchcraft, Love Philters, etc., in All Parts of the Globe.* Washington, D.C.: W. H. Lowdermilk and Co.

1892 The Medicine-Men of the Apache. *Ninth Annual Report of the Bureau of Ethnology, 1887–1888.* Pp. 443–603.

1980 Diary of John Gregory Bourke, 1872–1896. 124 vols.; 10 microfilm reels. Ann Arbor, Mich.: University Microfilms International.

Bowditch, Charles

1907 The Work of the Institute in American Archaeology. *American Journal of Archaeology* 11: 47–48.

Bowen, Thomas

1983 Seri. *Handbook of North American Indians. vol. 10 Southwest.* Pp. 230–49. Washington, D.C.: Smithsonian Institution Press.

Brack, Gene M.

1975 *Mexico Views Manifest Destiny, 1821–1846: An Essay on the Origins of the Mexican War.* Albuquerque: University of New Mexico Press.

Bradfield, Maitland

1973 *A Natural History of Associations: A Study in the Meaning of Community.* London: Duckworth.

Bradfield, Wesley

1921 Economic Resources of Chaco Canyon. *Art and Archaeology* 11(1–2): 36–38.

1931 *Cameron Creek Village: A Site in the Mimbres Area in Grant County, New Mexico.* Santa Fe: School of American Research Monographs 1.

Brainerd, George W.

1951 The Place of Chronological Ordering in Archaeological Analysis. *American Antiquity* 16(4): 301–13.

Brandes, Raymond

1965 Frank Hamilton Cushing: Pioneer Americanist. Ph.D. diss., University of Arizona, Tucson.

Breitbart, Eric

1997 *A World on Display: Photographs from the St. Louis World's Fair, 1904.* Albuquerque: University of New Mexico Press.

Bremer, Richard G.

1987 *Indian Agent and Wilderness Scholar: The Life of Henry Rowe Schoolcraft.* Mt. Pleasant: Clarke Historical Library, Central Michigan University.

Bremner, Robert H.

1988 *American Philanthropy.* 2d. ed. Chicago: University of Chicago Press.

Brew, J. O.

1941 Preliminary Report of the Peabody Museum Awatovi Expedition of 1939. *Plateau* 13(3): 37–48.

1946 *Archaeology of Alkali Ridge, Utah.* Papers of the Peabody Museum of American Archaeology and Ethnology, vol. 21.

1979 Hopi Prehistory and History to 1850. *Handbook of North American Indians, vol. 9, Southwest.*

Pp. 514–23. Washington, D.C.: Smithsonian Institution.

Briscoe, Virginia W.

1979 Ruth Benedict, Anthropological Folklorist. *Journal of American Folk-Lore* 92: 445–76.

Broder, Patricia J.

1990 *Shadows on Glass: The Indian World of Ben Wittick.* Savage, Md.: Rowman and Littlefield.

Brodie, Fawn M.

1971 *No Man Knows My History: The Life of Joseph Smith, the Mormon Prophet.* New York: Alfred A. Knopf.

Brody, J. J.

1991 *Anasazi and Pueblo Painting.* Albuquerque: University of New Mexico Press.

Brody, J. J., Catherine J. Scott, and Steven A. LeBlanc

1983 *Mimbres Pottery: Ancient Art of the American Southwest.* New York: Hudson Hills Press.

Brody, J. J., and Rina Swentzell

1996 *To Touch the Past: The Painted Pottery of the Mimbres People.* New York: Hudson Hills Press.

Brooke, John L.

1994 *The Refiner's Fire: The Making of Mormon Cosmology, 1644–1844.* New York: Cambridge University Press.

Brooks, Van Wyck

1955 *John Sloan: A Painter's Life.* New York: Dutton.

Browman, David L., and Douglas R. Givens

1996 Stratigraphic Excavation: The First "New Archaeology." *American Anthropologist* 98(1): 80–95.

Brown, David E.

1982 Biotic Communities of the American Southwest—United States and Mexico. *Desert Plants* 4(1–4): 1–341.

Brown, Donald N.

1979 Picuris Pueblo. In *Handbook of North American Indians. vol. 9 Southwest.* Pp. 268–77. Washington, D.C.: Smithsonian Institution.

Brugge, David M.

1983 Navajo Prehistory and History to 1850. *Handbook of North American Indians, vol. 10, Southwest.* Pp. 489–501. Washington, D.C.: Smithsonian Institution.

1994 *The Navajo-Hopi Land Dispute: An American Tragedy.* Albuquerque: University of New Mexico Press.

Brunhouse, Robert L.

1971 *Sylvanus G. Morley and the World of the Ancient Mayas.* Norman: University of Oklahoma Press.

Bryant, Keith L., Jr.

1974 *History of the Atchison, Topeka and Santa Fe Railway.* New York: Macmillan.

1978 The Atchison, Topeka and Santa Fe Railway and the Development of the Taos and Santa Fe Art Colonies. *Western Historical Quarterly* 9: 437–54.

Buel, J. W.

1894 *The Magic City: A Massive Portfolio of Original Photographic Views of the Great World's Fair.* St. Louis and Philadelphia: Historical Publishing Co.

Buel, J. W., ed.

1905 *Louisiana and the Fair: An Exposition of the World, Its People and Their Accomplishments.* 10 vols. St. Louis: World's Progress Publishing Co.

Bulmer, Martin

1984 *The Chicago School of Sociology: Institutionalization, Diversity, and the Rise of Sociological Research.* Chicago: University of Chicago Press.

Bumpus, Hermon C., and A. V. Kidder

1927 A Statement as of June 6, 1927—To the Members of the Committee on Outdoor Recreation and to Those Interested in the Establishment of an Anthropological Laboratory and Museum at Santa Fe, and to Those Who Have Already Assisted in the Project. ALAB.

Bunzel, Ruth L.

1929 *The Pueblo Potter: A Study in Creative Imagination in Primitive Art.* New York: Columbia University Press.

1932a Introduction to Zuñi Ceremonialism. *Forty-seventh Annual Report of the Bureau of American Ethnology, 1929–30.* Pp. 467–544.

1932b Zuñi Origin Myths. *Forty-seventh Annual Report of the Bureau of American Ethnology, 1929–30.* Pp. 545–609.

1932c Zuñi Ritual Poetry. *Forty-seventh Annual Report of the Bureau of American Ethnology, 1929–30.* Pp. 611–835.

1932d Zuñi Kachinas, An Analytical Study. *Forty-seventh Annual Report of the Bureau of American Ethnology, 1929–30.* Pp. 837–1086.

1952 *Chichicastenango, A Guatemalan Village.* Locust Valley, N.Y.: J. J. Augustin Publications.

Bunzl, Matti

1996 Franz Boas and the Humboldtian Tradition: From *Volkgeist* and *Nationalcharakter* to an Anthropological Concept of Culture. In *Volkgeist as Method and Ethic: Essays on Boasian Ethnography and the German Anthropological Tradition.* G. W. Stocking, Jr., ed. Pp. 17–78. History of Anthropology, vol. 8. Madison: University of Wisconsin Press.

Bureau of American Ethnology

1971 *List of Publications of the Bureau of American Ethnology.* Bureau of American Ethnology Bulletin no. 200. Washington, D.C.

Burg, David F.

1976 *Chicago's White City of 1893.* Lexington: University Press of Kentucky.

Burrus, Ernest J.

1971 *Kino and Manje, Explorers of Sonora and Arizona, Their Vision of the Future: A Study of Their Expeditions and Plans.* Sources and Studies for the History of the Americas, vol. 10. Rome and St. Louis: Jesuit Historical Institute.

Burrus, Ernest J., ed.

1969a *A History of the Southwest: A Study of the Civilization and Conversion of the Indians in Southwestern United States and Northwestern Mexico from the Earliest Times to 1700. Vol. I. A Catalogue of the Bandelier Collection in the Vatican Library.* Sources and Studies for the History of the Americas, vol. 7. Rome and St. Louis: Jesuit Historical Institute.

1969b *A History of the Southwest: A Study of the Civilization and Conversion of the Indians in Southwestern United States and Northwestern Mexico from the Earliest Times to 1700. Supplement to Volume I, Reproduction in Color of Thirty Sketches and of Ten Maps.* Sources and Studies for the History of the Americas, vol. 8. Rome and St. Louis: Jesuit Historical Institute.

Buschmann, Johann K.

1853 *Über die aztekischen Ortsnamen.* Berlin: F. Dümmler.

1859 *Die Spuren der aztekischen Sprache im nördlichen Mexico und höheren amerikanischen Norden . . .* Berlin: Academy of Sciences.

Bushnell, David I., Jr.

1925 John Mix Stanley, Artist-Explorer. *Smithsonian Institution Annual Report for 1924.* Pp. 507–12. Washington, D.C.

Bustamante, Adrian, and Marc Simmons, trans. and eds.

1995 *The Exposition on the Province of New Mexico, 1812 by Don Pedro Baptista Pino.* Santa Fe and Albuquerque: El Rancho de las Golondrinas and University of New Mexico Press.

Byers, Douglas S.
1965   Franz Blom, 1893–1963; Oliver La Farge,
        1901–1963. *American Antiquity* 35: 406–9.
Byrkit, James W.
1989   Introduction. In *Charles F. Lummis's Letters from
        the Southwest, Sept. 20, 1884 to March 14, 1885*. Pp.
        ii–xxii. Tucson: University of Arizona Press.
1992   Land, Sky, and People: The Southwest Defined.
        Journal of the Southwest 34(3): 257–386.
Caffey, David L., ed.
1988   *Yellow Sun, Bright Sky: The Indian Country Stories
        of Oliver La Farge*. Albuquerque: University of
        New Mexico Press.
Caffrey, Margaret M.
1989   *Ruth Benedict. Stranger in This Land*. Austin: Uni-
        versity of Texas Press.
Cahill, Holger
1933   *American Sources of Modern Art . . . the Museum of
        Modern Art*. New York: W. W. Norton.
Callaway, Donald G., Joel C. Janetski, and Omer C.
        Stewart
1986   Ute. *Handbook of North American Indians. vol. 11,
        Great Basin*. Pp. 336–67. Washington, D.C.:
        Smithsonian Institution.
Campbell, Lyle
1979   Middle American Languages. In *The Languages of
        Native America: Historical and Comparative Assess-
        ment*. L. Campbell and M. Mithun, eds. Pp.
        902–1000. Austin: University of Texas Press.
1997   *American Indian Languages: The Historical Lin-
        guistics of Native America*. New York: Oxford
        University Press.
Cannon, Cornelia J.
1926   *Pueblo Boy: The Story of Coronado's Search for the
        Seven Cities of Cibola*. Boston and New York:
        Houghton Mifflin.
1929   *The Pueblo Girl: The Story of Coronado on the Rio
        Grande*. Boston and New York: Houghton
        Mifflin.
Cantwell, Robert
1996   *When We Were Good: The Folk Revival*.
        Cambridge, Mass.: Harvard University Press.
Carleton, James H.
1854   Diary of an Excursion to the Ruins of Abó,
        Quarra, and Gran Quivira, in New Mexico. *Ninth
        Annual Report of the Smithsonian Institution for
        1854*. Pp. 296–317. Washington, D.C.
Carnegie, Andrew
1889   Wealth. *North American Review* 148: 653–64.

Carter, Denny
1978   *Henry Farny*. New York: Watson-Guptill
        Publications.
Carter, Edward C., II
1993   *"One Grand Pursuit": A Brief History of the Ameri-
        can Philosophical Society's First 250 Years, 1743–1993*.
        Philadelphia: American Philosophical Society.
Carvalho, Solomon Nunes
1857   *Incidents of Travel and Adventure in the Far West
        with Col. Fremont's Last Expedition Across the
        Rocky Mountains*. New York: Derby and Jackson.
Casanova, Frank E.
1968   General Crook Visits the Supais as Reported
        by John G. Bourke. *Arizona and the West* 10(3):
        253–76.
Cass, Lewis
1823   *Inquiries, Respecting the History, Traditions, Lan-
        guages, Manners, Customs, Religion, etc. of the Indi-
        ans Living within the United States*. Detroit: Shel-
        don and Reed. Copy in American Antiquarian
        Society Library, Worcester, Mass.
1826   Review of J. D. Hunter's "Manners and Customs
        of Several Indian Tribes . . . " *North American Re-
        view* 22: 37–90.
1840   Aboriginal Structures. *North American Review* 51:
        396–433.
Cassells, E. S.
1983   *The Archaeology of Colorado*. Boulder: Johnson
        Books.
Castillo, Edward D.
1978   The Impact of Euro-American Exploration and
        Settlement. *Handbook of the North American Indi-
        ans, vol. 8, California*. Pp. 99–127. Washington,
        D.C.: Smithsonian Institution.
Cater, Harold D., ed.
1947   *Henry Adams and His Friends: A Collection of Un-
        published Letters*. Boston: Houghton Mifflin.
Cather, Willa
1925   *The Professor's House*. New York: Alfred A. Knopf.
1927   *Death Comes for the Archbishop*. New York: Alfred
        A. Knopf.
Catlin, George
1857   *Illustrations of the Manners, Customs, and Condi-
        tion of the North American Indians . . .* 9th ed.
        2 vols. London: H. G. Bohn.
Caughey, John W.
1946   *Hubert Howe Bancroft, Historian of the West*.
        Berkeley and Los Angeles: University of Califor-
        nia Press.

Census Office, Dept. of the Interior

1883   *Compendium of the Tenth Census (June 1, 1880)
       Compiled Pursuant to an Act of Congress Approved
       August 7, 1882, Part I.* Washington, D.C.: Govern-
       ment Printing Office.

Chapin, Frederick H.

1889   *Mountaineering in Colorado: The Peaks about Estes
       Park.* Boston: Appalachian Mountain Club. Re-
       printed, Lincoln: University of Nebraska Press,
       1987.

1890   Cliff-dwellings of the Mancos Cañons. *American
       Antiquarian and Oriental Journal* 12(4): 193.

1892   *The Land of the Cliff-Dwellers.* Boston:
       Appalachian Mountain Club, W. B. Clarke and
       Co. Reprinted, Tucson: University of Arizona
       Press, 1988.

Chaplin, Joyce E.

1997   Natural Philosophy and an Early Racial Idiom in
       North America: Comparing English and Indian
       Bodies. *William and Mary Quarterly*, 3d ser. 54(1):
       229–52.

Chapman, Kenneth M.

1921   What the Potsherds Tell. *Art and Archaeology*
       11(1–2): 39–44.

1922   Life Forms in Pueblo Pottery Decoration. *Art and
       Archaeology* 13(3): 120–22.

1933–36 *Pueblo Indian Pottery.* 2 vols. Nice, France:
       Szwedzicki.

1938   *The Pottery of Santo Domingo Pueblo: A Detailed
       Study of Its Decoration.* Laboratory of Anthropol-
       ogy Memoirs 1. Reprinted, Santa Fe: School of
       American Research.

1970   *The Pottery of San Ildefonso Pueblo.* Albuquerque:
       University of New Mexico Press for the School of
       American Research.

n.d.   Memoirs. Typescript. KMCP.

Chauvenet, Beatrice

1983   *Hewett and Friends: A Biography of Santa Fe's
       Vibrant Era.* Santa Fe: Museum of New Mexico
       Press.

Chavez, Angelico, trans., and Ted J. Warner, ed.

1976   *The Domínguez-Escalante Journal: Their Expe-
       dition through Colorado, Utah, Arizona and New
       Mexico in 1776.* Provo, Utah: Brigham Young
       University Press.

Chinard, Gilbert

1943   Thomas Jefferson and the American Philosophical
       Society. *American Philosophical Society Proceedings*
       87(2): 270–88.

Clark, Ann N.

1964   From Basement to Basement: A History of the
       Indian Arts Fund (with annotations by K. M.
       Chapman). Unpublished Manuscript. Santa Fe:
       Indians Arts Research Center, School of
       American Research.

Clark, Harry

1973   *A Venture in History: The Production, Publication,
       and Sale of the Works of Hubert Howe Bancroft.*
       Berkeley: University of California Press.

Clark, L. D.

1964   *Dark Night of the Body: D. H. Lawrence's The
       Plumed Serpent.* Austin: University of Texas Press.

Clavigero, Francisco Javier

1979   *The History of Mexico.* 2 vols. New York and Lon-
       don: Garland Publishing. Originally published in
       1787.

Cline, Howard F.

1973   Hubert Howe Bancroft, 1832–1918. In *Handbook
       of Middle American Indians, vol. 13, Guide to Eth-
       nohistorical Sources*, Pt. 2. Pp. 326–47. Austin:
       University of Texas Press.

Cline, Howard F., ed.

1973   *Handbook of Middle American Indians, vol. 13,
       Guide to Ethnohistorical Sources*, Pt. 2. Austin:
       University of Texas Press.

Clissold, Stephen

1961   *The Seven Cities of Cibola.* London: Eyre and
       Spottiswoode.

Coe, Michael D.

1968   The Fall of the House of Ussher. *Midway, A
       Magazine of Discovery in the Arts and Sciences* 8(4):
       81–89.

1993   *Breaking the Maya Code.* New York: Thames and
       Hudson.

Coleman, A. D., and T. C. McLuhan

1972   *Portraits from the North American Indian by
       Edward S. Curtis.* New York: E. P. Dutton.

Colin, Susi

1987   The Wild Man and the Indian in Early Sixteenth
       Century Book Illustrations. In *Indians and
       Europe: An Interdisciplinary Collection of Essays.*
       C. W. Feest, ed. Pp. 5–36. Aachen: Rader Verlag.

Collier, Donald

1969   Chicago Comes of Age: The World's Columbian
       Exposition and the Birth of the Field Museum.
       Field Museum Bulletin 40(5): 2–7.

1972   Men and Their Work. *Field Museum Bulletin*
       43(8): 7–9.

Colton, Harold S.

1918   Geography of Certain Ruins Near the San Francisco Mountains, Arizona. *Bulletin of the Geographical Society of Philadelphia* 16(2): 37–60.

1938   Names of the Four Culture Roots in the Southwest. *Science* 87(2268): 551–52.

1939   *Prehistoric Culture Units and Their Relationships in Northern Arizona.* Museum of Northern Arizona Bulletin no. 17.

1953a History of the Museum of Northern Arizona. *Plateau* 26(1): 1–8.

1953b *Potsherds: An Introduction to the Study of Prehistoric Southwestern Ceramics and Their Uses in Historic Reconstruction.* Museum of Northern Arizona Bulletin 25.

1959   *Hopi Kachina Dolls; with a Key to Their Identification.* Rev. ed. Albuquerque: University of New Mexico Press.

Colton, Harold S., and Mary-Russell F. Colton

1918   The Little Known Small House Ruins in the Coconino Forest. *American Anthropological Association Memoirs* 5(4): 101–26.

Comparato, Frank E.

1979   *Chronicles of Genius and Folly. R. Hoe & Company and the Printing Press as a Service to Democracy.* Culver City, Calif.: Labyrinthos.

Conklin, Edwin G.

1940   Connection of the American Philosophical Society with Our First National Exploring Expedition. *American Philosophical Society Proceedings* 82: 519–41.

Connor, Seymour V., and Odie B. Faulk

1971   *North America Divided. The Mexican War, 1846–1848.* New York: Oxford University Press.

Connor, Seymour V., and Jimmy M. Skaggs

1977   *Broadcloth and Britches: The Santa Fe Trade.* College Station and London: Texas A&M University Press.

Cook, Harold L.

1925   Definite Evidence of Human Artifacts in the Pleistocene. *Science* 62: 459–60.

Cook, Sherburne F., and Cesare R. Marino

1988   Roman Catholic Missions in California and the Southwest. *Handbook of North American Indians, vol. 4, Indian-White Relations.* Pp. 472–480. Washington, D.C.: Smithsonian Institution.

Coolidge, Dane, and Mary Coolidge

1930   *The Navajo.* Boston and New York: Houghton Mifflin Co.

Coolidge, Mary.

1912   *Why Women Are So.* New York: Arno Press.

1929   *The Rain-Makers: Indians of Arizona and New Mexico.* Boston and New York: Houghton Mifflin Co.

Cooper, James F.

1954   *The Leatherstocking Tales.* New York: Pantheon Books.

Cope, E. D.

1879   Report on the Remains of Population Observed in Northwestern New Mexico. In *Archaeology.* F. W. Putnam, ed. Pp. 351–61, Vol. VII, *Report upon Geographical and Geological Explorations and Surveys West of the One Hundredth Meridian, in charge of Lt. George M. Wheeler, Corps of Engineers* Washington, D.C.: Government Printing Office.

Cordell, Linda

1997   *Archaeology of the Southwest.* 2d ed. San Diego: Academic Press.

Cosgrove, Harriet S., and Cornelius B. Cosgrove

1932   *The Swarts Ruin: A Typical Mimbres Site in Southwestern New Mexico.* Papers of the Peabody Museum of American Archaeology and Ethnology 51(1).

Cotter, John L.

1937   The Occurrence of Flints and Extinct Animals in Pluvial Deposits near Clovis, New Mexico, Pt. IV, Report on the Excavations in the Gravel Pit in 1936. *Philadelphia Academy of Natural Sciences Proceedings* 89: 2–16.

Coues, Elliott, ed. and trans.

1900   *On the Trail of a Spanish Pioneer: The Diary and Itinerary of Francisco Garcés in His Travels through Sonora, Arizona and California, 1775–1776.* 2 vols. New York: Francis P. Harper.

Crane, Leo

1925   *Indians of the Enchanted Desert.* Boston: Little, Brown.

1928   *Desert Drums: The Pueblo Indians of New Mexico, 1540–1928.* Boston: Little, Brown, and Co.

Crook, George

1946   *General George Crook, His Autobiography.* M. F. Schmitt, ed. Norman: University of Oklahoma Press.

Crosby, Alfred W.

1997   *The Measure of Reality: Quantification and Western Society, 1250–1600.* Cambridge, England: Cambridge University Press.

Crossette, George

1966   *Founders of the Cosmos Club of Washington, 1878: A Collection of Biographical Sketches and Likenesses of the Sixty Founders.* Washington, D.C.: The Cosmos Club.

Crown, Patricia L.

1994   *Ceramics and Ideology. Salado Polychrome Pottery.* University of New Mexico Press, Albuquerque.

Culin, Stewart

1903   America the Cradle of Asia. *American Association for the Advancement of Science Proceedings* 52: 493–500.

1907   Games of the North American Indians. *Twenty-fourth Annual Report of the Bureau of American Ethnology for 1902–3.* Pp. 3–809.

1958   *Games of the Orient: Korea, China, Japan.* Rutland, Vt. and Tokyo: C. E. Tuttle Co. Originally published in 1895.

Cullum, George W.

1868   *Biographical Register of the Officers and Graduates of the U.S. Military Academy, at West Point, New York, from Its Establishment, March 16, 1802 to the Army Reorganization of 1866–67.* 2 vols. New York: D. Van Nostrand.

Cummings, Byron

1910   The Great Natural Bridges of Utah. *National Geographic Magazine* 21(2): 157–67.

1926   Cuicuilco and the Archaic Culture of Mexico. *Scientific Monthly* 23: 289–304.

1927   Cochise's Yesterday *The Tombstone Epitaph* 449(4): 12, 25.

1933   *Cuicuilco and the Archaic Culture of Mexico.* Tucson: University of Arizona Social Science Bulletin no. 4.

Cummings Publication Council

1959   *The Discovery of Rainbow Bridge. The Natural Bridges of Utah and the Discovery of Betatakin.* Tucson: Cummings Publication Council Bulletin no. 1.

Curtis, Edward S.

1906   Vanishing Indian Types—The Tribes of the Southwest. *Scribner's Magazine* 39: 513–29.

1909a   Indians of the Stone Houses. *Scribner's Magazine* 45: 161–75.

1909b   Village Tribes of the Desert Land. *Scribner's Magazine* 45: 275–87.

1907–30 *The North American Indian; Being a Series of Volumes Picturing and Describing the Indians of the United States, and Alaska.* 20 vols. Vol. I–V, Cambridge, Mass.: University Press; Vol. VI–XX, Norwood, Conn.: Plimpton Press (reprinted, New York and London: Johnson Reprint Corp.) [Vol. I, 1907, Apaches, Jicarillas, Navaho; Vol. II, 1908, Pima, Papago, Qahatika, Mohave, Yuma, Maricopa, Walapai, Havasupai, Yavapai; Vol. XII, 1922, Hopi; Vol. XVI, 1926, Tiwa: Isleta and Taos; Keresan: Cochiti, Santo Domingo, Acoma, Laguna; Vol. XVII, 1926, Tewa: San Juan, San Ildefonso, Nambe; Zuni.])

Cushing, Frank H.

1875   Antiquities of Orleans County, N.Y. Annual *Report of the Board of Regents of the Smithsonian Institution, 1874.* Pp. 375–77. Washington, D.C.

1883   Zuñi Fetiches. *Second Annual Report of the Bureau of Ethnology, 1880–1881.* Pp. 3–45.

1884–85 Zuñi Breadstuff. *Millstone* 9 (1–12); 10 (1–4, 6–8). Book form edition 1920, with introduction by J. W. Powell, Indian Notes and Monographs. vol. 8. New York: Museum of the American Indian, Heye Foundation. Reprinted 1974.

1886   A Study of Pueblo Pottery Growth as Illustrative of Zuñi Cultural Growth. *Fourth Annual Report of the Bureau of Ethnology, 1882–1883.* Pp. 467–521.

1890   Preliminary Notes on the Origin, Working Hypothesis, and Primary Researches of the Hemenway Southwestern Archaeological Expedition. *Congrès International des Américanistes, Compte-Rendu, Berlin, 1888.* Pp. 151–94.

1893a   Frank Hamilton Cushing at the World's Columbian Exposition, 1893, transcribed by D. R. Wilcox from his unpublished diaries. National Anthropological Archives, Smithsonian Institution.

1893b   Monthly Report of Mr. Frank Hamilton Cushing, September 1893, CHP.

1895   The Arrow. *American Anthropologist,* o.s. 8: 307–49.

1896   Outlines of Zuñi Creation Myths. *Thirteenth Annual Report of the Bureau of Ethnology, 1891–1892.* Pp. 321–447.

1901   *Zuñi Folk Tales.* New York: G. P. Putnam's Sons.

1965   *The Nation of the Willows.* Flagstaff, Ariz.: Northland Press. Originally published in 1882.

1970   *My Adventures in Zuñi.* Palo Alto, Calif.: American West Publishing Co. Originally published in 1882–83.

1995   Itinerary of Reconnaissance to Casa Grande Ruins, December 31, 1887 to January 4, 1888. In

A Hemenway Portfolio: Voices and Views from the Hemenway Archaeological Expedition, 1886–1889. C. M. Hinsley and D. R. Wilcox, eds. *Journal of the Southwest* 37(4): 590–604.

Cutright, Paul R., and Michael J. Brodhead

1981 *Elliott Coues, Naturalist and Frontier Historian.* Urbana: University of Illinois Press.

Dall, Caroline H.

1896 Memorial: Professor William Wadden Turner, Jane Wadden Turner. Pamphlet, Biographical Files, National Anthropological Archives. Washington, D.C.: Smithsonian Institution.

Darnell, Regna

1970 The Emergence of Academic Anthropology at the University of Pennsylvania. *Journal of the History of the Behavioral Sciences* 6: 80–92.

1988 *Daniel Garrison Brinton: The "Fearless Critic" of Philadelphia.* Philadelphia: University of Pennsylvania Publications in Anthropology, no. 3.

1990 *Edward Sapir: Linguist, Anthropologist, Humanist.* Berkeley: University of California Press.

1998 *And Along Came Boas: Continuity and Revolution in Americanist Anthropology.* Amsterdam and Philadelphia: J. Benjamins Publishing Co.

Darrah, William C.

1951 *Powell of the Colorado.* Princeton, N.J.: Princeton University Press.

Darwin, Charles

1873 *The Expression of the Emotions in Man and Animals.* New York: D. Appleton and Co.

Dauber, Kenneth

1993 The Indian Arts Fund and the Patronage of Native American Arts. In *Paying the Piper. Causes and Consequences of Art Patronage.* J. H. Balfe, ed. Pp. 76–93. Urbana: University of Illinois Press.

Davis, Barbara A.

1985 *Edward S. Curtis: The Life and Times of a Shadow Catcher.* San Francisco: Chronicle Books.

Davis, Carolyn O.

1995 *My Heart is in the Work: Hattie Cosgrove's Mimbres Archaeology in the American Southwest.* Tucson: Sanpete Publications and Old Pueblo Archaeology Center.

Davis, Keith F.

1981 *Désiré Charnay, Expeditionary Photographer.* 1st ed. Albuquerque: University of New Mexico Press.

Dawdy, Doris O.

1993 *George Montague Wheeler: The Man and the Myth.* Athens [Ohio]: Swallow Press/Ohio University Press.

Deacon, Desley

1997 *Elsie Clews Parsons: Inventing Modern Life.* Chicago: University of Chicago Press.

Deacon, Richard

1966 *Madoc and the Discovery of America; Some New Light on an Old Controversy.* New York: George Braziller.

Debo, Angie

1976 *Geronimo: The Man, His Time, His Place.* 1st ed. Norman: University of Oklahoma Press.

Deegan, Mary Jo

1991 Mary Elizabeth Burroughs Roberts Smith Coolidge (1860–1945). In *Women in Sociology: A Bio-Bibliographical Sourcebook.* M. J. Deegan, ed. Pp. 100–109. New York: Greenwood Press.

DeHuff, John

1922 How We Should Educate the Indian. *El Palacio* 13(7): 61–62.

DeLeon, T. C.

1890 *Four Years in Rebel Capitals: An Inside View of Life in the Southern Confederacy, from Birth to Death.* Mobile, Ala.: The Gossip Printing Co.

1907 *Belles, Beaux and Brains of the Sixties.* New York: G. W. Dillingham Co.

Dellenbaugh, Frederick S.

1962 *A Canyon Voyage.* New Haven, Conn.: Yale University Press. Originally published in 1908.

Deloria, Philip J.

1998 *Playing Indian.* New Haven, Conn.: Yale University Press.

Deloria, Vine, Jr.

1969 *Custer Died for Your Sins: An Indian Manifesto.* New York: Macmillan.

Dewey, Mary E.

1995 Visit of the Zuni Indians to the Summer House of Mrs. Mary Hemenway in 1886. In *A Hemenway Portfolio: Voices and Views from the Hemenway Archaeological Expedition, 1886–1889.* C. M. Hinsley and D. R. Wilcox, eds. *Journal of the Southwest* 37(4): 551–65.

Dexter, Ralph W.

1965 Contributions of Frederic Ward Putnam to Ohio Archaeology. *The Ohio Journal of Science* 65(3): 110–17.

1971 The Putnam-Abbott Correspondence on Paleolithic Man in North America. *Actes XII Congrès Internationale d'Histoires des Sciences* 11: 17–21.

Dickason, Olive P.

1984   *The Myth of the Savage and the Beginnings of French Colonialism in the Americas.* Edmonton: University of Alberta Press.

Dicker, Laverne M.

1977   Laura Adams Armer. *California Historical Quarterly* 56(2): 129–39.

Diehl, Carl

1978   *Americans and German Scholarship, 1770–1870.* New Haven, Conn.: Yale University Press.

Dillehay, Tom D., and David J. Meltzer, eds.

1991   *The First Americans: Search and Research.* Boca Raton: CRC Press.

Dillon, Richard H.

1967   Stephen Long's Great American Desert. *American Philosophical Society Proceedings* 111(2): 93–108.

Dilworth, Leah

1996   *Imagining Indians in the Southwest: Persistent Visions of a Primitive Past.* Washington, D.C.: Smithsonian Institution Press.

Diner, Steven J.

1980   *A City and Its Universities: Public Policy in Chicago, 1892–1919.* Chapel Hill: University of North Carolina Press.

DiPeso, Charles C.

1974   *Casas Grandes: A Fallen Trading Center of the Gran Chichimeca.* 8 vols. Flagstaff, Ariz.: Amerind Foundation, Dragoon and Northland Press.

Dixon, Joseph K.

1913   *The Vanishing Race: The Last Great Indian Council: A Record in Pictures, with photographs by Rodman Wanamaker.* New York: Doubleday, Page.

D'Olwer, Luis N.

1987   *Fray Bernardino de Sahagún (1499–1590).* M. J. Mixco, trans. Salt Lake City: University of Utah Press.

Domenech, Emmanuel H. D.

1858   *Missionary Adventures in Texas and Mexico: A Personal Narrative of Six Years' Sojourn in Those Regions.* London: Longman, Brown, Green, Longman, and Roberts.

1860   *Seven Years' Residence in the Great Deserts of North America.* 2 vols. London: Longman, Green, Longman, and Roberts.

Domínguez, Francisco A.

1956   *The Missions of New Mexico, 1776.* E. B. Adams and A. Chavez, eds. and trans. Albuquerque: University of New Mexico Press.

Donohue, John A.

1969   *After Kino: Jesuit Missions in Northwestern New Spain, 1711–1767.* Rome: Jesuit Historical Institute.

Dorsey, George A.

1903   *Indians of the Southwest.* Chicago: Passenger Department, Atchison, Topeka and Santa Fe Railway System.

1925   *Why We Behave Like Human Beings.* London and New York: Harper and Bros.

1931   *Man's Own Show: Civilization.* London and New York: Harper and Bros.

Dorsey, George A., and H. R. Voth

1901   The Oraibi Soyal Ceremony. *Field Columbian Museum Publication* 55, *Anthropological Series* 3(1): 1–59.

1902   The Mishongnovi Ceremonies of the Snake and Antelope Fraternities. *Field Columbian Museum Publication* 55, *Anthropological Series* 3(3): 159–261.

Douglass, Andrew E.

1914   A Method for Estimating Rainfall by the Growth of Trees. *Carnegie Institution of Washington Publication* 192: 101–21.

1921   Dating Our Prehistoric Ruins: How Growth Rings in Timber Aid in Establishing Relative Ages of the Ruined Pueblos of the Southwest. *Natural History* 21(2): 27–30.

1929   The Secret of the Southwest Solved by Talkative Tree Rings. *National Geographic Magazine* 56(6): 736–70.

Downum, Christian E., and Todd W. Bostwick

1993   *Archaeology of the Pueblo Grande Platform Mound and Surrounding Features. Volume 1 Introduction to the Archival Project and History of Archaeological Research.* Pueblo Grande Museum Anthropological Papers no. 1.

Driver, Harold E., and Alfred L. Kroeber

1932   Quantitative Expression of Cultural Relationships. *University of California Publications in American Archaeology and Ethnology* 31(4): 211–56.

Driver, Harold E., and William C. Massey

1957   *Comparative Studies of North American Indians.* American Philosophical Society Transactions 47(2).

Dryden, John

1962   The Indian Queen, A Tragedy. *The Works of John Dryden* XIII: 182–231, 282–304. Berkeley: University of California Press.

1966   The Indian Emperour or the Conquest of Mexico

by the Spaniards. *The Works of John Dryden* IX: 1–112, 293–330. Berkeley: University of California Press.

1978 The Conquest of Granada. *The Works of John Dryden* XI: 1–218, 436–59. Berkeley: University of California Press.

Dunn, Dorothy

1968 *American Indian Painting of the Southwest and Plains Areas.* Albuquerque: University of New Mexico Press.

Dunne, Peter M., trans.

1955 *Jacobo Sedelmayr, Missionary, Frontiersman, Explorer in Arizona and Sonora. Four Original Manuscript Narratives, 1744–1751.* Tucson: Arizona Pioneers' Historical Society.

Du Ponceau, Peter S.

1838 *Mémoire sur le système grammatical des langues de quelques nations indiennes de l'Amérique du Nord.* Paris: A. Pihan de la Forest.

Du Ponceau, Peter S., et al.

1819 Heads of Enquiry and Observation among Each of the Indian Tribes of the Missouri. Original Manuscript in the American Philosophical Society Library, Philadelphia.

Dyk, Walter

1938 *Son of Old Man Hat: A Navaho Autobiography.* New York: Harcourt, Brace and Co.

Earle, Edwin, and Edward A. Kennard

1971 *Hopi Kachinas.* 2d rev. ed. New York: Museum of the American Indian, Heye Foundation.

Early, Frances H.

1997 *A World without War: How U.S. Feminists and Pacifists Resisted World War I.* Syracuse, N.Y.: Syracuse University Press.

Eggan, Fred

1950 *Social Organization of the Western Pueblos.* Chicago: University of Chicago Press.

1979a Pueblos: Introduction. *Handbook of North American Indians, vol. 9, Southwest.* Pp. 224–235. Washington, D.C.: Smithsonian Institution.

1979b H. R. Voth, Ethnologist. In *Hopi Material Culture: Artifacts Gathered by H. R. Voth in the Fred Harvey Collection.* B. Wright, ed. Pp. 1–7. Flagstaff, Ariz.: Northland Press, and Phoenix: The Heard Museum.

Eldredge, Charles C., Julie Schimmel, and William H. Truettner

1986 *Art in New Mexico, 1900–1945: Paths to Taos and Santa Fe.* New York: Abbeville Press.

Ellis, Bruce

1969 Kenneth Milton Chapman. *El Palacio* 75(2): 35–39.

Elliott, Melinda

1991 *Exploring Human Worlds: A History of the School of American Research.* Santa Fe: School of American Research.

1995 *Great Excavations: Tales of Early Southwestern Archaeology, 1888–1939.* Santa Fe: School of American Research.

Emory, W. H.

1848 *Notes of a Military Reconnaissance from Fort Leavenworth, in Missouri to San Diego in California, including Parts of the Arkansas, Del Norte, and Gila Rivers.* Pp. 1–126. 30th Cong., 1st sess. Senate Executive Doc. no. 7.

1857 *Report on the United States and Mexican Boundary Survey Made under the Direction of Secretary of the Interior.* Vol. 1. House of Representatives, 34th Cong., 1st sess., House Executive Doc. no. 135; Senate Executive Doc. no. 108. Washington.

1951 *Lieutenant Emory Reports: A Reprint of Lieutenant W. H. Emory's Notes of a Military Reconnaissance.* Introduction and notes by R. Calvin. Albuquerque: University of New Mexico Press.

Estergreen, M. Morgan

1962 *Kit Carson. A Portrait in Courage.* Norman: University of Oklahoma Press.

Ethnological Society of Paris

1841 *Instruciones générales addressées aux voyageurs.* Ethnological Society of Paris, Memoirs 1.

Euler, Robert C.

1965 Foreword to Frank Hamilton Cushing, *The Nation of the Willows.* Pp. 1–7. Flagstaff, Ariz.: Northland Press.

Ewers, John C.

1955 *The Horse in Blackfoot Indian Culture, with Comparative Material from Other Western Tribes.* Bureau of American Ethnology Bulletin no. 159.

Ezell, Paul H.

1983 History of the Pima. *Handbook of North American Indian Languages, vol. 10, Southwest.* Pp. 149–60. Washington, D.C.: Smithsonian Institution.

Fabian, Johannes

1983 *Time and the Other: How Anthropology Makes Its Object.* New York: Columbia University Press.

1991 *Time and the Work of Anthropology: Critical Essays 1971–1991.* Chur, Switzerland and Philadelphia: Harwood Academic Publishers.

Fagan, Brian M.

1984   *The Aztecs*. New York: W. H. Freeman.

Fagin, Nancy L.

1984   Closed Collections and Open Appeals: The Two
        Anthropology Exhibits at the Chicago World's
        Columbian Exposition of 1893. *Curator* 27(4):
        249–64.

Fane, Diana

1991a   The Language of Things: Stewart Culin as
        Collector. In *Objects of Myth and Memory: Ameri-
        can Indian Art at The Brooklyn Museum*. D. Fane,
        I. Jacknis, and L. M. Breen, eds. Pp. 13–27.
        Brooklyn: The Brooklyn Museum in association
        with University of Washington Press.

1991b   The Southwest. In *Objects of Myth and Memory:
        American Indian Art at The Brooklyn Museum*.
        D. Fane, I. Jacknis, and L. M. Breen, eds. Pp.
        45–159. Brooklyn: The Brooklyn Museum in asso-
        ciation with University of Washington Press.

1992   New Questions for "Old Things": The Brooklyn
        Museum's Zuni Collection. In *The Early Years of
        Native American Art History: the Politics of Schol-
        arship and Collecting*. J. C. Berlo, ed. Pp. 62–87.
        Seattle: University of Washington Press, and Van-
        couver: University of British Columbia Press.

1993   Reproducing the Pre-Columbian Past: Casts and
        Models in Exhibitions of Ancient America,
        1824–1935. In *Collecting the Pre-Columbian Past*.
        E. H. Boone, ed. Pp. 141–76. Washington, D.C.:
        Dumbarton Oaks Research Library and
        Collection.

Fane, Diana, Ira Jacknis, and Lise M. Breen

1991   *Objects of Myth and Memory: American Indian Art
        at the Brooklyn Museum*. Brooklyn: The Brooklyn
        Museum in Association with University of Wash-
        ington Press.

Farella, John R.

1984   *The Main Stalk: A Synthesis of Navajo Philosophy*.
        Tucson: University of Arizona Press.

Farington, A. C.

1972   Introduction. In *Desert Drums: The Pueblo Indi-
        ans of New Mexico, 1540–1928,* by Leo Crane, Pp.
        iii–xiv. Glorieta, N.M.: Rio Grande Press. Reprint
        of 1928 edition. [Introduction is only in reprint
        edition]

Faris, James C.

1990   *The Nightway: A History and a History of Docu-
        mentation of a Navajo Ceremonial*. Albuquerque:
        University of New Mexico Press.

Fawcett, David M., and Teri McLuhan

1988   Ruth Leah Bunzel. In *Women Anthropologists:
        A Biographical Dictionary*. U. Gacs, A. Khan,
        J. McIntyre, and R. Weinberg, eds. Pp. 29–36.
        New York: Greenwood Press

Fenton, William N.

1951   Iroquois Studies at Mid-Century. *American Philo-
        sophical Society Proceedings* 95: 296–310.

Fenton, William N., and Elizabeth L. Moore

1974–77 Introduction. In J. F. Lafitau, *Customs of the
        American Indians Compared with the Customs of
        Primitive Times*, 2 vols. 1: xxix–cxix. Toronto:
        Publications of the Champlain Society 48.

Ferdon, Edwin N., Jr.

1993   Introduction: Edgar L. Hewett. The Nature of
        the Man. In E. L. Hewett, *Ancient Communities
        in the American Desert*. Archaeological Society of
        New Mexico Monograph Series: 1: 11–19.

Ferguson, Adam

1966   *An Essay on the History of Civil Society*. D. Forbes,
        ed. Edinburgh: Edinburgh University Press. Orig-
        inally published in 1767.

Ferguson, T. J., and E. Richard Hart

1985   *A Zuñi Atlas*. Norman: University of Oklahoma
        Press.

Fergusson, Harvey

1930   *Footloose McGarnigal*. New York: Alfred A. Knopf.

Fewkes, Jesse W.

1890a   On the Use of the Phonograph among the Zuñi
        Indians. *American Naturalist* 24(283): 687–91.

1890b   A Contribution to Passamaquoddy Folk-lore.
        Journal of American Folk-Lore 3(11): 257–80.

1890c   A Study of Summer Ceremonials at Zuñi and
        Moqui Pueblos. *Bulletin of the Essex Institute*, July
        1890: pp. 89–113.

1891   A Few Summer Ceremonials at Zuñi Pueblo.
        Journal of American Archaeology and Ethnology 1:
        1–61.

1892a   A Few Summer Ceremonials at the Tusayan Pueb-
        los. *Journal of American Archaeology and Ethnology*
        2: 1–159.

1892b   On the Present Condition of a Ruin in Arizona
        Called Casa Grande. *Journal of American Archae-
        ology and Ethnology* 2: 181–93.

1894   Dolls of the Tusayan Indians. *Internationales
        Archiv für Ethnographie* 7: 45–74.

1895a   Catalogue of the Hemenway Collection in the
        Columbian Historical Exposition at Madrid. In
        Report of the United States Commission to the

Columbian Historical Exposition at Madrid in 1892–93. S. B. Luce, comp. Pp. 279–304. Washington, D. C.: Government Printing Office.

1895b The Bandelier Collection of Copies of Documents Relative to the History of New Mexico and Arizona. In *Report of the United States Commission to the Columbian Historical Exposition at Madrid in 1892–93*. S. B. Luce, comp. Pp. 305–26. Washington, D.C.: Government Printing Office.

1896a Preliminary Report of an Expedition to the Cliff Villages of the Red Rock Country and the Tusayan Ruins of Sikyatki and Awatobi, Arizona in 1895. *Smithsonian Institution Annual Report for 1895*. Pp. 537–88.

1896b The Tusayan Ritual: A Study of the Influence of Environment on Aboriginal Cults. *Smithsonian Institution Annual Report for 1895*. Pp. 683–700.

1897a Tusayan Kachinas. *Fifteenth Annual Report of the Bureau of Ethnology, 1893–94*. Pp. 245–313.

1897b Tusayan Snake Ceremonies. *Sixteenth Annual Report of the Bureau of American Ethnology, 1894–95*. Pp. 267–312.

1898a Archeological Expedition to Arizona in 1895. *Bureau of American Ethnology Annual Report, 1895–96*, Pt. 2: 519–744.

1898b Preliminary Account of an Expedition to the Pueblo Ruins near Winslow, Arizona in 1896. *Smithsonian Institution Annual Report for 1896*. Pp. 517–41.

1900a Tusayan Migration Traditions. *Nineteenth Annual Report of the Bureau of American Ethnology, 1897–98*, Pt. 2: 573–633.

1900b Tusayan Flute and Snake Ceremonies. *Nineteenth Annual Report of the Bureau of American Ethnology, 1897–98*, Pt. 2: 957–1011.

1903 Hopi Katcinas, drawn by Native Artists. *Twenty-first Annual Report of the Bureau of American Ethnology, 1899–1900*. Pp. 3–126.

1904 Two Summers' Work in Pueblo Ruins. *Twenty-second Annual Report of the Bureau of American Ethnology, 1900–1901*, Pt. 1: 3–195.

1907 Excavations at Casa Grande, Arizona in 1906–7. *Smithsonian Miscellaneous Collections* 50 (3): 289–329.

1909a *Antiquities of the Mesa Verde National Park: Spruce Tree House*. Bureau of American Ethnology Bulletin 41.

1909b *Antiquities of the Mesa Verde National Park: Cliff Palace*. Bureau of American Ethnology Bulletin 51.

1910 The Butterfly in Hopi Myth and Ritual. *American Anthropologist* 12: 576–94.

1914 Archaeology of the Lower Mimbres Valley, New Mexico. *Smithsonian Miscellaneous Collections* 63 (10): 1 53.

1915 Prehistoric Culture Centers in the West Indies. *Journal of the Washington Academy of Sciences* 5(12): 436–43.

1919a Designs on Prehistoric Hopi Pottery. *Thirty-Third Annual Report of the Bureau of American Ethnology, 1911–12*. Pp. 207–84.

1919b *Biography and Bibliography of Jesse Walter Fewkes: Bibliography compiled by Frances S. Nichols*. Washington, D.C.: National Research Service. Copy in Tozzer Library, Harvard University.

1919c *Prehistoric Villages, Castle and Towers of Southwestern Colorado*. Bureau of American Ethnology Bulletin 70.

1973 *Designs on Prehistoric Hopi Pottery*. New York: Dover Publications. Originally published in 1898.

Fewkes, Jesse W., and John P. Harrington

1925 *Hopi Katcina Songs and Six Other Songs by Hopi Chanters*. Gennett Records, nos. 5757–5761. Reissued, New York: Folkway Records FE 4394, 1964.

Fewkes, Jesse W., and Alexander M. Stephen

1892 The N-ác-nai-ya: a Tusayan Initiation Ceremony. *Journal of American Folk-Lore* 5(18): 189–217.

1893 The Pá-lü-lü-koñ-ti: a Tusayan Ceremony. *Journal of American Folk-Lore* 6(23): 269–82.

Fewkes, J. Walter, A. M. Stephen, and J. G. Owens

1894 The Snake Ceremonials at Walpi. *Journal of American Archaeology and Ethnology* 4.

Field, Stanley

1943 Fifty Years of Progress. *Field Museum News* 14(9–10): 3–10.

Figgins, J.

1927 The Antiquity of Man in America. *Natural History* 27: 229–39.

Findling, J. E., and K. D. Pelle, eds.

1990 *Historical Dictionary of World's Fairs and Expositions, 1851–1988*. New York: Greenwood Press.

Firchow, Peter E.

1984 *Aldous Huxley: Satirist and Novelist*. Minneapolis: University of Minnesota Press.

Fiske, Turbesé L., and Keith Lummis

1975   *Charles F. Lummis: The Man and His West.*
        Norman: University of Oklahoma Press.

Flack, J. K.

1975   *Desideratum in Washington: The Intellectual Com-
        munity in the Capital City, 1870–1900.* Cambridge:
        Schenckman Publishing Co.

Fletcher, Alice C.

1910   *Third Annual Report of the Managing Committee
        of the School of American Archaeology.* Boston: Ar-
        chaeological Institute of America.

Fletcher, John G.

1988   *The Autobiography of John Gould Fletcher: Origi-
        nally Life is My Song.* L. Carpenter, ed. Fayette-
        ville: University of Arkansas Press. Originally
        published in 1937.

Flinn, John J.

1893   *The Best Things to Be Seen at the World's Fair.*
        Chicago: Columbian Guide Co.

Fogelson, Raymond D.

1991   The Red Man in the White City. In *Columbian
        Consequences, vol. 3: The Spanish Borderlands in
        Pan-American Perspective.* D. H. Thomas, ed. Pp.
        73–90. Washington, D.C.: Smithsonian Institu-
        tion Press.

Fontana, Bernard L.

1983   Pima and Papago: Introduction. *Handbook of
        North American Indian Languages, vol. 10, South-
        west.* Pp. 137–48. Washington, D.C.: Smithsonian
        Institution.

1990   Church and Crown. *Journal of the Southwest*
        32(4): 451–61.

Force, Roland W.

1999   *Politics and the Museum of the American Indian:
        The Heye and the Mighty.* Honolulu: Mechas Press.

Fowler, Catherine S.

1978   Sarah Winnemucca, Northern Paiute, ca. 1844–
        1891. In *American Indian Intellectuals.* M. Liberty,
        ed. Pp. 33–42. 1976 Proceedings of the American
        Ethnological Society. St. Paul: West Publishing
        Co.

Fowler, Catherine S., and Don D. Fowler

1981   The Southern Paiute: A.D. 1400–1776. In *The Pro-
        tohistoric Period in the North American Southwest.*
        D. R. Wilcox and B. Masse, eds. Pp. 129–62.
        Tempe: Arizona State University Anthropological
        Research Papers 24.

Fowler, Don D.

1972   *In a Sacred Manner We Live: Photographs of the
        North American Indian by Edward S. Curtis.* Barre,
        Mass.: Barre Publications.

1975   Notes on Inquiries in Anthropology: A Biblio-
        graphic Essay. In *Toward a Science of Man: Essays
        in the History of Anthropology.* T. H. Thoresen, ed.
        Pp. 16–32. The Hague: Mouton.

1978   Models in Great Basin Prehistory. In *Selected Pa-
        pers from the Fourteenth Great Basin Anthropologi-
        cal Conference.* D. Tuohy, ed. Pp. 7–18. Ballena
        Press Publications in Archaeology, Ethnology, and
        History 11.

1986   Conserving American Archaeological Resources.
        In *American Archaeology Past and Future: A Cele-
        bration of the Society for American Archaeology,
        1935–1985.* D. J. Meltzer, D. D. Fowler, and J. A.
        Sabloff, eds. Pp. 135–62. Washington, D.C.:
        Smithsonian Institution Press.

1989   *The Western Photographs of John K. Hillers: Myself
        in the Water.* Washington, D.C.: Smithsonian In-
        stitution Press.

1990   Images of American Indians, 1492–1892. *Halcyon
        90: A Journal of the Humanities* 11: 75–100.
        Reno.

1992   Models of Southwestern Prehistory, 1840–1914. In
        *Rediscovering Our Past: Essays on the History of
        American Archaeology.* J. E. Reyman, ed. Pp.
        15–34. Aldershot, England, and Brookfield,
        U.S.A.: Avebury Press.

1999   Harvard versus Hewett: The Contest for Control
        of Southwestern Archaeology, 1904–1930. In *As-
        sembling the Past: Studies in the Professionalization
        of Archaeology.* A. Kehoe and M. B. Emmerichs,
        eds. Pp. 165–211. Albuquerque: University of
        New Mexico Press.

Fowler, Don D., ed.

1972   *"Photographed All the Best Scenery": Jack Hillers's
        Diary of the Powell Expedition, 1871–1875.* Salt
        Lake City: University of Utah Press.

Fowler, Don D., and Catherine S. Fowler

1969a   John Wesley Powell, Anthropologist. *Utah Histor-
        ical Quarterly* 37: 152–72.

1969b   John Wesley Powell's Second Colorado River Ex-
        pedition, 1871–1872. *Smithsonian Journal of
        History* 3(2): 1–44. Washington, D.C.

1991   The Uses of Natural Man in Natural History.
        In *Columbian Consequences, vol. 3. The Spanish
        Borderlands in Pan-American Perspective.* D. H.
        Thomas, ed. Pp. 37–71. Washington, D.C.:
        Smithsonian Institution Press.

Fowler, Don D., and Catherine S. Fowler, eds.

1971   *Anthropology of the Numa: John Wesley Powell's Manuscripts on the Numic Peoples of Western North America, 1868–1880.* Washington, D.C.: Smithsonian Contributions to Anthropology, no. 14.

Fowler, Don D., and Donald L. Hardesty, eds.

1994   *Others Knowing Others: Perspectives on Ethnographic Careers.* Washington, D.C.: Smithsonian Institution Press.

Fowler, Don D., and John F. Matley

1978   The Palmer Collection from Southwestern Utah, 1875. *University of Utah Anthropological Papers* 99: 19–42.

1979   *Material Culture of the Numa: The John Wesley Powell Collection, 1867–1880.* Washington, D.C.: Smithsonian Contributions to Anthropology, no. 26.

Fowler, Don D., and David R. Wilcox

1999   From Thomas Jefferson to the Pecos Conference: Changing Anthropological Agendas in the North American Southwest. In *Surveying the Record: North American Scientific Exploration to 1930.* E. C. Carter, II, ed. Pp. 197–223. American Philosophical Society Memoirs vol. 231.

Franch, José A.

1973   Juan de Torquemada, 1564–1624. *Handbook of Middle American Indians, vol. 13, Guide to Ethnohistorical Sources*, Pt. Pp. 256–75. Austin: University of Texas Press.

Francis, David R.

1913   *The Universal Exposition of 1904.* 2 vols. St. Louis: Louisiana Purchase Exposition Co.

Franciscan Fathers

1910   *An Ethnologic Dictionary of the Navaho Language.* St. Michaels, Ariz.: The Franciscan Fathers.

Frazer, Robert W.

1965   *Forts of the West: Military Forts and Presidios, and Posts Commonly Called Forts, West of the Mississippi River to 1898.* Norman: University of Oklahoma Press.

Freed, Stanley A., and Ruth S. Freed

1983   Clark Wissler and the Development of Anthropology in the United States. *American Anthropologist* 85(4): 800–825.

Freed, Stanley A., Ruth S. Freed, and Lawrence Williamson

1988   Capitalist Philanthropy and Russian Revolutionaries: The Jesup North Pacific Expedition (1897–1902). *American Anthropologist* 90(1): 7–24.

Freeman, John F.

1965   University Anthropology: Early Departments in the United States. *Kroeber Anthropological Society Papers* 32: 78–90.

Freire-Marreco, Barbara

1914   Tewa Kinship Terms from the Pueblo of Hano, Arizona. *American Anthropologist* 16(2): 269–87.

1930   Temperament in Native American Religion. *Journal of the Royal Anthropological Institute* 60: 363–87.

1931   Folk-history and its Raw Material: White Men's Raids on the Hopi Villages. *New Mexico Historical Review* 6(4): 376–82.

Frémont, John C.

1845   *Report on the Exploring Expedition to the Rocky Mountains in the Year 1842, and Oregon and north California in the Years 1843–'44.* Washington D.C.: Washington, Blair and Rives, Printers.

Frigout, Arlette

1979   Hopi Ceremonial Organization. *Handbook of North American Indians, vol. 9, Southwest.* Pp. 564–76. Washington, D.C.: Smithsonian Institution.

Frink, Maurice, and C. E. Barthelmess

1965   *Photographer on an Army Mule.* Norman: University of Oklahoma Press.

Frisbie, Theodore R.

1973   The Influence of J. Walter Fewkes on Nampeyo: Fact or Fancy? *El Corral de Santa Fe Westerners Brand Book 1973.* Pp. 231–43.

Frowe, Lida G.

1906   The Mesa Verde National Park. *The Modern World* 7(1): 7–12.

Fryer, Judith

1987   Desert, Rock, Shelter, Legend: Willa Cather's Novels of the Southwest. In *The Desert Is No Lady: Southwestern Landscapes in Women's Writing and Art.* V. Norwood and J. Monk, eds. Pp. 27–46. New Haven, Conn.: Yale University Press.

Fülöp-Miller, René

1963   *The Jesuits: A History of the Society of Jesus.* New York: Capricorn Books.

Gallatin, Albert H.

1836   A Synopsis of the Indian Tribes of North America . . . *Archaeologica Americana: Transactions and Collections of the American Antiquarian Society* 2: 1–422. New York.

1845   Notes on the Semi-Civilized Nations of Mexico,

Yucatán, and Central America. *American Ethnological Society Transactions* 1: 1–352.

1848a Ancient Semi-Civilization of New Mexico. *American Ethnological Society Transactions* 2: liii–xcvii.

1848b Hale's Indians of North-West America, and Vocabularies of North America. *American Ethnological Society Transactions* 2: xxiii– clxxxviii, 1–130.

Gallatin, Albert H. and Adams, Henry, ed.

1960 *Writings*, 3 vols. New York: Antiquarian Press. Originally published 1879.

Gallup Intertribal Ceremonial

1926 *Program of Events*. Gallup, N.M.: n.p. Copy in ALAB.

Galvin, John, ed.

1966 *Western America in 1846–1847: The Original Travel Diary of Lt. James W. Abert Who Mapped New Mexico for the United States Army*. San Francisco: John Howell-Books.

1970 *Through the Country of the Comanche Indians in the Fall of the Year 1845: The Journal of a U.S. Army Expedition Led by Lt. James W. Abert of the Topographical Engineers*. San Francisco: John Howell-Books.

Garcés, Francisco

1965 *A Record of Travels in Arizona and California, 1775–1776*. J. Galvin, ed., trans. San Francisco: John Howell-Books.

Garrard, Lewis H.

1938 *Wah-to-yah and the Taos Trail*. Glendale, Calif.: The Arthur H. Clark Co.

Gatschet, Albert S.

1879 Classification into Seven Linguistic Stocks of Western Indian Dialects Contained in Forty vocabularies. *Report upon U.S. Geographical Surveys West of the One-hundredth Meridian in Charge of First Lieut. Geo. M. Wheeler . . .* Volume VII, Appendix: Linguistics. Pp. 399–485. Washington, D.C.: Government Printing Office.

Gautier, Hippolyte

1889 *Les Curiosités de L'Exposition de 1889*. Paris: Librairie Charles Delagrave. Copy in Library of Victoria and Albert Museum, London.

Gennep, Arnold van

1960 *The Rites of Passage*. M. K. Vizedom and G. L. Caffe, trans. Chicago: University of Chicago Press. Originally published in 1909.

Gérando, Joseph-Marie, baron de

1883 Documents anthropologiques: l'ethnographie en 1800. *Revue d'Anthropologie*, 2d series, 6: 152–82.

1969 *The Observation of Savage Peoples*. F. C. T. Moore, ed. and trans. Berkeley: University of California Press.

Gerbi, Antonello

1973 *The Dispute of the New World: The History of a Polemic, 1750–1900*. Rev. ed. J. Moyle, trans. Pittsburgh: University of Pittsburgh Press.

Gerhard, Peter

1993 *The North Frontier of New Spain*. Rev. ed. Norman: University of Oklahoma Press.

Gibson, Charles

1947 Lewis Henry Morgan and the Aztec "Monarchy." *Southwestern Journal of Anthropology* 3(1): 78–84.

1966 *Spain in America*. New York: Harper and Row.

1971 *The Black Legend: Anti-Spanish Attitudes in the Old World and the New*. New York: Alfred A. Knopf.

Gidley, Mick

1998 *Edward S. Curtis and the North American Indian, Incorporated*. Cambridge: Cambridge University Press.

Gilbert, Grove K.

1877 *Report on the Geology of the Henry Mountains*. Washington, D.C.: U.S. Government Printing Office.

1890 *Lake Bonneville*. Washington, D.C.: U.S. Geological Survey Monograph no. 1.

Gill, Sam

1981 *Sacred Words: A Study of Navajo Religion and Prayer*. Westport, Conn.: Greenwood Press.

Gilliland, Marion S.

1975 *The Material Culture of Key Marco, Florida*. Gainesville: University Presses of Florida.

Gillmor, Frances, and Louisa Wade Wetherill

1953 *Traders to the Navajos: The Story of the Wetherills of Kayenta*. Albuquerque: University of New Mexico Press. Originally published in 1934.

Gilman, Benjamin I.

1891 Zuñi Melodies. *Journal of American Ethnology and Archaeology* 1(2): 65–91.

1908 Hopi Songs. *Journal of American Ethnology and Archaeology* 5(1): v–viii, 1–226.

Gilman, Benjamin I., and Katherine H. Stone

1908 The Hemenway Southwestern Expedition. *Journal of American Ethnology and Archaeology* 5(2): 227–35.

Gilpin, Laura

1926 Dream Pictures of My People. *Art and Archaeology* 22: 12–20.

1927   *The Mesa Verde National Park: Reproductions from a Series of Photographs.* Colorado Springs: The Gilpin Publishing Co.

1968   *The Enduring Navaho.* Austin: University of Texas Press.

Givens, Douglas R.

1986   Alfred Vincent Kidder, A Biography. Ph.D. diss., Washington University, St. Louis.

1992   *Alfred Vincent Kidder and the Development of Americanist Archaeology.* Albuquerque: University of New Mexico Press.

Gladwin, Harold S., Emil W. Haury, Edwin B. Sayles, and Nora Gladwin

1937   *Excavations at Snaketown, I: Material Culture.* Gila Pueblo. Medallion Papers no. 25. Globe, Ariz.

Gladwin, Winifred, and Harold S. Gladwin

1934   *A Method for Designation of Cultures and Their Variations.* Gila Pueblo, Medallion Papers no. 15. Globe, Ariz.

Glaser, Meg, Andrea Graham, and Barbara Mackey

1999   *Different Hairs on the Same Dog: the Work of a Public Folklorist.* Elko, Nev.: Western Folklife Center.

Goad, Edgar L.

1939   A Study of the Life of Adolph Francis Alphonse Bandelier, with an Appraisal of His Contributions to American Anthropology and Related Sciences. Ph.D. diss., University of Southern California, Los Angeles.

Goddard, Ives

1996a   Introduction. *Handbook of North American Indians, volume 17, Languages.* Pp. 1–16. Washington, D.C.: Smithsonian Institution.

1996b   The Description of the Native Languages of North America before Boas. *Handbook of North American Indians, volume 17, Languages.* Pp. 17–42. Washington, D.C.: Smithsonian Institution.

Goddard, Pliny E.

1913   *Indians of the Southwest.* New York: American Museum of Natural History.

1933   *Navajo Texts.* American Museum of Natural History Anthropological Papers 33, pt. 1.

Godoy, Ricardo

1977   Franz Boas and His Plans for an International School of American Archaeology and Ethnology in Mexico. *International Journal of the History of the Behavioral Sciences* 13: 22–42.

Goetzmann, William H.

1959   *Army Exploration in the American West, 1803–1863.* New Haven, Conn.: Yale University Press.

1966   *Exploration and Empire: The Explorer and the Scientist in the Winning of the American West.* New York: Alfred A. Knopf.

Goetzmann, William H., and William N. Goetzmann

1986   *The West of the Imagination.* New York: Norton.

Goetzmann, William H., and Kay Sloan

1982   *Looking Far North. The Harriman Expedition to Alaska, 1899.* New York: Viking.

Goldenweiser, Alexander

1933   *History, Psychology, and Culture.* New York: Alfred A. Knopf.

Goldfrank, Esther S.

1927   *The Social and Ceremonial Organization of Cochiti.* American Anthropological Association Memoir 33.

1967   *The Artist of "Isleta Paintings" in Pueblo Society.* Smithsonian Contributions to Anthropology 5.

1977   *Notes on an Undirected Life: As One Anthropologist Tells It.* Queens College Publications in Anthropology 3.

Goldfrank, Esther S. ed.

1962   *Isleta Paintings.* Introduction and Commentary by Elsie Clews Parsons. Bureau of American Ethnology Bulletin 181.

Goodman, David M.

1969   *Arizona Odyssey: Bibliographic Adventures in Nineteenth-Century Magazines.* Tempe: Arizona Historical Foundation.

Gosden, Christopher

1994   *Social Being and Time.* Oxford, England and Cambridge, Mass.: Blackwell.

Gould, L. L.

1990   Buffalo 1901, Pan-American Exposition. In *Historical Dictionary of World's Fairs and Expositions, 1851–1988.* J. R. Findling and K. D. Pelle, eds. Pp. 165–71. New York: Greenwood Press.

Gould, Stephen J.

1981   *The Mismeasure of Man.* New York: W. W. Norton and Co.

Graham, Ian

1977   Lord Kingsborough, Sir Thomas Phillips, and Obadiah Rich: Some Biographical Notes. In *Social Processes in Maya Prehistory.* N. Hammond, ed. Pp. 45–57. London: Academic Press.

Grant, Madison

1916   *The Passing of the Great Race, or the Racial Basis of European History*. New York: Charles Scribner.

Grattan, Virginia L.

1980   *Mary Colter: Builder upon the Red Earth*. Flagstaff, Ariz.: Northland Press.

Graves, Laura

1998   *Thomas Varker Keam, Indian Trader*. Norman: University of Oklahoma Press.

Graybill, Florence C., and Victor Boesen

1976   *Edward Sheriff Curtis. Visions of a Vanishing Race*. New York: Thomas Y. Crowell.

Grayson, Donald K.

1983   *The Establishment of Human Antiquity*. New York: Academic Press.

Green, Reverend C. H.

1893   *Catalogue of Unique Collection of Cliff Dweller Relics*. Privately printed for exhibit at Art Institute of Chicago. Chicago: n.p.

Green, Jesse

1990   *Cushing at Zuni: The Correspondence and Journals of Frank Hamilton Cushing, 1879–1884*. Albuquerque: University of New Mexico Press.

Green, Jesse, ed.

1979   *Zuñi: Selected Writings of Frank Hamilton Cushing*. Lincoln: University of Nebraska Press.

Greenberg, Joseph H.

1987   *Language in the Americas*. Stanford, Calif.: Stanford University Press.

Greene, John C.

1984   *American Science in the Age of Jefferson*. Ames: Iowa State University Press.

Greenhalgh, Paul

1991   *Ephemeral Vistas: The Expositions Universelles, Great Exhibitions and World's Fairs, 1851–1939*. Manchester: Manchester University Press.

Gregg, Josiah

1954   *Commerce of the Prairies*. M. L. Moorhead, ed. 2 vols. Norman: University of Oklahoma Press. Originally published in 1844.

Grey, Zane

1925   *The Vanishing American*. New York: Harper and Bros.

Grotius, Hugo

1962   *The Law of War and Peace*. Indianapolis: Bobbs-Merrill. Originally published 1625.

Gruber, Jacob W.

1986   Archaeology, History, and Culture. In *American Archaeology Past and Future*. D. J. Meltzer, D. D.

Fowler, and J. A. Sabloff, eds. Pp. 163–86. Washington, D.C.: Smithsonian Institution Press.

Gunnerson, Dolores A.

1974   *The Jicarilla Apaches: A Study in Survival*. De Kalb: Northern Illinois University Press.

Gunnerson, James H.

1969   *The Fremont Culture: A Study in Culture Dynamics on the Northern Anasazi Frontier*. Papers of the Peabody Museum of American Archaeology and Ethnology 59(2).

1979   Southern Athapaskan Archaeology. *Handbook of North American Indians, vol. 9, Southwest*. Pp. 162–69. Washington, D.C.: Smithsonian Institution.

Guthe, Carl E.

1925   *Pueblo Pottery Making: A Study at the Village of San Ildefonso*. Papers of the Phillips Academy Southwestern Expedition 2.

Gutiérrez, Ramón A.

1991   *When Jesus Came, the Corn Mothers Went Away: Marriage, Sexuality, and Power in New Mexico, 1500–1846*. Stanford, Calif.: Stanford University Press.

Haas, Mary R.

1969   Grammar or Lexicon? The American Indian Side of the Question from Duponceau to Powell. *International Journal of American Linguistics* 35: 239–55.

Hackett, Charles W.

1937   *Historical Documents Relating to New Mexico, Nueva Vizcaya, and Approaches Thereto, to 1773*, 3 vols. Washington, D.C.: Carnegie Institution of Washington Publication no. 330.

1942   *Revolt of the Pueblo Indians of New Mexico and Otermin's Attempted Reconquest, 1680–1682*. 2 vols. Coronado Cuarto Centennial Publications, 1540–1940, vols. 8–9. Albuquerque: University of New Mexico Press.

Haddon, Alfred C.

1906   Ethnology: Its Scope and Problems. In *Congress of Arts and Science, Universal Exposition, St. Louis, 1904*. H. J. Rogers, ed. 5:549–70. Boston: Houghton Mifflin.

Haeberlin, Herman K.

1916   *The Idea of Fertilization in the Culture of the Pueblo Indians*. American Anthropological Association Memoirs 3.

Hafen, Le Roy R., and Ann W. Hafen, eds.

1960   *Frémont's Fourth Expedition: A Documentary*

Account of the Disaster of 1848–1849 . . . Glendale, Calif.: Arthur H. Clark Co.

Hagan, William T.
1997   *Theodore Roosevelt and Six Friends of the Indian.* Norman: University of Oklahoma Press.

Haile, Berard
1981   *The Upward Moving and Emergence Way: The Gishin Biyé Version.* K. W. Luckert, ed. Lincoln: University of Nebraska Press.

Hale, Kenneth, and David Harris
1979   Historical Linguistics and Archaeology. *Handbook of North American Indians, vol. 9, Southwest.* Pp. 170–77. Washington, D.C.: Smithsonian Institution.

Hales, Peter
1988   *William Henry Jackson and the Transformation of the American Landscape.* Philadelphia: Temple University Press.

Hallman, Peter R.
1999   When Byron Cummings Discovered Arizona's "Ice Age." *Kiva* 65 (2): 125–42.

Hallowell, A. Irving
1960   The Beginnings of Anthropology in America. In *Selected Papers from the American Anthropologist, 1888–1920.* F. De Laguna, ed. Pp. 1–104. Evanston, Ill.: Row, Peterson Co.

Halpern, Katherine S., and Susan B. McGreevy, eds.
1997   *Washington Matthews Studies of Navajo Culture, 1880–1894.* Albuquerque: University of New Mexico Press, in cooperation with the Wheel-wright Museum of the American Indian, Santa Fe.

Hammond, George P., and Edgar F. Goad, eds.
1949   *A Scientist on the Trail: Travel Letters of Adolph F. Bandelier, 1880–1881.* Berkeley: The Quivira Society vol. 10.

Hammond, George P., and Agapito Rey, eds.
1928   *Obregón's History of Sixteenth Century Explorations in Western America . . . 1584.* Los Angeles: Wetzel Publishing.

Hampson, Norman
1983   *Will and Circumstance: Montesquieu, Rousseau and the French Revolution.* Norman: University of Oklahoma Press.

Handy, Moses P., ed.
1893   *World's Columbian Exposition, 1893: Official Catalogue.* Chicago: W. B. Conkey Co.

Hanke, Lewis
1970   *Aristotle and the American Indians: A Study in Race*

Prejudice in the Modern World. Bloomington: Indiana University Press.

Hanson, John W.
1905   *The Official History of the St. Louis World's Fair.* St. Louis: Louisiana Purchase Exposition Publishing Co.

Hardin, Margaret A.
1983   *Gifts of Mother Earth: Ceramics in the Zuni Tradition.* Phoenix: Heard Museum.

1993   Zuni Potters and The Pueblo Potter: The Contributions of Ruth Bunzel. In *Hidden Scholars: Women Anthropologists and the Native American Southwest.* N. J. Parezo, ed. Pp. 259–69. Albuquerque: University of New Mexico Press.

Hardy, R. W. H.
1829   *Travels in the Interior of Mexico, 1825, 1826, 1827, and 1828.* London: H. Colburn and R. Bentley.

Hare, Peter H.
1985   *A Woman's Quest for Science: Portrait of Anthropologist Elsie Clews Parsons.* Buffalo: Prometheus Books.

Haring, C. H.
1963   *The Spanish Empire in America.* New York: Harcourt, Brace, and World.

Harr, John E., and Peter J. Johnson
1988   *The Rockefeller Century.* New York: Charles Scribner's Sons.

Harrell, David
1992   *From Mesa Verde to The Professor's House.* Albuquerque: University of New Mexico Press.

Harrington, John P.
1910a Franz Nikolaus Finck. *American Anthropologist* 12: 724–28.

1910b The Language of the "Tano Indians" of New Mexico. *International Congress of Americanists, Buenos Aires 1910* 2: 321.

1916   The Ethnogeography of the Tewa Indians. *Twenty-ninth Annual Report of the Bureau of American Ethnology, 1907–8.* Pp. 29–618.

Harrington, Marie
1985   *On the Trail of Forgotten People: A Personal Account of the Life and Career of Mark Raymond Harrington.* Reno: Great Basin Press.

Harrington, Mark R.
1933   *Gypsum Cave, Nevada.* Southwest Museum Papers no. 8.

Harris, Marvin
1968   *The Rise of Anthropological Theory: A History of*

Theories of Culture. New York: Crowell Publications.

Harris, Neil

1962 The Gilded Age Revisited: Boston and the Museum Movement. *American Quarterly* 14: 546–66.

1981 Cultural Institutions and American Modernization. *Journal of Library History* 16: 28–47.

Harvey, Mark W. T.

1988 Adolph Bandelier. In *Historians of the American Frontier: a Bio-bibliographical Sourcebook.* J. R. Wunder, ed. Pp. 64–79. New York: Greenwood Press.

Harwell, Henry O., and Marsha C. S. Kelly

1983 Maricopa. *Handbook of North American Indians, vol. 10, Southwest.* Pp. 71–85. Washington, D.C.: Smithsonian Institution.

Hartley, Marsden

1920 Red Man Ceremonials: An American Plea for an American Esthetics. *Art and Archaeology* 9(1): 7–14.

Haury, Emil W.

1936 *The Mogollon Culture of Southwestern New Mexico.* Globe, Ariz.: Gila Pueblo Medallion Papers 20.

1945a The Problems of Contacts between Mexico and the Southwestern United States. *Southwestern Journal of Anthropology* 1(1): 55–74.

1945b *The Excavation of Los Muertos and Neighboring Ruins in the Salt River Valley, Southern Arizona.* Papers of the Peabody Museum, Harvard University 24(1).

1950 *The Stratigraphy and Archaeology of Ventana Cave, Arizona.* Tucson: University of Arizona Press.

1976a *The Hohokam, Desert Farmers and Craftsmen: Excavations at Snaketown, 1964–65.* Tucson: University of Arizona Press.

1976b Concluding Remarks. In E. B. Sayles, *The Cochise Cultural Sequence in Southeastern Arizona.* Pp. 158–66. University of Arizona Anthropological Papers 42.

1986 HH-39: Recollections of a Dramatic Moment in Southwestern Archaeology. In *Emil W. Haury's Prehistory of the American Southwest.* J. J. Reid and D. E. Doyel, eds. Pp. 55–60. Tucson: University of Arizona Press.

1995 Wherefore a Harvard Ph.D.? In *A Hemenway Portfolio: Voices and Views from the Hemenway Archaeological Expedition, 1886–1889.* C. M. Hinsley and D. R. Wilcox, eds. *Journal of the Southwest* 37(4): 710–33.

Haynes, James B.

1910 *History of the Trans-Mississippi and International Exposition of 1898.* Omaha: n.p.

Hays-Gilpin, Kelley A., Ann C. Deegan, and Elizabeth A. Morris

1998 *Prehistoric Sandals from Northeastern Arizona: The Earl H. Morris and Ann Axtell Morris Research.* University of Arizona Anthropological Papers 62.

Hecht, Robert A.

1991 *Oliver La Farge and the American Indian: A Biography.* Metuchen, N.J.: Scarecrow Press.

Hektoen, Ludwig

1929 Biographical Memoir of Theophil Mitchell Prudden (1849–1924). *National Academy of Sciences Biographical Memoirs* 12: 73–93.

Hellman, Geoffrey

1969 *Bankers, Bones and Beetles: The First Century of the American Museum of Natural History.* Garden City, N.Y.: Natural History Press.

Henderson, Alice C., ed.

1928 *The Turquoise Trail, An Anthology of New Mexico Poetry.* Boston: Houghton Mifflin.

Henderson, Junius, and John P. Harrington

1914 *Ethnozoology of the Tewa Indians.* Bureau of American Ethnology Bulletin no. 56.

Henige, David

1998 *Numbers from Nowhere: The American Indian Contact Population Debate.* Norman: University of Oklahoma Press.

Hennessy, C. A.

1978 *The Frontier in Latin American History.* London: Edward Arnold Publications.

Herder, Johann G.

1966 *Outlines of a Philosophy of the History of Man.* New York: Bergman Publishers. Originally published in 1800.

Herskovits, Melville J.

1953 *Franz Boas. The Science of Man in the Making.* New York: Charles Scribner's Sons.

Hewett, Edgar L.

1903 Archaeology [of New Mexico Territory]. In *Report of the Governor of New Mexico to the Secretary of the Interior.* Pp. 370–74. Washington, D.C.: U.S. Government Printing Office.

1904a Government Supervision of Historic and Prehistoric Ruins. *Science* 20 (517): 722–27.

1904b *Memorandum Concerning the Historic and Prehistoric Ruins of Arizona, New Mexico, Colorado and Utah, and their Preservation: General Land Office Circular Relating to Historic and Prehistoric Ruins of the Southwest and Their Preservation.* Washington, D.C.: U.S. Government Printing Office. Reprinted 1905 as A General View of the Archaeology of the Pueblo Region. *Smithsonian Institution Annual Report for 1904.* Pp. 583–605.

1905 Preservation of Antiquities. *American Anthropologist* 7: 164–66.

1906 Preservation of American Antiquities: Progress during the Last Year; Needed Legislation. *American Anthropologist* 8: 109–14.

1907–18 Organic Act and Annual Reports of the School of American Archaeology, 1906–1917. Santa Fe: Archives, School of American Research.

1908 Report on the Ruins of Mesa Verde, Colorado. Typescript, MVRCA.

1919–29 Compiled Annual Reports of the School of American Research. Santa Fe: Archives, School of American Research.

1921a The Chaco Canyon and Its Ancient Monuments. *Art and Archaeology* 11(1–2): 3–28.

1921b The Excavation of Chettro Kettle, Chaco Canyon, 1920. *Art and Archaeology* 11(1–2): 45–62.

1922a Art of the Earliest Americans. *El Palacio* 13(10): 124.

1922b The Chaco Canyon in 1921. *Art and Archaeology* 14(3): 115–31.

1929 *Preservation of the Scientific Resources of New Mexico.* Santa Fe: School of American Research.

1938 *Pajarito Plateau and Its Ancient People.* Albuquerque: School of American Research and University of New Mexico Press.

1943 *From Cave Dwelling to Mount Olympus.* Albuquerque: University of New Mexico Press.

1943 *Campfire and Trail.* Albuquerque: University of New Mexico Press.

1993 *Ancient Communities in the American Desert: Archaeological Research on the Distribution and Social Organization of the Ancient Populations of the Southwestern United States and Northern Mexico.* Archaeological Society of New Mexico Monograph Series: 1. Originally published 1908 as *Les Communautés Anciennes dans le Désert Américain* . . . Genéve: Librairie Kündig.

Hewitt, J. N. B.
1895 James Owen Dorsey. *American Anthropologist*, o.s. 8: 180–83.

Heÿink, Jac., and F. W. Hodge
1931 Herman Frederick Carel ten Kate. *American Anthropologist* 33: 415–18.

Hicb, Louis A.
1979 Hopi World View. *Handbook of North American Indians, vol. 9, Southwest.* Pp. 577–80. Washington, D.C.: Smithsonian Institution.

1993 Elsie Clews Parsons in the Southwest. In *Hidden Scholars: Women Anthropologists in the Native American Southwest.* N. J. Parezo, ed. Pp. 63–75. Albuquerque: University of New Mexico Press.

Higgins, C. A.
1905 *To California over the Santa Fe Trail.* Chicago: Passenger Dept., Santa Fe Railway.

Higinbotham, Harlow
1898 *Report of the President to the Board of Directors of the World's Columbian Exposition.* Chicago: Rand, McNally and Co.

Hilger, Michael
1986 *The American Indian in Film.* Metuchen, N.J.: Scarecrow Press.

Hine, Robert V.
1968 *Bartlett's West: Drawing the Mexican Boundary.* New Haven, Conn.: Yale University Press.

1982 *In the Shadow of Frémont: Edward Kern and the Art of Exploration, 1845–1860.* 2d. ed. Norman: University of Oklahoma Press.

Hinsley, Curtis M., Jr.
1981 *Savages and Scientists: The Smithsonian Institution and the Development of American Anthropology, 1846–1910.* Washington, D.C.: Smithsonian Institution Press.

1983 Ethnographic Charisma and Scientific Routine: Cushing and Fewkes in the American Southwest, 1879–1893. In *Observers Observed: Essays on Ethnographic Fieldwork.* G. W. Stocking, Jr., ed. Pp. 53–69. History of Anthropology, vol. 1. Madison: University of Wisconsin Press.

1985 From Shell Heaps to Stelae: Early Anthropology at the Peabody Museum. In *Objects and Others: Essays on Museums and Material Culture.* G. W. Stocking, Jr., ed. Pp. 49–74. History of Anthropology vol. 3. Madison: University of Wisconsin Press.

1986 Edgar Lee Hewett and the School of American Research in Santa Fe, 1906–1912. In *American Ar-*

chaeology Past and Future. D. J. Meltzer, D. D. Fowler, and J. A. Sabloff, eds. Pp. 217–36. Washington, D.C.: Smithsonian Institution Press.

1992a Collecting Cultures and Cultures of Collecting: the Lure of the American Southwest, 1880–1915. *Museum Anthropology* 16(1): 12–20.

1992b The Museum Origins of Harvard Anthropology 1866–1915. In *Science at Harvard University: Historical Perspectives*. C. A. Elliott and M. W. Rossiter, eds. Pp. 121–45. Bethlehem, Pa.: Lehigh University Press.

1996 Boston Meets the Southwest: The World of Frank Hamilton Cushing and Sylvester Baxter. In *The Southwest in the American Imagination: The Writings of Sylvester Baxter, 1881–1889*. C. M. Hinsley and D. R. Wilcox, eds. Pp. 3–33. Tucson: University of Arizona Press.

1999 Life on the Margins: the Ethnographic Poetics of Frank Hamilton Cushing. *Journal of the Southwest* 41(3): 371–382.

Hinsley, Curtis M., and David R. Wilcox, eds.

1995 *A Hemenway Portfolio: Voices and Views from the Hemenway Archaeological Expedition, 1886–1889*. In *Journal of the Southwest* 37(4): 519–744.

1996 *The Southwest in the American Imagination: The Writings of Sylvester Baxter, 1881–1889*. Tucson: University of Arizona Press.

Hispanic Society, The

1954 *A History of the Hispanic Society of America Museum and Library, 1904–1954*. New York: The Hispanic Society.

Hobbes, Thomas

1965 *Leviathan, or The Matter, Forme and Power of a Commonwealth, Ecclesiasticall and Civil*. M. Oakeshott, ed. New York: Washington Square Press.

Hoben, Patricia E.

1966 The Establishment of Mesa Verde as a National Park. Master's thesis, University of Oklahoma, Norman. Copy in MVRCA.

Hodge, Frederick W.

1896 John Gregory Bourke. *American Anthropologist* o.s. 9: 245–48.

1903 Frank Russell. *American Anthropologist* 5: 737–38.

1907 The Narrative of the Expedition of Coronado, by Pedro de Castañeda. In *Spanish Explorers in the Southern United States, 1528–1543*. F. W. Hodge and T. H. Lewis, eds. Pp. 273–387. New York: Charles Scribner's Sons.

1912 W J McGee. *American Anthropologist* 14: 683–87.

1924 Motion-Pictures at Zuni. *Indian Notes* 1: 29–30.

1932 Biographical Sketch and Bibliography of Adolphe Francis Alphonse Bandelier. *New Mexico Historical Review* 7(4): 353–70.

1937 *History of Hawikuh, New Mexico, One of the So-called Cities of Cíbola*. Los Angeles: Hodge Anniversary Fund, Publication no. 1.

1945 Foreword. In Emil W. Haury, *The Excavation of Los Muertos and Neighboring Ruins in the Salt River Valley, Southern Arizona*. Pp. vii–ix. Papers of the Peabody Museum of American Archaeology and Ethnology 24(1).

Hodge, Frederick W., ed.

1900 In Memoriam: Frank Hamilton Cushing ("Remarks" by W. J. McGee, W. H. Holmes, J. W. Powell, A. C. Fletcher, W. Matthews, S. Culin, and J. D. McGuire). *American Anthropologist* 2: 345–79.

1906 Recent Progress in American Anthropology. *American Anthropologist* 8: 441–558.

1907–10 *Handbook of American Indians North of Mexico*. Bureau of American Ethnology Bulletin 30, Pts. 1–2.

Hodge, Frederick W., and T. H. Lewis, eds.

1907 *Spanish Explorers in the Southern United States, 1528–1543*. New York: Charles Scribner's Sons.

Hodgen, Margaret T.

1964 *Early Anthropology in the Sixteenth and Seventeenth Centuries*. Philadelphia: University of Pennsylvania Press.

1977 *The Doctrine of Survivals: A Chapter in the History of Scientific Method in the Study of Man*. Folcraft, Pa.: Folcraft Library Editions. Originally published in 1936.

Hofstadter, Richard, and Walter P. Metzer

1955 *The Development of Academic Freedom in the United States*. New York: Columbia University Press.

Hoijer, Harry

1938 The Southern Athapaskan Languages. *American Anthropologist* 40(1): 75–87.

1956 The Chronology of the Athapaskan Languages. *International Journal of American Linguistics* 22(4): 219–32.

Hollcroft, Temple R., ed.

1953 The Diary of William Fellowes Morgan. *Scientific Monthly* 77(3): 119–28.

Hollinger, David A.

1975 Ethnic Diversity, Cosmopolitanism, and the

Emergence of the American Liberal Intelligentsia. *American Quarterly* 27: 133–51.

Hollon, W. E.

1949   *The Lost Pathfinder, Zebulon Montgomery Pike.* Norman: University of Oklahoma Press.

Holmes, William H.

1876   A Note on the Ancient Remains of Southwestern Colorado Examined during the Summer of 1875. *Bulletin of the Geological and Geographical Survey of the Territories* 2, no. 1: 3–24. Washington, D.C.

1886a   Pottery of the Ancient Pueblos. *Fourth Annual Report of the Bureau of Ethnology, 1882–83.* Pp. 210–360.

1886b   Origin and Development of Form and Ornament in Ceramic Art. *Fourth Annual Report of the Bureau of Ethnology,* 1882–83. Pp. 437–65.

1888   A Study of the Textile Art in Its Relation to the Development of Form and Ornament. *Sixth Annual Report of the Bureau of Ethnology, 1884–85.* Pp. 189–252.

1893a   Are There Traces of Man in the Trenton Gravels? *Journal of Geology* 1: 15–37.

1893b   The World's Fair Congress of Anthropology. *American Anthropologist* o.s. 6: 423–34.

1894   Natural History of Flaked Stone Implements. In *Memoirs, International Congress of Anthropology, Chicago, 1894* C. S. Wake, ed. Pp. 120–39. Chicago: Shulte Publishing Co., Chicago.

1902   Classification and Arrangement of the Exhibits of an Anthropological Museum. *Journal of the Anthropological Institute of Great Britain and Ireland* 32: 353–72.

1903   Classification and Arrangement of the Exhibits of the Anthropological Museum. *Annual Report of the U.S. National Museum for 1900–01.* Pp. 255–78.

1914   Areas of American Culture Characterization Tentatively Outlined as an Aid in the Study of the Antiquities. *American Anthropologist* 16: 413–46.

Honour, Hugh

1975   *The New Golden Land: European Images of America from the Discoveries to the Present Time.* New York: Pantheon Books.

Hooton, Earnest A.

1930   *The Indians of Pecos Pueblo, A Study of Their Skeletal Remains.* Papers of the Southwestern Expedition, Phillips Academy no. 4. Andover, Mass.: Yale University Press.

Horan, James D.

1966   *Timothy O'Sullivan: America's Forgotten Photographer.* Garden City, N.Y.: Doubleday

Horgan, Paul

1979   *Josiah Gregg and His Vision of the Early West.* New York: Farrar Straus Giroux.

Horn, Calvin

1963   *New Mexico's Troubled Years: The Story of the Early Territorial Governors.* Albuquerque: Horn and Wallace.

Hosmer, Charles B., Jr.

1981   *Preservation Comes of Age: From Williamsburg to the National Trust, 1926–1949.* 2 vols. Charlottesville: University Press of Virginia.

Hough, Walter

1892   Catálogo de la Colección Etnológica del Museo Nacional de los Estados Unidos. In *Catálogo de los Objetos expuestos por la Comisión de los Estados Unidos de America en la Exposición Histórico-Americana de Madrid, 1892.* S. B. Luce, comp. Pp. 3–120. Washington, D.C.: U.S. Government Printing Office.

1893   The Columbian Historical Exposition in Madrid. *American Anthropologist* o.s. 6: 270–77.

1908   Otis Tufton Mason. *American Anthropologist* 10: 661–67.

1917   A Revival of the Ancient Hopi Pottery Art. *American Anthropologist* 19: 322–23.

1931   Jesse Walter Fewkes. *American Anthropologist* 33: 92–97.

1932   Jesse Walter Fewkes (1850–1930). *National Academy of Sciences Biographical Memoirs* 15: 261–83.

Houlihan, Patrick T., and Betsy E. Houlihan

1986   *Lummis in the Pueblos.* Flagstaff, Ariz.: Northland Press.

Hovens, Pieter, trans.

1995   Ten Kate's Hemenway Expedition Diary, 1887–1888. In *A Hemenway Portfolio: Voices and Views from the Hemenway Archaeological Expedition, 1886–1889.* C. M. Hinsley and D. R. Wilcox, eds. Pp. 635–700. *Journal of the Southwest* 37(4): 519–744.

Hoving, Thomas

1993   *Making the Mummies Dance: Inside the Metropolitan Museum of Art.* New York: Simon and Schuster.

Howard, Kathleen L., and Diana F. Pardue

1996   *Inventing the Southwest: The Fred Harvey Company*

and Native American Art. Flagstaff, Ariz.: Northland Publishing.

Hoxie, Frederick E.

1979   Red Man's Burden. *Antioch Review* 37: 326–42.

Hrdlička, Aleš

1902   Ethnological Work in the Southwestern United States and Mexico. *American Museum Journal* 2(7): 68–72.

1908   *Physiological and Medical Observations among the Indians of the Southwestern United States and Northern Mexico.* Bureau of American Ethnology Bulletin 34.

1909   On the Stature of the Indians of the Southwest and Northern Mexico. In *Putnam Anniversary Volume.* Pp. 406–26. New York: G. E. Stechert and Co.

1917a   The Genesis of the American Indian. *Proceedings of the XIXth International Congress of Americanists (Washington).* Pp. 559–68.

1917b   The Most Ancient Skeletal Remains of Man. *Smithsonian Institution Annual Report for 1916.* Pp. 491–552.

1925a   *The Old Americans.* Baltimore: Williams and Wilkins Co.

1925b   The Origin and Antiquity of the American Indian. *Smithsonian Institution Annual Report for 1923.* Pp. 481–94.

1931   Catalogue of Human Crania in the United States National Museum Collections: Pueblos, Southern Utah Basket-Makers, Navaho. *U.S. National Museum Proceedings,* vol. 78, article 2. Pp. 1–95.

1935   The Pueblos, with Comparative Data on the Bulk of the Tribes of the Southwest and Northern Mexico. *American Journal of Physical Anthropology* 20: 235–460.

Huddleston, Lee E.

1967   *Origins of the American Indians: European Concepts, 1492–1729.* Austin: University of Texas Press.

Hughes, Dorothy B.

1939   *Pueblo on the Mesa: The First Fifty Years at the University of New Mexico.* Albuquerque: University of New Mexico Press.

Hughte, Phil

1994   *A Zuñi Artist Looks at Frank Hamilton Cushing.* Zuñi, N.M.: Pueblo of Zuñi Arts and Crafts; A:shiwi A:wan Museum and Heritage Center.

Humboldt, Alexander von

1814   *Researches Concerning the Institutions and Monuments of the Ancient Inhabitants of America.* 2 vols. Helen M. Williams, trans. London: Longman, Hurst, Rees, Orme, and Brown.

1858   Introduction to Balduin Möllhausen, *Diary of a Journey from the Mississippi to the Coasts of the Pacific with a United States Government Expedition.* 2 vols. Mrs. Percy Sinnett, trans. London: Longman, Brown, Green, Longmans & Roberts.

Hunt, Charles B.

1967   *Physiography of the United States.* San Francisco: W. H. Freeman and Co.

Hunt, David C., Marsha V. Gallagher, and William J. Orr

1984   *Karl Bodmer's America.* Lincoln: Joslyn Art Museum and University of Nebraska Press.

Huntington, Ellsworth

1912   The Fluctuating Climate of North America, Part I: The Ruins of the Hohokam. *The Geographical Journal* 40(3): 264–80.

Huseman, Ben W.

1995   *Wild River, Timeless Canyons: Balduin Möllhausen's Watercolors of the Colorado.* Fort Worth: Amon Carter Museum, and Tucson: University of Arizona Press.

Huxley, Aldous

1932   *Brave New World.* London: Chatto and Windus.

Hyatt, Marshall

1990   *Franz Boas, Social Activist: The Dynamics of Ethnicity.* New York: Greenwood Press.

Ingram, J. S.

1876   *Centennial Exhibition Described and Illustrated. . . .* Philadelphia: Hubbard Brothers.

Ives, Joseph C.

1861   *Report upon the Colorado River of the West, Explored in 1857 and 1858.* 36th Cong., 1st sess. House Executive Doc. no. 90. Washington, D.C.

Ives, Ronald L., trans. and ed.

1939   Sedelmayr's Relación of 1746. *Bureau of American Ethnology Bulletin 123, Anthropological Papers* no. 9. Pp. 97–117.

Jacknis, Ira

1985   Franz Boas and Exhibits: On the Limitations of the Museum Method of Anthropology. In *Objects and Others: Essays on Museums and Material Culture.* G. W. Stocking, Jr., ed. Pp. 75–111. History of Anthropology, vol. 3. Madison: University of Wisconsin Press.

1991a   Northwest Coast Indian Culture and the World's Columbian Exposition. In *Columbian*

Consequences, vol. 3, The Spanish Borderlands in Pan-American Perspective. D. H. Thomas, ed. Pp. 91–118. Washington, D.C.: Smithsonian Institution Press.

1991b The Road to Beauty: Stewart Culin's American Indian Exhibitions at the Brooklyn Museum. In *Objects of Myth and Memory: American Indian Art at The Brooklyn Museum.* D. Fane, I. Jacknis, and L. M. Breen, eds. Pp. 29–44. Brooklyn: The Brooklyn Museum in association with University of Washington Press.

1996 The Ethnographic Object and the Object of Ethnology in the Early Career of Franz Boas. In *Volksgeist as Method and Ethic: Essays on Boasian Ethnography and the German Anthropological Tradition.* G. W. Stocking, Jr., ed. Pp. 185–214. History of Anthropology, vol. 8. Madison: University of Wisconsin Press.

Jackson, Clarence S.
1947 *Picture Maker of the Old West: William Henry Jackson.* New York: C. Scribner's Sons.

Jackson, Donald
1981 *Thomas Jefferson and the Stony Mountains: Exploring the West from Monticello.* Urbana: University of Illinois Press.

Jackson, Donald, ed.
1978 *Letters of the Lewis and Clark Expedition, with Related Documents, 1783–1854.* 2d ed. 2 vols. Urbana: University of Illinois Press.

Jackson, Donald, and Mary Lee Spence, eds.
1970–84 *The Expeditions of John Charles Frémont.* Urbana: University of Illinois Press.

Jackson, Helen H.
1881 *A Century of Dishonor: A Sketch of the United States Government's Dealings with Some of the Indian Tribes.* 1st ed. New York: Harper and Brothers. 2d ed., 1885.

1884 *Ramona: A Story.* Boston: Roberts Brothers.

Jackson, William H.
1875 Ancient Ruins in Southwestern Colorado. *Bulletin of the United States Geological and Geographical Survey of the Territories* no. 1: 17–30. Washington, D.C.

1876 A Notice of Ancient Ruins in Arizona and Utah Lying about the Rio San Juan. *Bulletin of the United States Geological and Geographical Survey of the Territories* 2, no. 2: 25–45. Washington, D.C.

1940 *Time Exposure: The Autobiography of William Henry Jackson.* New York: G. P. Putnam's Sons.

Jacobs, Martina M.
1980 Hopi Kachina: Spirit of Life. *Carnegie Magazine* 54(9): 6–12. Pittsburgh: Carnegie Museum of Natural History.

Jameson, J. Franklin.
1907 Department of Historical Research. *Carnegie Institution of Washington Yearbook* no. 5, 1906: 186–201.

Janetski, Joel C.
1997 150 Years of Utah Archaeology. *Utah Historical Quarterly* 65(2): 100–133.

Jeançon, J. A.
1923 *Excavations in the Chama Valley, New Mexico.* Bureau of American Ethnology Bulletin 81.

Jefferson, Thomas
1944 Notes on Virginia. In *The Life and Selected Writings of Thomas Jefferson.* A. Koch and W. Peden, eds. Pp. 185–288. New York: The Modern Library. Originally published 1784.

Jefferson, Thomas, et al.
1799 Circular Letter. *American Philosophical Society Transactions* 4: xxxvii–xxxix. Reprinted 1809 in *Transactions*, vol. 5.

Jennings, Francis
1976 *The Invasion of America: Indians, Colonialism, and the Cant of Conquest.* New York: W. W. Norton.

Jeter, James, and Paula M. Juelke
1978 *The Saltillo Sarape.* Santa Barbara: New World Arts.

Jett, Stephen C.
1983 Precolumbian Transoceanic Connections. In *Ancient North Americans.* J. D. Jennings, ed. Pp. 557–613. San Francisco: W. H. Freeman.

1992 The Great "Race" to "Discover" Rainbow Natural Bridge in 1909. *The Kiva* 58(1): 3–66.

John, Elizabeth A. H.
1975 *Storms Brewed in Other Men's Worlds: The Confrontation of Indians, Spanish, and French in the Southwest, 1540–1795.* College Station: Texas A&M University Press.

Johnson, Alvin S.
1952 *Pioneer's Progress, an Autobiography.* New York: Viking Press.

Johnson, Tim, ed.
1998 *Spirit Capture: Photographs from the National Museum of the American Indian.* Washington, D.C.: National Museum of the American Indian in association with the Smithsonian Institution Press.

Judd, Neil M.

1922 Archeological Investigations at Pueblo Bonito, New Mexico. *Smithsonian Miscellaneous Collections* 72(15): 106–17.

1923 Pueblo Bonito, The Ancient. *National Geographic Magazine* 44(2): 99–108.

1925 Everyday Life in Pueblo Bonito. *National Geographic Magazine* 48(3): 227–62.

1926 *Archeological Observations North of the Rio Colorado.* Bureau of American Ethnology Bulletin 82.

1950 Pioneering in Southwestern Archaeology. In *For the Dean: Essays in Anthropology in Honor of Byron Cummings on his Eighty-Ninth Birthday, September 20, 1950.* E. K. Reed and D. S. King, eds. Pp. 11–27. Tucson: Hohokam Museums Association, and Santa Fe: Southwestern Monuments Association.

1954 *The Material Culture of Pueblo Bonito.* Smithsonian Miscellaneous Collections 124.

1959 *Pueblo del Arroyo, Chaco Canyon, New Mexico.* Smithsonian Miscellaneous Collections 138.

1964 The Architecture of Pueblo Bonito. *Smithsonian Miscellaneous Collections* 147(1).

1967 *The Bureau of American Ethnology: A Partial History.* Norman: University of Oklahoma Press.

1968 *Men Met along the Trail: Adventures in Archaeology.* Norman: University of Oklahoma Press.

Judd, Neil M., M. R. Harrington, and S. K. Lothrop

1957 Frederick Webb Hodge, 1864–1956. *American Antiquity* 22(4): 401–4.

Kafker, Frank A.

1996 *The Encyclopedists as a Group: A Collective Biography of the Authors of the Encyclopédie.* Oxford: Voltaire Foundation.

Kaufman, Edmund G.

1973 *General Conference Mennonite Pioneers.* North Newton, Kans.: Bethel College.

Kavanagh, Thomas W.

1990 A Brief Illustrated History of the Manikins, Statues, Lay-Figures, and Life-Groups Illustrating American Ethnology in the National Museum of Natural History. Manuscript on file, Mather Museum, Indiana University, Bloomington.

Keam, Thomas V.

1883 An Indian Snake Dance. *Chamber's Journal*, 4th series, vol. 20: 14–16. Keating, Margaret

1907 Knowledge of Ages is Buried in Mesa Verde. *The Modern World* 8(3): 149–54.

Keleher, William A.

1957 *Violence in Lincoln County, 1869–1881: A New Mexico Item.* Albuquerque: University of New Mexico Press.

Kelly, Isabel T., and Catherine S. Fowler

1986 Southern Paiute. *Handbook of North American Indians. vol. 11, Great Basin.* Pp. 368–97. Washington, D.C.: Smithsonian Institution.

Kelly, Lawrence C.

1988 United States Indian Policies, 1900–1980. *Handbook of North American Indians, vol. 4, History of Indian-White Relations.* Pp. 66–80. Washington, D.C.: Smithsonian Institution.

Kelly, Robert L.

1995 *The Foraging Spectrum: Diversity in Hunter-Gatherer Lifeways.* Washington: Smithsonian Institution Press.

Kennedy, David M.

1980 *Over Here: The First World War and American Society.* New York: Oxford University Press.

Kennedy, John M.

1968 Philanthropy and Science in New York City: The American Museum of Natural History, 1868–1968. Ph.D. diss., Yale University. Ann Arbor, Mich.: University Microfilms, 69–13, 347.

Kennedy, Roger G.

1994 *Hidden Cities: The Discovery and Loss of Ancient North American Civilization.* New York and Toronto: Maxwell Macmillan.

Kent, Kate P.

1985 *Navajo Weaving: Three Centuries of Change.* Santa Fe: School of American Research Press.

Kessell, John L.

1976 *Friars, Soldiers, and Reformers: Hispanic Arizona and the Sonora Mission Frontier, 1767–1856.* Tucson: University of Arizona Press.

1979 *Kiva, Cross, and Crown: The Pecos Indians and New Mexico, 1540–1840.* Washington, D.C.: National Park Service, U.S. Department of the Interior.

Kessell, John L., ed.

1989 *Remote Beyond Compare: Letters of don Diego de Vargas to His Family from New Spain and New Mexico, 1675–1706.* Albuquerque: University of New Mexico Press.

Kessler, Jascha

1959 Descent into Darkness: The Myth of the Plumed Serpent. In *A. D. H. Lawrence Miscellany.* H. T.

Moore, ed. Pp. 239–261. Carbondale: Southern Illinois University Press.

Kidder, Alfred V.

1910   Explorations in Southeastern Utah in 1908. *American Journal of Archaeology*, 2d series 14: 37–59.

1914   Southwestern Ceramics: Their Value in Reconstructing the History of Ancient Cliff Dwelling and Pueblo Tribes: An Exposition from the Point of View of Type Distinction. Ph.D. diss., Harvard University.

1915   The Pottery of the Pajarito Plateau and of Some Adjacent Regions in New Mexico. *American Anthropological Association Memoirs* 2(6): 407–62.

1916   Archaeological Explorations at Pecos, New Mexico. *Proceedings of the National Academy of Sciences* 2: 119–23.

1917   A Design Sequence from New Mexico. *Proceedings of the National Academy of Sciences* 3: 369–70.

1924   *An Introduction to the Study of Southwestern Archaeology with a Preliminary Account of the Excavation at Pecos*. Phillips Academy of Archaeology. Andover, Mass.: Yale University Press.

1927   Southwestern Archaeological Conference. *Science* 66(1716): 489–91.

1930   Division of Historical Research. *Carnegie Institution of Washington Yearbook* no. 29, 1930: 91–130.

1932   *The Artifacts of Pecos*. Papers of the Southwestern Expedition, Phillips Academy no. 6. New Haven, Conn.: Yale University Press.

1936   Speculations on New World Prehistory. In *Essays in Anthropology: Presented to A. L. Kroeber in Celebration of His Sixtieth Birthday, June 11, 1936*. R. H. Lowie, ed. Pp. 143–52. Berkeley: University of California Press.

1945   George Clapp Vaillant, 1901–1945. *American Anthropologist* 47(4): 589–602.

1957   Unpublished Memoirs, 3 vols. Harvard University, Peabody Museum Archives. Portions reproduced in Givens (1987).

1958   *Pecos New Mexico: Archaeological Notes*. Papers of the Robert S. Peabody Foundation for Archaeology 5.

1962   *An Introduction to the Study of Southwestern Archaeology*. New Haven, Conn.: Yale University Press. Originally published in 1924.

Kidder, Alfred V., and Samuel J. Guernsey

1919   *Archeological Explorations in Northeastern Arizona*. Bureau of American Ethnology Bulletin 65.

Kidder, Madeleine A., and Alfred V. Kidder

1917   Notes on the Pottery of Pecos. *American Anthropologist* 19(3): 325–60.

Kidder, Alfred V., and Anna O. Shepard

1936   *The Pottery of Pecos*. Papers of the Phillips Academy Southwestern Expedition no. 7. New Haven, Conn.: Yale University Press.

Kidder, A. V., et al.

1927   Preliminary Statement of ad interim Executive Committee of the Museum and Laboratory of Anthropology. N.p. ALAB.

Kincaid, Chris., ed.

1983   *Chaco Roads Project. Phase I: A Reappraisal of Prehistoric Roads in the San Juan Basin*. Albuquerque: Bureau of Land Management.

King, Clarence

1872   *Mountaineering in the Sierra Nevada*. Boston: Osgood Co.

1878   *Systematic Geology*. Report of the Geological Exploration of the Fortieth Parallel. Vol. 1. Washington, D.C.

Kingsborough, Lord [Edward King]

1831–48 *Antiquities of Mexico, Comprising Facsimiles of Ancient Mexican Paintings and Hieroglyphs . . .* 9 vols. London: R. Havell and Conaghi.

Kluckhohn, Clyde

1927   *To the Foot of the Rainbow, a Tale of Twenty-Five Hundred Miles of Wandering on Horseback Through the Southwest Enchanted Land*. New York and London: Century Co.

Kluckhohn, Clyde, and Dorothea C. Leighton

1946   *The Navaho*. Cambridge, Mass.: Harvard University Press, and London: C. Oxford University Press.

Koepping, K. P.

1983   *Adolph Bastian and the Psychic Unity of Mankind: the Foundations of Anthropology in Nineteenth Century Germany*. St. Lucia, Australia and New York: University of Queensland Press.

Kohlstedt, Sally G.

1980   Henry A. Ward: The Merchant Naturalist and American Museum Developer. *Journal of the Society for the Bibliography of Natural History* 9: 647–61.

Kramer, Barbara

1996   *Nampeyo and Her Pottery*. Albuquerque: University of New Mexico Press.

Krech, Shepard, III
1999   *The Ecological Indian: Myth and History.* New York: W. W. Norton and Co.

Kroeber, Alfred L.
1909   The Classificatory System of Relationship. *Journal of the Anthropological Institute* 34: 77–84.
1916a   Zuñi Culture Sequences. *Proceedings of the National Academy of Sciences* 2: 42–45.
1916b   Zuñi Potsherds. *American Museum of Natural History Anthropological Papers* 18(1): 1–37.
1916c   Thoughts on Zuni Religion. *Holmes Anniversary Volume.* Pp. 269–77.
1917a   The Superorganic. *American Anthropologist* 19: 163–213.
1917b   Zuñi Clan and Kin. *American Museum of Natural History Anthropological Papers* 18, Pt. II. Pp. 39–204.
1925   *Handbook of the Indians of California.* Bureau of American Ethnology Bulletin no. 78.
1928   Native Cultures of the Southwest. *University of California Publications in American Archaeology and Ethnology* 23(9): 375–398.
1929   Pliny Earle Goddard. *American Anthropologist* 31(1): 1–8.
1932   The Culture-Area and Age-Area Concepts of Clark Wissler. In *Methods in Social Science, A Case Book.* S. A. Rice, ed. Pp. 248–65. Chicago: University of Chicago Press.
1937   Thomas Talbot Waterman. *American Anthropologist* 39(3): 527–29.
1939   *Cultural and Natural Areas of Native North America.* University of California Publications in American Archaeology and Ethnology 38.
1943   Elsie Clews Parsons. *American Anthropologist* 45: 252–55.

Kroeber, A. L., et al.
1949   *Ruth Fulton Benedict: A Memorial.* New York: Viking Fund.

Kroeber, A. L., and C. Kluckhohn
1952   *Culture: A Critical Review of Concepts and Definitions.* Papers of the Peabody Museum of Archaeology and Ethnology 47(1).

Kroeber, Theodora
1961   *Ishi in Two Worlds: A Biography of the Last Wild Indian in North America.* Berkeley: University of California Press.
1970   *Alfred Kroeber: A Personal Configuration.* Berkeley: University of California Press.

Kuklick, Bruce
1996   *Puritans in Babylon: The Ancient Near East and American Intellectual Life, 1880–1930.* Princeton, N.J.: Princeton University Press.

La Farge, Oliver
1929   *Laughing Boy.* Boston: Houghton Mifflin.
1945   *Raw Material.* Boston: Houghton Mifflin.

Lafitau, J.-F.
1974–77 *Customs of the American Indians Compared with the Customs of Primitive Times.* 2 vols. W. N. Fenton and E. L. Moore, eds. and trans. Toronto: Champlain Society 48. Originally published 1724.

Laird, Carobeth
1975   *Encounter with an Angry God: Recollections of my Life with John Peabody Harrington.* Banning, Calif.: Malki Museum Press.
1976   *The Chemehuevis.* Banning, Calif.: Malki Museum Press.
1984   *Mirror and Pattern: George Laird's World of Chemehuevi Mythology.* Banning, Calif.: Malki Museum Press.

Lake, Sara E., and A. A. Gray, trans. and eds.
1937   *The History of [Lower] California by Don Francisco Javier Clavigero, S. J.* Stanford, Calif.: Stanford University Press.

Lamar, Howard R.
1966   *The Far Southwest 1846–1912: A Territorial History.* New Haven, Conn.: Yale University Press.

Lamb, Sydney M.
1964   The Classification of the Uto-Aztecan Languages: A Historical Survey. *University of California Publications in Linguistics* 34: 106–25.

Lamphere, Louise
1989   Feminist Anthropology: The Legacy of Elsie Clews Parsons. *American Ethnologist* 16: 318–33.
1993   Gladys Reichard among the Navajo. In *Hidden Scholars: Women Anthropologists and the Native American Southwest.* N. J. Parezo, ed. Pp. 157–81. Albuquerque: University of New Mexico Press.

Lange, Charles H., and Carroll L. Riley
1996   *Bandelier: The Life and Adventures of Adolph Bandelier.* Salt Lake City: University of Utah Press.

Lange, Charles H., and Carroll L. Riley, eds.
1966   *The Southwestern Journals of Adolph F. Bandelier, 1880–1882* [vol. 1]. Albuquerque: University of New Mexico Press, and Santa Fe: School of American Research, Museum of New Mexico Press.

Lange, Charles H., Carroll L. Riley, and Elizabeth
M. Lange, eds.

1970   *The Southwestern Journals of Adolph F. Bandelier, 1883–1884* [vol. 2]. Albuquerque: University of New Mexico Press.

1975   *The Southwestern Journals of Adolph F. Bandelier, 1885–1888* [vol. 3]. Albuquerque: University of New Mexico Press, and Santa Fe: School of American Research.

1984   *The Southwestern Journals of Adolph F. Bandelier, 1889–1892* [vol. 4]. Albuquerque: University of New Mexico Press, and Santa Fe: School of American Research.

Lange, Frederick W., and Diana Leonard, eds.

1985   *Among Ancient Ruins: The Legacy of Earl H. Morris*. Boulder, Colo.: Johnson Books.

Laut, Agnes C.

1913   *Through Our Unknown Southwest, the Wonderland of the United States*. New York: McBride, Nast and Co.

Laurie, Annie.

1928   *The Life and Personality of Phoebe Apperson Hearst*. Printed for W. R. Hearst by J. H. Nash, San Francisco.

Lavender, David S.

1970   *The Great Persuader*. Garden City, N.Y.: Doubleday.

Lawrence, D. H.

1926   *The Plumed Serpent [Quetzalcoatl]*. New York: Alfred A. Knopf.

1972   *Phoenix: The Posthumous Papers of D. H. Lawrence*. E. D. McDonald, ed. New York: Viking Press.

Leake, Harvey, and Gary Topping

1987   The Bernheimer Explorations in Forbidding Canyon. *Utah Historical Quarterly* 55(2): 137–66.

LeBlanc, Steven A.

1983   *The Mimbres People: Ancient Pueblo Potters of the Southwest*. New York: Thames and Hudson.

Lee, Ronald F.

1970   *The Antiquities Act of 1906*. Washington, D.C.: U.S. Department of the Interior, National Park Service.

Lehmann, William C., ed.

1979   *John Millar of Glasgow, 1735–1801*. New York: Arno Press. Originally published 1960.

Lekson, Stephen H.

1999   *The Chaco Meridian: Centers of Political Power in

the Ancient Southwest*. Walnut Creek, Calif.: AltaMira Press.

León-Portilla, Miguel

1972   The Norteño Variety of Mexican Culture: An Ethnohistorical Approach. In *Plural Society in the Southwest*. E. H. Spicer and R. H. Thompson, eds. Pp. 77–114. New York: Interbook.

Leone, Mark P.

1979   *Roots of Modern Mormonism*. Cambridge, Mass.: Harvard University Press.

Letterman, Jonathan

1856   Sketch of the Navajo Tribe of Indians, Territory of New Mexico. *Tenth Annual Report of the Smithsonian Institution for 1856*. Pp. 283–97.

Lévi-Strauss, Claude

1949   *Les Structures Élémentaires de la Parente*. Paris: Presses Universitaires de France.

1973   *Tristes Tropiques*. J. and D. Weightman, trans. New York: Atheneum.

Levy, Jerrold

1998   *In the Beginning: The Navajo Genesis*. Berkeley: University of California Press.

Liebersohn, Harry

1998   *Aristocratic Encounters: European Travelers and North American Indians*. Cambridge and New York: Cambridge University Press.

Liss, Julia E.

1995   Patterns of Strangeness: Franz Boas, Modernism and the Origins of Anthropology. In *Prehistories of the Future. The Primitivist Project and the Culture of Modernism*. E. Barkan and R. Bush, eds. Pp. 114–30. Stanford, Calif.: Stanford University Press.

1996   German Culture and German Science in the *Bildung* of Franz Boas. In *Volkgeist as Method and Ethic: Essays on Boasian Ethnography and the German Anthropological Tradition*. G. W. Stocking, Jr., eds. Pp. 155–84. History of Anthropology, vol. 8. Madison: University of Wisconsin Press.

Lister, Robert H., and Florence C. Lister

1968   *Earl Morris and Southwestern Archaeology*. Albuquerque: University of New Mexico Press.

1981   *Chaco Canyon, Archaeology and Archaeologists*. Albuquerque: University of New Mexico Press.

1987   *Aztec Ruins on the Animas, Excavated, Preserved, and Interpreted*. Albuquerque: University of New Mexico Press.

Lister, Robert H., and Florence C. Lister, eds.

1984 *Stones Speak and Waters Sing: The Life and Works of Gustaf Nordenskiöld* by Olof W. Arrhenius. Mesa Verde, Colo.: Mesa Verde Museum Association.

Llewellyn, Karl N., and E. Adamson Hoebel

1941 *The Cheyenne Way: Conflict and Case Law in Primitive Jurisprudence.* Norman: University of Oklahoma Press.

Locke, John

1960 *Two Treatises on Government.* Peter Laslett, ed. Cambridge: Cambridge University Press. Originally published in 1690.

Lockwood, Frank C.

1929 *The Life of Edward E. Ayer.* Chicago: A. C. McClurg and Co.

Lomatuway'ma, Michael, Lorena Lomatuway'ma, and Sidney Namingha, Jr.

1993 *Hopi Ruin Legends: Kiqötutuwutsi.* E. Malotki, trans. Published for Northern Arizona University by the University of Nebraska Press, Lincoln.

Long, Stephen H.

1823 *Account of an Expedition from Pittsburgh to the Rocky Mountains Performed in the Years 1819 and 1820.* London: Longman, Hearst, Rees, Orme, and Brown.

Longacre, William A.

1999 Why did the BAE Hire an Architect? *Journal of the Southwest* 41(3): 358–69.

Lovejoy, Arthur O.

1948 *Essays in the History of Ideas.* Baltimore: Johns Hopkins University Press.

Lovejoy, Arthur O., and George Boas

1935 *Primitivism and Related Ideas in Antiquity.* Baltimore: Johns Hopkins University Press.

Lowie, Robert H.

1914a Ernst Haeckel. *New Review* 2(6): 354–56.

1914b Some Recent Expressions of Racial Inferiority. *New Review* 2(9): 542–46.

1914c A Pro-German View. *New Review* 2(11): 642–44.

1915 Exogamy and the Classificatory System of Relationship. *American Anthropologist* 17: 223–39.

1920 *Primitive Society.* New York: Boni and Livewright.

1956 *The Crow Indians.* New York: Farrar and Rinehart, Inc.

1959 *Robert H. Lowie, Ethnologist: A Personal Record.* Berkeley: University of California Press

Lowitt, Richard

1992 *Bronson M. Cutting: Progressive Politician.* Albuquerque: University of New Mexico Press.

Lubbock, John [Lord Avebury]

1865 *Pre-historic Times, As Illustrated by Ancient Remains and the Manners and Customs of Modern Savages.* London: Williams and Norgate.

Luce, Stephen B., comp.

1895 *Report of the United States Commission to the Columbian Historical Expositions at Madrid, 1892–93.* Washington, D.C.: Government Printing Office.

Lumholtz, Carl

1987 *Unknown Mexico: Explorations in the Sierra Madre and Other Regions, 1890–1898.* 2 vols. New York: Dover Publications. Originally published 1902.

Lummis, Charles F.

1893 *The Land of Poco Tiempo.* New York: C. Scribner's Sons.

1900 The White Indian. *Land of Sunshine* 15(6): 11–13.

1904a Archaeological Institute of America, Southwest Society. *Out West* 20(2): 173–76.

1904b Archaeological Institute of America, Southwest Society. *Out West* 20(4): 369–73.

1904c The Sequoya League (inc.) To Make Better Indians. *Out West* 21(6): 578–83.

1905a Archaeological Institute of America, Southwest Society. *Out West* 23(1): 84–86.

1905b The Landmarks Club. *Out West* 23(1): 87–88.

1905c Archaeological Institute of America, Southwest Society. *Out West* 22(5): 343–46.

1905d Archaeological Institute of America, Southwest Society. *Out West* 23(5): 285–90.

1906a Archaeological Institute of America, Southwest Society. *Out West* 24(2): 238.

1925 *Mesa, Cañon and Pueblo: Our Wonderland of the Southwest.* New York and London: The Century Co.

1968 *Bullying the Moqui.* R. Easton and M. Brown, eds. Prescott, Ariz.: Prescott College Press. Articles from *Out West* magazine, originally published between April and October 1903.

1969 *A Tramp Across the Continent.* Albuquerque: Calvin Horn. Originally published 1892.

1989 *Letters from the Southwest, September 20, 1884 to March 14, 1885.* J. W. Byrkit, ed. Tucson: University of Arizona Press.

Lurie, Edward

1960   *Louis Agassiz: A Life in Science.* Chicago: University of Chicago Press.

1974   *Nature and the American Mind: Louis Agassiz and the Culture of Science.* New York: Science History Publications.

Lyman, Christopher M.

1982   *The Vanishing Race and Other Illusions: Photographs of Indians by Edward S. Curtis.* New York: Pantheon Books in association with the Smithsonian Institution Press.

Lyman, R. Lee, Michael J. O'Brien, and Robert C. Dunnell, eds.

1997a   *The Rise and Fall of Culture History.* New York: Plenum Press.

1997b   *Americanist Culture History: Fundamentals of Time, Space, and Form.* New York: Plenum Press.

Lyman, Stanford M.

1982   Two Neglected Pioneers of Civilizational Analysis: The Cultural Perspectives of R. Stewart Culin and Frank Hamilton Cushing. *Social Research,* Autumn: 690–729.

Lyon, William H.

1989   Gladys Reichard at the Frontiers of Navajo Culture. *American Indian Quarterly* 13: 137–63.

McClurg, Virginia

1930   The Making of Mesa Verde into a National Park. *The Colorado Magazine* 3(6): 216–19.

1933   *The Poems of Virginia Donaghe McClurg.* Colorado College Publications, Studies series no. 16.

McCown, S. M.

1904   Resume of Government's Indian Exhibit, L.P.E. *The Indian School Journal* 1(1): 39–60.

McCullough, Edo

1976   *World's Fair Midways: An Affectionate Account of American Amusement Areas from the Crystal Palace to the Crystal Ball.* New York: Arno Press.

MacCurdy, George G.

1902   The Teaching of Anthropology in the United States. *Science* 15: 211–16.

McGee, Emma R.

1915   *Life of W. J. McGee, Distinguished Geologist, Ethnologist, Anthropologist, Hydrologist, Etc.* Farley, Iowa: Private Printing.

McGee, W. J.

1896   1898 The Seri Indians. *Seventeenth Annual Report of the Bureau of American Ethnology, 1895–96,* Pt. 1. Pp. 1–128.

1903   Remarks. *World's Fair Bulletin* 4 (August): 29.

1904a   *Official Catalogue of Exhibits, Department of Anthropology.* Rev. ed. St. Louis: Universal Exposition.

1904b   Family Register of Indians at World's Fair Exhibit. McGee Papers, Box 28, Library of Congress.

1905a   Report of the Department of Anthropology to F. J. V. Skiff, Director, Universal Exposition of 1904. Louisiana Purchase Exposition files, file series III, subseries XI. St. Louis: Missouri Historical Society.

1905b   Department of Anthropology. In *Louisiana and the Fair: An Exposition of the World and its People and Their Achievements.* J. W. Buel, ed. Vol. 5. Pp. i–xv, 1567–1976. St. Louis: World's Progress Publishing Co.

1906   Anthropology and Its Larger Problems. In *Congress of Arts and Science, Universal Exposition, St. Louis, 1904.* H. J. Rogers, ed. Vol. 5. Pp. 449–467. Boston: Houghton Mifflin.

1912   Symptomatic Development of Cancer. *Science* n.s. 37(924): 348–50.

McGrane, Bernard

1989   *Beyond Anthropology: Society and the Other.* New York: Columbia University Press.

McGreevy, Susan B.

1993   Daughters of Affluence: Wealth, Collecting and Southwestern Institutions. In *Hidden Scholars: Women Anthropologists and the Native American Southwest.* Nancy J. Parezo, ed. Pp. 76–100. Albuquerque: University of New Mexico Press.

McGuire, Thomas R.

1983   Walapai. *Handbook of North American Indians, vol. 10, Southwest.* Pp. 25–37. Washington, D.C.: Smithsonian Institution.

McIntire, Elliot G., and Sandra R. Gordon

1968   Ten Kate's Account of the Walpi Snake Dance: 1883. *Plateau* 41(1): 27–33.

McKelvey, Susan D.

1991   *Botanical Exploration of the Trans-Mississippi West, 1790–1850.* Corvallis, Or.: Oregon State University Press.

McLaughlin, Andrew C.

1905   Historical Research. *Carnegie Institution of Washington Yearbook* no. 3, 1904: 65–67.

1906   Historical Research. *Carnegie Institution of Washington Yearbook* no. 4, 1905: 232–37.

McLennan, John F.

1865   *Primitive Marriage: an Inquiry into the Origin of*

the Form of Capture in Marriage Ceremonies. Edinburgh: Adam and Charles Black.

McLuhan, T. C.

1974 *The Shadow Catcher: Edward S. Curtis and the North American Indian: a Film.* New York: Shadow Catchers, Inc.

1985 *Dream Tracks: The Railroad and the American Indian, 1890–1930.* New York: Harry Abrams.

McNeley, James K.

1981 *Holy Wind in Navajo Philosophy.* Tucson: University of Arizona Press.

McNickle, D'Arcy

1971 *Indian Man: A Life of Oliver La Farge.* Bloomington: Indiana University Press.

McNitt, Frank

1964 Preface and Introduction. In *Navaho Expedition: Journal of a Military Reconnaissance from Santa Fe, New Mexico to the Navaho Country.* Pp. ix–lxxix. Norman: University of Oklahoma Press.

1966 *Richard Wetherill: Anasazi.* Rev. ed. Albuquerque: University of New Mexico Press.

McVicker, Donald

1992 The Matter of Saville: Franz Boas and the Anthropological Definition of Archaeology. In *Rediscovering Our Past: Essays on the History of American Archaeology.* J. E. Reyman, ed. Pp. 145–60. Aldershot, England, and Brookfield, U.S.A.: Avebury Press.

1993 The United States National Museum at the Louisiana Purchase Exposition. Manuscript in author's possession.

1999 Buying a Curator: Establishing Anthropology at the Field Columbian Museum. In *Assembling the Past: Studies in the Professionalization of Archaeology.* A. Kehoe and M. B. Emmerichs, eds. Pp. 37–52. Albuquerque: University of New Mexico Press.

McWilliams, Carey

1983 *Southern California Country: An Island on the Land.* Santa Barbara: Peregrine Smith Books.

Madeira, Percy C.

1964 *Men in Search of Man: The First Seventy-five Years of the University Museum of the University of Pennsylvania.* Philadelphia: University of Pennsylvania Press.

Mahood, Ruth I.

1961 *Photographer of the Southwest: Adam Clark Vroman, 1856–1916.* Los Angeles: Ward Ritchie Press.

Malkus, Alida

1928 *The Dragon Fly of Zuni.* New York: Harcourt Brace and Co.

Manuel, Frank

1959 *The Eighteenth Century Confronts the Gods.* Cambridge, Mass.: Harvard University Press.

1963 *Isaac Newton, Historian.* Cambridge, Mass.: Belknap Press of Harvard University Press.

Mardock, Robert W.

1971 *The Reformers and the American Indian.* Columbia: University of Missouri Press.

Mark, Joan

1980 *Four Anthropologists: An American Science in Its Early Years.* New York: Science History Publications.

1988 *A Stranger in Her Native Land: Alice Fletcher and the American Indians.* Lincoln: University of Nebraska Press.

Marrett, R. R.

1923 Review of *American Indian Life*, edited by E. C. Parsons. *American Anthropologist* 23: 266–69.

Marriott, Alice

1948 *María: The Potter of San Ildefonso.* Norman: University of Oklahoma Press.

Martin, Geoffrey J.

1973 *Ellsworth Huntington: His Life and Thought.* Hamden, Conn.: Archon Books.

Martin, Paul S.

1929 The 1928 Archaeological Expedition of the State Historical Society of Colorado. *Colorado Magazine* 6(1): 1–35.

1979 Prehistory: Mogollon. *Handbook of North American Indians, vol. 9, Southwest.* Pp. 61–74. Washington, D.C.: Smithsonian Institution.

Martin, Paul S., Lawrence Roy, and G. von Bonin

1936 *Lowry Ruin in Southwestern Colorado.* Field Museum of Natural History Anthropological Series 23(1).

Mason, Otis T.

1886 The Planting and Exhuming of a Prayer. *Science* 8(179): 24–25.

1887 The Occurrence of Similar Inventions in Areas Widely Apart. *Science* 9: 534–35.

1891 Anthropology at the Paris Exposition. *Smithsonian Institution Annual Report for 1890.* Pp. 31–122.

1894 Ethnological Exhibits of the Smithsonian Institution at the World Columbian Exposition. In *Memoirs of the International Congress of Anthropol-*

ogy, *Chicago, 1894.* C. S. Wake, ed. Pp. 206–16. Chicago: Schulte Publishing.

1896 Influence of Environment upon Human Industries or Arts. *Smithsonian Institution Annual Report for 1894–95.* Pp. 639–65.

Mathien, Frances J., and Randall H. McGuire, eds.

1986 *Ripples in the Chichimec Sea: New Considerations of Southwestern-Mesoamerican Interactions.* Carbondale: Southern Illinois Press.

Mathieu, Caroline

1989 Invitation au Voyage. In *1889: La Tour Eiffel et L'Exposition Universelle.* C. Mathieu et al, eds. Pp. 102–42. Paris: Éditions de la Réunion des Musées Nationaux.

Matthews, Washington

1873 *Grammar and Dictionary of the Language of the Hidatsa (Minnetarees, Grosventres of the Missouri).* Shea's Library of American Linguistics, series 2 (1). New York: Cramoisy Press.

1877 *Ethnography and Philology of the Hidatsa Indians.* U.S. Geological Survey of the Territories, Miscellaneous Publication no. 7. Washington, D.C.: Government Printing Office.

1883 Navajo Silversmiths. *Second Annual Report of the Bureau of Ethnology, 1880–81.* Pp. 167–78.

1884 Navajo Weavers. *Third Annual Report of the Bureau of Ethnology, 1881–82.* Pp. 371–91.

1885a Mythic Dry-Painting of the Navajos. *American Naturalist* 19(10): 931–39.

1885b Mythological Dry Painting of the Navajos. *Anthropological Society of Washington Transactions* 3: 139–40.

1887 The Mountain Chant: A Navajo Ceremony. *Fifth Annual Report of the Bureau of Ethnology, 1883–84.* Pp. 379–467.

1897 *Navajo Legends.* Memoirs of the American Folklore Society 5.

1902a *The Night Chant: A Navajo Ceremony.* Memoirs of the American Museum of Natural History, Anthropology, vol. 6.

1902b Review of Frank Hamilton Cushing, Zuni Folk Tales. *American Anthropologist* 4: 144–45.

1907 Navajo Myths, Prayers, and Songs with Texts and Translations, edited by P. E. Goddard. *University of California Publications in American Archaeology and Ethnology* 5: 21–63.

Matthews, Washington, Jacob L. Wortman, and John S. Billings

1893 *The Human Bones in the Hemenway Collection in the United States Army Medical Museum at Washington, by Dr. Washington Matthews.* Seventh Memoir of the National Academy of Sciences 6: 141–286.

Mead, Margaret

1959 Apprenticeship under Boas. In *The Anthropology of Franz Boas: Essays on the Centennial of His Birth.* W. Goldschmidt, ed. Pp. 29–45. American Anthropological Association Memoir 89.

Mead, Margaret, ed.

1959 *An Anthropologist at Work; Writings of Ruth Benedict.* Boston: Houghton Mifflin.

Meckier, Jerome

1969 *Aldous Huxley, Satire and Structure.* London: Chatto and Windus.

Meek, Ronald

1976 *Social Science and the Ignoble Savage.* Cambridge and New York: Cambridge University Press.

Meltzer, David J.

1983 The Antiquity of Man and the Development of American Archaeology. *Advances in Archaeological Method and Theory* 6: 1–51.

1993 *Search for the First Americans.* Montreal: St. Remy Press, and Washington, D.C.: Smithsonian Books, and Montreal: St. Remy's Press.

1998 Introduction: Ephraim Squier, Edwin Davis, and the Making of an American Archaeological Classic. In *Ancient Monuments of the Mississippi Valley.* Washington, D.C.: Smithsonian Institution Press.

Meltzer, David J., and Robert C. Dunnell, eds.

1992 *The Archaeology of William Henry Holmes.* Washington, D.C.: Smithsonian Institution Press.

Mera, Harry P.

1987 *Spanish-American Blanketry.* Santa Fe: School of American Research Press.

Meredith, Ellis

1906 What Colorado Women Have Done to Save the Remains of the Cliff Dwellers. *Pearson's Magazine* 31(5): 205–8.

Merk, Frederick

1963 *Manifest Destiny and Mission in American History: A Reinterpretation.* New York: Alfred A. Knopf.

Merriam, C. Hart, ed.

1900–1910 *Harriman Alaska Series.* 14 vols. Washington, D.C.: Smithsonian Institution.

Merrill, William L., and Richard E. Ahlborn

1997 Zuñi Archangels and Ahayu:da: A Sculpted Chronicle of Power and Identity. In *Exhibiting Dilemmas: Issues of Representation at the Smithson-*

ian. A. Henderson and A. L. Kaeppler, eds. Pp. 176–205. Washington, D.C.: Smithsonian Institution Press.

Merrill, William L., Edmund J. Ladd, and T. J. Ferguson

1993 The Return of the Ahayu:da: Lessons for Repatriation from Zuñi Pueblo and the Smithsonian Institution. *Current Anthropology* 34: 523–67.

Millar, John

1779 *The Origin of the Distinction of Ranks.* London: Murray.

Miller, Jimmy H.

1991 A Philadelphia Brahmin in Flagstaff: The Life of Harold Sellers Colton. Tsaile, Ariz.: Navajo Community College Press.

Miller, R. Berkeley

1975 Anthropology and Institutionalization: Frederick Starr at the University of Chicago, 1892–1923. *Kroeber Anthropological Society Papers* 51–52: 49–60.

Miller, Wick R.

1983 Uto-Aztecan Languages. *Handbook of North American Indian Languages, vol. 10, Southwest.* Pp. 113–24. Washington, D.C.: Smithsonian Institution.

Milton, John R.

1981 The Origin and Development of the Concept of the "Laws of Nature." *Archives of European Sociology* 22: 173–95.

Mindeleff, Cosmos

1897 The Repair of Casa Grande Ruin, Arizona, in 1891. *Fifteenth Annual Report of the Bureau of Ethnology, 1893–94.* Pp. 315–49.

1898 Navaho Houses. *Seventeenth Annual Report of the Bureau of American Ethnology, 1895–96,* Pt 2: 230–44.

1900 Tusayan Migration Traditions. *Nineteenth Annual Report of the Bureau of American Ethnology, 1897–98,* Pt. 2: 635–53.

Mindeleff, Victor

1891 A Study of Pueblo Architecture: Tusayan and Cibola. *Eighth Annual Report of the Bureau of Ethnology, 1886–87.* Pp. 3–228.

Mitchell, David J.

1981 *The Jesuits: A History.* New York and London: Franklin Watts.

Mithun, Marianne

1996 The Description of the Native Languages of North America: Boas and After. *Handbook of North American Indians, volume 17, Languages.*

Pp. 43–63. Washington, D.C.: Smithsonian Institution.

Modell, Judith S.

1983 *Ruth Benedict: Patterns of a Life.* Philadelphia: University of Pennsylvania Press.

Moffitt, John F., and Santiago Sebastián

1996 *O Brave New People: The European Invention of the American Indian.* Albuquerque: University of New Mexico Press.

Möllhausen, Balduin

1858 *Diary of a Journey from the Mississippi to the Coasts of the Pacific with a United States Government Expedition.* 2 vols. Mrs. Percy Sinnett, trans. London: Longman, Brown, Green, Longmans and Roberts.

Montaigne, Michel de

1947 *The Essays of Michel de Montaigne.* G. B. Ives, trans. New York: The Heritage Press.

Montesquieu, Charles de Secondat, Baron de

1949 *The Spirit of Laws.* T. Nugent, trans. New York: Hafner Press.

1985 *Persian Letters.* C. J. Betts, trans. New York: Penguin Books.

Moon, Grace

1925 *Chi-Weé: The Adventures of a Little Indian Girl.* Garden City, N.Y.: Doubleday, Page, and Co.

Mooney, James

1896 The Ghost-dance Religion and the Sioux Outbreak of 1890. *Fourteenth Annual Report of the Bureau of Ethnology. 1892–93.* Pp. 641–1110.

1899 The Indian Congress at Omaha. *American Anthropologist* 1: 126–49.

1905 In Memoriam: Washington Matthews. *American Anthropologist* 7: 514–23.

1907 In Memoriam: Albert Samuel Gatschet. *American Anthropologist* 9: 561–70.

Moorhead, Max L.

1968 *The Apache Frontier: Jacobo Ugarte and Spanish-Indian Relations in Northern New Spain, 1769–1791.* Norman: University of Oklahoma Press.

Morgan, Lewis Henry

1871 *Systems of Consanguinity and Affinity of the Human Family.* Washington, D.C.: Smithsonian Contributions to Knowledge 17.

1876a Montezuma's Dinner. *The North American Review* 122: 265–308.

1876b Houses of the Mound Builders. *The North American Review* 123: 60–85.

1877   *Ancient Society or Researches in the Lines of Human Progress from Savagery through Barbarism to Civilization.* New York: Henry Holt.

1880a   A Study of the Houses of the American Aborigines. *First Annual Report of the Archaeological Institute of America.* Pp. 29–80. Cambridge.

1880b   On the Ruins of a Stone Pueblo on the Animas River in New Mexico; with a Ground Plan. *Twelfth Annual Report of the Peabody Museum of American Archaeology and Ethnology,* II: 536–56.

1881   *Houses and House Life of the American Aborigines.* Contributions to North American Ethnology 4. Washington, D.C.: Government Printing Office.

1954   *League of the Ho-De-No Sau-Nee, or Iroquois.* New Haven, Conn.: Human Relations Area Files. Originally published 1851.

1959   *The Indian Journals, 1859–62.* L. A. White, ed. Ann Arbor: University of Michigan Press.

Morgan, William F.

1879   Description of a Cliff-House in the Cañon of the Mancos River. *Proceedings of the American Association for the Advancement of Science for 1878 (St. Louis).* Pp. 300–306.

Morley, Sylvanus G.

1908   The Excavations of Cannonball Ruins in Southwest Colorado. *American Anthropologist* 10: 598–610.

1915   Santa Fe Architecture. *Old Santa Fe Magazine* 2: 278–301.

Morris, Ann A.

1933   *Digging in the Southwest.* New York: Doubleday, Doran and Co.

Morris, Earl H.

1919a   Preliminary Account of the Antiquities of the Region between the Mancos and La Plata Rivers in Southwestern Colorado. *Thirty-Third Annual Report, Bureau of American Ethnology, 1911–12.* Pp. 155–206.

1919b   The Aztec Ruin. *American Museum of Natural History Anthropological Papers* 26(1): 1–108.

1921a   Chronology of the San Juan Area. *Proceedings of the National Academy of Sciences* 7: 18–22.

1921b   The House of the Great Kiva at the Aztec Ruin. *American Museum of Natural History Anthropological Papers* 26(2):109–38.

1924   Burials in the Aztec Ruin [and] The Aztec Ruin Annex. *American Museum of Natural History Anthropological Papers* 26(3–4): 139–257.

1928   Notes on Excavations in the Aztec Ruin: The Aztec Ruin Annex. *American Museum of Natural History Anthropological Papers* 26(5): 259–420.

1939   *Archaeological Studies in the La Plata District, Southwestern Colorado, and Northwestern New Mexico.* Washington, D.C.: Carnegie Institution of Washington Publications 519.

Morris, Earl H., and Robert F. Burgh

1941   *Anasazi Basketry—Basketmaker II through Pueblo III: a Study Based on Specimens from the San Juan River Country.* Washington, D.C.: Carnegie Institution of Washington Publications 533.

Morris, Elizabeth A.

1959   Basketmaker Caves in the Prayer Rock District, Northeastern Arizona. Ph.D. diss., University of Arizona, Tucson.

1980   *Basketmaker Caves in the Prayer Rock District, Northeastern Arizona.* University of Arizona Anthropological Papers 35.

Morss, Noel

1931   *The Ancient Cultures of the Fremont River in Utah.* Papers of the Peabody Museum of American Archaeology and Ethnology 12(2).

Moses, L. G.

1984   *The Indian Man: A Biography of James Mooney.* Urbana: University of Illinois Press.

1996   *Wild West Shows and the Images of American Indians, 1883–1933.* Albuquerque: University of New Mexico Press.

Murdock, George P.

1948   Clark Wissler, 1870–1947. *American Anthropologist* 50: 292–304.

1949   *Social Structure.* New York: Macmillan.

Museum of the American Indian

1956   *The History of the Museum.* Indian Notes and Monographs, Miscellaneous Series no. 55.

Nabokov, Peter

1989   Introduction to Victor Mindeleff, *A Study of Pueblo Architecture in Tusayan and Cibola,* pp. ix–xli. Washington, D.C.: Smithsonian Institution Press.

Nahohai, Milford, and Elisa Phelps

1995   *Dialogues with Zuni Potters.* Zuni, N.M.: Zuni A:shiwi Publishing.

Nash, Stephen E.

1999   *Time, Trees, and Prehistory: Tree-Ring Dating and the Development of North American Archaeology, 1914–1950.* Salt Lake City: University of Utah Press.

National Geographic Magazine
1921   A New National Geographic Expedition.
        National Geographic Magazine 39(6): 637–43.
National Park Service
1991   *The First Seventy-five Years.* Washington, D.C.:
        National Park Service.
Naylor, Thomas H., and Charles W. Polzer
1986   *The Presidio and Militia on the Northern Frontier
        of New Spain: A Documentary History, Volume
        One: 1570–1700.* Tucson: University of Arizona
        Press.
Nelson, Nels
1913   Ruins of Prehistoric New Mexico. *American Mu-
        seum Journal* 13: 389–94.
1914   Pueblo Ruins of the Galisteo Basin, New Mexico.
        *American Museum of Natural History Anthropolog-
        ical Papers* 15(1): 1–124.
1916   Chronology of the Tano Ruins, New Mexico.
        American Anthropologist 18: 159–80.
1948   Clark Wissler, 1870–1947. *American Antiquity* 13:
        244–47.
Nentvig, Juan
1980   *Rudo Ensayo: A Description of Sonora and Arizona
        in 1764 by Juan Nentvig.* A. F. Pradeau and R. B.
        Rasmussen, eds. and trans. Tucson: University of
        Arizona Press.
Newberry, John S.
1861   Geological Report. In Lt. J. C. Ives, *Report upon
        the Colorado River of the West, Explored in 1857 and
        1858,* Pt. III. 36th Cong. 1st sess. House Executive
        Doc. no. 90. Washington, D.C.
1876   Geological Report. In J. N. Macomb, *Report of
        the Exploring Expedition from Santa Fé, New Mex-
        ico, to the Junction of the Grand and Green Rivers
        of the Great Colorado of the West.* Pp. 47–118. Engi-
        neer Department, U.S. Army. Washington, D.C.:
        Government Printing Office.
Newcomb, Franc Johnson
1964   *Hosteen Klah: Navaho Medicine Man and Sand
        Painter.* Norman: University of Oklahoma Press.
New Mexican, The
1913   Animated Debate. Special Meeting of the Cham-
        ber of Commerce. Dr. Hewett is Discussed. *The
        New Mexican.* Nov. 19, 1913. Clipping in ELHP.
1920   Archaeologists Cover 2,000 Miles in Twenty
        Days. *The New Mexican.* Sept. 8, 1920. P. 2. Clip-
        ping in NMJP.
Newton, Isaac, Sir
1728   *The Chronology of Ancient Kingdoms Amended: To

Which Is Prefix'd, a Short Chronicle from the First
        Memory of Things in Europe, to the Conquest of
        Persia by Alexander the Great.* London: J. Tonson,
        J. Osborn and T. Longman. Facsimile reprint,
        London: Histories and Mysteries of Man.
New York Times
1912   Uncovering an Ancient City. Oldest in America is
        that of Quirigua, Guatemala, it is Thought—Dr.
        Hewitt [sic] Expects to Discover its Secret Next
        Summer. *The New York Times.* Jan. 21, 1912. Clip-
        ping in CHP.
1914–28 Various articles on Museum of the American
        Indian dated 7/22/1914: 18:4; 5/2/1916: 13:4;
        5/6/1916: 7:4; 6/4/1916: 4:3; 9/28/1916: 6:2;
        11/16/1922: 12:1; 1/30/1924: 5:5; 2/10/1926: 13:4;
        5/19/1928: 7:3
1997   Esther Goldfrank, 100, Dies; Studied Pueblos in
        the Southwest. *New York Times* Obituaries. May
        25, 1997.
Nichols, Frances S., comp.
1954   *Index to Schoolcraft's Indian Tribes of the United
        States.* Bureau of American Ethnology Bulletin
        152.
Nicholson, H. B.
1973   Eduard Georg Seler, 1849–1922. *Handbook of
        Middle American Indians vol. 13, Guide to Ethno-
        historical Sources,* pt. 2: 348–69. Austin: University
        of Texas Press.
Nietzsche, Friedrich W.
1927   *The Philosophy of Nietzsche: Thus Spake Zarathus-
        tra . . . The Birth of Tragedy.* New York: Random
        House. Originally published 1872–1891.
Nordenskiöld, Gustaf
1893   *The Cliff Dwellers of the Mesa Verde, Southwestern
        Colorado, Their Pottery and Implements.* D. L.
        Morgan, trans. Stockholm and Chicago: P. A.
        Norstedt and Söner. Facsimile reprint, Mesa
        Verde, Colo.: Mesa Verde Museum Association,
        1990.
1897   Recherches nouvelles dans les reines et les
        tombeaux de Mesa Verde [and] Discussion:
        M. M. Seler, Retzius, Virchow. *International
        Congress of Americanists Proceedings, Stockholm,
        1894.* Pp. 24–28.
1991   *Letters of Gustaf Nordenskiöld Written in the Year
        1991 and Articles from the Journals Ymer and The
        Photographic Times.* I. L. Diamond and D. M.
        Olsen, eds. Mesa Verde National Park, Colo.:
        Mesa Verde Museum Association.

Norton, Sara, and M. A. de Wolfe Howe

1913   *Letters of Charles Eliot Norton, with Biographical Comment.* 2 vols. Boston: Houghton Mifflin.

Nusbaum, Aileen

1926   *The Seven Cities of Cibola.* New York: G. P. Putnam's Sons.

Nusbaum, Deric

1926   *Deric in Mesa Verde.* New York: G. P. Putnam's Sons.

1927   *Deric with the Indians.* New York: G. P. Putnam's Sons.

Nusbaum, Jesse L.

1922   *A Basket Maker Cave in Kane County, Utah.* Indian Notes and Monographs, Miscellaneous Series no. 29.

1925   Mesa Verde National Park, Colorado. In *Annual Report of the Director of the National Park Service for 1924.* Pp. 39–42.

1926   Mesa Verde National Park, Colorado. In *Annual Report of the Director of the National Park Service for 1925.* Pp. 108–12.

1934   A Review of the Development of the Laboratory of Anthropology. Mimeo MS on file. ALAB.

1946   Confidential Memo for Director [of the National Park Service] Regarding J. D. Rockefeller, Jr., and Mesa Verde National Park. MVRCA.

1954   Memo to Freeman Tilden Regarding J. D. Rockefeller, Jr., Mesa Verde National Park and the Laboratory of Anthropology. MVRCA.

Nusbaum, Rosemary

1980   *Tierra Dulce: Reminiscences from the Jesse Nusbaum Papers.* Santa Fe: Sunstone Press.

O'Gorman, Edmundo

1942   *Fundamentes para la historia de America.* Imprenta universitaria, Mexico. Reprinted as *The Invention of America: An Inquiry into the Historical Nature of the New World and the Meaning of its History,* 1961. Bloomington: University of Indiana Press.

Opler, Morris E.

1983   The Apachean Culture Pattern and Its Origins. In *Handbook of North American Indians, vol. 10, the Southwest.* Pp. 368–92. Washington, D.C.: Smithsonian Institution.

Ortiz, Alfonso

1969   *The Tewa World: Space, Time, Being and Becoming in a Pueblo Society.* Chicago: University of Chicago Press.

Ortiz, Alfonso, ed.

1979   *Handbook of North American Indians, vol. 9, the Southwest.* Washington, D.C.: Smithsonian Institution.

1983   *Handbook of North American Indians, vol. 10, the Southwest.* Washington, D.C.: Smithsonian Institution.

Osborn, Henry F.

1918   *Men of the Old Stone Age: Their Environment, Life and Art.* 1st ed. New York: Charles Scribner's Sons.

1925   *The Hall of the Age of Man.* New York: American Museum of Natural History.

Owens, John G.

1892   Natal Ceremonies of the Hopi Indians. *Journal of American Archaeology and Ethnology* 2: 163–75.

Oxford English Dictionary

1971   *The Compact Edition of the Oxford English Dictionary.* 2 vols. Oxford: Oxford University Press.

1989   *The Oxford English Dictionary.* 20 vols., 2d ed. Oxford: Clarendon Press.

Packard, Gar, and Maggy Packard

1970   *Southwest 1880s with Ben Wittick: Pioneer Photographer of Indian and Frontier Life.* Santa Fe: Packard Publications.

Pagden, Anthony

1982   *The Fall of Natural Man: The American Indian and the Origins of Comparative Ethnology.* Cambridge: Cambridge University Press.

1993   *European Encounters with the New World: From Renaissance to Romanticism.* New Haven, Conn.: Yale University Press.

Panama-California Exposition

1915   *Official Guidebook to the Exposition.* San Diego: n.p.

Pan-American Exposition

1901   *Official Catalogue and Guide to the Pan-American Exposition.* Buffalo: C. Arhart.

Pandey, Triloki N.

1972   Anthropologists at Zuni. *American Philosophical Society Proceedings* 116(4): 321–37.

Parezo, Nancy J.

1983   *Navajo Sandpainting: From Religious Act to Commercial Art.* Tucson: University of Arizona Press.

1986   Now Is the Time to Collect. *Masterkey* 59(4): 11–18.

1987   The Formation of Ethnographic Collections: The Smithsonian Institution in the American Southwest. *Advances in Archaeological Method and Theory* 10: 1–46.

1993   Matilda Coxe Stevenson: Pioneer Ethnologist.

In *Hidden Scholars: Women Anthropologists and the Native American Southwest.* N. J. Parezo, ed. Pp. 38–62. Albuquerque: University of New Mexico Press.

1999   Collecting for Science and Gain: H. R. Voth and the Hopi. MS in the author's possession.

Parezo, Nancy J., ed.

1993   *Hidden Scholars: Women Anthropologists and the Native American Southwest.* Albuquerque: University of New Mexico Press.

Parmenter, Ross

1966   *Explorer, Linguist, and Ethnologist; a Descriptive Bibliography of the Published Works of Alphonse Louis Pinart, with Notes on his Life.* Frederick Webb Hodge Anniversary Publications 9. Los Angeles: Southwest Museum.

Parmentier, Richard J.

1979   The Pueblo Mythological Triangle: Poseyemu, Montezuma, and Jesus in the Pueblos. *Handbook of North American Indians, vol. 9, Southwest.* Pp. 609–22. Washington, D.C.: Smithsonian Institution.

Parsons, Elsie C.

1906   *The Family: An Ethnographical and Historical Outline with Descriptive Notes.* New York: G. P. Putnam's Sons.

1913a   *Religious Chastity: An Ethnological Study.* New York: Macauley Co. [published under pseudonym of John Main]

1913b   *The Old-Fashioned Woman: Primitive Fancies about Sex.* New York: G. P. Putnam's Sons.

1915a   *Social Freedom: A Study of the Conflicts between Social Classifications and Personality.* New York: G. P. Putnam's Sons.

1915b   War and the Elders. *New Review* 3(12): 191–92.

1916a   Ideal-Less Pacifism. *New Review* 4(4): 115–16.

1916b   The Zuñi La'mana. *American Anthropologist* 18(4): 521–28.

1920   A Hopi Ceremonial. *The Century Magazine* 101(2): 177–80.

1923   *Folk-Lore from the Cape Verde Islands.* Memoirs of the American Folk Lore Society 15, Pts. 1–2.

1932   Isleta, New Mexico. *Forty-seventh Annual Report of the Bureau of American Ethnology, 1929–30.* Pp. 193–466.

1936a   *Mitla: Town of the Souls and Other Zapoteco-Speaking Pueblos of Oaxaca, Mexico.* Chicago: University of Chicago Press.

1936b   Preface and Introduction. In *Hopi Journal of Alexander M. Stephen.* 2 vols. E. C. Parsons, ed. Pp. xx–lii. New York: Columbia University Contributions to Anthropology 23.

1939a   The Last Zuñi Transvestite. *American Anthropologist* 41(2): 338–40.

1939b   *Pueblo Indian Religion.* 2 vols. Chicago: University of Chicago Press.

1942   Anthropology and Prediction. *American Anthropologist* 44: 337–44.

Parsons, Elsie C., and Ralph L. Beals

1934   The Sacred Clowns of the Pueblo and Mayo-Yaqui Indians. *American Anthropologist* 36(4): 491–514.

Parsons, Elsie C., ed.

1922   *American Indian Life by Several of Its Students.* New York: B. W. Huebsch.

1936   *Hopi Journal of Alexander M. Stephen.* 2 vols. New York: Columbia University Contributions to Anthropology 23.

Pater, Walter

1899   *Greek Studies.* New York: Macmillan.

Patterson, Alex

1994   *Hopi Pottery Symbols, Based on Work by Alexander M. Stephen.* Boulder, Colo.: Johnson Books.

Pearce, Roy H.

1965   *Savagism and Civilization: A Study of the Indian and the American Mind.* Baltimore: Johns Hopkins University Press.

Peckham, Howard, and Charles Gibson, eds.

1969   *Attitudes of Colonial Powers toward the American Indian.* Salt Lake City: University of Utah Press.

Peckham, Stewart, Nancy Fox, and Marjorie Lambert

1981   The Laboratory's Modern Era: 1947–1981. *El Palacio* 87(3):32–42.

Penn, Arthur, director; Calder Willingham, writer

1970   *Little Big Man.* Film. Los Angeles: Stockbridge/Hiller/Cinema Center.

Pepper, George H.

1905   Ceremonial Objects and Ornaments from Pueblo Bonito, New Mexico. *American Anthropologist* 7: 183–97.

1909   The Exploration of a Burial Room in Pueblo Bonito, New Mexico. In *Putnam Anniversary Volume, Anthropological Essays Presented to Frederic Ward Putnam in Honor of His Seventieth Birthday.* Pp. 196–252. New York: G. E. Stechert and Co.

1920   *Pueblo Bonito.* American Museum of Natural History Anthropological Papers no. 27.

Peterson, Charles S.

1971   The Hopis and the Mormons. *Utah Historical Quarterly* 39(2): 179–98.

Peterson, Susan

1981   *The Living Tradition of María Martínez.* Tokyo and New York: Kodansha International.

Petrie, W. M. F.

1899   Sequences in Prehistoric Remains. *Journal of the Anthropological Institute of Great Britain and Ireland* 29: 295–301.

Phelan, John L.

1970   Neo-Aztecism in the Eighteenth Century and the Genesis of Mexican Nationalism. In *Culture in History: Essays in Honor of Paul Radin.* S. Diamond, ed. Pp. 760–70. Published for Brandeis University by Columbia University Press, New York.

Philadelphia Inquirer

1876   Fire Swept. A Score of Exhibition Side-Show Barnacles Burned Down on Saturday. Philadelphia Inquirer. Sept. 11, 1876. P. 2.

Phillips, Philip

1955   Alfred Marsten Tozzer: 1877–1954. *American Antiquity* 21: 72–80.

Pinkley, Frank

1925   The Southwestern Monuments. In *Annual Report of the Director of the National Park Service for 1924.* Pp. 148–150.

Pitts, Terance R.

1981   The Early Work of Laura Gilpin, 1917–1932. *Center for Creative Photography, University of Arizona Research Series* 13: 7–9.

Pickering, John

1820   On the Adoption of a Uniform Alphabet for the Indian Languages of North America. *American Academy of Arts and Sciences Memoirs* 4: 319–60. Cambridge.

Poling-Kempes, Lesley

1989.   *The Harvey Girls: Women Who Opened the West.* New York: Paragon House.

Pomeroy, Earl S.

1957   *In Search of the Golden West: The Tourist in Western America.* New York: Alfred A. Knopf.

Poor, Robert M.

1975   Washington Matthews: An Intellectual Biography. Master's thesis, University of Nevada, Reno.

Porter, Joseph C.

1986   *Paper Medicine Man: John Gregory Bourke and His American West.* Norman: University of Oklahoma Press.

Powell, John W.

1875a   The Cañons of the Colorado. *Scribner's Monthly* 9: 293–310, 523–37.

1875b   An Overland Trip to the Grand Cañon. *Scribner's Monthly* 10: 659–78.

1875c   The Ancient Province of Tusayan. *Scribner's Monthly* 11: 193–213.

1875d   *Explorations of the Colorado River of the West and Its Tributaries: Explored in 1869, 1870, 1871, and 1872, Under the Direction of the Secretary of the Smithsonian Institution.* Washington, D.C.: Government Printing Office.

1877   *Introduction to the Study of Indian Languages with Words, Phrases and Sentences to Be Collected.* Washington, D.C.: Government Printing Office.

1878a   *Geological and Geographical Surveys.* U.S. House of Representatives, 45th Cong., 2d sess., Executive Doc. no. 80. Washington. D.C.

1878b   *Report on the Lands of the Arid Region of the United States . . .* U.S. House of Representatives, 45th Cong., 2d sess., Executive Doc. no. 73. Washington, D.C.

1881a   Report of the Director. *First Annual Report of the Bureau of Ethnology, 1879–80.* Pp. xi–xxxiii.

1881b   Sketch of Lewis H. Morgan. *Popular Science Monthly* 18: 114–21.

1887   Museums of Ethnology and Their Classification. *Science* 9: 612–14.

1889   Report of the Director. *Sixth Annual Report of the Bureau of Ethnology, 1884–85.* Pp. xxiii–lviii. Washington, D.C.

1892a   Indian Linguistic Families of America North of Mexico. *Seventh Annual Report of the Bureau of Ethnology, 1885–86.* Pp. 1–142. Washington, D.C.

1892b   Comments by Major Powell on D. C. Brinton's "The Nomenclature and Teaching of Anthropology." *American Anthropologist* o.s. 5(3): 266–71.

1894   Report of the Director. *Eleventh Annual Report of the Bureau of Ethnology, 1889–90.* Pp. xxi–xlvii.

1895   The Soul. *The Monist* 5: 1–16.

1896   Relations of Primitive Peoples to Environment, Illustrated by American Examples. *Annual Report of the Board of Regents of the Smithsonian Institution for 1894–95.* Pp. 625–37.

1897   Report of the Director. *Fifteenth Annual Report of the Bureau of Ethnology, 1893–94.* Pp. xv–cxxi.

1898a *Truth and Error, or, the Science of Intellection.* Chicago: The Open Court Publishing Co.

1898b Report of the Director [the Five Categories of Human Activities—Esthetology, Technology, Sociology, Philology, and Sophiology]. *Sixteenth Annual Report of the Bureau of American Ethnology, 1894–95.* Pp. xv–xcix.

1900 Archaeology, Including the Stone Book, the Ruin Book, and the Tomb Book: Commencement Address for Limestone College. *Limestone College Studies* 1(6): 1–24.

Powell, John W., and George W. Ingalls

1874 *Report of Special Commissioners J. W. Powell and G. W. Ingalls on the Condition of the Ute Indians of Utah; the Paiutes of Northern Arizona, Southern Nevada, and Southeastern California* . . . Washington, D.C.: U.S. Government Printing Office.

Powell, Philip W.

1971 *Tree of Hate: Propaganda and Prejudices Affecting United States Relations with the Hispanic World.* New York: Basic Books.

Prem, Hanns J.

1997 *The Ancient Americas: A Brief History and Guide to Research.* K. Kurbjuhn. trans. Salt Lake City: University of Utah Press.

Prescott, William H.

1837 *History of the Reign of Ferdinand and Isabella, the Catholic.* 3 vols. Boston: American Stationers' Co.

1843 *History of the Conquest of Mexico, with a Preliminary View of the Ancient Mexican Civilization, and the Life of the Conqueror, Hernando Cortés.* 3 vols. New York: Harper Bros.

Price, Sally

1989 *Primitive Art in Civilized Places.* Chicago: University of Chicago Press.

Prudden, Lillian, ed.

1927 *Biographical Sketches and Letters of T. Mitchell Prudden, M.D.* New Haven, Conn.: Yale University Press.

Prudden, T. Mitchell

1896 A Summer among Cliff Dwellings. *Harper's New Monthly Magazine* 93: 545–61.

1897 An Elder Brother of the Cliff Dweller. *Harper's New Monthly Magazine* 95: 56–62.

1903 The Prehistoric Ruins of the San Juan Watershed of Utah, Arizona, Colorado and New Mexico. *American Anthropologist* 5: 224–88.

1906 *On the Great American Plateau: Wanderings Among Canyons and Buttes, in the Land of the Cliff-Dweller, and the Indian of To-day.* New York and London: G. P. Putnam's Sons.

1918 A Further Study of Prehistoric Small House Ruins in the San Juan Watershed. *American Anthropological Association Memoirs* 5(1).

Putnam, Frederic W.

1905 The Peabody Museum and the American Museum. *International Congress of Americanists, Thirteenth Session held in New York in 1902.* Pp. xxxix–xliv.

Putnam, Frederic W., comp. and ed.

1879 Pt. I, Reports Upon Archaeological and Ethnological Collections, pp. 1–314; and Pt. II, The Pueblo Ruins and the Interior Tribes. Pp. 315–97. *Report Upon U.S. Geographical Surveys West of the One Hundredth Meridian in Charge of First Lieut. Geo. M. Wheeler* . . . Washington, D.C.: Government Printing Office.

Pyne, Stephen J.

1980 *Grove Karl Gilbert: A Great Engine of Research.* Austin: University of Texas Press.

Quaife, Milo M., ed.

1921 *Alexander Henry's Travels and Adventures in the Years 1760–1776.* Chicago: Lakeside Press.

Rabineau, Phyllis

1981 North American Anthropology at the Field Museum of Natural History. *American Indian Art* 6(4): 30–37.

Radin, Paul

1942 *The Unpublished Letters of Adolphe F. Bandelier Concerning the Writing and Publication of The Delight Makers.* Southwestern Archaeologica, New York: C. P. Everitt.

Raymenton, H. K.

1962 *History of the San Diego Museum Association.* San Diego: San Diego Museum of Man.

Records

1903 Records Relating to the Investigation of the Bureau of American Ethnology, BAEC.

Redfield, Robert

1941 *The Folk Culture of Yucatán.* Chicago: University of Chicago Press.

Redman, Charles

1999 *Human Impacts on Ancient Environments.* Tucson: University of Arizona Press.

Reed, Erik K.

1951 Cultural Areas of the Pre-Hispanic Southwest. *New Mexico Quarterly* 21(4): 428–39.

Reed, Erik K., and Dale S. King, eds.

1950 *For the Dean: Essays in Anthropology in Honor of Byron Cummings on His Eighty-Ninth Birthday, September 20, 1950.* Tucson: Hohokam Museums Association, and Santa Fe: Southwestern Monuments Association.

Reed, Lori S., and Paul F. Reed, eds.

1992 *Cultural Diversity and Adaptation: The Archaic, Anasazi and Navajo Occupation of the Upper San Juan Basin.* Santa Fe: New Mexico Bureau of Land Management Cultural Resources Series no. 9.

Reeve, F. D.

1957 Seventeenth Century Navaho-Spanish Relations. *New Mexico Historical Review* 32: 36–52.

1958 Navaho-Spanish Wars. *New Mexico Historical Review* 33: 201–31.

1959 The Navaho-Spanish Peace, 1720s–1770s. *New Mexico Historical Review* 34: 9–40.

1960 Navaho-Spanish Diplomacy, 1770–1790. *New Mexico Historical Review* 35: 200–235.

1971 Navajo Foreign Affairs, 1795–1846. *New Mexico Historical Review* 46: 100–132.

Reff, Daniel T.

1992 Contact Shock in Northwestern New Spain, 1518–1764. In *Disease and Demography in the Americas.* J. W. Verano and D. H. Ubelaker, eds. Pp. 265–76. Washington, D.C.: Smithsonian Institution Press.

Reichard, Gladys A.

1925 *Wiyot Grammar and Texts.* University of California Publications in American Archaeology and Ethnology 22.

1928 *Social Life of the Navajo Indians.* New York: Columbia University Press.

1934 *Spider Woman: A Story of Navaho Weavers and Chanters.* New York: Macmillan.

1936 *Navaho Shepard and Weaver.* New York: J. J. Augustin.

1939 *Dezba, Woman of the Desert.* New York: J. J. Augustin.

1950a Another Look at the Navaho. Unpublished manuscript, Gladys Reichard Papers, Museum of Northern Arizona.

1950b *Navaho Religion: A Study in Symbolism.* 2 vols. Bollingen Series no. 18. Princeton, N.J.: Princeton University Press.

Resek, Carl

1960 *Lewis Henry Morgan, American Scholar.* Chicago: University of Chicago Press.

Resolutions

1913 List of Santa Fe Organizations Supporting E. L. Hewett against Charges made by Chamber of Commerce. MS in ELHP.

Rhees, William J.

1880 *James Smithson and His Bequest.* Smithsonian Miscellaneous Collections no. 330.

Rhees, William J., comp. and ed.

1901 *The Smithsonian Institution: Documents Relative to Its Origin and History, 1835–1889.* 2 vols. Washington, D.C.: Government Printing Office.

Rice, Prudence M.

1987 *Pottery Analysis: A Sourcebook.* Chicago: University of Chicago Press.

Richardson, Anna B.

1958 *Oral History Transcript: Anna Bourke Richardson and her Father, Captain John G. Bourke.* Omaha: Douglas County Historical Society.

Richter, Melvin

1977 *The Political Theory of Montesquieu.* Cambridge: Cambridge University Press.

Riggs, Stephen R.

1852 *Grammar and Dictionary of the Dakota Language.* Washington, D.C.: Smithsonian Contributions to Knowledge 4.

Riley, Carroll L.

1999 *The Kachinas and the Cross: Indians and Spaniards in the Early Southwest.* Salt Lake City: University of Utah Press.

Riley, Carroll L., and Basil C. Hedrick, eds.

1978 *Across the Chichimec Sea: Papers in Honor of J. Charles Kelley.* Carbondale: Southern Illinois University Press.

Rivers, W. H. R.

1907 On the Origin of the Classificatory System of Relationships. In *Anthropological Essays Presented to E. B. Tylor.* N. Balfour et al, eds. Pp. 309–23. Oxford: Oxford University Press.

1910 The Genealogical Method of Anthropological Inquiry. *Sociological Review* 3: 1–12.

Robbins, Jane

1901 The First Year at the College Settlement. *Survey* 24: 1801.

Robbins, Wilfred W., John P. Harrington, and Barbara Freire-Marreco

1916 *Ethnobotany of the Tewa Indians.* Bureau of American Ethnology Bulletin no. 55.

Roberts, Frank H. H., Jr.

1929 *Shabik'eshchee Village: a Late Basket Maker Site in*

the Chaco Canyon, New Mexico. Bureau of American Ethnology Bulletin 92.

1931   The Ruins at Kiatuthlanna, Eastern Arizona. Bureau of American Ethnology Bulletin 100.

1932   The Village of the Great Kivas on the Zuñi Reservation, New Mexico. Bureau of American Ethnology Bulletin 111.

1935   A Survey of Southwestern Archaeology. American Anthropologist 37(1): 1–35.

1937   The Folsom Problem in American Archaeology. In Early Man. G. MacCurdy, ed. Pp. 153–62. Philadelphia: Lippincott.

Roberts, Helen

1927   Indian Music from the Southwest. Natural History 27: 257–65.

Robertson, William

1840   History of America. In The Works of William Robertson, D. D. to Which is Prefixed an Account of His Life and Writings by Dugald Stewart, Book IV. Pp. 713–1080. London: William Ball.

Robinson, W. S.

1951   A Method for Chronologically Ordering Archaeological Deposits. American Antiquity 16(4): 293–301.

Robinson, W. W.

1960   The Story of the Southwest Museum. Los Angeles: Ward Ritchie Press.

Rodack, Madeleine T.

1985   Cibola Revisited. In Southwestern Culture History: Collected Papers in Honor of Albert H. Schroeder. C. H. Lange, ed. Pp. 163–82. Papers of the Archaeological Society of New Mexico, vol. 10.

1988   Adolph Bandelier's History of the Borderlands. Journal of the Southwest 30(1): 35–45.

Roessel, Robert A., Jr.

1983   Navajo History, 1850–1923. Handbook of North American Indians, vol. 10, the Southwest. Pp. 506–23. Washington, D.C.: Smithsonian Institution.

Rohner, Ronald, and Evelyn Rohner

1969   The Ethnography of Franz Boas. Chicago: University of Chicago Press.

Ronan, Charles E.

1973   Francisco Javier Clavigero, 1731–1787. In Handbook of Middle American Indians, vol. 13, Guide to Ethnohistorical Sources, pt. 2. Pp. 276–97. Austin: University of Texas Press.

Roosevelt, Theodore

1907   Introduction to Edward S. Curtis, The North American Indian, I: ii–xii. Cambridge, Mass.: University Press.

Roscoe, Will

1987   Bibliography of Berdache and Alternative Gender Roles among North American Indians. Journal of Homosexuality 14(3–4): 81–171.

1991   The Zuñi Man-Woman. Albuquerque: University of New Mexico Press.

Rosenberg, Rosalind

1982   Beyond Separate Spheres: Intellectual Roots of Modern Feminism. New Haven, Conn.: Yale University Press.

Rothman, Hal K.

1986   Forged by One Man's Will: Frank Pinkley and the Administration of the Southwestern National Monuments, 1923–1932. The Public Historian 8(2): 83–99.

1993   Ruins, Reputations, and Regulation: Byron Cummings, William B. Douglass, John Wetherill, and the Summer of 1909. Journal of the Southwest 35(3): 318–40.

Rowe, John H.

1954   Max Uhle, 1856–1944: A Memoir of the Father of Peruvian Archaeology. University of California Publications in American Archaeology and Ethnology 46(1): 1–134.

Rudisill, Richard

1973   Photographers of the New Mexico Territory, 1854–1912. Santa Fe: Museum of New Mexico Press.

Rudisill, Richard, comp. and ed.

1979   Frederick Monsen at Hopi. Museum of New Mexico Reprint Series no. 2.

Rushing, W. Jackson

1995   Native American Art and the New York Avant-Garde. Austin: University of Texas Press.

Russell, Frank

1898   The Jicarilla Apache. Manuscript 1302-a, National Anthropological Archives, Smithsonian Institution, Washington, D.C.

1908   The Pima Indians. Twenty-Sixth Annual Report of the Bureau of American Ethnology, 1904–5. Pp. 3–389.

Russell, [Frances] Theresa

1901   Sketch of a Pima Woman. Manuscript in F. T. Russell Papers, Special Collections, Stanford University Library, Stanford, Calif.

1906   In Pursuit of a Graveyard: Being the Trail of an Archaeological Wedding Journey. Out West Magazine 24: 39–49, 201–7, 300–307, 312–15,

405–14, 544–48; 25: 132–38, 247–57, 341–47, 511–17.

1920   *Satire in the Victorian Novel*. New York: Belle Lettres Victorian Novels; Macmillan.

1932   *Turning Utopia: The Realm of Constructive Humanism*. New York: Dial Press.

Ruxton, George F.

1950   *Ruxton of the Rockies, Collected by Clyde and Mae Reed Porter*. L. and A. W. Hafen, eds. Norman: University of Oklahoma Press.

1951   *Life in the Far West by George Frederick Ruxton*. L. Hafen and A. W. Hafen, eds. Norman: University of Oklahoma Press.

Rydell, Robert W.

1984   *All the World's a Fair*. Chicago: University of Chicago Press.

1989   The Culture of Imperial Abundance: World's Fairs in the Making of American Culture. In *Consuming Visions: Accumulation and Display of Goods in America, 1880–1920*. S. J. Bronner, ed. Pp. 191–216. New York: W. W. Norton and Co.

1992   *The Books of Fairs: Materials about World's Fairs, 1834–1916 in the Smithsonian Libraries*. Smithsonian Institution Libraries Research Guide no. 6. Chicago: American Library Association.

1993   *World of Fairs: The Century of Progress Expositions*. Chicago: University of Chicago Press.

Sabloff, Paula L. W.

1998   *Conversations with Lewis Binford: Drafting the New Archaeology*. Norman: University of Oklahoma Press.

Sahagún, Bernardino de

1932   *A History of Ancient Mexico*. Fanny Bandelier, trans. Vol. 1. Nashville: Fisk University Social Science Series.

St. Louis Globe-Democrat

1903   Untitled article, Aug. 14, 1903. In McGee Papers, Box 32, Newspaper scrapbook. Library of Congress, Washington, D.C.

St. Louis Post-Dispatch

1901   World Anthropology Exhibit, Aug. 27, 1901, n.p. Clipping in Louisiana Purchase Exposition files, Missouri Historical Society, St. Louis.

St. Louis Republic

1901   "To Cover the World." Reprinted in *Washington Post*, Aug. 30, 1901. n.p. James Mooney Collection, Folder 2214, BAEC.

Sánchez, Joseph P.

1997   *Explorers, Traders, and Slavers. Forging the Old Spanish Trail, 1678–1850*. Salt Lake City: University of Utah Press.

San Diego Union

1915   Priceless Busts of Primal Man at Fair. *San Diego Union*, Jan. 31, 1915. Clipping in Panama-California Exposition Papers, San Diego Historical Society.

Santa Fe Chamber of Commerce

1913   Resolution to AIA Regarding School of American Archaeology, Nov. 11, 1913. Copy in ELHP.

Sapir, Edward

1949   Time Perspective in Aboriginal American Culture: A Study in Method. In *Selected Writings in Language, Culture and Personality*. D. G. Mandelbaum, ed. Pp. 389–462. Berkeley and Los Angeles: University of California Press. Originally published in 1916.

Sauer, Carl O.

1971   *Sixteenth Century North America: The Land and the People as Seen by the Europeans*. Berkeley: University of California Press.

Saunders, Charles F.

1912   *Indians of the Terraced Houses: An Account of the Pueblo Indians of New Mexico and Arizona, 1902–1910*. New York: G. P. Putnam's Sons.

Sayles, E. B.

1983   *The Cochise Cultural Sequence in Southeastern Arizona*. University of Arizona Anthropological Papers no. 42.

Schaafsma, Polly, ed.

1994   *Kachinas in the Pueblo World*. Albuquerque: University of New Mexico Press.

Schmeckbier, L. F.

1904   *Catalogue and Index of the Publications of the Hayden, King, Powell, and Wheeler Surveys*. U.S. Geological Survey Bulletin no. 222; Series G, Misc., 26. Washington. Reprinted, Portland: Northwest Books, 1970.

Schoolcraft, Henry R.

1847   Inquiries Respecting the History, Present Condition and Future Prospects of the Indian Tribes of the United States. Washington, D.C.: Bureau of Indian Affairs. Reprinted in Schoolcraft 1851–57. I: 523–568.

1851–57 *Historical and Statistical Information Respecting the History, Condition and Prospects of the Indian Tribes of the United States, Collected and Prepared under the Direction of the Bureau of Indian Affairs, per Act of Congress of March 3rd, 1847.* 6 vols. Philadelphia: Lippincott.

Schroeder, Albert H.

1965   A Brief History of the Southern Ute. *Southwestern Lore* 30(4): 53–78.

1979   Pueblos Abandoned in Historic Times. *Handbook of North American Indians, vol. 9, Southwest.* Pp. 236–55. Washington, D.C.: Smithsonian Institution.

1993   Preface to this edition. In E. L. Hewett, *Ancient Communities in the American Desert.* Archaeological Society of New Mexico Monograph Series 1: xi–xvii.

Schroeder, John H.

1973   *Mr. Polk's War: American Opposition and Dissent, 1846–1848.* Madison: University of Wisconsin Press.

Schwartz, Douglas W.

1983   Havasupai. *Handbook of North American Indians vol. 10, Southwest.* Pp. 13–24. Washington, D.C.: Smithsonian Institution.

Scott, Ann H.

1968   *Census, U.S.A. Fact Finding for the American People, 1790–1970.* New York: Seabury Press.

Scott, David

1975   *John Sloan.* New York: Watson-Guptill Publications.

Sebastian, Lynne

1992   *The Chaco Anasazi: Sociopolitical Evolution in the Prehistoric Southwest.* Cambridge: Cambridge University Press.

Seed, Patricia

1993   "Are These Not Also Men?": The Indians' Humanity and Capacity for Spanish Civilisation. *Journal of Latin American Studies* 25(3): 629–52.

1995   *Ceremonies of Possession in Europe's Conquest of the New World, 1492–1640.* Cambridge: Cambridge University Press.

Seligman, E. R. A., John Dewey, Frank Fetter, A. O. Lovejoy, and H. C. Warren

1915   Preliminary Summary of Findings of the Committee of Inquiry of the American Association of University Professors on Conditions at the University of Utah, May 1915. Copy in Byron Cummings Papers, Arizona Historical Society, Tucson.

Seltzer, Carl C.

1944   *Racial Prehistory in the Southwest and the Hawikuh Zunis.* Papers of the Peabody Museum of American Archaeology and Ethnology 23(1).

Sergeant, Elizabeth S.

1934   The Santa Fe Group. *The Saturday Review of Literature,* Dec. 8, 1934. Pp. 352, 354.

Service, Elman R., Richard K. Beardsley, and Beth Dillingham

1976   Leslie Alvin White 1900–1975. *American Anthropologist* 78: 612–29.

Shakespeare, William

1978   The Tempest. In *The Annotated Shakespeare, vol. III, The Tragedies and Romances.* A. L. Rowse, ed. Pp. 860–907. New York: Clarkson N. Potter.

Sheets-Pyenson, Susan

1988   *Cathedrals of Science: The Development of Colonial Natural History Museums during the Late Nineteenth Century.* Kingston and Montreal: McGill-Queen's University Press.

Shelford, Victor E.

1963   *The Ecology of North America.* Urbana: University of Illinois Press.

Sheppard, Carl D.

1988   *Creator of the Santa Fe Style: Isaac Hamilton Rapp, Architect.* Albuquerque: University of New Mexico Press.

Shields, Robert H.

1945   The Enchanted City of the Caesars, El Dorado of Southern South America. In *Greater America: Essays in Honor of Herbert Eugene Bolton.* Pp. 319–40. Berkeley: University of California Press.

Shipek, Florence C.

1978   History of Southern California Indian Missions. *Handbook of North American Indians, vol. 8, California.* Pp. 610–18. Washington, D.C.: Smithsonian Institution.

Shipley, William F.

1978   Native Languages of California. *Handbook of North American Indians, vol. 8, California.* Pp. 80–90. Washington, D.C.: Smithsonian Institution.

Shishkin, J. K.

1968   *An Early History of the Museum of New Mexico Fine Arts Building.* Santa Fe: Museum of New Mexico Press.

Shoemaker, Nancy

1997   How Indians Got to be Red. *American Historical Review* 102(3): 625–44.

Silverberg, Robert

1968   *Mound Builders of Ancient America: The Archaeol-*

ogy of a Myth. Greenwich: New York Graphic Society.

1994   *The Pueblo Revolt.* Lincoln: University of Nebraska Press.

Simmons, Marc

1988   "Misery" as a Factor in New Mexican Colonial Life. In *Reflections: Papers on Southwestern Culture History in Honor of Charles H. Lange.* A. V. Poore, ed. Pp. 227–30. Santa Fe: Papers of the Archaeological Society of New Mexico vol. 14.

1991   *The Last Conquistador: Juan de Oñate and the Settling of the Far Southwest.* Norman: University of Oklahoma Press.

Simon, Charlie May

1953   *Johnswood.* New York: E. P. Dutton.

Simpson, James H.

1964   *Journal of a Military Reconnaissance from Santa Fe, New Mexico to the Navajo Country Made in 1849.* F. McNitt, ed. Norman: University of Oklahoma Press. Originally published 1850 in 31st Cong., 1st sess., Senate Executive Doc. 64, 55–168.

Sitgreaves, Lorenzo

1853   *Report of an Expedition Down the Zuñi and Colorado Rivers in 1851.* 32d Cong., 2d sess., Senate Executive Doc. no. 59, pp. 1–21.

Skiff, Frederick F. V.

1905   Introduction. In *Louisiana and the Fair: An Exposition of the World, Its People and Their Accomplishments.* J. W. Buel, ed. Vol. 9. Pp. i–xii. St. Louis: World's Progress Publishing Co.

Smith Company, H. Jay

1893   *The Cliff Dwellers* [Booklet guide to Cliff Dwellers exhibit, Chicago world's fair, 1893]. Chicago: n.p., CHP.

Smith, Jack E.

1985   *Mesas, Cliffs, and Canyons: The University of Colorado Survey of Mesa Verde National Park 1971–1977.* Mesa Verde Research Series Paper no. 3.

Smith, Watson, Richard B. Woodbury, and Nathalie F. S. Woodbury

1966   *The Excavation of Hawikuh by Frederick Webb Hodge. Report of the Hendricks-Hodge Expedition, 1917–1923.* New York: Contributions from the Museum of the American Indian, Heye Foundation. vol. 20.

Snead, James E.

1999   Science, Commerce and Control: Patronage and the Development of Anthropological Archaeology in the Americas. *American Anthropologist* 101(2): 256–71.

2001   *Competing for the Past: Ruins, Rivals, and the Making of Southwestern Archaeology.* Tucson: University of Arizona Press.

Snow, Dean R.

1994   *The Iroquois.* Cambridge: Blackwell.

Spencer, Frank

1979   Aleš Hrdlička, M.D., 1869–1943: A Chronicle of the Life and Work of an American Physical Anthropologist. Ph.D. diss., University of Michigan.

Spencer, Herbert

1857   Progress: Its Laws and Causes. *Westminster Review* 67: 445–85.

Spengler, Oswald

1926   *The Decline of the West.* 2 vols. New York: Alfred A. Knopf.

Spicer, Edward H.

1962   *Cycles of Conquest: The Impact of Spain, Mexico, and the United States on the Indians of the Southwest, 1533–1960.* Tucson: University of Arizona Press.

Spier, Leslie

1917a   Zuñi Chronology. *Proceedings of the National Academy of Sciences* 3: 280–83.

1917b   An Outline for a Chronology of Zuñi Ruins. *American Museum of Natural History Anthropological Papers* 18(3): 207–331.

1918   Notes on Some Little Colorado Ruins. *American Museum of Natural History Anthropological Papers* 18(4): 332–62.

1919   Ruins in the White Mountains, Arizona. *American Museum of Natural History Anthropological Papers* 18(5): 363–87.

1928   Havasupai Ethnography. *American Museum of Natural History Anthropological Papers* 29(3):81–392.

1931   N. C. Nelson's Stratigraphic Technique in the Reconstruction of Prehistoric Sequences in Southwestern America. In *Methods in Social Science, A Casebook.* S. A. Rice, ed. Pp. 275–83. Chicago: University of Chicago Press.

1959   Some Central Elements in the Legacy. In *The Anthropology of Franz Boas.* W. Goldschmidt, ed. Pp. 146–55. American Anthropological Association Memoir no. 89.

Spinden, Herbert J.

1915 Indian Dances of the Southwest. *American Museum Journal* 15(2): 103–15.

1922 *Ancient Civilizations of Mexico and Central America.* American Museum of Natural History Handbook Series no. 3.

Spitzka, Edward A.

1903 A Study of the Brain of the Late J. W. Powell. *American Anthropologist* 5: 585–643.

1913 A Death Mask of W J McGee. *American Anthropologist* 15: 536–38.

Springer, Frank

1901 *Uintacrinus: Its Structure and Relations.* Memoirs of the Museum of Comparative Zoology at Harvard College 25, no. 1.

1911 *Some New American Fossil Crinoids.* Memoirs of the Cambridge: Museum of Comparative Zoology at Harvard College 25, no. iii.

1926 *American Silurian Crinoids.* Washington, D.C.: Smithsonian Institution.

Squier, Ephraim G.

1848 New Mexico and California. *The American Review; A Whig Journal Devoted to Politics and Literature,* n.s. 3, whole vol. 9: 503–28.

1860 52 *Nicaragua: Its People, Scenery, Monuments, Resources, Condition and Proposed Canal.* New York: Harper and Bros.

Squier, E. G., and Edwin H. Davis

1848 *Ancient Monuments of the Mississippi Valley.* Smithsonian Contributions to Knowledge no. 1.

Stafford, Barbara M.

1984 *Voyage into Substance. Art, Science, Nature, and the Illustrated Travel Account, 1760–1840.* Cambridge: MIT Press.

Stanislawski, Michael

1979 Hopi-Tewa. *Handbook of North American Indians, vol. 9, Southwest,* pp. 587–602. Washington, D.C.: Smithsonian Institution.

Stark, Gregor, and E. Catherine Rayne

1998 *El Delirio: The Santa Fe World of Elizabeth White.* Santa Fe: School of American Research.

Starr, Kevin

1973 *Americans and the California Dream, 1850–1915.* New York: Oxford University Press.

1985 *Inventing the Dream: California through the Progressive Era.* New York: Oxford University Press.

1990 *Material Dreams: Southern California through the 1920s.* New York: Oxford University Press.

Stedman, Raymond W.

1982 *Shadows of the Indian: Stereotypes in American Culture.* Norman: University of Oklahoma Press.

Stegner, Wallace

1942 *Mormon Country.* New York: Duell, Sloan and Pearce.

1954 *Beyond the Hundredth Meridian: John Wesley Powell and the Second Opening of the West.* Boston: Houghton Mifflin.

Stephen, Alexander M.

1936 *Hopi Journal of Alexander M. Stephen.* 2 vols. E. C. Parsons, ed. New York: Columbia University Contributions to Anthropology 23.

Stephens, John Lloyd

1837 *Incidents of Travel in Egypt, Arabia Petraea, and the Holy Land.* New York: Harper and Bros.

1843 *Incidents of Travel in Yucatán.* New York: Harper and Bros.

Stephenson, Robert L.

1967 Frank H. H. Roberts, Jr., 1897–1966. *American Antiquity* 32(1): 84–94.

Stevenson, James

1881a Illustrated Catalogue of the Collections Obtained from the Indians of New Mexico and Arizona in 1879. *Second Annual Report of the Bureau of Ethnology, 1880–81.* Pp. 307–422.

1881b Illustrated Catalogue of the Collections Obtained from the Indians of New Mexico and Arizona in 1880. *Second Annual Report of the Bureau of Ethnology, 1880–81.* Pp. 423–65.

1891 Ceremonial of Hasjelti Dailjis and Mythical Sand Painting of the Navajo Indians. *Eighth Annual Report of the Bureau of Ethnology, 1886–1887.* Pp. 229–85.

Stevenson, Matilda Coxe

1894 The Sia. *Eleventh Annual Report of the Bureau of Ethnology, 1889–90.* Pp. 3–157.

1904 The Zuñi Indians: Their Mythology, Esoteric Fraternities, and Ceremonies. *Twenty-third Annual Report of the Bureau of Ethnology, 1901–2,* pp. 3–608.

1915 Ethnobotany of the Zuñi Indians. *Thirtieth Annual Report of the Bureau of Ethnology, 1908–9.* Pp. 31–102.

Stevenson, Tilly E., Mrs. [Matilda Coxe]

1887 The Religious Life of the Zuñi Child. *Fifth*

Annual Report of the Bureau of Ethnology, 1883–84.
Pp. 533–55.

Stevenson, Tilly Evans [Matilda Coxe]

1881   *Zuñi and the Zuñians.* Washington, D.C.:
Privately printed.

Steward, Julian H.

1961   Alfred Louis Kroeber 1876–1960. *American
Anthropologist* 63(4): 1038–87.

1973   *Alfred Lewis Kroeber.* New York: Columbia University Press.

Stewart, Kenneth M.

1983   Mohave. *Handbook of North American Indians,
vol. 10, Southwest.* Pp. 55–70. Washington, D.C.:
Smithsonian Institution.

Stewart, T. Dale

1940   The Life and Writings of Dr. Aleš Hrdlička
(1869–1939). *American Journal of Physical Anthropology* 26: 3–40.

Stirling, Matthew W., and Karlena Glemser

1963   John Peabody Harrington, 1884–1961. *American
Anthropologist* 65(2): 370–81.

Stocking, George W., Jr.

1968   *Race, Culture and Evolution: Essays in the History
of Anthropology.* New York: Free Press.

1971   What's in a Name? The Origins of the Royal
Anthropological Institute (1837–1871). *Man,
Journal of the Royal Anthropological Institute* 6:
369–90.

1974   Introduction: The Basic Assumptions of Boasian
Anthropology. In *The Shaping of American An-
thropology 1883–1911: A Franz Boas Reader.* G. W.
Stocking, Jr., ed. Pp. 1–20. New York: Basic
Books.

1981   Anthropological Visions and Economic Realities.
El Palacio 87(3): 14–17.

1982   The Santa Fe Style in American Archaeology: Regional Interest, Academic Initiative and Philanthropic Policy in the First Two Decades of the
Laboratory of Anthropology. *Journal of the
History of the Behavioral Sciences* 18: 3–19.

1985   Philanthropoids and Vanishing Cultures: Rocke-
feller Funding and the End of the Museum Era in
American Anthropology. In *Objects and Others:
Essays on Museums and Material Culture.* G. W.
Stocking, Jr., ed. Pp. 112–45. History of Anthro-
pology, vol. 3. Madison: University of Wisconsin
Press.

1989   The Ethnographic Sensibility of the 1920s and
the Dualism of the Anthropological Tradition. In
*Romantic Motives: Essays on Anthropological Sensi-
bility.* G. W. Stocking, Jr., ed. Pp. 208–76.
History of Anthropology, vol. 6. Madison: University of Wisconsin Press.

1995   *After Tylor: British Social Anthropology, 1888–1951.*
Madison: University of Wisconsin Press.

Stocking, George W., Jr., ed.

1974   *The Shaping of American Anthropology 1883–1911:
A Franz Boas Reader.* New York: Basic Books,
New York.

Stodder, Ann L. W., and Debra L. Martin

1992   Health and Disease in the Southwest Before
and After Spanish Contact. In *Disease and Demography in the Americas.* J. W. Verano and D. H.
Ubelaker, eds. Pp. 55–73. Washington, D.C.:
Smithsonian Institution Press.

Stolpe, Hjalmar

1897   Gustaf Nordenskiöld, Biographical Notice. *International Congress of Americanists Proceedings,
Stockholm (1894).* Pp. 245–48.

Strong, Pauline T.

1979   San Felipe Pueblo. *Handbook of North American
Indians, vol. 9, Southwest.* Pp. 390–97. Washington, D.C.: Smithsonian Institution Press.

Sullivan, Lawrence E., ed.

1989   *Native American Religions North America.* New
York: Macmillan.

Sunder, John E., ed.

1960   *Matt Field on the Santa Fe Trail, Collected by Clyde
and Mae Reed Porter.* Norman: University of
Oklahoma Press.

Sutherland, Edwin V.

1964   The Diaries of John Gregory Bourke: Their Anthropological and Folklore Content. Ph.D. diss.,
University of Pennsylvania, Philadelphia.

Swadesh, Morris

1967   Linguistic Classification in the Southwest. In
Studies in Southwestern Ethnolinguistics. D. H.
Hymes and W. E. Bittle, eds. Pp. 281–309. Paris
and The Hague: Mouton.

Swanberg, W. A.

1961   *Citizen Hearst: A Biography of William Randolph
Hearst.* New York: Scribner's.

Swanton, John R., and F. H. H. Roberts, Jr.

1931   Jesse Walter Fewkes. *Annual Report of the Smithsonian Institution for 1930.* Pp. 609–16.

Swarthout, William N.

1904   A Descriptive Story of the Philippine Exhibit.
World's Fair Bulletin 5(8): 48–56.

Swiggers, Pierre

1998 Americanist Linguistics and the Origin of Linguistic Typology: Peter Stephen Du Ponceau's "Comparative Science of Language." *American Philosophical Society Proceedings* 142(1): 18–46.

Tanner, Clara Lee

1954 Byron Cummings, 1860–1954. *The Kiva* 20(1): 1–20.

1968 *Southwest Indian Craft Arts.* Tucson: University of Arizona Press.

1973 *Southwest Indian Painting: A Changing Art.* 2d ed. Tucson: University of Arizona Press.

Taylor, W. W.

1948 *A Study of Archaeology.* American Anthropological Association Memoir 69.

Tedlock, Barbara

1992 *The Beautiful and the Dangerous: Encounters with the Zuñi Indians.* Viking Penguin, New York.

Tedlock, Dennis

1979 Zuñi Religion and World View. *Handbook of North American Indians, vol. 9, Southwest.* Pp. 499–508. Washington, D.C.: Smithsonian Institution Press.

Ten Broeck, P. G. S.

1854 Manners and Customs of the Moqui and Navajo Tribes of New Mexico. In *Historical and Statistical Information Respecting the History, Condition and Prospects of the Indian Tribes of the United States.* H. R. Schoolcraft, ed. Vol. 4: 72–98. Philadelphia: Lippincott, Grambo Co.

ten Kate, Herman F. C.

1892 Somatological Observations on Indians of the Southwest. *Journal of American Archaeology and Ethnology* 3: 119–44.

Ternaux-Compans, Henri, comp.

1837–41 *Voyages, Relations et mémoires originaux pour servir à l'histoire de la découverte de l'Amérique, puliiés pour la premiere fois en français.* Paris: A. Bertrand.

Thomas, Cyrus

1894 Report of the Mound Explorations of the Bureau of Ethnology. *Twelfth Annual Report of the Bureau of Ethnology, 1890–91.* Pp. 3–730.

Thomas, David H.

1991 Harvesting Ramona's Garden: Life in California's Mythical Mission Past. In *Columbian Consequences. vol. 3. The Spanish Borderlands in Pan-American Perspective.* D. H. Thomas, ed. Pp.

119–57. Washington, D.C.: Smithsonian Institution Press.

Thomas, Diane D.

1978 *The Southwest Indian Detours.* Phoenix: Hunter Publishers.

Thomas, Isaiah

1820 An Account of the American Antiquarian Society [and] Abstract of a Communication Made to the Society by the President. *Archaeologica Americana. Transactions and Collections of the American Antiquarian Society* 1: 24–40.

Thompson, Gerald

1983 *Edward F. Beale and the American West.* Albuquerque: University of New Mexico Press.

Thoreau, Henry D.

1980 *A Week on the Concord and Merrimack Rivers.* C. F. Hovde, ed. Princeton, N.J.: Princeton University Press.

Thoresen, Timothy H. H.

1975 Paying the Piper and Calling the Tune: The Beginnings of Academic Anthropology in California. *Journal of the History of the Behavioral Sciences* 11(3): 257–75.

Thorpe, James E.

1994 *Henry Edward Huntington: A Biography.* Berkeley: University of California Press.

Thorslev, Peter L., Jr.

1984 *Romantic Contraries: Freedom versus Destiny.* New Haven, Conn.: Yale University Press.

Thrapp, Dan L.

1967 *The Conquest of Apacheria.* Norman: University of Oklahoma Press.

Thwaites, Reuben G., ed.

1896–1901 *The Jesuit Relations and Allied Documents.* 73 vols. Cleveland: Burrows Brothers.

Titiev, Mischa

1944 *Old Oraibi: A Study of the Hopi Indians of Third Mesa.* Papers of the Peabody Museum of American Archaeology and Ethnology 22(1).

1972 *The Hopi Indians of Old Oraibi: Continuity and Change.* Ann Arbor: University of Michigan Press.

Tocqueville, Alexis de

1945 *Democracy in America,* 2 vols. New York: Alfred Knopf.

Tooker, Elisabeth

1978a History of Research. In *Handbook of North American Indians, vol. 15, Northeast.* Pp. 4–13. Washington, D.C.: Smithsonian Institution.

1978b The League of the Iroquois: Its History, Politics, and Ritual. In *Handbook of North American Indians, vol. 15, Northeast.* Pp. 418–41. Washington, D.C.: Smithsonian Institution.

1978c Iroquois since 1820. In *Handbook of North American Indians, vol. 15, Northeast.* Pp. 449–65. Washington, D.C.: Smithsonian Institution.

1994 *Lewis Henry Morgan on Iroquois Material Culture.* Tucson: University of Arizona Press.

Toulmin, Stephen

1992 *Cosmopolis: The Hidden Agenda of Modernity.* Chicago: University of Chicago Press.

Toulmin, Stephen, and June Goodfield

1965 *The Discovery of Time.* New York: Harper Torchbooks.

Toulouse, Betty

1981a Prelude: Founding of the Laboratory. *El Palacio* 87(3): 4–6.

1981b The Laboratory's Early Years: 1927–1947. *El Palacio* 87(3): 6–13.

Towner, Ronald H., ed.

1996 *The Archaeology of Navajo Origins.* Salt Lake City: University of Utah Press.

Tozzer, Alfred M.

1905 A Navajo Sand Picture of the Rain Gods and Its Attendant Ceremony. *International Congress of Americanists, Thirteenth Session Held in New York in 1902.* Pp. 147–56.

1908 A Note on Star-lore among the Navaho. *Journal of American Folklore* 21: 28–32.

1909 Notes on Religious Ceremonials of the Navaho. In *Putnam Anniversary Volume: Anthropological Essays Presented to Frederic Ward Putnam in Honor of His Seventieth Birthday, April 16, 1909.* F. Boas et al, eds. Pp. 299–343. New York: G. E. Stechert.

1912 Letter to the Editor, The New World's Oldest City? *The New York Times.* 1/25/1912. Clipping in CHP.

1915 Summary of the Work of the International School of American Archeology and Ethnology in Mexico, 1910–1914. *American Anthropologist* 17: 384–95.

1933 Zelia Nuttall. *American Anthropologist* 35: 474–482.

Trautmann, Thomas R., and Karl S. Kabelac

1994 *The Library of Lewis Henry Morgan.* Philadelphia: American Philosophical Society Transactions 84, pts. 6 and 7.

Trennert, Robert A., Jr.

1974 A Grand Failure: The Centennial Indian Exhibition of 1876. *Prologue: The Journal of the National Archives* 6(2): 118–29. Washington. D.C.

1987a Fairs, Expositions and the Changing Image of Southwestern Indians, 1876–1904. *New Mexico Historical Review* 62(2): 127–45.

1987b Selling Indian Education at World's Fairs and Expositions, 1893–1904. *American Indian Quarterly* 11: 203–20.

Trenton, Patricia, and Peter H. Hassrick

1983 *The Rocky Mountains: A Vision for Artists in the Nineteenth Century.* Norman: University of Oklahoma Press.

Treutlein, Theodore E., trans.

1949 *Ignaz Pfefferkorn, Sonora: A Description of the Provinces.* Albuquerque: University of New Mexico Press.

Troutman, John W., and Nancy J. Parezo

1998 "The Overlord of the Savage World": Anthropology at the 1904 Louisiana Exposition. *Museum Anthropology* 22(2): 17–34.

True, Frederick W., William H. Holmes, and George P. Merrill

1903 Report on the Exhibit of the United States National Museum at the Pan-American Exposition, Buffalo, New York, 1901. *U.S. National Museum Annual Report for 1900–01,* Pp. 177–231. GPO.

Truman, Benjamin C.

1893 *History of the World's Fair.* Chicago: Mammoth Publishing Co.

Turnbaugh, William A.

1980 Of Saints and Other Celebrated Savages. *Anthropology* 4 (1): 11–22.

Turner, Christy G., II

1962 *A Summary of the Archeological Explorations of Dr. Byron Cummings in the Anasazi Culture Area.* Flagstaff: Museum of Northern Arizona Technical Series no. 5.

Turner, Frederick J.

1894 The Significance of the Frontier in American History. *Annual Report, American Historical Association 1893.* Pp. 199–227. Washington, D.C.: Government Printing Office.

Turner, William

1852 The Apaches: A Paper Read before the American Ethnological Society. *Literary World* 272 (Apr. 17, 1852): 281–82.

Twitchell, Ralph E.

1909 *The History of the Military Occupation of the Territory of New Mexico from 1846 to 1851 by the Government of the United States.* Denver, Colorado: Smith-Brooks Co. Reprinted, Chicago: Rio Grande Press, 1963.

1919 *The City Different.* Santa Fe: Santa Fe Chamber of Commerce.

Tyler, David B.

1968 *The Wilkes Expedition: First United States Exploring Expedition (1838–1840).* American Philosophical Society Memoir 73.

Tylor, Edward B.

1888 On a Method of Investigating the Development of Institutions, Applied to Laws of Marriage and Descent. *Journal of the Anthropological Institute* 18: 245–72.

1958 *Primitive Culture: Researches into the Development of Mythology, Philosophy, Religion, Language, Art and Custom.* New York: Harper. Originally published in 1871.

Udall, Sharyn R.

1996 *Contested Terrain: Myth and Meanings in Southwest Art.* Albuquerque: University of New Mexico Press.

Upham, Steadman

1992 Population and Spanish Contact in the Southwest. In *Disease and Demography in the Americas.* J. W. Verano and D. H. Ubelaker, eds. Pp. 223–36. Washington, D.C.: Smithsonian Institution Press.

Urry, James

1972 Notes and Queries on Anthropology and the Development of Field Methods in British Anthropology, 1870–1920. *Proceedings of the Royal Anthropological Institute for 1972*: 45–57.

Ussher, James

1658 *The Annals of the World Deduced from the Origin of Time . . .* London: J. Crook and G. Bedell.

Van Gennep, Arnold

1960 *Rites of Passage.* Chicago: University of Chicago Press. Originally published in 1909.

Vaughan, Alden T.

1965 *New England Frontier: Puritans and Indians, 1620–1675.* Boston: Little, Brown.

1982 From White Man to Redskin; Changing Anglo-American Perceptions of the American Indian. *American Historical Review* 87: 917–53.

Vickery, John B.

1973 *The Literary Impact of The Golden Bough.* Princeton, N.J.: Princeton University Press.

Viola, Herman J.

1981 *Diplomats in Buckskins: A History of Indian Delegations in Washington City.* Washington, D.C.: Smithsonian Institution Press.

Vivian, R. Gordon

1964 *Gran Quivira: Excavations in a Seventeenth Century Jumano Pueblo.* Washington, D.C.: U.S. National Park Service Archeological Research Series 8.

Voegelin, Charles F., and Florence M. Voegelin

1957 *Hopi Domains: A Lexical Approach to the Problem of Selection.* Indiana University Publications in Anthropology and Linguistics, Memoir 14.

Voth, Henry R.

1901 The Oráibi Powamu Ceremony. *Field Columbian Museum Publication 61, Anthropological Series* 3(2): 67–158.

1903a The Oráibi Summer Snake Ceremony. *Field Columbian Museum Publication 83, Anthropological Series* 3(4): 262–358.

1903b The Oráibi Oáquöl Ceremony. *Field Columbian Museum Publication 84, Anthropological Series* 6(1): 1–46.

1905 The Traditions of the Hopi. *Field Columbian Museum Publication 96, Anthropological Series* 8: 1–319.

1912a The Oraibi Marau Ceremony. *Field Museum of Natural History Publication 156, Anthropological Series* 11(1): 1–88.

1912b Brief Miscellaneous Hopi Papers. *Field Museum of Natural History Publication 157, Anthropological Series* 11(2): 89–149.

Wade, Edwin L.

1976 The History of the Southwest Indian Ethnic Art Market. Ph.D. diss., University of Washington. Ann Arbor, Mich.: University Microfilms, 77–629.

1980 The Thomas Keam Collection of Hopi Pottery: A New Typology. *American Indian Art Magazine* 5(3): 55–61.

1985 The Ethnic Art Market in the American Southwest, 1880–1980. In *Objects and Others: Essays on Museums and Material Culture.* G. W. Stocking, Jr., ed. Pp. 167–91. History of Anthropology, vol. 3. Madison: University of Wisconsin Press.

Wade, Edwin L., and Katherine L. Chase

1996 A Personal Passion and Profitable Pursuit: The Katherine Harvey Collection of Native American Fine Art. In *The Great Southwest of the Fred Harvey Company and the Santa Fe Railway,* edited by Marta Wiegle and Barbara Babcock, Pp. 140–154. Phoenix: Heard Museum.

Wade, Edwin L., and Lea McChesney

1980 *America's Great Lost Expedition: The Thomas Keam Collection of Hopi Pottery from the Second Hemenway Expedition, 1890–1894.* Phoenix: Heard Museum.

1981 *Historic Hopi Ceramics: The Thomas V. Keam Collection of the Peabody Museum of Archaeology and Ethnology, Harvard University.* Cambridge, Mass.: Peabody Museum Press.

Wagner, Henry R.

1937 *The Spanish Southwest, 1542–1794: An Annotated Bibliography.* Quivira Society Publications vol. 7, pts. I–II.

1954 Henri Ternaux Compans: The First Collector of Hispanic-Americana. *Inter-American Review of Bibliography* 4(4): 283–98.

Walker, Franklin

1950 *A Literary History of Southern California.* Berkeley: University of California Press.

Wallace, Edward S.

1955 *The Great Reconnaissance: Soldiers, Artists and Scientists on the Frontier, 1848–1861.* Boston: Little, Brown and Company.

Wallace, Irving

1959 *The Fabulous Showman: The Life and Times of P. T. Barnum.* New York: Alfred A. Knopf.

Wallace, Lew

1873 *The Fair God, or, the Last of the 'Tzins: A Tale of the Conquest of Mexico.* Boston: James R. Osgood Co.

1880 *Ben Hur: A Tale of the Christ.* New York: Harper and Bros.

1906 *Lew Wallace: An Autobiography.* 2 vols. New York and London: Harper and Bros.

Wallace, Susan E.

1888 *The Land of the Pueblos.* New York: J. B. Alden.

Wallis, Wilson D.

1941 Alexander A. Goldenweiser. *American Anthropologist* 43: 250–55.

Walsh, Jane M.

1976 *John Peabody Harrington: The Man and His California Indian Fieldnotes.* Ballena Press Anthropological Papers no. 6.

Walters, Raymond, Jr.

1957 *Albert Gallatin: Jefferson Financier and Diplomat.* New York: Macmillan.

Ward, Albert E.

1975 Inscription House: Two Research Reports. *Museum of Northern Arizona, Technical Series* 16: 1–17.

Washburn, Dorothy K.

1995 *Living in Balance: The Universe of the Hopi, Zuni, Navajo and Apache.* Philadelphia: University of Pennsylvania Museum.

Washburn, Dorothy K., and Donald W. Crowe

1988 *Symmetries of Culture: Theory and Practice of Plane Pattern Analysis.* Seattle: University of Washington Press.

Washburn, Wilcomb E., ed.

1988 *Handbook of North American Indians, vol. 4, Indian-White Relations.* Washington, D.C.: Smithsonian Institution.

Waterman, T. T.

1929 Culture Horizons in the Southwest. *American Anthropologist* 31(3): 367–400.

Wauchope, Robert

1965 Alfred Vincent Kidder, 1885–1963. *American Antiquity* 31(2): 149–71.

Webb, George E.

1983 *Tree-Rings and Telescopes: The Scientific Career of A. E. Douglass.* Tucson: University of Arizona Press.

Weber, David J.

1979 "Scarce More Than Apes": Historical Roots of Anglo-American Stereotypes of Mexicans. In *New Spain's Far Northern Frontier. Essays on Spain in the American West, 1540–1821.* D. J. Weber, ed. Pp. 293–307. Albuquerque: University of New Mexico Press.

1985 *Richard H. Kern: Expeditionary Artist in the Far Southwest, 1848–1853.* Fort Worth: Amon Carter Museum, and Albuquerque: University of New Mexico Press.

1988 Turner, the Boltonians, and the Spanish Borderlands. In *Myth and the History of the Hispanic Southwest, Essays by David J. Weber.* Pp. 33–54. Albuquerque: University of New Mexico Press.

1992 *The Spanish Frontier in North America.* New Haven, Conn.: Yale University Press.

Weber, David J., ed.

1979 *New Spain's Far Northern Frontier: Essays on Spain in the American West, 1540–1821.* Albuquerque: University of New Mexico Press.

Webster's Dictionary
1974 *Webster's New World Dictionary of American English.* 3d college edition. New York: Prentice Hall.

Wedel, Waldo
1959 *An Introduction to Kansas Archaeology.* Bureau of American Ethnology Bulletin 174.

1961 *Prehistoric Man on the Great Plains.* Norman: University of Oklahoma Press.

1969 Washington Matthews: His Contribution to Plains Anthropology. *Plains Anthropologist* 14: 175–76.

Weigle, Marta
1976 1988 From Desert to Disney World: The Santa Fe Railway and the Fred Harvey Company Display the American Southwest. *Journal of Anthropological Research* 43: 115–37.

Weigle, Marta, and Barbara A. Babcock, eds.
1996 *The Great Southwest of the Fred Harvey Company and the Santa Fe Railway.* Phoenix: Heard Museum.

Weigle, Marta, and Kyle Fiore, eds.
1982 *Santa Fe and Taos: The Writer's Era, 1916–1941.* Santa Fe: Ancient City Press.

West, Richard S.
1988 *Satire on Stone: The Political Cartoons of Joseph Keppler.* Urbana and Chicago: University of Illinois Press.

Wetherill, Benjamin A.
1977 *The Wetherills of the Mesa Verde: Autobiography of Benjamin Alfred Wetherill.* Maurine S. Fletcher, ed. Lincoln: University of Nebraska Press.

Wetherill, Marietta
1992 *Marietta Wetherill: Reflections on Life with the Navajos in Chaco Canyon.* Boulder, Colo.: Johnson Books.

Wheeler, George M.
1872 *Preliminary Report Concerning Explorations and Surveys Principally in Nevada and Arizona . . . Conducted under the Immediate Direction of Lieut. George M. Wheeler, Corps of Engineers, 1871.* Washington, D.C.: Government Printing Office.

Whipple, A. W.
1855 *The Report of Lieutenant A. W. Whipple, Corps of Topographical Engineers, upon the Route near the Thirty-Fifth Parallel. Reports of Explorations and Surveys to Ascertain the Most Practicable and Economical Route for a Railroad from the Mississippi River to the Pacific Ocean . . . in 1853–4,* vol. III. 33d Cong., 2d sess., Senate Executive Doc. no. 78.

Whipple, A. W., T. Ewbank, and W. W. Turner
1855 Report upon the Indian Tribes, Pt. III. Pp. 1–127. In A. W. Whipple, *The Report of Lieutenant A. W. Whipple, Corps of Topographical Engineers, upon the Route near the Thirty-Fifth Parallel: Reports of Explorations and Surveys to Ascertain the Most Practicable and Economical Route for a Railroad from the Mississippi River to the Pacific Ocean . . . in 1853–4,* vol. III. 33d Cong., 2d sess., Senate Executive Doc. no. 78.

White, Charles A.
1893 Memoir of Ferdinand Vandeveer [*sic*] Hayden. *National Academy of Science Biographical Memoirs* 3: 395–413. Washington, D.C.

White, Leslie A.
1928 Summary Report of Field Work at Acoma. *American Anthropologist* 30(4): 559–68.

1932a The Acoma Indians. *Forty seventh Annual Report of the Bureau of American Ethnology, 1929–1930.* Pp. 17–192.

1932b *The Pueblo of San Felipe.* American Anthropological Association Memoirs 38.

1935 *The Pueblo of Santo Domingo, New Mexico.* American Anthropological Association Memoirs 43.

1942 *The Pueblo of Santa Ana.* Anthropological Association Memoirs 60.

1949 *Science of Culture: A Study of Man and Civilization.* New York: Farrar, Straus.

1959 Introductory Chapters and Notes. In *Lewis Henry Morgan, The Indian Journals, 1859–62.* Pp. 3–23, 201–29. Ann Arbor: University of Michigan Press.

1962 *The Pueblo of Sia.* Bureau of American Ethnology Bulletin 184.

1963 *The Ethnography and Ethnology of Franz Boas.* Austin: Texas Memorial Museum.

White, Leslie A., ed.
1937 Extracts from the European Travel Journal of Lewis H. Morgan. *Rochester Historical Society Publications* 16: 219–389.

1940 *Pioneers in American Anthropology: The Bandelier-Morgan Letters, 1873–1883.* 2 vols. Albuquerque: University of New Mexico Press.

1942 Lewis H. Morgan's Journal of a Trip to Southwestern Colorado and New Mexico, June 21 to August 7, 1878. *American Antiquity* 8: 1–26.

White, Leslie A., and Ignacio Bernal, eds.
1960 *Correspondencia de Adolfo F. Bandelier.* Instituto Nacional de Antropología e Historia, México.

Whiting, Lilian

1906   *The Land of Enchantment: From Pike's Peak to the Pacific.* Boston: Little, Brown.

Wilcox, David R.

1993   Pueblo Grande in the Nineteenth Century. In *Archaeology of the Pueblo Grande Platform Mound and Surrounding Features. Volume 1. Introduction to the Archival Project and History of Archaeological Research.* C. E. Downum and T. W. Bostwick, eds. Pp. 43–71. Phoenix: Pueblo Grande Museum Anthropological Papers no. 1.

Wilcox, David R., Jerry B. Howard, and Reuben Nelson

1990   *One Hundred Years of Archaeology at La Ciudad de Los Hornos.* Soil Systems Publications in Archaeology no. 16.

Wilcox, Donald J.

1987   *The Measure of Times Past: Pre-Newtonian Chronologies and the Rhetoric of Relative Time.* Chicago: University of Chicago Press.

Wilkins, Thurman

1958   *Clarence King, A Biography.* New York: Macmillan Co.

Willey, Gordon R., and Jeremy A. Sabloff

1980   *A History of American Archaeology.* 3d ed. San Francisco: W. H. Freeman.

Williams, Anita Alvarez de

1983   Cocopa. *Handbook of North American Indians, vol. 10, Southwest.* Pp. 99–112. Washington, D.C.: Smithsonian Institution.

Williams, David

1949   John Evans' Strange Journey, Part I: The Welsh Indians; Part II: Following the Trail. *American Historical Review* 54: 277–95, 508–29.

Williams, Gwyn A.

1979   *Madoc: The Making of a Myth.* London: Eyre Methuen.

Williams, Raymond

1976   *Keywords: A Vocabulary of Culture and Society.* New York: Oxford University Press.

Williams, Roger

1973   *A Key into the Language of America.* Detroit: Wayne State University Press. Originally published 1643.

Williams, Stephen

1991   *Fantastic Archaeology: The Wild Side of North American Prehistory.* Philadelphia: University of Pennsylvania Press.

Wilson, Carol G.

1955   *Alice Eastwood's Wonderland: The Adventures of a Botanist.* San Francisco: California Academy of Sciences.

Wilson, Chris

1997   *The Myth of Santa Fe: Creating a Modern Regional Tradition.* Albuquerque: University of New Mexico Press.

Wilson, E. O.

1998   *Consilience: The Unity of Knowledge.* New York: Knopf/Random House.

Winegrad, Dilys P.

1993   *Through Time, Across Continents: A Hundred Years of Archaeology and Anthropology at the University Museum.* Philadelphia: The University Museum, University of Pennsylvania.

Winship, George P.

1896   The Coronado Expedition, 1540–1542. *Fourteenth Annual Report of the Bureau of Ethnology, 1892–93.* Pp. 329–613.

Wislizenus, Frederick A.

1848   *Memoir of a Tour to Northern Mexico Connected with Col. Doniphan's Expedition in 1846 and 1847.* 30th Cong., 1st sess., Senate Misc. Doc. no. 26.

1912   *A Journey to the Rocky Mountains in the Year 1839.* St. Louis: Missouri Historical Society.

Wissler, Clark

1910   Material Culture of the Blackfoot Indians. *American Museum of Natural History Anthropological Papers* 5: 1–175.

1912   Ceremonial Bundles of the Blackfoot Indians. *American Museum of Natural History Anthropological Papers* 7: 65–289.

1913   Societies and Dances of the Blackfoot Indians. *American Museum of Natural History Anthropological Papers* 11: 359–460.

1914   Material Culture of the American Indians. *American Anthropologist* 16: 447–505.

1915   Explorations in the Southwest by the American Museum. *American Museum Journal* 15: 395–98.

1916   Correlations between Archaeological and Culture Areas in the American Continents. In *Holmes Anniversary Volume: Anthropological Essays.* Pp. 481–90. Washington. D.C.: J. W. Bryan Press.

1917a   *The American Indian.* New York: D.C. McMurtrie.

1917b   The New Archaeology. *American Museum Journal* 17: 100–101.

1921   Dating Our Prehistoric Ruins. *Natural History* 21(1): 13–26.

1923   *Man and Culture.* New York: Thomas Y. Crowell.

1926   *The Relation of Nature to Man in Aboriginal America.* New York: Oxford University Press.

1942   The American Indian and the American Philosophical Society. *American Philosophical Society Proceedings* 86(1): 189–204.

Witherspoon, Gary

1977   *Language and Art in the Navajo Universe.* University of Michigan Press, Ann Arbor.

1980   Language in Culture and Culture in Language. *International Journal of American Linguistics* 46(1): 1–13.

1983   Navajo Social Organization. *Handbook of North American Indians, vol. 10, Southwest.* Pp. 524–35. Washington, D.C.: Smithsonian Institution.

Wittfogel, Karl A.

1957   *Oriental Despotism.* New Haven, Conn.: Yale University Press.

Wittgenstein, Ludwig

1961   *Tractatus logico-philosophicus.* New York: Humanities Press.

Wolfe, Tom

1975   *The Painted Word.* New York: Farrar, Straus and Giroux.

Woodbury, Nathalie F. S., and Richard B. Woodbury

1988   Women of Vision and Wealth: Their Impact on Southwestern Anthropology. In *Reflections: Papers on Southwestern Culture History in Honor of Charles H. Lange.* Anne V. Poore, ed. Pp. 45–56. Santa Fe: Ancient City Press for the Archaeological Society of New Mexico.

Woodbury, Richard B.

1960a   Nels C. Nelson and Chronological Archaeology. *American Antiquity* 25: 400–401.

1960b   Nelson's Stratigraphy. *American Antiquity* 26: 98–99.

1973   *Alfred V. Kidder.* New York: Columbia University Press.

1979   Zuñi Prehistory and History to 1850. *Handbook of North American Indians, vol. 9, Southwest.* Pp. 467–73. Washington, D.C.: Smithsonian Institution.

1993   *Sixty Years of Southwestern Archaeology: A History of the Pecos Conference.* Albuquerque: University of New Mexico Press.

Worster, Donald

2000   *A River Running West: John Wesley Powell and His America.* New York: Oxford University Press.

Wright, Barton

1980   San Diego Museum of Man. *American Indian Art* 5(4): 48–53.

Wright, Barton, Marnie Gaede, and Marc Gaede

1986   *The Hopi Photographs, Kate Cory: 1905–1912.* La Cañada, Calif.: Chaco Press.

Wyman, Leland C.

1960   *Navaho Sandpainting: The Huckel Collection.* Colorado Springs.

1970   *Sandpaintings of the Navajo Shootingway and the Wolcott Collection.* Smithsonian Contributions to Anthropology, no. 13.

1970   *Blessingway.* Tucson: University of Arizona Press.

1975   *The Mountainway of the Navajo.* Tucson: University of Arizona Press.

1983   Navajo Ceremonial System. *Handbook of North American Indians, vol. 10, Southwest.* Pp. 536–57. Washington, D.C.: Smithsonian Institution.

Young, Robert W.

1983   Apachean Languages. *Handbook of North American Indian Languages, vol. 10, Southwest.* Pp. 393–400. Washington, D.C.: Smithsonian Institution.

Ziolkowski, Eric J.

1990   Heavenly Visions and Worldly Intentions: Chicago's Columbian Exposition and World's Parliament of Religions (1893). *Journal of Popular American Culture* 13: 9–15.

Zolbrod, Paul G.

1984   *Diné bahane': The Navajo Creation Story.* Albuquerque: University of New Mexico Press.

Zumwalt, Rosemary L.

1988   *American Folklore Scholarship: A Dialogue of Dissent.* Bloomington: Indiana University Press.

1992   *Wealth and Rebellion: Elsie Clews Parsons, Anthropologist and Folklorist.* Urbana: University of Illinois Press.

Index

Note: References to figures and maps are in boldface type. Footnotes have an "n" before the note number.

A. L. Bancroft & Company, 180
AAA (American Anthropological Association), 146, 263, 332–33
AAAS (American Association for the Advancement of Science), 80, 94–95, 222, 263; Section H, 240; Sub-Section D, 97–98
AAM (American Association of Museums), 368
Abbott, Charles C., 222, 228, 319; "The Stone Age in New Jersey," 227
abbreviations, listing of, 381
Abeita, Juan (pseudonym), 334
Abenaki Indians, 26
Abert, James W., 40–41; Abó watercolor, **41**
Abert, John James, 38
Abiquiu, New Mexico, 66
abnormality as culturally relative, 340
"Aboriginal American Mechanics" (Mason), 212
"An Aboriginal Pilgrimage" (Baxter), 125

Abó Ruin, 41, 56, 58; Abert watercolor, **41**
Abram (cook), 122
Account (Pike), 35
acculturation, 67, 252, 328, 331, 377
acequias, 66, 334
Ackman-Lowry Ruin, 306
Acoma Pueblo, 9, 41, 112, 175, 341; pottery, **110**
Acosta, Joseph de, 16
A.D. (*anno Domini*), 20, 384n31
Adams, Henry, 99
Adams, J. B., 287
Adams, J. P., 269, **269**
Adams, John, 24
Adler, Cyrus, 145
Adventures (Henry), 124
Adventures (Ruxton), 35
advertising of native cultures by Southwestern railroads, 206
African-American folklore, 331
Agassiz, Alexander, 161, 222
Agassiz, Louis, 221
Age-area hypothesis, 278
agriculture, 67–68, 159, 297, 315
Ahayu:da: Ma'a'sewi, 110, 158; Uyeyewi, 110, 157
AIA (Archaeological Institute of America), 100–102, 175–76,

254–55; development of new chapters, 256, 263–64
Alamo Ranch, 187, **188**, 189
Alarcón, Hernando, 32
Alaska expedition (Harriman expedition) photographs, 323
Albright, Horace, 306
Albuquerque, New Mexico, 248
Alkali Ridge, 257, 284
Alta California, 11–13
altars: Hopi, 225–26; replicas, 225, 305, 345–46; Zuni, 109
Alvarado Hotel, 345
Amazon women, 16
American Academy of Arts and Sciences, 24
American Anthropological Association (AAA), 146, 263, 332–33
American Anthropologist, 146, 240, 301, 317–18, 338; under Boasians' control, 333
American Antiquarian Society, 25, 27
American Association for the Advancement of Science (AAAS), 80, 94–95, 222, 263; Section H, 240; Sub-Section D, 97–98
American Association of Museums (AAM), 368

470

American Association of University Professors, 260
American Ethnological Society, 27–28, 30, 80
American Exploration Society, 226, 228, 241
American Folklore Society, 137, 328
American Geographical Society, 235
American Historical Review, 185
American Indian Life (Parsons), 327–28
American Museum of Natural History, 171, 177, 221, 233, 240, 278–79; collections: Chaco Canyon, 197; Grand Gulch, 193; Hopi, 225; Northwest Coast, 239; exhibits, 351; staff salaries, 327
American Philosophical Society (APS), 24–25
American Review, 67
Amerind Foundation, 60
Amsden, Monroe, **297**
Amsterdam International Industrial Exposition, 205
analogical savages, 16, 21, 23, 96. *See also* hunter gatherers
analogies, ethnographic, 298
Anasazi culture, 198, 300, 378
Ancient Monuments of the Mississippi Valley (Squier and Davis), 69
"Ancient Semi-Civilization of New Mexico" (Gallatin), 66
Ancient Society (Morgan), 97–98
Anderson, Arthur J. O., and Charles E. Dibble, on Spanish lust for gold, 8n15
Andrews, Roy Chapman, 284
Andrews's Third Asiatic Expedition, 284
Anglos: constructs of native peoples, ix; defined, viii
Animas River, 66
Annals of the World Deduced from the Origin of Time (Ussher), 20
anno Domini (A.D.), 20
Antelope society, 163
anthropological organizations, 240
Anthropological Society of Washington, 104, 115–16, 146
anthropologists, 113, 117–18, 171,

211–12, 336; accused of spying, 332–33; as ghostwriters, 283; jokes about, 129; museum-based, 204, 227–32; as novelists, 337; as poets, 146, 266–67, 270, 338; as short story writers, 327–28; territories of, 270, 282, 286–87, 294–96, 378–79; thrown out by Indians, 114, 135, 334
anthropology, 209, 327–28, 374, 377; development of, ix, 23–24, 67, 93; four-field approach, 240, 370; as gossip, 279; metamorphosis from ethnology, viii, 203, 282, 374; multidisciplinary, 106, 154; reorganization of, 240–41
"Anthropology and the Abnormal" (Benedict), 340
Anthropology Museum, University of California at Berkeley, 240
anthropology museums, 221, 240
anthropology reports, 47, 65–66, 89, 154; long delayed, 232
anthropometry, 153, 236
anti-Catholicism, 71
antiquities, as federal property, 370
Antiquities Act, 1906, 170, 190, 256, 263–64, 306
Anzá, Juan Bautista de, 13
Apache, Antonio, 211
Apache Gold (motion picture), 364
Apache Indians, 75, 134–38, 181–82, 239, 280; artifact exhibits, 231; at Bosque Redondo, 129; Chiricahuas, 213; on display, 205; Jicarillas, 321; languages, 4, 6; Mescaleros, 58; raiding-harvesting, 7, 10, 36–37, 56; using horses, 7; White Mountain, 213
Apollonians, 339
APS (American Philosophical Society), 24–25
Arapahoe Indians, 224, 242
Archaeological Institute of America (AIA), 100–102, 175–76, 254–55; development of new chapters, 256, 263–64
Archaeological Society of New Mexico, 262

"The Archaeologist" (Eakins), 229
archaeologists, self-taught, 144, 304
archaeology: sites, 57, 178; commercial exploitation of, 190; theories of the Southwest, 178
archaeology, reports, 50; Canyon de Chelly, 143; codas, 374; of Emory, 42; Hemenway Expedition, 154; lagging behind field-work, 145, 290, 293, 297, 304; left unwritten, 259, 303, 379; Marsh Pass, 289; Navajo Expedition, 42; New Mexico antiquities, 262; not published, 280; Pecos Pueblo, 318; scientific, 25, 190–92; unfinished manuscripts, 164; without synthesis, 318
architectural styles: Mission Revival, 251, 345; Santa Fe, 251, 345, 348–50, 373
archival documents. *See* historic documents
Archuleta, Ramos, 217
Aridian Indians, 156
Arid Lands Report (Powell), 99
Arikara Indians, 128
Aristotle, 15
Arizona, 84; statehood, 347
Arizona, University of, 260, 298–301
Arizona Archaeological and Historical Society, 260
Arizona Republic, 372
Arizona State Museum, 260, 373
Armer, Laura Adams, *Waterless Mountain*, 359
Armour, Allison V., 224
Army of the West, 40
Art and Archaeology, Chaco Canyon article, 296
Arthur, Chester A., 122
artifact collections: Grand Gulch, 198; Hazzard-Green, 228; Hemenway Expedition, 153, 159, 163, 207, 210, 377; Hopi House Ruin, 225; Indian Arts Fund, 367, 369; Laboratory of Anthropology pottery, 352; Mesa Verde, 188–89, 190; of Mimbres bowls, 171; Mummy Cave, 230

artifacts, 191, 196–97, 319; associated with time periods, 178; authenticity of, 159–60, 229, 230; "look-alike" forms, 281; proveniences, 191; reflecting cosmologies, 168; related to biogeographic areas, 209; removed from display, 226; returned to tribes, 111. *See also specific artifact types*

artifacts, collected, 138, 188–89, 192, 225, 228–29, 245–46; "complete" collections, 230; for export, 190, 372; of heirlooms, 168, 229; in return for annual support, 226; by trading, 112; without permission, 85, 107–11

Art Institute of Chicago, 210

arts and crafts, 252, 274, 345; fair prices for, 354; at world's fairs, 206, 214, 216–17. *See also* antiquities; artifacts

arts and crafts movement, 353

Arundel-Harcourt, T. (pen name), 181, 183

Ashiwi Indians. *See* Zuni Pueblo

assimilation, 205–6

astronomy, 67

Atchison, Topeka and Santa Fe Railway, 172, 272, 274, 344–45

Athapaskan Indians, 239; languages, 78

Atsidi Sani, 130

Atwater, Caleb, 27, 69

Audubon Terrace Museum group, 235, 245, 301

Austin, Mary, 350–52, 358

authenticity of artifacts, 159–60, 229, 230

Avanyu, 54

Avebury, Lord. *See* Lubbock, John

Awatovi (Hopi village), 9, 57, 112, 141, 165, 168

Awa Tsireh (Alfonso Roybal), 350–51

Ayer, Edward, 223–24

Aztec empire, 183

Aztec Indians: migration, 32–33, 50, 58; relation to Southwestern ruins, 8, 52, 61, 67–68, 181–82, 218

Aztec Ruins, 57, 66, 98, 290–91;

excavations, **290**; tree-ring specimens, 300

Aztec Ruins National Monument, 306

The Aztecs of Mexico (Vaillant), 287

BAAS (British Association for the Advancement of Science), 234

Babbitt, Benjamin, 192

Backus, Electus, 76

Baird, Spencer F., 81–82, 88, 91–92, 106; relationship with Cushing, 118–19

Baja California, 11

Baker, Frank, 145

Balcony House Ruin, 306, 309

Bancroft, Hubert Howe, 172, 180–84; *Native Races*, 181–84; photograph (Bradley and Rulofson), **180**

Bancroft Library, 184

Bandelier, Adolph Françoise Alphonse, 99, **99**, 172–80, 389n38, 395n1; and AIA, 102, 175–76; *The Delight Makers*, 174; Hemenway Expedition, 150–51, 176–78; history of the Spanish missions, 176; on looting of the Old Church of Zuni, 108; on Montezuma legends, 52; "On the Sources for Aboriginal History of Spanish America," 98; "An Outline of the Documentary History of the Zuni Tribe," 154; photograph (Bennett), **173**; relationship with Cushing, 173, 176; support of Morgan, 183; travel to Peru with Lummis, 249

Bandelier, Fanny Ritter, 177

Bandelier, Maria Josepha (Josephine) Huegy, 99, 175, 177

Bandelier National Monument, 173, 177, 306

Bannock Indians, 128, 134, 242

Bannon, John, 31, 185

Barber, E. A., 168

Barnes, Will, 175

Barnett, Frank, 145

Barrett, Samuel A., 243, 246

Barthelmess, Christian, 129

Bartlett, John Russell, 44–45, 77, 181; Buttre portrait of, **28**; Casas Grandes description, 60n31; *Dictionary of Americanisms*, 45; *Personal Narrative*, 45; "Progress of Ethnology," 27

Bartlett, Katherine, 372

Bartlett and Welford's Bookstore, 27–28, 44

Barton, Benjamin Smith, *New Views of the Origin of the Tribes and Nations of America*, 25

Basin and Range province, 1, **3**

Basket Dance, **355**

Basket Maker (Basketmaker) culture, 193, 197, 293, 313, 378, 397n24; classifications, 257, 310, 317; cranial data, 238–39; sites, 306

Basket Maker/Cliff-Dweller relationship, 289, 291

Bastian, Adolph, 175, 234

Battle Rock Mountain, 210

Baxter, Sylvester, 119–20, 149–50, **152**, 152–54, 158–59, 161; "An Aboriginal Pilgrimage," 125; "Father of the Pueblos," 125; Fort Wingate description, 121n11

B.C., 20, 384n31

B.C.E./C.E. (before current era/current era), 277, 384n31

Beale, Edward F., 48

Beals, Ralph, 331

Beam Expeditions, 299–300, 304

Bear Flag Revolt, 40

Beauregard, Donald, 257, **258**, 269, **269**

Becknell, William, 34

Beecher, Henry Ward, 234

before current era/current era (B.C.E./C.E.), 277, 384n31

belly dancing, 208

Benedict, A. L., 214

Benedict, Ruth Fulton, **330**, 333, 338–40, 371, 376; as Anne Singleton, 338; "Anthropology and the Abnormal," 340; "The Concept of the Guardian Spirit in North America," 338; *Patterns of Culture*,

340; "Psychological Types in the Cultures of the Southwest," 339–40; "The Vision in Plains Culture," 338
Benedict, Stanley R., 338
Benham, J. W., 199, 218
Ben Hur, A Tale of the Christ (Wallace), 173
Bennett, George C., 173; photograph of Pecos Pueblo and Bandelier, **173**
Benton, Thomas Hart, 36
berdaches, 114–15, 373
Berger, Thomas, *Little Big Man*, 124
Beringia, 238
Bering Strait, 67–68, 238
Berkhofer, Robert, 16
Bernheimer, Charles L., 291–92
Betatakin Ruin, 194, 257, 259, 295
Bible: as literal truth, 19–20; translations of, 23
bibliographies, 90
bibliophilia, 180
Billings, John S., 154
bison, 9; extinct, 319
Blackfeet Indians, 279
Black Legend, 71
blacksmithing, 130
Blair, Francis Preston, Jr., 84
Blair, Francis Preston, Sr., 84
blankets, Navajo, 6, 11, 182, 337, 345; as trade items, 130, 199, 211, 216
Blemmyae, 16
Blessingway, 232
Blom, Franz, 305, 360
Bloom, Lancing B., **316**, 351
Blumenbach, Johann Friedrich, 67, 236
Boas, Franz, 145–46, 208–9, 239–41, **330**, **333**; accusing anthropologists of spying, 332–33; American Museum of Natural History, 233–34, 278; on BAE staffing, 302; criticism of Curtis's volumes, 325; debate with Mason, 275–77; discredit of Hewett, 272; expelled from AAA, 333; Field Museum of Natural History, 223–24; *Handbook of American Indian Languages*, 241, 333;

"History of Anthropology," 240, 277; manuscripts purchased by McGee, 146, 224, 272; *Primitive Art*, 335; School of American Archaeology, 267–68; "The Occurrence of Similar Inventions in Areas Widely Apart," 275; University of California at Berkeley, 242
Boas-Hewett controversy, 272
Boasians, 241, 315, 332–40, 376
Boas-Mason debate, 275–77
Bolton, Herbert Eugene, 14, 172, 179–80, 184–86; *Guide to Mexican Archival Materials Relevant to United States History*, 185; relationship with Hodge, 184
Bonney, William ("Billy the Kid"), 173
Book of Mormon (Smith), 30, 55
Bosque Redondo, 10, 129
Boston Advertiser, 150
Boston Herald, 150
Boston Museum of Fine Arts, 241
Bostwick, Todd, 373
Boundary Commission, 42; survey, 44–45, 71–72
Bourke, John Gregory, 119, **120**, 133–37, 152, 159, 211; *On the Border with Crook*, 134, 136; and Indian artists, 350; *Scatologic Rites of All Nations*, 136; *The Snake Dance of the Moquis of Arizona*, 135; supporting Indian rights, 252
Bourke, Mary Horbach, 134
Bovard, George F., 254
Bowditch, Charles P., 263; and School of American Archaeology, 267–68
Bowles, George, 197–98
Bow Priest Society, 119
bows and arrows, 314
brachycephalic skulls, 193, 236, 239, 287, 314
Bradfield, Wesley, 352, 378; photograph of Jeançon and Chapman, **305**
Bradley, Luther, 120
brain sizes and intelligence, 236; Powell vs. McGee, 146–47

Brave New World (Huxley), 361–62
Breuil, Henri, 282
Brew, John Otis, 370, 378
Brinton, Daniel, 159, 211, 227–29
British Association for the Advancement of Science (BAAS), 234
Broca, Paul, 236
Brody, J. J., 170
Broken Flute Cave, 293
A Bronco Pegasus (Lummis), 255
Brooklyn Museum, 221, 229–31, 240
Brooks, Van Wyck, 265
Brosius, Samuel, 252
Brown, Barnum, 319
Brown, John Carter, 45, 180
Brown, William Henry, 173
Brown University, 185
Bryan, Kirk, **297**
Buchanan, James, 47
Buck, Orian, **197**
Buffalo, University of, 341
Buffalo Bill's Wild West Show, 208
Buffalo Museum of Science, 341
Buffon, Comte de, 24
Bumpus, Hermon, 240, 268, 278–79, 368–69, 372
Bunzel, Ruth, 304, 333, 335–36; called *Maiatitsa* ("Blue Bird"), 335; *Pueblo Potter*, 335
Bureau of American Republics, 137
Bureau of Ethnology (later Bureau of American Ethnology), ix, 80, 99, 105, 117, 221; investigation of, 145–46; and John Wesley Powell, 88, 91–94, 104–6, 144–47; merger with National Museum of American History, 305; purpose of, 92; staff on other payrolls, 93–94, 105. *See also* Corps of Ethnologists
Bureau of Indian Affairs, 81, 88, 122; exhibiting Indians, 205, 209, 215–16
burial mounds, excavated, 202
burial practices, 156
burials. *See* human remains
Burnham, Daniel, 222
Bursum, Holm O., 358–59
Burton, Charles E., 252–53
Buschmann, Johann Karl, 68

Buttre, J. C., portrait of Bartlett, **28**
Byers, Douglas S., 360
Bynner, Witter, 358, 361

Cabeza de Vaca, Alvar Núñez, 8; *Relation*, 32
calendars, Mesoamerican, 67
California at Berkeley, University of, 184, 240–44
Calusa Indians, 159–60
camel caravans, 48
camera lucida, 40
Camp Augustus, 151
Camp Hemenway, 151, **152**, 153
Campos, José Vincente, Father, 174
Canadian River, 40
Cannon, Cornelia James: *The Pueblo Boy*, 359; *Pueblo Girl*, 359
Cannonball Ruin, 266
Cañones Ruin, 66
Canyon de Chelly, 50, **57**, 63, 143, 287, **324**; artifact exhibits, 231; mapped, 141
Canyon de Chelly National Monument, 293, 306
Canyon del Muerto, 63, 292
Cape Verde Islands, 331
Capp, Al, 249
Cárdenas, Lopez de, 8
Carleton, James Henry, 56, 58, 129, 138
Carlyle, Thomas, 100
Carnegie, Andrew, 185; "Wealth," 220
Carnegie Institution of Washington, 177, 184–85, 284, 292–93, 318, 335–36
Carnegie Museum in Pittsburgh, 225
Carravahal (Mexican guide), 61–62
Carrizo Mountains, 292
Carson, Kit, 10, 129, 138
Carson, Levi, **197**
Cartailhac, Emile, 282
Casa Chiquita Ruin, **61**, 63
Casa Grande National Monument, 306, 309, 312
Casa Grande Ruin, 2, 33, **57**, 153, 170; Kino's description of, 12;

drawing (Stanley), **59**; mapped, 141; origin legend, 58–59; stabilization, 143
Casas Grandes Ruin (Paquimé Ruin), **57**, 60–61, 175
Cass, Lewis, **29**, 29–30, 96, 301; *Inquiries*, 29
Castañeda, Pedro de, 58, 185
Castillo, Alonso de, 8
Cataract Creek Canyon, 125
Cather, Willa: *Death Comes for the Archbishop*, 359; *The Professor's House*, 359
Catholic Church, 174, 332; parody of, 136; reintroduction of, 9
Catholic Encyclopedia, 176
Catholic theology vs. Protestant theology, 19
Catlin, George, 54
Caucasian race, 236
cemeteries, desecration of, 245
Cemetery Ridge, 291
Census Bureau, 93–94
censuses, 11, 91
Central America, 280
Central Asia, 284
Central Pacific Railroad, 234
Century Illustrated Monthly Magazine, 125
A Century of Dishonor (Jackson), 148, 250
cephalic index, 236
ceramic analyses and classifications, 191; in association with architectural types, 97–98, 178, 289, 317; nomenclature for, 315, 378; sherds vs. whole vessels, 288–89; temporal sequences, 283, 285–87, 300. *See also* pottery
"ceramic bacillus," 285
ceremonies: Christian preaching during, 225; cycles of, 169–70; as obscene, 332
Chacoan outliers, 63, 98
Chaco Canyon, 50, **57**, **61**, 170; Hyde Expedition, 194–200; mapped, 141; prehistoric roads, 198, 297; as Seven Cities of Cibola, 98; stratigraphy, 283; studied by archaeologists, 294–

98; visited by explorers, 42, 60–63, 83–84
Chaco Canyon National Monument, 306
Chaco Canyon National Park, 199
Chama River Valley, 65
Chamberlain, Alexander, 234, 240
Chamberlin, T. C., 223–24
Chandler, Harry, 249
Changing Woman, 126
chantways, 112, 129, 131–32, 202, 232
Chapin, Frederick H., 190; "Cliff Dwellings of the Mancos Canyon," 189; *The Land of the Cliff Dwellers*, 189
Chapman, Kenneth Milton, **269**, 274, **316**, 352–53; Museum of New Mexico, 268–69, 352; photograph (Bradfield), **305**; Rockefeller proposal, 367–69
"A Chapter in Zuni Mythology" (Stevenson), 211
Charnay, Désiré, 174
Chase, George, 285
Chase, Salmon P., 86
Chato, 136
chauvinism: male, 336; regional, 370, 372
Chavannes, Alexandre André, 27–28
Chaveyo, 74
Chemehuevi Indians, 13, 271
Cherokee Indians, 106
Chetro Ketl Ruin, **61**, 63, 84, 295
Cheyenne Indians, 36, 134, 224
Chicago, University of, 220, 223
Chicago Art Club, 351
Chicago Field Museum. *See* Field Museum of Natural History
Chicago Tribune, on ethnographic exhibitions, 208
Chicago World's Columbian Exposition, 137, 159, 192, 206–12, 307; congresses, 210–12
Chichén Itzá Ruin, 292
Chichicastenango, Guatemala, 336
Chichimeca Indians, 33
Chiishch'ilin Biye, 200
Chinook Jargon, 78
Chiricahua Apache Indians, 213

Havasupai Indians, 13, 48–49, 77, 112, 125, 136
Hawikuh Ruin, 295, 301–4, 314
Hayden, Ferdinand Vandiveer, 81–84, **82**, 91; photograph (Jackson), **82**
Hayden survey, 81–84
Hayes, Bartlett H., Jr., 360
Hayes, Rutherford, 134
Hazzard, Charles D., 210
Hazzard-Green collections, 228
Heard, Dwight B., 372–73
Heard, Maie Bartlett, 372–73
Heard Museum, 372–73
Hearst, George, 227
Hearst, Phoebe Apperson, 129, 159, 227; and AIA, 254; photograph (Prince), **241**; and University of California at Berkeley, 241–44
Hearst, William Randolph, 227
Heaton, Hal, **197**
Heluta, 148
Hemenway, Augustus, 148–49, 154, 161, 289
Hemenway, Mary Tileston, 148–49, **149**, 151, 153, 159, 161
"Hemenway House," 307–8
Hemenway Southwestern Archaeological Expedition, 148–58, 161, 164, 170, 239; artifact collections, 153, 159, 163, 207, 210, 377; reports, 154
Hemis Kachina, 73, 387n7
Henderson, Alice Corbin, 350
Henderson, Junius, 269, **269**, 290
Henderson, Mrs. Palmer: "The Cliff Dwellers of Southwestern America," 211
Henderson, William Penhallow, 350, 358, 373
Hendricks, Harmon W., 246, 302, **303**
Hendricks-Hodge Expedition, 302–4
Henige, David, 3
Henry, Alexander, *Adventures*, 124
Henry, Charleton, 75
Henry, Joseph, 80, 86
Henry, Mary, 83
Henshaw, Henry W., 105

Herder, Johann Gottfried, 158, 275–76
Hermann, Binger, 199
heroines, pathetic dusky, 18, 250, 343
Herrera, Antonio, *General History*, 32
Herrera, Velino Shije, 351
Herskovits, Frances, 331, 377
Herskovits, Melville, 331, 333, 377
Héshota Ruins, 153
Hewett, Edgar Lee, **258**, 261–74, **262**, **269**, 316, **367**; as AIA Director of Archaeology, 264–65; archaeological methods, 280–81, 288–89; called *El Toro*, 261; classroom manner, 271; discredit of, 272–73; dissertation of, 402–3n2; as "Doctor Archaeology," 268, 272; and Indian artists, 350; as lobbyist, 264, 307; New Mexico Normal School, 262–63; Pajarito Plateau ceramic types, 285; on pot hunters, 199; proposal for Rockefeller, 366–68; recreating Santa Fe, 347–48; regional chauvinism, 370; relationship with Tozzer, 267; School of American Archaeology director, 267; territory of, 282, 286–87, 294–96, 378–79
Heye, Blanche Williams, 245
Heye, George Gustav, 245–46, **303**; relationship with Hodge, 301–4
Heye, Thea Kowne Page, 245, 302, **303**
Heye Foundation, 245–46
hidalgos, 7
Hidatsa Indians, 128
Hieb, Louis A., on Hopi beliefs, 169n36
Higgins, Charles A., *To California over the Santa Fe Trail*, 345
High Desert province (Colorado Plateau), 1–2
High Plains, 1
Higinbotham, Harlow, 223–24
Hilder, Frank, 170
Hillers, John K., 87–89, 92, 105–6, 111, 141, 207; photograph of Powell, **87**; photograph of Taos

Pueblo, **111**; photograph of We'wha, **115**; photograph of Zuni schoolchildren, Hammaker, Ealy, and We'wha, **108**
Hinsley, Curtis M., 154, 162, 377
Hispanics, 11; defined, viii; relationships with Indian tribes, 8–14, 40
Hispanic Society of America, 177, 235
Hispanophobia, 71–72
Historical and Statistical Information (Schoolcraft), 88
historical particularism, 277–78, 374–76
historic documents, 172, 179, 185; American, 34–37; British, 33; German, 33; South American, 177; Spanish, 31–33
Historic Sites Act, 1935, 311–12
History of America (Robertson), 33
"History of Anthropology" (Boas), 240
The History of Mexico (Clavigero), 24, 32–33
Hobbes, Thomas, *Leviathan*, 18–19
Hodge, Frederick Webb, 144, 147, 150, **152**, 152–54, 165, **269**, 303; as an editor, 301, 323; Bureau of American Ethnology ethnologist-in-charge, 301; called Téluli, 304; Hewett agreement, 272; at the Heye Foundation, 246; and Museum of New Mexico, 268; Museum of the American Indian, 302; Pueblo Pottery Fund, 352; relationship with Bolton, 184; relationship with Cushing, 154, 159–60; relationship with Harrington, 271; relationship with Heye, 301–4
Hodge, Margaret Whitehead Magill, 122, 125, 148, 150–51, **152**, 152–53, 301
Hoe, Robert, III, 180
Hoebel, E. Adamson, 371
Hoffman, W. J., 105
hogans, 76
Hohokam culture, 151, 165, 322, 377
Hoijer, Harry, 370, 376
Holmes, William Henry, 83, 89, 140,

regional chauvinism, 370
Reichard, Gladys Amanda, 332–33, **336**, 336–37; *Dezba, Woman of the Desert*, 337; *Navaho Religion*, 337; *Navaho Shepherd and Weaver*, 337; *Social Life of the Navajo Indians*, 336; *Spider Woman*, 337
Reisner, George, 241, 282, 285
Relation (Cabeza de Vaca), 32
religious beliefs, 21, 130–32, 211, 331–32; anthropological studies thwarted, 114; covertly practiced, 9–10, 36; privacy of, 171; protected from outsiders, 51, 121, 174, 341; suppressed, 9, 252
Renaud, Etienne Bernardeau, 305, **316**
replicas: of altars, 225, 305, 345–46; of Cushing's Zuni costume, 230
reports, anthropology, 47, 65–66, 89, 154; long delayed, 232
reports, archaeological, 50; Canyon de Chelly, 143; codas, 374; of Emory, 42; Hemenway Expedition, 154; lagging behind fieldwork, 145, 290, 293, 297, 304; left unwritten, 259, 303, 379; Marsh Pass area, 289; Navajo Expedition, 42; New Mexico antiquities, 262; not published, 280; Pecos Pueblo, 318; scientific, 25, 190–92; unfinished manuscripts, 164; without synthesis, 318
research agendas, 29, 88, 177–78, 185, 280, 313; Fewkes's, 165–66; Morgan's, 95, 101–3, 106, 143; Parsons's, 328–29; Powell's, 89–91, 93, 101–3; ten Kate's, 153
research questions, 66–69, 239, 315
research standards, 296
research universities, 221
reservations, 23, 80–81, 251, 343; Hopi, 129–30; Seneca, 122; Ute, 190
Retzius, Anders, 193, 236
Retzius, Gustaf, 193
Rice, Allen Thorndike, 174
Rice, H. S.: photograph of Ethelyn Hobbs Nelson, **244**; photograph of Nels C. Nelson, **243**

Richards, W. A., 263
Ricketson, Edith Bayles, **316**
Ricketson, Oliver G., Jr., **316**
Riggs, Stephen Return, 134; *Grammar and Dictionary of the Dakota Language*, 96
The Rights of a Savage (motion picture), 364
Rinehart, Frank A.: "Geronimo and Apaches," **212**
Rio Arriba, 11
Rio Chama, 11
Rio Grande, 1–2
Rio Grande pueblos, 9; historic and abandoned, **6**
Rio Grande Valley, 9, 11
rites of passage, 117
Ritter, Fanny (Bandelier), 177
Rivers, W. H. R., 328
Robbins, Wilfred W., 269, **269**
Roberts, Frank H. H., Jr., 147, **297**, **316**, 318–19, 371, 378; Bureau of American Ethnology director, 305; Fewkes's obituary, 167n27
Roberts, Linda Butchart, 305, **316**
Robertson, William, 172; *History of America*, 33
Rockefeller, Abby Aldrich, 366
Rockefeller, John D., 220
Rockefeller, John D., Jr., 310–11, 352, 366–70, **367**
Rocky Mountains, 1–2, **3**, 86
romantic Indian-White motifs in literature, 123–25
Romantics, 339
Roosevelt, Theodore, 247, 252–53, 323, 325, 371; Antiquities Act of 1906 signed, 263; national monuments declared, 256, 308; on strange, simple, dead semi-civilizations, 307
Rowe Ruin, 287
Royal Ontario Museum of Toronto: agreement with Hewett, 294–95
Royal Society of London, 26
Roybal, Alfonso (Awa Tsireh), 350–51
Royce, Charles C., 93, 106
Rudisill, Richard, 363

"Ruins in Canon De Chelly [White House]" (Kern), **64**
Rules of the Aztec Language (Clavigero), 32
Ruppert, Karl, **297**
Russell, Frances Theresa Peet, 321–22, **322**
Russell, Frank, 114, 240, 307, **322**; Bureau of American Ethnology, 321–22
Russell, R. W., 173
Russell, Theresa, 307
Ruxton, George Augustus Frederick, 36, 55; *Adventures*, 35; *Life in the Far West*, 35

SAA-BAE research program, 271
SAA-BAE (School of American Archaeology, Bureau of American Ethnology) program, 269
The Sacred Turquoise of the Zuni (motion picture), 364
Sage, Russell, 220
Sahagún, Bernardino de, Fray, *General History of the Things of New Spain*, 32
Salem Academy (Peabody Academy of Science), 222
Salinas Pueblos, 50, **57**, 58, 175; legend of, 56
salt, 56
Salt River, 50
Salt River Valley: excavations, 156, 170; sites, 151–54
Sammons, Mrs. H. B., 296
San Cristóbal Pueblo, 282–83, **283**, 286
sandals, 293
San Diego Exposition, 272, 349
San Diego Museum of Man, 261, 274, 373
sandpaintings, 202, 346; on public display, 225, 305, 346, 359; as rug designs, 373
San Felipe Pueblo, 341
San Francisco Examiner, 227
San Francisco Mountains, 170
Sangre de Cristo Mountains, 1–2
San Ildefonso Pueblo, 112, 114, 248; blackware, 351–52; painters, 350

San Juan Mountains, 1

San Juan River, 66, 192; confluence with Colorado River, 192, 259

San Juan Triangle, 192

San Simon Valley, 58

Santa Ana Pueblo, 341

Santa Clara Pueblo, 112, 213; black-ware, 352; visited by Harvey Detours, **346**

Santa Fe, 9, 35, 248; architectural style, 251, 345, 348–50, 373; as the oldest city in the United States, 272, 348; reinvention of, 347–50, 353; as a tourist destination, 272

Santa Fe Archaeological Society, 199

Santa Fe Indian School, 350

Santa Fe Magazine, 346

Santa *Fe New Mexican*: Judd interview, 295–96

Santa Fe New Mexican, Boas's letters, 272

Santa Fe Railway, 172, 272, 274, 344–45

Santa Fe Trail, 34

Santo Domingo Pueblo, 72, 135, 174, 341

Santo Domingo Pueblo Church, **72**

San Xavier del Bac, 12–13, 153

Sapir, Edward, 224, 241; "Time Perspective in Aboriginal American Culture: A Study in Method," 278; University of Chicago, 376

Sarcilla Largo, 75

Sauer, Carl, 185

Saunders, Charles Francis, *The Indians of the Terraced Houses*, 358

savages: analogical, 16, 21, 23, 96 (*See also* hunter gatherers); ignoble, 16; managed, 23, 80–81, 88, 93, 251; noble (natural man), 16–19, 22, 339, 343; stereotypes of, 16–18, 182, 204–5, 211, 374; vanishing, 16, 93, 95, 209, 213–14, 254, 323

Saville, Marshall H., 208, 233–34, 246, 278

Sayles, E. B., 378

Scatologic Rites of All Nations (Bourke), 136

scatology, 136

Schiff, Esther (Goldfrank), 333–35, **334**

Schofield, C. S., **297**, 315

scholar-entrepeneurs, 247, 256, 261

Schoolcraft, Henry Rowe, 27, **28**, 29–30, 74–75, 95, 124; cyclopedia of American Indians, 79; *Historical and Statistical Information*, 88

School of American Archaeology, 177, 264–65, 267–69

School of American Archaeology, Bureau of American Ethnology (SAA-BAE) program, 269

School of American Archaeology and Ethnology, 267

School of American Research, 261, 352, 373

Schurz, Carl, 90, 92

Schweizer, Herman, 345

Schwemberger, Simeon, 231

Science, 145–46, 234, 275

science of man, ix, 203, 209. *See also* anthropology

Scott, Hugh L., 257

Scribner's Monthly, 87

The Secret of the Pueblo (motion picture), 364

seen vs. seen as, viii–ix, 374, 377

Seler, Eduard, 234

Seltzer, Carl, 314

semi-civilization, 68

Seneca Indian Reservation, 122

Seneca Indians, 95

septenary divisions, 156. *See also* six-direction spatial orientation

Sequoya League, 252–54

Sergeant, Elizabeth Shepley, 352, 357

seriation, 278, 280, 289, 302; defined, 281

Seri Indians, 145, 237, 321

Serra, Junípero, Fray, 12

Serrano Indians, 338

settlement movement, 326

The Seven Cities of Cibola (A. Nusbaum), 311

Seven Cities of Cibola legend, 8, 298

Seven Years' Residence in the Great Deserts of North America (Domenech), 69–70

Sevier, Ambrose, 44

Sevy, Milton, 260

Shabik'eschee Village, 305–6

Shaftesbury, Earl of, 19

Shakespeare, William, *The Tempest*, 18

Shalakos, 127, 304; drawing (Farny), **127**

Shapiro, Harry, 305

Shawnee Indians, 26

sheep, churro, 130

sheepherding, 11

Shelton, William T., 200

Shepard, Anna O., 319

sherds, stratigraphic sequence of, 286–87

Sherman, William Tecumseh, 129

Shipaulovi (Hopi village), 142

Shivwits, 87

Shiwian Indians, 156

Shoshoni Indians, 94, 134, 242

shovel-shaped incisors, 238

"show-biz" ethnography, 214, 217

Shuttleworth, Claire, 214

Sichomovi (Hopi village), 73, 142, 166

"The Significance of the Frontier in American History" (Turner), 211

sign languages, 128

Sihtaime, 329

Sikyatki pottery revival, 345

Sikyatki Ruin, 165–66, 168

silver jewelry, 345

silversmithing, 128, 130, 210–11, 230

Simpson, James Hervey, 42–44, 61–63, 73

Sinagua Indians, 378

Singleton, Anne (Ruth Benedict pseudonym), 338

sink-or-swim field schools, 266

Sioux Indians, 134

Sipapu, 169

"Site of the Latest Artifact and Bison Association, Folsom, New Mexico," **320**

Sitgreaves, Lorenzo, 44, 64, 73, 77

Siwatitsailu, 151

six-direction spatial orientation, 169. *See also* septenary divisions

skeletal collections, 237–38

Wetherill, Anna, 187–88
Wetherill, Benjamin Alfred, 187, **187**, 189, 191, 193–94, 198
Wetherill, Benjamin Kite, 187
Wetherill, Clayton, 187, **187**, 190, 194, **196**, 198
Wetherill, John, **187**, 187–88, 190, 192–94, 199, 257–59, **258**, 289; as Rainbow Bridge guide, 292
Wetherill, Louisa Wade, 199, 257–58, 289
Wetherill, Marietta Palmer, **196**, **197**, 198–200
Wetherill, Mary, **196**, 198
Wetherill, Richard, **187**, 187–90, 192–201, **196**, 210
Wetherill, Winslow, 187, **187**
We'wha, 123, 340; photograph (Hillers), **108**, **115**; relationship with M. Stevenson, 114–16
Wheeler, Benjamin Ide, 242–43, 254
Wheeler, George Montague, 81, 84–85
Wheeler, Lucy Blair, 84
Wheeler survey, 84–85
Wheelwright, Mary Cabot, 359, 373
Wheelwright Museum of the American Indian, 373–74
Whipple, Amiel Weeks, 44–47, 73, 78
Whipple Ruin, 300
White, Amelia Elizabeth, 350, 352, 369
White, Leslie A., 340–42, 371, **371**; "Medicine Societies in the Southwest," 341
White, Martha, 350, 369
White Anglo Saxon Protestants (WASPs), 237, 279
White Canyon, **57**, 256–57
White House Ruin, 50, 112, 141; drawing (Kern), **64**
White Mountain Apache Indians, 213
White River, 86
Whiteshell Woman, 126
Whitewater Draw, 319

Whiting, Lilian, *The Land of Enchantment: From Pike's Peak to the Pacific*, 344
Whitmore, C. E., 197–98
Whitmore, Teddy, **197**
Whitmore Exploring Expedition, **197**
Whitney, Asa, 46
Whitney, J. D., 81
Why We Behave Like Human Beings (Dorsey), 226
Why Women Are So (M. Coolidge), 359
Widener Library, 185
Wide Ruin, 141
Wijiji Ruin, **61**, 62
Wilcox, David R., 154, 377
Wilcox, Donald, 19
"wild" tribes, 72, 75
Wild West shows, 205–6, 208, 216, 217
Wilkes, Charles, 26
Williams, Gwyn, 54
Williams, Roger, *A Key into the Language of America*, 24
Wilson, Francis, 369
Winnemucca, Sarah, 122
Winship, George Parker, 185
Wintun Indians, 94
Wirtman, Jacob, 154
Wislizenus, Frederick Adolph, 35–37; "Memoir of a Tour in Northern Mexico," 36
Wissler, Clark, 200, 241, 244, 277–79, 282, 376; photograph (Kirschner), **279**; using tree ring dating, 299–300
Wissler's Southwest project, 244
Witherspoon, Gary, 129
Wittfogel, Carl, 334
Wittgenstein, Ludwig, viii–ix
Wittick, George Ben, 173, 363
Wiyot Indians, 336
Wolcott, Charles, 302
Wolfe, Tom, *The Painted Word*, 353
Woman's Indian Aid Association, 243
women: Anglo assumptions about,

326; discrimination against, 336, 370; feminist concerns, 211, 307, 326, 359; hiring of, 113; as members Anthropological Society of Washington, 115–16; rights of, 326; as university regents, 242
Women's Anthropological Society of America, 115, 145
women's clubs supporting archaeology, 254
women's knowledge, 112, 163
Woodbury, Nathalie, 304
Woodbury, Richard, 304
world history, invention of, 19
world's fairs, 203–19; midway entertainment zones, 204, 207–8, 213–14, 216; scholarly congresses, 205, 210–12, 240
World's Industrial and Cotton Exposition in New Orleans, 206
World War I, 326
Wormington, H. Marie, 305
Wortman, Jacob L., 152, **152**
Wounded Knee massacre, 343
Woy, Maude, 269, **269**
Wupatki National Monument, 44, 171
Wupatki Ruin, 50, **57**, 64–65
Wyman, Jeffries, 222
Wyman, Leland, 131

Yale University, 240
Yana Indians, 330
Yaqui Indians, 237, 331
Yarrow, Henry C., 106
Yavapai Indians, 13
yearners, 17, 120, 358–60, 374, 379; defined, 357; epitome of, 325; invading privacy of Indians, 135
Yeibichai dances, ersatz, 356; motion pictures of, 324–25, 346, 364
Yeibichai masks, 230–31
Yellow Jacket Canyon, 265
Yellow Jacket Ruin, **57**, 66
Yellowstone, 82–83
Yoruba Indians, 78
Young, Stuart, 257